Fifth Edition

CONSUMER BEHAVIOR
AND MARKETING ACTION

HENRY ASSAEL

New York University

SOUTH-WESTERN College Publishing

An International Thomson Publishing Company

Dedicated to Alyce

Acquisitions Editor:	Robert B. Jared
Production Editor:	Sharon L. Smith
Production House:	GTS Graphics
Cover Design:	Bruce Design/Annette Ross
Cover Illustrator:	Tony Novak
Internal Design:	Lesiak/Crampton Design
Photo Research:	Judy Feldman
Marketing Manager:	Stephen E. Momper

ST62EA
Copyright © 1995
by South-Western College Publishing
Cincinnati, Ohio

Library of Congress Cataloging-in-Publication Data

Assael, Henry.
  [Consumer behavior and marketing action]
  Consumer behavior & marketing action / Henry Assael. — 5th ed.
     p. cm.
  Includes bibliographical references.
  ISBN 0-538-84433-7
  1. Consumer behavior.   2. Motivational research (Marketing)
  I. Title.
  HF5415.3.A83   1994
  658.8'342—dc20   94-30946
                                                             CIP

  2 3 4 5 6 7 D 0 9 8 7 6 5
Printed in the United States of America

I(T)P
International Thomson Publishing

South-Western College Publishing is an ITP Company. The ITP trademark is used under license.

BRIEF CONTENTS

PART V

COMMUNICATIONS PROCESSES   *631*

CONTENTS

PART II

CONSUMER DECISION MAKING   *69*

3 Complex Decision Making   *71*

P R E F A C E

◆ KEY CHANGES IN THE FIFTH EDITION

The fifth edition of *Consumer Behavior and Marketing Action* is a marked departure from previous editions in three important respects.

1. *Greater macro/societal orientation and focus on consumerism.* Consumer rights and the societal/policy implications of consumer behavior and marketing strategy are now a more central focus of the text. Whereas in previous editions the chapter on consumerism was placed last, it is now the second chapter. Further, most chapters now have a section at the end titled "Societal Implications"; for example, Societal Implications of . . .

Brand and Store Loyalty (Chapter 4)
Low Involvement Decision Making (Chapter 5)
Information Processing (Chapter 7)
Attitude Change (Chapter 9)
Segmentation and Positioning Strategies (Chapter 12)

and so forth.

This focus on societal implications serves several objectives. First, it provides a balance between the strategic focus throughout the book and a focus on consumer rights. As before, the consumer's right to information, adequate choice, and product safety are discussed; however, these rights are now expanded to include a broader set of issues encompassing environmental protection, product labeling and health claims, advertising to children, and targeting minorities.

Second, the greater societal focus conforms to the current emphasis on ethical issues in the business curriculum. Ethical issues that relate to the ability of children to process information or to misleading labeling of food products can be more easily woven into conceptual discussions given their early introduction in the text.

Third, the societal focus reflects a greater macro orientation in the book. This is most evident in the chapter on culture (Chapter 13) which now reflects the latest emphasis on product symbolism, imagery, and purchase and consumption rituals. The chapter also provides a link to Chapter 14 which discusses differences in cultural values around the world and how they affect consumer behavior.

2. *Fuller integration of behavioral concepts with strategic applications.* When it was introduced in 1981, the text was recognized as the first consumer behavior book to take a marketing strategy approach to the topic by introducing applications of behavioral concepts. This was accomplished by citing strategic applications in each chapter, and also by having a signature section of the book entitled "Marketing Action." Each chapter in this section reflected one of the "four Ps" of marketing—promotion (marketing communications), product (segmentation and product positioning), place (store choice and shopping behavior), and price (pricing perceptions and influences).

The field has now matured to the point where a separate section on strategic applications is no longer necessary. The fifth edition integrates the material on the four Ps throughout the book. A good example is the treatment of the material from the chapter that covered Store Choice and Shopping Behavior in the fourth edition. The material has been moved as indicated below:

- store choice is discussed in the chapter on complex decision making
- store loyalty is discussed in the chapter on brand loyalty
- impulse purchasing is discussed in the chapter on low involvement
- shopping behavior is discussed in the chapter on market segmentation and
- store image is discussed in the chapter on perceptions.

Similarly, the material on price appears primarily in the chapter on perceptions, and the material on salesperson influences is in the chapter on word-of-mouth influence.

This edition, like prior editions, has strategic applications material integrated into every chapter. But the integration of the section on Marketing Action provides a more cohesive link between concept and strategy.

3. *A new section on Communications Processes.* In prior editions, chapters on communications were placed in different parts of the text. The fifth edition treats communications processes on an integrative basis in the last section. The three chapters in this section distinguish between communications from groups and from marketing organizations. Group communications are further divided between those that occur within groups (word-of-mouth communication) and those that occur across groups through a process of diffusion of information and influence.

 ADDITIONAL CHANGES

Another noteworthy change is the inclusion of the material on social class in the chapter on demographics. Including social class with demographics does not conform to the general convention of treating it as an environmental variable. But social class is defined by socioeconomic variables, and most research studies measure demographic variables as surrogates of social class. Further, social class does not deserve a separate chapter since it has not received much research attention in recent years. Therefore, it makes sense to deal with social class as a socioeconomic factor reflected in demographic variables.

Additional changes of note are:

- The use of a vignette to introduce each chapter. The vignettes provide a strategic foundation for the introduction of the chapter's material and are often interwoven throughout the chapter.

- A complete update of demographic trends in Chapter 10, particularly the growing importance of the teen and preteen markets, the results of an aging baby boomer segment, and the increasing clout of the mature market.

- A consideration of emerging life styles in Chapter 11, such as more emphasis on frugality and a trend toward de-emphasizing the organization and working at home.

- Placing the chapter on Market Segmentation and Product Positioning (Chapter 12) in the section on the individual consumer. In past editions this chapter was in the section on Marketing Action. The chapter is now better positioned in following the material on demographics and lifestyles since most segmentation strategies are based on these variables.

- Expanding the material on culture in Chapter 13 to include a consideration of
  - instrumental and terminal values in a means-end chain
  - semiotics and the role of product symbolism
  - consumption rituals
  - sacred and secular consumption.

- A focus on a "new reality" in consumption values, one which recognizes the limits of future economic growth and consequent earnings potential. The result is more price sensitivity and a greater emphasis on value.

- An update of cross-cultural and subcultural influences in Chapter 14 including the Americanization of consumption values worldwide and the growing importance of the Asian-American market in the United States.

This edition continues to feature a strategic applications box in each chapter. This additional integrative device was designed to further demonstrate strategic applications and was well received in the last edition. The research assignments at the end of each chapter continue to prove useful to students in applying behavioral principles. End-of-chapter questions and the glossary have been updated to reflect changes in the text.

The reception of the first four editions continues to confirm my belief that a consumer behavior text that is suitable for a business school must be applications oriented. Consumer behavior continues to be a dynamic and changing field that challenges the research interests of marketing scholars. I hope that students will continue to find this fifth edition of *Consumer Behavior and Marketing Action* useful and challenging in pursuing careers in marketing.

◆ ACKNOWLEDGEMENTS

I am indebted to a number of people for their help in completing the fifth edition. Russ Belk of the University of Utah provided a detailed review of the manuscript that was an invaluable guide, as it has been in past editions. Hal Kassarjian of UCLA was very helpful in reacting to key changes in the fifth edition. The perspectives of Rich Lutz of the University of Florida at Gainesville guided previous editions and are reflected in this one.

A number of other people provided insightful reviews and are owed a debt of thanks, particularly:

Louis M. Capella
Mississippi State University

Scott Dawson
Portland State University

Stephen J. Gould
Baruch College

I would also like to thank a highly impressive team of people at South-Western College Publishing for their assistance. Particular thanks go to Sharon Smith, my production editor, for overseeing every detail of the book and insuring it stayed on track. Thanks go to my editor, Rob Jared, for his support in every facet of the book. Thanks are also due to Debbie Kokoruda for the arduous task of obtaining innumerable permissions. Thanks also to Rhonda Eversole for an excellent job of copyediting and to Judy Feldman for an outstanding job as photo-researcher on this project. Thanks are also due to Chris Sofranko, the leader of this impressive team.

As in the first four editions, final thanks are reserved for my special partner, Alyce Assael for having spent long days reviewing periodicals and searching out references. As always, her help and support are invaluable.

Henry Assael

CONSUMER BEHAVIOR: A MANAGERIAL AND CONSUMER PERSPECTIVE

This introductory section views consumer behavior from both a manager's and a consumer's perspective. In Chapter 1, we establish both a managerial and a consumer orientation to the study of consumer behavior. The managerial perspective focuses on the link between satisfying consumer needs and developing marketing strategies. A consumer perspective seeks to ensure that when businesses pursue profits, consumer rights will be protected. The attempt to ensure consumer rights is known as consumerism and is the responsibility of the government, the business community, and consumers themselves.

Chapter 2 explores the pursuit of consumer rights in key areas such as environmental protection, product safety, ensuring minority rights, and protecting children from undue influence. This chapter provides a balanced perspective to ensure that we do not lose sight of these rights when we describe consumer behavior applications of marketing strategy.

1

Introduction

LEVI STRAUSS & CO. BEGINS TO FOCUS ON THE CONSUMER

Consumers determine the sales and profits of a firm by their purchasing decisions. As such, their motives and actions determine the economic viability of the firm.

In the past, many business firms were not overly concerned with consumer motives and actions. They focused more on sales results with little concern for why consumers did what they did. Today, however, business managers are more likely to realize that they must gain an understanding of consumers if their marketing strategies are to be successful. This awareness has created a new and more efficient focus in developing marketing strategies. Consider Levi Strauss & Co.: Until the mid-1980s, the company sold jeans to a mass market. But then, sales of jeans took a slide. Why? Basic demographic and social trends started affecting sales. Baby boomers (the 30- to 49-year-old group) were getting out of jeans, and teens—the most loyal of jeans purchasers—represented a shrinking proportion of the market.

Levi Strauss & Co.'s answer to this problem was a strategy of market segmentation. The company broadened its line to include slacks and then targeted different lines to different demographic segments. It first introduced baggy cotton slacks (the Dockers® line) for the baby boomers' expanding waistlines; then comfortable Action Slacks for the over-50 group; and in 1990, an ad was introduced for 501® buttonfly jeans with Spike Lee as a spokesperson for teens.[1] In 1988, the company targeted a line of jeans to women for the first time.[2] (See Exhibit 1.1.) Then, in 1992, Levi Strauss & Co. further segmented the market by bridging the gap between teens and baby boomers and introduced Loose jeans, a line of fashion-oriented denim slacks targeted to the "baby bust" generation (those between 18 and 30).[3]

The company has also followed a global strategy by recognizing the differing needs of consumers around the world. By using James Dean as the centerpiece of its advertising, under the tag line "Heroes Wear Levis," it caters to the desire of Japanese teenagers for American icons; and the company is poised to enter the Eastern European market.[4] However, in 1993, Levi Strauss & Co. rejected entry into China because it recognized that many of its loyal customers still resented the government's crackdown of the democracy movement four years before.[5]

Rapid changes in the marketing environment such as those experienced by Levi Strauss & Co. have led marketing managers to analyze more closely the factors that influence consumer choice. Managers are now concerned with delivering benefits to consumers, changing consumers' attitudes, and influencing consumer perceptions. They realize that marketing plans must be based on the psychological and social forces that are likely to condition consumer behavior—forces such as the aging of baby boomers, increasing concern with health and nutrition, more focus on a clean environment, and even the impact of foreign events on consumer purchasing attitudes.

The result of this realization is a new emphasis on consumer information. To paraphrase one marketing executive, the most successful companies will be those that get their hands on information that identifies and explains the needs and behavior of consumers.[6]

This introductory chapter establishes a managerial orientation to the study of consumer behavior. The chapter first considers the reasons why the study of consumer behavior is important and then reviews the organization of the text. It concludes by considering the study of consumer behavior from a consumer's, as opposed to a manager's, perspective. Such a consumer perspective of the field naturally leads to public policy questions that deal with protecting consumer rights in areas such as environmental protection and product safety.

◆ CONSUMER BEHAVIOR AND MARKETING ACTION

Much of this text will be devoted to a better understanding of terms such as consumer *benefits, perceptions,* and *attitudes* and how they influence development of successful marketing strategies. Because it recognized that jeans could

▶**EXHIBIT 1.1**
Levi Strauss & Co.'s market segmentation strategy

Source: Courtesy of Levi Strauss & Co.

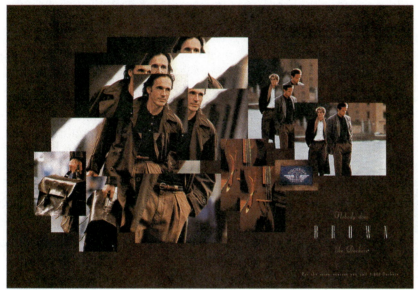

Targeting Baby Boomers

Targeting Women

Targeting Teens

no longer provide baby boomers with the *benefits* of a good fit, Levi Strauss & Co. was successful in introducing its Dockers® line of slacks. The company determined that baby boomers' *perceptions* linked Levi Strauss & Co. to jeans and that it would have to change these perceptions to market successfully the Dockers® line. Levi Strauss & Co. also had to change perceptions of jeans as a male-oriented product if it was to target females successfully with a new line of jeans. In changing consumer perceptions, Levi Strauss & Co. was trying to develop more positive *attitudes* toward its new product lines, thus increasing the chances that the targeted demographic groups would buy.

Companies that fail to recognize consumer needs are more likely to make costly mistakes. Consider Sears, the number one retailer in the United States until 1990, when it fell to third place. Before its slide, Sears had a clear focus on how to satisfy its customers—offer a wide variety of low-priced merchandise to middle America. However, Sears failed to see the implications of more working women and the greater affluence of dual-earning households. These demographic shifts meant that consumers wanted a greater variety of name brands at reasonable prices.

While other mass merchandisers were moving to specialty, name brand goods, Sears was slow to change. It continued to offer what consumers perceived as low-quality merchandise in aging stores with garish displays. By 1993, the company recognized it needed a drastic repositioning. Management is now remodeling Sears outlets and offering name brand merchandise in a more boutique-like environment. (See Exhibit 1.2.) Sears is climbing back to dominance by reinventing itself to better meet the needs of a more affluent customer base.[7]

As the Levi Strauss & Co. and Sears examples show, the basic philosophy required for successful marketing—the importance of satisfying consumers—may be simple; but its implementation is complex. It requires that the company:

- Define consumer needs.
- Identify consumer segments that have these needs.
- Position new products or reposition existing products to meet these needs.
- Develop marketing strategies to communicate and deliver product benefits.
- Ensure that such communications are not misleading or deceptive in any way.

Underlying these strategic requirements is the importance of obtaining information on consumer needs, consumer perceptions of new and existing brands, attitudes toward these brands, intentions to buy, and past purchasing behavior. This text attempts to provide an understanding of these components of consumer behavior within a strategic and managerial framework.

▶**EXHIBIT 1.2**

Sears redefines itself to better meet consumer needs

Source: Courtesy of Sears, Roebuck and Co.

Before

After

A HISTORICAL PERSPECTIVE

The philosophy that marketing strategies rely on a better knowledge of the consumer is known as the **marketing concept.*** The marketing concept states that marketers must first define the benefits consumers seek in the marketplace and gear marketing strategies accordingly. Acceptance of this concept has provided the impetus for studying consumer behavior in a marketing context.

———————

*All terms in bold type are defined in the Glossary at the back of the text.

Development of the Marketing Concept

First formulated in the early 1950s, the marketing concept seems so logical today that we may wonder why marketers did not turn to it sooner. There are two reasons. First, marketing institutions were not sufficiently developed before 1950 to accept the marketing concept. Consumer behavior research was in its infancy. Moreover, advertising and distributive facilities were more suited to the mass-production and mass-marketing strategies of that time. The implementation of the marketing concept requires a diversity of facilities for promoting and distributing products that meet the needs of smaller and more diverse market segments. This diversity in marketing institutions did not exist before 1950. Instead, the emphasis was on economies of scale in production and marketing. Before the '50s, for example, Coca-Cola was a one-product company; Chevrolet had only one model.

The second reason the marketing concept was not accepted until the 1950s is that prior to that time there was no economic necessity to do so. During the Depression, there was little purchasing power to spur an interest in consumer behavior. During World War II and immediately after, scarcities were prevalent. There was no competitive pressure to find out consumers' motives or to adjust product offerings to consumer needs. Manufacturers could sell whatever they made.

The end of the Korean War in 1953 changed this sales-oriented focus. The conversion to peacetime production was rapid and efficient. Different marketers brought out similar lines of refrigerators, ovens, and cars—but now they found consumers reluctant to buy. Consumers had become more selective in their purchasing habits after two major wars and a Depression, and they were now reluctant buyers. The economy experienced its first true buyers' market. For the first time, supply exceeded demand; and inventories built up in the face of consumer purchasing power.

Some marketers reacted by intensifying the old strategies: Push the existing line, heighten selling efforts, repeat selling themes, and push excess inventories on unwilling distributors and dealers. Others reacted with more foresight by recognizing that the right combination of product benefits would influence reluctant consumers to purchase. These manufacturers researched the market to identify consumer needs and to develop products to fit these needs. This newer approach resulted in an expanded set of product offerings. It also caused advertising strategy to shift from the repetitive campaigns designed to maintain brand awareness to more creative, diverse campaigns designed to communicate product benefits.

Marketers began talking in behavioral terms. In this new context, a product must be positioned to deliver a set of consumer benefits to a defined segment of consumers. Advertising's goals are to communicate symbols and images that show how the brand delivers these benefits, to create a favorable attitude toward the brand, and to induce trial. Advertising is also intended to reinforce the consumers' choices to influence them to repurchase. Using Ray Charles as a spokesperson singing "You got the right one, baby," PepsiCo's campaign for Diet Pepsi illustrates such reinforcement. (See Exhibit 1.3.) The slogan implied that the consumer choosing Diet Pepsi made the right decision and will be satisfied. The ads were so successful during their two-year run that Pepsi increased the campaign's budget from $70 million in 1991 to $120 million in 1992.[8]

Implications for Consumer Behavior

The shift from a sales orientation to a behavioral or consumer orientation did not occur overnight. It is still going on today. Avon Products reflects this shift. Before 1980, the company's sales-oriented management failed to see the potential impact of an increasing proportion of working women on its primary means of distribution—door-to-door sales of cosmetics. The simple fact was that fewer women were at home to open the door for the Avon salesperson. In addition, more affluent and aware female consumers were beginning to look down on Avon's low-price, bargain basement image.[9]

The shift to a consumer orientation required a new management team, which promptly commissioned a large-scale study of women's cosmetic needs and attitudes toward Avon products. On the basis of the study, the company acquired a line of high-priced prestige perfumes to appeal to the affluent working woman and began distributing them through department stores. It also sent its Avon sales reps to the office, rather than to the home, to reach less-affluent working women and to offer them traditional Avon products.[10] By 1990, Avon's management recognized that these shifts would not be sufficient. Since working women were requiring greater flexibility, the company began renewing emphasis on its long-standing catalog operation, but with one twist: It was encouraging its customers to call in their orders directly and even to fax them from the workplace. (See Exhibit 1.4.)

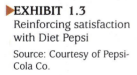

▶**EXHIBIT 1.3**
Reinforcing satisfaction with Diet Pepsi

Source: Courtesy of Pepsi-Cola Co.

The shift to a consumer orientation by companies such as Avon and Levi Strauss & Co. has changed the nature of marketing operations in several ways:

- *By providing a spur to consumer behavior research.* Both Levi Strauss & Co. and Avon conducted studies of consumer needs, attitudes, and purchasing behavior as a basis for their shift in strategy.
- *By creating a more customer-oriented framework for marketing strategies.* Levi Strauss & Co. could no longer rely on a mass-market approach. It recognized it had to broaden its line beyond jeans to satisfy baby boomers first and then baby busters. It also realized it would have to differentiate its appeals based on the needs of these segments—an appeal to baby boomers based primarily on fit and to baby busters based primarily on design.
- *By encouraging measurement of the factors that influence consumers to purchase.* Levi Strauss & Co. had to determine what factors influence choice of slacks among its various age segments.
- *By emphasizing market segmentation.* As we saw, Levi Strauss & Co. grouped its customers primarily into age segments. Avon also had to identify segments such as affluent working women (targets for more expensive perfumes), less-affluent working women (targets for sales calls at the workplace), and the traditional stay-at-home or work-at-home women (targets for sales calls at home).
- *By emphasizing product positioning to meet consumer needs.* Products are developed and advertised to establish qualities that set them apart from competition and to relate these qualities to the needs of a defined market segment. Based on the theme, "We're going to make you feel beautiful," Avon developed a campaign for its products positioned to the less-affluent working women. How did it arrive at this positioning strategy? Avon conducted research, showing that less-

affluent working women wanted to improve their feelings about themselves and to accept themselves more.

- *By creating greater selectivity in advertising and personal selling.* Emphasis is now on selective marketing rather than on mass marketing. Avon's separate strategies to target more-affluent working women, less-affluent working women, and women at home are examples.
- *By creating more selective media and distributive outlets.* There are now more specialized magazines, greater uses of catalogs and phone orders, and more specialized wholesalers and retailers. As we saw, Avon is broadening its base beyond door-to-door selling by relying more on direct customer orders.

In summary, in accepting the marketing concept, marketing management has recognized that the determinants of consumer behavior have a direct bearing on the formulation of marketing strategies.

Avon Products: Shifting from a Sales to a Consumer Orientation

An example of the shift from a sales to a consumer orientation is illustrated by the role of marketing research at Avon in 1975, when the company was sales-oriented, and in 1995 when it was more consumer-oriented.

The following hypothetical memos between the product manager for Avon's skin products line and the company's director of marketing research illustrate the sales-oriented nature of consumer information in 1975. Notice in particular (1) the reliance on sales data without determining the reasons behind consumer behavior and (2) the lack of a systematic approach to obtain reliable information on consumers.

TO: Director of Marketing Research

FROM: Product Manager, Skin Products

DATE: March 25, 1975

SUBJECT: Introduction of New Skin Moisturizer

What are your plans to obtain information from industry and consumer sources that might indicate the sales performance of the new skin moisturizer after its introduction?

TO: Product Manager, Skin Products

FROM: Director of Marketing Research

DATE: March 28, 1975

SUBJECT: Plans to Obtain Information on New Skin Moisturizer

The most important advantage of the new moisturizer as communicated by our laboratory people is that it is longer lasting and retains its moisturizing properties

in dry weather better than competitive moisturizers do. On this basis, I feel the prospects of success are good; but we cannot proceed on my judgment alone. Therefore, I plan to utilize the following sources of information:

- Sales figures on the introduction of competitive moisturizers
- Feedback from our Avon sales representatives on attitudes of women to competitive moisturizers. Do the sales reps think the new moisturizer will sell? Are they willing to give the product adequate attention in their door-to-door house calls?
- Tests with our employees (our products versus competitor's product)
- Tests on our panel of "expert" housewives to provide a check against results from our employee tests

Now, consider the following two memos under the same circumstances in 1995. These memos demonstrate the understanding that consumer feedback is central to evaluating new product opportunities. Notice in particular (1) the specific and detailed process of new product development that (2) requires reliable feedback from consumers (3) to ensure a sound information base for the development of marketing strategies.

TO: Director of Marketing Research

FROM: Product Manager, Skin Products

DATE: March 25, 1995

SUBJECT: Introduction of New Skin Moisturizer

What are your plans to obtain information from consumers on acceptability of the new skin moisturizer prior to launch?

TO: Product Manager, Skin Products

FROM: Director of Marketing Research

DATE: March 28, 1995

SUBJECT: Research Plans for New Skin Moisturizer

On the basis of our prior meeting with the advertising group and the VP of marketing, I believe that the positioning relies on two benefits: (1) longer moisturizing ability and (2) better performance in dry weather. The research plan calls for:

1. **Depth interviews** with four or five small groups of skin moisturizer users to discuss their reasons for purchasing moisturizers and the benefits they associate with moisturizers. [Depth interviews are informal, unstructured interviews to get consumers to talk freely and to express their feelings about a product or company.] From these interviews, we will identify a **vocabulary of consumer benefits** that might provide some indication of the importance of longer-lasting performance and of product performance in dry weather. This research should provide an indication of the types of needs that lead to the purchase of one brand of moisturizer over another.

2. **A product concept test** to evaluate several alternative positionings for the product. [Product concept tests attempt to obtain consumer reactions to a verbal description of the product before a company commits to producing the product.] Should long-lasting effectiveness be the primary appeal and effectiveness in dry weather be a secondary appeal, or vice versa? Three or four alternative descriptions will be provided to the consumer, and the products will be rated utilizing the need vocabulary defined in Step 1. This test will be conducted on 200 to 300 consumers.

   The concept test will identify consumers who consider the product's key benefits—long-lasting effectiveness and effectiveness in dry weather—most important. The key questions are: "What are the characteristics of this target group?" and "What positioning do they prefer most?"

3. An in-home **product use test** to evaluate the product in use. Moisturizer users will try the new product for one week and their regular moisturizer for one week on a rotating basis. The products will be rated utilizing the same need vocabulary identified in the depth interviews. Results of the in-home test will provide further refinement of the definition of the target segments and the positioning of the product. The in-home test will also indicate whether consumers felt the product delivered the promised benefits.

   By the way, I suggest we terminate our consumer panel and the use of company employees for testing. The company has been using this source of information for over thirty years. Results from the consumer panel and from company employees frequently contradict findings from the concept and in-home use tests. One obvious point is that our target group is no longer primarily housewives. My feeling is that in-home use tests are more reliable as a measure of consumer perceptions and attitudes toward brand offerings and as an indication of future purchase intent.

4. **Test marketing** the product in key cities and then projecting sales results on a national basis, assuming that results from the concept and in-home use tests are positive.

   Once the product is in test market for about six months, I suggest conducting a survey of consumers to determine their reactions to the product. The survey would determine the following:
   - Product characteristics consumers perceive our brand to have versus those of the competition (rich, smooth, not oily).
   - Product benefits consumers perceive our brand to have versus those of the competition (longer lasting, less irritating, more effective in dry weather)
   - Attitudes toward our brand versus those of the competition (prefer first, second, third)
   - Future buying intentions
   - Lifestyle and demographic characteristics of respondents
   - Advertising recall for our brand versus those of the competition

5. This survey would provide us with a basis for assessing our marketing strategy by focusing on the key to our success or failure—the consumer. Specifically, it would allow us to:
- Identify the market segments most likely to buy our brand
- Evaluate the positioning of the product to these target segments
- Assess our strengths and weaknesses relative to competition
- Measure the effects of specific components of our marketing strategy (price, advertising, packaging).

I have outlined a fairly comprehensive research plan. It will be costly, but I believe we must assess market opportunity first by determining the benefits consumers seek relative to our brand offering (Steps 1–3) and then by evaluating the consumers' reactions to our marketing plan (Step 4).

◆ STRATEGIC APPLICATIONS OF CONSUMER BEHAVIOR

A marketing manager faces three important tasks:

1. To identify new opportunities in the marketplace.
2. To evaluate the strengths and weaknesses of existing brand offerings.
3. To develop marketing strategies that influence consumers to buy.

Fulfilling these tasks requires information about the determinants of consumer behavior: consumers' needs, perceptions, attitudes, and intentions.

Marketing management requires information on the consumer in order to:

- Define and segment the market.
- In so doing, determine the needs of the target segment.
- Develop strategies based on customer needs, attitudes, and perceptions.
- Evaluate marketing strategies.
- Assess future customer behavior.

Defining and Segmenting Markets

In 1987, Sony introduced its new Mavica electronic photography system. Using a filmless camera, the system allows the user to take a picture on a disk that can be shown immediately by inserting it into a recorder connected to a video monitor. Consumer research on the camera, begun six years earlier, illustrated the consumer information required for effective strategy development.[11]

Sony's research was designed to investigate the potential for the Mavica. A preliminary survey identified a segment of 20 to 25 business markets with imaging needs that might use the new system. To better identify those target segments with the highest sales potential, the company conducted depth interviews with managers in each of these segments to determine (1) their imaging needs, (2) the benefits they saw in the Mavica, (3) how they would use it, and (4) their potential for purchasing it.

On this basis, the company identified the primary target segment as newspaper organizations with a need for electronic news gathering. Such definition of a target segment is essential because most products cannot be sold on a mass-market basis. Identifying individual segments that seek common product benefits allows marketing managers to develop strategies targeted to these segments.

Determining the Needs of the Target Segment

Next, Sony developed a detailed questionnaire based on information from the depth interviews and sent it to a sample of newspaper publishers across the country. The survey asked about publishers' current imaging needs, photographic procedures, film use, and number of staff photographers. This survey showed the need for higher-resolution pictures. As a result of this study, Sony improved the resolution of its camera.

Developing Marketing Strategies

Before introducing the product nationally, Sony developed 150 prototypes of the product, placed them with newspaper publishers, and interviewed the publishers two to four weeks later.[12] In addition, Sony interviewed 200 additional prospective users of the camera. Interviews with newspapers that used the prototypes found that users wanted a lighter-weight recorder so that pictures could be shown outside the office. As a result, Sony introduced a portable viewer.

Additional interviews with prospective users found that they placed heavy emphasis on the benefits of the total system, which included camera, recorder, and video monitor. This information resolved the question of how to position the Mavica. Sony was debating whether to advertise the camera and emphasize photography or to advertise the total system and emphasize imaging. Sony chose the latter positioning.[13]

As a result of this research, the elements of Sony's strategy were now in place:

- Position the Mavica as a total imaging system.
- In so doing, emphasize the benefits of high resolution and portable imaging.
- Introduce a new recorder to meet the need for portability.
- Advertise in media directed to newspaper publishers.

The Mavica was introduced in December 1987 based on this strategy.

Evaluating Marketing Strategies

Having introduced the Mavica, Sony then interviewed users in an attempt to answer the following questions:

- Is the product meeting the needs of the target segment?
- Are users' perceptions of the product consistent with the advertising message?
- Is the message reaching the target segment?
- Is the target segment purchasing the product?
- Are the attitudes of users positive enough to encourage buying more units?

With the information gathered from these questions, management evaluated its product positioning strategy, advertising plan, and media strategy. Initial sales results were positive. However, a negative answer to any of the above questions would have required changing promotional or media directions, adjusting product characteristics, or possibly taking the product off the market.

One survey of users is not enough, however. Sony currently tracks customer perceptions, attitudes, and behavior through ongoing surveys to refine the definition of its target segments and to determine whether additional changes in the product are warranted.

Assessing Future Customer Behavior

If needs, perceptions, and attitudes are closely related to consumer behavior, these characteristics can predict what consumers will do. For example, newspaper publishers who emphasize high resolution and portability in electronic news gathering are likely to buy the Mavica. Suppose, however, that a competitor such as Kodak comes out with an electronic photography system and that some newspaper publishers believe the Kodak system provides even better resolution than Sony's. The prediction would be that these companies might switch to Kodak's system based on their change in perception. Such a change might, therefore, forecast a decrease in purchases of the Mavica. On this basis, perceptions and attitudes toward brands and products can predict purchasing behavior.

There have been many attempts to use consumers' brand perceptions and attitudes to predict their purchasing behavior. The value of such predictions is that they assist management in estimating changes in consumer buying intentions. These studies have one common principle: Changes in consumers' brand perceptions or attitudes will influence future purchases.

Strategic Applications Summarized

What goes on in consumers' minds affects the planning of new marketing strategies and the evaluation of existing strategies. The development of new marketing strategies is influenced in several ways:

1. Marketing opportunity is identified by unmet needs (the need for higher-resolution pictures in newspaper photographs).
2. New products are developed and positioned to meet these needs (Sony's Mavica).
3. Successful positioning depends on consumer perceptions of the new product (perception of the Mavica as a total photography system).
4. Advertising strategy is based on communicating benefits that consumers desire (higher resolution and portability in viewing).
5. Media strategies are developed to ensure that the message reaches the target segment (newspaper publishers).

The success of marketing strategies depends on whether consumers see a brand as one that fulfills their needs, buy it as a result, and determine that the brand has met their expectations.

◆ A MODEL OF CONSUMER BEHAVIOR

The premise of this text is that marketing strategies must be based on the factors that influence consumer behavior. Figure 1.1, a simple model of consumer behavior, emphasizes the interaction between the marketer and the consumer. Consumer decision making—that is, the process of perceiving and evaluating brand information, considering how brand alternatives meet the consumer's needs, and deciding on a brand—is the central component of the model.

Two broad influences determine the consumer's choice. The first is the individual consumer whose needs, perceptions of brand characteristics, and attitudes toward alternatives influence brand choice. In addition, the consumer's demographics, lifestyle, and personality characteristics influence brand choice.

The second influence on consumer decision making is the environment. The consumer's purchasing environment is represented by culture (the norms of society and the influences of regional or ethnic subcultures), social class (the broad socioeconomic group to which the consumer belongs), and face-to-face groups (friends, family members, and reference groups). Marketing organizations are also part of the consumer's environment since these organizations provide the offerings that can satisfy consumer needs.

Communications from the environment to the consumer are necessary to influence consumer choice. These communications are primarily from face-to-face groups (friends and family) and from marketing organizations. Communications from marketing organizations are stimuli conveyed through product offerings, advertising, or by salespeople that are perceived and evaluated by the consumer in the process of decision making. Marketing research provides information to marketing organizations on consumer needs, perceptions of brand characteristics, and attitudes toward brand alternatives. From this information, marketing strategies are then developed and communicated to the consumer.

Once the consumer has made a decision, postpurchase evaluation, represented as feedback to the individual consumer, takes place. During evaluation, the consumer will learn from the experience and may change his or her pattern of acquiring information, evaluating brands, and selecting a brand. Consumption experience will directly influence whether the consumer will buy the same brand again.

A feedback loop also leads back to the environment. Consumers communicate their purchase and consumption experiences to friends and families. Marketers also seek information from consumers. They track consumer responses in the form of market share and sales data. However, such information neither tells the marketer why the consumer purchased nor provides information on the strengths and weaknesses of the marketer's brand relative to those of the competition. Therefore, marketing research is also required at this step to determine consumer reactions to the brand and to future purchase intent. This information permits management to reformulate marketing strategy to better meet consumer needs.

◆ ORGANIZATION OF THIS TEXT

The model in Figure 1.1 is an oversimplified representation of consumer behavior. The purpose of this text is to consider the components of the model in detail and, in so doing, emphasize consumer behavior applications to market-

▶**FIGURE 1.1**
Simple model of
consumer behavior

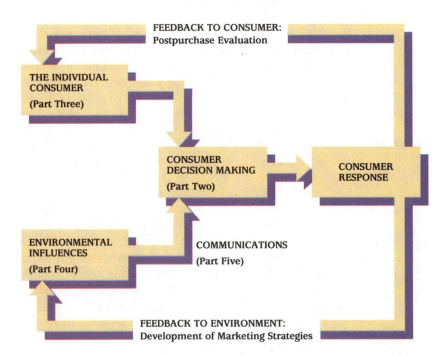

ing strategy. Figure 1.1 shows that we will consider a portion of the model in each of the remaining sections of this text. Part Two reviews consumer decision making, while Part Three discusses the individual consumer. Part Four covers the environmental factors influencing behavior, and Part Five considers communications from groups and marketing organizations to the consumer. Each of these sections is described in more detail here.

Part Two: Consumer Decision Making

The process by which consumers make purchasing decisions must be understood to develop strategic applications. Consumer decision making is not a single process. Deciding to buy a car is a different process from deciding to buy toothpaste. Figure 1.2 presents a typology of consumer decision making based on two dimensions: (1) the extent of decision making and (2) the degree of involvement in the purchase.

The first dimension represents a continuum from decision making to habit. Consumers can base their decisions on a cognitive (thought) process of information search and evaluation of brand alternatives. On the other hand, little or no decision making may take place when the consumer is satisfied with a particular brand and purchases it consistently.

The second dimension depicts a continuum from high to low involvement purchases. **High involvement purchases** are those that are important to the consumer. Such purchases are closely tied to the consumer's ego and self-image. They involve some risk to the consumer: financial (high-priced items), social (products important to the peer group), or psychological (the wrong decision might cause some concern and anxiety). In such cases, it is worth the consumer's time and energies to consider product alternatives carefully. **Low involvement purchases** are not as important to the consumer; and financial, social, and psychological risks are not nearly as great. In such cases, it may not

▶**FIGURE 1.2**
Consumer decision making

	HIGH INVOLVEMENT PURCHASE DECISION	LOW INVOLVEMENT PURCHASE DECISION
DECISION MAKING (information search, consideration of brand alternatives)	COMPLEX DECISION MAKING (autos, electronics, photography systems) Chapter 3	LIMITED DECISION MAKING (adult cereals, snack foods) Chapter 5
HABIT (little or no information search, consideration of only one brand)	BRAND LOYALTY (athletic shoes, adult cereals) Chapter 4	INERTIA (canned vegetables, paper towels) Chapter 5

be worth the consumer's time and effort to search for information about brands and to consider a wide range of alternatives. Therefore, a low involvement purchase generally entails a limited process of decision making.

Decision making versus habit and low involvement versus high involvement produce four types of consumer purchase processes. The first process, called **complex decision making,** takes place when involvement is high and decision making occurs (upper left-hand box). Examples might be the decision to buy an electronic photography system such as the Mavica or the decision to buy an automobile. In such cases, consumers actively search for information to evaluate and consider alternative brands by applying specific criteria such as resolution and portability for an electronic photography system or economy, durability, and service for an automobile.

Complex decision making will not occur every time the consumer purchases a brand. When choice is repetitive, the consumer learns from past experience and with little or no decision making buys the brand that is most satisfactory. Such **brand loyalty** is the result of repeated satisfaction and a strong commitment to a particular brand (lower left-hand box). Examples might be the purchase of Nike basketball sneakers or of Kellogg's Nutrific cereal. In each case, the purchase is important to the consumer (basketball shoes because of involvement in the sport; adult cereals because of the importance of nutrition). The consumer establishes brand loyalty based on satisfaction with past purchases. As a result, information search and brand evaluation are limited or nonexistent as the consumer has decided to buy the same brand again.

Figure 1.2 also illustrates two types of consumer purchase processes in which the consumer is not involved with the product. First, a decision in a low involvement condition is likely to be characterized by **limited decision making** (upper right-hand box). Consumers sometimes go through a decision process in buying, even if they are not highly involved, because they have little past experience with a product. For example, a new line of microwaveable snacks may be introduced. Not aware of or involved with the product category, the consumer examines the package in the store and purchases the product on a trial basis to compare to regular snack foods. In making this purchase, the consumer uses limited information search and evaluation of brand alternatives, as compared to those purchases that involve complex decision making.

Limited decision making is also likely to take place when consumers seek variety. When involvement is low, consumers are more likely to switch brands out of boredom and in a search for variety.[14] **Variety-seeking behavior** is likely to occur when risks are minimal and when the consumer has less commitment to a particular brand. Since the brand decision is not important enough to be preplanned, the consumer is likely to make the decision inside the store. For example, a consumer may decide to try a new brand of cookies or an adult cereal for variety's sake as there is little to lose.

Notice that adult cereals appear as products that could be characterized by both brand loyalty and limited decision making. This shows that the decision processes shown in Figure 1.2 are consumer-specific rather than product-specific. That is, the degree of involvement and decision making depends more on the consumer's attitude to the product than on the product's characteristics. One consumer might be involved with adult cereals because of their nutritional value; another might regard them as pretty much the same and switch brands in a search for variety.

The fourth choice process in Figure 1.2 is **inertia** (lower right-hand box), or low involvement with the product and no decision making. Inertia means the consumer is buying the same brand, not because of brand loyalty, but because it is not worth the time and trouble to search for an alternative. Robertson states that under low involvement conditions "brand loyalty may reflect only the convenience inherent in repetitive behavior rather than commitment to the brand purchased."[15] Examples might be the purchase of canned vegetables or paper towels.

Part Three: The Individual Consumer

The manner in which the individual consumer influences the decision process is central to an understanding of consumer behavior. The consumer's role in the decision process is presented in Figure 1.3.

The first influence on consumer choice is stimuli. Stimuli represent information consumers perceive. **Information processing** occurs when consumers evaluate information from advertising, friends, or their own product experiences by organizing and interpreting it.

The second and central influence on consumer choice is the consumer. The consumer is represented by thought variables and characteristics. **Consumer**

▶**FIGURE 1.3**
The individual consumer

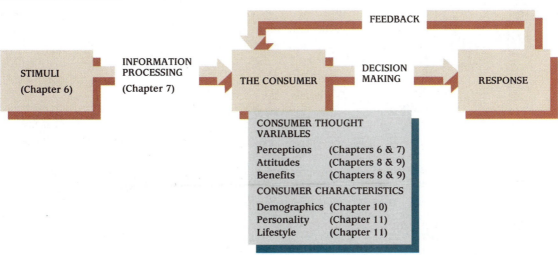

thought variables are the cognitive factors that influence decision making. Three types of thought variables play an essential role in decision making: perceptions of a brand's characteristics, attitudes toward the brand, and the benefits consumers desire.

Consumer characteristics are variables such as demographics, lifestyle, and personality characteristics that are used to describe consumers. The marketing manager first determines whether or not these characteristics are related to behavior and then tries to use this knowledge to influence behavior. If users of nutritionally oriented adult cereals tend to be young, high-income earners, and well educated, marketing managers can design advertising messages to appeal to this group. Media that are most likely to be read or seen by this target group will be selected. If heavy users of pain relievers tend to be compulsive, this knowledge can guide the advertiser in developing appeals to the compulsive personality. An appeal could suggest a strict routine in using analgesics and could portray the benefits received by regular and systematic use.

The third influence on consumer choice—consumer response—is the end result of the consumer's decision process and is an integral consideration throughout this text. Although consumer response most frequently refers to brand choice, there are other facets of consumer response such as choice of a product category (purchase of diet soda), choice of a store (purchase of a refrigerator in a department store), choice of a particular communications medium (a decision to read a magazine or listen to a salesperson to get information), or choice of a cause (contributions to the American Heart Association).

Part Four: Environmental Influences

Figure 1.3 accounts for only the internal influences on consumer behavior; that is, the consumers' characteristics and states of mind. As Figure 1.4 shows, consumers are also affected by **environmental variables:** culture, face-to-face groups, and situational determinants.

Culture refers to widely shared norms and patterns of behavior of a large group of people. For example, a generally accepted norm in American society is the emphasis on slimness as a sign of vitality and success. The consequent emphasis on diet foods is a cultural influence.

Subcultures refer to groups with norms and values that distinguish them from the culture as a whole. For example, Hispanics are considered a subculture within American society. **Cross-cultural influences** identify differences in cultural values between nations. Managers have given cross-cultural influences greater attention because of increased investments abroad as domestic markets stagnate. The consistent lesson American managers have learned is that they cannot export American strategies abroad. If they are to market their products successfully abroad, managers must adjust to the specific needs and cultural orientations of foreign consumers. (See Strategic Applications box.)

▶**FIGURE 1.4**
Environmental influences

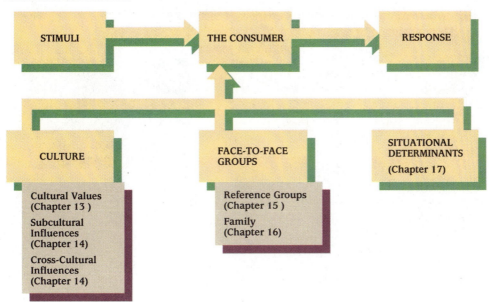

Face-to-face groups are important sources of information and influence for the consumer. Some face-to-face groups are called **reference groups** because they provide consumers with a means of comparing and evaluating their own brand attitudes and purchasing behavior. The most likely group to influence purchasing behavior is the family.

The final environmental variable to be considered in Part Three is situation. **Situational determinants** are important because brand preferences vary, depending on the reason for which the brand is purchased. When asked whether a certain beverage, perfume, or automobile is preferred, the consumer may quite logically say, "It depends on the situation." Preferences for coffee brands have been shown to vary, depending on situations such as "when alone," "feeling sleepy," or "after I wake up in the morning."[16] Preferences for snack products have also varied markedly, depending on whether they are purchased for parties or for afternoon or bedtime snacks.[17]

Part Five: Communications

Communications from the environment provide information to influence consumers. Figure 1.5 shows that communications can be from groups or from the marketing organization. Group communications can occur within or across groups. Within groups, communication is by word-of-mouth. For example, one friend tells another that a certain brand of cold tablets is most effective, or one

Lack of adequate knowledge of foreign consumers' needs and customs often results in American companies mismarketing abroad. Consider Procter & Gamble (P&G), a company renowned for its ability to meet the needs of American consumers with leading packaged goods such as Tide detergent, Crest toothpaste, Folgers coffee, and Pampers disposable diapers. Until recently, when it came to marketing in Japan, P&G appeared to be a novice. It made the basic mistake of assuming the marketing strategies that worked at home would also work abroad.

Its experience in disposable diapers was instructive. In the words of its current CEO, when P&G introduced Pampers in Japan in 1977, it used "American products, American advertising, and American sales methods and promotional strategies." The product was relatively thick and bulky, designed for American mothers who intended to leave diapers on their babies for longer periods. P&G did not realize that Japanese women are among the most compulsive cleaners in the world and change their babies' diapers twice as often as the average American mother. Japanese companies saw an opening and introduced a thinner, leak-resistant diaper better suited to the needs of Japanese mothers. As a result, Pampers' market share plummeted from 90 percent in 1977 to 7 percent in 1985.

At that point, a new head of international operations, Edward Artzt, recognized the fallacy of ignoring cross-cultural differences and encouraged development of an improved diaper with one-third the thickness of the original model. By 1990, the new diaper captured almost one-third of the Japanese market and became the prototype for Ultra Pampers in the United States.

P&G is now a company attuned to cross-cultural differences, especially since Artzt became CEO. From 1990 to 1993, under Artzt's leadership, the company became a world player in cosmetics. It is also aggressively moving into Eastern Europe. In each case, it is not doing so hesitantly, given its new-found confidence in defining and meeting the needs of foreign consumers.

Sources: "Procter & Gamble Is Following Its Nose," *Business Week* (April 22, 1991), p. 28; "At Procter & Gamble, Change Under Artzt Isn't Just Cosmetic," *The Wall Street Journal* (March 5, 1991), pp. A1 and A8; "Japan Rises to P&G's No. 3 Market," *Advertising Age* (December 10, 1990), p. 42; Edward Artzt, "Winning in Japan: Keys to Global Success," *Business Quarterly* (Winter, 1989), pp. 12–16.

▶**FIGURE** 1.5
Communications (Part Five)

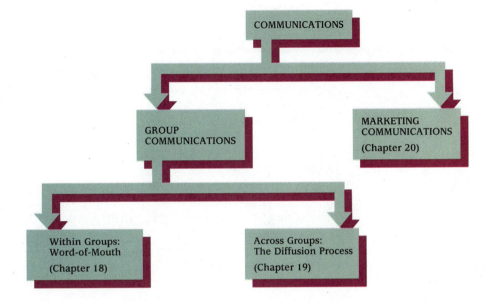

business associate tells another that a stock is a poor buy. The individual who influences the consumer is frequently an **opinion leader.**

Communication across groups occurs through a process of diffusion of information and influence. Marketers are most interested in diffusion of information about new products. The individual who is usually the first to buy new products and to influence others to buy is known as the **innovator.** The acceptance of new products across groups is particularly important to the marketer as new product development directly influences the firm's profit position.

Marketing communications occur primarily through advertising. However, other forms of information and influence may be equally or more important. New regulations requiring nutritional information on products have made packages a more important source of information. Salespeople are often the primary source of information and influence, particularly when consumers have a wide choice of alternatives for complex products such as computers or major appliances. In-store displays are also an important source of information about coupons, special offers, and prices.

◆ CONSUMER BEHAVIOR FROM A CONSUMER'S PERSPECTIVE

Until now, we have emphasized the managerial implications of studying consumer behavior. This is a logical perspective for current and future business managers. However, consumer behavior can take on a very different perspective through consumers' eyes.

Managerial Versus Consumer Perspectives

Managerial and consumer perspectives differ on at least three dimensions. First, most marketing strategies are product-specific. Managers introduce, price, advertise, and distribute individual brands. Consumers must make decisions across a range of brand alternatives. Further, consumers often view an individual product as part of a larger constellation that reflects their lifestyles. Buying health foods, wearing Levi jeans and Reebok sneakers, and owning a cellular telephone may not appear to be related; but they may reflect the lifestyle and desires of an individual consumer. These products are related in the consumer's mind, not in the marketer's.

Second, because of the profit motive, managers have a vested interest in presenting their products in the best light possible. Consumers are interested in evaluating information in light of their own needs. As a result, managers tend to view product information as a vehicle for influence. Consumers view information as a vehicle for making better choices.

Third, managers view competition as a threat. Consumers view competition as an opportunity to gain additional alternatives, frequently at lower prices.

Consumerism

The differences between the managerial and consumer views of consumer behavior could lead to potential abuses by marketers and suboptimal choices by consumers. The manager's product-specific, profit-oriented, anticompetitive perspective could lead to deceptive advertising, limited product choices, inadequate attention to product safety, and an attempt to skirt ecological responsibilities.

Fortunately, these inequities are the exception rather than the rule. In most cases, abuses of consumer rights do not occur because of the inherent protection of a free marketplace. Marketers can best maximize profits by offering consumers quality products and accurate information to ensure a loyal customer base. However, abuses have occurred with enough regularity to promote what has come to be known as **consumerism;** that is, the protection of consumer rights by consumer groups, government agencies, and at times even business organizations.

Consumerism, the public policy representation of the consumer perspective, attempts to ensure the consumer's right to product safety, accurate information, sufficient choice, and a clean environment. As such, it is the countervailing force to a managerial perspective of consumer behavior.

Much of this text is devoted to a study of the marketing strategy implications of consumer behavior; that is, the managerial perspective. In the next chapter, we consider consumerism and consumer rights to ensure that we do not lose sight of the consumer perspective.

SUMMARY

This introductory chapter has established the text's orientation by linking consumer behavior to marketing strategy. The need for consumer information to establish marketing strategies is recognized. Such consumer information permits marketing managers to:

- Define and segment markets.
- Identify the needs of these segments.
- Develop marketing strategies.
- Evaluate marketing strategies.
- Assess future customer behavior.

A historical perspective shows that a consumer orientation developed out of economic necessity in the 1950s. With the advent of a buyer's market, marketing managers began to identify consumer needs in a competitive environment and to gear marketing strategies accordingly. A better understanding of consumer needs, perceptions, attitudes, and intentions became necessary.

The text is organized after the model in Figure 1.1, which has four components: consumer decision making and the three elements that influence consumer decision making—the individual consumer, environmental influences, and communications from the environment to the consumer. In addition to the introductory section, these four components make up the four parts of the text.

Part Two describes the types of consumer decision making: complex decision making, habit, and high and low involvement decision making.

In Part Three, the individual consumer's brand perceptions, attitudes, and desired benefits are considered. They are referred to as consumer thought variables as they involve a consumer's cognitive assessment of brands and products. Part Three also examines the consumer's characteristics, demographics, lifestyle, and personality.

In Part Four, the environment in which the consumer makes decisions is considered. Culture provides the broadest environmental perspective. Face-to-face groups, particularly the family, are the most important sources of information and influence. Situational determinants describing when, where, and why a product is purchased or consumed represent another set of environmental influences.

Part Five provides the link between the consumer and his or her environment by describing communications from groups and from the marketing organization. Communications within groups take place by word-of-mouth and are influenced by opinion leaders. Communications across groups take place through a process of diffusion of information and are influenced by innovators. Marketing communications are primarily through advertising, but they may also occur by personal selling, sales promotion, and packaging.

Much of the text focuses on the managerial implications of consumer behavior. It is also important to recognize a consumer-oriented perspective that recognizes the consumer's rights to accurate information, adequate choices, safe products, and a clean environment. The next chapter takes such a consumer-oriented perspective.

QUESTIONS

1. Why did Levi Strauss & Co. switch from a mass-market strategy to a strategy of market segmentation?

2. A vice president of marketing for a large soft drink company often states that sales are the ultimate criterion of marketing effectiveness, and, therefore, one must look primarily at the relationship between marketing stimuli (price, advertising, deals, coupons) and sales. What arguments could you, as director of marketing research, present in support of behavioral research to demonstrate that sales figures alone are not sufficient to evaluate marketing strategies?

3. What do the hypothetical memos showing the differences in orientation at Avon in 1975 and 1995 imply for (a) marketing research, (b) product positioning, and (c) market segmentation?

4. What evidence is there that Sony's management subscribed to the marketing concept in its investigation of the opportunity to introduce an electronic photography system for newspaper publishers?

5. Could the research steps outlined in Sony's test of the new electronic photography system also be used as a prototype in testing (a) a new pain reliever that can be taken without water, (b) a high-potency vitamin for children, or (c) a portable cellular phone system designed for organizations? Why or why not?

6. The 1950s and 1960s are regarded as a time when the marketing concept and a consumer orientation were widely accepted.
   - What trends might occur in the 1990s?
   - What impact might greater emphasis on conservation have on acceptance of the marketing concept?
   - Will there be changes in consumer priorities (for example, performance vs. style, value and quality vs. lower price, or nutrition vs. taste)? If so, will marketing organizations adjust to these changes?

7. The distinction made in Figure 1.2 between decision making and habit is fairly commonplace. Less common is the distinction between decision making and variety seeking.
   - What is the nature of the distinction?
   - What are the marketing implications?
   - Do all purchases of a new brand or switches from one brand to another involve a process of extensive information search and brand evaluation? Why or why not?

8. Another distinction in Figure 1.2 is between brand loyalty and inertia.
   - What is the nature of this distinction?
   - What are the marketing implications?

9. In most cases, marketing studies are concerned with brand or product choice. However, in some cases, the focus may more appropriately be on store choice or even on the choice of media.
   • Under what conditions might store choice be more influential than brand or product characteristics in the consumer's final decision?
   • Under what circumstances might the media environment (types of magazines, TV shows, radio programs) be more influential than brand characteristics in the consumer's final choice?
10. What is the importance of consumerism? Why is it a countervailing force to a managerial perspective of consumer behavior?

RESEARCH ASSIGNMENTS

1. Do a content analysis of two issues of *Advertising Age,* one from about 1960 and one current issue, by determining the frequency of the appearance of certain basic marketing references.
   • How frequently mentioned in the 1960 and the current issues are (a) marketing research, (b) test marketing, (c) new product development, (d) market segmentation, (e) product positioning, (f) lifestyles, (g) advertising regulation, (h) environmental concerns, and (i) advertising to African-Americans and Hispanic-Americans?
   • What are the implications of the frequency of the references to these subjects in 1960 and currently?
2. Attempt to trace a large manufacturer's development of a marketing concept and evolution of a behavioral orientation for consumer packaged goods. Do so by tracing references to the company in business periodicals and, when possible, by interviewing company executives who have been with the company in marketing for ten years or more.
   • What has been the change in marketing research procedures, particularly in regard to (a) product testing, (b) advertising evaluation, (c) instore testing, and (d) utilization of concepts of market segmentation and product positioning?
   • What changes have occurred in the organization of the research function?
   • Do the changes in the company reflect the changes at Avon as depicted in the memos written in 1975 and 1995?

NOTES

1. "Slow Fade," *Marketing & Media Decisions* (October, 1990), p. 64; and "Levi Strauss & Co.'s Dockers Weigh Into Casuals," *Adweek's Marketing Week* (September 24, 1990), p. 26.

2. *Marketing & Media Decisions* (October, 1990), p. 64.

3. "Levi's Two New Campaigns Aim at Who Fits the Jeans," *The New York Times* (July 27, 1992).

4. "For Levi's, a Flattering Fit Overseas," *Business Week* (November 5, 1990), pp. 76–77.

5. "Levi Strauss, Leaving China, Passes Crowd of Firms Going the Other Way," *The Wall Street Journal* (May 5, 1993).

6. "Marketing: The New Priority," *Business Week* (November 21, 1983), p. 96.

7. "Sears Trims Operations, Ending an Era," *The Wall Street Journal* (January 26, 1993), p. B1; and "Sears Will Return to Retailing Focus," *The New York Times* (September 30, 1992), pp. A1 and D7.

8. "Affirmative Grunts," *Forbes* (March 2, 1992), pp. 90–91.

9. "Direct Selling Is Alive and Well," *Sales & Marketing Management* (August, 1988), p. 76; and "Fresher Face at Avon," *Management Today* (December, 1984), p. 60.

10. "Avon Answers Calling to Higher Scent Lines," *Advertising Age* (March 28, 1988), p. S-4.

11. "Sony: Sorting Out the Sales Suspects," *Business Marketing* (August, 1988), p. 44.

12. *Ibid.,* p. 46.

13. *Ibid.,* pp. 46, 48.

14. M. Venkatesan, "Cognitive Consistency and Novelty Seeking," in Scott Ward and Thomas S. Robertson, eds., *Consumer Behavior: Theoretical Sources* (Englewood Cliffs, N.J.: Prentice-Hall, 1973), pp. 354–384.

15. Thomas S. Robertson, "Low-Commitment Consumer Behavior," *Journal of Advertising Research,* 16 (April, 1976), p. 20.

16. Russell W. Belk, "Situational Variables and Consumer Behavior," *Journal of Consumer Research* (December, 1975), p. 162.

17. Private communication based on a study by a large food company.

2

Consumerism

THE BODY SHOP: A FOCUS ON CONSUMER RIGHTS AND CORPORATE RESPONSIBILITY

In Chapter 1, the focus was primarily on the strategic implications of consumer behavior. However, equally as important are considerations of consumer rights in the marketplace. Consumers have a right to accurate and full information, to safe products, to adequate product choices, and to products that do not harm the environment. Businesses have occasionally overlooked these rights in their zeal to maximize profits, though now firms are becoming more responsible in factoring them into a strategic focus. A cutting-edge example of this is Anita Roddick, an iconoclastic Londoner who is being hailed as a model for marketing in the 1990s.

Roddick, founder of The Body Shop, has tapped into a vein of environmentalism and corporate mistrust that runs deep among many of today's consumers. In her native Britain, for instance, one study suggests that 56 percent of shoppers are suspicious of environmental claims.[1] "Consumers crave information, not another bloody marketing hyperbole," says Roddick.[2] Roddick clings to a simple credo: Make sure your customers trust you to sell them products that are part of the solution, not the problem.

Roddick has been following her own advice since 1976, when she opened her first London store full of bottles filled with her handmade lotions and shampoos. Roddick drew a solid following among a new generation of consumers who were carefully scouring labels for proof that products they bought were all natural.[3]

The Body Shop's popularity really took off in the mid-'80s, when a wave of consumer protests were launched against companies accused of abusing animals for commercial profit. Widely publicized boycotts were organized against fur makers for inhumanely trapping minks and against cosmetics companies for testing their products on animals.[4] Roddick became one of the movement's most fiery supporters, going so far as to sell bath soaps in the shape of endangered animals and to label her products with the explicit promise that she did not engage in animal testing.[5]

That, however, would have been of little impact had her products not caught the imagination of shoppers. Blue corn oil made by indigenous Indian tribes from the American Southwest became a best-selling face lotion; mixtures from obscure African villages began appearing in bathrooms from Duluth to Dallas. By 1993, she was ringing up $266 million in sales from 900 stores.[6] That reach has led Roddick to attempt to influence how her shoppers act once they leave her stores. She encourages recycling, for instance, with an offer that gives a discount to those who bring back empty bottles for refilling.[7]

Roddick's critics accuse her of latching onto every cause to build her media celebrity status, thereby getting free advertising. Roddick waves off such criticism, saying that she is trying to create a new definition of corporate responsibility. "I thought it was very important that my business concern itself not just with hair and skin preparation, but also with the community, the environment, and the big wide world beyond cosmetics," she says.[8] (See Exhibit 2.1.)

Clearly, Roddick's business ethics are perfectly timed for the desires of a public that has begun to rebel against businesses that purposefully mislead, offer a restricted choice of alternatives, or sell unsafe products. The manifestation of this trend has come to be known as **consumerism.** Broadly defined, consumerism is activities by consumer groups, government agencies, and at times business organizations that are designed to protect the consumer.[9]

In this chapter, we explore consumerism, its historical antecedents, and its likely status in the rest of the 1990s. We focus on three trends that have defined consumerism in the 1990s:

1. Greater importance of environmental protection.
2. Greater control over health and nutritional claims.
3. Regulation of advertising directed to children.

In the rest of the chapter, we will explore the basic rights of consumers in the marketplace.

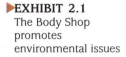

EXHIBIT 2.1
The Body Shop promotes environmental issues

◆ CONSUMERISM

The primary concern of consumerism is to ensure the consumer's rights in the process of exchange. These rights include the right to be informed, to be told the truth, to be given adequate alternatives, and to be assured of safety in the process of consumption. These activities have come to be known as the **consumer movement.**[10]

Three types of organizations make up the consumer movement: (1) consumer-oriented groups concerned primarily with increasing consumer consciousness and providing consumers with information to improve their basis for choice, (2) government through legislation and regulation, and (3) at times, business through competition and self-regulation. These forces are summarized in Figure 2.1.

Role of Consumer Activists and Organizations

The most visible forces in the consumer movement have been consumer activists. Upton Sinclair exposed the unsanitary conditions in Chicago's meat packinghouses in his book *The Jungle*. During the Depression in the 1930s, several authors continued to expose unsafe food and drug products. In the 1960s, Rachel Carson wrote about the dangers of pesticides and food additives in her book *Silent Spring*, and Ralph Nader wrote about the failure of the automobile

▶**FIGURE 2.1**

Agencies involved in consumerism

Source: Adapted from Jagdish N. Sheth and Nicholas Mammana, "Why Consumer Protection Efforts Are Likely to Fail," Faculty Working Paper No. 104, College of Commerce and Business Administration, University of Illinois at Urbana-Champaign, April 11, 1973, p. 3. Reprinted with permission from Jagdish N. Sheth, Emory University.

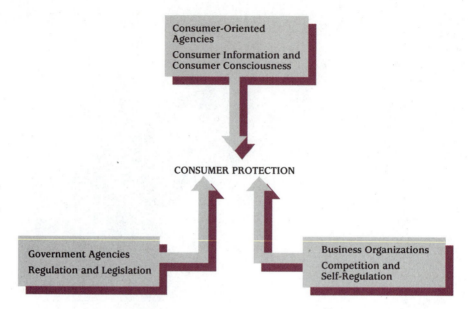

industry to maintain safety standards in *Unsafe at Any Speed*. In the 1980s, Dennis Hayes founded an environmental group, called Green Seal, to monitor environmental claims and to expose companies that use such claims to sell products without protecting the environment.

Consumer Organizations

Consumers Union, the oldest consumer group established in 1936 as a product-testing and consumer education agency, now has a membership of 2 million and publishes *Consumer Reports* magazine. It has undertaken broad consumer education programs regarding interest rates, life insurance, product safety, doctor selection, and the problems of low-income consumers. Consumers regard Consumers Union as an objective, impartial third party that can assess product quality and consumer complaints through its product-testing facilities.

Other groups such as the Sierra Club, the National Audubon Society, and Greenpeace have been active on environmental issues. In another area of concern, the Citizen Health Research Group and the Center for Science in the Public Interest monitor health claims. The latter is also active in monitoring cigarette and alcohol advertising to minorities and teens.

Consumer Boycotts

One primary means consumer activists and organizations have used to pressure business organizations is boycotts. Protesting higher prices, supermarket boycotts in 1966 and meat boycotts in 1973 received national attention. One of the most effective boycotts was of California grapes to protest grape growers' treatment of migrant workers.

In 1988, thousands of consumers joined Action for Corporate Accountability when it resumed a lapsed six-year boycott of Nestle S.A. for violating World Health Organization standards on marketing infant formula to developing nations.[11] Then, in 1990, a potential boycott of H. J. Heinz's Star-Kist tuna and Van Camp's Chicken of the Sea caused both companies to promote a plan to protect dolphins when fishermen net tuna.[12]

Overall, consumers' group action has been sporadic and uncoordinated. For instance, in 1991, Jesse Jackson's PUSH organization tried convincing the major sneaker companies to put their money in black-owned banks and to hire African-American executives, but the organization had few tangible results. The feminist organization Media Watch tried to boycott *Guess?* jeans for sexist advertising and had mixed results. On average, there are more than 100 national boycotts each year and most fail.[13] The reason is that consumers are difficult to organize and to represent because of their diverse interests.

The Role of Government

Government has a responsibility to protect consumer interests and does so through legislation and the actions of regulatory agencies. In the area of legislation, Congress has enacted safety standards for new and used automobiles, outlawed deceptive packaging, required warning labels on cigarettes, and mandated full disclosure of all finance charges in consumer credit agreements. States also have a legislative role in protecting consumer rights. State laws have required unit pricing on food products and open dating of perishable foods and drugs. States and local communities have also enforced laws regarding recycling and waste disposal.

Federal regulatory agencies play a critical role in ensuring consumer rights. The two most important are the **Federal Trade Commission (FTC)** and **Food and Drug Administration (FDA).** The FTC, established in 1914 to curb the monopoly powers of big business and unfair trade practices, is also a watchdog over deceptive advertising. The FDA, created in 1906 as a result of the outcry over Sinclair's *The Jungle*, sets product standards and requires disclosure of product contents. The **Federal Communications Commission (FCC),** oversees advertising directed to children.

Two other agencies, established in the 1970s, are important. The **Consumer Product Safety Commission (CPSC)** is empowered to set product safety standards to protect consumers from risk or injury. The **Environmental Protection Agency (EPA)** sets controls on industry emissions, toxic wastes, and automobile pollution.

The Role of Business Organizations

Business has acted to protect consumer rights in two ways: through responses to government regulation and through self-regulation. In reacting to government, businesses must conform to a variety of laws dealing with areas such as pollution controls, product safety, product labeling, truth in advertising, and controls over price fixing and antimonopoly activities. They must also conform to guidelines established by regulatory agencies such as the FTC's restrictions on deceptive advertising and health and the FDA's nutritional labeling requirements.

Since 1991, the FDA has been particularly active in controlling health claims and ensuring accurate labeling. Based on FDA actions in a two-year period, Kraft-General Foods had to stop exaggerating the calcium content of its Kraft Singles cheese;[14] Citrus Hill was made to take the word *fresh* off its orange juice label because it is made from concentrate; and restaurants have been ordered to begin backing up nutrition claims with hard data on their menus.[15]

More progressive companies have relied on self-regulation to gain advantage by acting before regulatory agencies tell them to do so or before consumers pressure them to do so. Many are adopting sophisticated antipollution policies, forthright labeling practices, and new channels for customers to exercise their rights. For example, Lever Brothers commits itself to using recycled plastics in packages for its household products; General Electric spends millions on reducing pollutants that deplete the ozone barrier; Procter & Gamble is advertising refills for its products to reduce waste by 25–35 percent (see Exhibit 2.2); and Wal-Mart is experimenting with an eco-store that features recycling as its wall-to-wall theme.[16]

 ## CONSUMERISM: A GLOBAL PERSPECTIVE

Consumerism is not just an American phenomenon. In fact, for much of the past 20 years, it has been a global one. The ecological focus of consumerism began in Western Europe, where the Green movement took root as a political movement in the early 1980s to protest acid rain's detrimental impact on Europe's forests. By decade's end, Greens had become establishment politicians, accounting for 14.5 percent of the parliamentary vote in the United Kingdom, 14 percent in Belgium, 8.4 percent in West Germany, and 10.5 percent in France.[17]

The Greens pressured federal, state, and local agencies in their countries to mobilize; and these agencies, in turn, made the message clear to industry. Non-pulp diapers were introduced in Britain; Germany's federal Environmental Protection Agency established a Blue Angel label for products declared environ-

▶**EXHIBIT 2.2**

Procter & Gamble advertises package refills to reduce waste

Source: ©The Procter & Gamble Company. Used with permission.

mentally sound (see Exhibit 2.3); an Ecover line of nonpolluting cleaning products was sold in Belgium; and a line of green products was unveiled in Canada.[18]

The cat food ad in Exhibit 2.3 shows that the concern of businesses in Europe can extend to ecological issues—in this case, the preservation of the Siberian Tiger. Overall, the public mood seems best summed by a 1990 poll that showed 75 percent of Western European consumers factored in the greenness of a product when making their decision.[19]

Unfortunately, in other parts of the globe, consumerism has received little emphasis. This is particularly true in Japan, where a powerful alignment between government and industry has all but ignored consumers' preferences by forming a protective barrier that has succeeded in excluding foreign competition.[20] While cooperation between government and industry may be suited to Japanese preferences for harmony and consensus, it leaves consumers with fewer brand alternatives. However, because of the first victory in 1993 of

▶EXHIBIT 2.3
Environmental issues
are a global concern

parties more sympathetic to free- trade principles and consumer rights, the pendulum may soon start swinging toward consumerism.

The same trend can be seen in some quarters of the former Soviet Union. Through much of this century, the chokehold of centralized planning and massive spending on arms led to one environmental crisis after another. The most famous was the nuclear meltdown at Chernobyl. As former EPA head William Reilly has written:

> To those who doubt the wisdom of pollution control . . . let them travel to Eastern Europe. Let them see the Vistula River in Poland, over 80 percent of it so corrosive that it is useless for even cooling machinery. Let them experience sulfur dioxide levels in Krakow, so high that 500-year-old monuments have crumbled in just 40 years. Let them confront Eastern Europe's high rate of infant mortality, lung disorders, worker absenteeism, and premature death. Poland, Hungary, Bulgaria, Romania and Czechoslovakia, not to mention Russia itself—these are entire nations living in the dark shadow of an environmental catastrophe.[21]

Though the going has been painfully slow and hampered by divisive fighting and internal squabbling, the Bush and Clinton administrations have attempted to furnish these countries with loans, technology, and education to correct the mistakes of the past 50 years. To quote Reilly, "There is such a thing as capitalism with a green thumb."

 ## THE HISTORY OF CONSUMERISM IN AMERICA

Three Periods of Consumerism from 1890 to 1980

The first recorded consumer protest in this country occurred in 1775 in Massachusetts where people who sold tainted food were sentenced to the pillory.[22] The real consumer movement started at the turn of the century and was followed by three distinct periods prior to 1980 when consumer protection became a national issue. Each of these periods was marked by rising consumer prices coupled with muckraking exposes, which resulted in consumer protection legislation.[23]

First Period of Consumerism

The first period came at the turn of the century, a time when huge corporations such as Standard Oil were amassing power. As a result, the Sherman Antitrust Act was passed in 1890 to limit big business from restraining competition. Also, national brands began gaining prominence and consumers were focusing on their performance. In 1906, the FDA was established to regulate these brands. That was also the year that Sinclair's *The Jungle* created such an outcry about unsanitary food processing that Congress passed the Meat Inspection Act. Another development in this period was passage in 1914 of the Federal Trade Commission Act, which established the FTC to curb monopoly and unfair trade practices.

Second Period of Consumerism

The Great Depression and the 1933 book *100,000,000 Guinea Pigs,* which exposed unsafe medicines, cosmetics, and foods, sparked the second period of consumerism. They led to other exposés of advertising through two books, *Our Master's Voice* and *The Popular Practice of Fraud,* and exposés regarding the preparation of foodstuffs through two other books, *Eat, Drink and Be Wary* and *American Chamber of Horrors: The Truth About Food and Drugs.* Thanks to such books, Consumers Union was formed in 1936 and the Wheeler-Lea Amendment to the Federal Trade Commission Act was passed in 1938. The amendment enlarged the powers of the FTC to prosecute unfair and deceptive trade practices, particularly advertising.

Third Period of Consumerism

The third period of consumerism began in the 1960s, when another series of exposés followed the relative quiet of the post-World War II years. In 1962, Rachel Carson's *Silent Spring* made consumers aware of the dangers of pesticides and other chemicals in foods and other products. In 1965, Ralph Nader's *Unsafe at Any Speed* exposed the automobile industry's disregard for even rudimentary safety precautions. Nader's study was instrumental in the passage of laws to set safety standards for cars.

Reilly described the 1970s as a period marked by an "astonishing record of legislation to protect the environment, with the passage of laws to restrict air pollution, control toxic substances, promote resource conservation, and protect drinking water."[24] From 1974 to 1978, federal expenditures on consumer safety, job safety, and other industry-specific regulation increased by 85 percent.[25] President Carter created a cabinet post to deal with energy conservation and the environment. Further, new agencies such as the EPA were formed and older regulatory agencies were rejuvenated. The FDA became more activist, requiring additional information on food labels. The FTC established clear rules to define deceptive advertising, made cigarette companies disclose harmful tar content on their packages, and energetically investigated TV advertising's effect on children.[26] By decade's end, the FTC's budget had increased by 500 percent.[27]

Predictably, the backlash from business interests was intense. Under massive lobbying, "regulation became a dirty word" in the nation's capital and beyond.[28] The deathblow to the third period came when the Carter Administration lost its bid to create an Office of Consumer Representation. Esther Peterson, President Carter's consumer adviser, has recalled that lobbying by big business was "all out of proportion to the issue."[29]

Decline in Consumerism in the 1980s

The Reagan Administration increased the drive to deregulation and de-emphasized consumer issues. The basic philosophy was stated in the President's 1982 economic report: "While regulation is necessary to protect such vital areas as food, health and safety, too much unnecessary regulation simply adds to the costs to businesses and consumers alike without commensurate benefits."[30]

To the Reagan Administration, self-regulation was preferable to government regulation in protecting consumer interests. Regulatory agencies were required to justify their actions with a cost-benefit analysis demonstrating the value of their proposals.[31] Unlike the 1970s, where the burden of proof was on industry to ensure consumer protection, the burden was now on the regulatory agencies.

Coinciding with this shift were severe cutbacks in most of the agencies' budgets. The greatest effect on marketing came from cutbacks at the FTC, which produced a one-third reduction of staff,[32] and resulted in a sharp reduction in the regulation of advertising activities.

Environmental control was also de-emphasized, and the EPA was weakened by a 50 percent staff cut.[33] The Administration also deregulated the airline industry, substantially reduced the enforcement powers of the Consumer Product Safety Commission, eliminated the nutritional educational program at the Department of Agriculture,[34] and rolled back automobile emission and pollution control standards.

By 1989, when the Bush Administration came to power, the marketing industry had grown used to relaxed rules on everything from children's advertising to nutritional labeling. Swinging the pendulum back toward consumerism yet again, the Bush Administration slowed the pace of deregulation and put more teeth into some of the agencies that were all but ignored during the Reagan years.

By 1990, for instance, the FTC's new chairperson said that the advertising industry would be held accountable for ads or practices regarded as unfair and deceptive.[35] The Bush Administration also:

- Instituted more controls to ensure airline safety.
- Embraced new rules by the FDA to curb health claims on foods.
- Gave its tacit approval to a law limiting the number of TV commercials allowed on children's programs.[36]

If there was a single reason for this course, it was that most surveys showed American consumers thought deregulation hurt them.

◆ THE REBIRTH OF CONSUMERISM IN THE 1990s

A rebirth of consumerism has occurred in the 1990s, primarily as a reaction to the deregulation of the Reagan years. The Bush Administration initiated this rebirth, and the Clinton Administration is carrying it forward.

Three issues have dominated the attention of consumer activists, government, and business in the 1990s: (1) the environment, (2) health claims, and (3) advertising to children.[37]

The New Environmentalism

The 1990s has seen greater enforcement of environmental controls and new initiatives to promote a clean environment. The impetus for these moves does not come from government but from an increased awareness among consumers for protecting the environment. Highly publicized environmental disasters such as the Exxon Valdez oil spill and the record oil spill Iraq caused during the Gulf War in 1991 have reinforced the notion among consumers that the environment is deteriorating.

Business Week magazine has labeled this awareness *the new environmentalism* and predicted it would be "the hottest issue of the 1990s demonstrated by suburban homeowners picketing incinerator plants, cities passing new anti-dumping and recycling statutes, teenagers refusing to use foam trays in the school cafeteria." The magazine went on to say that the new environmental-ism "is about radon, toxic-waste sites, undrinkable water, summer smog alerts, overflowing garbage dumps—and anger at the deteriorating quality of life in one's community."[38]

A 1992 Roper Poll found that consumers who considered themselves the most environmentally committed (or in the parlance of the poll, True-Blue Green) nearly doubled to 20 percent since 1990.[39] Another poll showed eco-logical concerns are at the same level as those about drugs and the AIDS virus. Also, a 1992 survey by *NBC News* and *The Wall Street Journal* found that four out of five consumers believe protecting the Earth is more important than keep-ing prices down.[40]

Surveys have also found that consumers are willing to take action based on their concerns. A 1990 survey found that 25 percent of consumers stopped buy-ing the product of at least one company because they believed it was not a "good environmental citizen." This same survey also found that 14 percent of consumers stopped buying Exxon products because of the Exxon Valdez oil spill.[41] Another survey found that three out of four disposable diaper purchasers said they would switch to a biodegradable brand, even if it cost more; and 41 percent said they would cancel their newspaper subscription if they knew the publisher did not use recycled paper.[42]

However, consumer actions on the environment are limited and defined by cost. Unless consumers consider environmental products to be the equal of reg-ular brands based on quality and purpose, they are unlikely to pay the higher prices environmentally sound products often require. (See Strategic Applications box.)

The new environmentalism of the 1990s has found a voice in each of the three parties to consumerism, as shown in Figure 2.1: the consumer, govern-ment, and business organizations.

Reaction of Consumer Activists and Agencies

Increased environmental concerns have led consumer groups and politi-cians to target marketers they believe produce needless pollutants and clog pre-cious landfill space. Because landfills receive 3 billion pounds of discarded dis-posable diapers annually, Procter & Gamble, the market leader, was a prime target. P&G fought a two-pronged attack. It tried mollifying conservationists by reducing the weight of its packaging and contributing $20 million for recy-cling.[43] In addition, P&G mounted a massive corporate image campaign to prove it was part of the solution and not the problem. Unfortunately for the company, unsatisfied environmentalists and the cloth diaper industry fought back with counter-ads. (See Exhibit 2.4.)

Such actions often center on consumer organizations that have played a public role in opposing business activities that harm the environment. The most prominent is the Sierra Club, an organization that seeks to protect land areas

Americans surveyed about their buying habits routinely tell interviewers that they prefer environmentally sound products or think green when they roll their shopping carts down supermarket aisles. As genuine as these sentiments are, however, a growing body of evidence suggests that many shoppers who talk green don't always buy green.

A 1992 *Wall Street Journal* article entitled "Green Product Sales Seem To Be Wilting" was among the first to announce that retailers have begun to lower their expectations about green products based on their customers' shopping patterns. "The consumer interest just has not been there," a Kmart spokesperson told the newspaper. One irony is that despite Kmart's program that identifies environmentally sound products with a green label, the chain continues to receive floods of letters from customers who voice concern about the environment.

Green products were introduced in the late 1970s and became so popular that they spawned an entire product niche. By the late 1980s, marketers thought skyrocketing sales of green products would continue unabated for years. However, while they were rushing out with one new green product after another, several factors were combining to make customers wary of products bearing environmental labels. One of those factors has to do with the initial flood of environmental claims, which left shoppers confused and cynical.

One way companies have attempted to restore trust with their customers is through third-party agreements with groups that have respectability in the green movement. One of the better-known examples was McDonald's highly publicized teaming with the Environmental Defense Fund. After years of being attacked by the EDF for its polystyrene packaging, the company did an about-face in 1989 and joined the group in a task force to study the issue. By 1992, McDonald's had banned the plastic boxes and converted entirely to recycled paper wrappings. It also launched a $100 million annual campaign to buy recycled materials for use in building franchises.

Such relationships do not combat another problem—consumers' perceptions of price in relation to the quality of green products. Green products tend to be more expensive because of higher manufacturing costs and the research and development that goes into creating the new goods. When green goods were a novelty, shoppers were willing to spend more to test them; but as time passed, they began to apply the same value and quality standards to green products as to any other product. Some recycled tissues, for instance, are not as soft; certain recycled paper is not appropriate for all uses.

These twin concerns—value and the believability of green claims—have caused marketers to realize that they have to give consumers of

STRATEGIC APPLICATIONS OF CONSUMER BEHAVIOR

What Consumers Say About the Environment Isn't Always What They Do

green products value plus green. Among the companies in the vanguard of this is Seventh Generation, a Vermont mail-order company that sells $10 million in "products for a healthy planet" annually. In 1992, *Consumer Reports* magazine rated its toilet paper best of all recycled brands and eighth of 44 overall. "We've proven that green does not have to cost more or work less effectively," says company president Jeffrey Hollender.

If the 1990s have taught marketers a lesson, it is that there are relatively few shoppers whose buying habits are shaped by environmental issues alone. When the majority of shoppers tell pollsters that they prefer to buy green, they mean that they will choose an environmentally friendly product if it can compete with their regular brand on the basis of quality and price.

Sources: "Green Commitment: Fading Out?" *Progressive Grocer* (December, 1992), p. 5; "The Color of Money," *Superbrands* (1992), p. 30; "Industry's Response to Green Consumerism," *Journal of Business Strategy*, pp.3–7; "Green Product Sales Seem to Be Wilting," *The Wall Street Journal* (May 18, 1992), p. B1; "The Green Revolution: McDonald's," *Advertising Age* (January 29, 1991), p. 32; "McDonald's to Drop Plastic Foam Boxes. . . ," *The Wall Street Journal* (November 2, 1990), p. A3.

▶**EXHIBIT 2.4**
Advertising cloth diapers as environmentally sound.

Source: Courtesy of the National Association of Diaper Services

NINETY DAYS AGO
THIS WAS A BEAUTIFUL TREE

FIVE HUNDRED YEARS FROM NOW
IT WILL STILL BE A DISPOSABLE DIAPER

Why do they call them *"disposable diapers"* if nobody knows how to get rid of them?

A typical baby will use 6,000 of the things. Once. And that's the problem. Each year, billions of single-use diapers are filling our nation's landfills.

To counter this, Procter & Gamble, with $3.5 billion in sales from single-use diapers, is advertising its experiments with waste disposal technology. Why worry about the environment if recycling and composting are the solution to the "diaper dilemma?"

Take a look at the facts and decide for yourself.

The much advertised disposable diaper recycling experiment in Seattle ended with both city officials and P&G spokespersons saying it was an "economic flop" (*Seattle Times, 1/24/91*). And industry proposals to encourage composting of soiled diapers have drawn serious opposition from environmental experts.

It turns out the real solution doesn't require multi-million dollar engineering projects.

It only takes common sense.

According to Environmental Action Foundation, "Parents should remember that reusing materials is the best way to prevent waste and conserve resources. Period."

And you'll be glad to know that with the new, pinless diaper covers, reusable cotton diapers are as easy on parents as they are on Mother Earth.

Choose reusable cotton diapers for your baby. It does make a difference.

National Association of Diaper Services
WE MAKE THE RIGHT CHOICE EASY.

REUSABLE COTTON DIAPERS
THEY'RE MAKING MORE SENSE THAN EVER

from development and publicizes negative environmental activities. Another, the Environmental Defense Fund, attempts to increase public awareness regarding issues such as waste disposal and encourages consumers to recycle trash. (See Exhibit 2.5.) The EDF was instrumental in influencing McDonald's to change its packaging from plastics to paper.

One consumer group that highlights the positive is California's Green Cross Certification program, which awards a stamp to products made from the highest possible percentage of recycled material. Clorox was the first to receive an award for the recycled content of its bleach boxes. Willamette Industries also received one for its 40 percent recycled grocery bags.[44]

Government Controls

The new environmentalism also has resulted in renewed activism by government. The Bush Administration gave the Environmental Protection Agency new life and enforcement powers. The EPA's budget increased from $85 million in 1984 to $343 million in 1990.[45] The appointment of William Reilly, former president of the Conservation Foundation, as head of the agency evidenced a commitment to environmental protection.

Legislative activity has kept apace in the 1990s. In 1990, the Clean Air Act was passed and required companies to conform to strict controls to avoid air pollution and acid-rain emissions. The bill will cost American companies an estimated $21 billion by the turn of the century.[46] By the end of the Bush

▶**EXHIBIT 2.5**
An environmentally oriented ad from a consumer organization

Source: Courtesy of Environmental Defense Fund

IF YOU'RE NOT RECYCLING YOU'RE THROWING IT ALL AWAY.

A little reminder from the Environmental Defense Fund that if you're not recycling, you're throwing away a lot more than just your trash. You and your community can recycle. Please write the

Environmental Defense Fund at: EDF-Recycling, 257 Park Avenue South, New York, NY 10010, for a free brochure that will tell you virtually everything you need to know about recycling.

EDF Ad

Administration, however, the President's commitment to the environment had become a source of debate. For one thing, Vice President Dan Quayle's Council on Competitiveness was exempting entire industries from laws like the Clean Air Act. In addition, during the 1992 presidential campaign, Bush promised to end all restrictions on logging in the virgin forests of the Pacific Northwest and called the Endangered Species Act "a sword aimed at the jobs, families and communities of entire regions like the Northwest."[47]

The Clinton Administration has strengthened the commitment to conservation by backing Vice President Gore's call for toughening environmental laws. On assuming office in 1993, Clinton dismantled Quayle's competitiveness council, replaced it with a new White House office of Environmental Policy, and placed a former aide to Gore at its helm. Clinton also tapped another Gore protege, Carolyn Browner, to head the EPA; made Hazel O'Leary, Minnesota utility company executive known for her promotion of conservation, the Secretary of Energy; and put Senator Bruce Babbitt, a staunch environmentalist, at the helm of the Interior Department.[48] Clinton also released 26 environmental measures that the previous administration had withheld.[49]

The federal government has not undertaken this mission alone. From coast to coast, local governments are recognizing that shrinking landfill space and finite resources make environmental policy good policy. In Texas, a law that went into effect in early 1994 requires 40 percent of all solid waste to be recycled. Other states are trying to lessen gasoline consumption by encouraging car pooling, mass transit, and even walking.[50] Some municipalities are even joining with business to educate consumers. The St. Lawrence County Solid Waste Disposal Authority, for instance, has teamed up with P&C Food markets of Syracuse, New York, to give environmental shopping tours to the chain's customers.[51]

Reaction of Business

The reaction of the third leg in the consumer movement, business organizations, has been mixed. On the positive side, some companies have begun to take steps to ensure environmentally responsible actions. In late 1993, the big three American automobile makers agreed to work with the White House to create jointly the technology that would produce a reliable and well-priced car that is three times more energy efficient than present models.[52] As Exhibit 2.6 shows, Japanese car makers such as Honda have begun using their fuel efficiency to appeal to environmentally minded consumers.

Companies have taken other actions to promote environmental controls; for example:

- Levi Strauss & Co. and Absolut vodka promote recycling, while Crane Papers advertises the natural content of its products. (See Exhibit 2.7.)
- McDonald's switched from plastic to paper wrapping and uses recyclable products to build its restaurants.

► **EXHIBIT 2.6**
Honda appeals to the
environmentally
conscious consumer

- Following McDonald's lead, six major paper users, among them Time Warner and Johnson & Johnson, agreed in 1993 to help the Environmental Defense Fund build a market for recycled paper by using second-hand pulp.[53]
- Sears, Roebuck & Co. has asked its 2,300 suppliers to cut packaging use 25 percent, while Pepsi-Cola has introduced 2-liter bottles made from 25 percent recycled materials.[54]
- Monsanto organized a task force of scientists and engineers to analyze the effects of any new materials and chemicals on the environment and on users. It views the task force as an "early warning system" that is intended to "blow the whistle on any new product concept that may introduce unacceptable hazards to users."[55]

Marketers have also unleashed a torrent of new products with environmental claims. In 1991, 13.4 percent of all consumer products introduced were positioned as green, up from 4.3 percent in 1989.[56]

On the negative side, many of these "green" claims are dubious at best. These questionable environmental claims relate primarily to two areas—biodegradability and recycling. Biodegradability is an issue because products that do not decompose will remain pollutants for years. Concern with plastics is greatest. As a result, Hefty, Glad, and Handi-Wrap trash bags have added chemicals to promote the decomposition of their products and have advertised them as degradable. The problem is that biodegradability requires the action of sunlight, and most of these products wind up in landfills where they do not

▶**EXHIBIT 2.7**
Promoting recycling

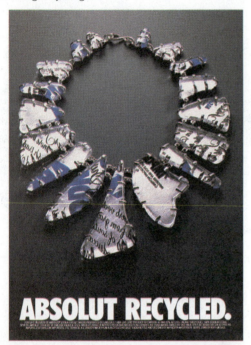

Source: Courtesy of Levi Strauss & Co.

Source: Courtesy of Crane & Co. Inc.

actually decompose. Companies producing products such as food wrap, cups, and fast-food foam containers have also advertised that their products are recyclable. This claim, however, assumes that consumers can bring products to recycling facilities; and few such facilities exist.

Such claims have led to a series of actions on the federal and state levels. The FTC and eight states are investigating whether recycling claims violate truth-in-advertising laws. In addition, the FTC has issued a set of guidelines on environmental labeling that, while voluntary, is expected to rein in the worst abusers. For example, calling a trash bag recyclable is now considered misleading because bags are not generally separated from other trash at landfills.[57]

Mobil Chemical decided to withdraw any reference to degradable from its Hefty trash bags because of a threat of FTC action. Although it paid $150,000 in damages to six states that accused it of misrepresentation,[58] the company cited "mounting confusion over the meaning and value of such claims."[59] As labeling requirements come into focus, more companies will attempt to position themselves as friends of the environment and the green movement.

Advertising Health Claims

A second issue that has generated consumer activism in the 1990s is concern with health claims on foods. Changing lifestyles have led to an increased focus on health and nutrition. Now, consumers are more aware of nutritional information in ads and on packages.

One survey recently found that over half of consumers interviewed said that health claims are an important factor in influencing their purchasing decision, and 44 percent said they read most health and nutritional information on the package.[60] The focus on health claims has been heightened by greater awareness of potential harm cigarettes, liquor, drugs, and even coffee can cause. This concern was shown in another poll that found three of four consumers support warnings on beer, wine, and liquor advertising and packaging.[61]

Reaction of Consumer Activists and Agencies

Protection of consumer rights in advertising health claims has been the primary responsibility of only one of the three legs of the consumer movement: government agencies. (See Figure 2.1.) Although they have begun to raise their voices, consumer activists and organizations have played a minor role in this area. In 1993, for example, the Center for Science in the Public Interest and 274 other consumer protection groups wrote to President Clinton, pushing for the resignation of the FTC's chairperson, a Bush appointee named Janet Steiger. The letter urged Clinton to draw from state and local consumer protection officials who are more concerned with health claims for future appointments.[62]

Government Controls

By 1990, studies casting doubt on many health claims caused Congress to pass the Nutrition Labeling and Education Act, which requires fuller disclosure of the nutritional content of foods in packaging. One study found that oat bran was no more effective in lowering a person's cholesterol or risk of heart disease than any other food with fiber such as whole wheat bread.[63]

The Bush Administration put new life into the regulatory powers of the Food and Drug Administration. Due to advertisers' unsubstantiated health claims, the FDA developed new rules in 1990. Now, advertisers must substantiate their claims for foods such as oat bran and high-fiber cereals with scientific evidence.[64] In 1991, the FDA forced Kellogg to withdraw its claim that Heartwise cereal helped reduce cholesterol. The company then changed the cereal's name to Fiberwise to avoid any connotation that the cereal fights heart disease. (See Exhibit 2.8.)

The FDA has also forced several food makers to eliminate no-cholesterol claims on vegetable oils. The agency said that such claims were misleading since they implied that no-cholesterol products are fat-free, which is not the case. Procter & Gamble immediately took no-cholesterol claims off its Crisco and Puritan oils.

▶**EXHIBIT 2.8**
The FDA prompts a name change: from Heartwise to Fiberwise

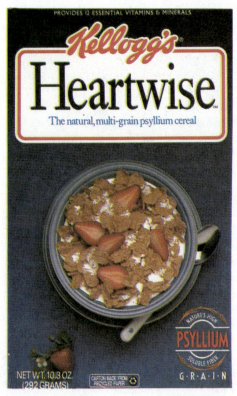

Individual states have also taken a more activist role in protecting consumer interests. In 1989, officials of several states stopped Campbell ads that promoted its soups as sources of calcium and fiber and prevented Nestle's Carnation unit from claiming that its Good Start formula is hypoallergenic.[65]

Reaction of Business

Food and drug companies have attempted to get on the nutritional bandwagon with a proliferation of products that have advertised fewer calories, less salt, lower fat, less cholesterol, more calcium, and higher vitamin content. Some companies have specialized in all-natural products. For instance, Tom's of Maine started with an all-natural toothpaste and is now branching out into other all-natural drug products. It saw sales increase by 55 percent in 1993.[66] However, with about 60 percent of foods sold in U.S. grocery stores having nutritional labels and one-third of all food advertising containing some kind of health message,[67] it is no wonder that consumers are confused. Consider the following:

- Klondike Lite ice cream bars, introduced in 1989, claimed to have half the calories and fat of the originals. Ads never cited the fact that the bars were only half the size of the originals.[68]
- Taco Lite, a product of Taco Bell, actually raises cholesterol more than the regular product, according to a spokesperson for the Center for Science in the Public Interest.[69]
- Best Foods' Mazola Light Corn Oil Spread promises no cholesterol and low sodium, with 50 percent fewer calories than margarine. Still, one tablespoon contains 50 calories and is 100 percent fat.[70]
- Entenmann Bakery's "no-cholesterol, low-calorie" cherry coffee cake must be served in tiny 1.3-ounce servings if it is to fulfill its low-calorie, low-fat claim.[71]

Companies are becoming more conscious of health and nutritional claims as a result of the FDA's more activist stance and new laws requiring fuller disclosure of nutritional contents. Kellogg's change in name from Heartwise to Fiberwise is an example.

Advertising to Children

A third issue that has been an increasing focus of consumer activists is advertising to children. Concern centers primarily on a child's inability to evaluate advertising, particularly the child's inability to understand that an advertiser's motive is to persuade and influence. Younger children may not be able to tell the difference between a TV program and a commercial and may regard anything said in a commercial message as truthful. This concern is heightened by the fact that children from ages 6 to 13 spend more time in front of the television than they do in school.[72]

Some have argued that exposing children to advertising permits them to become more informed consumers at an early age. They learn to discriminate claims and to process marketing information. Eliminating advertising would deprive them of such consumer socialization, and they would then become more vulnerable consumers later in life.

However, a number of studies support the position that excessive advertising to children is not in their best interest. Rubin found that younger children do not understand the purpose of a commercial as fully as older children.[73] In support of this study, Stephens and Stutts found that children between ages 3 and 5 had difficulty distinguishing between TV programming and commercials.[74] Roedder, Sternthal, and Calder found that preteens are likely to respond to the immediate influence of a commercial in buying decisions. They tend to ignore their own past experiences with products.[75] Similarly, Brucks, Armstrong, and Goldberg found that preteens do not refer to prior knowledge of products and brands when watching commercials. All of these studies support the notion that children may be unduly influenced by advertising because they have not developed abilities for perceptual discrimination and information processing.[76]

Both consumer organizations and government agencies have been active in controlling advertising to children. The response of business has been mixed.

Reaction of Consumer Activists and Organizations

Whereas government agencies have taken the lead in protecting consumer rights regarding nutritional claims, consumer organizations have taken a more active part regarding advertising to children. Advocacy groups such as the Action for Children's Television (ACT) have attacked advertising to children as unfair and deceptive for the reasons cited above.

Consumer agencies have singled out specific products and brands for criticism, particularly those that pose safety and health problems for children. For example, Hormel's Kid's Kitchen is the same product as the company's Top Shelf line of microwaveable entrees—except that it is positioned to children. Advertising touts the product as one that teaches children confidence and self-reliance. This implies that children can just pop it into the microwave. Parents are concerned that very young children might try to prepare the product.[77] Similarly, Banfi Vintners has been faulted for targeting its Riunite wines to young people. The vice president of marketing for Banfi described the goal as an effort to "win over entry-level drinkers to the product." Even though "entry-level drinkers" may be of legal drinking age, the ethics of aiming advertising to this group is questionable.[78]

Cigarette and liquor companies have also been criticized for subtly aiming pitches at youngsters. Cigarettes are promoted in products for young people such as Cool candy cigarettes, a Winston Cup racing newsletter with a Kids Korner section, and a Marlboro pack pictured on some video games.

No campaign has drawn more fire than the Joe Camel campaign, which R.J. Reynolds launched to resuscitate its ailing Camel brand. The campaign rescued Camel from obscurity to make it the sixth most popular brand in the nation. While Reynolds' stated intent is to appeal to smokers over the age of 21, antismoking activists insist that the cigarette maker's real desire is to attract teens with a likeable cartoon character. Camel's market share rose by 32 percent among teens since Joe Camel was introduced. Even more disturbing, one survey found that when asked to name a familiar cigarette, 90 percent of children 8 to 13 years old named Camel.[79] A coalition of groups, including ACT and the American Cancer Society, has lobbied the FTC to ban all cartoon characters to sell cigarettes because of their appeal to minors.

Government Controls

Concern about advertising and marketing practices to children has resulted in greater government controls in the 1990s. In 1990, Congress passed the Children's Television Act, which reduces the amount of commercials on children's television programming. When the Reagan Administration deregulated the broadcasting industry in 1984, guidelines for limiting commercial time to children were abandoned; and some stations showed as many as 14 minutes of ads per hour. The new bill reduces the amount of ad time allowed to about 10 minutes per hour on weekends and 12 minutes on weekdays. Broadcasters must also offer more educational programs for children.[80] Implementation of the Children's Television Act was so successful that at the end of 1992, Action for Children's Television decided to disband.[81]

Although guidelines limiting commercial time have been effective, government regulation has had less success in controlling commercial content. The Joe Camel experience demonstrates this difficulty. In 1992, Surgeon General Antonia Novello demanded that Reynolds stop using the Joe Camel promotion, only to be rebuffed by the company. Later, when she asked magazines to stop accepting the ads, Novello did not fare much better.[82] By August 1993, it appeared the FTC was preparing to recommend an outright ban of the campaign and was setting up a court challenge.[83]

Reaction of Business

The reaction of business to the issue of children's advertising has been mixed. Most advertisers avoid manipulating advertising claims to influence children unduly, and the Joe Camel experience seems to be the exception rather than the rule. Companies are particularly sensitive to the charge that they may be endangering the welfare of children or are acting in bad taste. While R.J. Reynolds has been stubbornly insistent that its Joe Camel character is not affecting children and seems to fuel the fires by including the character in catalogs featuring sports wear and other products, Kenner Products reacted differently to parents' concerns about a line of its toys. When parent groups railed at Kenner Products in 1993 for introducing a line of wheeled action toys called Savage Mondo Blitzers that had names such as Chunk Blowers, Puke Shooters, and Butt Kickers, the company did an about-face and discontinued the line.[84]

◆ ADDITIONAL CONSUMER RIGHTS

The recent trend toward greater consumer protection reflects certain basic rights that were first formulated in 1962. President John F. Kennedy sent a message to Congress titled *Special Message on Protecting the Consumer Interest*. This was the first message a President ever delivered on this topic. For the federal government to meet its responsibilities to consumers in the exercise of their rights, Kennedy stated that legislative and administrative action was required. He spelled out four rights that have served as a basis for consumer protection:

1. *The right to safety.*   To be protected against the marketing of goods that are hazardous to health or life.
2. *The right to be informed.*   To be protected against fraudulent or misleading information, advertising, labeling, or other practices and to be given the facts needed to make an informed choice.
3. *The right to choose.*   To be assured access to a variety of products and services at competitive prices.
4. *The right to be heard.*   To be assured that consumer interests will receive full and sympathetic consideration in the formulation of government policy.[85]

A fifth right should also be added to this list:

5. *The right to be a minority consumer without disadvantage.*   To ensure that minority groups or low-income consumers will not be at a disadvantage in relation to any of the above rights compared to other groups.

Marketing organizations have a responsibility to ensure each of these five consumer rights. The question is: Will they accept these responsibilities in the interest of furthering self-regulation? or Will they relegate these responsibilities to government in the expectation of further legislation, more controls, and the establishment of more regulatory bodies? The preference in a marketing society, on both pragmatic and ideological grounds, is for self-regulation rather than additional government regulation. However, the history of the past 30 years is not encouraging. The failure of large companies to recall unsafe products immediately, the imposition of excessive credit charges by inner-city retailers, and pollution of the waterways by the chemical industry are all indications of the need for continued government controls.

However, marketing organizations have been moving toward self-regulation. We have seen some companies take voluntary action to protect the environment. Many companies have also accepted self-imposed industry standards for labeling, product safety, and children's advertising. Of equal importance, many organizations have recently attempted to ensure consumer rights by providing better means to redress complaints through toll-free numbers and consumer service representatives. Some have also sought to improve communications with consumers through Consumer Affairs Offices that formulate policies for handling consumer complaints. Companies have also used Consumer Affairs offices to educate consumers by disseminating information on nutrition, product content, and product safety.

In this section, we will consider each of the five consumer rights that companies should be responsible for fulfilling.

The Right to Safety

Government agencies, businesspeople, and consumerists generally agree that abuses related to product safety must be eliminated. Most companies try to ensure product safety and reliability, but abuses occasionally exist.

The primary government agency responsible for eliminating these abuses is the Consumer Product Safety Commission. The Commission can ban the sale of products, require manufacturers to perform safety tests, and require repair or recall of unsafe products. It operates a hotline to report hazardous products and also runs the National Electronic Injury Surveillance System, a computer-based system that monitors 119 hospital emergency rooms across the country. On the basis of this system, the Commission computes a product Hazard Index. Among products with the highest hazard index are cleaning agents, swings and slides, liquid fuels, snowmobiles, and all-terrain vehicles (ATVs).[86]

The CPSC's action against manufacturers of ATVs demonstrated how the Commission tries to ensure product safety. All-terrain vehicles had been linked to over 900 deaths from 1982 to 1987. In 1987, the Commission filed suit against ATV manufacturers. In April 1988, all ATV manufacturers signed a consent decree agreeing not to sell any three-wheeled ATVs and to restrict sale of four-wheeled models to certain age groups.[87]

One of the positive outcomes of the Commission's work is its influence on firms such as Westinghouse to formalize their product safety procedures.[88] The CPSC also has been active in recalling products at an average of 200 per year. Another agency with recall powers is the National Highway Traffic Safety Administration, which in 1993 requested that General Motors recall 4.7 million C/K pickup trucks sold between 1973 and 1987 because of potential problems with the side-mounted gas tank. In late 1993, GM refused, setting the stage for a test of wills that might end up in court.[89]

The trend toward strengthening consumers' safety rights is spreading around the globe. Consumer activists are emerging in Asia to attack cigarette marketing methods, bolstered by a World Health Organization report that found U.S.-style tactics "caused immediate jumps in consumption among women and teens, traditionally non-smoking groups in less-developed countries."[90] Also, in Japan, the consumer movement may finally be loosening the stranglehold of monopolies that have left consumers powerless. Under current law, the consumer is the one who has to prove a product caused damage—the opposite of U.S. law. The Japanese have a term for the futility of trying to collect damages—*nakineiri*, or "crying one's self to sleep." Though a study by the

Ministry of International Trade and Industry recently concluded the time was not ripe for consumerist–style laws, the 1993 parliamentary victory of parties less committed to government protection of business may hasten change.[91]

The Right to Be Informed

President Kennedy's statement regarding the right to be informed covers two components: the right to be protected against misleading and deceptive information and the right to be given sufficient information to make an informed choice. The explosion of media outlets makes these rights even more important today. Statistics show the typical American spends 9 percent of his or her time watching commercials and gathering information about products.[92]

Deceptive Advertising

Over the years, the Federal Trade Commission has established a set of clearly defined guidelines for determining what is deceptive advertising under the Wheeler-Lea Amendment of the Federal Trade Commission. Advertising need only have the capacity to deceive to be considered deceptive. That is, the FTC does not need to prove deception actually occurred. Furthermore, the advertiser can be ignorant of any false claim and still be liable. Consumer researchers have tried to grapple with the question, Where does puffery end and deception begin?

Gardner identified three types of deceptive advertising.[93] The first is **fraudulent advertising;** that is, a straightforward lie. The second is **false advertising,** which involves a claim-fact discrepancy. That is, the product's claimed benefits are fulfilled only under certain conditions that may not be clear in the advertising. Or, the product must be used in a certain manner or with certain precautions. For example, Superior Rent A Car advertised a $69-a-week rate in Miami's Yellow Pages, but it never disclosed that the rate applies only to cars with manual transmissions.[94]

A third type of deception is **misleading advertising.** It involves a claim-belief interaction. In this case, an advertisement interacts with certain consumer beliefs and results in a misleading claim. For example, Nutri/System weight loss centers foster the belief through advertising that prospective customers will likely lose up to 100 pounds with its product. In fact, the results were so uncommon that the Federal Trade Commission sued the company in 1993 for making unsubstantiated claims.[95]

In the early 1990s, the FTC extended its interest to program-length commercials (known as infomercials), which rapidly multiplied across the cable TV airwaves. In one of its first actions, the agency won a $1.5 million settlement from the television production company Twin Star for hawking three products with bogus claims. The products were a baldness remedy, a skin patch that was supposed to be a diet suppressant, and a male impotence cure. As part of the

1990 settlement, the FTC required that claims in all future infomercials be based on "reliable scientific evidence."[96]

The FTC is also setting standards to regulate advertorials—advertisements in magazines meant to look like objectively written copy.[97] One set of standards states that ads with editorial appearance should be prominently labeled and in a different layout and typestyle than the publication.

In some cases, the FTC has asked certain companies not only to stop making deceptive claims, but also to correct these claims publicly. The rationale for requiring such *corrective advertising* was that deceptive claims have a residual effect and, if uncorrected, could remain in consumer memory for a period of time. Without corrective advertising, companies continue to benefit from such past claims. The FTC required corrective advertising in the following cases:

- Nutri/System, along with Physicians Weight Loss Centers of America and Diet Center Inc., was told that all future ads had to be backed with scientific evidence of weight loss and might have to carry disclaimers that read, "For many dieters, weight loss is temporary."[98]
- ITT-Continental had to correct past advertising that its Profile Bread was effective in weight reduction.
- Warner-Lambert had to correct the claim that Listerine helps prevent colds.
- Hawaiian Punch had to correct its claim that its drink was composed of natural fruit juices, when actually it contained only 11–15 percent fruit juice.[99]

One question that may be asked is whether corrected claims have an impact on consumer beliefs. One study found that the proportion of consumers who believed that Hawaiian Punch had little fruit juice went from 20 percent to 70 percent during the period of corrective advertising.[100]

As we saw, the FTC took a more activist role under the Bush Administration in controlling advertising and is continuing the same stance under the Clinton Administration. The criterion for taking action seems to have reverted to that used in the 1970s, namely, the capacity to deceive rather than actual deception.

Control of Other Deceptive Marketing Practices

So far, the discussion of deceptive information has focused on advertising. Deception can occur in other areas of marketing strategy as well. *Packaging* can be deceptive when misleading claims in regard to lowering cholesterol or the risk of heart disease are stated on a food package. As we saw, the Food and Drug Administration is developing guidelines to ensure full and truthful disclosure on food packages.

Another deceptive packaging practice is reducing the contents or size of the package while maintaining price. Such a practice would represent a deceptive price increase since consumers are getting less quantity for the same price. In the 1991–1992 recession, Star-Kist tuna decreased the contents of its cans by about 6 percent. Procter & Gamble and Kimberly Clark decreased the number of disposable diapers in a standard package by about 10 percent, and Lipton cut the weight of a jar of instant tea by about 7 percent. In each case, the company maintained the price of the product. The attorneys general in New York and Texas are examining these practices and pushing for a national bill that would require manufacturers to announce any such change in size directly on the package.[101]

Deception can also occur in *pricing* practices. One such practice, **bait-and-switch pricing,** involves a low-price offer intended to lure customers into a store where a salesperson tries to influence them to buy higher-priced items. Such practices are illegal, and the FTC and states' attorneys general police them. An example of this is the case of Craftmatic, which advertised low-priced therapeutic chairs on television. It then sent salespeople into the field to sell more expensive ones to the elderly. A Massachusetts judge barred the practice after the state's Attorney General's office revealed the scam.[102]

Selling practices can also be deceptive. For example, a realtor who glosses over defects in a home is being deceptive. However, government can do little to legislate fair sales practices. If the sales transaction is fraudulent, the consumer can take the seller to court; but few consumers do. In most cases, companies have become more sensitive to the need to maintain high standards in selling.

The Provision of Adequate Information

Does the right to information go beyond the right not to be deceived and include the right to adequate information to ensure a wise purchase? There are two positions on this issue. The view of most businesses is that the buyer should be guided by his or her judgment of the brand's quality. Consumer activists believe that business and impartial sources should provide full information and should reveal performance characteristics.

Regardless of the position one takes, the trend is toward more disclosure of information. An increasing number of states are requiring unit pricing of grocery products and open dating of perishables. Recent rules the Food and Drug Administration formulated require more information on certain food labels.

The question of the efficacy of providing more information to consumers does not resolve a basic question: Will consumers use the additional information provided? One study found that when consumers were given clear and concise performance information on carpeting, they used it because they regarded the information to be helpful and easy to employ.[103]

However, consumers do not always use the information marketers provide to make purchase decisions. If product involvement is low, informational requirements may be minimal. Adequate information is not as important a consumer rights issue for low involvement products such as toothpaste or paper towels.

The Right to Choose

Consumer satisfaction requires the ability to evaluate alternatives in the marketplace. Consumerists argue that large corporations restrict choice by discouraging market entry. The marketer of a leading brand may advertise heavily, preempt shelf space within the store, and offer frequent price deals and coupons. Such actions tend to make competitive entry more difficult and thus restrict choice. Carnation's entry into the infant formula market was initially thwarted by the dominance of Ross Labs and Mead Johnson Nutritionals, which together have 85 percent of the market.[104] Scott Paper's attempt to enter the disposable diaper market failed because of the dominance of P&G's Pampers. In the case of disposable diapers, supermarkets generally do not stock more than two brands because of space restrictions, and Scott had difficulty gaining adequate coverage.

The potential for market dominance may create monopoly powers that restrict consumer choice. The federal government has played an active role in preventing the restraint of competition by enforcing the antitrust laws. As we have seen, however, enforcement varies across political administrations. The Reagan Administration's emphasis on self-regulation prompted a proposal "to take the FTC out of the antitrust field entirely."[105] In the early 1980s, the Commission reduced antitrust enforcement activities by 50 percent and cut its antitrust and consumer protection staff by 25 percent.[106] Although the FTC has not been divorced totally from antitrust issues, its reduced powers prompted it to drop a ten-year-old "shared monopoly" case against the ready-to-eat breakfast cereal industry[107] and to accept large mergers such as Philip Morris's acquisition of General Foods and Kraft.

The Clinton Administration is less likely to condone such mergers and acquisitions. Clinton's new antitrust chief, Anne Bingaman, says, "The general philosophy is more active antitrust enforcement."[108] As a result, the Justice Department is questioning the proposed acquisition of McCaw Cellular by AT&T and the acquisition of Fisher-Price toys by Mattel. It also began investigating Microsoft, the computer software giant, as a possible monopoly. The philosophy is to try to "protect the little folk" by insuring adequate choice and competitive prices.

The Right to Be Heard

The consumer has the right to express dissatisfaction with a product and to have complaints resolved (redressed). Most surveys agree that the overall level of product dissatisfaction among consumers is low. A study by General Electric found that 6 percent of appliance customers were dissatisfied.[109] A survey of personal care products found dissatisfaction averaged less than 3 percent per product category.[110]

The level of product dissatisfaction has increased since these surveys were taken. The 1991–1992 recession has created greater consumer demand for product quality at fair prices. Consumers are increasingly dissatisfied with the higher prices of national brands relative to their quality. There has been a general decrease in loyalty to national brands and a significant move to lower-priced private labels (that is, retailer controlled) brands.

If not satisfied, consumers can react in three ways.[111] The first and most common is simply not to buy again. A second reaction is to express dissatisfaction to others. Such negative word-of-mouth is the most harmful effect of dissatisfaction because it goes beyond one consumer's reaction. One study found the average dissatisfied customer "bad-mouths" the product to 9 or 10 other people.[112]

A third reaction is to seek redress. Few dissatisfied customers actively bring their complaints to the marketer's attention. A study of personal care products found that among those consumers who were dissatisfied (a minority to begin with), only 8 percent returned the product to the store and 1 percent to the manufacturer. Another 12 percent complained to the store, the manufacturer, or the Better Business Bureau without returning the product. Therefore, only one-fifth of dissatisfied consumers took some overt action.[113] A study by A. C. Nielsen Co. of food products and health and beauty aids found that only 3 percent of all dissatisfied consumers brought their complaints to the attention of the manufacturer.[114] Both studies demonstrated that the manufacturer is almost totally cut off from direct consumer feedback regarding dissatisfaction with the product. As a result, the manufacturer may not be totally at fault for not adjusting products to consumer complaints.

Why do so few consumers bother to take action in expressing their dissatisfaction? The reason is that they are not sufficiently involved with the product to go out of their way to complain. The study of personal care products found that consumers said it was simply not worth the time and effort.[115] When financial risk and product involvement are higher, complaint behavior increases. Day studied a wide array of higher-priced products and found that one-third of all dissatisfied customers voiced complaints to manufacturers or retailers.[116] Goodman and Robinson studied industrial purchasers and found that the majority complained when they encountered inadequate service.[117]

Another possible explanation for the lack of consumer follow-up when dissatisfied is that there are no formal channels for redress. Letters of complaint are usually too much trouble to write and a minority of better-educated consumers are more likely to write them. Also, excessive red tape in retail stores frequently discourages product returns.

As we saw above, manufacturers have begun to provide consumers with direct channels to voice complaints through toll-free telephone numbers. Whirlpool was among the first to do so and was followed by Procter & Gamble, General Electric, Clairol, Pillsbury, General Mills, and many others. General Electric has programmed over 750,000 possible answers to customer inquiries and complaints. Thus, when consumers call, representatives will have a ready response.[118] A company's average cost to answer a complaint is about $3, often more than the cost of the product. However, the cost is generally worth it: One study found that quick and positive resolution of a complaint leads to repeat purchases 80 to 90 percent of the time.[119]

The Right to Be a Minority Consumer Without Disadvantage

The four consumer rights that have been discussed may have little relevance for low-income minority consumers. Consumers living in inner-city ghettos:

- Are more exposed to unsafe products.
- Have less access to information.
- Have fewer choices of alternative brands.
- Have less access to means of redress.

Therefore, being a low-income, minority consumer is likely to result in fewer consumer rights.

Various studies have confirmed that minorities in inner-cities pay more. Studies have found that African-Americans pay from 1 to 9 percent more on average for food products. The price differential for non-food products is even greater.[120] The inner-city poor are also victimized by merchant practices such as products with no price marks, the bait of a low-priced good to switch the customer to a higher-priced item, and exchange of goods after the sale.

The consistent finding is that compared to other consumers, low-income consumers do not always have the information necessary for a satisfactory choice. They often lack the freedom to go outside their local community to engage in comparison shopping and lack the means for redress if the product fails.[121]

Consumer activists also complain about marketing campaigns that they believe encourage unhealthy or unsafe product choices for minorities. They have been particularly forceful in their efforts to call attention to cigarette and alcohol advertising in minority neighborhoods, where incidents of lung cancer and liver damage are high. The Reverend Calvin Butts of Harlem, for one, has taken scores of his followers on marches through the neighborhood, where they paint over billboards selling cigarettes and alcohol. Some consumer organizations publish literature that attempts to educate minority consumers about how the major food, alcohol, and cigarette companies target them. The Center for Science in the Public Interest publishes two such books: *Marketing Disease to Hispanics* and *Marketing Booze to Blacks*.

Perhaps the most publicized protest involved R.J. Reynolds' 1989 launch of Uptown, a cigarette that was targeted specifically to African-Americans. The objective was to increase sagging sales by aiming at a segment that had a higher proportion of smokers. This was the first time that a new cigarette was designed especially for a minority group, instead of the usual practice of advertising existing brands across the racial spectrum. As a result, it drew a torrent of criticism, particularly since Uptown was very high in nicotine.[122] African-American leaders and consumer activists charged that the company was taking unfair advantage of inner-city minorities.

Further, the Secretary of Health and Human Services, Louis Sullivan, forcefully criticized Uptown. In 1990, he was quoted as saying, "Uptown's message is more disease, more suffering, and more death for a group already bearing more than its share of smoking-related illness and mortality."[123] The actions of Sullivan marked a more aggressive approach by federal health officials to regulate marketing to minorities.

R.J. Reynolds responded to the Uptown uproar by discontinuing the brand. Why the difference in its actions with Joe Camel and Uptown? Because the intended target saw the Uptown campaign as an affront, while the intended target for Joe Camel embraced the ads. By and large, cigarette and alcohol companies have not been overly responsive to complaints about their advertising tactics. The major beer companies, for example, continue to market their potent malt liquor brands almost exclusively to African-Americans despite outrage by health officials. As a result, this area will continue to provide fertile ground for consumerists for some time to come.

SUMMARY

Our marketing economy does not always afford the consumer an environment for making an optimal or even an adequate choice. The necessity to promote consumer rights relative to the powers of big business is known as the consumer movement or consumerism.

Consumerism is the set of activities of consumer organizations, government, and even business to promote the rights of the consumer. The consumer movement is not new. Three distinct periods in the last century have been marked by increased activities to protect consumer rights: 1890–1915, 1933–1940, and 1962–1977. Each of these periods was marked by increased prices and exposés of business practices leading to legislation protecting consumer rights. The 1980s saw a marked decrease in government activities to protect consumer rights as a result of the Reagan Administration's emphasis on self-regulation.

The 1990s is seeing a rebirth of the consumer movement under the Clinton Administration with a particular focus on three issues: (1) protection of the environment, (2) health and nutritional claims for food products, and (3) the influence of advertising on children.

Four consumer rights spelled out by President Kennedy in the early 1960s are of central concern to consumerists:

1. The right to safety protects consumers against the marketing of hazardous goods.

2. The right to be informed means protection from misleading information and the need for a sufficient amount of accurate information to make an informed choice.
3. The right to choose requires access to a variety of products and services at competitive prices.
4. The right to be heard requires provision of the channels of communication to permit consumers to register complaints to business.

An additional right is:

5. The right to be in the minority without disadvantage; that is, assurance that being a minority or low-income consumer does not mean deprivation of the foregoing rights.

Marketing organizations have a role in ensuring these rights. Some organizations have accepted their responsibilities by improving the means for registering complaints and by establishing consumer advisory boards and consumer affairs offices. However, there is still much to be done to encourage self-regulation to ensure consumer rights.

Having set the stage for the study of consumer behavior by considering consumer rights, in the next few chapters, we turn our attention to the process consumers use to make purchase decisions.

QUESTIONS

1. What is meant by "consumerism"? What are the reasons for the increasing awareness of consumer rights and greater current interest in the consumer movement?
2. What are the roles of the three groups in Figure 2.1 to ensure consumer rights?
3. Consumerism is a global movement. In what ways?
4. The 1980s did not see the emergence of another period of consumer activity parallel to that of the 1970s. Why not?
5. What changes took place in the role of the FTC after the Reagan Administration took office? What were the implications of these changes for advertising regulation? What changes occurred under the Bush Administration? What changes are likely to occur under the Clinton Administration?
6. What are the causes of the new environmentalism? How have governmental agencies reacted to this development?
7. What have been some of the more constructive responses of corporate America to the new environmentalism? Some of the less constructive responses? Provide examples.
8. Why do most consumers express increasing concern about the environment, yet show greater reluctance to buy green products?

9. Why have consumers been confused over health claims on food products? What is the government doing to control these claims? What is business doing?

10. What are the pros and cons of advertising to children? What are the findings from studies that support concerns about advertising to children?

11. What has been the role of the three forces in consumerism— consumer organizations, government, and business—regarding advertising to children?

12. In the mid-1970s, it was found that the Firestone radial 500 tire became damaged if driven for long periods in an underinflated condition, which increased the chances of an accident. Should the company have (a) recalled the tires, (b) stopped distribution without recall and informed current owners by mail, or (c) continued marketing the tire and informed customers of the need to keep the tires inflated at a certain pressure? Support your position.

13. What is the distinction between fraudulent, false, and misleading advertising? Cite an actual or hypothetical example of each. Clearly, the FTC should require advertisers to cease using fraudulent and false advertising. Should the agency require advertisers to cease using misleading advertising? Why or why not?

14. Why do most dissatisfied consumers fail to complain to manufacturers about products? Why should manufacturers encourage such complaints? How can they do so?

15. What actions can (a) businesspeople and (b) the federal government take to ensure the consumer rights of the inner-city poor?

16. Why did R. J. Reynolds withdraw Uptown, a cigarette positioned to African-Americans, but continue to use Joe Camel ads in the face of criticism that the character appeals to children?

RESEARCH ASSIGNMENTS

1. Conduct a survey among 40 to 50 consumers and identify those consumers who have taken some environmentally relevant action in the past month (for example, purchased recycled paper or brought materials to a recycling center). Identify the demographic and lifestyle characteristics of these consumers and their media habits.

   • What are the differences in demographics, lifestyle, and media habits between the more environmentally conscious consumers and the rest of the sample?

   • What are the implications for a campaign by the federal government to influence people to buy products that safeguard the environment?

2. Conduct a mail survey of 200 of the largest companies in the United States to determine the following information:

   a. Existence of a consumer affairs department

   b. Organization and objectives of the department

c. Existence of defined mechanisms for processing consumer complaints
What are the differences in organizational characteristics between companies that do and do not have consumer affairs departments?

NOTES

1. "Friendly to Whom?" *The Economist* (April 7, 1990), p. 83.
2. "What Selling Will Be Like in the '90s," *Fortune* (January 15, 1992), pp. 63–64.
3. *Ibid.*
4. "Who's Doing What to Animals in Manhattan," *The New York Observer,* p. 1.
5. "Whales, Human Rights, Rain Forests—and the Heady Smell of Profits," *Business Week* (July 15, 1991), pp. 114–115.
6. "Striving to Be Cosmetically Correct," *The New York Times* (May 27, 1993), pp. C1, C8.
7. *Fortune* (January 15, 1992), *loc. cit.*
8. "The Body Shop Club: Frequency Marketing for Politically Correct Cosmetics," *Colloquy* (Spring, 1993), p. 7.
9. George S. Day and David A. Baker, "A Guide to Consumerism," *Journal of Marketing,* 34 (July, 1970), p. 13.
10. See Robert O. Hermann, "Consumerism: Its Goals, Organizations and Future," *Journal of Marketing,* 34 (October, 1970), p. 56.
11. "Do Boycotts Work?" *Adweek's Marketing Week* (April 8, 1991), pp. 16–18; and "Facing a Boycott, Many Companies Bend," *The Wall Street Journal* (November 8, 1990), p. B1.
12. *Ibid.*
13. *New York Magazine* (February 11, 1991), p. 22.
14. "Suddenly, Green Marketers Are Seeing Red Flags," *Business Week* (February 25, 1991), p. 74.
15. "Cholesterol Crackdown," *Advertising Age* (May 20, 1991), pp. 1, 56; "P&G Gives In, Axes Its 'Fresh' Label," *Advertising Age* (April 29, 1991), p. 1; "U.S. Wants to Keep Menus Honest on Nutrition Claims," *The New York Times* (June 10, 1993), pp. A1, A23.
16. "Beware: Green Overkill," *Advertising Age* (January 29, 1991), p. 26; "Green Products Sprouting Again," *Advertising Age* (May 10, 1993), p. 12; "It's Green, It's Friendly, It's Wal-Mart 'Eco-store,'" *Advertising Age* (June 7, 1993), pp. 1, 4.
17. "How Green Is Your Market Basket?" *Across The Board* (January/February, 1990), p. 50.
18. "The Green Revolution: Loblaws," *Advertising Age* (January 29, 1991), p. 38.
19. *Across The Board* (January/February, 1990), *loc. cit.*
20. Marie Anchrdoguy, "A Brief History of Japan's Keiretsu," *Harvard Business Review,* 68 (July/August, 1990), pp. 58–59.
21. "Environment Inc.," *Business Horizons* (March-April, 1992), p. 9.
22. "A History of Consumer Protest," *The New York Times* (September 16, 1985), p. 46.
23. Hermann, "Consumerism . . . ," *loc. cit.*
24. "Earth Day '80 Dawns Tomorrow Amid Reflection and Plans for a New Decade," *The New York Times* (April 21, 1980), p. A16.
25. George A. Steiner, "New Patterns in Government Regulation of Business," *MSU Business Topics,* 26 (Autumn, 1978), pp. 53–61.
26. John S. Healey and Harold H. Kassarjian, "Advertising Substantiation and Advertiser Response: A Content Analysis of Magazine Advertisements," *Journal of Marketing,* 47 (Winter, 1983), pp. 107–117.
27. William L. Wilkie, Dennis L. McNeill, and Michael B. Mazis, "Marketing's 'Scarlet Letter': The Theory and Practice of Corrective Advertising," *Journal of Marketing,* 48 (Spring, 1984), p. 11.
28. "The Consumer Movement: Whatever Happened?" *The New York Times* (January 21, 1983), p. A16.
29. "Peterson Lists Alternatives to Defeated Consumer Bill," *Advertising Age* (February 13, 1978), p. 1.
30. *The New York Times* (January 21, 1983), *loc. cit.*
31. "Deregulation, Fast Start for the Reagan Strategy," *Business Week* (March 9, 1981), p. 62.
32. "It Sometimes Seems Like the Federal Tirade Commission," *The New York Times* (June 3, 1984), p. C5. See also, "Consumers Are Getting Mad,

Mad, Mad, Mad at Mad Ave," *Business Week* (April 30, 1990), pp. 70–71; and "F.D.A. Is Preparing New Rules To Curb Food Label Claims," *The New York Times* (October 31, 1989), p. A1.

33. "U.S. Environmental Agency Making Deep Staffing Cuts," *The New York Times* (January 3, 1982), p. 20.

34. *The New York Times* (January 21, 1983), *loc. cit.*

35. "FTC Warns Agencies; Eyes Tobacco, Cable," *Advertising Age* (March 12, 1990), p. 6.

36. "Deregulation Hindsight," *Research Alert* (January 20, 1989), p. 1.

37. "Green Consumerism: The Trend Is Your Friend," *Directors & Boards* (Summer, 1992), p. 47.

38. "Snap, Crackle, Stop," *Business Week* (September 25, 1989), p. 154.

39. "The Green Seal of Eco-Approval," *American Demographics* (January, 1993), p. 9.

40. "Blueprint for Green Marketing," *American Demographics* (April, 1992), p. 36.

41. "Green Concerns Influence Buying," *Advertising Age* (July 30, 1990), p. 19.

42. "P&G Gets Top Marks in AA Survey," *Advertising Age* (January 29, 1991), p. 10.

43. "The Green Revolution: Procter & Gamble," *Advertising Age* (January 29, 1991), p. 6.

44. "Ecology Seals Vie for Approval," *Advertising Age* (January 29, 1991), p. 30.

45. *Business Week* (April 23, 1990), p. 99.

46. *Ibid.*

47. "Clinton and Bush Show Contradictions in Balancing Jobs and Conservation," *The New York Times* (October 13, 1992), p. A18.

48. *Ibid.*

49. "From Conflict to Coexistence," *CQ* (February 13, 1993), p. 310.

50. *Business Week* (September 16, 1991), p. 86.

51. "Green Commitment: Fading Out?" *Progressive Grocer* (December 1992), p. 5.

52. "Government Dream Car," *The New York Times* (September 30, 1993), p. A1.

53. "An Alliance of 6 Big Consumers Vows to Use More Recycled Paper," *The New York Times* (August 19, 1993), p. A1.

54. "Tackling the Environment," *Progressive Grocer* (December, 1992), p. 9.

55. John W. Hanley, "Monsanto's Early Warning System," *Harvard Business Review,* 59 (November-December, 1981), pp. 107–122.

56. "Labeling More Than a One-Word Answer: Church & Dwight Exec," *Advertising Age,* p. GR-11.

57. "FTC Green Guidelines May Spark Ad Efforts," *Advertising Age* (August 3, 1992), p. 1.

58. "The Color of Money," *Superbrands* (1992), p. 30.

59. "Mobil Ends Environmental Claim," *The New York Times* (March 30, 1990), p. D1.

60. "Ad Claim Skeptics Still Bite," *Advertising Age* (May 7, 1990), p. S2.

61. "Alcohol Warnings Favored," *Advertising Age* (April 9, 1990), p. 1.

62. "Groups Put Heat on FTC," *The Wall Street Journal* (March 11, 1993).

63. *Advertising Age* (January 22, 1990), p. 1.

64. "Marketers Nervous Over Labeling Rules," *Advertising Age* (May 7, 1990), p. S8.

65. *Business Week* (September 25, 1989), pp. 42–44.

66. "Putting It Mildly, More Consumers Prefer Only Products That Are 'Pure,' 'Natural,'" *The Wall Street Journal* (May 11, 1993), p. B1.

67. "State Role in Labeling," *Advertising Age* (March 12, 1990), p. 73; and *The New York Times* (October 31, 1989), p. A1.

68. *The Wall Street Journal* (March 28, 1990), p. B1.

69. *Ibid.*, p. B5.

70. "How Low Is Low? How Free Is Free?" *Advertising Age* (May 7, 1990), p. S10.

71. *Ibid.*

72. Rita Weisskoff, "Current Trends in Children's Advertising," *Journal of Advertising Research,* 25 (February-March, 1985), pp. RC12–14.

73. Ronald S. Rubin, "The Effects of Cognitive Development on Children's Responses to Television Advertising," *Journal of Business Research,* 4 (1974), pp. 409–419.

74. Nancy Stephens and Mary Ann Stutts, "Preschoolers' Ability to Distinguish Between Television Programming and Commercials," *Journal of Advertising,* 11 (April-May, 1982), pp. 16–25.

75. Deborah L. Roedder, Brian Sternthal, and Bobby J. Calder, "Attitude-Behavior Consistency in Children's Responses to Television Advertising," *Journal of Marketing Research,* 20 (November, 1983), pp. 337–349.

76. Merrie Brucks, Gary M. Armstrong, and Marvin E. Goldberg, "Children's Use of Cognitive Defenses Against Television Advertising: A Cognitive Response Approach," *Journal of Consumer Research,* 14 (March, 1988), pp. 471–482; See

also Kenneth D. Bahn, "How and When Do Brand Perceptions and Preferences First Form? A Cognitive Developmental Investigation," *Journal of Consumer Research,* 13 (December, 1986), pp. 382–393; Alan R. Wiman and Larry M. Newman, "Television Advertising Exposure and Children's Nutritional Awareness," *Journal of the Academy of Marketing Science,* 17 (1989), pp. 179–188; and Deborah Roedder John and John C. Whitney, Jr., "The Development of Consumer Knowledge in Children: A Cognitive Structure Approach," *Journal of Consumer Research,* 12 (March, 1986), pp. 406–417.

77. "Kid's Kitchen May Face Safety Backlash," *Adweek's Marketing Week* (July 24, 1989), p. 25.

78. "Riunite Wine Isn't Afraid to Buck the Trends and Target the Young," *The Wall Street Journal* (April 4, 1990), p. B6.

79. "Poll Shows Camel Ads Are Effective with Kids," *Advertising Age* (April 27, 1992), p. 12.

80. "FCC Adopts Limits on TV Ads Aimed at Children," *The New York Times* (April 10, 1991), p. D7; and "White House Gets Bill Reducing Ads on Children's TV Programs," *The New York Times* (October 2, 1990), p. A1.

81. "Ms. Kidvid Calls It Quits," *Time* (January 20, 1992), p. 52.

82. "Top Health Official Demands Abolition of 'Joe Camel' Ads," *The New York Times* (March 10, 1992), pp. A1, D1.

83. "FTC Staff Recommends Ban of Joe Camel Campaign," *The Wall Street Journal* (August 11, 1993), p. B1.

84. "Tacky Toys With Crude Names," *Industry Week* (February 15, 1993), p. 26.

85. Executive Office of the President, Consumer Advisory Council, *First Report* (Washington, D.C.: U.S. Government Printing Office, 1963), pp. 5–8.

86. Consumer Product Safety Commission *Annual Report July 1, 1973–June 30, 1974* (Washington D.C.: U.S. Government Printing Office, 1975), p. 11.

87. "For Want of a Wheel," *Regulation* 12 (1988), p. 7.

88. Paul Busch, "A Review and Critical Evaluation of the Consumer Product Safety Commission: Marketing Management Implications," *Journal of Marketing,* 40 (October, 1976), p. 45.

89. "GM Gets Tough With Its Critics," *Fortune* (May 31, 1993), pp. 90–97.

90. "Even Overseas, Tobacco Has Nowhere to Hide," *Adweek's Marketing Week* (April 1, 1991), p. 4.

91. "Will Japanese Consumers Continue to Cry Themselves to Sleep?" *Tokyo Business Today* (November, 1991), p. 28.

92. "Consumers in the Information Age," *The Futurist* (January-February, 1993), p. 15.

93. David M. Gardner, "Deception in Advertising: A Conceptual Approach," *Journal of Marketing,* 39 (January, 1975), pp. 40–46. See also J. Edward Russo, Barbara L. Metcalf, and Debra Stephens, "Identifying Misleading Advertising," *Journal of Consumer Research*, 8 (September, 1981), pp. 119–131.

94. "Car-Rental Firms Leave Drivers Dazed by Rip-Offs, Options, Misleading Ads," *The Wall Street Journal* (June 1, 1990), p. B1.

95. "3 Diet Providers Settle with FTC," *New York Newsday* (October 1, 1993), p. 41.

96. "FTC Zaps Misleading Infomercials," *The Wall Street Journal* (June 19, 1990), pp. A1, B6.

97. Douglas Hausknecht, J. B. Wilkinson, George Prough, "Advertorials: Effective? Deceptive? Or Tempest in a Teapot?" *Akron Business & Economic Review* (Winter, 1991), pp. 41–52.

98. *New York Newsday* (October 1, 1993), *loc. cit.*

99. William L. Wilkie, Dennis L. McNeil, and Michael Vb. Mazis, "Marketing's 'Scarlet Letter': The Theory and Practice of Corrective Advertising," *Journal of Marketing,* 48 (Spring, 1984), pp. 11–31.

100. Thomas C. Kinnear, James Taylor, and Oded Gur-Arie, "Affirmative Disclosure: Long-Term Monitoring of Residual Effects," *Journal of Public Policy and Marketing,* 2 (1984), pp. 38–45.

101. "Critics Call Cuts in Package Size Deceptive Move," *The Wall Street Journal* (February 5, 1991), p. B1.

102. "Court Tells Craftmatic To Halt Deceptive Ads," *The New York Times* (February 12, 1992), p. D4.

103. Lawrence A. Crosby and Sanford L. Grossbart, "Voluntary Performance Information Disclosures: Economic Perspectives and an Experimental Test," in Andrew Mitchell, ed., *Advances in Consumer Research,* Vol. 9 (Ann Arbor, MI: Association for Consumer Research, 1982), pp. 321–326.

104. "Price-Fixing and Other Charges Roil a Once-Placid Market," *The New York Times* (July 28, 1991), p. D5.

105. "Transition Unit Tells Plan for FTC," *Advertising Age* (February 2, 1981), p. 3.

106. "Antitrust, Consumer-Law Enforcement by FTC Has Been Reduced, Report Says," *The Wall Street Journal* (November 10, 1983), p. 7.

107. *Marketing News* (April 30, 1982), p. 1.

108. "Clinton U-Turn on Antitrust," *Investor's Business Daily* (September 8, 1993), p. 1.

109. George S. Day, "The Mystery of the Dissatisfied Consumer," *Wharton Magazine* (Fall, 1977) p. 47.

110. Betty J. Diener and Stephen A. Greyser, "Consumer Views of Redress Needs," *Journal of Marketing,* 42 (October, 1978), p. 23.

111. See Jagdip Singh, "Consumer Complaint Intentions and Behavior: Definitional and Taxonomical Issues," *Journal of Marketing,* 52 (January, 1988), pp. 93–107, for a model of consumer complaint behavior.

112. "More Firms Use '800' Numbers to Keep Consumers Satisfied," *The Wall Street Journal* (April 7, 1983), p. 31.

113. Diener and Greyser, "Consumer Views of Redress Needs," *op. cit.,* p. 25.

114. Day, "The Mystery of the Dissatisfied Consumer," *loc. cit.*

115. Diener and Greyser, "Consumer Views of Redress Needs," *op. cit.,* p. 26.

116. Day, "The Mystery of the Dissatisfied Consumer," *op. cit.,* p. 59.

117. John A. Goodman and Larry M. Robinson, "Strategies for Improving the Satisfaction of Business Customers," *Business* (April–June, 1982), pp. 40–44.

118. "Customer Satisfaction Research Can Improve Decision Making," *Marketing News,* 4 (February 5, 1990), p. 13.

119. *The Wall Street Journal* (April 7, 1983), p. 31; see also Marsha L. Richins and Bronislaw J. Verhage, "Seeking Redress for Consumer Dissatisfaction: The Role of Attitudes and Situational Factors," *Journal of Consumer Policy,* 8 (March, 1985), pp. 29–44.

120. Donald E. Sexton, Jr., "Do Blacks Pay More?" *Journal of Marketing Research,* 8 (November, 1971), p. 423; Frederick D. Sturdivant and Walter T. Wilhelm, "Poverty, Minorities and Consumer Exploitation," in Frederick D. Sturdivant, ed., *The Ghetto Marketplace* (New York: The Free Press, 1969), pp. 108–117; and David Caplovitz, *The Poor Pay More* (New York: The Free Press, 1967).

121. Eric Schnapper, "Consumer Legislation and the Poor," *Yale Law Journal,* 76 (1967), pp. 745–768; and Louis G. Richards, "Consumer Practices of the Poor," in Sturdivant, *The Ghetto Marketplace, loc. cit.,* pp. 42–60.

122. "After Uptown, Are Some Niches Out?" *The Wall Street Journal* (January 22, 1990), p. B1.

123. *Ibid.*

P A R T II

CONSUMER DECISION MAKING

Part Two of the text sets the stage for the link between behavioral concepts and marketing strategies. The way consumers decide what brand to buy and where to buy it should impact on marketing strategy. If consumers want certain benefits in a brand, marketers should emphasize these benefits in the product and in advertising. Thus, the criteria consumers use in choosing brands should provide management with guidelines in developing strategies.

In Part Two, we recognize that consumer decision making is not a uniform process. There are distinctions between (1) decision making and habit and (2) high involvement decisions and low involvement decisions. Chapter 3 considers complex, high involvement decisions; Chapter 4 describes habit; and Chapter 5 reviews low involvement decision making. These chapters introduce behavioral concepts that are used throughout the text. They also set the stage for a consideration of market segmentation, product positioning, marketing communications, and marketing strategy applications in each succeeding chapter.

3

Complex Decision Making

WILL SATURN CHANGE CONSUMER ATTITUDES TOWARD GM CARS?

This chapter presents a model of complex decision making. A detailed example of a couple deciding on the purchase of a new car is used to describe this process. Then, the next chapter distinguishes between complex decision making and habit by describing behavior that involves little information search or brand evaluation.

The process of complex decision making includes many important behavioral concepts. For example, it involves an active search for information; therefore, consumer information processing is introduced. It also involves the evaluation of alternative brands; therefore, the process consumers use to assess brands in light of their needs is also considered. Finally, complex decision making involves the consumers' evaluation of the brand after purchasing it; therefore, concepts of consumer satisfaction and postpurchase evaluation are formulated. Thus, Chapter 3 sets the stage for many of the behavioral concepts used throughout the text.

General Motors' introduction of its Saturn car, designed to compete with lower-priced Japanese compacts, illustrates the importance of complex decision making for marketers. General Motors made a basic mistake in the 1980s: It did not pay sufficient attention to maintaining quality and lowering its costs, particularly for its compact line of cars. As a result, when consumers evaluated alternative brands, many found GM's compacts inferior to the imports. To lure Honda and Toyota buyers, GM designed the Saturn to change consumer beliefs and attitudes toward GM cars by "slashing costs and boosting quality."[1]

GM's success will depend on the consumers' process of complex decision making for the Saturn. As compact car buyers learn more about the Saturn, will they change their attitudes toward GM cars? The answer appears to be "yes." By 1993, the car had a waiting list and production was increased.[2] GM felt that Saturn was successfully challenging the imports by luring baby boomers and buyers in the Western states—prime markets for Japanese imports. As quality perceptions of GM's compacts and attitudes toward the Saturn became more positive, compact car buyers began regarding it as a viable alternative to Hondas and Toyotas.

◆ CONSUMER INVOLVEMENT AND COMPLEX DECISION MAKING

To understand complex decision making, we must first understand the nature of consumer involvement with the product. We will then describe the nature of the decision process in complex decision making.

When are consumers most likely to be involved with a product? When the product:

- *Is important to the consumer.*   The consumer's self-image is tied to the product (for example, a Piaget watch advertised as an "Expression of Personal Style," as in Exhibit 3.1).
- *Is continually of interest to the consumer.*   The fashion-conscious consumer, for example, has an interest in clothing.
- *Entails significant risks.*   Among these risks would be: the financial risk of buying a house, the technological risk of buying a personal computer, the social risk of changing one's wardrobe.
- *Has emotional appeal.*   For example, the avid skier buys a new pair of skis, and the music lover buys a new stereo system.
- *Is identified with the norms of a group.*   That is, the sign or "badge" value of a product such as a Vuitton bag that may be viewed as a mark of status for some upscale women (see Exhibit 3.2).[3]

These conditions are likely to result in complex decision making. As most brands lack significant self-identity, interest, risk, emotion, or badge value, it is not surprising that buying by inertia is more widespread than purchasing by complex decision making.

▶**EXHIBIT 3.1**
A product associated
with self-image

▶**EXHIBIT 3.2**
The badge value of
Vuitton bags

Types of Involvement

Behavioral researchers have identified two types of involvement with products: situational and enduring.[4] **Situational involvement** occurs only in specific situations and is temporary, whereas **enduring involvement** is continuous and is more permanent. Situational involvement generally occurs when a purchase decision is required. For example, an MBA graduate may not be particularly fashion-conscious, but she must buy a suit for job interviewing. This graduate will be highly involved with clothes only in that particular situation but not afterward. Another MBA graduate may be very fashion-conscious. She may also be looking for a suit for job interviews, but her interest in clothes is enduring, not situational. Such enduring involvement requires an ongoing interest in the product category, whether a purchase is required or not. According to Celsi and Olson, "The emphasis is on the product itself, and the inherent satisfaction its usage provides, rather than on some (situational) goal."[5]

Both situational and enduring involvement are likely to result in complex decision making. Whether the graduate is interested in clothes because of a job interview or on a more enduring basis, he or she will be aware of fashion information, consider alternative lines of clothing, and evaluate them carefully before making a decision.

The distinction between enduring and situational involvement is further illustrated by the two Godiva chocolate ads in Exhibit 3.3. The first ad is aimed at the individual with enduring involvement in the purchase of chocolates; one who can believe that "the rhythmic beauty of nature" can be preserved in a chocolate. The second ad is targeted to the individual who is situationally involved and is buying chocolates as a gift. Whereas the former individual may be a chocoholic who buys chocolates all year, the latter consumer is involved only on gift-giving occasions.

A Model of Consumer Involvement

A model of consumer involvement is shown in Figure 3.1. The figure shows that the basic conditions for *enduring involvement* are the product's importance to the consumer's self-image, continuous interest in the product, the product's emotional appeal, and its badge value to the consumer's reference group. The fashion-conscious consumer's interest in clothes would meet all of these conditions.

The primary conditions for *situational involvement* in a product are perceived risk and badge value to the reference group. One main reason why an otherwise uninvolved consumer becomes involved with a purchase is perceived risk in purchasing the product. By perceived risk, we mean the amount of risk consumers perceive in the purchase decision because of (1) uncertainty about the decision and/or (2) the potential consequences of a poor decision. The graduate buying clothes for the job interview may be uncertain about the criteria to use to evaluate alternative styles of clothing. She may also be uncertain about

▶**EXHIBIT 3.3**
Enduring versus situational involvement

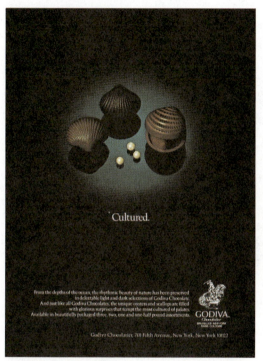

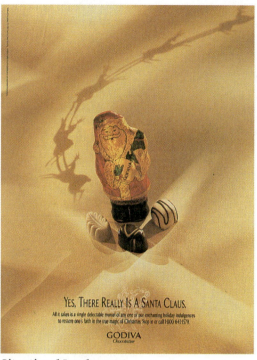

Enduring Involvement   *Situational Involvement*

the potential consequences of a poor decision; namely, the possibility of not looking good for a job interview. These risks increase her involvement with the purchase.

Badge value is a condition for both enduring and situational involvement. The otherwise uninvolved consumer might become involved with a purchase that his or her friends and business associates consider important. Appropriate dress for a job interview might obviously be important to business associates. Similarly, the badge value of clothing is one reason for the fashion-conscious consumer's continued interest in clothing.

The model shows that situational and enduring involvement can be independent; one does not necessarily have to lead to the other. However, a logical linkage exists: If it is frequent, situational involvement might lead to enduring involvement. Our MBA graduate who was not particularly clothes-conscious becomes aware of clothes not only for the job interview, but also in the work environment in general. As a result, clothes-consciousness becomes a permanent part of her life. Situational involvement becomes enduring involvement, as shown by the arrow between the two in Figure 3.1.

▶**FIGURE 3.1**
A model of consumer
involvement

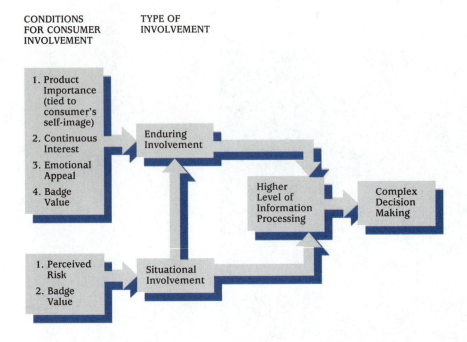

CONDITIONS
FOR CONSUMER
INVOLVEMENT

TYPE OF
INVOLVEMENT

1. Product Importance (tied to consumer's self-image)
2. Continuous Interest
3. Emotional Appeal
4. Badge Value

1. Perceived Risk
2. Badge Value

Enduring Involvement

Situational Involvement

Higher Level of Information Processing

Complex Decision Making

As noted, both types of involvement lead to higher levels of information processing, which means greater search for information and an evaluation of brand alternatives on a wider set of evaluative attributes. Such information processing defines complex decision making. In a study of involvement with tennis and tennis equipment, Celsi and Olson found that people who are more involved devote more attention to ads for tennis products and process the product information in the ads more extensively.[6] Similarly, Gensch and Javalgi found that farmers who were more involved with learning about farming methods were likely to use more attributes in evaluating alternative suppliers. Among involved farmers, 47 percent used three or more attributes in evaluating alternative retail stores. Among uninvolved farmers, only 15 percent used three or more attributes.[7] Both studies confirm that greater involvement results in consumers making choices by complex decision making.

Multidimensional Nature of Involvement

The five conditions for involvement, as shown in Figure 3.1, suggest that consumers can be involved with a product on several dimensions. In their study, Kapferer and Laurent[8] confirmed the multidimensional nature of involvement. They asked 800 women to agree or disagree with statements about 20 product categories. The statements were closely related to the five components of involvement: product importance, interest, risk, emotion, and badge value. Scales were developed for each component of involvement.

The scores for ten of the products are shown in Table 3.1 (with 100 as an average score). Clearly, for this sample of women, clothing and perfume were involving across all components, except for risk. This suggests that consumers are more likely to be involved with these items on an enduring, rather than a situational, basis. Champagne was involving for all components, except continuous interest, suggesting that consumers are involved with champagne on a situational basis (that is, for special occasions). Chocolate was involving only in its emotional appeal, suggesting possible pleasurable childhood associations with the product. Detergents and facial soap were not involving in any respect.

The value of the study is to show that products can be involving in different ways. For example, washing machines and vacuum cleaners were high in product importance, possibly because they serve a support role in the household. However, neither product had pleasure (emotional) or badge value because they necessitated the user's presence.[9] If the promotional objective is to create consumer involvement, advertisements for both washing machines and vacuum cleaners might emphasize their time-liberating value to increase their emotional appeal.

Cross-Cultural Nature of Consumer Involvement

The level of involvement with a product varies by individual. Some individuals may be highly involved with the purchase of toothpaste because they associate the product with personal appearance and social acceptance. However, most

▶**TABLE 3-1**
Product categories by components of involvement

Product	Components of Involvement				
	Interest	*Emotion*	*Budget Value*	*Product Importance*	*Risk*
Clothing	123	147	166	129	99
Perfume	120	154	164	116	97
Champagne	75	128	123	123	119
Washing Machine	130	111	104	136	102
Vacuum Cleaner	108	94	78	130	111
Detergent	80	44	77	75	94
Facial Soap	88	91	99	78	85
Shampoo	99	78	93	94	102
Yogurt	95	105	73	72	73
Chocolate	94	130	86	76	91

Source: Jean-Noel Kapferer and Giles Laurent, "Consumer Involvement Profiles: A New Practical Approach to Consumer Involvement," JOURNAL OF ADVERTISING RESEARCH, 25 (December, 1985–January, 1986), p. 51.

consumers are not highly involved because they view brushing their teeth as a necessary chore and see little difference between brands.

Differences in product involvement also occur on a cross-cultural basis. For example, bicycles are more important in China, where they are the primary means of transportation, than they are in the United States. A Chinese consumer might be as involved in buying a bicycle as an American consumer is in buying a car. Zaichkowsky and Sood surveyed business students in 15 countries to determine involvement levels for eight product categories.[10] Involvement in the purchase of beer among English and American students was significantly higher than that for students from South American countries. This difference probably reflects the cultural role of beer in these countries. English and American students associate beer with relaxation and social occasions, whereas no such association exists for students from South American countries. Students' involvement with soft drinks was uniformly low for all countries, except China. Apparently, soft drinks in China are a more valued commodity, particularly with the introduction of Western brands in the last ten years. Involvement with blue jeans was fairly uniform across countries, probably as a result of similar perceptions of the product among students worldwide.

These findings suggest that international marketers must adjust their strategies on a country-by-country basis, depending on the cultural role and importance of certain products.

◆ IMPORTANCE AND LIMITATIONS OF A CONSUMER MODEL

This chapter and the next two chapters describe models of consumer behavior—namely, complex decision making, habit, and low involvement decision making. A **model of consumer behavior** describes a sequence of factors that leads to purchase behavior and hypothesizes the relationship of these factors to behavior and to each other. Before describing these models, let us consider the importance and limitations of developing such models.

Importance

Why should management be interested in a sequence of steps leading to purchase behavior? There are at least five reasons:

1. *A model encourages a total and integrative view of consumer behavior.* Consumer behavior depends on many factors (multivariate relationships). Segmenting the car market into younger versus older purchasers, for example, would not be sufficient to guide GM's advertising, price, and product development strategies for the Saturn. Identifying compact car buyers as young singles who emphasize mobility and view compacts such as a Honda or Toyota as good values for the money would be a more relevant segment. These are the buyers GM would try to attract.

Management has recently begun to analyze consumer behavior in more multivariate terms. To do this, it needs a framework for relating consumer thought variables (that is, consumer perceptions, attitudes, and desired benefits) to behavior and to one another. This is exactly what a model of consumer behavior attempts to do.

2. *A model provides a basis for developing marketing strategies.* If attitudes toward a brand are related to behavior, reinforcing positive attitudes or changing negative ones might strengthen the brand's market position. GM's strategy regarding the Saturn is to try to change negative attitudes by influencing consumers that GM's compacts are equal to the imports. Creating more positive attitudes will increase purchases of GM cars.

3. *A model helps identify areas of information necessary to evaluate marketing strategies.* If brand attitudes are associated with behavior, these attitudes would be key variables for evaluating the effectiveness of marketing strategy. For example, a key variable in evaluating GM's success with the Saturn is the degree to which prospective buyers view the car as one that provides quality at a reasonable price.

4. *A model encourages quantification of these variables.* Relationships such as the one between attitudes and car purchase behavior must be demonstrated in a statistically reliable manner.

5. *A model provides a basis for segmenting markets.* If a model hypothesizes that consumers' lifestyles are likely to influence brand choice, these variables should be used to identify consumer segments. For instance, innovative consumers who like to try new products might be more willing to purchase the Saturn. Similarly, "couch potato" stay-at-home types might define the primary market for video rentals.

Limitations

The usefulness of a consumer model to marketing management has four limitations:

1. *The components of a model may not be equally important for all product categories.* Some may not even apply. For example, the level of information regarding product attributes is more important in purchasing a car than it is in buying a car radio. Brand attitudes may influence the purchase of cereals more than the purchase of frozen vegetables.

2. *The components of a model may not be equally important for all usage situations.* The purchase of a car for business use may produce a decision very different from one for the purchase of a car for family use. The number of alternatives may be much more restricted in buying a car for business reasons. Moreover, the criteria of selection may be very different; and, once again, a general model cannot identify these differences.

3. *A model will vary among individuals in the same market*.   Evaluating alternative brands of one product will be more important for those who like to switch brands than it is for those who stay loyal to one brand. Acquiring product information is more important for consumers who like to buy new products than it is for those who reduce risk by buying established brands.

4. *All purchase decisions are not equally complex*.   The purchase of a new car is more complex than the purchase of frozen orange juice. In buying a car, the consumer will carefully evaluate a number of alternatives, search for information, and assess the features of each make. The consumer may buy a brand of frozen orange juice by habit.

These limitations do not restrict the use of decision-making models. As we will see, there does not have to be one general model of consumer behavior. Marketing managers can develop models that vary by level of consumer involvement and complexity of the decision task. In addition, they can adapt a general model to particular circumstances. Adaptation from a consumer behavior model to specific markets requires research that will define the perceptions, attitudes, and desired benefits most likely to influence consumers' choices of particular brands. Therefore, a consumer behavior model is essential in defining the important variables in the consumer choice process.

◆ A MODEL OF COMPLEX DECISION MAKING

In **complex decision making,** consumers evaluate brands in a detailed and comprehensive manner. More information is sought and more brands are evaluated than in other types of decision-making situations. As we saw, such a process is most likely when consumers are involved with the product. Complex decision making is most likely for certain categories of products; namely:

- High-priced products.
- Products associated with performance risks (medical products, automobiles).
- Complex products (compact disc players, personal computers).
- Specialty goods (sports equipment, furniture).
- Products associated with one's ego (clothing, cosmetics).

Research on decision making has identified five phases in the decision process: (1) problem recognition, (2) search for information, (3) evaluation of alternatives, (4) choice, and (5) outcome of the choice.[11] These steps can be translated into those steps involved in consumers' complex decision making: (1) need arousal, (2) consumer information processing, (3) brand evaluation, (4) purchase, and (5) postpurchase evaluation. A model of complex decision making representing these five steps is presented in Figure 3.2. The model presents a process of complex decision making as follows:

1. *Need arousal.* A consumer begins with a particular state of mind that represents his or her perceptions of and attitudes toward known brands. For example, consider a business school student who is thinking of purchasing a personal computer. Need arousal occurs because she realizes she can never finish her work by the time the school's computer lab closes. She is involved with the purchase situation rather than being involved with the product on an enduring basis (as a computer buff might be). If she were to make a decision immediately, based on her own experience and the opinion of friends, she would probably buy a Compaq because of her perceptions of its reliability, processing speed, and price.

2. *Consumer information processing.* The immediate result of need arousal is gathering information about the product. Our consumer goes to several computer stores to investigate alternatives, becomes more aware of ads for computers, and examines several issues of *Consumer Reports* to determine how an impartial agency evaluates alternative brands. On the basis of this information, she begins to consider a notebook model because of portability and convenience. Price is an immediate factor, and she determines she can obtain a good notebook for under $2,000, a price she can afford because of some vacation money she has set aside and a graduation present her parents promised.

Two factors of concern are a smaller screen and keyboard compared to those of desktops and a smaller 3½-inch floppy disk than the standard 5¼-inch size used at school. Trying out several notebooks convinces her that the screen and keyboard are adequate. In addition, a knowledgeable friend assures her the smaller disk size will soon become standard.

▶**FIGURE 3.2**
A basic model of complex decision making

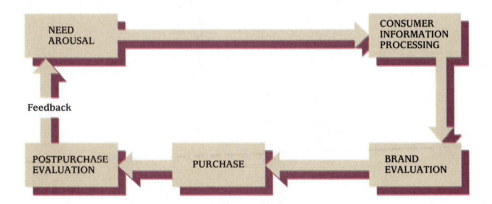

3. *Brand evaluation.*   Brand evaluation is the result of information processing. Based on her information search, our consumer is particularly impressed with three laptop brands—Toshiba, AST, and NEC. After further comparisons, she determines that the Toshiba's screen is the clearest and that the commands for the machine are executed somewhat faster than they are for the other two. However, the Toshiba costs $300 more than the other brands.

Barring constraints such as an unaffordable price or the product's lack of availability, the consumer will purchase the brand that comes closest to meeting her most important needs. All three brands fill her need for portability and convenience, so she uses secondary criteria such as speed and screen size. On this basis, our consumer decides the Toshiba is the best alternative for her needs and is worth the additional price.

4. *Purchase.*   Although our consumer has decided to purchase the Toshiba, various factors may delay her purchase (lack of funds, additional information on other makes, unavailability of the preferred brand). A consumer may decide not to buy immediately because existing brands do not sufficiently meet his or her criteria.

5. *Postpurchase evaluation.*   After a purchase, the consumer will evaluate the brand's performance. Satisfaction will reinforce the consumer's judgment and make him or her more likely to repurchase that brand in the future. Dissatisfaction will lead the consumer to reassess the choice and will decrease the likelihood of repurchase.

Consumers who receive negative information after the purchase (poor performance or communications from friends that the brand did not meet their expectations) may attempt to justify the purchase decision by ignoring such negative information or by perceiving it selectively. For example, our consumer might find the Toshiba's processing speed is slower than expected but concludes it is still pretty fast compared to older models. Regardless of the outcome, postpurchase evaluation is a learning process that provides feedback to the consumer who stores it as information for future reference.

In the remainder of this chapter, each of these five processes are considered in more detail to introduce some of the important behavioral concepts that will appear in later chapters. The model of complex decision making is illustrated by another example, that of a couple purchasing an automobile.

◆ NEED AROUSAL

Need arousal is outlined in Figure 3.3. The consumer's state of mind is described as the **psychological set** toward the prospective purchase—that is, the product benefits the consumer seeks and his or her attitudes toward various brands. The psychological set is represented in the figure at a given time,

▶FIGURE 3.3
Need arousal

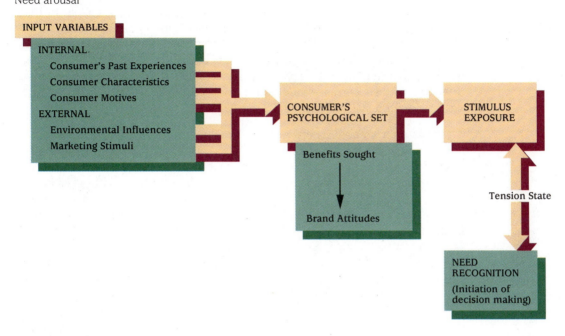

prior to decision making. It will change during decision making as the consumer processes new information.

The benefits a consumer seeks and his or her attitudes are a function of various input variables: (1) the consumer's past experiences, (2) consumer characteristics, (3) consumer motives, (4) environmental influences (face-to-face groups, culture, social class, and the buying situation), and (5) past marketing stimuli (product, price, promotion, and in-store strategies directed to the consumer). These input variables and the consumer's psychological set influence the types of stimuli the consumer perceives (seeing advertising, noticing the product on the shelf, hearing about it from friends or salespeople). The result could be recognition of a need for a product or brand.

The solid arrows, as shown in Figure 3.3 and in subsequent representations of models of consumer decision making, represent the hypothesized direction of causation. Thus, the various input variables influence the consumer's psychological set. Similarly, stimulus exposure influences need recognition; and need recognition influences stimulus exposure (as represented by a double arrow). This two-way influence exists because marketing stimuli may influence the consumer to recognize the need for a certain brand; and the nature of these needs, in turn, influences the stimuli the consumer selects. In this and other figures, boxes under a main variable list subvariables that further define the main variable. For instance, the consumer's psychological set is composed of benefits sought and brand attitudes.

Input Variables

Consider the following example. Rob and Linda Greene are a couple in their late-20s and live in a middle-class, suburban neighborhood of a large metropolitan area. They both work and use public transportation to get to their jobs. As a result, they are a one-car family. Rob inherited his parents' Oldsmobile when he married Linda three years ago. No longer satisfied with the economy or styling of their current model, both Rob and Linda are in the market for a new car. As a result, they recognize a need.

Consumer's Past Experiences

Rob and Linda are not involved in cars on an enduring basis. Their high level of involvement arose as a result of the situation—dissatisfaction with their current car. The status communicated by a car (badge value) is not very important to them. Since they are both starting out in careers—Rob as a financial analyst; Linda as a product manager for a food company—they see substantial financial and performance risks in buying. Highly involved in the purchase decision, they place more importance on economy, service dependability, performance, and comfort, in that order. They use their Olds primarily on weekends and for shopping needs, and it has served them well according to these benefit criteria. As a result, their past experiences with the car have been positive.

Rob and Linda have also developed a set of expectations regarding a car. They have come to expect good service and a car that performs consistently over time. Any deviations from these expectations might cause them to consider alternative models.

Consumer Characteristics

The benefits consumers seek and their brand attitudes are partially conditioned by their characteristics—their demographics, lifestyles, and personalities. Income may affect the type of car purchased—compact, standard, or luxury. Age, marital status, and number of children may affect the class of car—sports car, sedan, or station wagon. Lifestyle may affect the make. A socially oriented, outer-directed couple may want a car that impresses others and may stress styling and size of car. A family that travels a lot may emphasize the benefits of comfort at the expense of styling. Even personality has an influence. The power-oriented, aggressive individual may want a car with a great deal of acceleration. The compulsive individual may stress regular service benefits and the alleviation of anxieties with better warranty terms.

Consumer characteristics can play an important part in marketing strategy. We saw that Avon adjusted its marketing strategy because of the move of many women from the home to the workplace. Tupperware—famous for selling housewares through at-home "Tupperware parties"—saw its market shrink in the 1980s for the same reason. By 1993, the company was on the ropes because of its failure to adjust to this significant demographic shift and was a candidate for divestment.[12]

Consumer Motives

Past experiences and consumer characteristics may create particular motives in consumers. Motives are general drives that define consumers' needs and direct their behavior toward attaining these needs. Common motives include factors such as possession, economy, curiosity, dominance, status, pleasure, and imitation. These motives are not specific to any product. Economy or possession could apply equally well to buying a car or a compact disc.

Motives directly affect the specific benefit criteria consumers use to evaluate brands. If Rob is motivated by status, his two important benefit criteria will be the size and styling of the car. If economy is Rob's important motive, then his most important benefit criteria may be gas mileage, service costs, and initial price.

Abraham Maslow developed a theory based on a *hierarchy of motives*.[13] According to Maslow, motives operate from a lower to a higher level in a systematic order. An individual will satisfy the lowest motivational level first before the next higher set of motives becomes activated. Once these have been satisfied, the individual then attempts to satisfy the next higher level, and so on. Thus, the unfulfilled motives lead to action. Maslow defined five levels of motives, from lowest to highest:

1. Physiological (food, water, shelter, sex).
2. Safety (protection, security, stability).
3. Social (affection, friendship, acceptance).
4. Ego (prestige, success, self-esteem).
5. Self-actualization (self-fulfillment).

Marketers can appeal to a range of motives within Maslow's five levels. For example, they can appeal to:

- Physiological needs through sexual appeals, as in ads for personal grooming products.
- Safety needs, as in messages advertising safer cars or promoting a safer environment.
- Social needs, by showing group acceptance as a result of wearing certain types of clothing or using a brand of soap or deodorant.
- Ego needs, by linking a product to success in business (credit cards) or in sports activities (athletic shoes).
- Self-actualization needs, by showing self-fulfillment through travel, education, or cultural pursuits.

According to Maslow, few people satisfy their social and ego needs and move to the fifth level. In fact, most advertising appeals focus on social and ego needs, whether it is an appeal for the status of a luxury car or the more mundane appeal for the social protection a deodorant affords.

One researcher equates Maslow's theory to three stages in a family's life cycle.[14] In the first stage, young adults acquire material possessions primarily to gain acceptance and to emulate their peers (Level 3 above). Having established themselves in their middle years, consumers view possessions as a means of demonstrating success and gaining self-esteem (Level 4.) As adults reach older age, possessions are no longer important. They now seek experiences that provide emotional satisfaction and self-realization (Level 5).

Environmental Influences

Consumers purchase and use many products in a social setting. The purchase of a car is frequently a family decision, and each member of the family influences the decision. Neighbors and business associates may also be important sources of information and influence. It is clear that cultural norms and values affect consumers' attitudes toward cars. The automobile is the prime means of transportation in the United States, but it is also a prime means of socialization and represents socioeconomic status.

A study by Vinson, Scott, and Lamont found a marked difference in the perception of automobiles among college students from liberal and conservative universities.[15] Students from the liberal university emphasized performance and engineering, whereas students from the more conservative university emphasized prestige and luxury. Apparently, cultural norms at the two universities affected students' perceptions of automobiles.

Past Marketing Stimuli

Past information about brand characteristics and prices will affect consumers' beliefs and brand attitudes. Consumers obtain such information from advertising, in-store stimuli, and sales representatives.

Consumer's Psychological Set

In the context of consumer decision making, the consumer's psychological set is directed to brand, product, or store evaluations. The psychological set is made up of two components: benefits sought and brand attitudes.

Benefits Sought

Benefit criteria are the factors consumers consider important in deciding on one brand or another. Rob's and Linda's most important criteria are economy and service dependability; but other criteria such as road performance, comfort, styling, and safety are also relevant. Marketers identify **benefit segments** by consumers that emphasize the same benefit criteria. Identifying consumer segments who emphasize benefits such as economy, performance, and style, marketers try to develop product characteristics that satisfy these benefits. The car manufacturer that appeals to a performance segment might advertise product characteristics such as quick acceleration and a smooth ride.

Consumers regard product characteristics as goal objects that may or may not satisfy desired benefits. Thus, the goal object consumers use to evaluate economy may include gas mileage and service costs.

Brand Attitudes

Brand attitudes are consumers' predispositions to evaluate a brand favorably or unfavorably. They are represented by three factors: beliefs about brands, evaluation of brands, and tendency to act.[16] The assumption is that these components operate in sequence as follows:

1. Beliefs are formed about the brand that influence
2. attitudes toward the brand, which then influence
3. an intention to buy (or not to buy).

That is, if brand beliefs result in positive attitudes, there is a greater chance the consumer will buy the brand.

This sequence has been referred to as a **hierarchy of effects** model of consumer decision making. It stipulates the sequence of stages consumers go through in purchasing, a sequence involving thinking (beliefs), feelings (evaluations), and actions (the intention to buy the brand).[17] Interestingly, the first person to theorize this decision-making sequence of thinking, feeling, and acting was Plato in ancient Greece.

The hierarchy of effects is particularly important to marketers because it provides a basis for defining the factors that influence consumer behavior. The sequence was implicit in the description at the beginning of the chapter of the strategic issues related to the Saturn. In this case, GM knew that a large segment of car buyers emphasize economy because of budgetary constraints and want value for their money as defined by quality and dependability. These desired benefits (economy, quality, dependability) drive their decision process. Compact car buyers will evaluate alternative makes primarily on these criteria. Beliefs about the extent to which cars have these attributes will determine their evaluation of the car. Thus, the belief that a Saturn is economical, dependable, and high-quality will result in a positive evaluation of the car, which in turn will increase the likelihood that consumers will decide to buy it. That is, needs influence the nature of beliefs about the Saturn; and these beliefs determine how consumers will evaluate it and whether they are likely to buy.

Returning to the Greenes, Rob and Linda believe their Olds provides performance and comfort but question its economy because of the increasing costs of maintenance. Consumers attribute characteristics to brands whether they have used them or not. Because of advertising and comments from friends, Linda suggests they consider a Toyota Corolla and General Motors' Saturn because both are nicely styled, provide comfort, and are not expensive to maintain.

An important link exits between benefits and attitudes. When beliefs about a brand conform to the benefits consumers desire, consumers will evaluate the brand favorably. Favorable brand evaluation is more likely to lead to an intention to buy the brand. Given that Rob's and Linda's primary benefit criteria are economy and service dependability, they will prefer a car (brand evaluation) that has these characteristics (their beliefs) and will probably plan to buy such a car (their tendency to act).

Stimulus Exposure

In the market for a new car, Rob and Linda are more likely to notice stimuli related to cars such as advertisements, comments friends make about their cars, and cars in showrooms and on the street. They are also more likely to be aware of information that affects the cost of owning and operating a car such as sticker prices, trade-in allowances, gasoline, and service and parts.

Rob and Linda are more likely to notice these stimuli because they need a car. Their attitudes about makes of cars will also influence stimulus exposure. Their interest in an Olds, a Saturn, and a Corolla will make them take more notice of ads for these makes than those for others. The needs and attitudes of consumers, therefore, directly influence the stimuli they will notice.

Consumers' exposure to stimuli is often selective. People tend to choose friends who support their views, reinforce their egos, and parallel their lifestyles. They often seek commercials that support recent purchases in an attempt to justify them. They also frequently tune out information that conflicts with their needs or beliefs. The recent car buyer may ignore the negative experiences of a friend with the same make or may rationalize poor performance by thinking the car is not yet broken in.

Therefore, stimulus exposure is a selective process that is directed by the need to reinforce existing brand attitudes and perceptions and to seek additional information.

Need Recognition

When consumers recognize a need, a state of tension occurs and causes them to search for information that will help in decision making. Figure 3.3 shows an interaction between need recognition and stimulus exposure. New stimuli cause someone to recognize a need, and need recognition makes that person more aware of relevant stimuli.

Stimuli external to consumers can initiate decision making. Such stimuli include marketing communications (information about a new product) or environmental influences (seeing a friend use a product, information about the economy, a shift in cultural norms away from usage of certain products). Also, stimuli internal to consumers, specifically their needs and brand evaluations, can initiate decision making. These internal stimuli include recognition of poor product performance or, more basically, physical needs such as hunger and thirst.

Rob and Linda were motivated to consider a new car by internal as well as external stimuli. Rob learned that his Oldsmobile needs a transmission overhaul. This fact, in addition to poor gas economy, caused him to begin considering alternative makes. He was also prompted to begin a decision-making process by awareness of several more economical foreign compact cars. One additional factor prompted a consideration of makes other than an Olds. Both Rob and Linda believed the Olds had a stodgy image and agreed they should consider getting a sportier, more up-to-date-looking car. Rob remembered a recent ad campaign meant to counteract the Olds' image. Rob had found that campaign, based on the theme "This is not your father's car," amusing since the Olds used to be his father's car. The ad had done little to counter Rob's perception of Olds.

◆ CONSUMER INFORMATION PROCESSING

Consumer information processing involves the exposure to, organization of, and search for information. These processes are represented in Figure 3.4. To influence consumers' psychological set, stimuli must gain the consumers' attention, be comprehended, and be retained in the consumers' memory for a certain period of time. As we will see in Chapter 5, information processing may be quite different when consumers are not very involved. Consumers could become aware of a stimulus with little interpretation or comprehension on their part, but that stimulus could still influence their behavior.

▶**FIGURE 3.4**
Consumer information processing

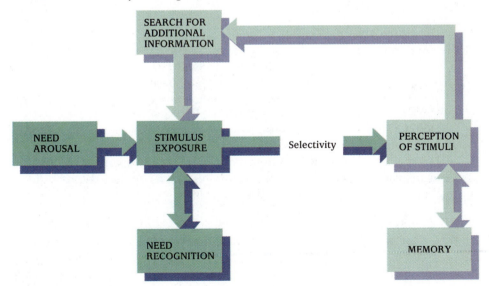

Perception of Stimuli

Perception is the process by which consumers select, organize, and interpret stimuli to make sense of them. Stimuli are more likely to be perceived when they:

- Conform to consumers' past experiences.
- Conform to consumers' current beliefs about a brand.
- Are not too complex.
- Are believable.
- Relate to a set of current needs.
- Do not produce excessive fears and anxieties.

It is clear that consumers' perceptions of stimuli, as well as their exposure to stimuli, are selective. Ads that reinforce consumers' beliefs and experiences are more likely to be noticed and retained. Also, consumers are more likely to dismiss or reinterpret those ads that contradict past experiences and current beliefs about a brand. By perceiving stimuli selectively, consumers attempt to achieve a state of psychological equilibrium; namely, a state that lacks conflict and avoids contradictory information.

Once exposed to the stimulus, consumers' perceptions go through three distinct phases: attention, comprehension, and retention. Selectivity takes place in each phase.

Attention
Attention is the process of noticing a stimulus or certain portions of it. Attention is selective; that is, consumers are more likely to notice the portion of a stimulus that relates to their needs and conforms to their experiences.

Comprehension
Comprehension is understanding and interpreting the message. It, too, is a selective process; consumers are more likely to interpret a message to agree with their beliefs. Two consumers may interpret the same ad differently because of differences in beliefs, attitudes, and experiences regarding the product being advertised.

Rob's interpretation of various messages is selective because he accepts certain stimuli and discounts others. He was particularly aware of compacts' claims of better gas mileage and more economical service costs. He generally discounted claims regarding comfort because, being over six feet tall, he believed that compact cars cannot be very comfortable.

Retention
A message can be noticed, interpreted, and quickly forgotten. Consumers are more likely to **retain** (that is, remember) in their memory those messages that are most relevant to their needs. In their initial information search, Rob and Linda decided to consider seriously an economy car as a replacement for

the Oldsmobile. They retained information on the types of economy cars on the market and the alternative features of these makes.

Memory

Retained information is stored in consumers' **memory,** which is composed of past information and experiences. New information on brands and products may stimulate recall of past information, and is then retained in memory. Once stored in memory, information can be recalled for future use, as shown by the double arrow in Figure 3.4 between memory and perception of stimuli. (Memory processes are described in Chapter 7 as part of a detailed discussion of consumer information processing.)

Search for Additional Information

Consumers may not have enough information to make adequate decisions. In such cases, they will search for additional information. Such a search is most likely when consumers:

- Believe that alternative brands being considered are inadequate.
- Have insufficient information about the brands under consideration.
- Receive information from friends or media sources that conflicts with past experiences and current information.
- Are close to deciding on a particular brand and would like to confirm expectations regarding its performance.

Studies have shown that consumers do not engage in extensive information search unless they consider the benefits gained from additional information to be worth the time and cost of such a search. One study found that when consumers were presented with information on 16 alternative brands, they used only 2 percent of the information available in making a decision.[18] Another study found that one-half of all consumers studied visited only one store or showroom when buying cars and major appliances.[19] A limited search does not necessarily reflect consumers' lack of concern about the purchase. It may mean that many consumers rely on past experience in deciding on a brand or believe they have enough information at the time of purchase.

About two weeks after deciding to purchase a new car, Linda visited several showrooms and obtained figures from dealers on gas mileage, service costs, and resale value of various makes of cars. She took several copies of *Consumer Reports* out of the library to determine ratings of various makes from an impartial source. On occasion, Rob and Linda asked friends who owned one of the makes under consideration about their experiences. On the basis of this information search, they narrowed their choice to four cars—Toyota Corolla, Honda Accord, Saturn, and Oldsmobile.

Figure 3.4 shows that the search for additional information feeds back to stimulus exposure, as additional information may stimulate further search. This process illustrates the dynamic nature of consumers' decision-making process. The components of information processing and brand evaluation are not discrete; they occur on an ongoing basis until consumers reach a final decision.

◆ BRAND EVALUATION

Brand evaluation is illustrated in Figure 3.5. As a result of information processing, consumers will use past and current information to associate brands they are aware of with their desired benefits. Consumers will prefer the brand they expect will give the most satisfaction based on the benefits they seek.

Benefit Association

In benefit association, one must develop a priority of desired benefits and relate a brand's characteristics to these benefits. Rob's and Linda's priorities are, by order of importance, economy, service dependability, performance, comfort, safety, and styling. Rob and Linda use these benefit criteria to evaluate the characteristics of the four makes they are considering. While they give greater weight to benefits they regard as most important, they also include other benefits in assessing the relative merits of each car. On this basis, Rob and Linda determine that the Saturn and Corolla do best on economy, the Saturn and Accord score best on service dependability, and all four makes are rated close to equal on performance. However, the Saturn scores worst on styling. Rob and Linda select the Saturn, despite the negative rating on styling, because it scored highest on the most important benefits.

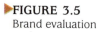
FIGURE 3.5
Brand evaluation

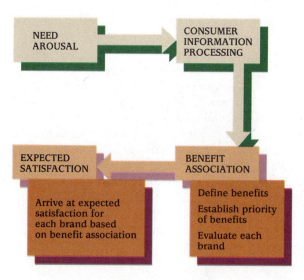

This evaluative procedure is known as a compensatory method of evaluation because a negative rating on one criterion can be made up by a positive rating on another. Thus, even though the Saturn scored lowest on styling, its high ratings on economy and service dependability resulted in Rob and Linda choosing the car.

In the **compensatory method,** consumers evaluate each brand across all benefit criteria. The alternative is a **noncompensatory method** of evaluation in which consumers rate brands one criterion at a time. For example, Rob and Linda might first evaluate the four cars by economy and eliminate the Olds on this basis. They would then evaluate the three remaining cars by the next most important criterion, service dependability, and might eliminate the Accord. Using performance as a criterion they might next eliminate the Corolla, leaving the Saturn as the choice. Thus, consumers may use different decision rules in evaluating brands.[20]

Consumers are more likely to use a compensatory method of evaluation in complex decision making because it guarantees that all brands will be evaluated by all of the most important criteria. The decision is too important to eliminate a brand based on a "one strike and you're out" criterion. On the other hand, consumers are more likely to use noncompensatory methods for less involving decisions such as those for detergents and toothpaste, which take less time and effort to choose.

Expected Satisfaction

Both the compensatory and noncompensatory models agree that consumers develop a set of expectations based on the degree to which a brand or product satisfies the benefits consumers desire. The brand that comes closest to satisfying the most important benefits is expected to provide the most satisfaction. For Rob and Linda, the Saturn had the highest expected satisfaction because it did best on their most important benefit criterion, economy.

◆ PURCHASE AND POSTPURCHASE EVALUATION

The outcome of brand evaluation is an intention to buy (or not to buy). The final sequence in complex decision making involves purchasing the intended brand, evaluating the brand during consumption, and storing this information for future use (that is, feedback). These steps are outlined in Figure 3.6.

Intention to Buy

Once consumers evaluate brands, they intend to purchase those achieving the highest level of expected satisfaction. Purchasing in complex decision making is not likely to be immediate. Rob and Linda may still have some shopping to

▶**FIGURE 3.6**
Purchase and postpurchase evaluation

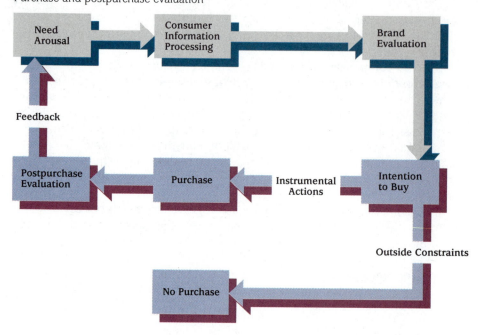

do to obtain the best trade-in value on their present car, and they may have to obtain financing. Therefore, a period of time will ensue before Rob and Linda purchase the Saturn. To purchase the car, they must do several things called **instrumental actions:** select a dealer; determine when to purchase; go to the place of purchase; and, as is often the case with an automobile purchase, arrange for financing. Moreover, they may have to decide on options such as air conditioning or a tape deck.

No Purchase

The consumer decision-making model shows that a decision might be made to delay purchase or not to buy. Rob and Linda may decide not to buy a new car because they estimate that, in the long run, it would be cheaper to fix the Olds. Or, having evaluated the various brands, they may decide to wait and see if some additional options may be introduced in next year's models.

Figure 3.6 demonstrates that the decision-making process may be terminated at any stage because of outside constraints. For example, the Saturn may not be available when expected, or the price of the Saturn may increase unexpectedly due to cost overruns in production.

Purchase

Figure 3.6 demonstrates that the link between intention to buy and actual purchase requires instrumental action. The time lag between intention and purchase is likely to be greater in complex decision making because of the greater number of actions required for a purchase to take place.

Of the instrumental actions required for a purchase, store selection is most important. In fact, store selection may require a decision-making process of its own. Where to purchase a suit or dress may be more critical than what brand to buy. The act of purchasing may also require Rob and Linda to negotiate to get the best terms regarding price, used car allowance, and financing. Rob and Linda will select the dealer that gives them the best terms.

In this case, Rob and Linda made their decision to buy a certain car prior to the purchase. For many goods, decision and purchase are almost simultaneous because consumers make the brand decision in the store. For example, by a glance at the supermarket shelf, a consumer may be reminded of a need for canned peas. With no strong brand loyalties, the consumer examines two or three brands for price, ingredients, and brand name, and makes a decision.

Postpurchase Evaluation

Once the product is purchased, the consumer will evaluate its performance in the process of consumption.

Purchasing Versus Consuming

It is important to distinguish between purchase and consumption for three reasons. First, the product may be purchased by one person and consumed by another. The consumer, not the purchaser, determines product satisfaction. Second, the purchase depends on consumer expectations of the degree to which brands are likely to satisfy needs. Consumption determines whether these expectations are confirmed. Third, a consumer's postpurchase evaluation determines whether the brand is likely to be repurchased. It is unlikely that any brand can survive over time without some degree of loyalty. The consumer's dissatisfaction will lead to no further purchases, negative word-of-mouth communication about the brand, and lost sales.

Satisfaction Versus Dissatisfaction

Satisfaction occurs when consumer expectations are met or exceeded and the purchase decision is reinforced. Such reinforcement is represented in Figure 3.6 as feedback from postpurchase evaluation. Satisfaction reinforces positive attitudes toward the brand, leading to a greater likelihood that the consumer will repurchase the same brand. Dissatisfaction results when consumer expectations are not met. Such disconfirmation of expectations is likely to lead to negative brand attitudes and lessens the likelihood that the consumer will buy the same brand again.

Postpurchase Dissonance

In many cases, a decision involves two or more close alternatives and could go either way. Having made their decisions, consumers may feel insecure, particularly if substantial financial or social risks are involved. Any negative information about the chosen product causes **postpurchase dissonance;** that is, conflict resulting from two contradictory beliefs.

Assume in Rob's and Linda's decision-making process that the Oldsmobile was a close second to the Saturn. The likelihood of postpurchase dissonance increases. The financial risks of purchasing the car make dissonance even more likely. There are also the social risks of buying a car that may not conform to the norms of friends and neighbors, and there is the psychological risk that the wrong decision may have been made.

Suppose that shortly after the purchase, Rob meets a friend who also purchased a Saturn and who relates some negative experiences such as lower than expected gas mileage and mechanical failures. Rob also learns that Oldsmobile will be introducing a smaller, more economical model next year. This information produces postpurchase doubt, as Rob believes he should have perhaps delayed the purchase. Such doubt is psychologically uncomfortable. The tendency is to reduce doubt by confirming the purchase. Consumers do this in several ways:

1. By ignoring the dissonant information.
2. By selectively interpreting the information, saying, for example, that any brand will have an occasional lemon.
3. By lowering the level of expectations, saying that even if there are a few problems with the car, it still is an acceptable choice.
4. By seeking positive information about the brand.
5. By convincing others you made a good choice, and in doing so convincing yourself.

In each case, dissonance is reduced.[21]

Now assume that after six months, Rob finds the Saturn's gas mileage is about 20 percent lower than dealer and advertising claims and that service costs are somewhat higher than expected. In other respects (styling, comfort, performance), the car meets expectations. The theory of postpurchase dissonance says that Rob will focus on the positive performance and tend to dismiss or rationalize the negative performance. If, as is true with Rob and Linda, the disparity between prior expectations and subsequent product performance is not great, an **assimilation effect** occurs. That is, consumers ignore the product's defects and their evaluation of the product remains positive.

If there is a great disparity between prior expectations and performance, however, a **contrast effect** is likely to take place in which consumers recognize and magnify poor performance.[22] Thus, if the Saturn's gas mileage is half of that claimed in the advertising, it is unlikely that Rob would focus solely on the positive aspects of performance. He would probably be extremely dissatisfied, have negative attitudes toward the selected brand, and be unlikely to consider that brand next time.

This description of complex decision making has focused on the individual consumer. The complexities of group decision making were not emphasized in this chapter. For example, what occurs when spouses have different objectives, different sources of information, or different preferences? What is the nature of word-of-mouth influence from friends and relatives in the decision process? What is the impact of differing roles such as influencer, information gatherer, purchasing agent, decision maker, and consumer in the process of group decision making? These considerations will be incorporated into the model of complex decision making in Part Four of the text.

◆ SYMBOLIC PURCHASING BEHAVIOR

The model of complex decision making in Figure 3.2 and the example of Rob's and Linda's purchase of a car assume that consumers make decisions objectively by collecting information on utilitarian product attributes such as service costs, gas mileage, repairs, and performance. This is not always the case. As we all know, we sometimes make decisions based on emotional factors that are the result of our more innate desires and fantasies. A study of motorcycle owners found that many buy not because of the bike's performance, but because of the feeling of independence and power they get while riding and the feeling of kinship with fellow riders at bike rallies.[23] Similarly, rather than buying jeans based on comfort or durability, a consumer might buy them because he or she feels the product enhances self-image. (See Exhibit 3.4.)

In many of these cases, the product is purchased for its symbolic, rather than its utilitarian, value. Such purchases are termed **symbolic purchasing behavior** because, as Hirschman and Holbrook note, products so purchased "are viewed not as objective entities but rather as subjective symbols."[24] Putting it another way, "People buy products not only for what they can *do,* but also for what they *mean.*"[25] As a result, our purchases are a reflection of who we are—our values, aspirations, and social connections.

In symbolic purchases, consumers frequently use emotional, rather than utilitarian, criteria in evaluating alternative brands. (We use the term "emotional" rather than "irrational" and the term "utilitarian" rather than "rational" because emotional criteria such as "feel behind the wheel" could be as rational as utilitarian criteria such as "service costs.") Buying a Gucci scarf for twice as much as the same scarf with a store label cannot be justified based on the functional benefits of a scarf, but it can certainly be justified based on its symbolic value.

Most symbolic purchases are highly involving for consumers because they reflect their self-image. As a result, the model of complex decision making

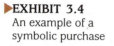

An example of a
symbolic purchase

shown in Figure 3.2 is essentially the same for symbolic purchases. The distinct nature of symbolic purchasing behavior is reflected in the nature of information processing and brand evaluation. Information processing is likely to hinge on the tie between the symbols consumers see in the product and the association of these symbols to the consumers' self-images and social roles. Brand evaluation is more likely to be based on the experiences and emotions that are likely to result from using the brand rather than on the brand's utilitarian performance and economic value.[26] Such evaluations are likely to be the result of consumer impressions and images rather than observable product characteristics.

The marketer's perspective will be very different in symbolic purchasing behavior. In this case, marketing research is concerned not so much with what the product is as with what it means to consumers.[27] As a result, advertising tries to associate the product with the symbols that generate positive emotions and fantasies. Kawasaki was successful in developing such symbolism for its motorcycles by an ad showing a lone rider rounding a bend on a deserted country road with his knee almost touching the ground. The ad captured the feeling of freedom, speed, danger, and contact with the elements—in short, emotion, not performance.

Product characteristics and price become less important elements in marketing strategy for such products. The overriding concern is establishing a brand image that is linked to positive consumer emotions. As we shall see in the next chapter, if product symbols become strongly linked with positive emotions, consumers may eventually purchase by habit rather than by decision making.

A viewing of television advertising on any given day demonstrates the importance of product symbolism in purchasing behavior. Advertisements for cars, cosmetics, clothing, sports equipment, and a range of other products frequently use symbols meant to evoke positive emotional associations. Even when utilitarian product characteristics dominate in brand evaluation, as was the case with Rob's and Linda's purchase of a car, symbols are likely to influence purchases. Although Rob and Linda selected the Saturn primarily on performance criteria, an important symbolic factor was its "new wave" image among many of their friends. As such, the Saturn was a symbol of innovativeness and independence from traditional alternatives for Rob, Linda, and their peer group.

At times, advertisers attempt to appeal to both the symbolic motives of consumers through emotional themes and the more utilitarian motives through product information. The ad for Saab, shown in Exhibit 3.5, is an example. The first page is clearly informational; the second page relies on a direct appeal to the car buyer's emotions.

▶**EXHIBIT 3.5**
Ad appealing to both utilitarian and symbolic motives

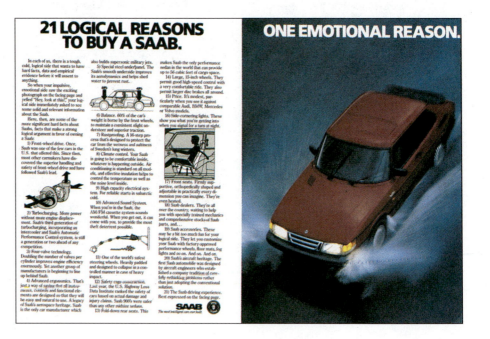

In summary, complex decision making should incorporate consumer evaluations of brands as both objective entities and subjective symbols. Since consumers frequently employ products as symbols in a social setting, the role of product symbolism in consumer behavior will become more evident in Chapters 11 and 13, which cover consumer lifestyles and cultural values.

STRATEGIC APPLICATIONS OF CONSUMER BEHAVIOR

From Heavy Metal to Cologne: Harley-Davidson Changes Its Symbols

Harley-Davidson has long recognized that bikers choose motorcycles for their symbolism as much as their performance. (See Exhibit 3.6.) Until the 1980s, Harley's symbols were the heavy metal and black leather associated with big bikes—a throwback to the days of James Dean and Marlon Brando. Harley had a virtual monopoly of the big bike market. However, by the 1980s, the black leather crowd was dwindling; and Harley knew it would have to look to a new customer base.

The new customer base Harley went after—baby boomers—was a complete reversal of form. By the mid-1980s, many baby boomers were heading toward mid-life crises and were looking for some escape from everyday cares. The stock market crash of 1987 further fueled the search for fantasy. Harley felt big bikes might provide it.

But the symbolism would have to change, and with it, Harley's image. Harley changed its image to appeal to a more affluent, white-collar market in several ways. Out went the heavy metal look in its advertising; in came a softer approach. One ad featured a baby in a Harley T-shirt with the tag line, "When did it start for you?" Harley also began to use celebrities such as Kurt Russell and Elizabeth Taylor in its advertising. The company even began to sell items such as cologne and wine coolers with the Harley name in its dealerships.

By 1990, Harley's success in attracting baby boomers was reflected in the fact that over 60 percent of its buyers attended college with a median income of $45,000, and the company could boast of a three-fold rise in revenues and earnings.

Buying a Harley may still be a good example of symbolic purchasing behavior, but the symbolism has certainly changed.

Sources: "After Nearly Stalling, Harley-Davidson Finds New Crowd of Riders," *The Wall Street Journal* (August 31, 1990), pp. A1 and A6; "Bikers Ride Into Middle Age," *American Demographics* (December, 1991), p. 15.

▶**EXHIBIT 3.6**
Harley-Davidson: A product that emphasizes both symbolism and performance

◆ COMPLEX DECISION MAKING AND STORE CHOICE

Until now, we have focused on decision making for brands. However, consumers also make decisions regarding in what stores they will shop. In buying a car, consumers will determine the make of car first and then choose the dealer to buy from. But frequently, consumers' choice of a store comes first and influences their choice of the brand. For example, we generally make a decision regarding the store first and then the brand when we shop for clothes. Similarly, we often make a brand decision in the store when we shop for appliances or electronics. In these cases, store choice conditions brand choice.

A Model of Store Choice

Consumers' decision making process for a store is similar to that for a brand. The model of store choice in Figure 3.7 is an adaptation of the basic model of complex decision making in Figure 3.2. Consider the business school student, introduced in the beginning of the chapter, who was purchasing a notebook computer. One of the first decisions she had to make was what stores to visit to gather information about alternative brands.

The model in Figure 3.7 shows that there are two components to *need arousal* in store choice: first, a purchasing need (recognition of a need to buy a computer) and, second, a shopping need (need to search for alternatives in various stores). Shopping needs can be complex. Some consumers consider the process of shopping time-consuming and not particularly enjoyable. Others like to search for bargains and enjoy interacting with salespeople.

Need arousal will establish certain priorities as to the store or stores that consumers will select. Assume our student is time-oriented and does not enjoy shopping. Based on her purchase and shopping needs, she is looking for conveniently located stores with knowledgeable salespeople and competitive prices. *Information search* involves asking friends which stores are reliable and searching for store ads with information on prices and models.

On this basis, our consumer will *evaluate stores* and choose several to visit. In the process, she will develop an image of each store. The closer the store is to her needs (knowledgeable and helpful salespeople, good service, competitive prices), the more likely she will buy the computer from that store. Therefore, *store choice* depends on the degree to which the consumer's image of the store is related to his or her purchasing and shopping needs.

As we saw, our consumer decided to purchase a Toshiba. Once having made the brand decision, she selected the store based on price, service, and convenience. In *postpurchase evaluation*, she will evaluate both the brand and the store. The two are closely related; satisfaction with the brand will lead to satisfaction with the store. However, some components of postpurchase evaluation are specific to the store; for example, a car buyer who is satisfied with the purchase but dissatisfied with the service the dealer offers.

▶**FIGURE 3.7**
A model of store choice

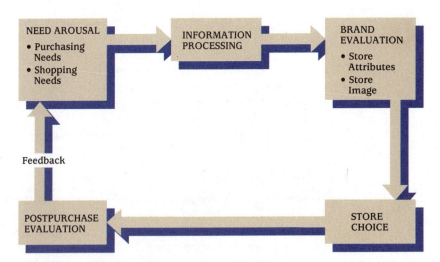

Store Choice and Brand Choice

In the preceding example, our consumer selected the brand first and then the store. It is possible that a consumer might make a computer decision in the store (that is, store choice preceded brand choice).

Under what circumstances is store choice most likely to influence brand choice?

- *When store loyalty is high.*   Consumers loyal to a particular department store are more likely to shop there first for desired items.
- *When brand loyalty is low.*   Consumers with no strong loyalties to a particular brand are more likely to select the store first and make a brand decision within the store.
- *When brand information is inadequate.*   Consumers who have little brand experience or information are more likely to rely on sales personnel for assistance. Brand choice is, therefore, more likely to be made in the store.

SUMMARY

The purpose of this chapter has been to present a comprehensive model of complex decision making. Complex decision making occurs when consumers are involved with the product and go through an extensive decision process to arrive at a choice.

To understand better the nature of complex decision making, consumer involvement with products and purchases was discussed. Two types of involvement are enduring (involvement with the product on a continuing basis) and situational (involvement with the product only during the purchase situation). Consumers are involved on an enduring basis if the product is important, has emotional appeal, and has badge value. Situational involvement is likely to occur when consumers see risk in purchasing the product.

A model of complex decision making has several phases:

1. *Need arousal* initiates a decision process. Consumers' needs may be stimulated by receiving new information about brands, economic conditions, advertising claims, or simply by recognizing an out-of-stock situation. In addition, the consumers' lifestyles, demographics, and personality characteristics are likely to influence their purchase decisions.

2. *Consumer information processing* involves a search for and organization of information from various sources. Information processing is selective; consumers choose information that is (1) most relevant to the benefits they seek and (2) likely to conform to their beliefs and attitudes. Processing of information involves a series of steps—exposure, attention, comprehension, retention in memory, and search for additional information.

3. In the process of *brand evaluation,* consumers will evaluate the characteristics of various brands and choose the brand that is most likely to fulfill their desired benefits.

4. Consumers *purchase* the brand most likely to satisfy their desired benefits. In so doing, various instrumental actions are required such as selecting a store, determining when to purchase, and possibly obtaining financing.

5. Once consumers have made purchases, *postpurchase evaluation* occurs. If performance has met the consumers' expectations, consumers are likely to be satisfied with the product. If not, dissatisfaction will occur, reducing the probability that consumers will repurchase the same brand. In cases in which consumers had difficulty making up their minds, dissonance is likely. Dissonance or postpurchase conflict results from doubts about the decision. As dissonance is not a desirable state, consumers may seek to reduce it by ignoring negative information or by seeking positive information about the brand.

The model of complex decision making assumes an objective process of evaluation in which consumers evaluate alternative products based on utilitarian attributes. However, consumers often purchase products for their symbolic value. Symbolic purchasing behavior is dominated more by emotional, rather than by utilitarian, criteria in evaluating brands. Consumers purchase products for what they mean rather than for what they can do. Examples are motorcycles, perfume, and clothing. Marketing strategies attempt to associate products with symbols that generate positive feelings for such products.

Although most of the chapter was devoted to brand decision making, we noted that consumers also make store decisions. At times, the store decision may determine brand choice. A model of store decision making is essentially the same as that for brands, except that consumers are evaluating store attributes and selecting stores according to shopping as well as purchasing needs.

The next chapter shifts the focus from complex decision making to habit.

QUESTIONS

1. An auto manufacturer is trying to distinguish between consumers who are and those who are not involved with cars. What conditions would identify a consumer who is involved with cars? What are the strategic implications of these conditions?

2. The auto manufacturer further distinguishes between consumers who are involved with cars on an enduring basis and those involved on a situational basis. Cite an example of a consumer who is involved with cars on an enduring basis and one who is involved on a situational basis. What are the distinctions between the two types of involvement?

3. A large auto manufacturer conducted a survey of recent car purchasers to determine their needs in buying new cars and their perceptions of the com-

pany's makes to evaluate possible new product offerings. Information the company collected can be classified into information dealing with each of the four stages of the decision-making model, namely:

a. Need arousal

    1. Consumer thought variables

    2. Consumer characteristics

b. Information processing

    1. Exposure to marketing stimuli

    2. Perceptions of marketing stimuli

c. Evaluation of alternative brands of cars

d. Purchase and postpurchase evaluation

- Specify the types of information the auto manufacturer might collect from consumers for each of the four stages described above.
- Specify the strategic applications of such information.

4. Use the model of complex decision making in this chapter to describe the steps in the decision-making process for the following cases:
   - A businessperson considers adopting a new Picturephone for communication between branches of the firm.
   - A college student considers purchasing a personal computer.
   - A consumer considers purchasing a headache remedy that is advertised as stronger and more effective.

5. What are the implications for marketing strategy based on your description of the decision-making process for each of the three cases in Question 4, particularly implications (where applicable) for: (a) market segmentation, (b) advertising, (c) pricing, (d) distribution, and (e) development of new products?

6. What are the limitations of the model of complex decision making in deriving strategic implications?

7. Of what use might the model of complex decision making be to a marketing manager in the following situations?
   - Kellogg's introduces a new line of adult cereals.
   - General Motors introduces its new line of Saturn cars.
   - Procter & Gamble introduces an improved version of Pampers disposable diapers with better absorbency.

8. What differences in the decision-making process might exist for Rob and Linda Greene in the following situations?
   - They have never purchased a car before.
   - They are in a lower-income group.
   - They are buying a car for business purposes.

9. In some cases, consumers buy almost immediately after reaching a decision. In other cases, there might be a gap between intention and purchase. What are implications of such a gap for advertising and selling strategies?

10. What is meant by symbolic purchasing behavior? What types of products are consumers most likely to purchase based on symbolism? Why?

11. Select a product category that consumers are more likely to purchase on a utilitarian basis and a product category that consumers are more likely to purchase on a symbolic basis.
    - What types of attributes are consumers likely to use in evaluating alternative brands for the utilitarian product? for the symbolic product?
    - What are the implications for advertising the utilitarian product? the symbolic product?
12. A large retailer of sports equipment in an urban area finds sales slipping. As a result, the retailer wishes to conduct a study to determine (a) how consumers decide on a store for sports equipment and (b) the image of the store relative to that of the competition. Specify how the model of store choice in Figure 3.7 might help in determining the required information.

RESEARCH ASSIGNMENTS

1. Select an electronics product that is likely to cost several hundred dollars or more (a video cassette recorder, compact disc player, or personal computer, for example). Conduct depth interviews with consumers who have purchased the item within the past year or who are currently considering purchasing.*
    - Describe the decision-making process for both the decision to buy the product and the particular brand to be purchased.
    - Does the decision-making process conform to the model in Chapter 3?
    - What are the implications of the decision-making process for (a) market segmentation, (b) product positioning, and (c) advertising strategy?
2. Now select an electronics product that is likely to cost under $100 (portable headphones, telephone answering machine, calculator). Conduct depth interviews with consumers who have purchased the item within the past year or who are currently considering purchasing.
    - How does the decision-making process differ from that described in the first assignment?
    - What are the implications of the decision-making process for (a) market segmentation, (b) product positioning, and (c) advertising strategy?

---

* Many of the research assignments proposed in this text will involve conducting depth interviews. **Depth interviews** are unstructured interviews designed to provide the researcher with general insights into consumers' motives and behavior. They can be conducted with individual consumers, or the researcher can bring a group of five to ten consumers together for a group discussion (known as **focus group interviews**). In both cases, the researcher does not ask specific questions; rather, he or she acts as a moderator or passive listener. The researcher may develop a list of areas to be covered in the discussion and may steer the conversation to these topics. Generally, focus group interviews tend to be more insightful and productive because of the stimulation of group interaction. At the end of a series of depth interviews, the researcher should have developed sufficient hypotheses regarding consumer behavior to permit the formulation of a more structured and empirically based research design.

3. Select a product category in which the choice of a store is particularly important (for example, clothing, furniture, rugs and carpets). Identify consumers who have bought an item in the category within the past six months. Conduct seven or eight depth interviews with the consumers to identify the process of store choice.

- Describe the decision process.
- Does the process of store choice conform to the model described in Figure 3.7?
- What are the strategic implications of the decision process for the retailer?

NOTES

1. "Here Comes GM's Saturn," *Business Week* (April 9, 1990), pp. 56–62.
2. "Saturn Turnabout Doubles Ad Budget," *Advertising Age* (January 17, 1994), pp. 1, 44.
3. For a similar clarification of the components of involvement, see Giles Laurent and Jean-Noel Kapferer, "Measuring Consumer Involvement Profiles," *Journal of Marketing Research,* 22 (February, 1985), pp. 41–53.
4. Michael J. Houston and Michael L. Rothschild, "Conceptual and Methodological Perspectives on Involvement," in Subhash C. Jain, ed., *1978 Educators' Proceedings* (Chicago: American Marketing Association, 1978), pp. 184–187.
5. Richard L. Celsi and Jerry C. Olson, "The Role of Involvement in Attention and Comprehension Processes," *Journal of Consumer Research,* 15 (September, 1988), pp. 210–224.
6. *Ibid.*
7. Dennis H. Gensch and Rajshekhar G. Javalgi, "The Influence of Involvement on Disaggregate Attribute Choice Models," *Journal of Consumer Research,* 14 (June, 1987), pp. 71–82.
8. Jean-Noel Kapferer and Gilles Laurent, "Consumer Involvement Profiles: A New Practical Approach to Consumer Involvement," *Journal of Advertising Research,* 25 (December, 1985–January, 1986), pp. 48–56.
9. Laurent and Kapferer, *loc. cit.*
10. Judith L. Zaichowsky and James H. Sood, "A Global Look at Consumer Involvement and Use of Products," *International Marketing Review,* 6 (February, 1988), pp. 20–34.

11. See John Dewey, *How We Think* (New York: Heath, 1910), and Orville Brim *et al.*, *Personality and Decision Processes* (Stanford, CA: Stanford University Press, 1962).
12. "Families Have Changed But Tupperware Keeps Holding Its Parties," *The Wall Street Journal* (July 21, 1992), pp. A1, A4.
13. Abraham H. Maslow, *Motivation and Personality* (New York: Harper & Row, 1954).
14. "Marketing to Mature Adults Requires a State of Being," *Marketing News* (December 9, 1991), p. 10.
15. Donald E. Vinson, Jerome E. Scott, and Lawrence M. Lamont, "The Role of Personal Values in Marketing and Consumer Behavior," *Journal of Marketing,* 41 (April, 1977), pp. 44–50.
16. Michael L. Ray, "Attitudes in Consumer Behavior," in Leon G. Schiffman and Leslie L. Kanuk, *Consumer Behavior* (Englewood Cliffs, NJ: Prentice-Hall, 1978), pp. 150–154.
17. R. Lavidge and Gary A. Steiner, "A Model for Predictive Measurements of Advertising Effectiveness," *Journal of Marketing,* 25 (October, 1961), pp. 59–62; and Michael L. Ray, "Marketing Communication and the Hierarchy of Effects," in P. Clarke, ed., *New Models for Mass Communication Research* (Beverly Hills, CA: Sage Publications, 1973), pp. 147–175.
18. Jacob Jacoby *et al.*, "Pre-Purchase Information Acquisition," in Beverlee B. Anderson, ed., *Advances in Consumer Research* Vol. 3 (Atlanta: Association for Consumer Research, 1975), pp. 306–314.

19. Joseph W. Newman and Richard Staelin, "Prepurchase Information Seeking for New Cars and Major Household Appliances," *Journal of Marketing Research,* 9 (August, 1972), pp. 249–257.

20. For a good review of compensatory and noncompensatory models, see William L. Wilkie and Edgar A. Pessemier, "Issues in Marketing's Use of Multi-Attribute Attitude Models," *Journal of Marketing Research,* 10 (November, 1973), pp. 435–438.

21. For a review of the literature on postpurchase dissonance, see William H. Cummings and M. Venkatesan, "Cognitive Dissonance and Consumer Behavior: A Review of the Evidence," in Mary Jane Schlinger, ed., *Advances in Consumer Research,* Vol. 2 (Ann Arbor: Association for Consumer Research, 1975), pp. 21–31.

22. For a description of assimilation versus contrast theories, see Rolph E. Anderson, "Consumer Dissatisfaction: The Effect of Disconfirmed Expectancy on Perceived Product Performance," *Journal of Marketing Research,* 10 (February, 1973), pp. 38–44.

23. *A Case Study in Understanding Consumer Behavior* (Fountain Valley, CA: Coast Telecourses, 1988).

24. Elizabeth C. Hirschman and Morris B. Holbrook, "Hedonic Consumption: Emerging Concepts, Methods and Propositions," *Journal of Marketing,* 46 (Summer, 1982), pp. 92–101.

25. Sidney Levy, "Symbols for Sale," *Harvard Business Review,* 37 (July–August), pp. 117–124; and Sidney Levy, "Symbolism and Lifestyle," in Steven Greyser, ed., *Toward Scientific Marketing,* Proceedings of the American Marketing Association Educators' Conference, 1964.

26. John C. Mowen, "Beyond Consumer Decision Making," *Journal of Consumer Marketing,* 5 (Winter, 1988), pp. 15–25.

27. James H. Leigh and Terrance G. Gabel, "Symbolic Interactionism: Its Effects on Consumer Behavior and Implications for Marketing Strategy," *Journal of Consumer Marketing,* 9 (Winter, 1992), pp. 27–38; and Hirschman and Holbrook, "Hedonic Consumption," *loc. cit.*

4

Consumer Learning, Habit, and Brand Loyalty

This chapter describes the opposite of complex decision making—habit. A consumer's prior satisfaction with a brand leads to repeat purchases and may result in purchasing by habit. For such purchases, the consumer finds little need for evaluating brand alternatives; recognizing a need will lead directly to a purchase. Therefore, habit is a way of ensuring satisfaction based on past experience and of simplifying decision making by reducing the need for information search and brand evaluation.

Understanding habit requires understanding the principles of consumer learning, as learning theory focuses on the conditions that produce consistent behavior over time. Habit leads to brand loyalty or inertia. Brand loyalty is repeat buying because of commitment to a certain brand, whereas inertia is repeat buying without commitment to the brand. Prior satisfaction with an unimportant product leads the consumer to buy the same brand because it is not worth the time and trouble to go through a decision process.

The strategic importance of habit and brand loyalty is illustrated by one of the most successful and longest-running advertising campaigns in history, the Marlboro Cowboy campaign. Although some might rightfully object to cigarette advertising, there is no denying that until recently, the campaign was highly effective. Why?

In the mid-1950s, Philip Morris, the brand's producer, decided to reposition Marlboro from an elite cigarette aimed at women smokers to a new filtered cigarette aimed at men who were heavier smokers. Needing a symbol to attract blue-collar males who were the heaviest-smoking group, the company decided on the cowboy. The choice of symbol proved to be a stroke of genius because male smokers associated the figure with dominance and masculinity. As the advertising campaign ran, smokers began to *learn* to associate Marlboro with the cowboy. In associating the product with the cowboy, consumers established a positive attitude toward Marlboro; and many decided to try the brand and to purchase it. Repetitive advertising *reinforced* their continued use. As a result, many consumers became brand loyal.

However, the Marlboro Cowboy isn't what he used to be. Many Marlboro smokers are switching to cheaper, low-priced cigarettes, a reflection of greater price consciousness resulting from the 1991–1992 recession. By 1993, Philip Morris began putting more emphasis on price cuts than on the Marlboro Cowboy to retain its consumers.[1] (See the Strategic Applications box on page 121.) The decreasing effectiveness of the Marlboro Cowboy campaign after almost 40 years in the saddle demonstrates that habit and brand loyalty are transitory. Satisfaction can lead to dissatisfaction; reinforcement, to extinction.

In this chapter, we elaborate on many of the terms used above: learning, habit, reinforcement, extinction, and brand loyalty. We first describe learning as a process leading to repetitive behavior. Then, we describe habit and consider two possible outcomes of habitual purchase behavior: brand loyalty and inertia.

◆ CONSUMER LEARNING

Consumers learn from past experience, and their future behavior is conditioned by such learning. In fact, **learning** can be defined as a change in behavior occurring as a result of past experience. As consumers gain experience in purchasing and consuming products, they learn not only what brands they like and do not like, but also the features they like most in particular brands. They then adjust their future behavior based on past experience. After wearing the brand repeatedly, a consumer might determine that a pair of Reebok running shoes is the most comfortable and provides the best support. Continued satisfaction with the brand leads this consumer to buy Reeboks every time he needs new athletic shoes. Thus, continued satisfaction reinforces past experience and increases the probability that the consumer will buy the same brand the next time.

There are two schools of thought in understanding the process of consumer learning: the behaviorist and the cognitive. The **behaviorist school** is concerned with observing changes in an individual's responses as a result of exposure to stimuli. Behaviorist psychologists have developed two types of learning theories: classical conditioning and instrumental conditioning. Classical conditioning views behavior as the result of a close association (contiguity) between a primary stimulus (social success) and a secondary stimulus (a brand of toothpaste, deodorant, or soap). Instrumental conditioning views behavior as a function of the consumer's actions (purchase behavior) and the consumer's assessment of the degree of satisfaction obtained from the action. Satisfaction leads to reinforcement and to an increase in the probability of repurchasing.

The **cognitive school** views learning as problem solving and focuses on changes in the consumer's psychological set (the consumer's attitudes and desired benefits) as a result of learning. In this respect, the cognitive school more closely describes learning within a framework of complex decision making. However, the concepts are relevant to habit, since complex decision making may lead to habit when the consumer is satisfied with the brand and repurchases it over a period of time.

Figure 4.1 illustrates the cognitive and the behaviorist schools of learning and, within the behaviorist school, classical and instrumental conditioning. These three theories of learning will be considered next.[2]

Classical Conditioning

In **classical conditioning,** a secondary stimulus is paired with a primary stimulus that already elicits a particular response. As a result of this pairing, an association is formed. Eventually, the secondary stimulus will elicit the same reac-

▶**FIGURE 4.1**
Types of learning theories

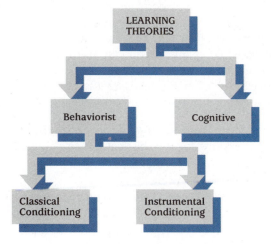

tion as the primary stimulus. An effective advertising campaign may link a product to a stimulus that evokes a positive feeling. For example, the basis for the Marlboro Cowboy campaign was the fact that many people viewed a cowboy as conveying strength, masculinity, and quiet security. The cowboy is the **primary** or **unconditioned stimulus.** The positive feeling that the cowboy evokes (strength, masculinity) is the **unconditioned response.**

Consumers associate the product (Marlboro cigarettes) with the cowboy through (1) repetitive advertising and (2) contiguity (cowboy always linked to Marlboro). The product then becomes a **secondary** or **conditioned stimulus** because it will evoke the same positive feeling as does the cowboy. The Marlboro campaign was successful because of this positive link. As a result, the cowboy influenced smokers to buy Marlboro and reminded Marlboro smokers to repurchase. The brand purchase is the **conditioned response.**

Theories of classical conditioning[3] are reflected in Pavlov's famous experiments.[4] Pavlov reasoned that because his dogs salivated (unconditioned response) at the sight of food (unconditioned stimulus), a neutral stimulus such as a bell could also cause the dogs to salivate if it was closely associated with the unconditioned stimulus (food). To test his theory, Pavlov rang a bell when presenting food to the dogs. After a number of trials, the dogs learned the connection between bell and food; and when they heard the bell (conditioned stimulus) even in the absence of food, they salivated (conditioned response).

These associations are represented at the top of Figure 4.2. The association between the conditioned stimulus and unconditioned stimulus is represented as a dotted arrow because it is a learned association. The association between conditioned stimulus and conditioned response is also learned. The two key concepts are repetition and contiguity. To establish a conditioned response, the conditioned stimulus must be frequently repeated in close contiguity to the unconditioned stimulus.

Classical conditioning can be applied to marketing in an effort to associate a product with a positive stimulus. For example, Miller Lite Beer is frequently advertised during exciting sports events. Because of the repetitive pairing of the product with sports events, the excitement the sports event produces may eventually carry over to Miller Lite. This association may influence people to buy the brand. Similarly, companies frequently use celebrities who are associated with social or financial success as spokespersons to establish a positive link with their products (for example, Julius Erving advertising Dr. Scholl's foot powder or Chris Evert advertising tennis shoes. (See Exhibit 4.1.)

Requirements for Utilizing Classical Conditioning

If advertisers are to use classical conditioning concepts to influence consumers, several conditions must occur. McSweeney and Bierley cite four conditions:[5]

1. *There should be no other stimuli that could overshadow the unconditioned stimulus.* For example, assume the Marlboro Cowboy was always

▶**FIGURE 4.2**
Summary of three
learning theories
Source: Reprinted with the
permission of Macmillan
College Publishing
Company from *Consumer
Behavior and the Practice of
Marketing*, 3/e by Kenneth
E. Runyon and David W.
Stewart. Copyright © 1987
by Macmillan College
Publishing Company, Inc.

CLASSICAL CONDITIONING

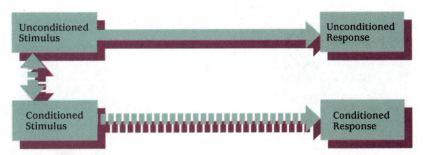

Emphasis: Association through repetition and contiguity

INSTRUMENTAL CONDITIONING

Emphasis: Reinforcement; dependence of outcome on learner's actions

COGNITIVE LEARNING THEORY

Emphasis: Problem solving; understanding relationships

portrayed on a white horse. It is possible the white horse might have over-shadowed the cowboy as a stimulus, thus weakening the association between the cowboy and the product. This is known as the **overshadowing effect.** The overshadowing effect purposefully occurs in advertising Marlboro cigarettes in Hong Kong, where the cowboy is shown in a white hat on a white horse to create an association with the positive cultural significance of the color white in the Far East.

▶**EXHIBIT 4.1**
Using a spokesperson to establish a positive link with the product

2. *Unconditioned stimuli should have no previous associations to other brands or product categories.* Assume a beer company decides to use a cowboy in its advertising to convey a macho image to its target group. The campaign would be ineffective because of the association already established by the Marlboro Cowboy. This is referred to as the **blocking effect.**

3. *The unconditioned stimulus should not be overly familiar and presented alone.* Consumers could become oversaturated with certain stimuli that frequently appear in the mass media (known as a **preexposure effect**). Such stimuli are unlikely to be effective as the unconditioned stimulus. For example, the tuxedo has been shown so often as a symbol of luxury that it has probably lost its effectiveness. Similarly, Michael Jordan appearing as a spokesperson for Nike may wear thin as a result of his frequent exposure. He has also served as a spokesperson for McDonald's, Hanes, Wheaties, and Gatorade. (See Exhibit 4.2.)

4. *Classical conditioning is more effective when the conditioned stimulus is new.* Consumers have established associations for well-known products. Given Pillsbury's strong association with the Doughboy, it would be difficult for the

► **EXHIBIT 4.2**
An example of the preexposure effect

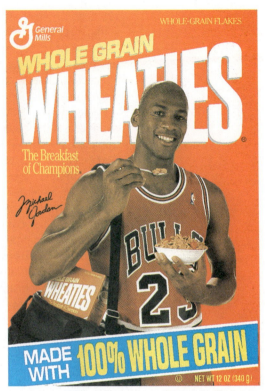

Source: Used with the permission of General Mills, Inc.

company to link its products with a new unconditioned stimulus. When Philip Morris introduced the Marlboro Cowboy, it repositioned the brand as a new product entry. First introduced in the 1920s as an elite cigarette aimed at women smokers, Marlboro had a rose tip so the red imprint of women's lipstick would not show; and its advertising slogan was "Mild as May." Performance was lackluster.[6] In repositioning the brand, Philip Morris wanted to make a clean break with these past associations.

Additional support for the greater effectiveness of new stimuli comes from research by Shimp, Stuart, and Engle. They associated colas with various background scenes and found that conditioning was strongest for relatively unknown cola brands with names like Elf, Cragmont, and Target. When it came to Pepsi and Coke, they "are so well-known that little opportunity remains for additional learning."[7]

Applications of Classical Conditioning

Advertisers accepted classical conditioning concepts of repetition and contiguity on a more widespread basis before 1950. At that time, advertisers used jingles and themes frequently in radio commercials. The advent of television lent a new dimension to advertising by providing more variability through the video component. In addition, a more consumer-oriented approach to advertising resulted in greater variation as advertisements were directed to particular consumer segments. A mass advertising approach based on a single repeated theme was not as viable a strategy. As a result of these developments, attempts to establish associations through frequent repetition have decreased since the 1950s.

The shift in advertising emphasis away from classical conditioning also implied a shift toward principles of cognitive learning. Measures of recall are still used in evaluating ads to determine whether basic brand associations have been established. However, measures of attitude change (changes in brand beliefs, preferences, and intention as a result of advertising) are also used as criteria for advertising effectiveness. This change means that criteria of effectiveness have shifted from measures of association (such as recall) to measures of change in the consumer's psychological set (for example, brand perceptions and attitude change).

Today, advertisers still recognize the importance of principles of classical conditioning and attempt to associate products with positive symbols and images. One such application is the recent swing back to using past advertising themes and symbols that were so successfully bonded to the product through advertising that consumers still associate the brand with the theme.

An example was the reintroduction in 1993 of Elsie the Cow as the symbol for Borden after a 20-year hiatus.[8] The past contiguity between Elsie and the Borden name is so strong that most consumers have no trouble making the association, even after 20 years. Borden found it more economical to resurrect the old symbol than to attempt to build new associations through untested advertising campaigns. The simple rationale was that Elsie created positive associations with the product in the past, and bringing her back would reinforce these positive associations. Other companies have brought back past advertising themes for the same reason; for example, Timex (It takes a lickin' and keeps on tickin'); Memorex tapes (Is It Live or Is It Memorex?) (see Exhibit 4.3.); and Campbell's Soup (Mmm, Mmm, Good!).

Few advertisers believe that such associations are strong enough to result in automatic responses of the type Pavlov created. Instead, the attempt is to create a mood or image that is positively associated with a brand to induce consumers to purchase.

Instrumental Conditioning

Instrumental conditioning also requires the development of a link between a stimulus and response. However, the individual determines the response that provides the greatest satisfaction. That is, no previous stimulus-response connection is required; response is within the conscious control of the individual. In classical conditioning, the unconditioned stimulus is already linked to a response; response is automatic or involuntary. Instrumental conditioning can best be illustrated by a hypothetical experiment. Suppose Pavlov had provided

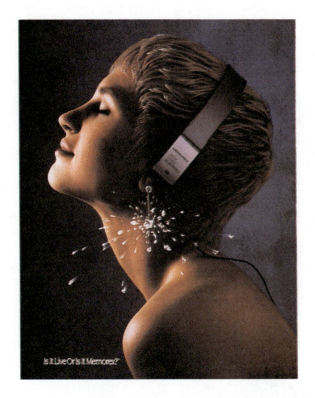

his dogs with two levers instead of one. When pushed, one lever would produce food; the other, a shock. The dogs would have quickly learned to press
the lever that produced food and to avoid the lever that produced a shock.
Learning occurs because the same act is repeatedly rewarded or reinforced.

The foremost proponent of instrumental conditioning was B. F. Skinner. In
Skinner's experiments, the subject was free to act in a variety of ways.[9] The
consequences of the act (degree of satisfaction or dissatisfaction) will influence
future behavior. These associations are summarized in the middle of Figure 4.2.
Behavior results in an evaluation of degree of reward or punishment obtained
from past behavior. Reward will increase the probability of repeating the behavior; punishment will decrease that probability.

Antismoking commercials rely on principles of instrumental conditioning
by linking smoking to a shortened life span. This link, which is meant to create avoidance, would be analogous to the lever producing an electric shock. In
contrast, Philip Morris was relying on principles of classical conditioning by trying to condition smokers' responses based on the positive association of the
cowboy with the product.

Reinforcement

Instrumental conditioning comes closer than classical conditioning to
describing the formation of habit in consumer purchasing. The consumer has

control over his or her purchasing behavior. Continuous **reinforcement** (repeated satisfaction) resulting from product usage increases the probability that the consumer will purchase the same brand. Initially, the consumer undergoes a decision process; but with continuous reinforcement, the probability of buying the same brand increases until the consumer establishes a habit.

The role of reinforcement in producing habit is illustrated in a study by Bennett and Mandel.[10] They asked a sample of recent car purchasers to recall the cars they had purchased in the past and to determine the amount of information seeking in their most recent purchase. Although Bennett and Mandel found that information seeking did not decrease with the number of car purchases made in the past, it did decrease if the consumer purchased the same car repeatedly. In other words, past experience alone will not reduce information seeking. Rather, it is reduced only by past experience that leads to satisfaction and repeat purchase of the same brand. Therefore, a necessary condition for the formation of habit is reinforcement of past purchase behavior.

Continued satisfaction with a product means that the product becomes a positive reinforcer of past behavior. Other stimuli can also be positive reinforcers. For example, if a consumer regularly buys a favorite brand of clothing in a particular store, not only the product but also the store becomes a positive stimulus in reinforcing past behavior. Other reinforcers may be a special sale on the consumer's regular brand, a new, improved version of it, or positive word-of-mouth communication about the brand from friends and relatives.

Extinction and Forgetting

Theories of instrumental conditioning also help us understand the events that may lead a consumer to cease buying by habit. If a consumer is no longer satisfied with the product, a process of **extinction**—that is, the elimination of the link between stimulus and expected reward—takes place. Extinction will lead to a rapid decrease in the probability that the consumer will repurchase the same brand. Successful antismoking commercials will create extinction by eliminating the link between a cigarette and the pleasure of smoking.

Forgetting differs from extinction. **Forgetting** occurs when the stimulus is no longer repeated or perceived. If a product is not used or if its advertising is discontinued, consumers may forget that product. At the turn of the century, Sapolio soap was on a par with Ivory as a leading brand. When the company decided that Sapolio was so well known that a reduction in advertising was warranted, both the company and the product began their demise. In this case, extinction did not occur because the brand still satisfied consumers. Rather, the company's action resulted in forgetting and a long-term decline in sales repetition. Another cause of forgetting is competitive advertising, which causes interference with receipt of the message. The consumer may become confused by advertising clutter, and the link between stimulus and reward weakens.

Marketers can combat forgetting by repetition. By simply maintaining the level of advertising expenditures relative to competition, a company can generally avoid any serious forgetting on the consumer's part. However, repetition, in itself, is of limited use because showing the same ad again and again may merely irritate the consumer. It is more important to avoid extinction since lack of sufficient reward can mean the quick end of any brand. The most important vehicle for avoiding extinction is to deliver sufficient benefits to a defined target segment, The problem Marlboro faces is that many former users do not see sufficient benefits compared to those of lower-priced alternatives.

Figure 4.3 presents learning curves that reflect processes of reinforcement, extinction, and forgetting as related to *advertising exposure*. Reinforcement occurs if repetitive exposures to an ad campaign increase the probability of repurchase. Extinction quickly decreases that probability because of a negative stimulus, even if the consumer continues to see the ad campaign for the product. Forgetting results in a longer-term decline in the probability of repurchase due to a decrease in advertising frequency.

The importance of these concepts is illustrated by the Federal Trade Commission's decision to force Listerine to undertake corrective advertising to counter its long-advertised claim that its mouthwash helped stop colds. The FTC could have merely asked Listerine to stop making the claim, but it chose corrective advertising because of the cumulative effects of past reinforcement. As the campaign had run for many years, consumers' memories of it would die slowly; and positive association between stimulus and response would continue. In other words, the consumer would be on the forgetting portion of the curve. Corrective advertising, however, would force extinction between the stimulus and response. As *Ad Age* reported, "The FTC said it believed it had ample evidence to demonstrate that the effects of Listerine advertising will carry over into future consumer buying decisions unless corrective advertising is implemented."[11]

▶**FIGURE 4.3**
Reinforcement, extinction, and forgetting

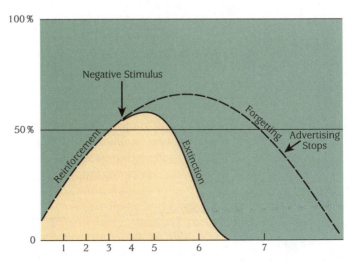

PROBABILITY OF PURCHASING ON THE NEXT TRIAL

NUMBER OF REPETITIVE EXPOSURES OVER TIME

In a similar situation, the FTC chose not to force Ocean Spray to correct the impression that cranapple juice has more vitamins than apple juice. The FTC was satisfied with having Ocean Spray cease advertising the claim. One possible reason for the difference in the two cases is that Ocean Spray's claim was not advertised as long as Listerine's. As a result, consumers more easily forgot it.

An unforeseen potential for extinction occurred in 1990 when Perrier found traces of benzene, a possible carcinogen, in its bottled water. The company recalled its inventory (representing 72 million bottles in the United States) and immediately launched a $25 million marketing campaign to avoid product extinction and to re-establish the product's credibility. The tag line "Perrier. Worth waiting for" was meant to reassure loyal users that the link between the product and customer satisfaction would be maintained once the product returned.[12]

Applications of Instrumental Conditioning to Marketing

Instrumental conditioning is important in marketing because the theory focuses on reinforcement. Quite simply, consumers will repurchase when they are satisfied. Therefore, the objective of all marketing strategy should be to reinforce the consumer's purchase through product satisfaction. This thesis is the very basis of the marketing concept: Develop marketing strategies that deliver known consumer benefits. Only in this manner can a brand achieve repeat purchases and a core of loyal users.

Principles of instrumental conditioning can be applied to advertising and sales promotional strategy. The role of advertising is to increase consumers' expectation of reinforcement. This can be done by communicating product benefits to convince consumers that they will be satisfied if they buy the product. The role of sales promotion is to create an initial inducement to try the product by offering free samples, coupons, or price deals. If the product is satisfactory, many consumers will continue to buy, even if the incentives are withdrawn. Coupons and price deals should be withdrawn gradually, however.[13] These strategies can be successful only if the product is a source of satisfaction and reinforcement. Advertising and price inducements cannot support a poor product for very long.

Cognitive Learning

Cognitive psychology views learning as a problem-solving process rather than the development of connections between stimulus and response. Cognitive learning for consumers is a process of perceiving stimuli, associating stimuli to needs, evaluating alternative brands, and assessing whether products meet expectations. Learning is equated to a process of complex decision making because of the emphasis on problem solving.

Cognitive Learning Theory

Markin compares the cognitive orientation to learning with the behaviorist orientation:

The behaviorist is inclined to ask, "What has the subject learned to do?" The cognitivist, on the other hand, would be inclined to ask, "How has the subject learned to perceive the situation?" The cognitivist is interested in

---

STRATEGIC APPLICATIONS OF CONSUMER BEHAVIOR

From Reinforcement to Extinction: The Marlboro Cowboy Falls Off His Saddle

It was Friday, April 2, 1993, and Philip Morris had just announced a steep price cut for its flagship brand, Marlboro. The reaction on Wall Street was immediate, an almost 15-point drop in Philip Morris's stock price, representing a loss of $13 billion in market value. In the coming week, other producers of packaged goods would experience a similar drop in their stock prices—PepsiCo, Coca-Cola, P&G, Gillette.

What happened? Investors were reacting to a change in consumer buying habits that were building for a decade. The 1991-1992 recession hit the bastion of brand loyalty—the middle class—hardest. In moving from the free-spending '80s into the '90s, this group became more price- and value-conscious. Higher-priced national brands were out. Lower-priced private brands (that is, brands sponsored by retailers or wholesalers) and lower-priced manufacturers' brands were in because they were often of equal quality to the national brands. (In 1993, 50 percent of consumers in a survey said private brands equalled national brands in quality, up from 31 percent in 1985.)

Marlboro was particularly hard hit by the shift. The brand lost 5 share points from 1989 to 1993, representing a loss of close to $2 billion a year in sales. Lower-priced brands such as Doral, Viceroy, and Bucks were stealing Marlboro loyalists in droves because these brands cost as much as a dollar a pack less. By 1993, 39 percent of cigarette sales were going to private brands.

Once the company decided to satisfy the consumer's greater price sensitivity, the Marlboro Cowboy was doomed. Philip Morris is now relying more on coupons, price promotions, and special offers to sell Marlboro than on advertising. (See Exhibit 4.4.) As one analyst said, "Today a campaign [such as the Marlboro Cowboy] won't have much impact on puffers who want to snag a bargain." [*The Wall Street Journal* (June 23, 1992), p. B1.]

The result is a clear weakening of any conditioning effect and outright extinction of the positive association between the Marlboro Cowboy and the brand for many smokers. The Marlboro Cowboy's days in the saddle may be numbered.

Sources: "Up in Smoke," *Adweek* (June 21, 1993), pp. 24-32; "Brands on the Run," *Business Week* (April 19, 1993), pp. 26-28; "Marlboro's 2-Fisted Pitch," *The New York Times* (April 6, 1993), pp. D1 and D22; and "More Shoppers Bypass Big-Name Brands and Steer Carts to Private-Label Products," *The Wall Street Journal* (October 20, 1992), pp. B1 and B5.

▶**EXHIBIT 4.4**
An example of
extinction: Marlboro's
shift away from the
Cowboy

Before

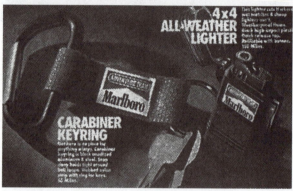

After

examining a learning situation in terms of such factors as motivation, the perceived goals, the overall nature of the situation, and the beliefs, values, and personality of the subject—in short, the entire range of the subject's psychological field. The cognitivist, as opposed to the behaviorist, contends that consumers do not respond simply to stimuli but instead act on beliefs, express attitudes, and strive toward goals.[14]

In other words, cognitive theory emphasizes the thought process involved in consumer learning. Classical and instrumental conditioning emphasize the results based on the stimulus associations.

Cognitive learning theory is an outgrowth of Kohler's experiments on apes conducted in the early 1920s.[15] In one experiment, Kohler placed a chimpanzee in a cage with several boxes, and bananas were hung from the roof. After trying to reach the food and failing, the chimp solved the problem by placing a box under the bananas. Learning was not a result of contiguity between stimulus and response or reinforcement; it was the result of insight. The cognitive approach to learning is presented at the bottom of Figure 4.2 as recognition of a goal, purposive behavior to achieve the goal, insight as to a solution, and goal achievement. Reinforcement is a recognized part of cognitive learning, as there must be an awareness of goal achievement for learning to take place. However, the nature of the goal is understood from the beginning, and the reward (such as eating the bananas) is anticipated. In instrumental conditioning, the reward is not apparent until after behavior takes place.

Marketing Applications of Cognitive Learning

Cognitive learning is relevant in understanding the process of consumer decision making. The model of complex decision making in Chapter 3 describes a process of cognitive learning. Consumers recognize a need, evaluate alternatives to meet that need (purposive behavior in Figure 4.2), select the product they believe will most likely satisfy them (insight), and then evaluate the degree to which the product meets the need (goal achievement).

Cognitive learning is particularly important in understanding the adoption process for an innovation. Consumers learn of innovations from advertising, friends and relatives, and impartial sources such as *Consumer Reports* magazine. To consider a new product, the consumer goes through a series of cognitive stages—awareness, interest, and evaluation—before deciding whether to adopt the product. For an innovation to be adopted widely, knowledge must be diffused across groups (that is, learning must be widespread). The introduction of the videodisc is an example. Until RCA introduced its version of the product, SelectaVision, the level of knowledge and rate of diffusion of information was fairly low. Afterward, consumers became more aware of the product alternatives because of RCA's heavy advertising campaign. However, consumers were reluctant to adopt the product because it did not have recording capabilities and because of confusion about competing videodisc technologies.[16] A cognitive process of problem solving led many consumers to reject the product because it did not meet their in-home entertainment needs.

A study of the purchasing patterns of recent residents of a community also reflects a process of cognitive learning. Andreasen and Durkson studied the purchasing patterns of three groups of households, selected according to the time they had been living in the Philadelphia area: less than three months, one and a half to two years, and three years or more.[17] The researchers believed there would be little difference among the three groups for national brands. However, for local brands, they predicted that the longer a family lived in the area, the closer brand awareness and purchasing would be to those of established residents. Results confirmed their hypothesis. The families living in the area one and a half to two years were closer to the purchase patterns of the established residents than were families living in the area three months or less.

Andreasen and Durkson identified three learning tasks in a new market environment: (1) brand identification, (2) brand evaluation, and (3) establishment of regular behavioral patterns with respect to the evaluated brands. This perspective clearly reflects a cognitive orientation to learning.

Relevance of the Cognitive Versus the Behaviorist Perspective

It is apparent that the cognitive and behaviorist approaches to learning are very different. Therefore, it is reasonable to ask in what marketing situations one is more likely to be relevant than another.

As the behaviorist approach places little emphasis on thought processes and consumer attitudes, it might be most relevant when the consumer's cognitive activity is minimal. As we will see in the next chapter, this is most likely to occur when the consumer is not involved with the product. Taking an instrumental conditioning perspective, consumers in a passive, uninvolved state may be more receptive to buying what they purchased before as long as it is reasonably satisfactory. Perhaps if they spent more time searching for information on soap, toothpaste, or paper towels, they might find a better brand. However, for many products, it is simply not worth the effort. Positive reinforcement produces a satisfactory but by no means optimal choice.

Principles of classical conditioning can also be applied to low involvement purchasing behavior. According to Allen and Madden, when the consumer is in a passive state, it is easier to establish a link between a product and a positive stimulus.[18] For example, a brand of toothpaste might be linked to a nice smile or a brand of disposable diapers to a contented baby, with little thought on the part of the consumer. If the link is repeated frequently enough, the consumer may see the brand in the store and buy it based on these positive associations.

Cognitive learning theory is more relevant for important and involving products. In these cases, a consumer's problem solving takes place through a process of information search and brand evaluation. Goal achievement through purposive behavior is more descriptive of decisions for buying cars, clothing, or furniture than those for toothpaste, paper towels, or detergents.

Vicarious Learning

A type of consumer learning that has important marketing applications is **vicarious learning;** that is, people change their behavior as a result of observing the behavior of others. Vicarious learning affects people's behavior in two ways:

1. If they see positive consequences from the behavior of others, they will imitate it.
2. If they see negative consequences, they will avoid the behavior.

Advertisers often promote vicarious learning by showing people using their products and having positive results or by showing the negative results if people do not use their products. Praise for clean clothes as a result of using a laundry detergent or social approval after using a hair coloring product are appeals that attempt to stimulate positive vicarious learning. In contrast, the social embarrassment of not using a deodorant or a denture adhesive stimulate negative vicarious learning.

◆ HABIT

Habit can be defined as repetitive behavior resulting in a limitation or absence of (1) information seeking and (2) evaluation of alternative choices. Learning leads to habitual purchasing behavior if the consumer is satisfied with the brand over time. After repetitive purchases, the consumer will buy the brand again with little information seeking or brand evaluation. In this section, we consider the nature of habit. We then consider brand loyalty as a likely result of habitual purchasing behavior.

A Model of Habitual Purchasing Behavior

A model showing the process of habitual purchasing behavior is presented in Figure 4.4. The consumer has settled on a regular brand, for example, Coca-Cola Classic (hereafter, Coke), based on past experience and has become a loyal purchaser. Stimulus exposure is limited primarily to a reminder of the need to purchase (the consumer is out of stock) or to simple internal stimuli such as thirst. As a result, the consumer recognizes a need; but information processing is limited or nonexistent. That is, recognition of a need is likely to lead directly to an intention to buy. Being out of the brand may be sufficient reason to add Coke to the shopping list, or perhaps the loyal consumer will be reminded by seeing Coke on the store shelf. The consumer evaluates the brand after purchase and expects to receive the same satisfaction from the brand as experienced

▶**FIGURE 4.4**

A model of habitual purchasing behavior

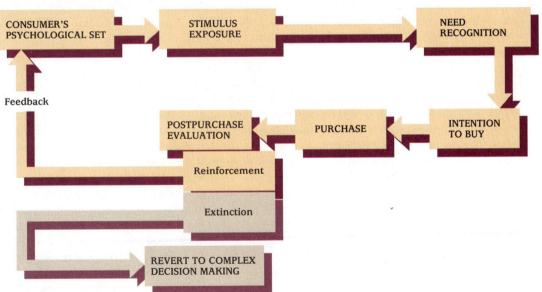

previously. This is very likely, since prepackaged products generally ensure standardization. Continued satisfaction results in a high probability that the consumer will repurchase the brand.

However, the possibility exists that the product will not meet the consumer's expectations, resulting in extinction of the link between brand usage and positive rewards. For example, the consumer may find a box of cereal is half-empty when purchased or may not like the taste of a reformulation of a brand of toothpaste. As a result, the consumer considers alternative brands, initiating a process of decision making.

Other factors besides dissatisfaction may cause extinction and a change from habit to complex decision making. For instance, a new product comes on the market; the consumer becomes aware of it and considers purchasing. Information search and brand evaluation result. In another case, additional information may cause a change in needs and may result in decision making. Information on the negative effects of smoking might cause a smoker to reassess the favored brand of cigarettes in terms of tar and nicotine content.

Also, boredom with a brand may prompt the consumer to look for something new. Howard and Sheth state that at times consumers get tired of buying by habit: "The buyer, after attaining routinization of his decision process [habit], may find himself in too simple a situation. He is likely to feel monotony or boredom associated with such repetitive decision making. . . . He feels a need to complicate his buying situation by considering new brands."[19] The result, once again, is a move away from habit to more complex decision making.

Finally, extinction may result because of constraints on purchasing the same brand. For example, if the store was out of the preferred brand, the consumer then considers other brands and finds a preferred alternative. There may also be a change in price. If the price of a less-preferred brand is reduced or that of the regular brand increased, the consumer may consider other alternatives.

Habit and Information Seeking

Several studies have examined the relationship between habit and information seeking. Newman and Werbel evaluated habitual purchasing according to information sought and classified purchases as (1) habit, (2) approaching habit, and (3) decision making.[20] They used this scheme to analyze the purchase of major appliances. One would assume the incidence of habit would be very low for major appliances as they are infrequently purchased and carry high financial risk. Newman and Werbel found that 15 percent of the purchases could be characterized as habit and another 12 percent as approaching habit. Therefore, over one-fourth of the purchases of major appliances are routinized despite the potential risks.

In their study, Lehmann, Moore, and Elrod further illustrate the link between habit and information seeking. They asked consumers to choose five different types of bread over a six-week period.[21] Before making a choice, consumers were able to acquire as much or as little information as they desired. The study found a decline over time in the desire for information. In fact, for a substantial number of respondents, choice became so routinized that they selected no information at all.

Functions of Habit

Purchasing by habit provides two important benefits to the consumer. First, it reduces risk; second, it facilitates decision making. When consumers are highly involved with the product, habit is a means of reducing purchase risk. Buying the same brand again and again reduces the risk of product failure and financial loss for important purchases. Frequently, when information is limited, consumers buy the most popular brand as the safest choice. Several studies cite such brand loyalty as a means of reducing risk. Roselius questioned consumers on ways of reducing purchase risk and found that brand loyalty and buying a well-known brand were mentioned most frequently.[22]

Habit also simplifies decision making by minimizing the need for information search. When consumers are not involved with a product, they try to minimize search because it is not worth the time and energy involved. A typical shopping list may easily include 20 items or more, many of which are relatively unimportant. Consider the amount of time the consumer would spend in prepurchase deliberation or in-store selection if each item required an examination of brand alternatives.

A study by Kass examined the role of habit in new mothers' purchases of baby products.[23] As mothers became more experienced and knowledgeable, the number of information sources they used in evaluating alternative baby products and the amount of information they sought decreased. Clearly, habit formation was taking place. The findings also showed that as habit develops not only is information reduced, but the type of information also changes. For example, purchasing by habit resulted in:

1. A shift in the type of information sought from general product information to specific brand information.
2. More reliance on information on price or availability, with less reliance on product-specific information such as freshness and vitamin content.

Consumers were learning to be more efficient purchasers by selecting a favorite brand. However, they were also watching for price specials on competitive brands and for the appearance of new brands.

Strategic Implications of Habit Versus Complex Decision Making

Complex decision making and habit are two extremes of a continuum. In between is what might be described as limited decision making. The top of Figure 4.5 presents complex decision making, limited decision making, and habit on a continuum based on the probability of repurchase. Consumers purchase

▶**FIGURE 4.5**
As the probability of purchasing the same brand increases, the amount of information search and prepurchase deliberation decreases.

PROBABILITY OF PURCHASING SAME BRAND AGAIN

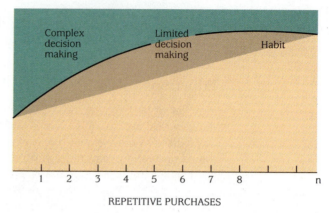

REPETITIVE PURCHASES

TIME SPENT IN PREPURCHASE INFORMATION SEARCH

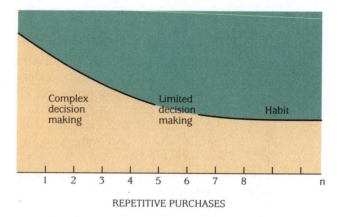

REPETITIVE PURCHASES

more frequently those products bought by habit. With each successive purchase of the same brand, the chances of buying again increase until there is a high probability consumers will continue to repurchase. As the probability of repurchasing increases, the time consumers spend on information search and prepurchase deliberation decreases, as shown on the bottom half of Figure 4.5.

The curve at the top of Figure 4.5 is a **learning curve** because it shows that over time consumers learn which brand satisfies them. The result is an increase in the probability that consumers will continue to purchase the brand. It is important for marketing management to identify the position of a brand on the continuum from habit to complex decision making. The strategic implications of this position apply to every facet of marketing strategy.

Distribution

As brands consumers purchase by habit are likely to be high-turnover, low-margin items, they should be distributed extensively. Widespread distribution is important for those consumers who purchase by habit because seeing the item reminds them to buy. The classic example is Hershey's sole reliance, until the early 1970s, on intensive distribution rather than on advertising to promote its chocolate bar. Since consumers do not purchase as frequently those products characterized by complex decision making, manufacturers are more likely to distribute them selectively or exclusively.

Product

Products consumers purchase by complex decision making, primarily appliances and durables, tend to be technically more complex. Personal selling is more important for these products, and service is more likely to be required. Products consumers purchase by habit are generally packaged goods involving few service requirements and little direct selling.

Advertising and In-Store Promotions

The nature of advertising and promotions differs according to the product's position on the decision-making continuum. Products with a high incidence of consumers' habitual purchases are more likely to use advertising as a reminder. In such cases, frequent advertising is most important. In contrast, markets characterized by consumers' complex decision making are more likely to use advertising selectively to convey information to specific audiences. (See Exhibit 4.5.) In-store stimuli will also be more important for products consumers purchase by habit. Because they show the product, displays and shelf position become important vehicles to induce purchasing. In contrast, products that involve consumers' complex decision making require promotions that will influence the purchaser to evaluate the brand before entering the store. Marketers rely more on informational advertising and personal selling for this purpose.

Pricing

Pricing policies are also likely to differ. When consumers purchase brands by habit, frequently the only way a competitor can get a brand-loyal consumer to try an alternative brand is to introduce a price deal or special sale. Another method of inducing trial among brand loyalists is to provide free samples in the hope the loyal consumer will consider buying the alternative brand. Price deals or free samples are less effective in consumers' complex decision making because the risks of buying just to save money may be too great. In addition, the marketer's costs for free samples or price deals for specialty items may be prohibitive.

Inducing a Switch from Habit to Decision Making

Generally, consumers are more likely to purchase the market leader in a product category by habit. This is true because repeat purchase and satisfaction are likely to increase market share and many consumers buy the leading brand to avoid risk and the need to search for information. Buying the market leader is a safe way to routinize purchase behavior.

▶**EXHIBIT 4.5**

Advertising used to inform versus to remind consumers

Source: Courtesy of Apple Computer Inc.

Advertising to inform

Advertising to remind

Marketers who want their brands to challenge the leading brand must induce consumers to switch from habit to decision making. Various marketing strategies can induce consumers who buy by habit to consider other brands:

- *Create awareness of an alternative to the leading brand.*   MCI advertises "800 reasons to leave AT&T" to create awareness of an alternative for long distance service. (See Exhibit 4.6.)
- *Advertise a new feature in an existing brand.[24]*   Plaque-fighting properties in toothpaste or hexachlorophene in soap may induce consumers to switch brands.
- *Try to change consumer priorities by introducing a feature consumers had not previously considered.*   Toothpaste in pump dispensers appealed to many consumers.
- *Use free product samples, coupons, or price specials to get consumers to switch from their favored brand.*
- *Introduce a line extension of an existing brand that offers a new benefit.* Colgate in gel form provides better taste.

▶EXHIBIT 4.6
Encouraging a switch
from habit to decision
making

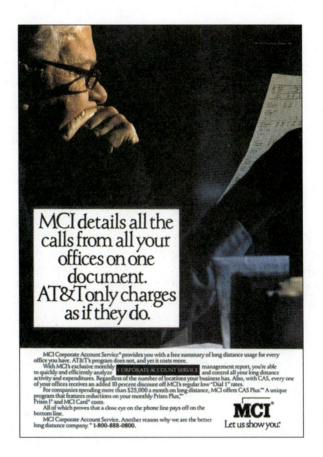

Conversely, marketers of the market leader try to retain habitual purchasers by repetitive advertising that reinforces satisfaction and attempts to simplify the choice process. Coke's former advertising slogan "Coke Is It" implied that once consumers choose Coke, they are satisfied and further information search is not necessary. Some marketers regarded the subsequent introduction of a new Coke formula as a mistake for the simple reason that it prompted many habitual Coke users to reassess their choice (that is, to switch from habit to decision making).

◆ BRAND LOYALTY

A close link exists among learning, habit, and brand loyalty. **Brand loyalty** represents a favorable attitude toward a brand resulting in consistent purchase of the brand over time. It is the result of consumers learning that one brand can satisfy their needs.

Two approaches to the study of brand loyalty have dominated marketing literature. The first, an instrumental conditioning approach, views consistent purchasing of one brand over time as an indication of brand loyalty. Consumers' repeat purchasing behavior is assumed to reflect reinforcement and a strong stimulus-to-response link. Research that takes this approach uses probabilistic models of consumer learning to estimate the probability of consumers buying the same brand again, given a number of past purchases of that brand. The shape of the learning curve in Figure 4.5 determines this probability. Thus, ten consecutive purchases of Minute Maid frozen orange juice might mean a 92 percent probability the consumer will buy the same brand again on the next purchase. Since the prediction is always in probability terms, this is a **stochastic model** of consumer behavior.

The second approach to the study of brand loyalty is based on cognitive theories. Some researchers believe that behavior alone does not reflect brand loyalty. Loyalty implies a commitment to a brand that may not be reflected by just measuring continuous behavior. A family may buy a particular brand because it is the lowest-priced brand on the market. A slight increase in price may cause the family to shift to another brand. In this case, continuous purchasing does not reflect reinforcement or loyalty. The stimulus (product) and reward links are not strong. An attitudinal measure combined with a behavioral measure is required to identify true loyalty.

Cognitive theorists are more likely to develop deterministic models of consumer choice. **Deterministic models** demonstrate the linkages between variables that influence behavior and attempt to predict behavior based on these linkages. The models of complex decision making in the previous chapter and habitual purchasing behavior in this chapter (Figure 4.4) are examples of deterministic models.

The differences between a behavioral and a cognitive orientation in defining brand loyalty and habit are best illustrated by the statements of two researchers. Tucker takes a strong behavioral position: "No consideration should be given to what the subject thinks or what goes on in his central nervous system; his behavior is the full statement of what brand loyalty is."[25] Jacoby takes a clear cognitive position: "To exhibit brand loyalty implies repeat purchasing behavior based on cognitive, affective, evaluative and predispositional factors— the classical primary components of an attitude."[26] And, "brand loyalty is a function of psychological (decision-making, evaluative) processes."[27] In this discussion, behavioral (instrumental conditioning) and attitudinal (cognitive) approaches to understanding brand loyalty will be considered.

Behavioral Approach to Brand Loyalty

Recent developments in data collection have given more spur to the behavioral as opposed to the cognitive school in measuring brand loyalty. The availability of electronically recorded purchases through in-store **scanners** has made it possible to provide managers with quick information on what people do. As a result, marketers are relying more on behavioral data generated through scanners and less on attitudinal and perceptual data generated through surveys.

The problem with relying primarily on behavioral data in developing and assessing marketing strategies is, in the words of one marketing expert, that "what people do does not say anything about why they do it. There is no surrogate available for talking to the consumer."[28]

Behavioral Measures of Loyalty

Behavioral measures have defined loyalty by the sequence of purchases (purchased Brand A five times in a row) and/or the proportion of purchases (Brand A represents 80 percent of all purchases of frozen orange juice). In one of the earliest studies in this area, Brown defined brand loyalty as five purchases in a row of the same brand. He analyzed a panel of consumers for frequently purchased items such as coffee, orange juice, soap, and margarine and found that from 12 percent to 73 percent of the families studied were loyal to the same brand, depending on the product.[29] Tucker defined loyalty as three purchases in a row,[30] while Lawrence defined loyalty to a new brand as four purchases in a row.[31] Blattberg and Sen used proportion of purchases, rather than sequence, as the behavioral measure of loyalty and identified consumers loyal to national and private label (retailer-owned) brands.[32]

These varying definitions illustrate the fact that no consistent measure of behavioral loyalty has been accepted in consumer research.

Limitations of Behavioral Measures of Loyalty

Several limitations of a strictly behavioral approach to identifying brand loyalty should be recognized. First, measurement of loyalty based on past behavior may be misleading. Consider the consumer who buys one brand of coffee for personal consumption, another brand for the spouse, and occasionally a third, higher-priced brand to have available for guests. The purchase sequence would not indicate loyalty; however, the consumer may be highly loyal to the preferred brand.

Second, consumer purchases may not reflect reinforcement. Lawrence studied the sequence of purchases after a consumer switched his or her regular brand.[33] He found four patterns of purchasing:

1. Reversion (switching back to the original brand).
2. Conversion (remaining loyal to the new brand).
3. Vacillation (characterized by random switching between brands).
4. Experimentation (characterized by further systematic trial of other brands).

Only the reversion and conversion patterns would conform to instrumental conditioning since, in both cases, previous purchases are clearly increasing the probability of buying the same brand again. For vacillation and experimentation, no specific sequence is established, making it difficult to predict behavior from past purchases. However, Lawrence found that over 50 percent of the consumers studied conformed to a pattern of vacillation or experimentation.

Third, brand loyalty is not merely a function of past behavior. It is a multidimensional concept that must incorporate the consumer's commitment to the brand. The very term loyalty implies commitment, rather than just repetitive behavior, which suggests that there is the need for a cognitive as well as a behavioral view.

Cognitive Approach to Brand Loyalty

Some of the limitations of a strictly behavioral approach in measuring brand loyalty are overcome when loyalty includes both attitudes and behavior. Day states that to be truly loyal, the consumer must hold a favorable attitude toward the brand in addition to purchasing it repeatedly.[34] Day recognizes that consumers might continue to buy the same brand because other brands are not readily available, a brand offers a long series of price deals, or consumers want to minimize decision making. Day defines these conditions as spurious loyalty because they do not reflect commitment.

Evidence suggests that utilizing both the attitudinal and behavioral components provides a more powerful definition of brand loyalty. In his study, Day found that when he attempted to predict brand loyalty, the predictive power of the model using both attitude and behavior measures was almost twice as good as the model using behavior alone. Furthermore, if the behavior measure alone were used, over 70 percent of the sample would have been defined as brand loyal. Adding the attitudinal component reduced the proportion of brand-loyal consumers to under 50 percent. In other words, defining loyalty based only on repeat purchasing overstates the degree of loyalty.[35]

Brand-Loyal Consumer

Several researchers have attempted to define the characteristics of a brand-loyal consumer. Their studies have uniformly shown that there is no general, brand-loyal consumer; that is, a consumer who tends to be loyal regardless of product category.[36] Brand loyalty is product-specific. Consumers will be loyal to brands in one category and will have little loyalty to brands in other categories.

Despite the product-specific nature of brand loyalty, some generalizations can be made about those who tend to be brand loyal:

1. *The brand-loyal consumer tends to be more self-confident in his or her choice.* Both Day[37] and Carman[38] found this relationship to be true in separate studies of consumer packaged goods.

2. *Brand-loyal consumers are more likely to perceive a higher level of risk in the purchase* and use repeat purchasing of a single brand as a means of reducing risk.[39]

3. *The brand-loyal consumer is more likely to be store loyal.* Carman states that the consumer who restricts the number of stores visited thereby restricts

the opportunity to be disloyal to the brands the store sells. Therefore, "store loyalty is a regulator of brand loyalty."[40]

4. *Minority group consumers tend to be more brand loyal.* Some studies have found that African-American and Hispanic-American consumers tend to be more brand loyal.[41] Loyalty may be the result of greater financial risk in purchases and a desire to "play it safe."

Brand Loyalty and Product Involvement

The cognitive definition of brand loyalty means that loyalty represents commitment and, therefore, involvement with the purchase. (See Exhibit 4.7 for the ultimate example of commitment resulting in brand loyalty.) A study by J. Walter Thompson, a large advertising agency, found that brand loyalty is highest when consumers are personally involved with the brand and find the purchase risky.[42] In these cases, the brand is a source of self-identification (cosmetics, automobiles, cigarettes).

Inertia—that is, repeat purchasing of a brand without commitment—represents habitual purchasing with a low level of involvement. In this case, the consumer has no strong opinions or feelings about the brand. The consumer bases purchasing on what is most familiar. Repeat purchase of a brand does not represent commitment; it merely represents acceptance.

Decrease in Brand Loyalty in the 1990s

The lack of commitment to many products is demonstrated by a steady decrease in brand loyalty during the 1980s and 1990s. Lower brand loyalty was

▶**EXHIBIT 4.7**
An example of commitment and brand loyalty
Source: © Bill Whitehead

"Brand loyalty isn't just an empty phrase to Arthur!"

partially triggered by greater price consciousness as a result of inflation in the 1970s and a deep recession in the early 1980s and was further fueled by the 1991-1992 recession. The recent recession is likely to have a longer lasting effect on consumer behavior than previous ones did because consumers have become more value conscious. Many no longer equate well-known national brands to value. As a result, they are less likely to pay the price premium the leading brands demand. Private brands have made inroads during the 1990s in cigarettes, disposable diapers, over-the-counter medicines, and cosmetics.

The decrease in brand loyalty is not restricted to the United States. The recent recession also turned European shoppers to private brands. In England, private brands represent 31 percent of packaged food sales, up from 23 percent in 1982. Similar increases have occurred in Germany, France, Holland, and Switzerland.[43] The erosion of brand loyalty is likely to become a global trend.

◆ STORE LOYALTY

Consumers are loyal to stores just as they are to brands. At times, store loyalty may be stronger than brand loyalty. A young lawyer may religiously shop at one particular department store because it conforms to his self-image as being upwardly mobile and achievement-oriented. Given this link between his self-image and his image of the store, our shopper's loyalties to this department store are likely to be stronger than his loyalty to any of the items of merchandise it carries.

Store-Loyal Consumer

In the previous section, we noted that brand-loyal consumers also tend to be store loyal. It is possible that consumers who wish to reduce the time and effort in brand selection also seek to minimize time and effort in store selection. Another possibility is that shopping in the same store fosters loyalty for brands carried by that store, particularly private (retailer-controlled) brands.

Reynolds, Darden, and Martin related lifestyle characteristics to store loyalty.[44] They identified store loyalty by the willingness of a sample of women to shop in the same stores and to avoid the risk of shopping in new stores. They found that the store-loyal woman tends to be older and more downscale (lower income, less educated) than one who is not loyal.

Goldman supported these findings in his study.[45] He found that store-loyal consumers engaged in less prepurchase search, knew about fewer stores, and were less likely to shop even in stores known to them. Goldman concluded that store-loyal behavior appears to be "part of a low search, low knowledge and low utilization level shopping style" and that this shopping style is more likely to exist among low-income consumers because they are constrained by their inability to shop much.[46] The clear implication is that store loyalty is an inefficient mode of shopping and is more likely to exist among low-income consumers because of limited information and less discretionary income.

The two studies just cited also found that store-loyal consumers see more risk in shopping..[47] The lower income and educational level of the store-loyal consumer may heighten the sense of risk in shopping behavior. The careful and conservative nature of these customers suggests that store loyalty may be a means of reducing the risk of shopping in unknown stores. One obvious strategy in reducing risk in store choice is to shop in one or a select number of stores.

Level of Store Loyalty

Consumers' greater price sensitivity as a result of the two recent recessions has led to an erosion of store as well as brand loyalty. A study by Yankelovich, Skelly, and White, a marketing research firm, found that almost 50 percent of all shoppers said they switched from their favorite supermarket to one with lower prices during the 1980-1982 recession.[48] The 1991-1992 recession promoted comparison shopping and further discouraged store loyalty.

The Yankelovich study also found a countervailing trend. The increase in the number of working women increased the premium on convenience and reduced the time for comparison shopping. For these consumers, the additional cost of being store or brand loyal is worth the time saved.

Overall, store loyalty is likely to erode in the 1990s, along with brand loyalty, as shoppers place more emphasis on economy than on time-saving conveniences.

◆ SOCIETAL IMPLICATIONS OF BRAND AND STORE LOYALTY

The above description of brand and store loyalty suggests that it may not be the most efficient mode of decision making for consumers. On the positive side, brand and store loyalty save consumers time and effort in evaluating alternatives. However, such loyalty may lead consumers to repurchase the same brand even if it is higher priced or of inferior quality.

Implications for Brand Loyalty

Name brands often trade on their national reputation and frequent advertising to charge higher prices. Many consumers are swayed by the name appeal alone and establish strong brand loyalties based on image. Blind taste tests have shown that many consumers cannot tell the difference between Pepsi and Coke or Miller and Budweiser. However, when the name is revealed, the consumers exhibit strong preferences. Clearly, loyalty is a function of brand name and image rather than any functional brand attributes. Similarly, bleach is a fairly standardized product; however, Clorox can charge more than other brands because it is a known commodity.

Consumers have a right to develop brand loyalties based on image alone. However, the fact that brand and store loyalties tend to be higher for minority consumers and older, downscale consumers is disturbing. These consumers are often the ones who can least afford the higher prices of national brands.

In this respect, the recent move to private brands may be beneficial from a societal standpoint. Increasingly, consumers are moving away from established patterns of behavior and are showing more willingness to shop around for value. Shopping for value could mean trying a lower-priced brand of toothpaste or a private brand of disposable diapers. As a result, we are witnessing the development of more efficient and economical consumers.

Unfortunately, this move to more effective modes of brand choice is more characteristic of middle-income consumers, not lower-income consumers. Because lower-income consumers are less likely to be aware of brand and price alternatives, a key question is whether there should be a governmental role in increasing price and brand awareness for these consumers.

Implications for Store Loyalty

The same considerations apply to store loyalty. Store loyalty may be a convenient mode of shopping and does save time and effort, but it inhibits comparisons of brand alternatives by restricting choice to one store.

As with brand loyalty, the erosion of store loyalty may be beneficial from a societal viewpoint in encouraging consumers to shop for alternatives. As a result, consumers are more likely to find lower-priced alternatives of similar quality to their preferred brands. Here again, the problem is that older, downscale consumers and disadvantaged minorities continue to be the most store loyal. As noted in Chapter 2, low-income consumers often lack the mobility to engage in comparison shopping. Goldman's description of store-loyal consumers as exhibiting a low knowledge and low utilization style of shopping most applies to downscale consumers.[49] However, these are the consumers who can most benefit by increasing their range of alternatives.

In this regard, government could have a role in increasing the mobility of lower-income, disadvantaged consumers through improved modes of transportation to facilitate comparison shopping.

SUMMARY

Consumer learning, habit, and brand loyalty are closely linked concepts. Habitual purchasing behavior is the result of consumer learning from reinforcement. Consumers will repeatedly buy what satisfies them best. This behavior leads to brand loyalty.

Concepts of learning are necessary to understand habit. The distinction is made between behavioral and cognitive approaches to learning. Behavioral learning focuses on the stimuli that affect behavior and on behavior itself. Cognitive learning focuses on problem solving and emphasizes the consumer thought variables that influence learning. Within the behavioral school, the distinction is also made between classical and instrumental conditioning. Classical conditioning explains behavior based on the establishment of a close association between a primary and a secondary stimulus. Instrumental conditioning views behavior as a function of the consumer's actions. Satisfaction leads to reinforcement and to an increase in the probability of repurchasing.

Learning leads to repetitive buying and habit. In a model representing habitual purchasing behavior, a consumer's need arousal leads directly to an intention to buy, a subsequent purchase, and postpurchase evaluation. Information search and brand evaluation are minimal.

Habit serves two important functions. It reduces risk for high involvement purchases and saves time and energy for low involvement products.

Habit frequently leads to brand loyalty; that is, repetitive buying based on a commitment to the brand. The different learning theories describe two views of brand loyalty. An instrumental conditioning approach suggests that a consumer's consistent purchase of a brand is a reflection of brand loyalty. But such loyalty may lack commitment to the brand and reflect repeat buying based on inertia. The cognitive school believes that behavior is an insufficient measure of loyalty. Attitudinal commitment to the brand is also required.

Brand-loyal consumers also tend to be store loyal. But store loyalty is an inefficient mode of shopping since it is likely to result in the consumer paying more because of a lack of search for alternatives.

Chapter 5 focuses on the low involvement conditions that encourage inertia, often in the form of brand and store loyalty.

QUESTIONS

1. Why is the Marlboro Cowboy advertising campaign a good example of concepts of habit, learning, and brand loyalty? What other product categories are consumers likely to purchase by habit? What do these categories have in common?

2. Why was the Marlboro campaign less effective in the early 1990s compared to its success in previous years? How can learning theory explain this development?

3. If habit is based on reinforcement and an increased likelihood of consumers buying the same product, why have certain dominant brands, once purchased by habit, become extinct or experienced a substantial loss in market share (for example, Sapolio soap)?

4. This chapter suggests that consumers' boredom and desire for variety may result in a change from habit to decision making.
   - Is this more likely for certain product categories than for others?

- Is this more likely for certain consumers than for others? That is, is there a "stick with it" type as opposed to a "novelty seeker" type?

5. Habit serves two different purposes for high and low involvement situations.
   - What are they?
   - Can you cite examples of habit in a high involvement situation? in a low involvement situation?

6. How can principles of classical conditioning be applied to advertising? What are the shortcomings of such applications?

7. What conditions are necessary for classical conditioning to work in advertising? Provide examples.

8. The implication in this chapter is that the emphasis in advertising strategy has shifted from an adherence to classical learning theory before 1950 to an adherence to cognitive theories of learning after 1950.
   - How would such a shift be reflected in advertising strategy?
   - Do you agree that such a shift has taken place in advertising in the past 30 years?

9. How can principles of instrumental conditioning be applied to advertising? In what ways do applications of instrumental conditioning differ from those of classical conditioning?

10. As a member of the Federal Trade Commission, what principles of conditioning would you use in deciding whether a company engaging in misleading advertising should either correct its advertising or simply stop it? If corrective advertising were ordered, what principles of conditioning would you use to determine if this action had the desired effects?

11. A good example of the operation of cognitive learning is to determine how new residents in a community learn about new products not available in their previous community. What evidence might demonstrate that a process of learning is taking place among new residents of a community?

12. A brand manager for a brand with frequent deals and coupons assumes that consumers who repeatedly buy the brand are loyal purchasers.
    - What are the dangers of such an assumption?
    - What marketing errors might result in (a) advertising strategy, (b) pricing, and (c) in-store promotions?

13. What are the strategic implications of the erosion of brand loyalty in the 1990s?

14. Under what circumstances are brand and store loyalty inefficient models of consumer choice? What are the societal implications?

RESEARCH ASSIGNMENTS

1. Develop an experiment in which you ask consumers to evaluate three brands in a product category. Each brand should be placed in a separate room with background music. Make sure the brands are in the same price range and of the same quality. Play rock music in one room, classical in the second, and

country and western in the third. Ask consumers to state their preference for one of the three brands. Ask consumers their musical preferences, as well.

- Are brand preferences related to preferences for the background music played?
- What learning theories could you use to explain your results?
- What are the implications of your results for marketing strategy?

References for this assignment: M. Elizabeth Blair and Terence Shimp, "Consequences of an Unpleasant Experience with Music: A Second-Order Negative Conditioning Perspective," *Journal of Advertising,* 21 (March, 1992), pp. 35–43; and Gerald Gorn, "The Effects of Music in Advertising on Choice Behavior: A Classical Conditioning Approach," *Journal of Marketing,* 46 (Winter, 1982), pp. 94-101.

2. Develop a measure of brand loyalty using either a behavioral or a cognitive approach. Interview a sample of from 30 to 50 consumers of a frequently purchased packaged product (coffee, toothpaste, frozen orange juice). Identify those who are loyal to a brand versus those who are not.
   - Are there any differences between the two groups in terms of (a) demographic characteristics, (b) importance placed on need criteria in selecting brands, (c) brand attitudes, (d) advertising recall, and (e) price paid?
   - What are the implications of the differences between loyalists and non-loyalists for (a) attempts at increasing the number of loyal users, (b) product positioning, and (c) utilization of deals and coupons?
3. Develop a measure of loyalty incorporating both behavior and brand attitudes. Interview a sample of consumers of a frequently purchased packaged good. Distinguish between true loyalists and those who buy regularly out of inertia.
   - What are the differences between the two groups according to the criteria in Question 2?
   - According to your findings, should marketers try to influence consumers who buy their brand out of inertia to become truly loyal? What are the advantages and disadvantages of such a strategy?
   - What other marketing implications emerge from your findings?

NOTES

1. "Marlboro's 2-Fisted Pitch," *The New York Times* (April 6, 1993), pp. D1, D22.
2. For a good summary of these three learning theories, see Michael L. Ray and Peter H. Webb, "Three Learning Theory Traditions and Their Application in Marketing," in Ronald C. Curhan, ed., *Combined Proceedings of the American Marketing Association,* Series No. 36 (1974), pp. 100–103.
3. E. L. Thorndike, *The Psychology of Learning* (New York: Teacher's College, 1913); and J. B. Watson and R. Rayner, "Conditioned Emotional Reactions," *Journal of Experimental Psychology,* 3 (1920), pp. 1–14.
4. Ivan Pavlov, *Conditioned Reflexes. An Investigation of the Physiological Activity of the Cerebral Cortex,* G. V. Anrep, ed. (London: Oxford University Press, 1927).

5. Frances K. McSweeney and Calvin Bierley, "Recent Developments in Classical Conditioning," *Journal of Consumer Research,* 11 (September, 1984), pp. 619–631.

6. "Enduring Brands Hold Their Allure by Sticking Close to Their Roots," *The Wall Street Journal* (Centennial Edition, 1989), p. B4.

7. Terence A. Shimp, Elnora W. Stuart, and Randall W. Engle, "A Program of Classical Conditioning Experiments Testing Variations in the Conditioned Stimulus and Context," *Journal of Consumer Research,* 18 (June, 1991), pp. 1–12.

8. "Elsie and Family Return to Help Revive Borden's Flagging Dairy Fortunes," *The New York Times* (March 10, 1993).

9. B. F. Skinner, *The Behavior of Organisms: An Experimental Analysis* (New York: Appleton-Century-Crofts, 1938).

10. Peter D. Bennett and Robert M. Mandel, "Prepurchase Information Seeking Behavior of New Car Purchasers—The Learning Hypothesis," *Journal of Marketing Research,* 6 (November, 1969), pp. 430–433.

11. *Advertising Age* (September 13, 1976), p. 124.

12. "Perrier Sets Slow Pace for U.S. Relaunch," *The Wall Street Journal* (March 7, 1990), pp. B1, B6; and "Perrier's Back," *Advertising Age* (April 23, 1990), pp. 1 and 84.

13. Michael L. Rothschild and William C. Gadis, "Behavioral Learning Theory: Its Relevance to Marketing and Promotions," *Journal of Marketing,* 45 (Spring, 1981), pp. 70–78.

14. Rom J. Markin, Jr., *Consumer Behavior, A Cognitive Orientation* (New York: Macmillan, 1974), p. 239.

15. Wolfgang Kohler, *The Mentality of Apes* (New York: Harcourt Brace & World, 1925).

16. "RCA Blaming Excessive Optimism for Slow Sales of Videodiscs Player," *The Wall Street Journal* (January 26, 1982), p. 37.

17. Alan R. Andreasen and Peter G. Durkson, "Market Learning of New Residents," *Journal of Marketing Research,* 5 (May, 1968), pp. 166–176.

18. Chris T. Allen and Thomas J. Madden, "A Closer Look at Classical Conditioning," *Journal of Consumer Research,* 12 (December, 1985), pp. 301–315.

19. John A. Howard and Jagdish Sheth, *The Theory of Buyer Behavior* (New York: John Wiley, 1969), pp. 27–28.

20. Joseph W. Newman and Richard A. Werbel, "Multivariate Analysis of Brand Loyalty for Major Household Appliances," *Journal of Marketing Research,* 10 (November, 1973), pp. 404-409.

21. Donald R. Lehmann, William L. Moore, and Terry Elrod, "The Development of Distinct Choice Process Segments Over Time: A Stochastic Modeling Approach," *Journal of Marketing,* 46 (Spring, 1982), pp. 48–59.

22. Ted Roselius, "Consumer Rankings of Risk Reduction Methods," *Journal of Marketing,* 35 (January, 1971), pp. 56–61.

23. Klaus Peter Kass, "Consumer Habit Forming, Information Acquisition, and Buying Behavior," *Journal of Business Research,* 10 (March, 1982), pp. 3–15.

24. Lehmann, Moore, and Elrod, "The Development of Distinct Choice Process Segments," *op. cit.,* p. 57.

25. W. T. Tucker, "The Development of Brand Loyalty," *Journal of Marketing Research,* 1 (August, 1964), p. 32.

26. Jacob Jacoby, "A Model of Multi-Brand Loyalty," *Journal of Advertising Research,* 11 (June, 1971), p. 26.

27. Jacob Jacoby and David B. Kyner, "Brand Loyalty vs. Repeat Purchasing Behavior," *Journal of Marketing Research,* 10 (February, 1973), p. 2.

28. "What Do People Want, Anyway?" *The New York Times* (November 8, 1987), p. F4.

29. "Brand Loyalty—Fact or Fiction?" *Advertising Age* (June 19, 1952), pp. 53–55; (June 30, 1952), pp. 45–47; (August 11, 1952), pp. 56–58; (September 1, 1952), pp. 80–82; (October 6, 1952), pp. 82–86; (December 1, 1952), pp. 76–79; (January 25, 1953), pp. 32–35.

30. Tucker, "The Development of Brand Loyalty," *loc. cit.*

31. Raymond J. Lawrence, "Patterns of Buyer Behavior: Time for a New Approach?" *Journal of Marketing Research,* 6 (May, 1969), pp. 137–144.

32. Robert C. Blattberg and Subrata K. Sen, "Market Segments and Stochastic Brand Choice Models," *Journal of Marketing Research,* 13 (February, 1976), pp. 34–45.

33. Lawrence, "Patterns of Buyer Behavior . . . ," *loc. cit.*

34. George S. Day, "A Two-Dimensional Concept of Brand Loyalty," *Journal of Advertising Research,* 9 (September, 1969), pp. 29–36.

35. *Ibid.*

36. See *Are There Consumer Types?* (New York: Advertising Research Foundation, 1964); and Ronald E. Frank, William F. Massy, and Thomas M. Lodahl, "Purchasing Behavior and Personal Attributes," *Journal of Advertising Research,* 9 (December, 1969), pp. 15–24.

37. Day, "A Two-Dimensional Concept . . . ," *loc. cit.*

38. James M. Carman, "Correlates of Brand Loyalty: Some Positive Results," *Journal of Marketing Research,* 7 (February, 1970), pp. 67–76.

39. Roselius, "Consumer Rankings . . . ," *loc. cit.*; and Jagdish Sheth and M. Venkatesan, "Risk-Reduction Processes in Repetitive Consumer Behavior," *Journal of Marketing Research,* 3 (August, 1968), pp. 307–311.

40. Carman, "Correlates of Brand Loyalty . . . ," *loc. cit.*

41. "Traditional Brand Loyalty," *Advertising Age* (May 18, 1981), p. S2; and "Hispanics: All for One?" *Advertising Age* (September 13, 1984), p. 3.

42. "Brand Loyalty Beats Price in Some Product Categories," *Marketing News* (November 28, 1980), p. 1.

43. "Europeans Witness Proliferation of Private Labels," *The Wall Street Journal* (October 20, 1992), pp. B1, B5.

44. Fred. D. Reynolds, William R. Darden, and Warren S. Martin, "Developing an Image of the Store-Loyal Customer," *Journal of Retailing,* 50 (Winter, 1974–1975), pp. 73–84.

45. Arieh Goldman, "The Shopping Style Explanation for Store Loyalty," *Journal of Retailing,* 53 (Winter, 1977–1978), pp. 33–46.

46. *Ibid.*

47. Robert D. Hisrich, Ronald J. Dornoff, and Jerome B. Kernan, "Perceived Risk in Store Selection," *Journal of Marketing Research,* 9 (November, 1972), pp. 435–439; and Joseph F. Dash, Leon G. Schiffman, and Conrad Berenson, "Risk and Personality Related Dimensions of Store Choice," *Journal of Marketing,* 40 (January, 1976), pp. 32–39.

48. *Supermarket Shoppers in a Period of Economic Uncertainty* (New York: Yankelovich, Skelly, and White, Inc. 1982), p. 16.

49. Goldman, "The Shopping Style Explanation for Store Loyalty," *loc. cit.*

5

Low Involvement Decision Making

KELLOGG'S INCREASES INVOLVEMENT WITH CEREALS

In describing complex decision making and brand loyalty in the last two chapters, we assumed that consumers are involved with the purchasing decision. However, when we consider the variety of more mundane products purchased on an everyday basis— toothpaste, detergents, cereals, deodorants—it is not surprising that most purchases are low in consumer involvement.[1] A **low involvement purchase** is one in which consumers do not consider the product important to their belief system and do not strongly identify with the product.

Marketers like to think that consumers are involved with their products because involved consumers are more likely to pay attention to their advertising, to evaluate carefully their products, and to become brand loyal. Where consumer involvement is lacking, marketers try to create it by differentiating their brands and equating advertising appeals to consumer needs.

Kellogg's followed such a strategy in the 1980s when it created the adult cereal market. Until then, cereals were primarily a children's product; but by 1980, the market was stagnating because of a declining birth rate. Kellogg's saw an opportunity for targeting cereals to nutritionally oriented baby boomers. To do so, however, it would have to get these consumers more involved in cereals by convincing them it is not just kid stuff.

Kellogg's did so in the most direct way. In 1984, it began touting the high-fiber content of its All-Bran cereal as helping to prevent cancer. (See Exhibit 5.1.) It followed by targeting a new line of cereals—Common Sense, Just Right, Mueslix—to diet-conscious, health-oriented, and fitness segments. As a result, adults began seeing cereals as part of a healthier lifestyle, a highly involving issue. Kellogg's success in transforming cereals from a less to a more involving product doubled the growth rate for cereals. Today, adult cereals represent one-third of the company's sales.

▶**EXHIBIT 5.1**
Kellogg's increases the level of involvement with cereals

However, Kellogg's might have gone too far when it introduced Heartwise as a cereal that helped reduce cholesterol. When the Food and Drug Administration forced Kellogg's to withdraw the claim as insupportable, the company reintroduced Heartwise as Fiberwise in 1991 to avoid the connotation the product fights heart disease.[2]

Marketers accept the fact that consumers are not involved with their products and try to attract them through price promotions and other incentives. The proliferation of coupons and price promotions for products such as paper towels, household cleaners, coffee, and detergents attests to the low involvement nature of these product categories.

This chapter focuses on purchase decisions in which consumers are not highly involved. The importance of a low involvement perspective is considered first. Next, consumer decisions are classified by level of product involvement. Several theoretical bases for low involvement purchase behavior are described. Strategic implications of high versus low involvement situations are considered, with special emphasis on advertising strategy.

◆ IMPORTANCE OF A LOW INVOLVEMENT PERSPECTIVE

Most consumers' purchases are not involving, either situationally or on an enduring basis. Kassarjian supports the view that most purchase decisions do not greatly involve consumers: "Subjects just do not care about products; they are unimportant to them. Although issues such as racial equality, wars and the draft may stir them up, products do not."[3]

There is support for Kassarjian's low involvement perspective. Hupfer and Gardner conducted a study in the early 1970s and asked college students to rate 20 issues and 20 products on a 7-point scale from very important (7) to not important at all (1).[4] Some of the relative ratings are listed in Table 5.1. Although students rated some of the products as fairly important (automobiles and houses), it is apparent that in most cases students considered the product categories as relatively unimportant when compared to the issues. Vietnam and Watergate dominated the early 1970s, and the importance of products paled in comparison to these issues. Product choice was not one of the most important concerns in consumers' lives then, and it is probably not now.

Involvement and the Hierarchy of Effects

If low involvement characterizes so much of purchasing, why have marketers focused on high involvement decisions (that is, complex decision making and brand loyalty)? There are two reasons. First, since marketers are highly involved with their products, they easily assume consumers are also highly involved. Tyebjee notes the reluctance of product and advertising managers to consider an uninvolved consumer:

▶TABLE 5-1

Relative importance of products and issues

Product or Issue	Rating
The draft	6.71
Vietnam War	6.28
World peace	6.17
Automobiles	4.52
Houses	4.17
Beer	3.00
Coffee	2.61
Fraternity membership	2.38
Toothpaste	1.95
Bicycles	1.39
Facial tissues	1.19

SOURCE: Nancy T. Hupfer and David M. Gardner, "Differential Involvement with Products and Issues: An Exploratory Study," in David M. Gardner, ed., PROCEEDINGS OF THE 2ND ANNUAL CONFERENCE OF THE ASSOCIATION FOR CONSUMER BEHAVIOR (College Park, MD: Association for Consumer Research, 1971), pp. 262–269.

These individuals [product and advertising managers] spend a major part of their waking hours thinking about their brand. Therefore, when they evaluate the advertising strategy they do so as highly involved individuals, unlike the target consumer. Highly cluttered, complex advertising copy is often a result of agency and brand group decision makers who are unable to view the product from the perspective of the [uninvolved] consumer.[5]

Exhibit 5.2 is a good illustration of the marketer's assumption that consumers are involved with mundane products.

A second reason why marketers tend to focus on high involvement decisions is that it is easier for them to understand and influence consumers if they assume consumers employ a cognitive process of brand evaluation. Complex decision making assumes a sequence in the consumers' choice process (referred to as a **hierarchy of effects**), which stipulates that consumers think before they act. That is, they first form brand beliefs (the cognitive component of attitudes), then evaluate brands (the affective component), and then make a purchase decision (the behavioral or conative component). The beliefs/evaluation/behavior hierarchy assumes involved consumers. The assumption that such a high involvement hierarchy of effects describes consumer choice has dominated marketing thought since consumer behavior became an integrated field of study.

▶**EXHIBIT 5.2**
The involved marketer
and the uninvolved
consumer

Source: Drawing by H.
Martin; ©1983 The New
Yorker Magazine, Inc.

*"And now a message of importance to those of you who
have been giving serious thought to the purchase of a
new tube of toothpaste."*

Low Involvement Hierarchy

In the past ten years, consumer behavior researchers have directed more attention to a low involvement hierarchy of effects. This hierarchy stipulates that consumers may act without thinking. For example, when purchasing table salt, it is unlikely that the consumer will initiate a process of information search to determine brand characteristics. Nor is the consumer likely to evaluate alternative brands to identify the most favored one.

Rather than searching for information, the consumer will receive information passively. The consumer sits in front of the television and sees an advertisement for Morton salt that describes it as "easy to pour." Stifling a yawn, the consumer is thinking about anything but salt. The consumer is not really evaluating the advertisement. Rather, in just seeing the ad, the consumer is storing information in a few bits and pieces without any active cognitive process. However, over time, the consumer establishes an association of Morton salt with ease in pouring. Lastovicka refers to this process as *information catching* rather than information processing.[6]

A need arises simply because the amount of salt in the house is running low. The consumer buys Morton salt because of familiarity that repetitive advertising produces. The consumer sees the brand on the store shelf, associates it with the advertising theme, and has sufficient stimulus to purchase Morton salt. Under these conditions, the consumer does not form an attitude toward the brand and has no favorable or unfavorable reaction. Instead, the consumer regards the brand as relatively neutral, since it is not associated with any important benefits tied to self or group identification.

Therefore, the hierarchy of effects for low involvement products is quite different from that for high involvement, as indicated in Table 5.2. Consumers become aware of the product and form beliefs about it passively. They make a purchase decision with little brand information and then evaluate the brand after the purchase to determine the level of satisfaction. At this point, consumers may develop weak attitudes toward the brand—for example, if a new feature such as a convenient spout is introduced (favorable evaluation) or if the brand performs poorly (sticks to the container, producing an unfavorable reaction). If such attitudes develop, they occur after the purchase and are weakly held.[7]

Several studies have supported the distinction between a high and a low involvement hierarchy. Joseph E. Seagram & Sons and Time, Inc., jointly conducted a study of consumer choice of liquor brands and found that an increase in brand awareness was related to a subsequent purchase of the advertised brand. However, there was no change in attitudes toward the brand as a result of brand evaluation. The study concluded that the findings "tend to contradict the long-accepted belief that first you change people's attitudes, then you change their buying habits."[8] The findings supported a beliefs/behavior/attitude hierarchy.

In a later study, Beatty and Kahle distinguished between consumers who are and who are not involved with soft drinks. The more involved consumers evaluated brand alternatives more extensively and tended to make choices based on favorable attitudes toward the preferred brands. For less involved consumers, attitudes did not play an important role in the decision for less involved consumers.[9]

Low Involvement Decision Criteria

The Morton salt example cited above suggests that in low involvement decision making, consumers do very little brand evaluation or information processing.

▶TABLE 5-2

A comparison of low and high involvement hierarchies

Low Involvement Hierarchy	High Involvement Hierarchy
1. Brand beliefs are formed first by *passive* learning.	1. Brand beliefs are formed first by *active* learning.
2. A purchase decision is made.	2. Brands are evaluated.
3. The brand may or may not be evaluated afterward.	3. A purchase decision is made.

If this is true, then how do consumers make decisions? They follow relatively simple decision rules that minimize the time and effort in shopping and decision making.

One rule cited in the Morton salt example is to pick the most familiar brand. Our consumer saw Morton salt on the shelf, recognized the name, associated it with the advertising, and picked it because it was most familiar. A study by Hoyer and Brown support this type of decision making in low involvement purchases. They found that consumers who are aware of one brand in a product category will repeatedly choose it, even if it is lower in quality compared to that of other brands.[10]

Another simple decision rule is to pick the brand used the last time if it was adequate. A study by Lynch, Marmorstein, and Weigold found that uninvolved consumers will make decisions on this basis by recalling previously formed brand evaluations.[11] Finally, if uninvolved consumers have few prior associations with brands, the simplest expedient is to pick the least expensive alternative.

In each of these cases, consumers are making quick decisions (generally in the store) with little or no brand evaluation.

◆ FOUR TYPES OF CONSUMER BEHAVIOR

In Chapter 1, we described four types of consumer choice processes based on the level of involvement and decision making: complex decision making, brand loyalty, limited decision making, and inertia. Figure 5.1 shows that each of these processes is described by a different hierarchy of effects.[12] The high and low involvement processes are also described by different learning theories based on these decision hierarchies.

Complex Decision Making and Brand Loyalty

The upper left-hand box of Figure 5.1 represents the process of complex decision making described by the traditional "think before you act" hierarchy. The learning theory that best describes this process is cognitive learning; that is, a process that requires the consumers' development of brand attitudes and a detailed evaluation of brand alternatives.

The lower left-hand box describes brand loyalty; that is, consumers make purchases with little deliberation because of past satisfaction and a strong commitment to the brand as a result. The learning theory that best describes brand loyalty is instrumental conditioning (positive reinforcement based on satisfaction with the brand leading to repetitive behavior). Both high involvement processes are described by a beliefs/evaluation/behavior hierarchy, except that forming beliefs and evaluating brands are not a necessary part of the choice

▶FIGURE 5.1
Four types of consumer
behavior

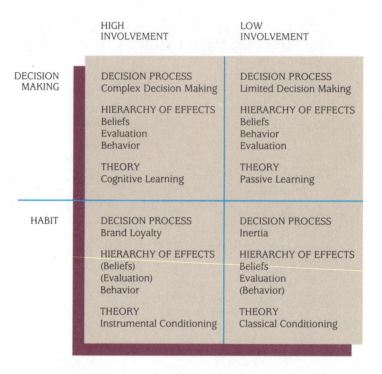

	HIGH INVOLVEMENT	LOW INVOLVEMENT
DECISION MAKING	DECISION PROCESS Complex Decision Making HIERARCHY OF EFFECTS Beliefs Evaluation Behavior THEORY Cognitive Learning	DECISION PROCESS Limited Decision Making HIERARCHY OF EFFECTS Beliefs Behavior Evaluation THEORY Passive Learning
HABIT	DECISION PROCESS Brand Loyalty HIERARCHY OF EFFECTS (Beliefs) (Evaluation) Behavior THEORY Instrumental Conditioning	DECISION PROCESS Inertia HIERARCHY OF EFFECTS Beliefs Evaluation (Behavior) THEORY Classical Conditioning

process in brand loyalty. Complex decision making was described in Chapter 3 and brand loyalty in Chapter 4. In this chapter, we focus on the two low involvement processes shown in Figure 5.1—inertia and limited decision making.

Inertia

The lower right-hand box represents the Morton salt example—buying based on **inertia.** As we saw, when a low involvement hierarchy operates, a consumer forms beliefs passively, makes a decision with little information processing, and then evaluates the brand after the purchase. As inertia involves repetitive buying of the same brand to avoid making a decision, the consumer does not make a subsequent brand evaluation until after the first few purchases. If the brand achieves a certain minimum level of satisfaction, the consumer will repurchase it. This process is sometimes referred to as *spurious loyalty* because repetitive purchases may make it appear that the consumer is loyal to the brand when actually no such loyalty exists.

The learning theory that best describes inertia is classical conditioning. When the consumer is not involved with the product, contiguity between a stimulus and a response could be established more easily through repetitive advertising because the consumer is in a passive state. The consumer forms the association without thinking. When the consumer goes into a store, the association may be triggered by seeing the product; and the easiest thing to do is to buy the product with little deliberation. Thus, repetitive exposure to a theme like "The quicker, thicker picker upper" for Bounty paper towels might create an association between absorbency and the product for a low involvement product category.

Various studies have demonstrated the effectiveness of repeating advertising themes in low involvement conditions. Batra and Ray showed that repeating an advertising message will result in more favorable brand attitudes for low involvement purchases.[13] In the high involvement case, repetition had an initial favorable impact; but after a while, repetition became counterproductive. Similarly, Hawkins and Hoch found that for low involvement purchases, repetition resulted in greater acceptance of the truth of advertising claims.[14] In both cases, repetition created familiarity, allowing consumers to more easily associate known claims with a particular brand.

The study by Hoyer and Brown cited above supports these findings by reinforcing the importance of creating brand awareness for low involvement products.[15] The study found that if consumers were aware of a particular brand of peanut butter (a low involvement product), this awareness was sufficient to make a brand choice. Consumers would choose the known brand of peanut butter, even if taste tests suggested it was of lower quality. These consumers were not motivated to process information on alternative brands of peanut butter. They demonstrated inertia by simply selecting the brand they knew best. Such brand awareness is best created by repetitive advertising.

Because of the dominance of low involvement products, inertia is probably much more common than most marketing managers would like to admit. Product managers and advertisers sometimes use marketing strategies that assume consumers care. Most consumers do not.

Limited Decision Making

Occasionally, low involvement purchases warrant some decision making (upper-right box in Figure 5.1). The introduction of a new product, a change in the existing brand, or a desire for variety might cause a consumer to switch from buying based on inertia to limited decision making. For example, assume a new, thicker paper towel is introduced and is advertised as being so strong, it can be reused. A consumer who consistently buys Bounty notices the ad. Involvement with the category is low, but introduction of the new product is enough to arouse mild interest and curiosity. The decision process conforms to a low involvement hierarchy, as there is little information seeking and brand evaluation. The consumer forms beliefs about the brand (thick, strong, can be reused), purchases the brand, and then evaluates it based on initial trial.

Although limited decision making involves cognitive processes, the relevant learning process is described as passive, rather than cognitive, because no active information search and brand evaluation takes place. The consumer receives information about the new paper towel passively and puts it in the back of his or her mind. Seeing the brand in the store triggers recall; the consumer examines the package and purchases the product for trial.

An important form of limited decision making is **variety seeking.** Consumers often try a variety of brands out of boredom simply because many low involvement products are ordinary and mundane. It is unlikely that consumers develop strong preferences for a brand of salad dressing. However, a consumer may consciously experiment by buying a variety of brands. Purchases are made without brand evaluation or changes in brand attitude. The chosen brand will be evaluated while being consumed.

In their study, R. H. Bruskin, a large marketing research firm, found evidence of variety-seeking behavior. Bruskin found that for certain low involvement products such as toothpaste, potato chips, and salad dressing, most consumers who switched to other brands continued to have favorable attitudes toward their former brand. The study concluded that consumers do not switch to other brands because of dissatisfaction but "just to try something new."[16] Since the level of involvement is low, the consumer is not likely to be seriously dissatisfied. Rather, the motivation to switch brands is a desire for change and a search for novelty.

◆ UNPLANNED PURCHASING BEHAVIOR

Both limited decision making and inertia generally result in **unplanned purchases;** that is, purchases that consumers do not plan before going to the store. In contrast, complex decision making assumes a preplanning process. There are two basic reasons for an unplanned purchase. First, the time and effort involved in searching for alternatives outside the store may not be worth the trouble, and consumers buy largely on a reminder basis (that is, by inertia). Second, consumers may seek variety or novelty and thus buy on impulse (that is, by limited decision making).

The influence of in-store stimuli such as displays, shelf position, packaging, and price become more important for unplanned purchases than preplanned purchase decisions. This does not mean that advertising and in-store stimuli are separate. As we know, advertising can reinforce in-store stimuli by reminding consumers of the brand once they see it on the shelf. Conversely, displays and good shelf position are a necessity if advertising is to be effective. As a result, the role of advertising will differ markedly, depending on the type of purchase. For preplanned purchases, advertising attempts to create demand beforehand. For unplanned purchases, advertising is meant to tie in with in-store stimuli that influence consumers at the point of sale.

Types of Unplanned Purchases

Unplanned purchasing is often **impulse buying,** which is a tendency to buy on whim or an action based on a "powerful and persistent urge."[17] However, there are other types of unplanned purchases. By seeing the product on the supermarket shelf, a parent may be reminded that there is no breakfast cereal in the house. The parent then decides to examine nutritional information on various packages and selects that cereal judged to be most nutritious. This is an unplanned purchase, not an impulse purchase, as the parent did not made it on whim or base it on some persistent urge.

There are five types of unplanned purchases:[18]

1. *Pure impulse* for variety or novelty. This type of behavior represents a departure from the normal set of products or brands purchased.

2. *Suggestion effect* for a new product based on in-store stimuli. For example, a consumer was not aware of a nondetergent laundry product. Seeing it on the shelf or in a counter display, the consumer purchases it because the product is related to the consumer's needs.

3. *Planned impulse* refers to a consumer's intention to go to a specific store because of a sale but with no plan to buy particular products. Buying on special sale or by coupon is planned, but purchasing the item itself is not.

4. *Reminder effect* because the consumer needs the item but did not include it in shopping intentions prior to entering the store. The trigger is seeing the product on the shelf or on display.

5. *Planned product category* refers to a consumer who plans to buy a particular product category (for example, paper towels) but does not preplan the brand decision. This consumer conducts an in-store search to decide on the brand and then selects the brand that is often the lowest price option.

Scope of Unplanned Purchases

Several studies document the scope of unplanned purchases. DuPont Inc. conducted a study of consumer purchasing of toiletries, health care, and pharmaceutical products in supermarkets.[19] Among consumers' decisions for health care and beauty aid items, 61 percent were unplanned. Among their decisions for pharmaceuticals and vitamins, 51 percent were unplanned. A more recent study of supermarket items found that from 65 to 70 percent of consumers' purchases of dinners, entrees, and soups were unplanned.[20] Even purchases consumers make outside of supermarkets and drugstores are frequently unplanned. Prasad found that 39 percent of department store shoppers and 62 percent of discount store shoppers purchased at least one item on an unplanned basis.[21]

The last two recessions have probably increased unplanned purchases but have reduced pure impulse buying. The decrease in brand loyalty, cited in the last chapter, has caused more consumers to shop for bargains and to make brand decisions in the store. Most of these purchases are unplanned and are frequently based on price. On the other hand, pure impulse purchases (that is, purchases for variety or novelty) have probably decreased as a result of the last two recessions. A study by Yankelovich, Skelly, and White, the marketing research firm, found that almost one-fourth of the shoppers surveyed after the 1980-1982 recession said they made fewer impulse purchases.[22] Since impulse purchases are largely discretionary, shoppers' greater price sensitivity has tended to reduce impulse buying.

◆ THREE THEORIES OF LOW INVOLVEMENT CONSUMER BEHAVIOR

A better understanding of low involvement choice has evolved in marketing because of three theories: the theory of passive learning developed by Krugman,[23] the theory of social judgment developed by Sherif,[24] and the elaboration likelihood model developed by Petty and Cacioppo.[25]

Krugman's Theory of Passive Learning

Much of the work on low involvement consumer behavior is based on Krugman's perspective of television as an uninvolving medium. Krugman sought an answer to why television advertising produced high levels of brand recall yet little change in consumers' attitudes toward brands. He hypothesized that television is a low involvement medium that results in **passive learning.** The viewer is in a relaxed state and does not pay attention to the message. In this low involvement environment, the viewer does not link the message to his or her needs, brand beliefs, and past experiences (as is assumed in the high involvement case). The viewer retains information randomly because of repetition of the message. As a result, a respondent can show a high level of recall for a particular television advertisement, but the advertisement has little influence on brand attitudes.

Why is television a low involvement medium? First, television advertising is animate, while the viewer is inanimate (passive). Second, the pace of viewing is out of the viewer's control, and the viewer has little opportunity for reflection or making connections.[26] In contrast, print media (magazines and newspapers) are high involvement media because advertising is inanimate, while the reader is animate. The pace of exposure is within the reader's control because the reader has more opportunity to reflect on the advertising.

Krugman predicts that television would be more effective for low involvement cases and print advertising for high involvement cases. In their study, Grass and Wallace confirmed this view.[27] They found that for unmotivated consumers television was more effective in conveying a message than print ads were. For motivated consumers, print ads were somewhat more effective. A study by Childers and Houston concluded that verbal messages (such as print ads) are best for high involvement audiences, and visual messages (such as TV ads) are best for low involvement audiences.[28]

Krugman summarized his view of television by saying, "The public lets down its guard to the repetitive commercial use of television. . . . It easily changes its ways of perceiving products and brands and its purchasing behavior without thinking very much about it at the time of TV exposure."[29] In other words, consumers can change beliefs about a brand, leading to a purchase decision with very little thought and deliberation involved.

Krugman's theory of passive learning also has implications for the nature of advertising. If consumers are passive and disinterested, brand evaluation is unlikely to occur. Therefore, conveying product benefits through an informational approach is unlikely to work. Advertising must use noninformational means such as symbols and imagery to convey the message.

Consumer Behavior Implications of Passive Learning

Krugman's view of a passive consumer has stood many of the traditional behavioral concepts in marketing on their head. Table 5.3 lists the traditional behavioral concepts associated with an involved, active consumer and the parallel concepts of an uninvolved, passive consumer.

▶**TABLE 5-3**
The low involvement, passive consumer versus the high involvement, active consumer

Newer, Low Involvement View of a Passive Consumer	Traditional, High Involvement View of an Active Consumer
1. Consumers learn information at random.	1. Consumers are information processors.
2. Consumers are information gatherers.	2. Consumers are information seekers.
3. Consumers represent a passive audience for advertising. As a result, the effect of advertising on the consumers is strong.	3. Consumers represent an active audience for advertising. As a result, the effect of advertising on the consumer is weak.
4. Consumers buy first. If they do evaluate brands, it is done after the purchase.	4. Consumers evaluate brands before buying.
5. Consumers seek some acceptable level of satisfaction. As a result, consumers buy the brand least likely to give them problems and buy based on a few attributes. Familiarity is the key.	5. Consumers seek to maximize expected satisfaction. As a result, consumers compare brands to see which provide the most benefits related to needs and buy based on multiattribute comparisons of brands.
6. Personality and lifestyle characteristics are not related to consumer behavior because the product is not closely tied to the consumer's identity and belief system.	6. Personality and lifestyle characteristics are related to consumer behavior because the product is closely tied to the consumer's identity and belief system.
7. Reference groups exert little influence on product choice because products are unlikely to be related to group norms and values.	7. Reference groups influence consumer behavior because of the importance of the product to group norms and values.

The newer low involvement view holds that:

1. *Consumers learn information at random.*   Krugman views uninvolved consumers as those who learn from repetitive advertising, much as children learn nonsense syllables, by just picking up random stimuli and retaining them. The traditional view is of involved consumers who actively processes information in a cognitive manner by going through stages of awareness, comprehension, and retention. Hollander's and Jacoby's study supports the low involvement view of nonsense learning. They overlaid the audio portion of one commercial on the video portion of another, producing a nonsense TV commercial. Recall of the nonsense commercial was higher than the recall of the normal commercial.[30]

2. *Consumers are information catchers.*   In the low involvement case, consumers are information catchers; that is, passive receivers of information. High involvement consumers are regarded as information seekers, actively searching for information from alternative sources and engaging in shopping behavior. Studies by Celsi and Olson and by Gensch and Javagali have confirmed that less involved consumers seek less information and consider fewer product alternatives in evaluating brands.[31] The limited amount of information search for most consumer products is demonstrated in studies that show that many consumers typically visit one store and consider only one brand.[32]

3. *Consumers represent a passive audience for advertising.*   The low involvement perspective views advertising as most effective when it deals with unimportant matters. Under these conditions, advertising is a much more effective medium for inducing purchasing behavior in low involvement conditions. In Krugman's view, just being exposed to a commercial is persuasive and may lead consumers to purchase without the intervening step of comprehension.

The traditional active audience view is tied to the assumption that consumers are involved information seekers with strongly held brand attitudes. Under such conditions, consumers are likely to resist advertising that does not conform to prior beliefs (selective perception). This view logically leads to the conclusion that advertising is a weak vehicle for changing people's minds and is better suited to confirming strongly held beliefs. Bauer summarizes the active audience view in describing advertising as a "most difficult business. . . Typical communication experiments, including advertising tests, show that only a few percentages of the people exposed to the communication ever change their mind on anything important."[33]

On balance, when consumers are passive and the message is relatively unimportant, the low involvement view considers advertising a more powerful medium than does the traditional active audience view.

4. *Consumers evaluate brands after buying.*   Krugman states that uninvolved consumers may buy simply due to a reminder effect since most such purchases are unplanned. As a result, consumers often make the connection between a need and the brand in the store. Brand evaluation occurs after the purchase. For example, consumers select a lower-priced brand of paper towels in the store and then evaluate the brand after using it. The traditional view holds that consumers evaluate alternative brands before purchasing them.

5. *Consumers seek an acceptable rather than optimal level of satisfaction.* In the low involvement case, consumers do not seek to maximize brand satisfaction. The energy required in search of the best product is not worth the expected benefits. A lower level of satisfaction is acceptable. Active consumers seek to maximize satisfaction by extensively evaluating brands. Comparing brand attributes, consumers select the brand that best meets their needs.

6. *Personality and lifestyle characteristics are not related to consumer behavior.* There is no reason to assume that personality variables such as compulsiveness and lifestyle variables such as sociability are related to behavior for uninvolved consumers. Most products consumers purchase are not central to their beliefs or self-identity. As Kassarjian said, "Personality variables may be related to racial prejudice, suicide, violent crimes, or the selection of a spouse. But turning to unimportant, uninvolving, low-commitment consumer products such as brands of beer, chewing gum, t-shirts, and magazine exposure, the correlations [of personality to behavior] are extremely low."[34]

In contrast, the traditional view assumes that the consumer's personality and lifestyle will be related to the purchase decision. Such relationships are assumed to exist because a high level of involvement assumes the product is important to the consumer's belief system and self-identity. Since self-identity is reflected in the consumer's personality and lifestyle, it makes sense to relate these characteristics to products with high consumer involvement.

7. *Reference groups exert little influence on consumers.* The low involvement perspective holds that reference groups have little influence on consumers. A study by Cocanougher and Bruce supports this view.[35] Products such as salt, toothpaste, paper towels, and plastic wrap have little visibility and are not relevant to group norms. Since reference groups are not very important for low involvement products, much of the advertising portraying social approval in the use of products such as floor wax or room deodorizers may be misplaced. The more relevant approach may be to portray the problems such products can eliminate.

Involved consumers are more likely to be influenced by reference groups because a high involvement product is likely to reflect the norms and values of the group. Products such as automobiles, homes, and stereo sets are visible and have important status connotations.

Sherif's Theory of Social Judgment

A second theory that sheds additional light on uninvolved consumers is Sherif's **social judgment theory.** Sherif described an individual's position on an issue according to his or her involvement with the issue.[36] He identified a latitude of acceptance (the positions the individual accepts), a latitude of rejection (positions the individual rejects), and a latitude of noncommitment (positions toward which the individual is neutral). A highly involved individual who has a definite opinion about an issue would accept very few other positions and would reject a wide number of positions (narrow latitude of acceptance and wide latitude of rejection). An uninvolved individual would find more positions acceptable (wide latitude of acceptance) or would have no opinion about the issue (wide latitude of noncommitment).

A highly involved individual who agrees with a message (within his or her latitude of acceptance) will interpret it more positively than it actually is. This reaction represents an **assimilation effect.** A message that the individual disagrees with (within the latitude of rejection) will be interpreted as more negative than it actually is. This reaction represents a **contrast effect.** For example, a car buff who just bought a Chevy Blazer and is very satisfied with the car might recall some comments a friend made about it as more positive than they were (assimilation). However, if very disappointed with the Blazer, the car buff may recall the same comments by the friend as more negative than they actually were (contrast). Therefore, the highly involved individual is more likely to perceive messages selectively based on his or her preconceptions and biases. The uninvolved individual is less likely to perceive the message selectively, and an assimilation or contrast effect is less likely to occur.

Sherif's theory as applied to consumer behavior is illustrated in Figure 5.2. Active, involved consumers would find fewer brands acceptable and would

▶**FIGURE 5.2**
Social judgment theory applied to consumer behavior

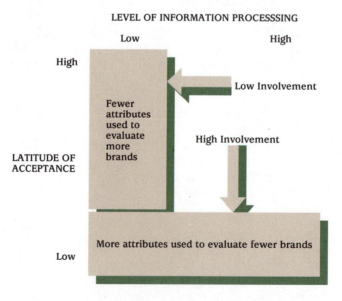

actively process information, whereas less involved consumers would find many brands acceptable and would engage in less information processing.

Sherif's theory conforms well to Krugman's concept of passive learning and provides more insight into passive consumers. Uninvolved consumers are willing to consider a wider number of brands because of a lack of commitment to one or several brands, but they do not search for alternatives. Given a lack of commitment, they are less willing to spend time interpreting advertising messages and evaluating brands. As a result, they perceive advertising with little cognitive activity and purchase brands in the easiest way possible—by purchasing the most familiar brand and buying the same brand repetitively. On this basis, social judgment theory and the theory of passive learning both agree that uninvolved consumers seek a satisfactory solution to problem solving, whereas involved consumers seek a more optimal solution.

Rothschild and Houston extend Sherif's theory to predict that highly involved consumers will use more attributes to evaluate fewer brands (horizontal bar in Figure 5.2), while less involved consumers will use fewer attributes to consider more brands (vertical bar in Figure 5.2).[37] This assumption makes sense, since more involved consumers' latitude of acceptance is narrower (fewer brands considered) and level of information processing is greater (more attributes used in evaluation), while the reverse is true for less involved consumers.

Several studies have supported Sherif's social judgment theory. Rothschild and Houston applied Sherif's measures of involvement to political choice.[38] They identified two types of political choices: a Presidential election (high involvement) and a state assembly race (low involvement). They found the latitude of acceptance of issues was narrower and the number of issues used to evaluate the candidates was greater for the Presidential race than in the state assembly race.

A study by Gensch and Javagali of farmers' selection of sources of supply found that less involved farmers evaluated more suppliers and did so on fewer attributes.[39] Both studies support the likelihood that less involved consumers process less information with a broader latitude of acceptance.

Elaboration Likelihood Model

Petty and Cacioppo's **elaboration likelihood model** (ELM) is a third theory that provides insight into uninvolved consumers. Illustrating how consumers process information in high and low involvement conditions,[40] the model presents a continuum from elaborate (central) processing to nonelaborate (peripheral) processing. The degree of elaboration depends on the relevance of the message to consumers. The more relevant the message in meeting consumer needs, the more likely consumers will be to develop thoughts in support of or counter to its content (that is, the more consumers will elaborate on the message). Thus, the arthritic consumer viewing a commercial for a pain reliever that claims to relieve the pain of arthritis is more likely to elaborate on the message by injecting his or her thoughts (such as, "This product might help me" or "This product could upset my stomach") compared to the consumer who rarely encounters such pain. Such elaboration is most likely when consumers are involved. Uninvolved consumers are unlikely to develop such message-relevant thoughts. Elaboration is minimal because consumers are passive recipients of information.

Petty and Cacioppo's distinction between high and low elaboration is similar to Krugman's distinction between active and passive consumers, shown in Table 5.3. The difference is that ELM focuses on the consumers' response to the message (in support of or against) and the nature of the stimuli that are most likely to persuade the active or passive information processor, whereas Krugman's model focuses on message exposure and comprehension.

Several studies support the elaboration likelihood model. Petty, Cacioppo, and Goldman found that involved consumers are more likely to be influenced by the quality and strength of the message (central cues). In contrast, less involved consumers are more likely to be influenced by stimuli that are peripheral to the message—for example, the use of color in the ad, the nature of the background, or the use of an expert spokesperson.[41] Such peripheral cues had little influence on involved consumers.

Schumann, Petty, and Clemons found that less involved consumers are likely to be influenced by cosmetic variations in the ad (print type, layout, a picture of a spokesperson), whereas more involved consumers are likely to be influenced by substantive variations (changes in message content regarding product attributes and benefits).[42] Here again, less involved consumers were engaging in peripheral processing, and more involved consumers were engaging in central processing.

Another study supports the use of message cues with involved consumers and nonmessage cues with uninvolved consumers. Gardner, Mitchell, and Russo found that involved consumers are more likely to retain and organize advertising messages that help them in their brand choice.[43] On the other hand, uninvolved consumers view advertising more for form than content. They are more likely to notice elements of the ad such as music, characters, and scenery, without linking these elements to the brand.

These studies imply that advertising to involved consumers should emphasize central message cues dealing with performance. Advertising to uninvolved consumers should use peripheral cues that might create a positive environment to stimulate the passive receipt of information. The ad in Exhibit 5.3 for a BMW motorcycle, a highly involving product, focuses on message cues dealing with performance. The ad for Parfum Bic takes a less involving approach because the brand is disposable. It uses peripheral cues in the background (the Eiffel Tower, a couple on a bicycle) with a simple tag line, "Paris in Your Pocket." The danger is that the message might be lost in a barrage of peripheral cues.

▶**EXHIBIT 5.3**
Use of central versus peripheral cues in advertising

*Central message cues for a high
involvement product*

Source: Courtesy of BMW of North
America Inc.

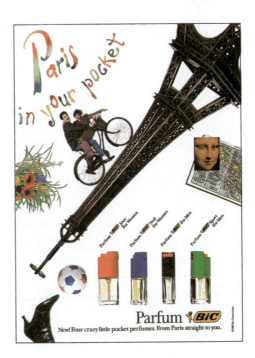

*Peripheral message cues for a low
involvement product*

◆ STRATEGIC IMPLICATIONS OF LOW INVOLVEMENT DECISION MAKING

The low involvement perspective and the theories of Krugman, Sherif, and Petty and Cacioppo have implications for every facet of marketing strategy. This section reviews the strategic implications of low involvement decision making and some strategic issues that arise from this perspective.

Marketing Strategy

The most important implications of a low involvement perspective are for advertising strategy. Important implications apply to other facets of marketing strategy as well.

Advertising

Advertising strategy should be very different for a low involvement product than for a high involvement product. Differences in advertising approaches, as reflected in the theories cited, suggest the following strategies for low involvement products:

1. *Advertising dollars should be spent in a campaign of high repetition and should use short-duration messages.*[44]   As Krugman notes, repetition is necessary to gain exposure, even though processing the message may be minimal.[45] High repetition and short messages encourage passive learning and ensure brand familiarity.

These principles apply concepts of classical conditioning. Repetition is required to create consumers' contiguity between advertising theme or symbol and brand use. An example is the constant repetition of Diet Pepsi's theme over a two-year period sung by Ray Charles "You Got the Right One, Baby," followed by an "Uh Huh" refrain. The message was short, did not require the consumers' attention, and could, therefore, be processed passively. However, consumers remembered and easily linked it to the brand once they were in the store. In-store promotions and print ads with the same theme reinforced the television campaign.

In the high involvement case, advertising should do more than create awareness and contiguity. It should influence consumers by communicating a persuasive message. Repetition is not the key; rather, it is the content of the message. Messages are likely to be more complex and varied and are likely to deal more directly with desired product benefits. Such ads can utilize an emotional or an informational appeal. The ads for car stereos in Exhibit 5.4 illustrate both approaches. The ad for the Coustic car radio takes an informational approach by detailing the characteristics and performance of the product. The ad for the Clarion creates involvement through emotion but has little informational content.

▶**EXHIBIT** 5.4
Ads for high involvement products

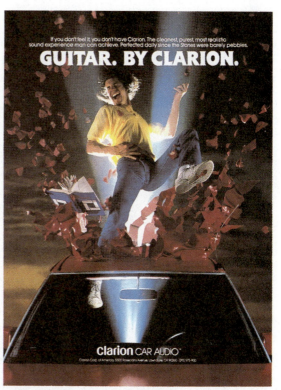

This Coustic ad for car stereos reflects consumer involvement by supplying detailed information on product performance.

This Clarion ad, also for car stereos, reflects consumer involvement by showing emotional attachment to the product.

2. *Advertising should focus on a few key points rather than on a broad-based information campaign.* Where there is little consumer interest or attention, there is limited ability to process and assimilate information. A proper campaign in the low involvement case "utilizes short messages emphasizing a few key points."[46] The Parfum Bic ad in Exhibit 5.3 is short and to the point. It has only two messages—disposability and a Parisian flavor.

3. *Visual and nonmessage components should be emphasized.*[47] Since uninvolved consumers learn passively and forget quickly, it is important to keep the product visually in front of them. In-store displays and packaging are important communications tools. Television advertising is more likely to be effective than print media because of the active visual component in television commercials. Where print is used, the product should be in the foreground and any peripheral cues in the background. Again, the Parfum Bic ad in Exhibit 5.3 is illustrative.

4. *Advertising should be the primary means of differentiating the product from that of the competition.* Because there are no substantial brand differences for many low involvement products, advertising becomes a primary means of competitive differentiation. Advertisers use symbols and imagery as substitutes for actual product differences and to maintain interest in undifferentiated brands. In this respect, symbols that can be positively identified with the brand such as the Pillsbury Doughboy should be used. As Tyebjee states, "Communication differentiation rather than product differentiation is the strategic role of the sales proposition of low involvement advertising."[48]

5. *Television rather than print media should be the primary vehicle for communication.* If less product information is required, a low involvement medium such as television is more suitable. This is because television does not require consumers to evaluate the content of the communication as closely as for print. Print media are more suitable if the audience is active in seeking information and evaluating it.

Product Positioning

Low involvement products are more likely to be positioned to minimize problems, whereas high involvement products are more likely to be positioned to maximize desired benefits. This is true because uninvolved consumers seek acceptable, not optimal, products.

Taking a high involvement view, a product such as plastic wrap might be positioned to stress benefits such as extra strength and the protection it affords food. A low involvement positioning might emphasize problem minimization such as a wrap that is less likely to shred or one that avoids freezer burn. (See Exhibit 5.5.) Frequent reference to avoiding problems such as dirty floors, stained glasses, or "ring around the collar" suggests the prevalence of a problem minimization approach for low involvement products.

Price

Consumers buying low involvement products are likely to be more price sensitive. They frequently purchase on the basis of price alone, since brand comparisons are unimportant and there are few differences between brands. Therefore, a decrease in price or a coupon offer may be enough to influence the consumer to buy.

A study by Gotlieb, Schlacter, and St. Louis confirmed the greater price sensitivity of less involved consumers.[49] They found that it took less of a price difference to get uninvolved consumers to switch from their current brand. In his study of margarine purchasers, Lastovicka also demonstrated the importance of price for uninvolved consumers. Among those who said the purchase was unimportant, 52 percent said price was the determining factor. Among those who thought the purchase important, only 22 percent said that price was the determinant.[50]

▶**EXHIBIT 5.5**
Advertising the solution
to a problem for a low
involvement product

In-Store Stimuli

Since most low involvement purchases are unplanned, in-store stimuli such as coupons, displays, or price deals are more likely to be important when consumers are not involved. Consumers may purchase the brand at eye level or the one with the largest shelf space simply because of the reminder effect. The package may be more influential for low involvement goods because it is encountered in the store.

Distribution

Widespread distribution is particularly important for low involvement products because consumers are not motivated to search for a brand. If a favored brand is not in the store, consumers are likely to make another choice. Marketing strategy must ensure in-store availability to discourage the likelihood of a brand switch.

Product Trial

Attempts at inducing trial are particularly important for low involvement products, since consumers may form a favorable attitude toward the brand after the purchase.[51] For instance, a consumer may try a free sample of toothpaste,

Several advertising agencies have begun to utilize the concept of involvement in developing advertising strategy. Foote Cone & Belding (FCB) classifies products on two dimensions: level of involvement (high versus low) and motives for purchasing (think versus feel). Think (or cognitive) motives are utilitarian and are related to product performance. Feel (or affective) motives are more self-expressive and sensory. They are related to a product's badge value and its ability to arouse emotion. A consumer buying a car based on criteria such as handling and acceleration reflects utilitarian motives and would be in the "think" category. A consumer who buys a car based on style and status criteria would reflect self-expressive motives and would be in the "feel" category.

STRATEGIC APPLICATIONS OF CONSUMER BEHAVIOR

Advertising Agencies Utilize the Involvement Concept

The matrix shown in Figure 5.3 classifies products into four categories. Products in Quadrant 1 are generally high in involvement, and consumers evaluate them based on utilitarian motives. Examples are life insurance, cameras, and credit cards. Products in Quadrant 2 are high involvement categories that consumers evaluate based on more emotional criteria. Examples are sports cars, perfume, and wine. Products in Quadrant 3 are low in involvement, and consumers evaluate them based on utilitarian criteria. Examples are razors, liquid bleach, and suntan lotion. Products in Quadrant 4 are uninvolving, and consumers usually buy them based on sensory criteria. FCB describes these products as "life's little pleasures." Examples are beer, soft drinks, pizza, and cigarettes.

Foote Cone & Belding has developed advertising strategies for each of these four categories. Products in Quadrant 1 should be advertised using an informational approach that emphasizes performance, while products in Quadrant 2 should be advertised through emotional appeals linked to the consumer's self-image. Quadrant 3 products should be advertised by repetitive appeals that maintain brand awareness and encourage repeat buying. Quadrant 4 products should be advertised by utilizing principles of classical conditioning: repetitive appeals that develop contiguity between a symbol or theme (such as the Marlboro Cowboy) and the product.

As stereo components straddle the think-feel dimension, there is probably a place in Figure 5.3 for both the informationally oriented Coustic car stereo ad and the emotionally oriented Clarion ad in Exhibit 5.4. The two products probably appeal to different segments of the car stereo market—Coustic to performance-oriented consumers and Clarion to consumers who view the product as an extension of their self-image.

Another advertising agency, Lintas USA, has adopted a remarkably similar classification. The only difference is that instead of think versus feel, they classify products into those that consumers purchase for negative versus positive motives. Negatively motivated products are almost always in the think category—credit cards and insurance for high involvement products; razors and sun-tan lotion for low involvement products. These are products designed to solve problems. Positively motivated products are almost always in the feel category. They are related to taste (soft drinks, wine) or self-enhancement (perfumes, sports cars). Advertising for less involving, negatively motivated products should demonstrate clear solutions to a problem. (See the ad for Ziploc freezer bags in Exhibit 5.5.) Ads for less involving, positively motivated products should emphasize positive sensory experiences (the Parfum Bic ad in Exhibit 5.3).

Sources: "What's in a Brand?" *American Demographics* (May, 1993), pp. 26-32; Brian T. Ratchford, "New Insights About the FCB Grid," *Journal of Advertising Research,* 27 (August-September, 1987), pp. 24-38; and Richard Vaughn, "How Advertising Works: A Planning Model Revisited," *Journal of Advertising Research,* 26 (February-March, 1986), pp. 57-66.

▶**FIGURE 5.3**
The FCB involvement grid

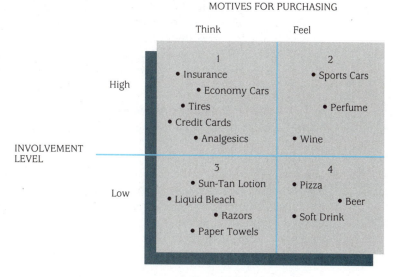

like the taste, and purchase it. Not seeking to maximize satisfaction, the consumer may continue to purchase the toothpaste just because the brand is adequate.[52] Information search and further brand evaluation are not warranted. Due to inertia, trial may be sufficient to induce the consumer to continue purchasing the brand.

What strategies can the marketer use to encourage trial under low involvement conditions? Free samples, deals and coupons, joint promotions with other products, in-store displays, and intensive distribution are all useful. Under high involvement conditions, consumers are unlikely to switch brands because of a price deal or coupon incentives, so these strategies are unlikely to induce trial. Trial under high involvement conditions can be encouraged only by demonstrating that the brand can deliver desired product benefits.

Strategic Issues

Several strategic issues dealing with low involvement decision making remain to be considered:

- Should marketers attempt to get consumers more involved with a low involvement product? If so, how?
- Given low involvement, should marketers attempt to shift consumers from a pattern of repetitive buying that reflects inertia to variety-seeking behavior?
- Should marketers segment markets by degree of involvement so that different strategies are directed to high involvement and low involvement consumers for a particular product category?

Shifting Consumers from Low to High Involvement

It would make sense for a marketer to try to get consumers more involved in a product. Because involvement means commitment, involved consumers are more likely to remain loyal to the marketer's brand in the face of competitive activity. What strategies can the marketer use to involve consumers with the product?

1. *Link the product to an involving issue.* Rothschild and Houston use Sherif's theory in citing one strategy as an attempt to widen the latitude of rejection of competitive brands. This can be done by linking the advertised brand to an involving issue.[53] Clorox initiated a campaign to link bleach (an uninvolving product) to the prevention of Salmonella poisoning (a highly involving issue as a result of a series of such cases early in 1993). The ad in Exhibit 5.6 suggests sanitizing kitchen appliances and surfaces with Clorox to kill germs. Other examples of linking low involvement products with high involvement issues are associating toothpaste with cavity prevention and disposable diapers with biodegradability.

2. *Link the product to an involving personal situation.* Another strategy is to associate a low involvement product with an involving situation. Tyebjee suggests relating the product to an activity in which the consumer is engaged.[54] He cites examples such as an early morning coffee commercial, advertisements of automobile products on radio during rush hours, and messages about sleep aids on nighttime television shows. In each case, involvement with the product increases because of the situation's relevance. The ad in Exhibit 5.6 for Reebok portrays an athlete reflecting on her involvement with the sports activities of her children.

▶**EXHIBIT 5.6**
Three strategies to increase involvement for uninvolving products

Linking the product to an involving issue

Linking the product to involving advertising

Source: ©The Procter & Gamble Company. Used with permission.

Linking the product to an involving situation

3. *Link the product to involving advertising.*   A third strategy is to create involvement with the advertising in the hope that consumers will establish some link with the product. Lutz said that just because "some products may be inherently low in involvement, their advertising need not be."[55] He cites two types of ads that may create involvement. An ego defensive ad would help consumers defend themselves against inadequacy (for example, Marlboro smokers are masculine). A value expressive advertisement expresses the consumers' values and beliefs. The ad for Tide in Exhibit 5.6 is an example. It shows two young girls trying to act like women. It tries to create an emotional attachment for an uninvolving product.

A third approach is to give an uninvolving product badge value through advertising. A Häagen-Dazs ad, for example, shows the product in the middle of an elegant table setting with the statement, "It is now socially acceptable to eat Häagen-Dazs ice cream with your fingers." The ad tries to increase involvement with an uninvolving product category by a tongue-in-cheek attempt at creating snob appeal.

4. *Change the importance of product benefits.*   A more difficult strategy is to try to change the importance consumers attach to product benefits. An example is Seven Up advertising its flagship brand as having no caffeine. Actually, the brand never did have caffeine, but the company did not advertise it because it did not think the presence or absence of caffeine made any difference to its buyers. However, with the greater health-consciousness of American consumers, Seven Up felt it could increase the importance attached to caffeine content in soft drinks and, thereby, increase the involvement with its product.

5. *Introduce an important characteristic in the product.*   Boyd, Ray, and Strong cite the possibility of introducing into a product an attribute that had not been considered important or that did not previously exist.[56] Examples include using additives in gasoline, adding bran to cereals, and introducing automatic rewinds in cameras.

These five strategies would assist the marketer in creating more product involvement—but involvement is relative. Creating greater involvement for toothpaste or ice cream does not mean that consumers are likely to engage in complex decision making when they evaluate brands. It means only that a moderate amount of cognitive activity may be stimulated through advertising and product policies.

Shifting Consumers from Inertia to Variety Seeking

Under a condition of low involvement, another question is whether marketers should encourage consumers to switch brands in a search for variety or to avoid product search and stay with the same brand (inertia) because of familiarity. (See Exhibit 5.7 for an example of switching from inertia to variety seeking.)

If a brand is a market leader, it would be in the brand's interest for the marketer to encourage inertia. If it is a less-known brand, the marketer should

▶**EXHIBIT 5.7**
Switching from inertia
to variety seeking
Source: ©Bill Whitehead.

"I've been faithful to this brand for 27 years. . . . Maybe it's time for a little fling!"

encourage variety seeking. In a low involvement situation, consumers may purchase the market leader because of familiarity. In such conditions, the marketer should use advertising as a reminder. In-store conditions would also be important to maintain brand familiarity. To keep the brand in front of consumers, the market leader would place the brand in the dominant shelf space in the store. For less familiar brands, the marketer would attempt to encourage variety seeking by using deals, lower prices, coupons, and free samples to encourage trial. The objective is to induce consumers to switch brands and gain wider experience. Sherif's theory would support this view. In a low involvement condition, the consumer has a wide latitude of acceptance, which suggests a greater willingness to try a diversity of brands.

Campbell's Soup is a good example of a market leader in a low involvement category. Campbell's strategy has consistently been to advertise frequently to maintain familiarity and to dominate shelf space within the store. Other canned soups have occasionally been introduced. Competitors' strategies have reflected attempts to induce trial by lower prices, free samples, and appeals to variety in advertising. However, Campbell's high-frequency advertising campaigns and in-store dominance have made entry into the canned soup market difficult for other brands.

Segmenting Markets by Degree of Consumer Involvement

The concept of involvement is consumer-related, not product-related. It is defined in terms of consumers' evaluation of the importance of and identity with the product. Although most consumers may have little involvement with toothpaste, some consumers may be more highly involved.

Because involvement can be measured on an individual level, markets can be segmented by consumer involvement. Purchasers of toothpaste can be categorized as high, medium, and low involvement consumers. Therefore, should marketing strategies for a given product category be differentiated by the degree of consumer involvement? Is it feasible to direct different advertising strategies to a high versus a low involvement segment for the same product? Such an approach would be expensive and could confuse consumers. A more realistic approach would be to differentiate product rather than advertising strategy.

A good example is cereal. Ordinarily, cereal is regarded as a low involvement product; however, to consumers concerned with nutritional and health benefits, it is more involving. A company would introduce a cereal brand to more involved consumers through print as well as TV advertising by communicating the benefits of the brand in an informationally oriented campaign. Deals and coupons would not be emphasized, but nutritional information would be prominently displayed in the ads and on the package.

To direct a brand to the low involvement segment, marketers would use deals and coupons to induce trial and place less emphasis on nutritional information. The marketer would also seek in-store displays and eye-level shelf space for the brand to encourage impulse buying.

In short, where it is possible to identify high and low involvement segments, marketers should consider differentiating their strategies by offering different brands.

◆ SOCIETAL IMPLICATIONS OF LOW INVOLVEMENT DECISION MAKING

Consumers are involved with issues as well as with products. Some consumers are more highly involved than others with issues such as environmental protection, drug abuse, teenage drinking, and prevention of AIDS. Whereas it would not necessarily benefit society to increase consumer involvement with bleach, toothpaste, or cars, it would be of benefit to increase involvement with the above societal issues.

The problem is that consumers that are not involved reflect the profile of Krugman's passive consumer—low awareness of the issues, little processing of information regarding these issues, and little or no consideration of alternative solutions. What kind of consumers are least likely to be involved with societal issues? There have been few studies to identify these consumers. Webster's study of the ecologically conscious consumer found that those least likely to be involved with ecological issues were older, less educated, and less likely to be upwardly mobile.[57] Studies of political involvement indicate that those least involved have the exact same profile—older, less educated, lower income.[58]

Reinforcing this profile of the low involvement consumer is Hyman's study of involvement with the selection of a phone company after the deregulation of telephone service. Hyman found that the least involved consumers had essentially the same profile.[59] These studies suggest that those least likely to be involved with key societal issues and perhaps even with their own well-being may be older, downscale consumers.

A key question is how to increase involvement with societal issues among those least involved. The three groups cited in Chapter 2—business, government, and consumer groups—have a role. At times, companies have played a constructive role. For example, Anheuser-Busch has run ads in magazines such as *Parenting* to increase awareness of problems of teenage drinking and driving. (See Exhibit 5.8.) Consumer groups have played an active role in trying to increase awareness of and involvement in key issues. For example, the Environmental Defense Fund has mounted advertising campaigns to increase awareness of recycling (see Exhibit 5.9); the Association for a Drug Free America has run a nationwide campaign to increase awareness of drug abuse; and organizations such as Momentum have been instrumental in increasing awareness of AIDS prevention.

Government plays an indirect role in increasing involvement by trying to encourage participation in the political process and by publicizing legislation and activities at the federal, state, and local levels regarding issues such as pol-

▶**EXHIBIT 5.8**
The role of business in increasing involvement with a societal issue

▶**EXHIBIT 5.9**
The role of consumer groups in increasing involvement with a societal issue

Source: Courtesy of Environmental Defense Fund.

lution control. A key question is whether the federal government should do more to provide information to those who might be most at risk—for example, providing more effective information on AIDS prevention to drug abusers or increasing awareness of the dangers of drinking and driving among teenagers.

SUMMARY

This chapter has focused on consumer choice in low involvement situations. Four types of consumer behavior were identified using two dimensions: level of consumer involvement and level of decision making.

1. *Complex decision making* requires high consumer involvement and extensive information processing. Consumers form beliefs about brands, evaluate them, and then choose. This think-before-you-act model conforms to a traditional hierarchy of effects.
2. *Brand loyalty* requires high involvement but little information processing. Positive reinforcement results in the consumers' purchase of the same brand repetitively.
3. *Inertia* assumes a low level of involvement and little information processing. The consumer has found a reasonably satisfactory brand and will stick with it. There is little incentive to search for information and to evaluate alternative brands. Brand switching may be induced by price deals and coupons.

4. *Limited decision making* assumes a low level of involvement but a moderate amount of information processing. Consumers may switch from inertia to limited decision making because of the introduction of a new product or changes in the existing product. Variety seeking because of boredom is an important example of limited decision making.

Unplanned purchases are an important manifestation of low involvement purchasing behavior since consumers make most unplanned purchase decisions in the store. As a result, in-store stimuli such as displays, coupons, and price specials are more likely to be influential.

Three theories were presented as a basis for understanding low involvement decision making. Krugman's theory of passive learning suggests that when consumers are not involved, they do not cognitively evaluate advertising messages. Exposure to advertising could occur without recall and comprehension. Sherif's theory of social judgment suggests that in conditions of low involvement, consumers are willing to consider many brands; however, they are likely to use only a few attributes to evaluate them. Petty and Cacioppo's elaboration likelihood model suggests that uninvolved consumers are more likely to react to nonmessage stimuli in communications than they are to the message itself.

The implications of low involvement decision making for the development of marketing strategy were described. Several important strategic questions were raised:

- How can marketers get consumers more involved with low involvement products?
- How can marketers of less-known brands get consumers to switch from inertia to variety-seeking behavior?
- Should marketers segment markets by consumers' degree of involvement?

The chapter closed by considering the societal implications of a lack of involvement in key issues such as environmental control, teenage drinking, and drug abuse and the role of business, consumer agencies, and government in increasing awareness and involvement.

Having focused on consumers' decision processes in Chapters 3 to 5, we now turn our attention to the individual consumer and how the consumer's psychological set and characteristics influence behavior.

QUESTIONS

1. This chapter suggests that many consumers are not involved with the brand purchased and that they make decisions frequently based on inertia.
   - If this is true, why do most marketing strategies assume an involved consumer?

- Why is it hard for a marketing manager to believe that most consumers might not be involved in the purchase of the company's brand?

2. • Design a general marketing strategy for a new brand of paper towel that is positioned as more economical because it has more sheets at the same price, yet has the same level of quality as other towels. (In most cases, consumers would regard paper towels as a low involvement product.)
   • Now assume that the same manufacturer has identified a segment of paper towel users who are more involved with the product because they recognize many usage situations that require a high-quality towel. The company decides to introduce a heavier-weight/high-quality towel to this involved segment. How would this marketing strategy differ from the previous strategy?

3. One group of consumers usually determines what cereal it will buy in advance and then goes to the store and buys it. Another usually makes its decision in the store. What differences might be employed in marketing to each group?

4. Develop a profile of the involved consumer for paper towels (the segment in the second part of Question 2) versus the uninvolved consumer (the segment in the first part of Question 2). Use Table 5.3 as a basis for profiling these two segments.

5. What strategies can a retailer use to encourage the five types of unplanned purchasing behavior specified in the chapter?

6. • What is the FCB grid?
   • What are the advertising implications of the FCB grid for each of the following product categories: (a) life insurance, (b) detergents, (c) beer, and (d) perfume?

7. The elaboration likelihood model suggests that nonmessage cues in advertising are more influential in low involvement conditions.
   • Why is this true?
   • How can nonmessage cues be used in advertising strategies?

8. Discuss the two arguments that (a) advertising is a weak communications medium because of consumer involvement resulting in selective exposure (the active audience view) versus (b) advertising is a strong communications medium because of a lack of consumer involvement resulting in retention of the message with little cognitive activity (the passive audience view).
   • What is the predominant view in advertising today? Why?
   • Can you cite advertising examples that tend to support recognition on the part of advertisers of a passive audience?

9. Pick a low involvement product category. Assume you are introducing a new brand in this category. Devise a strategy for attempting to create higher involvement with the brand by utilizing the five strategies for shifting consumers from low to high involvement described in the chapter.

10. Consider the product you selected in Question 9.
   - Under what conditions would a marketer of a brand encourage variety seeking?
   - Under what conditions would the marketer encourage inertia?
11. Is it realistic to develop separate brand and marketing strategies for high and low involvement segments of a product category?
12. Should business, government, and consumer groups have a role in increasing consumer involvement with societal issues such as pollution control or teenage drinking? If so, what should that role be?

RESEARCH ASSIGNMENT

Select what you regard as a high involvement and a low involvement product category. Develop a means of measuring degree of consumer involvement for these two product categories using a consumer's rating of (a) the importance of the product, (b) the risk associated with the product, and (c) the emotional appeal of the product. Interview a small sample of consumers applying this measure.
   - Was your assumption correct? That is, are significantly more consumers involved in what you identify as the high involvement category compared to the low?
   - Determine the following information for each consumer:
     1. Number of brands considered
     2. Number of attributes cited as important in evaluating brands for each product
     3. Advertising recall for key brands

Now categorize the sample into those above and below average on level of involvement for each product category.
   - Are there differences in characteristics between those more and less involved according to the three areas of information listed above?
   - Do your findings conform to the theories of (a) passive learning, (b) social judgment, and (c) elaboration likelihood?

NOTES

1. For a review of low involvement consumer behavior, see Scott A. Hawkins and Stephen J. Hoch, "Low Involvement Learning: Memory Without Evaluation," *Journal of Consumer Research*, 19 (September, 1992), pp. 212–225; John C. Maloney and Bernard Silverman, eds., *Attitude Research Plays for High Stakes* (Chicago: American Marketing Association, 1979); and William L. Wilkie, ed., *Advances in Consumer Research*, Vol. 6 (Ann Arbor: Association for Consumer Research, 1979), pp. 174–199. See also the following sources: Ruth Lynne Zaichowsky, "Measuring the Involvement Construct," *Journal of Consumer Research*, 12 (December, 1985), pp. 341–352; Marsha L. Richins and Peter H. Bloch, "After the New Wears Off: The Temporal Context of Product Involvement," *Journal of Consumer Research*, 13 (September, 1986), pp. 280–285; Banwari Mittal and Myung-Soo Lee,

"Separating Brand-Choice Involvement from Product Involvement via Consumer Involvement Profiles," in Michael J. Houston, ed., *Advances in Consumer Research,* Vol. 15 (Provo, UT: Association for Consumer Research, 1987), pp. 43–49; Sharon E. Beatty, Lynn R. Kahle, and Pamela Homer, "The Involvement-Commitment Model: Theory and Implications," *Journal of Business Research,* 16 (March, 1988), pp. 149–168; Carolyn L. Costley, "Meta Analysis of Involvement Research," in Houston, *Advances in Consumer Research,* Vol. 15, pp. 554–562; Richard L. Celsi and Jerry C. Olson, "The Role of Involvement in Attention and Comprehension Processes," *Journal of Consumer Research,* 15 (September, 1988), pp. 210–224; Dennis H. Gensch and Rajshekhar G. Javalgi, "The Influence of Involvement on Disaggregate Attribute Choice Models," *Journal of Consumer Research,* 14 (June, 1987), pp. 71–82; and Jean-Noel Kapferer and Gilles Laurent, "Consumer Involvement Profiles: A New Practical Approach to Consumer Involvement," *Journal of Advertising Research,* 25 (December, 1985–January, 1986), pp. 48–56.

2. "How King Kellogg Beat the Blahs," *Fortune* (August 29, 1988), pp. 55–64.

3. Harold H. Kassarjian and Waltraud M. Kassarjian, "Attitudes Under Low Commitment Conditions," in Maloney and Silverman, *Attitude Research Plays for High Stakes, op. cit.,* p. 8.

4. Nancy T. Hupfer and David M. Gardner, "Differential Involvement with Products and Issues: An Exploratory Study," in David M. Gardner, ed., *Proceedings of the 2nd Annual Conference of the Association for Consumer Research* (College Park, MD: Association for Consumer Research, 1971), pp. 262–269.

5. Tyzoon T. Tyebjee, "Refinement of the Involvement Concept: An Advertising Planning Point of View," in Maloney and Silverman, *Attitude Research Plays for High Stakes, op. cit.,* p. 106.

6. John L. Lastovicka, "Questioning the Concept of Involvement Defined Product Classes," in Wilkie, *Advances in Consumer Research,* Vol. 6, pp. 174–179.

7. See Michael L. Rothschild, "Advertising Strategies for High and Low Involvement Situations," in Maloney and Silverman, *Attitude Research Plays for High Stakes, op. cit.,* pp.74–93. Recent research has suggested that attitudes are formed in low involvement conditions on a noncognitive basis. Yet these attitudes are likely to be weaker than those formed on a cognitive basis in high involvement conditions. See Chris Janiszewski, "Preconscious Processing Effects: The Independence of Attitude Formation and Conscious Thought," *Journal of Consumer Research,* 15 (September, 1988), pp. 199–209.

8. "Major Study Details Ads' Effects on Sales," *Advertising Age* (June 21, 1982), pp. 1, 80.

9. Sharon E. Beatty and Lynn R. Kahle, "Alternative Hierarchies of the Attitude-Behavior Relationship: The Impact of Brand Commitment and Habit," *Journal of the Academy of Marketing Science,* 16 (Summer, 1988), pp. 1–10.

10. Wayne D. Hoyer and Steven P. Brown, "Effects of Brand Awareness on Choice for a Common, Repeat-Purchase Product," *Journal of Consumer Research,* 17 (September, 1990), pp. 141–148.

11. John G. Lynch, Howard Marmorstein, and Michael F. Weigold, "Choices from Sets Including Remembered Brands: Use of Recalled Attributes and Prior Evaluations," *Journal of Consumer Research,* 15 (September, 1988), pp. 169–184.

12. For a similar four-part classification, see F. Steward DeBruicker, "An Appraisal of Low-Involvement Consumer Information Processing," in Maloney and Silverman, *Attitude Research Plays for High Stakes, op. cit.,* p. 124.

13. Rajeev Batra and Michael L. Ray, "Situational Effects of Advertising Repetition: The Moderating Influence of Motivation, Ability, and Opportunity to Respond," *Journal of Consumer Research,* 12 (March, 1986), pp. 432–445.

14. Hawkins and Hoch, "Low Involvement Learning . . . ," *loc. cit.*

15. Hoyer and Brown, "Effects of Brand Awareness . . . ," *loc. cit.*

16. "Former Customers are Good Prospects," *The Wall Street Journal* (April 22, 1982), p. 31.

17. Dennis W. Rook, "The Buying Impulse," *Journal of Consumer Research,* 14 (September, 1987), pp. 189–199.

18. The first four types of unplanned purchasing behavior were proposed by Hawkins Stern, "The Significance of Impulse Buying Today," *Journal of Marketing,* 26 (April, 1962), pp. 59–62.

19. "Marketing Emphasis," *Product Marketing* (February, 1978), pp. 61–64.

20. "Study Confirms Impulse Buying on Rise," *Promote* (October 12, 1987), pp. 6–8.

21. V. Kanti Prasad, "Unplanned Buying in Two Retail Settings," *Journal of Retailing,* 51 (Fall, 1975), pp. 3–12.

22. *Supermarket Shoppers in a Period of Economic Uncertainty* (New York: Yankelovich, Skelly, and White, Inc., 1982), p. 53.

23. Herbert E. Krugman, "The Impact of Television Advertising: Learning Without Involvement," *Public Opinion Quarterly,* 29 (Fall, 1965), pp. 349–356.

24. C. W. Sherif, M. Sherif, and R. W. Nebergall, *Attitude and Attitude Change* (Philadelphia: Saunders, 1965).

25. Richard E. Petty and John T. Cacioppo, *Attitudes and Persuasion: Classic and Contemporary Approaches* (Dubuque, IA: William C. Brown, 1981); and Richard E. Petty, John T. Cacioppo, and David Schumann, "Central and Peripheral Routes to Advertising Effectiveness: The Moderating Role of Involvement," *Journal of Consumer Research,* 10 (September, 1983), pp. 135–146.

26. Herbert E. Krugman, "The Measurement of Advertising Involvement," *Public Opinion Quarterly,* 30 (Winter, 1966), pp. 584–585.

27. Robert C. Grass and Wallace H. Wallace, "Advertising Communication: Print vs. TV," *Journal of Advertising Research,* 14 (October, 1974), pp. 19–23.

28. Terry L. Childers and Michael J. Houston, "Conditions for a Picture-Superiority Effect on Consumer Memory," *Journal of Consumer Research,* 11 (September, 1984), p. 652.

29. Krugman, "The Impact of Television Advertising . . . ," *op. cit.,* p. 354.

30. Stephen W. Hollander and Jacob Jacoby, "Recall of Crazy, Mixed-Up TV Commercials," *Journal of Research,* 13 (June, 1973), pp. 399–42.

31. Celsi and Olson, "The Role of Involvement. . . ," *loc. cit.;* and Gensch and Javagali, "The Influence of Involvement. . . ," *loc. cit.*

32. W. P. Dommermuth, "The Shopping Matrix and Marketing Strategy," *Journal of Marketing Research,* 2 (May, 1965), pp. 128–132; and Joseph W. Newman and Richard Staelin, "Prepurchase Information Seeking for New Cars and Major Household Appliances," *Journal of Marketing Research,* 9 (August, 1972), pp. 249–257.

33. R. A. Bauer, "The Obstinate Audience," *American Psychologist,* 19 (May, 1964), pp. 319–328.

34. Kassarjian and Kassarjian, "Attitudes Under Low Commitment Conditions . . . ," *op. cit.,* p. 10.

35. A. Benton Cocanougher and Grady Bruce, "Socially Distant Reference Groups and Consumer Aspirations," *Journal of Marketing Research,* 8 (August, 1971), pp. 378–381.

36. Sherif, Sherif, and Nebergall, *Attitude and Attitude Change;* and M. Sherif and C. E. Hovland, *Social Judgment* (New Haven, CN: Yale University Press, 1964).

37. Michael L. Rothschild and Michael J. Houston, "The Consumer Involvement Matrix: Some Preliminary Findings," in Barnett A. Greenberg and Danny N. Bellenger, *Proceedings of the American Marketing Association Educators' Conference,* Series. No. 41 (1977), pp. 95–98.

38. *Ibid.*

39. Gensch and Javagali, "The Influence of Involvement . . . ," *loc. cit.*

40. Petty, Cacioppo, and Schumann, "Central and Peripheral Routes to Advertising Effectiveness," *loc. cit.*

41. Richard E. Petty, John T. Cacioppo, and Rachel Goldman, "Personal Involvement as a Determinant of Argument-Based Persuasion," *Journal of Personality and Social Psychology,* 41 (November, 1981), pp. 847–855; and Petty, Cacioppo, and Schumann, "Central and Peripheral Routes to Advertising Effectiveness," *loc. cit.*

42. David W. Schumann, Richard E. Petty, and D. Scott Clemons, "Predicting the Effectiveness of Different Strategies of Advertising Variation: A Test of the Repetition-Variation Hypotheses," *Journal of Consumer Research,* 17 (September, 1990), pp. 192–203.

43. Meryl Gardner, Andrew Mitchell, and J. Edward Russo, "Strategy-Induced Low Involvement with Advertising," paper presented at the first Consumer Involvement Conference, New York University, June, 1982.

44. Rothschild, "Advertising Strategies for High and Low Involvement Situations," *op. cit.,* p. 84.

45. Krugman, "The Measurement of Advertising Involvement," *loc. cit.*

46. Rothschild, "Advertising Strategies for High and Low Involvement Situations," *op. cit.,* p. 84.

47. Krugman, "The Measurement of Advertising Involvement," *loc. cit.*

48. Tyebjee, "Refinement of the Involvement Concept . . . ," *op. cit.,* p. 97.

49. Jerry B. Gotlieb, John L. Schlacter, and Robert D. St. Louis, "Consumer Decision Making: A Model of the Effects of Involvement, Source Credibility, and Location on the Size of the Price Difference Required to Induce Consumers to Change Suppliers," *Psychology & Marketing,* 9 (May/June, 1992), pp. 191–206.

50. John L. Lastovicka, "The Low Involvement Point-of-Purchase: A Case Study of Margarine Buyers," paper presented at the first Consumer Involvement Conference, New York University, June, 1982.

51. Thomas S. Robertson, "Low-Commitment Consumer Behavior," *Journal of Advertising Research,* 16 (April, 1976), p. 23; and Henry Assael, "The Conceptualization of a Construct of Variety-Seeking Behavior," Working Paper Series #79–43, Stern School of Business, New York University, May, 1979, p. 5.

52. Peter L. Wright, "The Choice of a Choice Strategy: Simplifying vs. Optimizing," Faculty Working Paper No. 163, University of Illinois, Department of Business Administration, 1974.

53. Rothschild and Houston, "The Consumer Involvement Matrix . . . ," *op. cit.,* p. 95–98.

54. Tyebjee, "Refinement of the Involvement Concept . . . ," *op. cit.,* p. 100.

55. Richard J. Lutz, "A Functional Theory Framework for Designing and Pretesting Advertising Themes," in Maloney and Silverman, *Attitude Research Plays for High Stakes, op. cit.,* p. 47.

56. Harper W. Boyd, Jr., Michael L. Ray, and Edward C. Strong, "An Attitudinal Framework for Advertising Strategy," *Journal of Marketing,* 36 (April, 1972), p. 31.

57. Frederick E. Webster, Jr., "Determining the Characteristics of the Socially Conscious Consumer," *Journal of Consumer Research,* 2 (December, 1975), pp. 188–196.

58. Lester W. Milbrath and M.L. Goel, *Political Participation,* 2nd ed. (New York: New York University Press, 1982).

59. Drew Hyman, "The Hierarchy of Consumer Participation: Knowledge and Proficiency in Telecommunications Decision Making," *The Journal of Consumer Affairs,* 24 (Summer, 1990), pp. 1–23.

PART III

THE INDIVIDUAL CONSUMER

Part Three focuses on the individual consumer's role in the purchasing process. Chapters 6-9 are concerned with the consumers' thought variables—namely, perceptions, attitudes, and desired benefits—and the way consumers process marketing information. The thought variables are central to consumer behavior because they affect the development of product and promotional strategies. Perceptions determine the way consumers select and organize marketing stimuli such as prices and advertising. Desired benefits define areas of marketing opportunity for new products and the possible repositioning of existing products. Brand attitudes provide a basis for determining whether the marketer is positively influencing consumers.

Chapters 10 and 11 describe the second component of the consumer: demographic, lifestyle, and personality characteristics. These factors are important in describing consumers and are used to segment markets and to develop promotional strategies. In Chapter 12, we discuss identifying market segments—groups of consumers with common needs, attitudes, and characteristics—and the implications of targeting these segments.

6

Consumer Perceptions

CONSUMER PERCEPTIONS: CLEAR PRODUCTS ARE IN, COLOR IS OUT

One of the key elements of a successful marketing strategy is the development of product and promotional stimuli that consumers will perceive as relevant to their needs. In Chapter 3, we defined consumer **perceptions** as the selection, organization, and interpretation of marketing and environmental stimuli into a coherent picture. In this chapter, consumer perceptions are considered in more detail.

Consumer perceptions are the reason why an increasing number of consumer packaged goods companies are coming out with clear products. Consumers associate clear products with benefits such as mild, light, and natural ingredients. In 1992, Procter & Gamble replaced Liquid Ivory, formerly a white liquid in a white bottle, with a clear liquid in a clear bottle to highlight purity and mildness.[1] The contradiction between the name Ivory and a clear product does not seem to bother P&G as long as the consumers *perceive* these benefits.

Similarly, in 1992, Colgate-Palmolive came out with Palmolive Sensitive Skin in a clear bottle to reinforce its mildness claim (see

Exhibit 6.1); Bristol Myers, with Ban clear deodorant; and Mennen with Lady Speed Stick Crystal. Also, far afield from soaps and deodorants, Amoco has begun heavily touting a product around since 1915, Crystal Clear Amoco, because it found that the product is more environmentally pure than that of its competitors.[2] Apparently, consumer perceptions of natural ingredients apply to gasoline as well as to packaged goods.

Perhaps the greatest impact of the trend toward clear has been in "new age" soft drinks. Pepsi led the way with the introduction of Crystal Pepsi. (See Exhibit 6.1.) By 1993, Crystal Pepsi had captured 2 percent of the soft drink market, making it a $1 billion brand and the biggest success story since Diet Coke.[3] Advertising the benefits of light, natural flavorings and no preservatives appealed to health-conscious young adults. Competitors quickly followed suit; Coke was ready to introduce Tab Clear, and Seagram Co. tested a clear, low-calorie soft drink called Quest.[4]

Marketers face a risk in relying on consumer perceptions to introduce clear products. Many consumers associate clear with water rather than with health benefits. Also, taste experiences may be at variance with the lack of color. For example, some consumers were disappointed with Crystal Pepsi because it did not have a "cola" taste; and the brand dipped in sales after its initial success. However, given the greater health orientation of American consumers, it is likely that clear is here to stay.

In this chapter, we first focus on what consumers are perceiving—stimuli. Next, we consider the three processes by which consumers perceive stimuli— selection, organization, and interpretation—and their strategic implications for marketing. We then focus on one of the most important applications of perceptions—consumer perceptions of prices and association of price with product quality.

◆ MARKETING STIMULI AND CONSUMER PERCEPTIONS

Stimuli are any physical, visual, or verbal communications that can influence an individual's response. The two most important types of stimuli influencing consumer behavior are marketing and environmental (social and cultural influences). In this chapter, we consider marketing stimuli. Environmental stimuli are considered in Parts Four and Five.

Marketing stimuli are any communications or physical stimuli that are designed to influence consumers. The product and its components (package, contents, physical properties) are **primary** (or **intrinsic**) **stimuli**. Communications designed to influence consumer behavior are **secondary** (or **extrinsic**) **stimuli** that represent the product either through words, pictures, and symbolism or through other stimuli associated with the product (price, store in which purchased, effect of salesperson).

The trend toward clear products

Source: (left) Courtesy of Pepsi-Cola Co.; (right) Courtesy of Colgate-Palmolive Co.

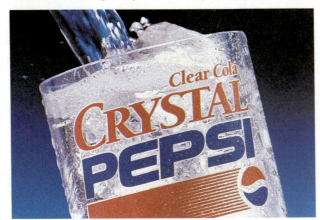

To survive in a competitive market, manufacturers must constantly expose consumers to secondary marketing stimuli. Continuous advertising would not be profitable, however, unless enough consumers were to buy again. Therefore, the ultimate determinant of future consumer actions is experience with the primary stimulus, the product. At times, manufacturers attempt to introduce such product experience prior to a purchase by giving consumers free samples. Before introducing their products to the general market, some manufacturers may offer samples to provide consumers a direct and risk-free product experience. However, distributing free samples as a primary stimulus to influence consumers to buy products is the exception. The dominant element in marketing strategy is communication about the product.

The key requirement in communicating secondary stimuli to consumers is the development of a product concept. A **product concept** is a bundle of product benefits that can be directed to the needs of a defined group of consumers through messages, symbolism, and imagery. The product concept represents the organization of the secondary stimuli into a coordinated product position that can be communicated to consumers. For example, Nestle developed the concept for its freeze-dried coffee entry, Taster's Choice, as a product that provides the convenience of instant but the taste and aroma of regular coffee. Nestle geared the secondary stimuli to the intended concept. The brand name implied taste, and the advertising demonstrated the taste benefits of a good instant coffee for the head of the family. Nestle even tested the shape of the jar and determined that a deep square jar would provide more of an image of hefty taste than would the traditional cylindrical jar. Clearly, definition of the product concept must precede development of the secondary stimuli in the marketing plan.

Two key factors determine which stimuli consumers will perceive and how they will interpret them: the characteristics of the stimulus and the consumers' ability to perceive the stimulus. These two influences interact in determining consumer perceptions. Assume a company producing a leading deodorant subtly changes ingredients to give the deodorant a "cleaner" smell (a stimulus characteristic). If many consumers cannot distinguish between the new and the old smell (a consumer characteristic), the change in stimulus will be ineffective. We will consider stimulus and consumer characteristics in the following sections.

Stimulus Characteristics Affecting Perception

Several characteristics of marketing stimuli affect the way consumers perceive products. These characteristics can be divided into sensory elements and structural elements. Both have implications for product development and advertising.

Sensory Elements

Sensory elements are composed of color, smell, taste, sound, and feel.

Color.   *Color* has important sensory connotations. One study tested the same roll-on deodorant packaged in three different colors.[5] Respondents said the product in one color scheme dried quickly and was effective, the product in the second had a strong aroma, and the product in the third was irritating and ineffective. Differences in consumers' reactions to the identical product were caused solely by differences in the color of the packaging. Mary Kay, the second largest direct seller of skin care products in the United States, has always associated its products and logo with pink—a color that reinforced an old-fashioned image. In an attempt to appeal to the contemporary woman, the company has begun to use a more sophisticated off-white.[6] Even in Spain, a more traditional country, Mary Kay uses new color schemes to depict a contemporary woman but retains its basic pink as background. (See Exhibit 6.2.)

The importance of color perceptions is further illustrated by P&G's attempt to change Prell shampoo from its traditional green to blue. An outcry arose among loyal Prell users, forcing the company to change Prell back to its traditional green. One analyst concluded that "Challenging [long-standing] consumer perceptions is very tricky and is generally a mistake."[7]

Color perceptions are likely to differ among countries. A study by Jacobs *et al.* of consumers in the Far East and in the United States found that consumers in China and Japan associate purple with expensive products and grey with inexpensive products. The associations are exactly the opposite for American consumers, who associate purple with inexpensive products and grey with expensive ones.[8] As we saw in Chapter 4, in Hong Kong, Marlboro uses cross-cultural differences in color perceptions by depicting the Cowboy in a white hat on a white horse because white is culturally significant in China.

Taste. Taste is another sensory factor that will condition consumers' brand perceptions. One of the problems with Crystal Pepsi is that many consumers expect it to taste like regular Pepsi, but it has a distinctly lighter taste. The company is now trying to communicate the taste difference with the ad theme, "You've never seen a taste like this." The importance of taste is illustrated by P&G's blunder when it first introduced Pringles potato chips. Its main focus was the novel packaging in an easy-to-stack cylindrical can that avoided contents breakage. Not only did the package look like a tennis can, but the chips also tasted like tennis balls. P&G had to spend hundreds of million of dollars to reformulate the product and successfully reintroduce it.

Taste can be an elusive perception. A study by Allison and Uhl found that when consumers were asked to taste three unlabelled brands of beer, they rated all three brands similarly; and most consumers could not identify their regular brand.[9] However, when shown the labels, consumers had a strong preference for their regular brand. The result shows that taste is not an objective criterion. It is inextricably linked to the brand's image in the consumer's mind. Without brand identification, the consumer's taste experience is entirely different. This fact was illustrated when Coca-Cola tried to change the formula of its flagship brand. Blind taste tests showed that New Coke was superior to the original. When the company tried to change the formula, consumer resistance was so great it had to bring back the original as Coca-Cola Classic. The strong association with a brand that was part of many consumers' heritage went beyond taste.

Smell. Smell is particularly important for cosmetics and food products. In one study, two different fragrances were added to the same facial tissue. Consumers perceived one facial tissue as elegant and expensive and the other as a product to use in the kitchen.[10] Smell can be a factor even in car purchases. Car dealers have been known to use a spray inside cars so they smell "new." Rolls Royce included scent strips in advertisements in *Architectural Digest* to convey the smell of its leather upholstery. In another application, Procter & Gamble used scratch and sniff stickers on its detergent packaging so consumers could more easily smell the products in the store.[11]

Smell also has cross-cultural dimensions. The social role of perfumes and colognes in Western society was never established in Japan. Because of crowding and small living spaces, Japanese consumers value cleanliness and never felt the need for using these products as a means of avoiding body odor. In fact, many Japanese regard perfumes and colognes as intrusive to other people's privacy.

Sound. Sound is another important sensory stimulus. Advertisers have traditionally used English accent voice-overs to convey status and authority. This was one reason why Commander Whitehead was an effective spokesperson for Schweppes beverage mixers. Advertisers also frequently use music through jingles or as background themes to create positive associations with brands. Marketers must pretest such stimuli to ensure that they will create positive associations with a brand. Gorn demonstrated the importance of such associations in an experiment. Consumers were asked to choose among several pens, one of which they saw advertised with background music. Consumers were more likely to choose the pen if they liked the background music.[12]

Feel. The *feel* of certain products will also influence consumers' perceptions. Softness is considered a desirable attribute in many paper products. The former theme "Don't squeeze the Charmin" suggests the importance of feel. Feel is also a means of determining quality. Consumers often use the feel of textile fabrics, clothing, carpeting, or furniture to evaluate quality.

Structural Elements

A number of findings have emerged from studies of structural elements applied primarily to print advertising. For example:

- The larger the *size* of the ad, the more likely it is to be noticed.[13]
- A *position* in the first 10 pages of a magazine or in the upper half of a printed page produces more attention.[14]
- *Contrast*—for example, the picture of a product on a stark white background is likely to produce attention.
- *Novelty* is another attention-getting device. The Panasonic ad in a Saudi Arabian magazine (Exhibit 6.3) is an example under the heading "Mood music on the move."

Consumer Characteristics Affecting Perception

Two characteristics are important in determining consumers' perception of stimuli: ability to discriminate between stimuli and propensity to generalize from one stimulus to another.

▶**EXHIBIT 6.3**
Attracting attention through novelty

Source: Courtesy of Al DahLawi Co., Sole Agent-National/ Panasonic/Technics, Jeddah, Saudi Arabia

Stimulus Discrimination

One of the basic questions regarding the effect of marketing stimuli on perceptions is whether consumers can discriminate among differences in stimuli. Do consumers perceive differences between brands in taste, in feel, in price, in the shape of the package?

The ability to discriminate among stimuli is learned. Generally, frequent users of a product are better able to notice small differences in product characteristics between brands. However, in many cases, the consumers' ability to discriminate sensory characteristics such as taste and feel is small. As a result, marketers rely on advertising to convey brand differences that physical characteristics alone would not impart. They attempt to create a brand image that will convince consumers that one brand is better than another.

Threshold Level. The ability of consumers to detect variations in light, sound, smell, or other stimuli is determined by their **threshold level.** Some consumers are more sensitive to these stimuli than others. Arthur D. Little, a management consulting firm, has identified expert taste testers for products such as cigarettes and coffee. Since their level of sensory discrimination is much greater than the average consumer's, these experts can detect subtle differences in coffee or cigarette blends and are used by marketers to evaluate various test products and to screen out potential losers. Once these experts identify the best prospective blends, the products are then tested on consumers in standard taste tests.

Just-Noticeable Difference. A basic principle in determining a consumer's threshold level is that a differential threshold exists in comparing two stimuli. The consumer will not be able to detect any difference between stimuli below his or her differential threshold. The differential threshold, therefore, represents the **just-noticeable difference (j.n.d.).** For example, if a private label detergent is five cents below the consumer's regular brand, the consumer may not notice the difference. However, if the private label brand is ten cents below the regular brand, the consumer is likely to notice the difference. Therefore, ten cents is the differential threshold, or j.n.d., for this consumer.

Marketers sometimes seek to make changes in marketing stimuli that will *not* be noticed (a decrease in package size or an increase in price). A good example of the need to change a marketing stimulus without notice is the periodic updating of existing packaging. For instance, General Mills has subtly changed one of the most enduring symbols in advertising, Betty Crocker, who was first introduced in 1921, to give her a more contemporary look.[15] (See Exhibit 6.4.) Most consumers would not notice the more subtle changes (for example, the one between 1965 and 1968) because they are below their j.n.d.

Of even more direct application to marketing strategy is the need to differentiate a brand from that of the competition so it will be noticed. In this case, the marketer seeks to develop product characteristics and advertising messages that are easily detectable (differences in size, taste, color, ingredients, and so on).

▶**EXHIBIT 6.4**
Changes in Betty Crocker's appearance below the just-noticeable-difference
Source: Courtesy of General Mills Inc .

1936   1955   1965   1968

1972   1980   1986

Weber's Law.   As most consumers cannot detect small changes in a product's price, package size, or physical characteristics, a relevant question for marketers is the degree of change required for consumers to take notice. A principle developed by a German physiologist over a hundred years ago, known as Weber's law, provides some insight into this question. **Weber's law** says that the stronger the initial stimulus, the greater the change required for the stimulus to be seen as different. In marketing terms, this would mean that the higher the price, the greater the change in price required for consumers to take notice. The price of a $500 stereo set would have to increase more significantly than that of a $100 tape deck in order to be noticed. Moreover, Weber's law says that the increase in the difference required to reach the differential threshold (the j.n.d.) is constant. That is, if price had to increase by a minimum of $10 to be noticed for a $100 tape deck, it would have to increase by a minimum of $50 to be noticed for a $500 stereo set. In both cases, the j.n.d. is a constant 10 percent.

The Federal Trade Commission implicitly recognized the nature of Weber's law when it required that the surgeon general's warning in cigarette advertising had to be a certain size.[16] The bigger the ad, the bigger the warning's typeface had to be to be noticed. If the typeface size fell below the specifications the FTC set, it might fall below the j.n.d. for many consumers who would thus not perceive it.

The most direct applications of Weber's law are in regard to price. One important implication is that the higher the original price of an item, the greater the markdown required to increase sales. The required markdown on a designer suit would be greater than that on a regular suit.

Subliminal Perceptions.   The differential threshold was identified as the minimum difference between two stimuli that consumers can detect. Thus, a consumer may be able to tell the difference between two cordials of 40 proof and 60 proof; but if the difference between the two is smaller, a consumer will not detect it (60 minus 40, or 20 proof, is the j.n.d.). There is also an **absolute threshold** below which consumers cannot detect the stimulus at all. Thus, a consumer can detect alcohol in a cordial that is 10 proof; but below that, a consumer can detect no alcoholic content in the beverage. Therefore, the differential threshold is 20 proof, and the absolute threshold is 10 proof.

One of the major controversies regarding consumer perceptions is whether consumers can actually perceive marketing stimuli below their absolute threshold. **Subliminal perception** means perception of a stimulus below the conscious level.[17] The threshold level at which perceptions occur is referred to as the **limen.** Thus, perception below the absolute threshold level is subliminal. It may seem contradictory that consumers can perceive a message below their minimum level of perception, but experiments conducted in the 1950s suggest that exposure may actually occur without attention and comprehension. That is, consumers do not see the message, but they register it.

Vicary conducted a test in 1957 in which two messages, "Eat popcorn" and "Drink Coca-Cola," were shown in a movie theater for 1/3,000 of a second (well below the absolute threshold) at intervals of every five seconds.[18] Popcorn sales in the theater increased by 58 percent and Coca-Cola sales by 18 percent compared to periods in which there was no subliminal advertising. These results immediately raised serious ethical questions, as consumers could be influenced by messages without their approval or knowledge. The *New Yorker* magazine said that "minds had been 'broken and entered.' "[19]

The controversy over subliminal advertising proved shallow because there was little proof that it influenced consumer actions.[20] Subsequent attempts to replicate Vicary's findings did not succeed.[21] Although the Federal Communications Commission took an immediate interest in the implications of subliminal advertising, it could not confirm the conclusion that subliminal advertising influences the receiver's responses.[22] Later studies by Moore and Saegert found little influence resulting from subliminal advertising.[23] However, at least one study by Janiszewski did find that consumers process advertising information on a subliminal level and that such processing may in fact interfere with communication of the intended advertising message.[24]

The controversy over subliminal advertising has extended to print as well as to TV advertising. Some writers have claimed that print ads use **subliminal embeds,** that is, tiny figures inserted into magazine ads by high-speed photography or by airbrushing.[25] As evidence, a Gilbey's Gin ad was cited in which the ice cubes spell out the letters SEX. However, a study by Rosen and Singh found little evidence that such embeds exert a subconscious influence on unaware consumers.[26]

Overall, the evidence suggests it would be extremely difficult at best to exert influence through subliminal stimuli. Variations among consumers in perceptual ability, the difficulty of implementing advertising themes at low threshold levels, and the lack of evidence of any effect of subliminal advertising on purchasing behavior have effectively eliminated subliminal advertising as a marketing tool.

Adaptation Level. **Adaptation level** is the level at which consumers no longer notice a frequently repeated stimulus. An individual walking into an air-conditioned room, a kitchen full of fragrances, or a noisy party will not notice these stimuli after a period of time. **Advertising wearout** is the consumers' adaptation to an advertising campaign over time due to boredom and familiarity. Consumers reduce their attention level to frequently repeated ads and eventually fail to notice them.

Consumers differ in their level of adaptation. Some tune out more quickly than others. Certain consumers have a tendency to be more aware of the facets of information and communication, even if they are repeated frequently. Because of the advertiser's desire to gain attention and maintain distinctiveness, the objectives of the typical advertising campaign are to decrease the adaptation level by introducing attention-getting features. Novelty, humor, contrast, and movement are all stimulus effects that may gain consumers' attention and reduce their adaptation. The most effective means of reducing the adaptation level, however, is to ensure that the message communicates the benefits consumers desire.

Stimulus Generalization

Consumers develop not only a capacity to discriminate between stimuli but also a capacity to generalize from one similar stimulus to another. The process of **stimulus generalization** occurs when two stimuli are seen as similar (contiguous); and the effects of one, therefore, can be substituted for the effects of the other.

Discrimination allows consumers to judge brands selectively and to evaluate one brand over another. Generalization allows consumers to simplify the process of evaluation because they do not have to make a separate judgment for each stimulus. Brand loyalty is a form of stimulus generalization. The consumer assumes that positive past experiences with the brand will be repeated. Therefore, a consumer does not need to make a separate judgment with each purchase. Perceptual categorization is also a form of stimulus generalization. As new products are introduced, consumers generalize from past experience to categorize them. When the automobile was first introduced at the turn of the century, it was called the horseless carriage. People generalized from their experience with the best-known mode of transportation, the horse and carriage, and put the automobile in the same general category.

Strategic Applications of Generalization.   It may appear that marketers seek to avoid consumers' generalization because they are attempting to distinguish their brands from those of the competition. However, in some cases, generalization may be a conscious and productive strategy. Heinz uses a strategy of generalization by advertising "57 varieties." The hope is that consumers will generalize the positive experience with one of the company's brands to other brands. General Electric also follows this policy of family branding. On the other hand, Procter & Gamble avoids a policy of generalization, preferring to position each brand in a unique way without reference to the company name. Whereas Heinz and General Electric employ stimulus generalization, Procter & Gamble employs stimulus discrimination.

A related form of stimulus generalization is **brand leveraging.** (See Strategic Applications box.) Companies often use a successful brand name on a product-line extension (Diet Coke and Ivory Liquid, for example) or on a different product category (Arm & Hammer detergents, Jell-O Pudding Pops).

Advertisers also use generalization in positioning brands to compete with the market leader. A brand may be introduced with the same basic benefits but at a lower price or in a larger package. The hope is that consumers will generalize the known benefits of the leading brand to the new entry and thus accept it. Some private (retailer-controlled) brands use a principle of generalization by making their package look as similar as possible to the leading brand in the category. One problem with these attempts at generalization is that they may be infringing on the trademark of the better-known brand. Companies zealously guard their package design and brand name, and they can sue imitators. For example, Toys "R" Us successfully sued a children's clothing chain called Kids "R" Us for trademark infringement and then introduced its own line of children's clothing under that name.

◆ PERCEPTUAL SELECTION

Having described the nature of stimuli and the factors that affect stimulus perception, we can now turn to describing the process of perception. The steps in the perceptual process, selection, organization, and interpretation, are shown in Figure 6.1.

The first component of perception, **selection,** requires consumers to be exposed to marketing stimuli and to attend these stimuli. Consumers will pick

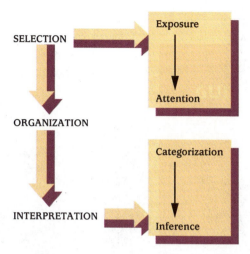

▶**FIGURE 6.1**
The perceptual process

and choose marketing stimuli based on their needs and attitudes. The car buyer will be more attentive to car ads; the fashion-conscious consumer will be more attentive to ads for clothing; the consumer who is loyal to Budweiser beer will be more attentive to Budweiser advertising. In each case, the consumer is processing stimuli selectively by picking and choosing them based on his or her psychological set. However, for such selective perception to occur, the consumer must first see or hear the stimulus and then respond to it. Therefore, three processes define selection, exposure, attention, and selective perception.

Exposure

Exposure occurs when consumers' senses (sight, hearing, touch, smell) are activated by a stimulus. Exposure to a stimulus either occurs or it does not. Consumers' interest in and involvement with the stimulus is reflected in the level of attention they devote to it.

Consumers will pick and choose the stimuli they are exposed to. A consumer in the market for a new car is more likely to look for car ads. The consumer shopping for a laptop computer is more likely to ask friends and business associates about their experiences with various brands.

Consumers are also likely to avoid exposure to stimuli that are unimportant and uninteresting. The advent of remote control devices for TV sets has permitted "zapping" of TV commercials by switching channels. Another manifestation of stimulus avoidance is known as the "flush factor." When the first Superbowl game was held between the Green Bay Packers and the Kansas City Chiefs in 1967, at halftime the water pressure in Kansas City reached a record low.

Attention

Attention is the momentary focusing of a consumer's cognitive capacity on a specific stimulus. When consumers notice a TV ad, a new product on a shelf, or a car in a showroom, attention has taken place.

STRATEGIC APPLICATIONS OF CONSUMER BEHAVIOR

Brand Leveraging: An Application of Stimulus Generalization

Brand leveraging is one of the most direct and popular applications of stimulus generalization in marketing. Companies have utilized the strategy with increasing frequency because of the growing expense of introducing new products and the fact that such introductions are 40 percent to 80 percent less expensive when a product is given an existing name. A study by Aaker and Keller found two perceptual requirements for brand leveraging to work. First, consumers must associate the brand with high quality. Second, there must be a perception of fit between the two products—that is, a logical transference from the old to the new product—for stimulus generalization to take place. A quality name and positive transference through stimulus generalization led Eastman Kodak to introduce a battery line. Research showed that a significant number of consumers thought the company already sold batteries, even before it introduced them.

There are two types of brand leveraging: a simple line extension (Diet Coke) and a transference of the name from one product category to another (Bic pens to Bic disposable lighters). Park, Milberg, and Lawson studied these types of brand leveraging and found that successful line extensions require *product feature similarity,* whereas successful category extensions require *concept consistency*. That is, Coca-Cola could leverage its flagship brand to Diet Coke because both brands had similar features to permit name transferability (for example, carbonation, colas, color, and so forth). Bic was able to leverage its name from pens to disposable lighters despite a lack of similarity in product features because there was concept consistency between the two categories—disposability.

When concept consistency is lacking, brand leveraging will fail because consumers will not be able to generalize from one product category to another. When Bic attempted to introduce perfumes it failed. Consumers could not generalize the Bic name to perfume because the category was not consistent with disposability.

Sources: C. Whan Park, Sandra Milberg, and Robert Lawson, "Evaluation of Brand Extensions: The Role of Product Feature Similarity and Brand Concept Consistency," *Journal of Consumer Research,* 18 (September, 1991), pp. 185–193; David A. Aaker and Kevin Lane Keller, "Consumer Evaluations of Brand Extensions," *Journal of Marketing,* 54 (January, 1990), pp. 27–41.

Advertisers can use many of the structural factors described previously to get consumers' attention—for example, size through larger ads, position by placing an ad in the upper half of a page, and novelty by using eye-catching photos or illustrations. These factors apply to in-store stimuli as well. For example, one study found that brands on the upper shelf in a supermarket received 35 percent more attention than those on the lower shelf and that increasing the number of packages for a particular brand on the shelf from two to four increased attention by 34 percent.[27] Sensory factors can also increase consumers' attention—for example, sound such as the use of a jingle or voice-overs of famous people in a commercial, or smell such as scratch and sniff print ads for perfume.

An important principle of attention is that the greater the consumers' adaptation level, the less likely it is that attention will take place. Many consumers have become so adapted to repetitive TV commercials that they "tune out"; that is, they are exposed to the commercial but do not notice it.

The opposite of adaptation is **contrast,** a change from the constant conditions consumers are used to. Advertisers try to achieve contrast by varying their campaigns, by using attention-getting stimuli, or by introducing new stimuli. This will reduce advertising wearout. Brand repositioning is an example of moving from adaptation to contrast by introducing new stimuli. When Philip Morris bought Miller Brewing Co., it changed the theme of its leading brand, Miller High Life, from "The champagne of bottled beers" to a "Miller Time" campaign targeted to the heavy beer drinking segment. The contrast between the elite beer drinking group in the older campaign and the male-oriented, blue-collar group pictured in the later ads was sharp and drew attention to the campaign. As time passes, consumers adapt to any campaign, and further attempts at introducing contrast to maintain consumer attention are required.

Selective Perception

Consumers perceive marketing stimuli selectively because each individual is unique in the combination of his or her needs, attitudes, experiences, and personal characteristics. **Selective perception** means that two consumers may perceive the identical advertisement, package, or product very differently. One consumer may believe a claim that Clorox gets clothes whiter than other bleaches; another may regard such a claim as untrue and may believe that all bleaches are the same.

Selective perception occurs at every stage in the perceptual process as illustrated in Figure 6.1. *Selective exposure* occurs because people's beliefs influence what they choose to listen to or read. *Selective organization* occurs because people organize information to be consistent with their beliefs. Also, *selective interpretation* occurs so that perceptions conform with prior beliefs and attitudes. For example, Arm & Hammer's claim that its baking soda toothpaste is healthier for teeth and gums was consistent with consumers' beliefs that toothpaste makes a difference, even though it usually does not. As a result, many consumers chose to believe the claim, despite statements from dentists that baking soda does not affect dental hygiene one way or the other.[28]

Such selective perception operates for both high and low involvement purchases. In the high involvement case, consumers selectively choose information that (1) helps them evaluate brands that meet their needs and (2) conforms to their beliefs and predispositions. In the low involvement case, consumers selectively screen out most information in an attempt to avoid cognitive activity and informational clutter.

There is ample evidence of selective perception of marketing stimuli. We noted the research by Allison and Uhl that found consumers perceived taste differences between brands of beer only when they were shown the brand label. These consumers' perceptions were based on brand name associations derived from advertising and social stimuli, associations that tended to conform to the consumers' current knowledge and past experiences.

Functions of Selective Perception

Selective perception ensures that consumers will receive information most relevant to their needs. This process is called **perceptual vigilance.** In a marketing study demonstrating the operation of perceptual vigilance, Spence and Engel found that consumers recognize names for preferred brands more quickly than they do names for other brands.[29] Individuals were more likely to perceive preferred stimuli.

In high involvement purchases, perceptual vigilance guides consumers to necessary information. Consumers are directed to information that is instrumental in attaining desired benefits. In low involvement purchases, perceptual vigilance acts by screening out information because consumers want to minimize information processing. It filters out unnecessary stimuli. It has been estimated that the average consumer is exposed to 300 to 600 advertisements in a normal day.[30] Therefore, the less involved consumer must be selective in screening out information.

Consumers sometimes perceive information to conform to their beliefs and attitudes. This second function of selective perception is called **perceptual defense** because it protects the individual from threatening or contradictory stimuli. For example, the cigarette smoker may avoid antismoking advertisements or play down their importance. Accepting the message may mean recognizing that the smoker's actions are detrimental to his or her health. The recent purchaser of a poorly insulated home may ignore unexpectedly high fuel bills or rationalize the situation by saying fuel costs are high for everyone.

Perceptual defense tends to operate when consumers are involved. Involved consumers have strong beliefs and attitudes about a brand. In terms of Sherif's social judgment theory, firmly held beliefs reflect a narrow latitude of acceptance.[31] Messages in agreement with the consumers' beliefs will be accepted and distorted in the direction of those beliefs (an assimilation effect). Messages that do not conform to the consumers' strongly held beliefs will be rejected or distorted to contrast with the consumers' opinions (a contrast effect).

Perceptual defense is more likely in anxiety producing situations because it leads consumers to avoid stimuli that produce fears and anxieties. For example, the heavy smoker avoids the anxiety of viewing an antismoking commercial. A current example of perceptual defense is the many misconceptions people have formed about AIDS. The ad in Exhibit 6.5 tries to break down these perceptual defenses by correcting misconceptions and educating individuals about the realities of AIDS.

▶**EXHIBIT 6.5**

An attempt to break down perceptual defense

Source: Courtesy of U.S. Department of Health and Human Services/Public Health Service/Centers for Disease Control and Prevention

You won't get AIDS from everyday contact.
You won't get AIDS from being a friend.
You won't get AIDS from a mosquito bite.
You won't get AIDS from a kiss.
You won't get AIDS by talking.
You won't get AIDS by listening.
You won't get AIDS from a public pool.
You won't get AIDS from a pimple.
You won't get AIDS from a toilet seat.
You won't get AIDS from a haircut.
You won't get AIDS by donating blood.
You won't get AIDS from an airplane.
You won't get AIDS from tears.
You won't get AIDS from food.
You won't get AIDS from a hug.
You won't get AIDS from a towel.
You won't get AIDS from a telephone.
You won't get AIDS from a crowded room.

You won't get AIDS from an elevator.
You won't get AIDS from a greasy spoon.
You won't get AIDS from a bump.
You won't get AIDS by laughing.
You won't get AIDS by watching a movie.
You won't get AIDS from a cat.
You won't get AIDS from a schoolyard.
You won't get AIDS from going to a party.
You won't get AIDS from taking a trip.
You won't get AIDS from a dog bite.
You won't get AIDS from visiting a city.
You won't get AIDS from a cab.
You won't get AIDS from a bus.
You won't get AIDS at a play.
You won't get AIDS by dancing.
You won't get AIDS because someone is different from you.
You won't get AIDS from a classroom.

Stop Worrying About How You Won't Get AIDS. And Worry About How You Can.

You *can* get AIDS from sexual intercourse with an infected partner.
You *can* get AIDS from sharing drug needles with an infected person.
You *can* get AIDS by being born to an infected mother.

AMERICA RESPONDS TO AIDS

1-800-342-AIDS
Deaf access:
1-800-AIDS-TTY
1-800-342-7889

U.S. DEPARTMENT OF HEALTH AND HUMAN SERVICES/PUBLIC HEALTH SERVICE/Centers For Disease Control

Perceptual Equilibrium

The underlying principle in the operation of selective perception is that consumers seek **perceptual equilibrium;** that is, consistency between the information they receive about a brand and their prior beliefs about that brand. Such consistency ensures that the consumers' psychological set is in equilibrium. Three cognitive theories are based on principles of selective perception and perceptual equilibrium.

- *Sherif's social judgment theory* (discussed in Chapter 5) states that consumers process information to ensure consistency by either rejecting contradictory information (contrast) or by interpreting acceptable information to fit more closely with their views (assimilation).[32]
- *Heider's balance theory* states that when information about an object conflicts with the consumers' beliefs, consumers will achieve balance by changing their opinion about the object, about the source of information, or both.[33] The result is a balance in beliefs about the information and the object. For example, if a close friend expresses the view that your favorite camera takes poor pictures, you can doubt the credibility of your friend as a source of information about cameras, form a more negative attitude toward your favorite camera, or do a little bit of both to obtain balance between information and object.
- *Cognitive dissonance theory* states that when postpurchase conflicts arise, consumers will seek balance in the psychological set by seeking supporting information or by distorting contradictory information.

Each of these theories results in consistency between consumers' perceptions of marketing stimuli and their beliefs and attitudes.

Perceptual Disequilibrium

Consumers not only accept information consistent with their beliefs, but they will also accept discrepant information about a selected product. If they did not, it would mean that every time a consumer was dissatisfied, he or she would make some attempt to rationalize the purchase and would never switch brands. Both learning and cognitive dissonance theories predict different outcomes from dissatisfaction.

- *Learning theory* says that when a brand does not meet expectations, consumers learn from the negative experience and adjust beliefs and attitudes accordingly. The result is a reduction in the probability of repurchase. For example, even though 80 percent of nonsmokers accept the link between smoking and cancer, over half of heavy smokers also accepted this link. These smokers must be in a state of perceptual disequilibrium. Many will accept this dissonant information and attempt to stop smoking to change their behavior to conform to the information.

- *Cognitive dissonance theory* says that when a brand does not meet expectations, consumers will discount the negative information—for example, heavy smokers discounting the link between cancer and smoking and rationalizing their smoking behavior.

Selective Perception and Marketing Strategy

Marketing messages can be clear-cut or ambiguous. If consumers engage in perceptual defense, then ambiguous messages are more likely to be effective because the marketer is giving consumers latitude to interpret the message to accord with their beliefs about the brand. If consumers engage in perceptual vigilance, then clear-cut messages are more likely to be effective because it is apparent whether the information is supportive of or contradictory to the consumers' beliefs.

Using Perceptual Defense.   Ambiguity should be used in advertising when the product is important to consumers but its benefits are not clear-cut. Since consumers are introducing beliefs that are consistent with their needs, the operating principle is perceptual defense. The ad for Ziari sunglasses in Exhibit 6.6 illustrates this well. The purpose is to link the sunglasses with the wearer's self-image by projecting almost any motive into the advertisement. The photo and

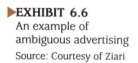

▶**EXHIBIT 6.6**
An example of
ambiguous advertising
Source: Courtesy of Ziari

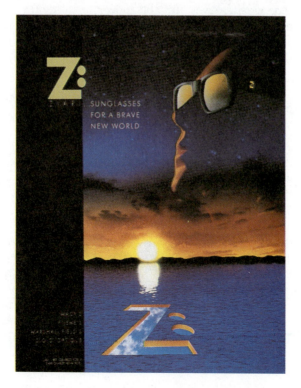

theme "Sunglasses for a Brave New World" and the imagery can mean many different things to different people. Consumers can selectively perceive what is desired with a minimum of informational content. Ambiguity, therefore, permits different consumers to perceive selectively a message in line with their needs and to project a desired self-image.

Generally, a moderate amount of ambiguity is optimal. If the message is too explicit, consumers have little room for projecting; and the marketer may be unnecessarily restricting the potential market. On the other hand, if the message is too ambiguous, consumers will have difficulty understanding it or relating to it. Some might question whether the Ziari ad is too ambiguous.

Using Perceptual Vigilance.   Marketers should be explicit in their advertising if the product's benefits are clear-cut and if the product is targeted to a well-defined segment. In such cases, the informational content of the advertisement dominates and ambiguity is held to a minimum. Industrial advertising tends to be less ambiguous because it is more heavily balanced toward informational content than toward symbolism. Since consumers are seeking information directed to their needs and avoiding unnecessary information, the operating principle is perceptual vigilance.

Performance-oriented autos use unambiguous ads with straightforward informational content. An ad for the Pontiac Grand Prix refers to a turbocharged V6 engine creating over 200 horsepower, a cross-ram intake, GT + 4 radial tires, and so on. There is little left to the imagination. The information is clear and readily perceived. It is also easily filtered out by those who are not interested in the intricacies of a car's performance.

◆ PERCEPTUAL ORGANIZATION

In being exposed to 300-600 commercials a day, the typical consumer apparently uses some form of perceptual organization of disparate, and at times conflicting, stimuli. **Perceptual organization** means that consumers group information from various sources into a meaningful whole to comprehend it better and to act on it.

The basic principle of organization is **integration,** which means that consumers perceive various stimuli as an organized whole. Such an organization simplifies information processing and provides an integrated meaning for the stimuli. These principles have been derived from **Gestalt psychology.** (Gestalt is roughly translated from German as total configuration or whole pattern.) Since they provide a framework for interpreting advertising messages as an integrated whole, principles of Gestalt psychology directly apply to marketing strategy. The advertising campaign, price level, distribution outlet, and brand characteristics are not disparate elements of the marketing plan. They are viewed in concert and produce an overall brand image. In short, the whole is greater than the sum of the parts.

The principles of perceptual integration are based on Gestalt psychologists' basic hypothesis that people organize perceptions to form a complete picture of an object. Perceptual integration is a process of forming many disparate stimuli into an organized whole. The picture on a television screen is a good example. In actuality, it is made up of thousands of tiny dots, but we integrate these dots into a cohesive whole so that there is little difference between the picture on the screen and the real world.

The most important principles of perceptual integration are those of closure, grouping, and context.

Closure

Closure refers to a perceiver's tendency to fill in the missing elements when a stimulus is incomplete. Consumers have a desire to form a complete picture and derive a certain amount of satisfaction in completing a message on their own. This principle operates when consumers develop their own conclusions from moderately ambiguous advertisements. A study by Heimbach and Jacoby showed that an incomplete ad may increase attention to and recall of the message.[34] They presented one group of consumers with a complete commercial and another group with a commercial cut at the end. The incomplete commercial generated 34 percent more recall than did the complete version.

The principle of closure is shown in the J&B ad in Exhibit 6.7. The desire to produce closure causes the viewer to visualize putting the earring the model is wearing in the left of the ad to complete Justerini & Brooks.

Grouping

Consumers are more likely to perceive a variety of information as chunks rather than as separate units. They integrate various bits and pieces of information into organized wholes. **Chunking** or **grouping information** permits consumers to evaluate one brand over another by using a variety of attributes. Principles of grouping that have emerged from Gestalt psychology are proximity, similarity, and continuity. These principles are represented in Figure 6.2.

The tendency to group stimuli by **proximity** means that one object will be associated with another because of its closeness to that object. Because of their vertical proximity, the twelve dots in Figure 6.2 are seen as three columns of four dots rather than four rows of three dots. Most advertising uses principles of proximity by associating the product with positive symbols and imagery that are close to the product. For example, an L.A. Gear ad positions sneakers in proximity to a guitar and a picture of James Dean. The attempt is to associate the product with rock music and with a symbol of antiestablishment culture.

Consumers also group products by **similarity.** The eight squares and four circles in Figure 6.2 are grouped in three sets because of their similarity—two sets of four squares and one set of four circles. The ad for Reynolds Plastic

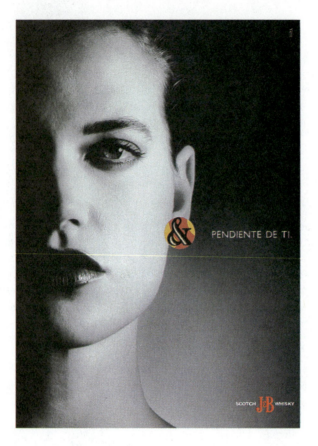

Wrap in Exhibit 6.8 demonstrates a principle of grouping by similarity. The tendency is to group the products together because of similarity in name, color, and design. The intention is to view the set of products as an integrated whole.

Consumers also group stimuli in uninterrupted forms, rather than into discontinuous contours, to attain **continuity.** The dots in the third part of Figure 6.2 are more likely to be seen as an arrow projecting to the right than as columns of dots. Applying continuity to a retail store means that there should be no sharp breaks from one sales station to the next by type of merchandise. The transition should be reasonably continuous.

Context

Consumers will tend to perceive an object by the **context** in which it is shown. The setting of an advertisement will influence the perception of a product. For example, consumers may perceive one advertisement quite differently in two different media. In a study by Fuchs, identical advertisements were placed in high-prestige magazines (*Harper's, New Yorker*) and in low-prestige magazines

▶**FIGURE 6.2**
Principles of
organization

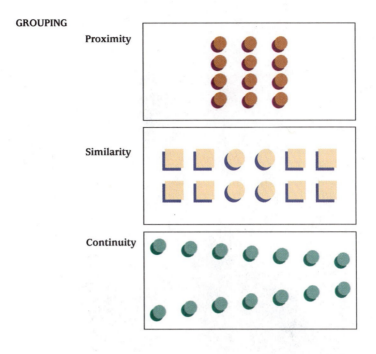

(*True, Detective*). Not surprisingly, consumers rated advertisements in the high-prestige magazines much higher than the identical ads in low-prestige magazines, showing that media context will directly influence the perception of the ad.[35]

The most important principle of context is **figure and ground.** Gestalt psychologists state that in organizing stimuli into wholes, individuals will distinguish stimuli that are prominent (the figure that is generally in the foreground) from stimuli that are less prominent (those in the ground or background). The lower part of Figure 6.2 illustrates the principle of figure and ground. The picture can be seen as a goblet (figure) with a dark background or as two profiles (figure) with a lighter background. Advertisers seek to ensure that the product is the figure and the setting is the background.

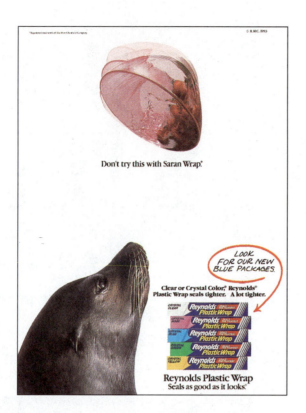

The determination of what part of the whole is the figure and what part is ground will greatly affect the way consumers perceive stimuli. Utilizing Snoopy cartoon figures, MetLife's advertising campaign used figure and ground. (See Exhibit 6.9.) The Snoopy campaign was successful in changing MetLife's image from a faceless and friendless company to a warmer and friendlier one. The campaign has not increased sales, however.[36] The campaign should convey the product, MetLife, as the figure and the Snoopy characters as the ground. However, the advertisement in Exhibit 6.9 raises the question of whether Snoopy is the figure and the company is the background. If so, the campaign may be placing too much attention on Snoopy at the company's expense.

◆ PERCEPTUAL INTERPRETATION

Once consumers select and organize stimuli, they interpret them. Two basic principles help consumers interpret marketing information. The first principle involves a tendency to place information into logical categories. **Categorization** helps consumers process known information quickly and efficiently. ("This is another ad for Bounty. I know what they are going to say, so I don't have to

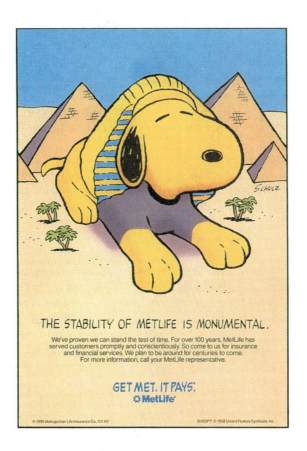

pay much attention.") Categorization also helps consumers classify new information. ("This is an ad for a new breakfast food that is probably like Carnation
Slender.")

Inference involves the development of an association between two stimuli.
For example, consumers might associate a high price with quality or blue suds
in a detergent with cleansing power.

Perceptual Categorization

Marketers seek to facilitate the process of perceptual categorization. They want
to make sure consumers recognize a brand as part of a product class, but do not
want their brand to be a direct duplicate of other brands. Product positioning
attempts to establish both product categorization and product uniqueness.

Monsanto's Starch-Eze is an example of a new product that failed because
it was not correctly categorized. A starch concentrate, Starch-Eze had to be
diluted and was meant to be used only every 10 or 12 washings.[37] The product
was advertised as a starch, and the name implied it was easy to use. Consumers

categorized it as another brand of starch and used it in every wash cycle. The result was a cardboard shirt. According to Day, "Once a new object is placed in an existing category, it becomes the focus of the existing repertory of behaviors which are appropriate to the overall category."[38] The problem was not with Starch-Eze itself but how consumers placed the product in the traditional category of starch. The existing repertory of behaviors required using the product frequently, which resulted in the product's failure.

Category Levels

When consumers first learn about a product, they classify it at the most basic level. As they process more information, they then develop a capacity to use refined classifications.[39] For example, when computers were first introduced in the 1950s, they were one category. By the 1970s, consumers could distinguish between mainframes, microcomputers, and then later, personal computers (PCs). (See Figure 6.3.) By the 1980s, PCs could be categorized into desktops, portables, and laptops. Then, by the 1990s, as laptops became more widespread, they could be further categorized as notebooks or pen computers.

The more involved the consumer, the greater the likelihood that he or she will classify stimuli at more refined levels. Thus, the typical consumer might say, "I rode to work in my neighbor's car," whereas the car buff might say, "I rode to work in my neighbor's new Chevy Blazer." Categorization based on usage will also vary across cultures. Chinese consumers are likely to have many

▶**FIGURE 6.3**
Category levels for computers

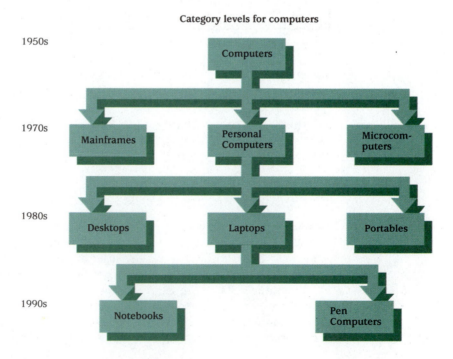

Category levels for computers

1950s		Computers
1970s	Mainframes	Personal Computers	Microcomputers
1980s	Desktops	Laptops	Portables
1990s	Notebooks		Pen Computers

more categories for bicycles, but they may view computers as one category. Conversely, most American consumers view bicycles as one category but recognize several categories for computers.

Process of Categorization

The process of establishing subcategories within a broader product category can be better understood by introducing two concepts—schema and subtyping.

Schema.   When consumers first gather information about a new product like computers, they store bits and pieces of information about the category in their memory.[40] As they gain more knowledge of the category, they recall information in clusters of thoughts, ideas, and symbols known as a **schema**.[41] The consumers' original schema for computers in the 1950s might have equated them to desk calculators and more generally to business machines. By the 1960s, their schema for computers was more detailed, probably involving ideas and objects such as "punch cards," "mainframes," and "automatic processing."

Subtyping.   As the computer industry developed new technologies and consumers gained more information, a process of subtyping began. **Subtyping** involves developing a subcategory of a broader category. By the 1970s, consumers could distinguish between mainframes and microcomputers based on characteristics such as size, speed, interfaces, terminals, and so forth. The schema (that is, words, ideas, and symbols) associated with microcomputers became the definition of a subcategory of computers in consumers' minds. By the 1980s, personal computers became the dominant subtype based on a schema that included hard disks, floppies, memory, portability, and other features.

When marketers offer unique benefits in a new product they encourage consumers to subtype.[42] If successful, marketers have established a dominant position in a new subcategory. When PepsiCo introduced Slice, it was successful in establishing a new schema in consumer minds—fruit-based soft drinks. It did so with the campaign theme "We've Got the Juice" and with the name Slice. The entry of Coca-Cola and P&G with juice-enriched products firmly established the subcategory.

Research on Categorization

Several studies have considered the role of schema and subtyping in the process of categorization. Stayman, Alden, and Smith found that schema tend to be more important for consumers who are not highly knowledgeable about product categories.[43] A typical consumer buying a computer might first determine the category of computer to be purchased and then think of the schema associated with the category (memory, speed, disk capacity) to determine the criteria by which to evaluate brands. Computer buffs tend to think more in terms of what they want from computers across categories.

Another study by Meyers-Levy and Tybout also sheds some light on the process of subtyping.[44] They found that consumers subtype products that are moderately different from existing products. Slice had common attributes with the soft drink schema, but the fruit-based feature warranted developing a sub-category within the broader category of soft drinks. If PepsiCo were to introduce a calcium-based breakfast drink, it is likely consumers would establish a totally new schema to incorporate this product.

Perceptual Inference

Consumers develop inferences about brands, prices, stores, and companies.[45] These inferences are beliefs consumers form about objects from past associations. Consumers may associate a Rolex watch with quality. This inference is based on word-of-mouth communications from friends and on advertising for the watch.

Semiotics

The inferences consumers draw are largely based on the signs and symbols they associate with an object. To some, the Mercedes symbol connotes quality and status; the Arm & Hammer trademark, freshness; the Pillsbury Doughboy reliability and home-baked; the Polo logo, casual elegance. The fact that some may view the Mercedes emblem as representing ostentation or the Polo logo as passé means that marketers must study the association consumers make between objects and the signs and symbols attached to them. A field of study called **semiotics** has been established to study the interrelationship among these three components—namely the object (brand), the signs and symbols associated with the object, and the consumer who does the associating.[46]

An example of the application of semiotics is a study of the association consumers make with corporate logos.[47] The study found little association between the level of advertising and the strength of the logo's association with the company, suggesting that consumer perceptions vary widely, depending on how they interpret these signs and symbols. For example, the heavily advertised Centurion American Express used was not strongly associated with the company. However, the much less advertised Michelin Man had a stronger and more positive association with the company.

Symbols like the Michelin Man or the Pillsbury Doughboy are clearly related to the products the company produces, thus facilitating inferences of quality and reliability. However, since the Centurion is not a clear symbol of anything that American Express does, making positive inferences is difficult.

Marketing Implications of Perceptual Inference

Consumers tend to form images of brands, stores, and companies based on the inferences they draw from marketing and environmental stimuli. An **image** is a total perception of the object that consumers form by processing information from various sources over time. Gestalt psychology suggests that forming an image is a natural process of developing a total perception of the object. An important objective of marketing strategy is to influence the perception of a brand, store, or company. Thus, marketers are constantly trying to influence consumers' images.

Brand Image.   Brand images represent the overall perception of the brand and are formed based on the inferences consumers make and the schema consumers associate with the brand. The importance of brand image is also reflected in the record $25 billion purchase price for RJR Nabisco. This figure was based primarily on the value of the company's brand names rather than on its physical facilities.

The key ingredient in influencing consumers' brand image is **product positioning.** Marketers try to position their brands to meet the needs of defined customer segments. They do so by developing a product concept that can communicate the desired benefits through advertising and by utilizing media that will reach the target segment. When Schweppes first came on the market in the United States, it could have been positioned as a soft drink or as a mixer. Positioning it as a mixer guided the promotional direction. The use of Commander Whitehead as the dapper Englishman referring to "Schweppervescence" produced an image of prestige for a product category that consumers might have otherwise regarded as commonplace. This positioning also required the selection of media for an older, more conservative, and more upscale (higher socioeconomic) group than the group that Schweppes would have targeted to position the product as a soft drink.

Store Image.   Consumers develop store images based on advertising, merchandise in the store, opinions of friends and relatives, and shopping experiences. Store image often influences brand image. Consumers will perceive the identical product quite differently in Woolco or Kmart than in Nieman-Marcus or Bloomingdale's. In one study, four identical samples of carpet were given to consumers to evaluate.[48] Each sample was labeled with a more or less prestigious store. Even when prices were identical, consumers rated the same samples higher in a prestigious store than those in a less prestigious one. A positive store image thus produced a positive brand image, even though product and price were identical.

Retailers have a particular stake in establishing a positive store image, as their image is directly tied to sales results. J. C. Penney has upgraded its image by repositioning its line to higher-quality merchandise.[49] It deleted appliances, garden supplies, and automotive products and put more emphasis on designer clothing.

Corporate Image.   Consumers also organize the variety of information about companies and experiences with a company's products into corporate images. Companies spend millions of dollars to improve their images with the public for several reasons. First, a positive corporate image will reinforce positive perceptions of the company's products. Such a link between corporate and

brand image is particularly important when the brand name is closely associated with the company. General Electric will advertise itself as innovative and
forward-looking in the hope that consumers will carry over the association to
its brands. Such advertising is not as important for Procter & Gamble because
that company does not link its brands closely to the corporate name.

Companies also seek to maintain a favorable image regarding public issues
that may directly affect consumers. For example, the Toyota ad in Exhibit 6.10
cites the company's $5 billion investment in the American economy through
manufacturing facilities in Kentucky and California and the creation of 16,000
U.S. jobs. The purpose is to show that Toyota's presence in America is having
a positive effect.[50]

◆ PRICE PERCEPTIONS

One of the most important applications of consumer perceptions to marketing
strategy is in the area of price. Consumers' price perceptions directly influence
their perceptions of brand quality and frequently determine their purchasing
behavior.

▶EXHIBIT 6.10
An attempt to influence
corporate image
Source: Courtesy of Toyota

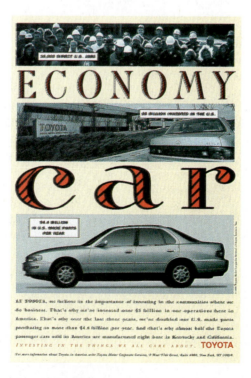

Companies must establish pricing strategies based on consumer price perceptions. In the early 1980s, Parker Pen repositioned its pens based on price. It decided to move away from its line of expensive, hand-finished pens to low-priced pens because of the explosive growth of cheap ballpoints. The results were disastrous because the company's image was not consistent with its price. In 1989, it moved back to its strength, high-priced fountain pens, with an ad campaign featuring style and luxury. The shift made the company profitable once again.[51]

Consumers' price perceptions may appear to be a simple matter of determining a product's price based on an ad or on observation in a store. However, it is not that simple because (1) consumers have certain expectations about what prices are or should be, (2) these expectations may or may not reflect the actual price, and (3) consumers frequently associate price level with the product's quality. We will consider each of these components of consumer price perceptions.

Price Expectations

When deciding whether to replace an old nineteen-inch color TV set, a consumer may expect to pay about $400 for a comparable set. This price is the consumer's **reference price** (also known as a **standard price**); that is, the price the consumer expects to pay for a certain item. The reference price serves as a standard or frame of reference by which consumers compare prices for alternative brands.[52]

Consumers do not have just one price point when they consider buying a product. Generally, they are willing to accept a range of prices, known as an **acceptable price range,** for a particular product. The reference price and the acceptable price range for the consumer buying a TV set are shown at the top of Figure 6.4. The acceptable price range is from $250 on the lower end (a set priced below $250 might arouse suspicions about its quality) to $500 on the higher end. The higher end of the acceptable price range is known as the **reservation price** and is the "upper limit above which an article would be judged too expensive." The lower end of the acceptable price range is the "lower limit below which the quality of the item would be suspect."[53]

The acceptable price range is likely to vary widely, depending on consumer characteristics and attitudes toward a brand. For example, Rao and Sieben found that when consumers were not knowledgeable about a product, they put a lower limit on the acceptable price range.[54] These consumers had lower price expectations because they had little basis for making quality judgments.

One other measure of price expectations is shown in Figure 6.4. The **expected price range** is the range of prices the consumer expects to find in the marketplace.[55] This range is almost always wider than the acceptable price range. In our example, the consumer expects to find nineteen-inch color TV sets priced as high as $600 and as low as $200, but anything above or below the acceptable price range is unlikely to influence the consumer's behavior.

▶**FIGURE 6.4**
Measures of consumers'
price expectations

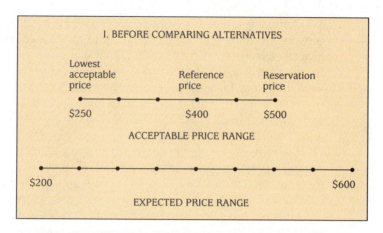

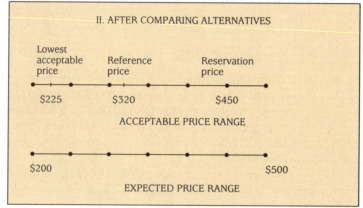

Actual Versus Reference Prices

An important consideration for marketers is the relationship between consumers' reference prices and the actual prices they encounter in the marketplace. Consumers' reference prices are rarely exactly the same as the actual
prices of items. How do consumers react to a difference between their reference price and the actual price?

Researchers have used assimilation-contrast theory (see Chapter 5) to
explain consumer reactions. If the difference between actual and reference price
is within the consumer's acceptable price range, an assimilation effect occurs.
Suppose our consumer evaluates three TV brands and finds that nineteen-inch
sets are priced at $299, $320, and $350. These are within the consumer's
acceptable range. Our consumer is likely to shift her reference price from $400
down toward the actual price of one of these brands (say $320) as a result of
comparing alternatives. Furthermore, both the acceptable price range and the

expected price range are likely to be lower, as shown at the bottom of Figure 6.4.

Urbany, Bearden, and Weilbaker confirmed such a shift. They found that a difference between reference and actual prices resulted in a move by reference prices closer to actual prices as long as the actual prices were acceptable. What happens when actual prices are not acceptable? For example, our consumer encounters brands at prices of $550 and $600 as well as at prices of $299, $320, and $350. In such a case, a contrast effect is likely to occur. That is, our consumer is likely to reject those brands priced higher than $500.[56]

Price-Quality Relationship

An important question for marketers is whether consumers perceive a price-quality association. Generally, when consumers do not have sufficient information about product quality, they use price as an indication of quality. Since these consumers know little about the product, they are less likely to be involved. Conversely, consumers with information about product characteristics are less likely to make price-quality inferences. These consumers are more likely to be involved with the product category.[57]

Various studies have supported this view. Rao and Monroe found that price-quality associations are strongest for consumers who have less product information.[58] Similarly, Monroe found that when respondents had experience with a brand, that experience overcame price as the dominant factor in brand choice.[59]

Price is more likely to be a reflection of quality if consumers have confidence in the source of the price information. Gotlieb and Sarel found that when consumers felt the source of price information was trustworthy and credible (for example, an electrical engineer evaluating a VCR), they were more likely to associate a higher price with quality.[60]

Price is also more likely to be a surrogate for quality when consumers believe that quality and price differences exist between product alternatives. Such variations allow for price-quality inferences. Consumers are unlikely to attribute higher quality to products that are standardized or that differ by only a few cents. A price range permits quality inferences. In support of these views, Obermiller found that price-quality associations are more likely for product lines than they are for single brands because product lines are more likely to have a wide range in prices.[61] Similarly, Zeithaml found that when products are standardized (salt or gasoline), consumers view prices as reflecting cost rather than quality.[62]

On this basis, if the consumer shopping for the nineteen-inch color TV set believes there are significant price and quality differences among brands and has little knowledge about TV sets, she will tend to use high price as an indicator of quality.

SUMMARY

A product's success depends largely on the way consumers perceive and process marketing stimuli designed to promote it. In this chapter, we considered the nature of marketing stimuli and how consumers perceive them.

Marketing stimuli were classified into the primary stimulus (the product) and the secondary stimuli (symbols, imagery, and information representing the product). A key question is the degree to which consumers can discriminate between marketing stimuli. Marketers attempt to create such discrimination by informing consumers about the differences between their brands and competitors' brands. Consumers also generalize from one similar stimulus to another. By using existing brand names for new products, marketers use strategies of stimulus generalization through brand leveraging. Positive associations with the existing brand helps launch the new product. The chapter also recognized that consumers differ in their ability to perceive marketing stimuli.

Selection, organization, and interpretation are the three basic processes underlying consumer perceptions. Selection involves being attentive to stimuli and selectively perceiving them. Selective perception serves two purposes: (1) It guides consumers in selecting information that is relevant and in screening out information that is not relevant to their needs. This process is known as perceptual vigilance. (2) It permits consumers to select information that conforms to their beliefs and predispositions about brands, products, and companies. This function is known as perceptual defense.

The organization of marketing stimuli depends on the principle of integration. Integration permits consumers to perceive many different stimuli and to organize them into a cohesive whole. Consumers are able to integrate information by processes of closure, grouping, similarity, continuity, and context.

Interpretation of stimuli also depends on two processes: categorization and inference. Categorization simplifies information processing by permitting consumers to classify brands into product categories. Inference is a belief about objects that consumers develop from past associations.

Consumers form total perceptions or images of brands, stores, and companies based on inferences. Marketers try to influence brand image by communicating desired product benefits through positioning strategies. The store image will also influence the brand image, particularly for brands that are distributed in selective stores. The corporate image affects consumers' purchasing behavior, particularly for brands that are tied to the company name.

Consumer perceptions of prices are particularly important to marketers because they often influence perceptions of quality. Consumers also form expectations regarding price levels that influence their behavior.

The next chapter focuses on how consumers process the information they perceive.

QUESTIONS

1. Can you cite applications of the differential threshold to changes in (a) package size and (b) advertising duration and intensity?

2. Some studies have shown that sensory perceptions (taste, smell, and so on) play a minimal role in the selection of major national brands in such categories as tea, coffee, cigarettes, and perfumes. How does Coca-Cola's experience when it had to reintroduce old Coke relate to this finding?

3. What are the implications of the concept of stimulus discrimination for the changes in the packaging of Ivory Soap in the 100-plus years it has been in existence?

4. What are the implications of the concept of stimulus generalization for (a) using the GE name on refrigerators, (b) Colgate introducing cold tablets and antacids under its name, and (c) Bic introducing perfumes?

5. What is the distinction between perceptual vigilance and perceptual defense? Which is most likely to operate when (a) a consumer buys the same brand of frozen orange juice because of inertia and (b) a consumer buys the same perfume because of brand loyalty?

6. What are the implications of principles of proximity and similarity for (a) product-line policies and (b) in-store product organization?

7. What are some of the implications of principles of context for (a) media selection, (b) advertising layout, and (c) positioning of brands to specific usage situations?

8. Do consumers have a schema for brands such as the Macintosh computer as well as categories such as PCs? What is the purpose of a brand-related schema? What might be some logical components of a Macintosh schema?

9. Cite a product category and trace the subtyping that has occurred over time for the category. Why does such subtyping take place?

10. Why are certain companies that do not sell directly to the final consumer concerned with the corporate image they project to the consuming public?

11. Apply the concept of reference price and acceptable price range to explain a rationale for the decrease in the price of Macintosh computers in 1993.

12. How are consumers' price perceptions likely to change if there is a difference between their reference price and the actual price for a product? How can assimilation-contrast theory explain the consumer reactions to such a difference?

13. Under what conditions is price likely to be used as an indicator of quality? Are consumers more likely to establish a price-quality association for certain products? If so, what products?

RESEARCH ASSIGNMENTS

1. Pick two closely competing brands in two product categories: a high involvement category (such as cars) and a low involvement category (such as toothpaste). Identify a number of consumers who own or regularly use each brand. Ask consumers to rate the two competing brands (their own and the

close competitor) on a number of need criteria (for cars it might be economy, durability, and style). If consumers perceive brands selectively, they are likely to rate their own brand much higher than they do the competitive brand. This selective perception is more likely for the high involvement than it is for the low involvement category.

- Do your findings show this to be true? That is, (a) are brand ratings for the consumer's own brand much higher than those of the competitive brand, and (b) are the differences in ratings between the regular and competitive brands greater for the high involvement product category?
- Do consumers rate their own brand much higher on certain attributes but not on others?
- Do these differences reflect a process of selective perception?

2. Test the consumers' ability to discriminate between the taste of alternative brands in one of the following product categories: soft drinks, coffee, or tea. Run the following experiment: Identify three leading brands in the category. (Make sure the brands tested are in the same class for the product; for example, colas or noncolas for soft drinks, regular or instant for coffee.) Select an equal number of respondents who pick one of the three brands as their regular brand. Ask all respondents how often they purchase their regular brand. Then have each respondent taste the three unidentified brands. (Make sure to rotate the order of tasting so the same brand is not always presented first.) Ask the respondent to identify his or her preferred brand. On the basis of chance, one would expect one-third correct identification.

- Was the proportion of correct identification significantly more than chance?
- Were those who correctly identified their preferred brand different from those who did not? Were they more frequent users of the category? Did they use a certain brand?

3. Select two advertising campaigns that are informationally oriented and two that rely on symbolism and imagery and can be regarded as more ambiguous. Select a sample of consumers and measure (a) unaided advertising awareness for the four brands and (b) awareness of key points in the advertising message.

- Was awareness of the informationally oriented campaign more accurate than that of the more ambiguous campaign?
- Were consumers more likely to project themes and messages not actually in the ads into the more ambiguous communications? If so, what was the nature of these projections?
- Did you detect any misperception or misinterpretation of the advertising messages? Did these misperceptions reflect perceptual defense?

4. Select a frequently purchased consumer good (such as toothpaste, detergents, or analgesics). Select a sample of 50 consumers who buy the product. Determine each consumer's acceptable price range by identifying a standard size and by asking consumers the price below which they would not

trust the product's quality and the price above which they would not buy. In addition:

a. Ask consumers to identify their regular brand. Then ask them to assume there is a price increase in their regular brand. At what price increase would they switch to a competitive brand?

b. Determine the strength of the consumer's preference for the regular brand by asking if it is the best brand on the market, one of the best brands, or the same as other brands.

c. One would expect that the higher the price required for the consumer to switch to another brand, the greater the degree of brand loyalty. Was this confirmed in your study?

NOTES

1. "Transparent Brands Are Clearly Trendy," *The Wall Street Journal* (May 21, 1992), p. B1.
2. "Behind the 'Clear' Trend," *The New York Times* (June 6, 1993), p. F11.
3. "Pepsi's Future Could Be Less Crystal Clear," *The Wall Street Journal* (April 30, 1993), pp. B1, B10.
4. "Crystal Pepsi, A Clear, Colorless Cola Is Being Launched in 3 Test Markets," *The Wall Street Journal* (April 13, 1992), p. B7; and "Coke Hopes to Revive Tab as a Clear Cola," *The Wall Street Journal* (December 15, 1992), pp. B1, B8.
5. "Design Research: Beauty or Beast," *Advertising Age* (March 9, 1981), p. 43.
6. "Mary Kay Puts On a New Face," *Adweek's Marketing Week* (July 3, 1989), p. 4.
7. "P&G Discovers a New Look to an Old Product," *The New York Times* (January 28, 1993), p. D20.
8. Laurence Jacobs, Charles Keown, Reginald Worthley, and Kyung-Il Ghymn, "Cross-Cultural Colour Comparisons: Global Marketers Beware!" *International Marketing Review*, 8 (1991), pp. 21–30.
9. R. I. Allison and K. P. Uhl, "Influence of Beer Brand Identification on Taste Perception," *Journal of Marketing Research*, 1 (August, 1964), pp. 36–39.
10. William Copulsky and Katherine Marton, "Sensory Cues," *Product Marketing* (January, 1977), pp. 31–34.
11. "Finding New Ways to Make Smell Sell," *The New York Times* (July 23, 1988).
12. Gerald J. Gorn, "The Effects of Music in Advertising on Choice Behavior: A Classical Conditioning Approach," *Journal of Marketing*, 46 (Winter, 1982), pp. 94–101.
13. R. Barton, *Advertising Media* (New York: McGraw-Hill, 1964), p. 109.
14. "Position in Newspaper Advertising: 2," *Media Scope* (March, 1963), pp. 76–82.
15. Lucy A. McCauley, "The Face of Advertising," *Harvard Business Review* (November-December, 1989), pp. 155–159.
16. John Revett, "FTC Threatens Big Fines for Undersized Cigarette Warnings," *Advertising Age* (March 17, 1975), p. 1.
17. For additional references on subliminal advertising, see Timothy E. Moore, "The Case Against Subliminal Manipulation," *Psychology and Marketing*, 5 (1988), pp. 297–316; Anthony Pratkanis and Anthony Greenwald, "Recent Perspectives on Unconscious Processing: Still No Marketing Applications," *Psychology and Marketing*, 5 (1988), pp. 337–354; Philip M. Marikle and Jim Chessman, "Current Status of Research on Subliminal Perception," in Melanie Wallendorf and Paul Anderson, eds., *Advances in Consumer Research*, Vol. 14 (Provo, UT: Association for Consumer Research, 1987), pp. 298–302.
18. See H. Brean, "What Hidden Sell Is All About," *Life* (March 31, 1958), pp. 104–114.
19. *New Yorker* (September 21, 1957), p. 33.
20. Timothy E. Moore, "Subliminal Advertising: What You See Is What You Get," *Journal of Marketing*, 46 (Spring, 1982), pp. 38–47.

21. M. L. DeFleur and R. M. Petranoff, "A Television Test of Subliminal Persuasion," *Public Opinion Quarterly* (Summer, 1959), pp. 170–180.

22. "Subliminal Ad Okay If It Sells: FCC Peers into Subliminal Picture on TV," *Advertising Age* (1957).

23. Moore, "The Case Against Subliminal Manipulation," *loc. cit.*; and Joel Saegert, "Why Marketing Should Quit Giving Subliminal Advertising the Benefit of the Doubt," *Psychology and Marketing,* 4 (Summer, 1987), pp. 107–120.

24. Chris Janiszewski, "Preconscious Processing Effects: The Independence of Attitude Formation and Conscious Thought," *Journal of Consumer Research,* 15 (September, 1988), pp. 199–209.

25. Wilson Bryan Key, *Media Sexploitation* (Englewood Cliffs, NJ: Prentice-Hall, 1976).

26. Dennis L. Rosen and Surendra N. Singh, "An Investigation of Subliminal Embed Effect on Multiple Measures of Advertising Effectiveness," *Psychology & Marketing,* 9 (March/April, 1992), pp. 157–172.

27. "Packaging Research Probes Stopping Power, Label Reading, and Consumer Attitudes Among the Targeted Audience," *Marketing News* (July 22, 1983), p. 8.

28. "Tooth-Brushers Take a Shine to Baking Soda," *The Wall Street Journal* (March 2, 1992), pp. B1, B6.

29. Homer E. Spence and James F. Engel, "The Impact of Brand Preference on the Perception of Brand Names: A Laboratory Analysis," in David T. Kollat, Roger D. Blackwell, and James F. Engel, eds., *Research in Consumer Behavior* (New York: Holt, Rinehart & Winston, 1970), pp. 61–70.

30. Stuart Henderson Britt, Stephen C. Adams, and Alan S. Miller, "How Many Advertising Exposures Per Day?" *Journal of Advertising Research,* 12 (December, 1972), pp. 3–10.

31. M. Sherif and C. E. Hovland, *Social Judgment* (New Haven, CT: Yale University Press, 1964).

32. *Ibid.*

33. Fritz Heider, *The Psychology of Interpersonal Relations* (New York: John Wiley, 1958).

34. James T. Heimbach and Jacob Jacoby, "The Zerganik Effect in Advertising," in M. Venkatesan, ed., *Proceedings, 3rd Annual Conference* (Association for Consumer Research, 1972), pp. 746–758.

35. Douglas A. Fuchs, "Two Source Effects in Magazine Advertising," *Journal of Marketing Research,* 1 (August, 1964), pp. 59–62.

36. "What Have Snoopy and Gang Done for Met Life Lately?" *Adweek's Marketing Week* (November 13, 1989), pp. 2–3.

37. Kenneth E. Runyon, *Consumer Behavior and the Practice of Marketing* (Columbus, OH: Charles E. Merrill, 1977), pp. 302–303.

38. George S. Day, "Theories of Attitude Structure and Change," in Scott Ward and Thomas S. Robertson, eds., *Consumer Behavior: Theoretical Sources* (Englewood Cliffs, NJ: Prentice-Hall, 1973), p. 341.

39. Joseph W. Alba and J. Wesley Hutchinson, "Dimensions of Consumer Expertise," *Journal of Consumer Research,* 13 (March, 1987), pp. 411–454. For additional references on categorization, see Mita Sujan and Christine Dekleva, "Product Categorization and Inference Making: Some Implications for Comparative Advertising," *Journal of Consumer Research,* 14 (December, 1987), pp. 372–378; Joel B. Cohen and Kunal Basu, "Alternative Models of Categorization: Toward a Contingent Processing Framework," *Journal of Consumer Research,* 13 (March, 1987), pp. 455–472; Craig Thompson, "The Role of Context in Consumers' Category Judgments," in Thomas K. Srull, ed., *Advances in Consumer Research,* Vol. 16 (Provo, UT: Association for Consumer Research, 1989), pp. 542–547; and Eloise Coupey and Kent Nakamoto, "Learning Context and the Development of Product Category Perceptions," in Michael J. Houston, ed., *Advances in Consumer Research,* Vol. 15 (Provo, UT: Association for Consumer Research, 1987), pp. 77–82.

40. Bobby J. Calder and Paul H. Schurr, "Attitudinal Processes in Organizations," *Research in Organizational Behavior,* 3 (1981), pp. 283–302.

41. For additional references on schema, see Lawrence W. Barsalou and J. Wesley Hutchinson, "Schema Based Planning of Events in Consumer Contexts," in Wallendorf and Anderson, *Advances in Consumer Research,* Vol. 14, *op. cit.,* pp. 114–118; and Meera Venkatraman and Angelina Villarreal, "Schematic Processing of Information: An Exploratory Investigation," in Thomas C. Kinnear, ed., *Advances in Consumer Research,* Vol. 11 (Provo, UT: Association for Consumer Research, 1984), pp. 355–360.

42. Mita Sujan and James R. Bettman, "The Effect of Brand Positioning Strategies on Consumers' Brand and Category Perceptions: Some Insights from Schema Research," *Journal of Marketing Research,* 26 (November, 1989), pp. 454–467.

43. Douglas M. Stayman, Dana L. Alden, and Karen H. Smith, "Some Effects of Schematic Processing on Consumer Expectations and Disconfirmation Judgments," *Journal of Consumer Research,* 19 (September, 1992), pp. 240–255.

44. Joan Meyers-Levy and Alice M. Tybout, "Schema Congruity as a Basis for Product Evaluation," *Journal of Consumer Research,* 16 (June, 1989), pp. 39–54.

45. For additional references on perceptual inference, see Jeen-Su Lim, Richard W. Olshavsky, and John Kim, "The Impact of Inferences on Product Evaluations," *Journal of Marketing Research,* 25 (August, 1988), pp. 308–316; Valerie S. Folkes, Susan Koletsky, and John L. Graham, "A Field Study of Causal Inferences and Consumer Reaction," *Journal of Consumer Research,* 13 (March, 1987), pp. 534–539; Frank R. Kardes, "Spontaneous Inference Processes in Advertising," *Journal of Consumer Research,* 15 (September, 1988), pp. 225–233; and Gary T. Ford and Ruth Ann Smith, "Inferential Beliefs in Consumer Evaluation," *Journal of Consumer Research,* 14 (December, 1987), pp. 363–371.

46. David Mick, "Consumer Research and Semiotics: Exploring the Morphology of Signs, Symbols, and Significance," *Journal of Consumer Research,* 13 (September, 1986), pp. 196–213.

47. "Firm's Eye-Catching Logos Often Leave Fuzzy Images in Minds of Consumers," *The Wall Street Journal* (December 5, 1991), pp. B1, B8.

48. Ben M. Enis and James E. Stafford, "Consumers' Perception of Product Quality as a Function of Various Informational Inputs," in Phillip R. McDonald, ed., *Marketing Involvement in Society and the Economy* (Proceedings of the American Marketing Association, Series No. 30, 1969), pp. 340–344.

49. "Penney Moves Upscale in Merchandise But Still Has to Convince Public," *The Wall Street Journal* (June 7, 1990), pp. A1, A8.

50. "A Corporate Campaign Tries Selling Toyota's U.S. Presence," *The New York Times* (July 21, 1993), p. D24.

51. "Penmanship with a Flourish," *Forbes* (April 3, 1989), p. 152.

52. See Robert Jacobson and Carl Obermiller, "The Formation of Expected Future Price: A Reference Price for Forward-Looking Consumers," *Journal of Consumer Research,* 16 (March, 1990), p. 420; and James E. Hegelson and Sharon E. Beatty, "Price Expectation and Price Recall Error: An Empirical Study," *Journal of Consumer Research,* 14 (December, 1987), p. 379.

53. Andre Gabor and C. W. J. Granger, "Price as an Indicator of Quality: Report on an Enquiry," *Economica,* 46 (February, 1966), pp. 43–70.

54. Akshay R. Rao and Wanda A. Sieben, "The Effect of Prior Knowledge on Price Acceptability and the Type of Information Examined," *Journal of Consumer Research,* 19 (September, 1992), pp. 256–270.

55. See Joel E. Urbany, William O. Bearden, and Dan C. Weilbaker, "The Effect of Plausible and Exaggerated Reference Prices on Consumer Perceptions and Price Search," *Journal of Consumer Research,* 15 (June, 1988), pp. 95–110.

56. *Ibid.*

57. Donald R. Lichtenstein, Peter H. Bloch, and William C. Black, "Correlates of Price Acceptability," *Journal of Consumer Research,* 15 (September, 1988), pp. 243–252.

58. Akshay R. Rao and Kent B. Monroe, "The Moderating Effect of Prior Knowledge on Cue Utilization in Product Evaluations," *Journal of Consumer Research,* 15 (September, 1988), pp. 253–264.

59. Kent B. Monroe, "The Influence of Price Differences and Brand Familiarity on Brand Preferences," *Journal of Consumer Research,* 3 (June, 1976), pp. 42–49.

60. Jerry B. Gotlieb and Dan Sarel, "Effects of Price Advertisements on Perceived Quality and Purchase Intentions," *Journal of Business Research,* 22 (1991), pp. 195–210.

61. Carl Obermiller, "When Do Consumers Infer Quality from Price?" *Channel of Communication* (Summer, 1988), pp. 1–2.

62. Valerie A. Zeithaml, "Consumer Perceptions of Price, Quality, and Value: A Means-End Model and Synthesis of Evidence," *Journal of Marketing,* 52 (July, 1988), pp. 2–22.

7

Consumer Information Processing

To make purchasing decisions, consumers acquire and process information from advertising, from their experience with products, from friends and neighbors, and from other sources. Processing requires that consumers perceive and remember information. Perception is, therefore, a key component of information processing. However, processing also requires that consumers go beyond the selection, organization, and interpretation of information described in the last chapter. Consumers must also retain information in memory and retrieve it when evaluating brands.

Marketers have a direct interest in the way consumers process information. If consumer information processing does not result in positive brand evaluation and purchase behavior, companies can lose millions of dollars on ineffective advertising. Eveready learned this lesson when it introduced the Eveready Bunny to sell batteries. The campaign was designed to poke fun at Eveready's main competitor, Duracell, whose ads showed toys with Duracell batteries winning endurance contests. The series of Eveready ads (launched in 1989) developed into a parody of typical TV commercials, with each commercial being interrupted by the drumming Eveready Bunny and a voice-over saying "Still Going."

Consumers loved the ads, and their recall of the Bunny was very high. However, there was one problem. In one study, fully 40 percent of consumers recalled seeing a Duracell ad.[1] Why? Since the ads parodied prior Duracell commercials, they appeared to be an extension of Duracell's theme of endurance. There was another problem. The Bunny, rather than the product, was the centerpiece of the ad. The humor of the ad seemed to be dominating the message.

By 1991, Eveready claimed that recall of the ads was up 50 percent.[2] Clearly, consumers were processing the ad and recalling the message. But many consumers were getting the wrong message—Duracell and a funny bunny. Eveready's long-lasting batteries seemed to have been lost in the shuffle.

In this chapter, we extend our discussion of perception by focusing on how consumers process information. We first discuss how information is acquired from marketing and nonmarketing sources. We then consider information processing, with particular emphasis on the role of memory, and conclude by considering limitations consumers face in processing information.

◆ CONSUMER INFORMATION ACQUISITION

Consumers must acquire information before they can process it. The role of information acquisition in consumer decision making is shown in Figure 7.1. To illustrate, consider the business school student cited in Chapter 3 who is in the market for a laptop computer. She is involved in the decision, perceives some risk in the purchase, and has little past experience in buying a computer. These factors encourage information search.

Figure 7.1 shows the three different processes leading to information acquisition. Ongoing search for computer information might characterize the consumer with enduring involvement in the product. For example, the computer buff who subscribes to computer magazines is aware of a wide variety of options. Purchase-specific search is characteristic of the consumer with situational involvement who collects information when making a purchase decision (for example, visiting a retail store or asking a friend about personal computers).

The third process does not require an active search for information; instead, it involves the passive acquisition of information. For example, our business school student happens to notice a computer ad in a magazine. In this case, she did not search for information but noticed it in passing. Such passive acquisition of information is more typical of uninvolved consumers. However, since our consumer is situationally involved, she acquires most of her information through a purchase-specific search process.

▶**FIGURE 7.1**

Role of information acquisition in consumer decision making

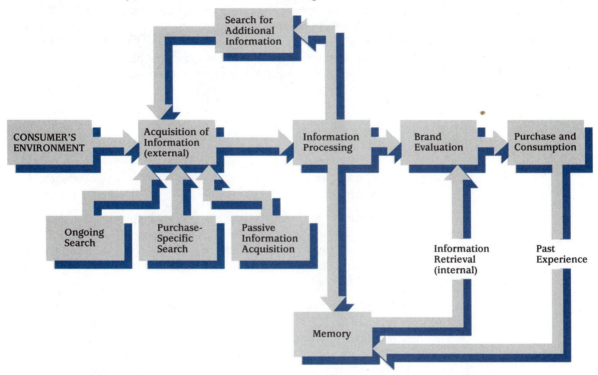

After acquiring the information, consumers process it. In the course of information processing, consumers may believe more information is necessary to evaluate alternative brands or to determine product features. In seeking additional information about product or price alternatives, consumers reduce the risk of making a poor choice. They will retain the more important information in memory to retrieve in the process of brand evaluation. You will recall that our business school student was most concerned about the laptop's screen size, keyboard flexibility, and storage capacity. She stores in memory information on these three attributes for each brand being considered and will retrieve it when she compares the brands. She also stores in memory her product and consumption experiences, which allows her to learn based on past experience.

Figure 7.1 shows that retrieving information from memory is regarded as *internal* information acquisition because the source of information is the consumer. In contrast, information from advertising, salespeople, or friends and relatives is obtained through a process of *external* acquisition because these are sources of information from the consumer's environment.

Several studies have found that, other things being equal, consumers tend to rely more on external than memory-related sources of information. For example, Biehal and Chakravarti found that consumers are more likely to choose a brand that they can see in a store (external information source) rather than one they might remember from a previous shopping trip (internal source.)[3] However, Alba and his colleagues found this to be true only if recall about brands is poor.[4] For example, our student will tend to rely more on external sources of information about computers if she has little recall about her past experiences with computers (that is, internally derived information). If her past experiences are memorable and persuasive, then these experiences might outweigh the influence of advertising, salespeople, or even friends and relatives.

Determinants of Information Search

A key component of information acquisition in Figure 7.1 is the search for additional sources of external information. Several factors encourage consumers to acquire more information:

1. *High consumer involvement.*   As we saw in Chapter 3, the higher the level of involvement, the greater the amount of information acquired. That is, information search is greater if consumers' self-images are tied to the product, if the product has emotional appeal or badge value, or if consumers have ongoing interest in the product.

2. *High perceived risk.*   The higher the perceived risk in purchasing, the greater the amount of information search. Locander and Hermann found that when risk was high, consumers searched for more information from neutral sources such as *Consumer Reports* and from personal sources such as friends and neighbors.[5] Murray also found that perceived risk increases information search, particularly for services compared to products. This is because services tend to be harder to evaluate, and collecting more information on them is instrumental in reducing risk.[6]

3. *Little product knowledge and experience.*   In a study of purchases of TVs, VCRs, and home computers, Beatty and Smith found that consumers with less knowledge of these products were more likely to search for information.[7] Conversely, Srinivasan and Ratchford found that past experience with a product reduces information search because consumers with experience learn how to search for information more efficiently.[8] However, if past experience is negative, it may increase the search for information.[9]

4. *Less time pressure.*   Time pressure to make a decision will discourage information search. Beatty and Smith found that if consumers have more time available, their information search will increase.[10] This is probably true for high rather than low involvement products.

5. *High price.*   The higher the price, the greater the information search. This was found to be true for women's apparel, appliances, and cars.[11] A higher price means that the economic benefits of information search are greater; therefore, consumers are more likely to devote more effort to search.

6. *More product differences.* There is a higher payoff in searching for information when substantial differences exist between brands. Claxton, Fry, and Portis found that furniture and appliance buyers who saw more differences between brands visited more stores.[12]

Another determinant of information search is its cost. There are monetary and nonmonetary costs associated with information search. Information search frequently involves the monetary costs of traveling to various retail stores. Another cost is the time involved in traveling, shopping, reading advertisements, asking the advice of friends, and so on. Consumers must weigh search time against alternatives such as leisure or business pursuits. A third cost is psychological. Information search may not be desirable to individuals who dislike shopping.

If these costs are too high, consumers will avoid information search, even if the six conditions encouraging search are operating. Generally, consumers operate by weighing the costs of information search against the benefits of additional information. One economist suggested that consumers probably operate at the margin; that is, they will continue to collect information until the incremental benefits of the additional information no longer exceed the incremental cost of collecting that information.[13] Although consumers may not consciously operate at the margin, they do choose information sources with some cost-benefit principle in mind.

Sources of Information

Consumers can utilize several sources of information from their environment. Figure 7.2 shows these sources categorized on two dimensions: personal versus impersonal sources and marketer-controlled versus non-marketer-controlled sources.

In evaluating alternative laptop computers, our student utilizes all four types of sources shown in Figure 7.2. She talks to salespeople in retail stores about alternatives, prices, and peripherals (personal marketer-controlled sources). She is aware of advertising in magazines for laptops (impersonal marketer-controlled sources). She also talks to friends and business associates about their experiences with laptops (personal non-marketer-controlled sources). Finally, she uses neutral sources such as *Consumer Reports* magazine, a publication that impartially tests and rates products, to determine its evaluation of laptop brands (impersonal non-marketer-controlled source).

Figure 7.2 shows the sources of information for external search. As we noted, consumers also undertake a process of internal search by retrieving information from memory. In trying out several laptop models her friends owned, our consumer stored her past experiences in memory and retrieved them in the process of brand evaluation.

The consumers' stage in the decision process affects their use of information sources. Marketer-controlled sources tend to be more important in the early

▶**FIGURE 7.2**

Sources of consumer information

Source: Adapted from CONSUMER BEHAVIOR by Thomas S. Robertson, Joan Zielinski, and Scott Ward. Copyright © 1984 by Scott, Foresman and Company. Reprinted by permission of HarperCollins College Publishers.

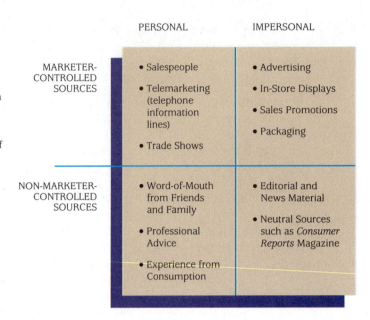

	PERSONAL	IMPERSONAL
MARKETER-CONTROLLED SOURCES	• Salespeople • Telemarketing (telephone information lines) • Trade Shows	• Advertising • In-Store Displays • Sales Promotions • Packaging
NON-MARKETER-CONTROLLED SOURCES	• Word-of-Mouth from Friends and Family • Professional Advice • Experience from Consumption	• Editorial and News Material • Neutral Sources such as *Consumer Reports* Magazine

stages of decision making when consumers are obtaining information on product alternatives. The opinions of friends and associates[14] and the consumers' own experiences become more important as they move closer to the final decision because they regard these sources as more trustworthy.

Use of information sources also varies according to the conditions for information search. In their study of VCRs, TVs, and home computers, Beatty and Smith found that consumers with little product knowledge are more likely to rely on friends and associates for information because they are regarded as more credible than a salesperson.[15] On the other hand, more knowledgeable consumers are likely to rely on their past experiences because they are confident of their evaluations and judgments.

Amount of Information Search

Despite consumers' reasons for undertaking a search for information, their amount of information search for all but the most expensive products is very limited.[16] In most cases, they consider the search for additional information simply not worth the time and money.

The limited nature of consumer search is illustrated in an experiment by Jacoby and his colleagues.[17] They presented consumers of breakfast cereals with information in a matrix of 16 brands by 35 product characteristics—560 pieces of information in all. On average, consumers selected 11 pieces of information, or less than 2 percent of the information available, before making a decision. Capon and Burke studied appliance purchasers and found that consumers used

24 percent of available information.[18] The higher level of information utilization is due to the higher price and greater risk of purchasing appliances compared to those of cereals. Even so, information use was low.

Other studies have focused on the number of retail stores consumers visited.[19] Most purchasers of toys and small appliances visit only one store. Purchasers of refrigerators and furniture are more likely to visit three or more stores. Half of the purchasers of cars and major appliances, however, visited only one showroom. The amount of shopping for these products is not as great as one might expect, given the risks involved.

Studies have also considered the number of alternative brands. One study[20] found the following proportions of consumers considering more than one brand:

- 59 percent for refrigerators
- 53 percent for cars and household appliances[21]
- 39 percent for washing machines
- 29 percent for vacuum cleaners

These figures suggest that the number of brands consumers consider is typically small. Although the evidence points to limited information search, this does not mean buyers are uninvolved. A prospective consumer may be entering the decision-making process with a large amount of past experience and purchase information stored in memory.[22] Therefore, for such consumers, the necessity for extensive information search may be low.

Limits of Information Acquisition

Some consumer advocates and government agencies assume that consumers should be supplied with as much information as possible to permit a comparison of brand alternatives. The same assumption underlies economic theory: Optimal choice requires access to information on all alternatives. The reality, however, is that consumers rarely seek all of the available information. They find the cost of search and the complexity of processing just too great to attempt to consider all brand alternatives. Therefore, more information is not necessarily better. In fact, too much information may create **information overload;** that is, confusion in the decision task resulting in an ineffective decision.

Jacoby, Speller, and Kohn found that information overload exists.[23] They provided consumers with a range of 8 to 72 items of information on alternative laundry detergents by varying the number of brands consumers could consider and the number of pieces of information per brand. They then related the amount of information to the effectiveness of brand choice. Effectiveness of choice was determined by the degree to which consumers chose brands that were similar to their ideal laundry detergent. If consumers used up to 24 pieces of information, the "more is better" notion seemed to hold. However, more than 24 pieces of information seemed to cause consumers to choose brands that were not similar to their ideal. Thus, having too much information and too many brands to choose from complicated the consumers' decision task and resulted in less effective choices.

A more recent study by Hutchinson and Alba provides further confirmation of information overload. They varied the number of comparisons consumers had to make to evaluate stereo speakers. They found that when comparative brand information increased, the consumers' ability to classify and evaluate brands correctly was reduced.[24]

The possibility that at some point too much information may have negative consequences on decision tasks suggests that both advertisers and public agencies must be careful not to provide consumers with irrelevant information. The problem is aggravated by the sheer number of commercials on the air. (It is estimated that the average consumer is exposed to from 300 to 600 print and broadcast advertisements per day.) Simplifying information on complex decisions would be a step in the right direction.

Another factor contributing to information overload is the large number of alternative brands available to consumers. A decade ago, the average supermarket carried 9,000 items; today, it carries an average of 25,000. American consumers buying cereal face a choice of over 200 products. Further, the number of variations of existing products (known as *brand extensions*) has increased tremendously because marketers are finding it safer and cheaper to rely on such extensions rather than on new products.

Increasing evidence suggests that many consumers see little added value from such brand extensions and regard them as sources of confusion. One survey found that 44 percent of consumers agree that the increasing number of product introductions makes selection more difficult, not easier.[25] As Alvin Toffler concluded in his book *Future Shock*, "We are racing toward 'overchoice'— the point at which the advantage of diversity and individualization are canceled by the complexity of the buyer's decision-making process."[26]

Strategic Implications of Information Acquisition

The way consumers acquire information has direct implications for marketing strategy.

Determinants of Information Acquisition

The factors encouraging information search cited above indicate that consumers want more information for product categories that involve risk, are high priced, and have significant differences between brands. Therefore, products such as cars, personal computers, and compact discs must have an informational base.

Communicating information does not always mean the straight recitation of product characteristics, however. Information can also be conveyed by images and symbols. When IBM first introduced personal computers, it used the Charlie Chaplin character in its ads to convey information both through the written word and by symbol. (See Exhibit 7.1.) IBM conveyed product features such as speed, storage, software availability, and compatibility of its personal computers. However, even more importantly, IBM conveyed information visually by using Charlie Chaplin to communicate a user-friendly image. This image reinforced the product characteristics the ad communicated.

Cost of Information Acquisition

Marketers must consider ways to reduce the costs of information search for consumers. Offering free samples is one method of reducing search by providing consumers product experience. Apple Computer's offer to "test drive a MacIntosh" in a recent ad campaign (see Exhibit 7.2) had a similar objective—to provide consumers with direct experience to reduce the need for additional information. Intensive distribution of products is also a means of reducing information search, as consumers do not have to travel as far to inspect products. For marketers who can identify prospects and provide relevant information directly, direct mail is another means of reducing the costs of information search. In-store information can also reduce search costs. Unit pricing has helped some consumers reduce the time spent in in-store brand comparisons.

Marketers might also try to direct product information more effectively to groups who have higher costs of information search. For instance, AT&T realized that the groups who were taking the best advantage of off-peak rates were higher-income, better-educated consumers. As a result, AT&T attempted to direct its message to the lower-income groups to facilitate information acquisition. Because the marginal cost of information is higher for low-income consumers, AT&T's strategy was designed to lower the cost of search by directing information more effectively to this segment.

▶**EXHIBIT 7.1**
Conveying information through symbols and the printed word

▶**EXHIBIT 7.2**
An example of a
strategy to reduce
information search

Source: Courtesy of Apple
Computer Inc.

The "Test Drive a Macintosh" promotion prompts 200,000 people to take a Macintosh home for a free 24-hour trial.

Type of Information Search

The type of information search also has important ramifications for marketers. A company selling motorcycles is probably dealing with a target market that has enduring, rather than situational, interest in the product because most motorcycle owners are involved with their machines on an ongoing basis. This group will notice information on motorcycles whether they are in the market for one or not. As a result, marketers will try to generate interest in their products by providing information on product features and performance in specialty magazines or through feature articles in newspapers. In this case, marketers will use advertising more in a support role to convey the image of a bike as part of the rider's identity.

If the product is in a low involvement category, marketers realize that consumers will acquire information passively and must encourage such passive receipt of information. For example, in introducing a new product, they might use repeat advertising on TV to establish a sufficient level of awareness. Television is the best medium to ensure passive acquisition because consumers' exposure to TV commercials does not require information search.

Passive acquisition points to the importance of trial as a means of obtaining information.[27] It may actually be cheaper for consumers to buy an inexpensive product for trial than it is to search for additional information. Marketers who recognize the limits of information search may decide to put more money into inducing trial than in trying to convey information to consumers. That is, it might be more cost-effective to put additional dollars into free samples and price promotions than to increase advertising budgets. For this reason, marketers of consumer packaged goods have been shifting more money from advertising to sales promotions.

◆ CONSUMER INFORMATION PROCESSING

Once they acquire information, consumers must process it. Marketers are interested in information processing because it determines which information consumers remember, which information they use in the process of brand evaluation, and how they use it.

An Information Processing Model

The way consumers process information depends largely on their level of involvement with the product decision. As we saw, when consumers are involved in a product, they actively search for information and analyze it to assess alternative brands effectively. For low involvement products, consumers are more likely to receive information passively; and they will process this information in detail.

Figures 7.3 and 7.4 present models of information processing for high and low involvement decisions, respectively. The two processes differ primarily in the extent of processing and in their effect on brand evaluation.

High Involvement Information Processing

The high involvement model in Figure 7.3 is an extension of the description of information processing in complex decision making in Chapter 2. Let us pursue the example of the business school student in the market for a laptop computer. Figure 7.3 shows that processing takes place as information is acquired. In the process of information search, our consumer has noticed an ad for a Toshiba, decides to visit several stores to try one out, and realizes the speed of the machine is faster than anticipated. This information is perceived; that is, it receives the consumer's attention and is then organized and interpreted.

The next step in processing is determining what information will be retained in memory to be retrieved in the process of brand evaluation. Our consumer first processes information in her short-term memory, which acts as a filter to determine the information she will store and the information she will ignore. Such a filter is necessary because no consumer can retain everything that is seen (and no consumer would want to). The principle of selective retention states that only the most important and relevant information to the brand decision will be stored in long-term memory.

Our consumer was interested in information obtained on the Toshiba from advertising and from several salespeople. She organized information on the Toshiba and other laptops by product features to facilitate future comparison (that is, she compared brands by speed, by price, and so on). She retained the information on the Toshiba's speed in long-term memory. However, other information such as the size of the screen and necessary attachments to the printer were passed through short-term memory and not retained.

▶**FIGURE 7.3**
A model of high-involvement information processing

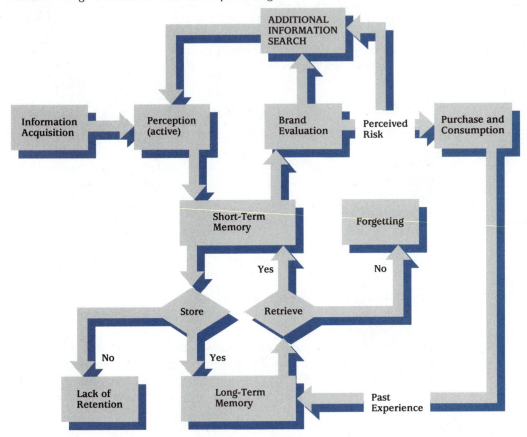

Our consumer retrieves information in long-term memory in the process of brand evaluation. Information on the Toshiba causes our consumer to change her beliefs about the characteristics of the brand and to develop a more positive attitude toward it and thus increase the chance that she may select it.

In the process of brand evaluation, consumers assess the degree of risk involved in the purchase. Such perceived risk may be because of high price, product complexity, the importance of the product to the consumers' peer groups, or the consumers' emotional attachment to the product. Such risk encourages consumers to seek additional information before making a purchase decision. Our student sees both financial and performance risks in the purchase of the laptop. As a result, she continues her information search by obtaining information on two additional brands, the AST and the NEC, to ensure that she is not overlooking better or more economical makes than the Toshiba.

Once the purchase is made and the product is used, consumers will remember and learn from the purchase and usage experience. Our student decides to

▶FIGURE 7.4

A model of low involvement information processing

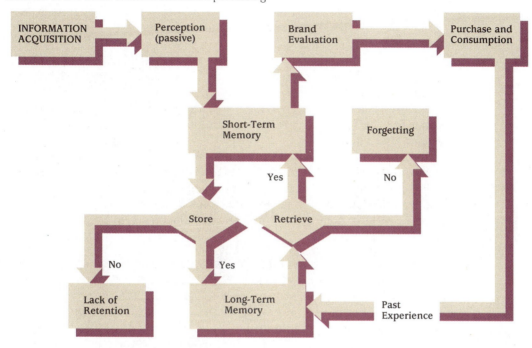

buy the Toshiba. She stores her experience with the machine in long-term memory and may use it if and when she decides to upgrade to a more powerful PC. She also stores her experiences in deciding on the Toshiba in memory. This information will be useful when she goes back into the market for another machine. Based on these experiences, she will be a more effective information searcher, shopper, and brand evaluator.

Low Involvement Information Processing

Figure 7.4 presents a model of information processing in low involvement decisions. Several aspects of the model differ from those of the high involvement processing model.

First, since consumers process information passively, they can store this information in memory with little attention to it.[28] For instance, the consumer seeing an advertisement for Diet Pepsi may remember two things: the brand name and a theme such as "You got the right one, baby." However, the theme is almost like a series of nonsense syllables and has little immediate meaning, although the message that Diet Pepsi is the right choice may sink in eventually. The consumer organizes the ad and places it in the category of information relating to soft drinks. However, the message is not interpreted. Instead, the consumer filters it through short-term memory and stores some part of it, probably just the basic theme, in long-term memory. Diet Pepsi promotions in supermarkets with the same theme provide an in-store context for the consumer to link the ad to the product. The next time the consumer goes to the store, the sight of Diet Pepsi on the shelf may evoke an association with "You got the right one, baby," and may remind the consumer of a need to purchase a diet soft drink.

A second contrast with the high involvement model is that here, brand evaluation is minimal. The consumer's belief that Diet Pepsi is the right choice may lead to a decision to buy without formation of any strong brand attitudes. The sequence in Figure 7.4 is consistent with the low involvement hierarchy in Chapter 5: beliefs leading to behavior with the possible development of brand attitudes after the fact.

The third difference between the two models is that perceived risk is not an outcome of information processing in low involvement purchases. Given the low level of involvement, financial, performance, or social risks are unlikely to come into play. Fourth, it is unlikely that consumers will seek additional information to make a brand choice in low involvement decisions. It is not worth the time and effort to do so.

Information Processing and the Elaboration Likelihood Model (ELM)

The elaboration likelihood model (ELM), described in Chapter 5, provides further insight into the distinction between high and low involvement processing. ELM says that in high involvement cases, consumers are more motivated to process information because of the importance of the product and the risk associated with its purchase.[29] The model refers to such high involvement processing as taking a *central route;* that is, consumers process information that directly links product features and benefits to their needs.

In low involvement cases, consumers have little motivation to search for and process information because product interest and perceived risk are low. In such cases, consumers are likely to process information by a *peripheral route.* Such a route means focusing on elements in the communication that may not be central to the message—for example, the music, the voice of the announcer, the attractiveness of a spokesperson, or the background in an ad.

The strategic implication is that message cues related to product benefits should be the primary means of persuasion in high involvement communications; non-message (peripheral) cues should be the primary means of persuasion in low involvement communications.

Memory Processes

In both the high and the low involvement cases, processing information requires that it, first, be filtered through short-term memory, second, stored in long-term memory, and, third, retrieved for purposes of brand evaluation.

Filtering Information Through Short-Term Memory

When consumers perceive information, they briefly evaluate it in **short-term memory** to determine whether to store it in long-term memory or to filter it out as unimportant or undesirable information. Consumers decide whether to retain information or to filter it out by relating it to information they already have stored in memory. If the information is important enough, then consumers will store it.

For example, when our consumer learned about the Toshiba's fast processing speed, she briefly retained this information in short-term memory. Information from long-term memory based on her past experience told her to expect short processing times for laptops; and since the new information regarding Toshiba's processing speed was important enough, she stored this in her long-term memory. That is, the interaction between the new information and information from memory resulted in retention of this information in long-term memory.

Short-term memory has a limited capacity to process information. In terms of time and pieces of information, short-term memory capacities can be measured in seconds (certainly less than one minute) or an average of seven pieces of information at any one time. Individuals react to this restriction by chunking information. For example, a social security number is composed of nine figures; but people usually chunk it into three groups of figures to recall it more easily. A brand image represents the beliefs consumers associate with a brand and is an information chunk. It may be composed of 20 different components, but it can be retrieved as one general impression.

Once they filter the information through short-term memory, consumers will either store it in long-term memory or choose not to retain it. Most information is not retained for a variety of reasons: It might be irrelevant, not important enough, confusing information that is difficult to interpret, or undesirable information that consumers choose to ignore.

Storing Information in Long-Term Memory

Information in **long-term memory** is stored as images that reflect our memory of past events (**episodic memory**) or as words and sentences that reflect facts and concepts we remember (**semantic memory**).[30]

Consumers' memories of brands are in the form of both words and images. The word *McDonald's* may evoke other words such as *fast food* and *Big Mac*. It also may evoke images learned from advertising and from past experience such as golden arches and the Ronald McDonald character. Words and images in long-term memory are linked to other words or images in an information network. Each word or image in long-term memory is called a **node.** An example of a particular consumer's information network is shown in Figure 7.5. The nodes fast service, good for the family, good food, clean surroundings, Ronald McDonald, and Big Mac are all linked to the McDonald's node. (See Exhibit 7.3.) These nodes represent beliefs about McDonald's in the consumer's mind.

As we saw in the last chapter, such a cluster of beliefs is called a *schema*. In the context of memory processes, a schema occurs when a certain node (such as a brand) elicits a cluster of other nodes.[31] In marketing terms, such a schema is a consumer's brand or company image. McDonald's is a schema because

▶FIGURE 7.5
An example of a consumer's information network

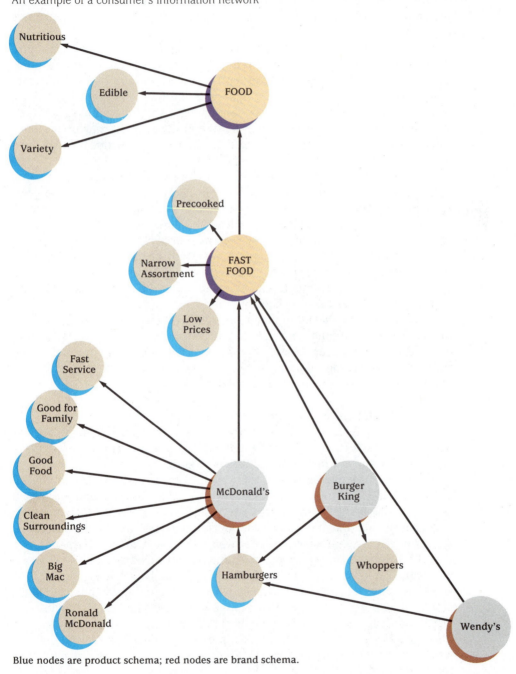

Blue nodes are product schema; red nodes are brand schema.

▶**EXHIBIT 7.3**
The images (or nodes) that are associated with the McDonald's schema
Source: Courtesy of McDonald's Corporation

when the word *McDonald's* is activated by either an ad, a food outlet, or in conversation, a group of associated nodes is elicited in the consumer's mind.

Figure 7.5 also shows broader nodes such as fast food and food in general, each of which is associated with various other beliefs. This consumer associates fast foods with precooked food, a narrow assortment, and low prices, but also associates fast food with the McDonald's, Burger King, and Wendy's nodes. Activating fast foods in this consumer's mind might bring up McDonald's and its related nodes.

From a strategic perspective, the fact that McDonald's has many more nodes associated with it means that it has a fuller brand image for this consumer. The positive associations in Figure 7.5, if true for the general market, would indicate a strong market position for McDonald's based on an image of family values and good food.

Marketing strategy has two important objectives in the context of long-term memory: first, *establishing linkages* between the brand and other positive nodes, and, second, *activating* these linkages once they are established. As we saw in Chapter 4, positive associations are established through consumer learning. The most important element in establishing associations in memory is consumers' experience with the product, but advertising has a key role in maintaining positive linkages over time. For example, although this consumer may be satisfied with the experience the linkages show in Figure 7.5, repetitive advertising reinforces these linkages; and this consumer does not forget them.

Marketing strategy also activates the associations in a brand's schema so consumers can use them in the purchase decision. Advertising the brand name or the symbols and images associated with the brand may trigger other associations. For example, a picture of golden arches may be enough to trigger the association to a McDonald's schema. McDonald's advertising has been successful in establishing such associations. Its past theme, "It's a good time for the great taste of McDonald's" was the basis for communicating an image of good food and family values, important nodes in McDonald's schema. The high level of awareness of the campaign and the positive associations it produced meant that consumers were likely to retain it in long-term memory.

In contrast, Burger King has had a long-standing problem establishing a positive brand image. Illustrative is a past campaign, "Where's Herb?" that was designed to encourage consumers to find a character called Herb who had never tasted a Whopper. Most consumers never comprehended the message. The focus on Herb as a balding eccentric in glasses, white socks, and gaudy plaids did little to promote retention in long-term memory. The campaign turned out to be a $40 million fiasco.[32] As a result of its problems in establishing a strong brand image, nodes associated with Burger King are weak.

Retrieval

Once consumers filter information through short-term memory and store it in long-term memory, it is available for retrieval. When retrieving information from long-term memory, consumers briefly store it in short-term memory and use it to evaluate brands. (See Figures 7.3 and 7.4.) In evaluating a brand, consumers will activate some key pieces of information. The activation of the schema for McDonald's and its related nodes will determine how consumers evaluate McDonald's relative to Wendy's or Burger King.

Three factors are required for retrieval of information from long-term memory: activation, transfer, and placement. The linkages between nodes must be **activated** for retrieval to take place. For the consumer in Figure 7.5, McDonald's advertising will activate various nodes associated with the McDonald's schema. Sales promotions also play an important role in activation. McDonald's frequently runs sweepstakes that provide an incentive for consumers to visit a McDonald's outlet. Such an incentive will also activate the McDonald's schema. More indirectly, any of the nodes in the McDonald's schema—for example, the words *Big Mac*—might activate it. Keller found that when consumers were provided with cues related to a brand (such as a picture of a Big Mac or of Ronald McDonald) recall for the brand was increased.[33] The brand's schema could be activated by these related nodes without the brand name.

By constantly reminding consumers of the positive linkages related to a brand, repetitive advertising plays an essential role in encouraging activation. Such repetition strengthens the linkages between nodes over time and reinforces positive brand images (schema).

A second process necessary for retrieval is **placement,** which determines which other nodes consumers will connect the activated node to. The student buying a laptop computer may connect Toshiba to processing speed based on new information. The consumer seeing an ad for Lean Strips may connect it to bacon or may establish a new node called "bacon substitute" if the product is regarded as new and different.

A third factor required for retrieval is a **transfer** process that determines the information consumers will retrieve from long-term to short-term memory.

Generally, consumers will transfer information that is most important in making a decision—that is, information with the highest potential utility.

Certain factors inhibit retrieval. The three most important are forgetting, interference, and extinction. The student buying a laptop may retrieve information such as the quoted prices for several models, the capacity of these models, and screen and keyboard facility. At one time, she remembered data on processing speed of alternative models; but after a few days, she could no longer retrieve that information. She had forgotten it. **Forgetting** is the inability to retrieve information from long-term memory. If a consumer does not retrieve information for a period of time, any subsequent attempt to do so may fail.

Interference occurs when a related information node blocks the recall of the relevant information. An advertisement by Burger King for a Whopper may cause a consumer to lose the connection in long-term memory between Big Mac and McDonald's because of the strength of the Burger King-Whopper connection. Competitive advertising often causes consumers to be unable to recall advertising for a related brand. At times, consumers confuse one brand with another. Some consumers may even recall an advertisement for a Whopper as a McDonald's ad because of the strength of the McDonald's schema in their long-term memory. In the first case, interference helped Burger King; in the second case, interference hurt it.

Three studies have shown how interference effects inhibit retrieval of information from long-term memory. Keller[34] and Burke and Srull[35] found that the greater the number of competitive claims, the less the recall was for the advertised brand. Keller also found that advertising the target brand at the same time as competitive brands reduces such interference.[36] Consumers' recall of correct claims for the advertised brand improves but is still not as good as if there were no competitive advertising. The logical conclusion is that interference from competitive advertising is partially offset if the target brand continues to advertise. Such repetitive advertising ensures continued activation of the linkages consumers associate with the brand in long-term memory, despite competitive advertising. (See Strategic Applications box.)

Whereas forgetting and interference result in consumers' inability to recall linkages in long-term memory, **extinction** is a change in these linkages. Assume that a consumer reads that McDonald's hamburgers have been criticized for being fatty and having little nutritional value. For this consumer, the linkage between McDonald's and "good for the family" as shown in Figure 7.5 is broken. The McDonald's schema also changes. As we saw in Chapter 4, the FTC may order corrective advertising to correct past erroneous linkages that misleading advertising establishes such as Listerine's claim that it fights colds.

Brand Evaluation

The final step in information processing in Figures 7.3 and 7.4 is brand evaluation. Information on brands comes from many sources. As a result, consumers

One proven method to increase retention of messages in consumers' long-term memory is repetition. Long-lasting symbols such as Betty Crocker or the Pillsbury Doughboy are examples of the benefits of repetition.

STRATEGIC APPLICATIONS OF CONSUMER BEHAVIOR

Advertising Repetition Can Work For or Against You

When companies lose sight of the benefits of repetition, they can run into trouble. Heineken is an example. It slashed its advertising budget from $13.2 million in 1985 to $2.9 million in 1987 in the face of intense competition from brews such as Corona. Ads on network radio and television were cut entirely. The result? Market share went down from 38 percent to 23 percent. The moral? "Out of sight, out of mind." The company has since increased advertising expenditures to remain competitive.

However, there are several risks to repetition. One risk is that consumers learn to expect an advertising theme after many repetitions and pay less attention to it. *Advertising wearout* takes its toll by decreasing consumers' attention level to repetitive ads. A recent study supports this effect. It found that when advertising repeats well-known themes or symbols—McDonald's arches or Pillsbury's Doughboy, for example—information processing decreases. If the ad theme is unique and unexpected, consumers are motivated to process the information in the ad in more detail. To be effective, however, such unique advertising must be directed to consumer needs. As we saw with the Eveready Bunny, uniqueness alone does not guarantee message delivery.

A second risk of repetition is that it creates such an ingrained image of a brand or company that any subsequent attempt to change it will be difficult. In processing terms, repetition establishes strong linkages in consumers' long-term memory (that is, the schema associated with the brand node). If advertising messages are at variance with the established brand image, consumers might reject them. For example, repetition established associations of low cost and no frills with the People Express Airlines node. Repetition established associations of luxury, large, and expensive with Cadillac. People Express ran into trouble when it tried to be a regular airline offering services. Cadillac ran into trouble when it introduced a medium-sized car.

Rolling Stone magazine had a similar problem. Its image, originally reinforced by repeated advertising and editorial content, was that of a magazine for "hippies." This image began to inhibit marketers from placing ads in the magazine. However, the magazine's readership had changed over the years to a younger and more urbane group. *Rolling Stone* launched an effective campaign, titled "Perception/Reality," to change its image. (See Exhibit 7.4.) The ad pictured a stereotypical "hippie" and, in contrast, a hip-looking young man to characterize the magazine's true readership. The campaign was effective in changing consumers' image of *Rolling Stone* by effectively communicating the change in readership.

One possible reason *Rolling Stone* was successful in changing its image whereas People Express and Cadillac were not is that *Rolling Stone*'s schema was not as strongly entrenched in consumers' long-term memory. Another reason might be that *Rolling Stone*'s change in image from hippie to yuppie was more believable than People Express's change from no frills to frills or Cadillac's from large- to medium-sized cars.

Sources: Ronald C. Goodstein, "Category-Based Applications and Extensions in Advertising: Motivating More Extensive Ad Processing," *Journal of Consumer Research*, 20 (June, 1993), pp. 87–99; "The Message, Clever as It May Be, Is Lost in a Number of High-Profile Campaigns," *The Wall Street Journal* (July 27, 1993), pp. B1, B4; "Heineken Learns the Pitfalls of Cutting Advertising Expenditures," *Forbes* (February 8, 1988), pp. 128–130; and "Defamiliarization," *Marketing Insights* (Fall, 1990), pp. 87–90.

▶ **EXHIBIT 7.4**

An attempt to counteract the effects of repetitive advertising: *Rolling Stone* changes its image

Source: Courtesy of Wenner Media

Perception.   Reality.

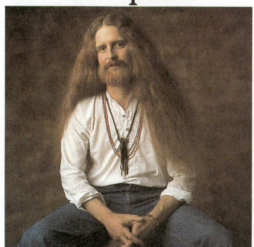 

If your idea of a Rolling Stone reader looks like a holdout from the 60's, welcome to the 80's. Rolling Stone ranks number one in reaching concentrations of 18-34 readers with household incomes exceeding $23,000. When you buy Rolling Stone, you buy an audience that sets the trends and shapes the buying patterns for the most affluent consumers in America. That's the kind of reality you can take to the bank.

need a set of guidelines or decision rules for evaluating brands. These decision rules are the information-processing strategies consumers use in evaluating brands.

Consumers use a variety of such strategies, depending on the level of involvement with the brand, amount of knowledge about the brand, and whether the information is new or already stored in memory. These strategies are classified in Figure 7.6.

▶**FIGURE 7.6**
Processing strategies for brand evaluation

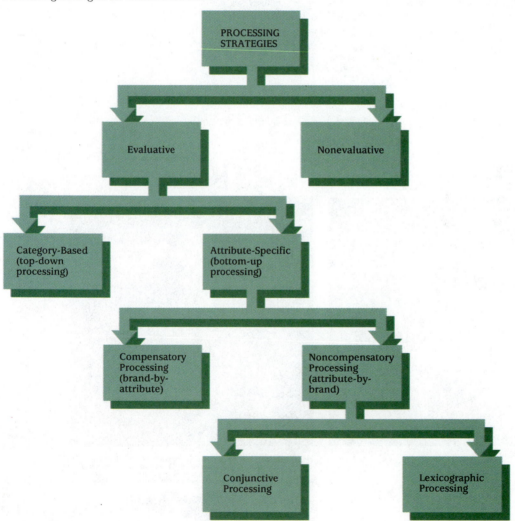

Evaluative vs. Nonevaluative Processing

The most basic distinction is whether an evaluative process takes place or not. **Evaluative strategies** require the organization of information about alternative brands. **Nonevaluative strategies** involve the use of a simple decision rule to avoid the necessity of evaluating brands—for example, buying the most popular brand, the cheapest brand, the same brand as your best friend, or the brand a salesperson recommends. In each case, brand evaluation is avoided.

Gardner and her colleagues found that consumers most likely use evaluative strategies when involvement is higher and nonevaluative strategies when involvement is lower. People using a nonevaluative strategy try to avoid the effort involved in active information processing. They do not actively seek brand information. When they view ads, they do not focus on message content; rather, they might view ads for enjoyment or curiosity.[37] As a result, peripheral cues such as color or music might be more effective in influencing consumers who use nonevaluative strategies, whereas message cues communicating product attributes and benefits are most effective in influencing consumers who use evaluative strategies. On this basis, evaluative strategies closely parallel the central processing route in the ELM model; nonevaluative strategies, the peripheral route.

Category-Based vs. Attribute-Specific Processing

Evaluative strategies can be divided into **category-based strategies** and those that are **attribute-specific.**[38] A category-based strategy involves evaluation of a brand as a totality rather than on specific attributes. Such brand evaluation requires development of a schema for the brand so that consumers can retrieve a set of associations as a whole from long-term memory. On this basis, they can quickly compare brands and establish a preference. On the other hand, attribute-specific strategies require comparison of each brand alternative on specific attributes such as quick service, good taste, or nice atmosphere; and then consumers decide which brand to choose.

When are consumers most likely to use category-based processing? They use it when they have some knowledge about the brand and, therefore, have a brand schema that they can call up readily from memory. Consumer awareness of brands such as Coke, Pepsi, McDonald's, or Ivory suggests that these brands are evaluated on a category rather than on attribute basis. Consumers who objected to Coca-Cola's withdrawal of old Coke did not base their objections on an analysis of specific attributes but on an overall feeling about the brand.

Attribute-specific processing is required when a new product is introduced or when new information is provided about existing products. When consumers started becoming aware of the effects of tartar and plaque on teeth, they began to move from category to attribute processing in evaluating toothpaste. This processing shift is one reason why new tartar and plaque-fighting toothpastes were successful.

Attribute-specific processing is also more likely when the consumer is (1) involved with the brand[39] and (2) knowledgeable about the product category.[40] Involved consumers are unlikely to be satisfied with an overall judgment of brands based on past information. They are likely to seek additional information about brands and to evaluate them based on specific attributes. A consumer in the market for a new car, personal computer, or stereo system is unlikely to make a decision based on an overall brand image formed from past experience and information. This consumer will seek additional information and specifically evaluate it. Similarly, knowledgeable consumers do not have to rely on an overall schema to make brand judgments. They have the ability and confidence to evaluate brands on an attribute-by-attribute basis.

If consumers use category-based processing, marketers should emphasize the brand name and positive symbols associated with it such as the McDonald's arch or the Pepsi-Cola red and blue logo. In doing so, they trigger the schema associated with the brand. If processing is attribute-specific, marketers should focus more on communicating specific information on product characteristics.

Compensatory vs. Noncompensatory Processing

The bottom of Figure 7.6 shows that if consumers use an attribute-specific evaluation strategy, two additional strategies are possible. Consumers can evaluate brands one at a time across a range of attributes (compensatory evaluation) or evaluate specific attributes across the range of brands being considered (noncompensatory evaluation).

The student comparing various laptop models could consider a Toshiba by evaluating its processing speed, memory capacity, screen display, keyboard, and other attributes and come up with an overall evaluation. Such a compensatory method of evaluation is additive: The evaluation of the Toshiba is the sum of all the attributes, and a good rating on one attribute such as processing speed can *compensate* for a poor rating on another attribute such as screen display.

The student could also consider one attribute at a time and evaluate all brands being considered by each attribute. In this case, the student will compare the Toshiba, NEC, and AST models on processing speed, then on price, then on memory capacity, and so on until she has evaluated each brand on all important attributes. This strategy is noncompensatory because a consumer can eliminate a brand as a result of a deficiency on one attribute. For example, if the student finds the NEC to be significantly more expensive than the AST or Toshiba, she might rule it out even before she considers the brands on other attributes. In the compensatory approach, the student would consider the AST on all attributes first before making a decision.

Use of compensatory strategies requires marketers to communicate a broad set of product attributes to allow consumers to make comparisons between brands. If consumers use noncompensatory strategies, the marketer can focus on a few key attributes that consumers are likely to use in brand evaluation.

Figure 7.6 shows two types of noncompensatory strategies. These are further described in Table 7.1. Assume our consumer rates four laptop brands on three attributes. She uses a 7-point scale, with 7 being the best rating. Using a **conjunctive strategy,** a consumer considers a brand only if it meets acceptable standards on key attributes. Assume an acceptable rating is one that scores 5 or higher. In this case, NEC is eliminated because our consumer rated it below the acceptable level on processing speed, and AST is eliminated because of a poor rating on keyboard/display features and on storage capacity. The choice is then between the Toshiba and the Compaq.

Using a **lexicographic strategy,** consumers first evaluate brands on the most important attribute. If there is a tie, consumers next evaluate brands on the second most important attribute, and so on until a brand is selected. Assume the most important attributes are listed in the same order as in Table 7.1. Toshiba and AST are tied for first based on ratings on the most important criterion, processing speed. The consumer then goes to the second most important criterion, storage capacity, and chooses Toshiba over AST on this basis.

Several studies have examined the use of compensatory and noncompensatory strategies. Lussier and Olshavsky found that consumers frequently use a combination of both noncompensatory and compensatory approaches.[41] They use noncompensatory strategies to screen out certain brands and then use compensatory strategies to evaluate the final candidates. This is a good strategy for reducing the number of brands under consideration and ensuring that the amount of information to be processed is manageable. In the above example, using a conjunctive strategy, our consumer eliminated NEC and AST because

▶**TABLE 7.1**

Noncompensatory processing strategies

	NEC	Toshiba	AST	Compaq
Processing speed	2	7	7	5
Storage capacity	6	6	4	6
Keyboard/display	7	5	3	7

Conjunctive Processing
- NEC is eliminated because of poor rating on processing speed.
- AST is eliminated because of poor rating on keyboard/display and on storage capacity.
- Select between Toshiba and Compaq.

Lexicographic Processing
- Assume most important attributes are listed in same order as in table above.
- Toshiba and AST are tied for first. Go to next most important attribute and select Toshiba on this basis.

of poor ratings on processing speed. The selection between the Toshiba and Compaq then might have been made on a compensatory basis by evaluating each brand across all attributes. The consumer selects the make that is rated best.

A study of the strategies consumers use in selecting stereo systems supported this dual strategy.[42] Consumers first eliminated systems that were not competitively priced and did not have a knowledgeable sales force to back them up. Consumers then evaluated the remaining makes by considering attributes such as quality, style, warranty, and other product features on a compensatory basis.

Measuring Brand Evaluation

Researchers who study how consumers evaluate brands seek to measure (1) the amount of information consumers acquire, (2) the processing strategies they use, and (3) the way they evaluate information. Three methods have been used to measure these aspects of brand evaluation: information display boards, observation, and controlled experimentation.

Jacoby and his colleagues developed a means of tracing the way consumers process information through the use of *information display boards*.[43] A board is developed that lists a number of brands across the top and attribute information for each brand (price, ingredients, and so on) down the side. Information on the board is not openly displayed; consumers must "acquire" it by some action such as turning over a tab or pressing a button. Consumers are asked to place themselves in a shopping situation in which they will buy one brand and can select as much or as little information from the display board as they like. This procedure permits the researcher to determine the way consumers process information (that is, by object or by attribute) and the amount of information acquired.

Another way to trace brand evaluation is by observation. For example, Hoyer placed observers in various stores to determine the way consumers use in-store information when shopping for laundry detergents.[44] Observers recorded the brands consumers examined, whether they also examined the shelf tag, the amount of time they spent examining brands, and the brand they selected.

A third approach in measuring brand evaluation is controlled experimentation. Marketing stimuli are presented to consumers in controlled conditions, and the nature of processing is inferred by determining the effect of these stimuli on brand preferences or behavior. For example, consider the hypothesis that message-related advertising stimuli are more likely to influence brand choice in high involvement conditions, and peripheral stimuli such as layout or color are more influential in low involvement conditions.[45] The researcher can develop two sets of ads, one set in which message-related stimuli dominate and another in which peripheral stimuli dominate. A high and a low involvement condition can be created. Respondents are assigned to one of four groups on a random basis:

- High involvement/message stimuli
- High involvement/peripheral stimuli
- Low involvement/message stimuli
- Low involvement/peripheral stimuli

The researcher can then infer the way consumers process message-related or peripheral stimuli in high and low involvement conditions by determining the effects of these stimuli on brand preferences.

Each of these methods has its advantages. Information display boards provide a means of determining the information consumers use in brand choice. Controlled experiments permit researchers to test specific hypotheses about the way information affects brand choice. Both of these methods, however, test consumer reactions in artificial laboratory conditions. While observation allows the researcher to study brand evaluation in a realistic setting, it does not permit control over what the consumer is reacting to.

Perceived Risk

One other component of information processing shown in Figure 7.3 is **perceived risk.** The perception that a purchase might be risky is actually an outcome of information processing that could lead consumers to acquire additional information.

When consumers see potential risk in a purchase, they may be uncertain about the outcome of the decision (What are the chances my new car will break down in the first six months?), or they may be concerned about the consequences of the decision (What will the results of a breakdown be in terms of cost, inconvenience, and some personal anxiety?). Thus, the two components of perceived risk are uncertainty about the outcome of the decision and concern about the consequences of the decision.

Factors Associated with Perceived Risk

Several factors are likely to increase the risk consumers see in purchasing. Perceived risk is likely to be greater when:

- There is little information about the product category.
- The product is new.
- The product is technologically complex.
- Consumers have little self-confidence in evaluating brands.
- There are variations in quality among brands.
- The price is high.
- The purchase is important to consumers.[46]

Perceived risk in purchasing a laptop is high because most of the listed criteria will be met. As the product category is still relatively new for many consumers, they have little experience with alternatives. Moreover, the product is technologically complex, making evaluation more difficult. As a result, consumer confidence in selecting one brand over another is low. Furthermore, substantial variations among brands and incompatible systems heighten risk. A high price will also contribute to perceived risk. Finally, such a purchase is probably important to consumers.

Perceived risk is also likely for well-established products. Self-confidence in purchasing products such as cameras, stereo equipment, and carpeting is low because most consumers lack knowledge of the criteria by which to judge variations among brands and price. To reduce risk, consumers tend to rely on sources of information with a high degree of credibility such as friends who have purchased the brand or impartial sources such as *Consumer Reports*.

Types of Risk

Consumers may face several different types of risk in purchasing decisions:

1. *Financial risk* is a function of the cost of a product relative to consumers' disposable incomes. For example, the consumer who has saved for four years to buy a high-priced car runs a greater risk than the individual who can buy the same car out of discretionary income every two years.
2. *Social risk* means that a purchase may not meet the standards of an important reference group. Visible items (clothing, cars, household furnishings) and items designed to enhance social attractiveness (cosmetics, mouthwash) are particularly subject to social risk.
3. *Psychological risk* is the chance that a product important to consumers does not conform to their self-image (for example, a suit does not look quite right or the automobile does not have the right feel in driving).
4. *Performance risk* is associated with the possibility that the product will not work as anticipated or may fail. It is greatest when the product is technically complex or when ego-related needs are involved.
5. *Physical risk* is the risk of bodily harm as a result of product performance; for example, faulty brakes that could lead to a car crash or an adverse reaction to a pharmaceutical product.

Consumer Strategies to Reduce Risk

Consumers use various strategies to try to reduce risk. These strategies are designed either to increase the certainty of the purchase outcome or to reduce the consequence of failure.

The most direct means of increasing the certainty of the purchase outcome is to *acquire additional information* that will allow consumers to better assess risk. By searching for additional information on laptops, our student attempts to reduce the financial risk of her purchase and the risk of buying a computer with inadequate storage capacity or processing speed. Another strategy to increase certainty is to engage in *more extensive information processing* to better evaluate alternatives. More detailed brand evaluation can ensure that consumers will avoid products that fail. Involved consumers are more likely to use these strategies because these consumers are more motivated to acquire and process information to increase the certainty of the purchase outcome.

A third strategy is *brand loyalty.* Buying the same brand repeatedly increases the certainty of the purchase outcome because consumers know what to expect from the product. The best way to avoid the possibility of dissatisfaction is to stay with a reasonably acceptable alternative. This strategy is apparent in industrial as well as in consumer buying behavior. Risk reduction frequently results in staying loyal to the same vendor for years, even though other sources of supply may be less costly. For instance, a purchasing agent perceives the risk of change that involves associations with new vendors and greater uncertainty.

Buying the most popular brand is also a safe strategy. For consumers who lack information, purchasing the most popular brand is the best means of increasing the certainty of the outcome. Johnson & Johnson relies on the recognition of its name as the leading producer of baby products. In so doing, it seeks to reduce any uncertainty new parents may have in buying baby products. (See Exhibit 7.5.) Consumers purchasing appliances, television sets, or stereos also may lack confidence in comparing brands. Claims that a certain brand is the largest seller or a leading brand are attempts to influence prospective buyers by assuring them that millions of fellow consumers cannot be wrong.

▶**EXHIBIT 7.5**

Johnson & Johnson reduces the uncertainty of buying baby products

Source: Johnson & Johnson

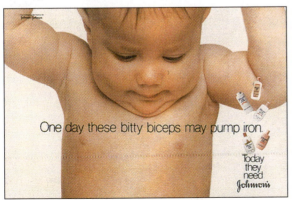 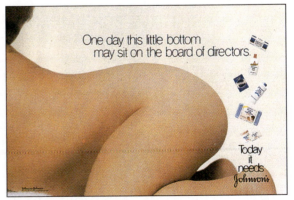

Less involved consumers are more likely to use strategies that involve buying the same or the most popular brand because these strategies minimize the time and effort involved in information processing.

Other strategies attempt to reduce the consequences of failure. Consumers' most common means of reducing the consequence of product failure is to *buy the lowest-priced item* or *the smallest size*. These strategies reduce the financial risk but not the psychological risk. A strategy to reduce the psychological risk of making the wrong decision is to *reduce the level of expectation* before making the purchase. Consider a purchaser who decides that cars are a necessary evil that inevitably produce mechanical failures and repair bills. This purchaser is not going to be terribly disappointed if his or her car does not perform well; he or she expects it.

The various strategies consumers use to reduce risk suggest two types of consumers. Risk avoiders are more likely to buy the lowest-priced brand, the same brand, or the most popular brand. This type of consumer is willing to forego taking a chance on a riskier alternative that might or might not provide better performance in favor of the "safe bet." A second type of consumer is more of a risk taker. He or she will search for more information and will process information in more detail to find the best product. The risk taker is more likely to buy new products before they are well established. Studies have found that risk takers are likely to be higher-income consumers, to have upward social mobility, and to exhibit personality traits such as needs for achievement, dominance, and change.[47]

In his study, Roselius found that the most common strategy consumers use to reduce risk is brand loyalty.[48] On this basis, it appears that increasing the certainty of the outcome is more important to consumers than reducing the consequences of failure. Such brand loyalty might mean buying a higher-priced item just because it is a known commodity. If this is the case, consumers are merely trading off one risk for another—that is, increasing financial risk to reduce psychological risk.

◆ STRATEGIC IMPLICATIONS OF INFORMATION PROCESSING

This chapter has described two key components of information processing—storing information in memory and evaluating brands. An important outcome of information processing, perceived risk, was also described. Important marketing implications emerge in each of these three areas.

Memory Processes

A primary objective of advertising strategy is to ensure that consumers will retain the message in memory. The most obvious means of increasing retention is through repetition of the advertising message. A study by Ray and

Sawyer found that advertising recall almost tripled as the number of repetitions went from one to six.[49] The study also shows the diminishing returns of additional repetitions. As advertising is repeated, the incremental gains in consumer retention become smaller.

There is another problem with frequent advertising repetition: a wearout effect. Consumers may become so familiar with an ad campaign that they no longer notice it. The campaign can be revitalized only by introducing new and fresher ideas to communicate product benefits. Constant repetition, in fact, may start irritating consumers, as was the case with the frequent repetition of the theme "ring around the collar." Another important implication of memory processes is for marketers to develop sets of associations with a brand that will lead to a positive and consistent brand image. In establishing a positive image, advertising must link the brand to nodes with positive associations in consumers' memory.[50]

Once consumers establish a strong brand image, marketers should reinforce it by all elements of marketing strategy. This is best achieved by a marketing campaign that coordinates advertising, packaging, and in-store stimuli. McDonald's marketing strategy promotes a strong image because various elements of its campaign such as Ronald McDonald, playgrounds, sales promotions, and in-store decor promote the image of good service and family values. Elements at variance with an established image cause confusion and a weakening of associations in consumers' memory, as when Cadillac introduced a medium-sized car.

Brand Evaluation

The manner by which consumers evaluate brands also has strategic implications. Evaluative processing, which suggests a more involved consumer, requires the marketer to develop a message closely related to consumer needs. Nonevaluative processing suggests a less-involved consumer. Here, advertisers can use simpler themes and peripheral cues and rely primarily on TV to communicate them.

There are also strategic implications for the types of evaluative processing consumers use. If consumers evaluate brands on an attribute-specific basis, advertising should be informational and present product characteristics that consumers can evaluate easily. Category-based evaluation lends itself more to image-oriented advertising since consumers evaluate the brand as a whole. Symbols and images such as the Marlboro Cowboy or the Apple Computer logo can be used as a shorthand for the brand. These symbols evoke the brand image without having to specify particular attributes of the brand.

Perceived Risk

Marketers often seek competitive advantage by reducing consumers' risk of purchasing their brand. In all cases, marketers attempt to reduce risks by (1) lowering the consequences of a loss or (2) increasing the certainty of the outcome.

Marketers can reduce the consequence of failure by offering warranties, money-back guarantees, and liberal return policies for defective merchandise. Offering products at lower prices or in smaller packages also minimizes consumers' risk in trying a product for the first time. Shimp and Bearden found that these strategies tended to reduce the perception of financial risk but not the perception of performance risk.[51] Apparently, consumers must have experience in using the product to reduce perceived performance risk.

Marketers can attempt to increase the certainty of the purchase outcome in several ways. Endorsements by experts might assure consumers of the certainty of product performance when consumers are not sure of the purchase. Free samples give consumers the opportunity to try new products before a purchase commitment. One reasonable strategy to increase certainty is to convey sufficient information to provide consumers with a sound basis for choice. Technical specifications on performance, complete labeling of ingredients, and nutritional information are all means of providing consumers with more information to judge product performance better.

◆ SOCIETAL IMPLICATIONS OF INFORMATION PROCESSING

As we saw in Chapter 2, consumers have the right to adequate information to give them the capability to make reasonable decisions. Three societal issues emerge in this regard. First, should consumers be given more information? This is what consumer activists propose. Or, in some cases, should consumers be given less? Some researchers who have found that consumers are subject to information overload have proposed this. Second, do consumers sometimes use poor strategies to process complex brand information, and if so, can anything be done to encourage them to use more optimal strategies? Third, evidence of less efficient information processing among younger and older consumers raises the question whether government and/or business organizations have a role in increasing the information processing capabilities of these two groups.

More or Less Information?

Several studies have found that, for some product categories, more information increases consumer confusion and leads to less efficient choice. This may suggest that product information should be limited and kept simple.

Consumer activists would argue that product information such as contents, performance, and price should be made available to consumers on a uniform basis, and consumers should then decide how much information to use. These activists believe it is better to run the risk of too much information and consumer confusion than too little information and a poor choice.

As we saw in Chapter 2, government is taking an increasingly activist view in supporting additional information. The Food and Drug Administration has established rules requiring more information on ingredients and nutritional value and clearer warning labels on packaging. More states are requiring unit pricing information in stores and open dating of perishable items. Business organizations are also showing more willingness to supply detailed product information in ads, brochures, and by direct mail. Some retailers such as Jewel and Shop-Rite stores have introduced in-store consultants to inform shoppers of price and brand alternatives.

There are several compelling reasons to support this trend to more information. First, some consumers will use such information. Unfortunately, older and less-educated consumers are least likely to use product information. Government and business can do more to increase information acquisition by these groups—for example, providing comparative price information for key product categories such as pharmaceuticals and improving transportation to shopping areas.

Second, when consumers use information, they often make more efficient purchases. Several studies have found that consumers who use unit pricing information shift their purchases toward lower-priced goods.[52] Third, providing more information increases consumer confidence. One study found that although only 10 percent of consumers used credit information in buying a durable good, 54 percent said they felt better about knowing the rates and charges.[53]

Compensatory or Noncompensatory Processing?

A second issue is whether consumers use adequate processing strategies, regardless of the amount of information available. Hutchinson and Alba found that in selecting stereo speakers, most consumers used only two or three criteria, despite the availability of a full complement of product information.[54] Similarly, we noted a study by Capon and Burke that found consumers using only 24 percent of available information in buying appliances.[55] Unless consumers are knowledgeable about the product category, such noncompensatory strategies may lead to suboptimal decisions, particularly for expensive and high-risk items like stereo speakers and appliances.

A strong case could be made to encourage consumers to use a wider set of criteria in making decisions for expensive, high-risk products, particularly if consumers lack knowledge and confidence in their choices. Companies can do more to educate consumers in criteria for comparing brands by product features. For example, a computer company could provide prospective buyers an informational brochure explaining how to use criteria such as memory, capacity, and speed in selecting a computer.

Age-Related Information Processing

Sufficient evidence of reduced processing capacities among the very young and very old raises some serious societal issues. Chapter 2 noted that young children generally fail to understand the purpose of commercials and often cannot distinguish between TV programming and commercials. The focus was on ensuring responsible actions by business to avoid taking advantage of children based on their reduced processing abilities.

A related issue is whether responsible advertising strategies can be geared to improving childrens' acquisition of information. For example, Peracchio studied the ability of kindergarten children to learn how to return defective merchandise. She found that their acquisition of information regarding the procedures for such returns was as efficient as older children's when the younger children (1) were repetitively exposed to a single story line, and (2) the information was very explicit.[56] The study suggests that advertisers could use repetitive and explicit information to improve children's acquisition of information as long as there is some assurance that such information is accurate and responsible.

There is also evidence that older consumers process information less efficiently. Studies have found that older consumers cannot retain as many alternatives in memory as can younger consumers and tend to use fewer attributes in evaluating brand alternatives.[57] A study by Cole and Balasubramanian found that when elderly consumers were instructed to select a cereal according to specific nutritional criteria, they were less likely than younger subjects to search for information and to select a cereal based on their needs.[58]

The latter study also found that when elderly consumers were asked to write down information, their processing abilities improved. Further, visual symbols that integrated information such as a Good Housekeeping seal of approval improved the elderly's information processing abilities. The implications are that stores can provide checklists of information that should be considered in buying nutritional or drug items to facilitate information processing by the elderly. Further, companies can develop symbols to connote chunks of information. For example, they could develop a symbol for cholesterol-free food products or use a common symbol to indicate a generic drug item.

SUMMARY

An important part of any consumer's decision process is the acquisition and processing of information. Consumers will acquire more information about products if they are involved in the purchase, see risk in purchasing, have little product knowledge, and see differences among products. Information acquisition is limited by the amount of information consumers can reasonably process. Studies have shown that consumers sometimes are subjected to information overload—that is, too much information—which results in confusion.

Once consumers acquire information, they must process it. To process information, consumers must be able to retain it in and retrieve it from memory. The memory process has short-term and long-term components. Short-term memory acts as a filter to determine what information will be retained in long-term memory. Information stored in long-term memory is organized into schemas, which represent the sets of associations consumers have with brands, products, or companies. Such schemas are the basis for brand or company images.

Consumers retrieve information from long-term memory to evaluate brands. Brand evaluation requires a set of decision rules for comparing brands. Using category-based processing, consumers evaluate brands as a whole and make judgments based on associations in long-term memory. Attribute-specific processing requires consumers to compare brands on specific attributes. A possible outcome of the brand evaluation process is the perception that the purchase will involve financial, social, or performance risks. Consumers seek to reduce risks by buying the same brand, a low-priced brand, or the most popular brand. They can also reduce risk by seeking more information to increase the certainty of a purchase outcome.

Strategic applications were developed from the two key components of information processing—storing information in memory and evaluating brands. Strategic applications from perceived risk were also described.

The chapter concluded by considering the societal implications of information processing. Three issues were considered. First, should more information be provided to consumers, and if so, what should be the role of government and business in providing such information? Second, can consumers be encouraged to use processing strategies that evaluate brands on a wider set of criteria? Third, given the reduced processing abilities of the very young and very old, can business or government play a role in improving their abilities?

In the next two chapters, we consider the results of information processing; namely, the formation of consumer attitudes toward brands and products.

QUESTIONS

1. Which of the following situations would you describe as either (a) ongoing search, (b) purchase-specific search, or (c) passive information acquisition? Why?
   - A consumer listening to a radio ad for life insurance
   - A consumer shopping for a suit to wear to a job interview
   - A consumer reading several magazines dealing with antique furniture
2. What types of sources of information are most likely to be important for each of the following consumers and why?
   - A business school student close to a final decision in purchasing a laptop computer
   - An industrial buyer purchasing electrical cable
   - A consumer first considering various alternatives in selecting life insurance
3. What are the limits of consumers' ability to acquire and process information?
4. How can marketers attempt to overcome the limits you cited in Question 3 above?

5. Consider the two purchasing situations below:
   • A consumer regards cereals as a source of bran and other nutritional ingredients and is aware of brand alternatives and their ingredients. This consumer regards the brand decision for cereals as important, as it is related to health and fitness.
   • Another consumer sees little difference among brands of cereal and buys primarily for taste. This consumer has a low level of information regarding brand alternatives and ingredients and does not associate the purchase of cereals with health and fitness.

   A new brand of cereal containing raisins and nuts and advertised as a product with all-natural ingredients is introduced. What differences might occur between the two consumers in acquiring and processing information on the new cereal?

6. How does short-term memory operate for:
   • The prospective car buyer who first becomes aware of GM's Saturn line?
   • The consumer who sees an ad for Pampers disposable diapers while watching an early evening quiz show?

7. When are consumers most likely to use:
   • Evaluative processing versus nonevaluative processing?
   • Category-based processing versus attribute-specific processing?

8. What are the advertising implications if consumers use category-based processing? Attribute-specific processing?

9. What strategies have you used in buying a car and in selecting a college or business school to:
   • Reduce the consequences of failure?
   • Increase the certainty of the outcome?

10. What are the differences between risk takers and risk avoiders in the ways they deal with perceived risk in the purchasing process?

11. What type of measure of brand evaluation—display boards, observation, or controlled experimentation—would be most appropriate for each of the following studies and why?
    • A cereal company would like to determine the average amount of time shoppers take to look at various brands of cereals before purchasing them.
    • A computer manufacturer would like to determine the types of product attributes consumers use in selecting a laptop computer and the average number of attributes they use in the selection process.
    • A car manufacturer would like to test the hypothesis that informationally oriented advertising is more effective for consumers who are highly involved in car purchases and symbolic or imagery-oriented advertising is more effective for those who are less involved.

12. What are the pros and cons of providing consumers with more information? Under what circumstances should business and government be encouraged to provide consumers with more information?

13. What are the societal issues regarding age-related differences in acquiring and processing information? What are the public policy implications of these differences?

RESEARCH ASSIGNMENTS

1. Develop an information board for automobiles and another information board for cereals. The boards should list at least four brands or models across the top and eight attributes down the side. Show the boards to about ten consumers for each product category. Ask consumers to describe aloud their process of evaluating the brands on each board. On this basis, try to determine if processing is by category or by attribute and, if by attribute, whether it is compensatory or noncompensatory processing.

   At the end of the process of evaluation, ask consumers to complete a short questionnaire to determine (a) demographics, (b) selected lifestyle items, (c) brand or model used, and (d) frequency of usage or number of miles driven in a year.
   - What are the differences in evaluation between the cereals and the autos? Specifically, are consumers more likely to evaluate autos and cereals by category-based or by attribute-based processing? If the latter, are consumers more likely to evaluate each product category by compensatory or noncompensatory processing?
   - Are there differences in evaluation between types of consumers? That is, are certain consumers more likely to evaluate by category and others by attribute? If so, are there differences in the characteristics of category versus attribute evaluators?

2. Some studies have compared perceived risk across product categories. For example, Jacoby and Kaplan studied the risk college students perceive in the purchase of 12 product categories such as cars, life insurance, color TV sets, clothing items, and pharmaceutical products.[59] Using the references in this chapter, develop a measure of perceived risk that incorporates (a) the uncertainty of product performance and (b) the consequences when a product does not meet consumer expectations. In addition, measure the respondent's self-confidence in selecting a brand in the product category. Select a sample of college students and apply the measure of perceived risk and self-confidence to four or five product categories.
   - What are the variations in perceived risk among product categories?
   - What are the variations in perceived risk among students? That is, do certain individuals (risk takers) see less risk than others? If so, are there any differences in characteristics (for example, frequency of use of the product categories, brands purchased, needs emphasized) between those who tend to see more risk and those who tend to see less risk?

NOTES

1. "Too Many Think the Bunny Is Duracell's, Not Eveready's," *The Wall Street Journal* (July 31, 1990), p. B1.

2. "How the Bunny Charged Eveready," *Advertising Age* (April 9, 1990), p. 20.

3. Gabriel Biehal and Dipankar Chakravarti, "Information Accessibility as a Moderator of Consumer Choice," *Journal of Consumer Research,* 10 (June, 1983), pp. 1–14; see also Carolyn L. Costley and Merrie Brucks, "Selective Recall and Information Use in Consumer Preferences," *Journal of Consumer Research,* 18 (March, 1992), pp. 464–474.

4. Joseph W. Alba, Howard Marmorstein, and Amitava Chattopadhyay, "Transitions in Preference Over Time: The Effects of Memory on Message Persuasiveness," *Journal of Marketing Research,* 29 (November, 1992), pp. 406–416.

5. William B. Locander and Peter W. Hermann, "The Effect of Self-Confidence and Anxiety on Information Seeking in Consumer Risk Reduction," *Journal of Marketing Research,* 16 (May, 1979), pp. 268–274.

6. Keith B. Murray, "A Test of Services Marketing Theory: Consumer Information Acquisition Activities," *Journal of Marketing,* 55 (January, 1991), pp. 10–25.

7. Sharon E. Beatty and Scott M. Smith, "External Search Effort: An Investigation Across Several Product Categories," *Journal of Consumer Research,* 14 (June, 1987), pp. 83–95.

8. Narasimhan Srinivasan and Brian T. Ratchford, "An Empirical Test of a Model of External Search for Automobiles," *Journal of Consumer Research,* 18 (September, 1991), pp. 233–241.

9. Peter D. Bennett and Robert M. Mandell, "Prepurchase Information Seeking Behavior of New Car Purchasers—The Learning Hypothesis," *Journal of Marketing Research,* 6 (November, 1969), pp. 430–433.

10. Beatty and Smith, "External Search Effort . . . ," *loc. cit.*

11. W. P. Dommermuth and E. W. Cundiff, "Shopping Goods, Shopping Centers, and Selling Strategies," *Journal of Marketing,* 31 (October, 1967), pp. 32–36; and Joseph W. Newman and Richard Staelin, "Prepurchase Information Seeking for New Cars and Major Household Appliances," *Journal of Marketing Research,* 9 (August, 1972), pp. 249–257.

12. John D. Claxton, Joseph N. Fry, and Bernard Portis, "A Taxonomy of Prepurchase Information Gathering Patterns," *Journal of Consumer Research,* 1 (December, 1974), pp. 35–42.

13. G. Stigler, "The Economics of Information," *Journal of Political Economy,* 69 (1961), pp. 213–225; and Brian T. Ratchford, "Cost-Benefit Models for Explaining Consumer Choice and Information Seeking Behavior," *Management Science,* 28 (February, 1982), pp. 197–212.

14. Thomas S. Robertson, *Innovative Behavior and Communications* (New York: Holt, Rinehart and Winston, 1971).

15. Beatty and Smith, "External Search Effort . . . ," *loc. cit.*

16. Howard Beales, Michael B. Mazis, Steven C. Salop, and Richard Staelin, "Consumer Search and Public Policy," *Journal of Consumer Research,* 8 (June, 1981), pp. 11–22.

17. Jacob Jacoby *et al.* "Pre-Purchase Information Acquisition," in Beverlee B. Anderson, ed., *Advances in Consumer Research,* Vol. 3 (Atlanta: Association for Consumer Research, 1975), pp. 306–314.

18. Noel Capon and Marian Burke, "Individual, Product Class, and Task-Related Factors in Consumer Information Processing," *Journal of Consumer Research,* 7 (December, 1980), pp. 314–326.

19. Compiled from five studies by David L. Loudon and Albert J. Della Bitta, *Consumer Behavior* (New York: McGraw-Hill, 1979), p. 463.

20. W. P. Dommermuth, "The Shopping Matrix and Marketing Strategy," *Journal of Marketing Research,* 2 (May, 1965), pp. 128–132.

21. Newman and Staelin, "Prepurchase Information Seeking . . . ," *loc. cit.*

22. Girish Punj, "Presearch Decision Making in Consumer Durable Purchases," *Journal of Consumer Marketing,* 4 (Winter, 1987), pp. 71–82.

23. Jacob Jacoby, Donald E. Speller, and Carol A. Kohn, "Brand Choice Behavior as a Function of Information Load," *Journal of Marketing Research,* 11 (February, 1974), pp. 63–69.

24. J. Wesley Hutchinson and Joseph W. Alba, "Ignoring Irrelevant Information: Situational Determinants of Consumer Learning," *Journal of Consumer Research,* 18 (December, 1991), pp. 326–345.

25. Kerr, Kevin. "Do Americans Have Too Many Brands?" *Adweek's Marketing Week,* December 9, 1991, p. 14.

26. "Free Choice: When Too Much Is Too Much," *The New York Times* (February 14, 1990), p. C1.

27. C. Whan Park and Henry Assael, "Has the Low Involvement View of Consumer Behavior Been Overstated?" Working Paper, University of Pittsburgh, 1983.

28. Herbert E. Krugman, "Memory Without Recall, Exposure with Perception," *Journal of Advertising Research,* 17 (August, 1977), pp. 7–12.

29. Richard E. Petty, John T. Cacioppo, and David Schumann, "Central and Peripheral Routes to Advertising Effectiveness: The Moderating Role of Involvement," *Journal of Consumer Research,* 10 (September, 1983), pp. 135–146; see also Scott B. Mackenzie and Richard A. Spreng, "How Does Motivation Moderate the Impact of Central and Peripheral Processing on Brand Attitudes and Intentions?" *Journal of Consumer Research,* 18 (March, 1992), pp. 519–529.

30. E. Tulving, "Episodic and Semantic Memory," in E. Tulving and W. Donaldson, eds., *Organization of Memory* (New York: Academic Press, 1972).

31. See Joan Meyers-Levy, "The Influence of a Brand Name's Association Set Size and Work Frequency on Brand Memory," *Journal of Consumer Research,* 16 (September, 1989), pp. 197–207.

32. "Burger King Hypes Ads, but Many People Are Fed Up," *The Wall Street Journal* (January 23, 1986), p. 33.

33. Kevin Lane Keller, "Memory and Evaluation Effects in Competitive Advertising Environments," *Journal of Consumer Research,* 17 (March, 1991), pp. 463–476.

34. Kevin Lane Keller, "Memory Factors in Advertising Evaluations," *Journal of Consumer Research,* 14 (December, 1987), pp. 316–333.

35. Raymond R. Burke and Thomas K. Srull, "Competitive Interference and Consumer Memory for Advertising," *Journal of Consumer Research,* 15 (June, 1988), pp. 55–68.

36. Keller, "Memory and Evaluation Effects . . . ," *loc. cit.*

37. Meryl P. Gardner, Andrew A. Mitchell, and J. Edward Russo, "Strategy-Induced Low Involvement with Advertising," *Journal of Advertising Research.* See also Wayne D. Hoyer, "An Examination of Consumer Decision Making for a Common Repeat Purchase Product," *Journal of Consumer Research,* 11 (December, 1984), pp. 822–828.

38. For a similar distinction, see Mita Sujan, "Consumer Knowledge: Effects on Evaluation Strategies Mediating Consumer Judgments," *Journal of Consumer Research,* 12 (June, 1985), pp. 31–46; see also John G. Lynch, Jr., Howard Marmorstein, and Michael F. Weigold, "Choices from Sets Including Remembered Brands: Use of Recalled Attributes and Prior Overall Evaluations," *Journal of Consumer Research,* 15 (September, 1988), pp. 169–184.

39. Sujan, "Consumer Knowledge . . . ," *loc.cit.*

40. Douglas M. Stayman, Dana L. Alden, and Karen H. Smith, "Some Effects of Schematic Processing on Consumer Expectations and Disconfirmation Judgments," *Journal of Consumer Research,* 19 (September, 1992), pp. 240–255.

41. For example, Denis A. Lussier and Richard W. Olshavsky, "Task Complexity and Contingent Processing in Brand Choice," *Journal of Consumer Research,* 6 (September, 1979), pp. 154–165.

42. Naelm H. Abougomaah, John L. Schlacter, and William Gaidis, "Elimination and Choice Phases in Evoked Set Formation," *Journal of Consumer Marketing,* 4 (Fall, 1987), pp. 67–73.

43. Robert W. Chestnut and Jacob Jacoby, "Behavioral Process Research: Concept and Application in Consumer Decision Making," in G. R. Ungson and D. N. Braunstein, eds., *Decision Making: An Interdisciplinary Inquiry* (Boston: Kent Publishing, 1982), pp. 232–248.

44. Hoyer, "An Examination of Consumer Decision Making for a Common Repeat Purchase Product," *loc. cit.*

45. Petty, Cacioppo, and Schumann, "Central and Peripheral Routes to Advertising Effectiveness . . . ," *loc. cit.*

46. James R. Bettman, "Perceived Risk and Its Components: A Model and Empirical Test," *Journal of Marketing Research,* 10 (May, 1973), pp. 184–190.

47. Thomas S. Robertson, "The Touch-Tone Telephone: Diffusion of an Innovation," in Roger D. Blackwell, James F. Engel, and David T. Kollat, eds., *Cases in*

Consumer Behavior (New York: Holt, Rinehart & Winston, 1969), pp. 274–297.

48. Ted Roselius, "Consumer Rankings of Risk Reduction Methods," *Journal of Marketing,* 35 (January, 1971), pp. 56–61.

49. Michael L. Ray and Alan G. Sawyer, "Repetition in Media Models: A Laboratory Technique," *Journal of Marketing Research,* 8 (February, 1971), pp. 20–29.

50. John Deighton, "How to Solve Problems That Don't Matter: Some Heuristics for Uninvolved Thinking," in Thomas C. Kinnear, ed., *Advances in Consumer Research,* Vol. 11 (Provo, UT: Association for Consumer Research, 1984), pp. 314–319.

51. Terence A. Shimp and William O. Bearden, "Warranty and Other Extrinsic Cue Effects on Consumer's Risk Perceptions," *Journal of Consumer Research,* 9 (June, 1982), pp. 38–46.

52. Clive W. Granger and Andrew Billson, "Consumers' Attitudes Toward Package Size and Price," *Journal of Marketing Research,* 9 (August, 1972), pp. 239–248; and J. Edward Russo, Gene Dreiser, and Sally Miyashita, "An Effective Display of Unit Price Information," *Journal of Marketing,* 39 (April, 1975), pp. 11–19.

53. George S. Day, "Assessing the Effects of Information Disclosure Requirements," *Journal of Marketing,* 40 (April, 1976), pp. 42–52.

54. Hutchinson and Alba, "Ignoring Irrelevant Information . . . ," *loc. cit.*

55. Capon and Burke, "Individual, Product Class, and Task-Related Factors . . . ," *loc. cit.*

56. Laura A. Peracchio, "How Do Young Children Learn to Be Consumers? A Script-Processing Approach," *Journal of Consumer Research,* 18 (March, 1992), pp. 425–440.

57. Irving Janis and Leon Mann, *Decision Making* (New York: Free Press, 1977); and Charles Schaninger and Donald Sciglimpaglia, "The Influence of Cognitive Personality Traits and Demographics on Consumer Information Acquisition," *Journal of Consumer Research,* 8 (September, 1981), pp. 208–216.

58. Catherine A. Cole and Siva K. Balasubramanian, "Age Differences in Consumers' Search for Information: Public Policy Implications," *Journal of Consumer Research,* 20 (June, 1993), pp. 157–169.

59. Jacob Jacoby and Leon B. Kaplan, "The Components of Perceived Risk," in M. Venkatesan, ed., *Proceedings, Third Annual Conference* (Association for Consumer Research, 1972), pp. 382–393.

8

Consumer Attitudes

CHANGING ATTITUDES: CAN AT&T REDEFINE ITSELF AMONG YOUNGER CONSUMERS?

The past two chapters have dealt with how consumers perceive and process information. In this chapter, we explain how consumers develop beliefs about and preferences for brands based on the information they have processed. These beliefs and preferences define consumers' attitudes toward a brand. In turn, their attitudes toward a brand often directly influence whether they will buy it.

The strategic importance of attitudes is illustrated by marketers' attempts to reposition their brands. Such repositioning requires a change in attitudes on the consumers' part. In past chapters, we saw how difficult it can be to reposition a brand when consumer attitudes are fairly entrenched. People Express went under because it failed to change the established attitude that the airline was a low-cost, no-frills alternative to the major carriers. Oldsmobile's attempt to reposition itself as a car for the younger generation with the theme "This is not your father's Olds" only succeeded in alienating its older customer base. However, there have also been classic success stories in repositioning brands—for example, Philip Morris's success in repositioning Miller High Life from an elite beer to a product with a mass-market appeal targeted to heavier beer drinkers with the theme "It's Miller time."

More recently, AT&T is trying to reposition itself among its younger consumers. Whereas older consumers still view AT&T as *the* phone company, attitudes of younger consumers (those under 40) are not nearly as positive. Many have flocked to alternative providers such as Sprint and MCI because they view AT&T as less innovative with fewer service options. AT&T's objective is similar to that of Oldsmobile's—improve attitudes among the younger set without alienating AT&T's older customer base. The stakes in repositioning itself are particularly high, because AT&T's share of the long-distance market slipped from more than 90 percent in 1984 to just over 60 percent in 1992, a sales decrease of over $14 billion per year![1]

The key thrust in changing attitudes among the under 40 group is a new advertising campaign, introduced in 1993, that defines AT&T as an innovative computer and communications company. Whereas past advertising took a very soft image approach in positioning AT&T (consumers shown using the phone in meaningful, personal moments), the newer ads are more modernistic and high-tech. Whether AT&T will be successful in improving attitudes among the younger set while maintaining its loyal customer base remains to be seen.

In this chapter, we consider brand attitudes from the perspectives of the consumer and the marketing manager. The nature, function, and development of brand attitudes are described. Research that establishes a relation between brand attitudes and purchasing behavior is cited. Finally, we consider attitude models that provide a basis by which marketers can evaluate a brand's strength or weakness relative to consumer needs and develop guidelines for advertising and product positioning.

◆ NATURE OF CONSUMER ATTITUDES

Over 50 years ago, Gordon Allport formulated the most frequently used definition of attitudes. He wrote: "Attitudes are learned predispositions to respond to an object or class of objects in a consistently favorable or unfavorable way."[2] **Attitudes** toward brands are consumers' learned tendencies to evaluate brands in a consistently favorable or unfavorable way; that is, consumers' evaluation of a particular brand on an overall basis from poor to excellent.

Brand attitudes are based on the schema of a brand consumers store in long-term memory. A schema of AT&T as being stodgy and old-fashioned has led many younger consumers to choose other long-distance providers. Older consumers are more likely to have a schema of the company associated with reliability, security, and good service. Since these attributes constitute the beliefs many older consumers have of AT&T, they are likely to lead to a positive evaluation of the company and to selection of AT&T as the long-distance provider. As a result, brand beliefs (AT&T provides good service) lead to brand evaluations (I like AT&T) and thus to intended behavior (I plan to use AT&T for long-distance service).

Three Components of Attitudes

The link among brand beliefs, evaluations, and intended behavior will be a main focus of this chapter.[3] Brand beliefs, brand evaluations, and intention to buy define the three components of attitudes shown in Figure 8.1. Brand beliefs are the **cognitive** (or **thinking**) component of attitudes; brand evaluations, the **affective** (or **feeling**) component; and intention to buy, the **conative** (or **action**) component. The link among these three components illustrates the high involvement hierarchy of effects: brand beliefs influence brand evaluations, which influence intention to buy. The assumption in this hierarchy is that these components are then related to behavior; thus, note the dotted line from intention to buy to behavior in Figure 8.1.

As these three attitudinal components play such a central role in marketing strategy, it would be helpful to have a fuller understanding of each of them.

Beliefs

Consumers' beliefs about a brand are the characteristics they ascribe to it. Through marketing research, marketers develop a **vocabulary of product attributes and benefits** similar to the vocabulary a large food company develops for a beverage. (See Table 8.1.) These types of vocabularies are based on the results of a series of **depth interviews** with consumers. Once marketers establish a vocabulary of product attributes and benefits, they include it in a questionnaire and conduct a consumer survey in which they ask respondents to rate brands utilizing the vocabulary. Thus, a study of soft drinks may involve asking consumers to rate various brands on the criteria listed in Table 8.1.

On this basis, consumers may be asked whether a soft drink is sweet, carbonated, nutritional, or thirst-quenching. Such ratings provide the marketer with the means to identify the strengths and weaknesses of the company's brand

▶**FIGURE 8.1**
Three components of attitudes

COGNITIVE COMPONENT

Brand Beliefs

AFFECTIVE COMPONENT

Brand Evaluation

CONATIVE COMPONENT

Intention to Buy

BEHAVIOR

▶**TABLE 8-1**
Vocabulary of brand beliefs for a beverage product

Product Attributes	Product Benefits
Caloric content	Restores energy
Vitamin content	Nutritional
Natural ingredients	Good for the whole family
Sweetness	Gives a lift
Aftertaste	Good at mealtimes
Carbonation	Thirst-quenching

relative to that of the competition. For example, beliefs may show that teenagers regard Pepsi as a sweeter and more carbonated beverage than Coke. If beliefs show weakness, then the marketer might consider a repositioning strategy, similar to what AT&T is doing in attempting to strengthen attitudes among younger consumers.

The vocabulary of attributes in Table 8.1 provides the marketer with only half the equation in understanding beliefs. A consumer may rate a soft drink very sweet, but this rating does not mean the consumer wants a sweet drink. The other half of the beliefs equation requires determining the value a consumer places on attributes such as sweet and refreshing. Two consumers can rate a soft drink "very sweet," but one puts a high value on sweetness, whereas the other does not. As a result, the first consumer will have a more positive attitude toward the brand compared to that of the second consumer, despite similar beliefs.

This evaluative component is important in segmenting consumers because it shows what they want. In this case, it would be logical to define a "sweet" segment in the soft drink market.

Overall Brand Evaluation

The second attitude component, the affective or feeling component, represents consumers' overall evaluation of the brand. Beliefs about a brand are multidimensional because they represent the brand attributes consumers perceive. The affective component, however, is one-dimensional. Consumers' overall evaluation of a brand can be measured by rating the brand from "poor" to "excellent" or from "prefer least" to "prefer most." If we accept the basic attitudinal model in Figure 8.1, brand evaluations result from brand beliefs. The reason teens have a positive attitude toward Pepsi is their belief that it is a sweeter drink *and* the high value most teens put on sweetness.

Of the three components, brand evaluation is central to the study of attitudes because it summarizes consumers' predisposition to be favorable or unfavorable to the brand. Brand beliefs are relevant only to the extent that they influence brand evaluations, which are the primary determinants of intended behavior. In fact, brand evaluation conforms to the definition of brand attitudes as a "tendency to evaluate brands in a favorable or unfavorable way."

Therefore, rather than speaking of three components of attitudes in the remainder of this chapter, we will refer to brand attitudes as the overall evaluation of a brand. Brand beliefs influence attitudes, and attitudes influence intention to buy.

Intention to Buy

The third attitude component, the conative dimension, is consumers' tendency to act toward an object; and this is generally measured in terms of intention to buy. Measuring buying intent is particularly important in developing marketing strategy.

Marketing managers frequently test the elements of the marketing mix—alternative product concepts, ads, packages, or brand names—to determine what is most likely to influence purchase behavior. Tests of these alternatives are conducted under artificially controlled circumstances that try to hold all factors constant except the marketing stimuli being tested. Consumers viewing alternative ads or trying various product formulations are asked about their intentions to buy after experiencing these marketing stimuli. Marketers regard the alternative producing the highest buying intent as the best choice. In the absence of actual buying behavior, management uses the closest substitute, intention to buy, to determine the effectiveness of the components of the marketing mix.

As we will see, there are times when the linkages in Figure 8.1 may not hold. However, these relationships occur frequently enough to make them important determinants of marketing strategy. Much of this chapter focuses on these linkages.

Strategic Implications of the Three Components

Figure 8.1 suggests that marketers should influence consumer beliefs to encourage positive brand attitudes and to increase the chances consumers intend to buy. Most marketing strategies adhere to this hierarchy by advertising product features and benefits to influence beliefs. That is the case with AT&T's attempt to convey the belief that it is a progressive and innovative computer and communications company. As we noted, younger consumers adopting these beliefs are more likely to have positive attitudes about the company and to use AT&T.

Marketers can also directly appeal to brand evaluations without necessarily influencing beliefs. An attempt to influence brand evaluations requires the use of symbols and imagery to evoke positive feelings and emotions about the brand. In contrast, influencing beliefs tends to be more informationally based because such strategies focus on product features.

Toyota uses both approaches as shown in Exhibit 8.1. The ad for the Corolla is informationally based and tries to influence beliefs about the brand. The ad for the Celica is strictly image oriented. It makes no reference to product features. Rather, it tries to influence a consumer's evaluation of the brand by establishing a mood of luxury. In this case, belief formation is not a prerequisite for developing positive attitudes.

The 1980s and 1990s have seen an increase in the use of such feeling oriented as opposed to informational ads. Why? Because when marketers have no unique claims to make based on features and benefits, they can rely on feelings to sway consumers. Toyota might have decided it could say little new and unique about the Celica, so it decided to use image and symbolism to try to create positive attitudes. In the last ten years, we have seen greater standardization in many product categories. Marketers find it increasingly difficult to gain a competitive advantage by making unique claims about their products. Thus, direct appeals to the affective component of attitudes have increased.

▶**EXHIBIT 8.1**
Influencing beliefs and brand evaluations
Source: Courtesy of Toyota

Influencing beliefs   *Influencing brand evaluations*

Marketers can also try to appeal to the third component of attitudes—the intention to buy—without influencing beliefs and brand evaluation. A sharp reduction in price or a special coupon offer may be inducement enough for consumers to try a less-favored brand. Beliefs and attitudes about the chosen brand do not have to change for consumers to establish an intention to buy.

Measuring the Attitudinal Components

The components of attitudes must be measured reliably if they are to form the basis for marketing strategies. Since these are qualitative variables, this is a difficult task. The most common approach is to develop rating scales so consumers can identify the degree to which they think a brand has certain attributes (beliefs), the degree to which they prefer certain brands (brand evaluations), and their intentions.

Using colas as an example, Table 8.2 shows one or more rating scales to measure these attitudinal components.

▶**TABLE 8-2**
Measures of Attitudinal Components*

Brand Beliefs (b)

b_1: How likely is it that I will get a highly carbonated cola if I buy Brand A?
Very likely   — — — — — — — —   Very unlikely

b_2: Rate Brand A by the following characteristics:
Highly carbonated   — — — — — — — —   Not at all carbonated

b_3: Indicate how well Brand A is described by the following characteristics:
Highly carbonated
Describes very well   — — — — — — — —   Does not describe at all

---

Attribute Evaluations (e)

e_1: Indicate how you would evaluate the following:

A highly carbonated cola:
Very good   — — — — — — — —   Very bad

e_2: Indicate the degree of satisfaction you would get from the following:
Highly carbonated
Very satisfying   — — — — — — — —   Not at all satisfying

e_3: Think of your ideal brand of cola and rate it on the characteristics listed below:
Highly carbonated   — — — — — — — —   Not at all carbonated

Overall Brand Evaluations (A)

A_1: Rate Brand A as follows:
I like it very much   — — — — — — — —   I don't like it at all

A_2: Rate Brand A as follows:
Very favorable   — — — — — — — —   Very unfavorable

A_3: Which of the following brands do you prefer most? Which of the brands do you prefer second, third, (and so forth)?
[Key brands of cola would be listed.]

A_4: Suppose you could pick ten free cans of cola and had the choice of any combination of brands. Which brands would you pick? How many of each brand? (Make sure the total adds up to ten cans.)
(Key brands would be listed and respondents instructed to place any number of cans next to each brand so the total allocated equals ten.)

Intention to Buy (BI)

What is the likelihood you would buy Brand A the next time you purchase cola?
Definitely will buy   ____
Probably will buy   ____
Might buy   ____
Probably will not buy   ____
Definitely will not buy ____
(Key cola brands will be listed and respondents asked their intention to buy.)

---

*Scales for brand beliefs and attribute evaluations are developed for a number of characteristics such as sweet, carbonated, good to serve guests, and so forth.

Brand Beliefs (b)

Measuring beliefs first requires determining the attributes and benefits that might make up consumers' schema for soft drinks (such as those in Table 8.1). Typically, 10 to 15 attributes will be identified in depth interviews such as carbonation and sweetness.

Three measures of beliefs (b) are shown. Measure b_1 rates brand attributes on a probability basis using a seven-point scale. Measure b_2 is a scaling device known as the **semantic differential**. It uses bipolar adjectives on a seven-point scale to measure brand beliefs. The third scale measures beliefs about the accuracy of a brand's description—for example, whether it is accurate to describe a brand as highly carbonated.

Each of these rating scales approaches the measurement of beliefs differently, suggesting there is no standard measure. The semantic differential scale (b_2) is the most widely used because it is easy to construct and administer. Marketers can quickly determine the image of their brand by how consumers position it on various bipolar adjectives.

Attribute Evaluations (e)

Although attribute evaluations are not cited as one of the three components of attitudes in Figure 8.1, they must be measured to understand brand beliefs. As we noted, rating a brand on degree of carbonation must be coupled with measuring the consumer's desire for carbonation. Three scales are shown to rate attribute evaluations. The first (e_1) asks consumers to rate each attribute from "very good" to "very bad"; the second (e_2) from "very satisfying" to "not at all satisfying." The third scale asks consumers to visualize an ideal cola. A semantic differential scale is used to rate this ideal brand.

Overall Brand Evaluations (A)

The affective component of attitudes—overall brand evaluations—can be measured in various ways. The first scale measures the likability of the brand; the second, the degree to which it is favored. A third possibility is to rank the preferences for various brands from most to least preferred (measure A_3). This scale, known as a **rank order of preference scale**, is *nonmetric*. That is, the values have *ordinal* meaning in the sense of "better than" or "more than." The other scales cited above have *metric* meaning in the sense that a rating of "2" is equidistant from "1" and "3." As a result, they are known as **equal interval scales**.

The fourth measure of brand evaluations asks consumers to assume they will be given ten free cans of cola and can select any combination of brands they want. The degree to which consumers select a brand is a measure of preference. This scale is known as a **constant sum scale** because the amount selected must always add to the same number—in this case, ten. The constant sum scale is known as a *ratio* scale because it permits ratio comparisons. A consumer who picks six cans of Pepsi and three of Coke has selected twice as much Pepsi as Coke. The question is whether one can assume that this rating means the consumer prefers Pepsi twice as much as Coke.

The constant sum scale, semantic differential, and rank order of preference are the three major categories of scales. The constant sum scale has ratio properties, the semantic differential is an equal interval scale, and the rank order of preference is an ordinal scale.

Buying Intentions

Buying intentions are generally measured on a scale from "definitely will buy" to "definitely will not buy." The percent of consumers saying they will definitely buy is a closely watched figure because studies have shown a close relationship between this percentage and subsequent trial of a new product.

Behavior

Since the attitudinal components are assumed to be related to behavior, it is important to consider how consumers' behavior is measured. In the past, behavior was measured in consumer surveys on a self-reported basis. The question asked was "What brand did you last purchase?" with additional details on quantity and price paid.

The increasing availability of scanner data (bar-coded merchandise that is laser-scanned at the checkout counter) has made it possible to use more objective measures of behavior. Research companies have established scanner panels—that is, a sample of consumers who use an identification card when they purchase. These same consumers can then be asked attitudinal questions like those in Table 8.2, thus linking survey-derived attitudinal questions to scanner-derived background data.

Attitudes and Consumer Involvement

The influence of beliefs on attitudes and attitudes on behavior largely depends on consumers' involvement with the purchase. The greater the consumers' involvement, the stronger these linkages are.

In Chapter 5, we saw that when consumers are involved, attitudes are part of a hierarchy of effects that lead to a purchase decision: Consumers first form beliefs about a brand, then develop a brand attitude, and then decide whether or not to buy it. Figure 8.1 depicts a high involvement hierarchy.

Much of the discussion in this chapter assumes an involved consumer. That is because attitudes do not have as central a role in low involvement as in high involvement decisions. As we saw in Chapter 5, consumers frequently buy low involvement products without forming a definite attitude about the brand. Instead, they form beliefs about a brand in a passive way. Therefore, any link between beliefs and attitudes is weak. There is also a weak relationship between attitudes and behavior for low involvement purchases. If consumers buy, they frequently evaluate the brand after the fact. Attitudes do not predict behavior as well in low involvement purchases as in the high involvement case because well-defined attitudes do not generally precede behavior.

Several studies have found support for a diminished role of attitudes for less involved consumers. Beatty and Kahle identified consumers who were more and less involved with soft drinks. Attitudes influenced behavior for the more involved individuals, but they did not play any significant role in influencing behavior for less involved consumers.[4] In another study, MacKenzie and Spreng motivated consumers to process advertising information and thereby increased these consumers' involvement in the task. They found that attitudes were more closely related to purchase intentions for the motivated group as compared to those of the unmotivated group.[5]

Although the attitudes consumers form after a low involvement purchase may be weakly held, they may still influence future purchases. A consumer who tries a new paper towel and decides it is not as good as his or her regular brand is unlikely to buy it again. This overall evaluation is important information for the marketer, even if this consumer is not very involved with the brand.

Attitude Development

To understand the role of attitudes in consumer behavior, we must understand how they develop and the functions they play. Attitudes develop over time through a learning process affected by family influences, peer group influences, information, experience, and personality.

Family Influences

The family is an important influence on purchase decisions. Regardless of their tendency to rebel in teenage years, children have a high correlation between their attitudes and those of their parents. As Bennett and Kassarjian note, "Attitudes toward personal hygiene, preferences for food items, attitudes toward boiled vegetables or fried food, and beliefs about the medicinal value of chicken soup are similarly acquired (from parents)."[6]

This influence is demonstrated in some advertising themes. For instance, Johnson & Johnson once advertised its baby powder by portraying a mother using it on her daughter's wedding day and tearfully reminiscing about its earlier use. Parental influence is especially apparent in attitudes toward candy. If parents used candy as a punishment or reward for their children, in later years those children as adults have subconscious guilt feelings about eating candy.[7] Thus, some advertising tries to alleviate guilt feelings by making positive associations with candy.

Peer Group Influences

Many studies have shown pervasive group influence on purchasing behavior. Katz and Lazarsfeld found peer groups are much more likely than advertising to influence attitudes and purchasing behavior.[8] Coleman found that socially integrated doctors who valued peer group norms accepted a new drug faster.[9] Arndt found that socially integrated consumers accepted a new coffee product sooner.[10] In each of these studies, group norms influenced product attitudes.

Information and Experience

Consumers' past experiences influence their brand attitudes. According to learning theory, such experiences condition future behavior, but brand loyalty will quickly end if the brand does not perform well enough. Therefore, information is also an important attitude determinant. For example, knowing that a pain reliever has a newer, faster-acting formula may result in a more favorable evaluation of the brand and may induce consumers to switch.

Personality

Consumers' personalities affect their attitudes. Traits such as aggression, extroversion, submissiveness, or authoritarianism may influence attitudes toward brands and products. An aggressive individual may be likely to be involved in competitive sports and will buy the most expensive equipment in an attempt to excel. In such a case, attitudes toward sports equipment are a function of personality.

Functions of Attitudes

Understanding the **functions of attitudes** means understanding how they serve the individual. Daniel Katz proposed four classifications of attitude functions:[11]

- Utilitarian function.
- Value-expressive function.
- Ego-defensive function.
- Knowledge function.

Utilitarian Function

The utilitarian function of attitudes guides consumers in achieving desired benefits. For example, a consumer who considers safety and immediate relief the most important criteria in selecting a pain reliever will be directed to brands that fulfill these benefits. Conversely, in their utilitarian role, attitudes will direct consumers away from brands unlikely to fulfill their needs. Auto advertising reflects the utilitarian function of attitudes when it features performance characteristics.

Exhibit 8.2 shows examples of advertising's use of each of the four functions of attitudes. The ad for Pirelli is an example of the utilitarian function. If a consumer values high-performance tires, this appeal will enhance the brand's utility.

▶**EXHIBIT 8.2**

Use of attitudinal functions in advertising

Sources: (upper left) Courtesy of Pirelli Armstrong Tire Corporation; (upper right) Courtesy of AT&T; (lower left) © The Procter & Gamble Company. Used with permission.

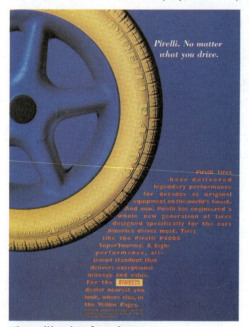

The utilitarian function

The knowledge function

The ego-defensive function

The value-expressive function

Value-Expressive Function

Attitudes can express consumers' self-images and value systems, particularly for a high involvement product. The self-image of an individual purchasing a sports car, for example, may be of a hard-driving, domineering person who likes to gain the upper hand. Aggressiveness may manifest itself in purchasing a car that fits this image. Likewise, the individual who dresses conservatively like everyone else where he or she works has accepted the values of conservatism and wealth as expressions of success.

Advertisers often appeal to the value-expressive nature of attitudes by implying that use or purchase of a certain item will lead to self-enhancement, achievement, or independence. In this manner, advertisers are appealing to a large segment who value these self-expressive traits. The ad in Exhibit 8.2 for That Man cologne by Revlon is an example. It suggests that the user is a confident, self-aware, warm individual.

Ego-Defensive Function

Attitudes protect the ego from anxieties and threats. Consumers purchase many products, like mouthwashes, to avoid anxiety-producing situations. Most individuals use mouthwashes to avoid bad breath rather than to cure it. Advertising capitalizes on the fears of social ostracism by demonstrating greater social acceptance through use of certain products. As a result, consumers develop positive attitudes toward brands associated with social acceptance, confidence, and sexual desirability. The ad for Head and Shoulders in Exhibit 8.2 is an example. Using Head and Shoulders avoids the embarrassment of flaking from dry scalp.

Knowledge Function

Attitudes help consumers organize the mass of information they are exposed to daily. Consumers sort all of the messages, ignoring the less-relevant information. The knowledge function also reduces uncertainty and confusion. Advertising that provides information about new brands or new characteristics of existing brands is valuable for the information it provides. The ad for AT&T in Exhibit 8.2 informs business customers of three new plans: one that provides discounts on calls, another that helps prevent unauthorized calling card usage, and a third that helps track phone charges more easily.

In summary, attitudes have different functions. The function that is served will affect the individual's overall evaluation of an object.[12] For example, two individuals having equally favorable attitudes toward Listerine mouthwash will vary markedly in the nature of these attitudes, depending on whether they reflect a utilitarian function (Listerine freshens my mouth) or an ego-defensive function (Listerine avoids bad breath). Trying to influence the utilitarian consumer that Listerine avoids bad breath would be as ineffective as trying to influence the ego-oriented consumer that Listerine freshens one's mouth.

Further, it is important to realize that attitudes can fulfill more than one function. For example, brand attitudes can help consumers judge the value of information while at the same time guide consumers to achieve desired benefits. A consumer who evaluates alternative VCR models by the number of events that can be programmed will be guided to such information (the knowledge function) and will evaluate brand attitudes based on this information (the utilitarian function).

◆ ROLE OF ATTITUDES IN DEVELOPING MARKETING STRATEGY

Marketers define and measure attitudes toward their brands because attitudes can help them identify benefit segments, develop new products, and formulate and evaluate promotional strategies.

Define Benefit Segments

Market segments can be defined by the benefits consumers desire. These benefits identify the key product attributes marketers should use to influence consumers. Kellogg's successfully segmented the cereal market into nutrition, taste, and weight-watcher segments and positioned brands such as Common Sense Oat Bran, All Bran, and Special K to these segments.

In the car market, segments are defined by economy, performance, and luxury. Marketers attempt to influence consumer attitudes in the performance segment by citing key features such as acceleration, horsepower, and fuel efficiency. While price and service costs are the primary criteria to emphasize for the economy segment, marketers cannot ignore performance criteria.

Develop New Products

Attitudes are crucial in evaluating alternative positionings for new products. For example, when Motorola was developing cellular phones, it could have positioned them as an improvement over existing carphones (less static and interference), as a means of providing mobile communication (both as a hand-held device and in a car), or as a cost-effective means of communication compared to other alternatives. The proper positioning depends on the benefits the defined target group desires—whether it is salespeople on the road, top corporate executives in transit, or doctors requiring immediate communications with medical staff.

The key question is what attributes each group emphasizes and how they rate cellular phones on these attributes. For example, doctors might emphasize hand-held portability, whereas salespeople might emphasize static-free communication while in a car. The target group must rate a new product or concept on such key evaluative criteria, and the marketer tries to position the new product based on those criteria that the target group emphasizes. If the product's most favorable ratings are from doctors because of its portability, this segment would be a logical target for the product.

Similarly, marketers must rate products on these same evaluative criteria when they are introduced into a test market prior to launch as well as when they have been on the market for some time. When a company tests a new product, it does so first by presenting a description of the product in words and pictures. Evaluating a description of a product is very different from evaluating the product in use. Motorola would have to determine whether expectations were met on key criteria such as portability, clarity of communication, and convenience after doctors used cellular telephones. The product's evaluation may change over time as desired benefits change and new products enter the market, so periodic reassessment of brand attitudes is essential.

Develop and Evaluate Promotional Strategies

Attitudes are important in developing promotional strategies. If doctors emphasize portability and convenience as desired benefits of cellular telephones, these are the benefits marketers must emphasize in advertising and promotional literature to create favorable attitudes among the target group. Communication of these benefits as well as their subsequent fulfillment by the product will result in positive attitudes toward Motorola's cellular telephone. Advertising's role is to communicate the benefits the product can deliver.

Attitudes are also important in evaluating the effectiveness of advertising messages. Television commercials and print ads are frequently judged by how large and how favorable an attitude shift they produce. Brand attitudes are measured before and after exposure to a commercial in a controlled environment. Marketers use any changes in brand attitudes to evaluate the commercial's effectiveness.

Marketers also use attitudes to evaluate advertising campaigns over time to determine whether the attitudes are being maintained or whether they are changing favorably or unfavorably. Advertising campaigns may have attitude change as a specific objective. Cadillac's introduction of a medium-sized car required careful tracking by the company to determine whether such a change would alienate its core market by weakening associations with prestige. The ad campaign required a modification of beliefs (Cadillac is no longer a large car) while maintaining current favorable attitudes (I like Cadillac because it represents prestige and luxury).

◆ RELATIONSHIP BETWEEN BELIEFS AND ATTITUDES

The key concern of marketers is the relationships shown in Figure 8.1; namely, how consumer beliefs influence brand attitudes and how consumer attitudes influence behavior.[13] The relationship among beliefs, attitudes, and behavior is important to marketers because it indicates the success of marketing strategies. If advertising is successful in establishing positive beliefs about a brand, consumers are more likely to evaluate the brand positively and to buy it. Satisfaction with the brand strengthens positive attitudes and increases the probability that consumers will repurchase it.

STRATEGIC APPLICATIONS OF CONSUMER BEHAVIOR

Volvo: Doing Too Good A Job In Forming Consumer Attitudes

Can a company do too good a job in forming consumer attitudes and molding its brand image? Volvo seems to think so. Since 1968, it has used a singular theme in positioning its cars—safety. However, the safety image has begun to be counterproductive for Volvo for two reasons. First, whereas the safety theme was unique to Volvo in the 1970s, this was no longer the case in the 1980s and 1990s. Other car makers began positioning their models based on safety, particularly with the advent of air bags.

A second problem was that Volvo's safety theme was so persistent that consumers saw little else and began associating Volvo with attributes such as "plodding" and "sluggish." Safety became a two-sided sword in forming consumer attitudes. Partly as a result, Volvo's 1992 sales in the United States were half what they were in 1986.

Volvo's answer is to lampoon its safety image. The company introduced its sporty 850 model in 1993 with a commercial showing a couple driving a sturdy tank and the tag line "Driving a Volvo usually inspires a certain sense of safety." (See Exhibit 8.3.) Other ads appeal directly to consumer feelings by showing a red Volvo zooming along a desert field (an approach similar to the Celica ad in Exhibit 8.1). Volvo is not trying to negate its association with safety; rather, it is trying to establish a broader image (that is, a broader schema) in consumers' minds.

However, there is a risk in Volvo's strategy. In lampooning its image Volvo may in fact be reminding consumers of associations with plodding and sluggish. Further, if Volvo's image is too entrenched, it may face the same hard lesson learned by People Express Airlines and Oldsmobile: that changing entrenched attitudes is difficult. Volvo may just have done too good a job in linking its cars to safety.

Source: "Volvo Seeks to Soft-Pedal Safety Image," *The Wall Street Journal* (March 16, 1993), p. B7.

In this section, we discuss the relationship between beliefs and brand attitudes by considering two theories that focus on this relationship: Heider's balance theory and Fishbein's multiattribute theory. In the next section, we consider the relationship between attitudes and behavior.

Heider's Balance Theory

Heider's **balance theory** is so named because it maintains that people seek to achieve balance between their thoughts (beliefs) and feelings (evaluations).[14]

A good illustration of how the balance theory operates occurred when J. C. Penney attempted to upgrade its image by contracting to carry Halston's designer line of clothes. Many consumers had a positive image of Halston but a negative image of Penney (as shown in the top left triangle in Figure 8.2). When Halston began selling at Penney's (represented by a plus between Halston and Penney), this relationship created an imbalance (a positive object linked to a more negative object). Two pluses and a minus produce a minus, leaving an imbalance in consumers' minds. Penney hoped that consumers would resolve this imbalance by developing a more favorable image of its stores (the triangle in the upper right). What actually happened was that many consumers maintained their image of Penney but developed a more negative image of Halston (lower triangle). This image shift created balance in consumers' cognitive system (two minuses and a plus produce a plus), but not the balance Penney intended.

One of the problems with balance theory is that it presents attitudes in absolute, rather than relative, terms. What actually happened in the above example is that many consumers developed somewhat more positive attitudes toward Penney and much more negative attitudes toward Halston, which created balance. The actual result was similar to the bottom triangle in Figure 8.2.

Balance theory conforms to a basic behavioral principle of **cognitive consistency**. This principle states that consumers value harmony between their

EXHIBIT 8.3
Volvo debunks its safety image

▶**FIGURE 8.2**
Illustration of balance
theory

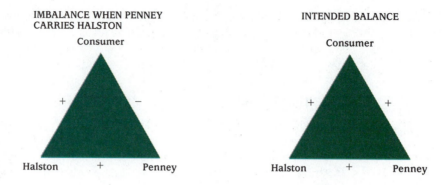

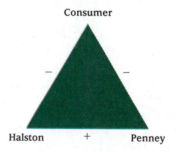

beliefs and evaluations. If one is inconsistent with the other, consumers will
change their attitudes to create harmony in their cognitive structure. Research
supports the idea that consistency exists between beliefs and brand evaluations.
In a study of six consumer goods, Sheth and Talarzyck found that brand ratings on specific attributes such as taste, price, nutrition, and packaging were
closely related to overall evaluation of the brand.[15] Other studies have also
found a link between brand beliefs and overall evaluations.[16]

However, there are cases when beliefs and overall evaluations may not be
related—for example, if beliefs are not relevant to consumers' decisions. The
belief that McDonald's is a good place for the family and has quick service is
not particularly relevant for the single consumer who likes leisurely dining.
These beliefs may be positive, but they do not enter into this consumer's evaluation of restaurant alternatives. This lack of association between beliefs and
evaluations does not violate balance theory, since balance theory assumes that
beliefs have to be relevant if consumers want to achieve balance.

Fishbein's Multiattribute Model

Fishbein's **multiattribute model** of attitudes[17] describes attitude formation as
a function of consumer beliefs about the attributes and benefits of a brand.
Fishbein's model allows marketers to diagnose the strengths and weaknesses

of their brands relative to those of the competition by determining how consumers evaluate brand alternatives on important attributes. In so doing, marketers can apply multiattribute models directly to vocabularies of attributes used to evaluate specific brands.

Fishbein's model is shown in Figure 8.3. It states that an attitude (*A*) toward an object (*O*) depends on consumers' beliefs (*b*) that the object has certain attributes (*i*) and on the evaluation (*e*) of these product attributes (*i*). That is,

$$A_O = \Sigma b_i \times e_i$$

As shown in Figure 8.3, consumers start with the evaluation of certain attributes (a medicinal tasting mouthwash is good for you). Consumers then form beliefs as to whether an object has that attribute (Listerine has a medicinal taste). Attitudes toward the object are the sum total of beliefs and values for not just one attribute, but for all relevant attributes. Thus, a consumer might rate Listerine more favorably because it has a medicinal taste and gives the

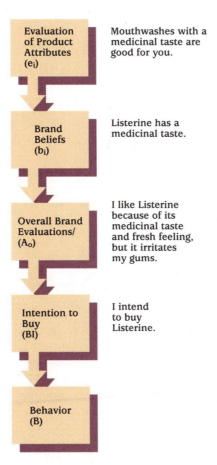

▶**FIGURE 8.3**
Fishbein's multiattribute model

mouth a fresh feeling, both of which this consumer considers desirable attributes. At the same time, the consumer might rate Listerine less favorably on certain other important attributes such as irritation to the gums.

As a result, Fishbein's model is a compensatory model of brand attitudes. That is, consumers can compensate the weakness of a brand on one attribute by the strength on another. All of the attributes are summed to determine the favorability or unfavorability of the attitude toward the brand. On balance, the fact that Listerine is rated positively based on its medicinal taste and refreshing feeling but negatively because of irritation to the gums should produce a somewhat positive overall evaluation of the brand.

As an example of the application of Fishbein's model, assume that consumers are first asked to rate the value of two attributes in selecting a soft drink, sweetness and carbonation, using a semantic differential scale (measure e_2 in Table 8.2) as follows:

Indicate how satisfied you would be with:

A strongly carbonated cola:

| Very satisfied | X | __ | __ | __ | __ | __ | __ | Very dissatisfied |

A sweet cola:

| Very satisfied | __ | X | __ | __ | __ | __ | __ | Very dissatisfied |

They are then asked to rate two brands on these same attributes, again using a semantic differential scale (rating b_2 in Table 8.2) as follows:

BRAND A

| Strong carbonation | __ | __ | __ | __ | __ | X | __ | Weak carbonation |
| Sweet | __ | __ | X | __ | __ | __ | __ | Not sweet |

BRAND B

| Strong carbonation | __ | X | __ | __ | __ | __ | __ | Weak carbonation |
| Sweet | __ | __ | __ | __ | X | __ | __ | Not sweet |

The X's above show one consumer's ratings. This consumer likes a strongly carbonated, sweet cola (evaluation of attributes). Fishbein's model would predict that Brand B is preferred over Brand A (evaluation of brands) because it is more carbonated, even though it is less sweet (beliefs about Brands A and B). In other words, the carbonation of Brand B compensated for its lack of sweetness, which produces a positive attitude and a preference for Brand B over Brand A.

Fishbein's multiattribute model is linked to the traditional hierarchy of effects shown in Figure 8.1. The sum total of desired attributes (e_i) and brand beliefs (b_i) influence brand evaluations (A_O). Fishbein's model also states a linkage between brand evaluations and intended or actual behavior: A positive (negative) attitude toward a brand will increase (decrease) the likelihood that consumers intend to buy it. Positive buying intentions are likely to lead to actual behavior. Therefore:

$BI \sim A_O$ That is, buying intentions are a function of brand attitudes (evaluations).

$B \sim BI$ That is, behavior is a function of buying intentions.

Although the attitude-to-behavior link completes the model, the key is not so much this link but, rather, the link between beliefs and evaluations that explains attitude formation. Nonetheless, without a link between attitude and behavior, Fishbein's model would be irrelevant for marketers.

In the next section, we consider the key attitude-to-behavior link.

◆ RELATIONSHIP BETWEEN ATTITUDES AND BEHAVIOR

If attitudinal models are to be strategically relevant, they must show some link between attitudes and behavior. Both the traditional hierarchy of effects and Fishbein's model link attitudes to behavioral intentions. (See the link between the affective and conative components in Figure 8.1.)

Fishbein's Theory of Reasoned Action

In an attempt to better explain the link between attitudes and behavior, Fishbein modified his multiattribute model. The resulting **theory of reasoned action** proposes that to predict behavior more accurately, it is more important to determine the person's attitude to that behavior than to the object of behavior.[18] That is, it is more important to determine an individual's attitude toward buying a Pepsi, a Saturn car, or a Zenith TV than it is to measure attitudes toward these individual brands. The appropriate attitude measurement should be based on the act of purchasing or using a brand (A_{act}), not on the brand itself (A_o). It is the consumer's act of purchasing and, ultimately, consuming the product that determines satisfaction. The attitude toward the object may not be a valid basis for gauging attitudes. A consumer may have a very positive attitude toward a Rolls-Royce but a negative attitude toward buying one because of the price. In Fishbein's words:

A woman might believe that "high pile" carpeting is "warm," "comfortable," "luxurious," and "prestigious," and since she positively evaluates those attributes, she is likely to have a positive attitude toward "high pile carpeting." However, what do you think the consequences of buying high pile carpeting are for that woman if she has two dogs, a cat, and three children under nine?[19]

A second modification in the model was to define beliefs as the perceived consequences of an action rather than the perceived attributes of a brand. Rather than rating a toothpaste brand on attributes such as "whitens teeth" and "freshens breath," consumers would rate a brand based on the likelihood that their teeth would be whiter or their breath fresher *if they used it*. The distinction is subtle—the difference between rating a brand in general and rating it if you use it—but it could be important. For example, a person might rate a certain car as safe. However, if asked if it was safe enough for her to drive with her baby as a passenger, she might say no. Consumers' beliefs are likely to differ when asked to rate a product in the context of their own personal use rather than in general.

Fishbein developed a third modification in his model because of mixed results in relating beliefs and evaluation to behavior. He concluded that other elements must also influence behavior. Since family and peer group norms are so important in shaping attitudes, he introduced social influences into his model. Two social elements were introduced: normative beliefs and the motivation to comply with them. Normative beliefs may be represented by the following measure:

My family thinks I:

| Should buy | | | | | | | Should not |
| Brand X | __ | __ | __ | __ | __ | __ | __ | buy Brand X |

The motivation to comply could be measured by this scale:

I want to							I do not want
do what my							to do what my
family thinks							family thinks
I should							I should do
do regarding							regarding
Brand X	__	__	__	__	__	__	__	Brand X

Figure 8.4 illustrates the theory of reasoned action, which predicts intentions and behavior better than does the original model. In a review of studies, Ryan and Bonfield concluded that attitudes toward purchasing a brand were more highly correlated with behavior than were attitudes toward the brand itself.[20] Wilson, Matthews, and Harvey measured intentions and behavior for toothpaste purchases using the original and extended Fishbein models.[21] They also found that attitudes toward the purchase of a brand were more closely related to behavior than were attitudes toward the brand. A study by Knox and Chernatony of buyers of mineral water confirmed that using attitudes toward purchasing was a good predictor of subsequent behavior.[22]

▶**FIGURE 8.4**
Fishbein's theory of
reasoned action

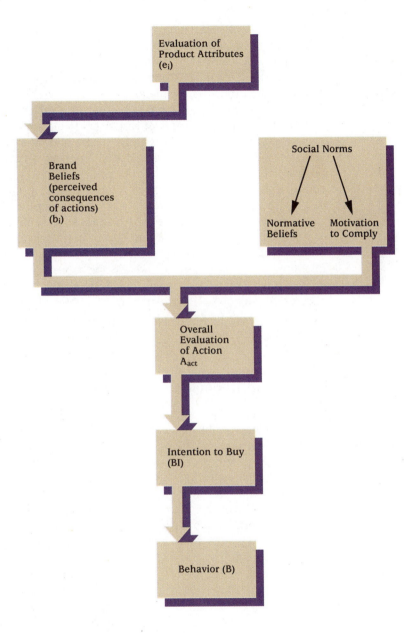

Studies of the Relationship
of Attitudes to Behavior

Various studies have confirmed an association between attitudes and behavior.
One study involved consumer attitudes toward and consumption of 19 brands
in 7 product categories.[23] The study found a strong relationship among changes

in beliefs, overall evaluation of the brand, and changes in a brand's market share. For example, a 4-percent increase in the rating of a brand on economy (a belief) was followed by a 2.5-percent increase in the overall rating of the brand (evaluation) and a 5-percent increase in the brand's share of users (behavior). The study supports the hierarchy of effects, as beliefs about economy influenced overall brand evaluations, which in turn influenced behavior.

American Express's study of card users found a strong relationship between changes in the overall evaluation of the card and intended usage. Among those consumers whose attitudes toward the American Express card became more positive, about 60 percent said they would increase card usage. Among those consumers with no attitude change, only 2 percent said they would increase card usage. Among those consumers with a more negative attitude toward American Express, over three-fourths said they would decrease card usage.[24]

In another study, Mitchell and Olson found that beliefs and evaluations of brands of facial tissue were related to intention to buy.[25] Interestingly, they found that attitudes toward the advertising as well as attitudes toward the brand influence the likelihood of buying. A basic principle in marketing is that good advertising cannot sell a bad product. The Mitchell and Olson study suggests that the opposite might also be true: Bad advertising (that is, advertising that creates negative attitudes) can turn people off of an otherwise good product.

Relationship Between Intention to Buy and Behavior

Intention to buy in the attitudinal models in Figures 8.3 and 8.4 is shown as an intervening variable between attitudes and behavior. Both marketers and economists have used intentions to predict future behavior. Marketers use consumer buying intentions to evaluate alternative new product concepts and advertising themes. Economists use consumer intentions to predict future economic trends.

Marketers should confirm the relationship between intention and subsequent behavior if purchase intention is to be regarded as a valid measure of action tendency. In a study of magazine readership, Bagozzi and Baumgarten found that intentions were closely related to behavior for six of the seven magazines studied.[26] McQuarrie's study of purchasers of computer systems found intentions were more closely related to behavior for heavy computer users. The implication was that greater knowledge and higher involvement produce a closer link between intentions and behavior.[27]

In an earlier study of seven product categories, Banks found that 62 percent of respondents who said they would buy actually did so.[28] Among those who did not intend to buy, 28 percent purchased the product. The greatest fulfillment rate (correspondence between intention and actual purchase) occurred for coffee and scouring cleanser. The lowest fulfillment rate was for ice cream, which reflects the impulsive nature of ice cream purchases.

The Survey Research Center at the University of Michigan provided the most extensive confirmation of the relationship between intentions and purchase. George Katona, former director of the Center, used consumer buying intentions to forecast economic trends. He reported on the close relationship between intentions and behavior for automobiles.[29] Among those consumers who said they planned to or might buy a new car, 63 percent bought in the next year. Among those consumers who did not intend to buy, 29 percent purchased a new car. These fulfillment rates were almost identical to those in Banks's study. Both studies showed that the majority of consumers who intended to buy a product fulfilled their intentions.

Katona conducted his studies before 1970. Since then, consumer intentions have proved to be a less reliable predictor of behavior. Energy shortages and two severe recessions in the early 1980s and 1990s have made the relationship between intentions and behavior less certain. During the energy crisis, most consumers said they would cut back on driving but did not. After the stock market crash of 1987, many consumers said they would cut back on purchases of high-ticket items but did not. Interestingly, the Survey Research Center now asks consumers not what they intend to buy, but what their expectations are regarding their economic situation.[30] The latter measure seems to be more predictive of total consumer expenditures.

Another factor inhibiting the fulfillment of consumer intentions is a long repurchase cycle. The University of Michigan study interviewed consumers to determine actual car purchases one year after determining intentions. Many factors, such as a change in needs, economic circumstances, or alternatives available, can intervene in the space of a year to change intentions.

Relationship of Behavior to Attitudes

Not only do consumer attitudes influence behavior, but behavior can also influence subsequent attitudes. There are three situations in which behavior is likely to influence attitudes: during cognitive dissonance, during passive learning, and when there is a disconfirmation of expectations.

Theories of cognitive dissonance, passive learning, and disconfirmation of expectations have reduced the importance of attitudes in explaining consumer behavior by showing that attitude change is not a necessary condition for a change in purchasing behavior.

Cognitive Dissonance

According to dissonance theory, consumer attitudes sometimes change to conform to previous behavior, thus reducing postpurchase conflict. Several studies have confirmed these relationships. For example, Knox and Inkster interviewed bettors at a racetrack before bets on a horse were made.[31] On the average, bettors gave their horse little better than a fair chance of winning. The researchers then interviewed the same bettors after they made their bets but before the race. Predictions about the performance of the horse became substantially more positive after they made the decision. Apparently, bettors sought to reduce the potential for postdecisional conflict by enhancing the evaluation of the chosen alternative. This finding indicates that individuals tend to reinforce their decision after the fact by changing their attitudes in favor of the chosen brand.

Passive Learning

The theory of passive learning provides another basis for downplaying the importance of consumer attitudes as determinants of behavior.[32] As we have seen, under conditions of low involvement, a change in attitude is not necessary to influence a change in behavior. The awareness of a new brand may be sufficient reason for consumers to switch in a search for variety, and consumers may form attitudes toward the new brand after using it. Ginter's study of a low involvement category, household cleaning products, found that consumers tended to rate brands more favorably after they made the purchase.[33]

Disconfirmation of Expectations

When expectations regarding product performance are not met, such **disconfirmation of expectations** may give consumers more negative attitudes toward the product after the purchase. According to **assimilation/contrast theories,** when consumers are only slightly disappointed, attitudes will adjust to expectations since the experience is accepted and assimilated. When consumers are very disappointed, however, a negative change in attitudes is likely to occur after the purchase, and they may exaggerate this change.

◆ FACTORS INHIBITING THE RELATIONSHIP AMONG BELIEFS, ATTITUDES, AND BEHAVIOR

As the preceding section suggests, many factors may intervene to cause little or no relationship among beliefs, attitudes, and behavior.

One study showing a lack of association between beliefs and attitudes found that people prefer Pizza Hut to McDonald's, even though McDonald's outsells Pizza Hut by two to one. Why the disparity? Because people like pizza better than hamburgers (higher evaluation of pizza), but beliefs about McDonald's (quick service, better variety) lead them to go there.[34]

Likewise, the relationship between consumer attitudes and intentions is also not always consistent. There are two reasons for this disparity. First, as we saw, such evaluations may not play a role in low involvement purchases because consumers may simply buy what is best known or most convenient without going through a process of evaluation. Consumers may be reminded to buy a brand in the store. A previously favorable attitude toward the brand leads to an immediate purchase without a prior intention to buy.

A second reason for inconsistency between attitudes and intentions is that consumers may have a very positive attitude toward the brand, but it may not be one of the brands consumers can feasibly purchase. For example, a consumer may evaluate a Rolls-Royce very positively, but the car is not a realistic alternative for most consumers because of its price.

Marketers must also recognize occasions when consumer attitudes are unlikely to be related to behavior. The following conditions may cause a lack of association between beliefs, attitudes, and behavior:

1. *Lack of involvement.* As we saw in Chapter 5, consumer attitudes are less likely to be related to behavior for low involvement products.

2. *Lack of direct product experience.* Berger's and Mitchell's study found that when consumers have direct product experience, their attitudes are more likely to be related to subsequent behavior.[35] Lack of product experience may result in weakly held attitudes that are not related to behavior.

3. *Lack of relation between values and beliefs.* Attitudes are unlikely to be related to behavior if brand beliefs are not tied to consumer values. The fact that consumers believe a brand of cereal has fewer calories is not going to predict behavior if consumers have no interest in losing weight.

4. *Changing market conditions.* An increase in the price of the favored brand may cause consumers to switch with no change in attitudes. Special price promotions or better credit terms for competitive brands may cause consumers to buy a less-preferred brand. The unavailability of the preferred brand may lead consumers to purchase a less-preferred brand with no change in attitudes.

5. *Poor attitude accessibility.* As we saw in the last chapter, consumers retain brand beliefs in memory as schema representing their associations with the brand. For these beliefs to affect brand evaluations, they must be accessible from memory. Fazio and his associates suggest that lack of a relationship between attitudes and behavior may be due to the fact that some attitudes are so weakly held that they are not accessible.[36] If consumers have strongly held attitudes, they often spontaneously retrieve them when they encounter the object. If a consumer has a strong positive attitude toward McDonald's, the consumer could spontaneously retrieve the McDonald's schema by the mere mention of a Big Mac or by the sight of the golden arches.

SUMMARY

This chapter focused on one of the most important consumer thought variables—attitudes. In a marketing context, attitudes are predispositions toward specific brands, products, or companies that cause consumers to respond favorably or unfavorably toward them. The development and function of attitudes were discussed.

Brand attitudes are composed of consumer beliefs about a brand, an overall evaluation of the brand, and an action tendency. These components are important to marketers because they (1) influence consumers' behavior, (2) enable marketers to define attitudinal segments toward which strategies can be directed, and (3) help marketers evaluate strategies.

The focus of this chapter was on the relationships between brand beliefs and brand attitudes and between brand attitudes and behavior. Two theories best describe the link between brand beliefs and attitudes. Heider's balance theory posits that consumers always strive for cognitive balance between beliefs and evaluations. Fishbein's multiattribute model describes attitudes as a function of beliefs that a brand has certain attributes and the desirability of these attributes.

The link between brand attitudes and behavior was also examined. Fishbein's theory of reasoned action proposes that the appropriate focus of research is consumer attitudes toward the purchase of a brand rather than attitudes toward the brand itself. Research suggests that such a focus increases the strength of association between attitudes and behavior.

The final sections of the chapter considered various factors that might inhibit the relationships among consumer beliefs, attitudes, and behavior and the role of attitudes in developing marketing strategies.

The next chapter focuses on the strategic applications of attitudes; namely, strategies for attitude reinforcement and change.

QUESTIONS

1. What are some of the difficulties AT&T faces in changing attitudes of younger consumers toward the company?

2. How can marketers attempt to change consumer brand evaluations without changing brand beliefs? Why have such attempts increased in recent years?

3. Why are attitudes more closely related to behavior for consumers who are involved with the purchase? Does this mean that consumer attitudes play no strategic role for low involvement products? Explain.

4. Two manufacturers of men's clothing launch a national advertising campaign. One directs the campaign to value-expressive attitudes toward men's clothing. The other directs advertising to ego-defensive attitudes.
   • What differences may result from the two campaigns?
   • To what types of consumers would each ad appeal?

5. How do the ads in Exhibit 8.2 reflect each of the four functions in Katz's functional theory of attitudes?

6. Why did Volvo do too good a job in shaping consumer attitudes toward the car? Do you agree with its current strategy? Why or why not?

7. A consumer has a positive attitude toward his gas-guzzling car and values environmental protection. Apply balance theory in resolving this apparent conflict.

8. A food company is considering introducing an artificial bacon product that is leaner and has less cholesterol than bacon. How can it use Fishbein's multiattribute model to evaluate the new product? What strategic implications might it derive by applying the model?

9. One study linking attitudes to behavior suggested that an ongoing marketing information system designed to track changes in attitudes may benefit management. Of what use would a system that tracks consumer attitudes be for (a) new product development and (b) evaluating advertising effectiveness?

10. Consider the statement: "Consumer attitudes toward the act of using or purchasing a brand are more closely related to behavior than are consumer attitudes toward the brand itself." Assume you are a marketer considering repositioning a breakfast food so that it will also appeal to the snack market. What are the implications of the statement for repositioning strategy?

11. Under what circumstances is consumer behavior likely to influence subsequent attitudes? What are the strategic implications of attitude change occurring after behavior?

12. Under what circumstances are consumer brand attitudes unlikely to be related to purchase behavior? If attitudes are not related to behavior, should marketers continue to measure them? Why or why not?

RESEARCH ASSIGNMENTS

1. According to the theory of cognitive dissonance, recent purchasers of important items such as cars or appliances are more likely to have positive attitudes toward their brands than those who have owned the brand for a longer period of time. The reason for this is that once they make a purchase, recent purchasers are likely to seek positive information about the brand to reinforce the choice they have made.

   Test this hypothesis by selecting both recent purchasers of a major durable good (car, stereo set, microwave oven) and consumers who have owned the item for a longer period of time. Measure (a) beliefs about the brand utilizing a vocabulary of need criteria and (b) overall evaluation of the brand.
   - Do recent purchasers have more positive attitudes?
   - Are there differences in beliefs about brands between recent purchasers and long-time owners?
   - What are the strategic implications of your findings, particularly for (a) advertising and (b) service policies?

2. Select a particular brand to study (preferably a consumer packaged good). You would like to evaluate the strengths and weaknesses of the brand relative to the competition. To do so, you decide to utilize a multiattribute approach.

   Conduct a number of depth interviews with consumers to develop a vocabulary of attributes that consumers use in evaluating brands. Construct scales to measure (a) how consumers evaluate each attribute in the vocabulary and (b) beliefs about the brand under study and two or three other key competitive brands, based on the vocabulary of attributes. Select a sample of users of the product category so that at least one-third of your sample uses the brand under study.

- What are the brand's strengths and weaknesses based on a comparison of the brand to (a) desired attributes and (b) competitive brands?
- How do brand ratings differ between users and nonusers of the brand?
- What are the implications of your findings for (a) possible repositioning strategies for the brand, (b) identification of unmet needs, and (c) formulation of new product concepts to meet consumer needs?

3. Some marketers believe that a significant proportion of consumers develop images of brands based on the advertising rather than on product experience. If this is true, one would expect beliefs about brands to reflect advertising themes. Select a product category in which different advertising themes can be associated with brands (for example, pain relievers, airlines, paper towels). Construct a vocabulary of product attributes, including the advertising themes. Ask consumers to rate the brands in the product category utilizing the vocabulary.

- Are brands rated higher on criteria used in the brand's advertising?
- Do both heavy and light users of the product category rate brands in accordance with the advertising themes? Do both users and nonusers of the brand?

NOTES

1. "Ma Bell Faces Up to Her Generation Gap," *Adweek's Marketing Week* (June 22, 1992), pp. 18–19.

2. Gordon W. Allport, "Attitudes," in C. A. Murchinson, ed., *A Handbook of Social Psychology* (Worcester, MA: Clark University Press, 1935), pp. 798–844.

3. For a good review of attitudinal theories, see Richard J. Lutz, "The Role of Attitude Theory in Marketing," in Harold H. Kassarjian and Thomas S. Robertson, eds., *Perspectives in Consumer Behavior* (Glenview, IL: Scott, Foresman and Co., 1991).

4. Sharon E. Beatty and Lynn R. Kahle, "Alternative Hierarchies of the Attitude-Behavior Relationship: The Impact of Brand Commitment and Habit," *Journal of the Academy of Marketing Science,* 16 (Summer, 1988), pp. 1–10.

5. Scott B. Mackenzie and Richard A. Spreng, "How Does Motivation Moderate the Impact of Central and Peripheral Processing on Brand Attitudes and

Intentions," *Journal of Consumer Research,* 18 (March, 1992), pp. 519–529.

6. Peter D. Bennett and Harold H. Kassarjian, *Consumer Behavior* (Englewood Cliffs, NJ: Prentice-Hall, 1972), p. 81

7. Intercollegiate Clearing House Case; *Young and Rubicam* (A) (Cambridge, MA: Harvard Graduate School of Business Administration, 1957).

8. Elihu Katz and Paul F. Lazarsfeld, *Personal Influence* (New York: The Free Press, 1955).

9. James S. Coleman, Elihu Katz, and Herbert Menzel, *Medical Innovation: A Diffusion Study* (New York: Bobbs-Merrill, 1966).

10. Johan Arndt, "Role of Product-Related Conversations in the Diffusion of a New Product," *Journal of Marketing Research,* 4 (August, 1967), pp. 291–295.

11. Daniel Katz, "The Functional Approach to the Study of Attitudes," *Public Opinion Quarterly,* 24 (Summer, 1960), pp. 163–204.

12. Richard J. Lutz, "A Functional Theory Framework for Designing and Pretesting Advertising Themes," *Attitude Research Plays for High Stakes* (Chicago: American Marketing Association, 1979), pp. 37–49; and William B. Locander and W. Austin Spivey, "A Functional Approach to Attitude Measurement," *Journal of Marketing Research,* 15 (November, 1978), pp. 576–587.

13. For research on attitude formation and structure, see Mark P. Zanna, "Attitude-Behavior Consistency: Fulfilling the Need for Cognitive Structure," in Thomas K. Srull, ed., *Advances in Consumer Research,* Vol. 16 (Provo, UT: Association for Consumer Research, 1989), pp. 318–320; Michael D. Johnson, "On the Nature of Product Attributes and Attribute Relationships," in Srull, *Advances in Consumer Research,* Vol. 16, pp. 598–604; Morris B. Holbrook and William J. Havlena, "Assessing the Real-to-Artificial Generalizability of Multiattribute Attitude Models in Tests of New Product Designs," *Journal of Marketing Research,* 24 (February, 1988), pp. 25–35; Punam Anand, Morris B. Holbrook, and Debra Stephens, "The Formation of Affective Judgments: The Cognitive-Affective Model Versus the Independence Hypothesis," *Journal of Consumer Research,* 15 (December, 1988), pp. 386–391; Michael D. Johnson and Claes Fornell, "The Nature and Methodological Implications of the Cognitive Representation of Products," *Journal of Consumer Research,* 14 (September, 1987), pp. 214–228; and Robert E. Smith and William R. Swinyard, "Attitude-Behavior Consistencies: The Impact of Product Trial Versus Advertising," *Journal of Marketing Research,* 20 (August, 1983), pp. 257–267.

14. See Fritz Heider, *The Psychology of Interpersonal Relations* (New York: John Wiley, 1958).

15. Jagdish N. Sheth and W. Wayne Talarzyk, "Perceived Instrumentality and Value Importance as Determinants of Attitudes," *Journal of Marketing Research,* 9 (February, 1972), pp. 6–9.

16. See Richard J. Lutz, "An Experimental Investigation of Causal Relations Among Cognitions, Affect, and Behavioral Intentions," *Journal of Consumer Research,* 3 (March, 1977), pp. 197–208; Jagdish N. Sheth, "Brand Profiles from Beliefs and Importances," *Journal of Advertising Research,* 13 (February, 1973), pp. 37–42; Frank M. Bass and William L. Wilkie, "A Comparative Analysis of Attitudinal Predictions of Brand Preference," *Journal of Marketing Research,* 10 (August, 1973), pp. 262–269; and David E. Weddle and James R. Bettman, "Marketing Underground: An Investigation of Fishbein's Behavioral Intention Model," in Scott Ward and Peter Wright, eds., *Advances in Consumer Research,* Vol. 1 (Urbana, IL: Association for Consumer Research, 1973), pp. 310–318.

17. Martin Fishbein, "An Investigation of the Relationships Between Beliefs About an Object and the Attitude Toward That Object," *Human Relations,* 16 (1963), pp. 233–240. For a good review of multiattribute models, see William L. Wilkie and Edgar A. Pessemier, "Issues in Marketing's Use of Multiattribute Models," *Journal of Marketing Research,* 10 (November, 1983), pp. 428–441.

18. Martin Fishbein, "Attitudes and the Prediction of Behavior," in Martin Fishbein, ed., *Readings in Attitude Theory and Measurement* (New York: John Wiley, 1967), pp. 477–492.

19. Martin Fishbein, "Some Comments on the Use of 'Models' in Advertising Research," in *Proceedings: Seminar on Translating Advanced Advertising Theories into Research Reality* (Amsterdam: European Society of Marketing Research, 1971), p. 301.

20. Michael J. Ryan and E. H. Bonfield, "The Fishbein Extended Model and Consumer Behavior," *Journal of Consumer Research,* 2 (September, 1975), pp. 118–136.

21. David T. Wilson, H. Lee Matthews, and James W. Harvey, "An Empirical Test of the Fishbein Behavioral Intention Model," *Journal of Consumer Research,* 1 (March, 1975), pp. 39–48.

22. S. Knox and L. de Chernatony, "The Application of Multiattribute Modeling Techniques to the Mineral Water Market," *Quarterly Review of Marketing* (Summer, 1989), pp. 14–20.

23. Alvin A. Achenbaum, "Advertising Doesn't Manipulate Consumers," *Journal of Advertising Research,* 12 (April, 1972), pp. 3–13; and Alvin A. Achenbaum, "Knowledge Is a Thing Called Measurement," in Lee Adler and Irving Crespi, eds., *Attitude Research at Sea* (New York: American Marketing Association, 1966), pp. 111–126.

24. Richard Garfein, presentation to American Marketing Association Conference on Forging Change in Service Organizations, New York, April 1, 1987.

25. Andrew A. Mitchell and Jerry C. Olson, "Are Product Attribute Beliefs the Only Mediator of Advertising Effects on Brand Attitude?" *Journal of Marketing Research,* 18 (August, 1981), pp. 318–332.

26. Richard P. Bagozzi and Johann Baumgarten, "An Investigation into the Role of Intentions as Mediators of the Attitude-Behavior Relationship," *Journal of Economic Psychology,* 10 (1989), pp. 35–62.

27. Edward F. McQuarrie, "An Alternative to Purchase Intentions: The Role of Prior Behavior in Consumer Expenditures on Computers," *Journal of the Marketing Research Society,* 30 (October, 1988), pp. 407–437.

28. Seymour Banks, "The Relationship Between Preference and Purchase of Brands," *Journal of Marketing,* 15 (October, 1950), pp. 145–157.

29. George Katona, *The Powerful Consumer* (New York: McGraw-Hill, 1960), pp. 80–83.

30. "Recession Coming? Ask the Consumer," *The New York Times* (April 4, 1990), p. D6.

31. Robert E. Knox and James A. Inkster, "Post-Decision Dissonance at Post Time," *Journal of Personality and Social Psychology,* 8 (1968), pp. 319–323.

32. Herbert E. Krugman, "The Impact of Television Advertising: Learning Without Involvement," *Public Opinion Quarterly,* 29 (Fall, 1965), pp. 349–356.

33. James L. Ginter, "An Experimental Investigation of Attitude Change and Choice of a New Brand," *Journal of Marketing Research,* 11 (February, 1974), pp. 30–40.

34. "Glitzy Brands Make Small Impressions," *The Wall Street Journal* (December 15, 1989), p. B4.

35. Ida E. Berger and Andrew A. Mitchell, "The Effect of Advertising on Attitude Accessibility, Attitude Confidence, and the Attitude-Behavior Relationship," *Journal of Consumer Research,* 16 (December, 1989), pp. 269–279. See also Smith and Swinyard, "Attitude-Behavior Consistencies . . . ," *loc. cit.*

36. Russell H. Fazio, Martha C. Powell, and Carol J. Williams, "The Role of Attitude Accessibility in the Attitude-to-Behavior Process," *Journal of Consumer Research,* 16 (December, 1989), pp. 280–288.

9

Attitude Reinforcement and Change

CHANGING ATTITUDES AT KMART: FROM THE POLYESTER PALACE TO HIGH-FASHION RETAILER

Marketers can use their knowledge of consumer attitudes to develop two types of strategies. One strategy reinforces existing attitudes; another tries to change them. There is no question that reinforcing existing attitudes is easier than changing them.

Most advertising for well-known brands attempts to maintain and reinforce positive attitudes. Successful themes such as Chevrolet's "Heartbeat of America" or Miller Lite's "Less Filling/Tastes Great" reinforced consumer attitudes through long-running campaigns. Even when these campaigns change, as they must over time, advertising continues to reinforce positive attitudes. McDonald's may have changed its campaign from the slogan "You Deserve a Break Today," to "It's a Good Time for the Great Taste of McDonald's," but the intent is the same: to reinforce an image of family values and good food.

Strategies that reinforce attitudes may be easier to implement, but there may be compelling reasons to try to change attitudes. A good example is Kmart, the number two retailer in the country. In the 1980s, Kmart came up against the baby boom generation. These consumers wanted greater quality and value than Kmart was giving them. Kmart could not afford to ignore this group, given their numbers and purchasing power. The trouble was that many baby boomers viewed Kmart as a purveyor of low-quality merchandise. These negative attitudes earned Kmart the nickname "The Polyester Palace."[1]

In 1987, a new management team embarked on a strategy to reposition Kmart as a high-fashion discount store and thereby change negative attitudes of baby boomers. The company introduced a high-quality clothing line, the Jacklyn Smith Signature Collection, by using the former star of the TV show "Charlie's Angels" to promote the line. In a further attempt to leave its polyester image behind, Kmart signed on Martha Stewart, a stylish hostess, as its spokesperson in its advertising.

By 1990, flat sales were showing Kmart the difficulty of moving out of its polyester image. So management initiated a five-year, $3 billion chainwide store renovation program to improve its in-store decor. Then, in 1993, it embarked on a new advertising campaign to try to get working women to think of Kmart as a source of fashion.[2] The campaign used a "soft-image" approach to try to show that Kmart is in tune with consumers' feelings. One ad shows a working mother relaxing, with the copy: "You put yourself through a lot. Between the kids, the home, and your job, it seems there's no time left for you."

Has Kmart's attempt at attitude change been successful? The Jacklyn Smith line is doing well, and by mid-1992 Kmart sales started increasing.[3] However, there is little evidence that the company is attracting fashion-oriented baby boomers. Kmart still has a long way to go to convince consumers it has transformed itself from polyester to high fashion.

In this chapter, we show how marketers use consumer attitudes to develop strategies of attitude reinforcement and change. Attitudes are reinforced or changed through product positioning strategies that communicate brand attributes and images. To understand this process, the first section presents a basic communications model. We then consider the conditions when change strategies are most likely to be successful and the theories that provide guidelines for attitudinal change both before and after a purchase. We conclude by describing the nature of product positioning strategies and how marketers can use them for reinforcement or change.

◆ COMMUNICATIONS PROCESS

When marketers try to reinforce or change consumer attitudes, they are communicating information about their products. A basic communications model is presented in Figure 9.1. Any type of communication requires a source, message,

▶**FIGURE 9.1**
The communications process

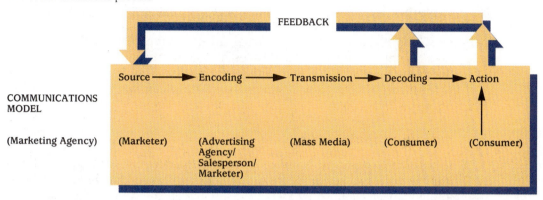

means of transmitting the message, receiver who might act on the message, and feedback to the source. Figure 9.1 also shows the marketing agencies responsible for each stage of the communications process and the consumer's role in the process.

Source

The **source** of the message (the marketer) develops communications objectives and identifies a target for its communications. For example, when Polaroid developed its Spectra camera, its communications objective was to convince its target group that the camera was the equal of 35mm cameras. With a price tag of $225, the Spectra was targeted to a younger, more upscale segment than Polaroid's traditional customer base.[4] This definition of the target segment influenced message development and media strategy.

Encoding

The process of translating these objectives into a message is known as **encoding.** Advertising agencies develop messages that are encoded into ads. Salespeople encode messages in developing a sales presentation for customers.

Polaroid's ad agency decided to use Ben Cross, the actor, as a spokesperson for the Spectra because it believed he conveyed a younger, upscale image. Ads showed him comparing results of the Spectra to shots from a 35mm camera. Polaroid also developed a direct-mail catalog that emphasized the same message.

Transmission

Advertising agencies select media designed to reach the intended audience. Transmission might also involve word-of-mouth communication from a salesperson or direct mail literature sent to targeted households.

The primary medium Polaroid used to transmit messages regarding the Spectra was network TV. Print ads were also placed in upscale magazines to reach higher-income baby boomers, and the Spectra was advertised on billboards in 25 markets.

Decoding and Action

In **decoding,** consumers translate a message to understand and possibly retain it in memory. Two key questions are whether consumers interpret the message in the manner intended by the advertiser and whether the message positively influences consumer attitudes and behavior. Since most marketing communications are designed to influence consumers to act, purchasing behavior is the key variable in assessing communications effectiveness.

Polaroid hoped that a substantial number of consumers in the target audience would (1) notice Spectra ads, (2) decode them to mean that the Spectra produced comparable pictures to a 35mm camera, (3) remember the message, and (4) act on it by considering Spectra an alternative to a 35mm camera.

Feedback

The final step in the communication process is **feedback;** that is, evaluating the effectiveness of the communication. Feedback is represented in Figure 9.1 as a loop going from action to the source. Marketers try to assess the effectiveness of their communications by evaluating sales results. However, determining the effects of advertising on sales is difficult because marketers do not know if consumers purchased primarily because of the advertising or because of a host of other factors that might have influenced their purchase behavior.

Difficulties in relating advertising to sales results have caused researchers to evaluate advertising effectiveness by studying consumers' decoding process. That is, research attempts to measure whether consumers are aware of the advertising message, how they interpret the message, whether they retain it, and if their brand attitudes change after being exposed to the message. The reliance on decoding, as well as action in evaluating marketing communications, is shown in Figure 9.1 as a feedback loop from decoding to the source.

The Spectra campaign was judged a success based on the way the target group decoded it. Awareness of the campaign was high among the target group of younger, upscale consumers. A significant proportion recalled and retained the main theme of parity between Spectra and 35mm cameras. Most important, sales exceeded expectations in the first year.[5]

Communications will be considered further in Part Five of the text when we discuss personal and marketing communications.

◆ CONDITIONS FOR ATTITUDE REINFORCEMENT AND CHANGE

Several studies show that when communications conform to, rather than contradict, existing brand attitudes, consumers are more easily influenced. McCullough, MacLachlan, and Moinpour found that communicating toothpaste attributes known to be important to consumers was more effective than attempting to change the importance of these attributes.[6] A study by Raj found that reinforcing users' positive attitudes of a brand was more effective in increasing consumption of the brand than trying to change the attitudes of nonusers.[7]

Given the greater difficulty in changing consumer attitudes than in reinforcing them, marketers must know when attitude change is feasible. The conditions for attitude change are particularly important, as there are times when marketers must attempt to change consumer attitudes about their companies or brands. However, a certain irony exists in attempting such changes: Attitudes are easiest to change when they are least likely to influence behavior (for example, when product involvement is low and when attitudes are weakly held). As a result, strategies of attitude change may take much longer than expected (for example, Kmart's attempt to develop a more upscale image) or they may not produce the payoff that marketers expect.

Despite the difficulty in changing brand attitudes, a significant portion of advertising expenditures is devoted to such change by providing additional information and persuasive appeals. The question marketers must ask is: "Under what conditions should changes in attitudes be attempted?" A number of conditions reflecting the product category, market environment, and nature of consumers make it easier to produce changes in attitudes through marketing strategies. These principles may change consumer beliefs about a brand, brand attitudes (evaluations), or intention to buy.

1. *Beliefs are easier to change than desired benefits.* Marketers could seek to change beliefs about a brand. They could also attempt to change the benefits consumers desire by changing the value consumers place on brand attributes. Desired benefits are more enduring, ingrained, and internalized than beliefs because they are more closely linked to consumer values. For instance, a manufacturer of pain relievers produces a brand that consumers regard as significantly stronger and as providing more immediate relief. However, most consumers put more value on the benefits of a mild, safe brand that doctors recommend. The manufacturer could try to convince consumers that pain relievers are nonprescription items that do not need a doctor's recommendation, that safety should be of no concern, and that a stronger product is perfectly acceptable. Alternatively, the manufacturer could tone down the emphasis on strength in the advertising, continue to emphasize quick relief, and point out the safety of the product based on FDA approval. The latter strategy is going to be more effective than the former because the marketer is trying to change beliefs about the brand within the consumers' existing value structure.

Lutz tested the effectiveness of changing beliefs versus benefits. He introduced a fictitious laundry soap to consumers in a test situation.[8] After receiving a description of the brand, consumers were asked to read an article in *Consumer Reports* that was designed to change their beliefs about the brand. A second message attempted to change their values by convincing them that high sudsiness was not a valuable attribute. Lutz found that a change in beliefs changed the overall evaluation of the brand, but an attempted change in values did not cause any change in evaluation. This finding conforms to the principle stated in the previous section that changing beliefs about a brand is easier than changing the value of these beliefs.

2. *Brand beliefs are easier to change than brand attitudes.* Cognitions (beliefs) are easier to change than affect (attitudes). The traditional high involvement hierarchy of effects states that a change in beliefs precedes a change in brand attitudes. Therefore, when consumers are involved, changing their beliefs should be easier than changing their brand attitudes. The information that a car has fast acceleration will change the beliefs about the brand, but the evaluation of the car will not necessarily change unless consumers see a benefit in fast acceleration. Most advertising implicitly follows the principle that beliefs are easier to change because advertising generally communicates the attributes of a brand.

If consumer beliefs inhibit purchase, advertisers sometimes try to change their attitudes without changing their beliefs. For example, the belief that Rolls-Royce is a high-priced car inhibits attitudes toward purchasing the car (A_{act}). As a result, Rolls tried to change consumer attitudes toward purchasing without changing beliefs. It identified its target as affluent consumers who have positive beliefs about the car but who are intimidated by the price and its image. Rolls ran a campaign comparing its cars to other luxury cars such as the BMW, Mercedes, and Cadillac. The campaign does not try to change beliefs, since little is said about the characteristics of the car. Rather, it attempts to change attitudes toward purchasing a Rolls among owners of other luxury cars. The campaign is unlikely to succeed because beliefs about the car have not changed and the initial price resistance has not been overcome.

3. *Attitudes are easier to change when there is a low level of involvement with the product.* The principle that consumer beliefs are easier to change than their attitudes is more applicable for high involvement purchases. Attitudes toward uninvolving products are easier to change because consumers are not committed to the brand. This principle is true for the three key components of involvement: That is, consumer attitudes are easier to change if there is little self-identification with the product, little emotional attachment to it, and no badge value associated with it. Sherif's theory of social judgment supports this view.[9] When consumers have a high level of involvement with a product, they will accept messages only if the messages agree with their beliefs. When involvement is low, consumers are more likely to accept a message even if it does not agree with prior beliefs.

The California Milk Advisory Board, a marketing association representing the State's 2,200 dairy families, has instituted a campaign to convince teens and young adults that milk has nutritional value for them as well as for kids. (See Exhibit 9.1.) The Board has been fairly successful in its campaign, primarily because milk lacks badge value and is not a source of self-identity.

4. *Weak attitudes are easier to change than strong ones.* If consumer brand attitudes are not strong, marketers can more easily establish new associations with the brand. Lubriderm®, a skin care product, had the image among nonusers of a heavy, greasy product. Nonusers viewed Lubriderm® more as a medicinal product for serious skin problems than as a general cosmetic product, and marketers knew the attitudes of nonusers would have to change if the brand was to increase sales. The company began advertising the brand as an everyday product that softens the skin (see Exhibit 9.2) and tried to put as many free samples in the hands of potential users as possible to prove that Lubriderm® was not greasy. One of the reasons that nonusers were open to the campaign is that their attitudes were not strongly held. They were weakly formed impressions that were not based on direct product experience.[10] However, weakly held attitudes make it easier for competitors to convince consumers to switch to their brands by changing attitudes.

When company or brand attitudes are strongly held, as with Rolls Royce and Kmart, they are much more difficult to change.

5. *Attitudes held by consumers who have less confidence in their brand evaluations are easier to change.* Consumers who are unsure of their evaluation of a brand will be more receptive to the informational content of advertising and more subject to attitude change. Confusion about the criteria to use in evaluating a brand can cause consumers to lack self-confidence in making a decision. A number of years ago, the Carpet Institute hired a research firm to study the purchasing process for rugs and carpets. They concluded, "There is a great deal of confusion and misconception about the characteristics, features and terminology in carpeting. Even the terms rug vs. carpet, the type of rug

▶**EXHIBIT 9.1**
Changing attitudes for a low involvement product

Source: Courtesy of California Milk Advisory Board

►**EXHIBIT 9.2**
An attempt to overcome negative brand attitudes

Lubriderm® is a registered trademark of Warner-Lambert Company. © Copyright by Warner-Lambert Company. Reproduced with permission.

construction vs. company names are confused. It would seem on the surface that too wide a variety of features are pressed upon the housewife with her rather simple needs in floor covering."[11]

In a case like this, consumers would be receptive to a brand that provides information on a few key product attributes. The strategy would be to change beliefs about the product category and to capitalize on these attitudinal changes by associating them with the manufacturer's brand name.

6. *Attitudes are easier to change when they are based on ambiguous information.* Consumers faced with ambiguous claims about competitive products or with highly technical information they cannot assess seek clarifying information that may produce attitude change. When information is highly ambiguous, any clarifying information may cause a change in attitudes. One study found that high informational ambiguity consistently produced greater attitude change over a wide variety of products.[12]

In presenting a clear-cut message of the user-friendly nature of its machines, Apple was successful in introducing its personal computers to schools in the late 1970s. At this time, PCs were in a product category that first-time users found highly technical and ambiguous. For many students, the symbolism of the Apple was meant to alleviate uncertainty of using a PC.

◆ ATTITUDE CHANGE BEFORE A PURCHASE

Given the frequency with which marketers attempt to change consumer brand and product attitudes and the frequent difficulty in doing so, a fuller understanding of the process of attitude change is warranted. The attitudinal theories discussed in the previous chapter provide a basis for marketers to attempt to change attitudes to induce consumers to try a brand before a purchase. Some of these theories also provide a basis for changing attitudes after the purchase to convince consumers they made the right choice.

Two types of theories influence attitude change strategies before a purchase: attitudinal theories and theories of information processing. The processing model with the greatest relevance for attitude change is Petty and Cacioppo's elaboration likelihood model (ELM). Whereas the attitudinal models provide strategic implications primarily for high involvement conditions, ELM provides separate strategic implications for attitude change for high and low involvement purchases.

Attitudinal Theories and Attitude Change

The attitudinal theories described earlier—Fishbein's multiattribute models, Katz's functional theory of attitudes, and Sherif's social judgment theory—provide a good framework for considering strategies of attitude change before a purchase. Each model assumes a link between attitudes and behavior.

Multiattribute Models and Attitude Change

In Fishbein's multiattribute model, consumer beliefs based on brand attributes (the b_i component) and the value placed on these beliefs (the e_i component) influence the overall evaluation of the brand (A_o or A_{act}), which, in turn, influences behavioral intent (BI) and, ultimately, behavior (B).

On this basis, marketers can consider four strategies to influence behavior based on the multiattribute models:

1. Change the values placed on particular product attributes (a change in an e_i component).
2. Change beliefs (a change in a b_i component).
3. Change brand attitudes—i.e., evaluations (a change in A_o) or toward buying the brand (a change in A_{act}).
4. Change behavioral intentions (a change in BI) or behavior (a change in B).

1. *Change the values placed on particular product attributes.* This strategy requires convincing consumers to reassess the value of a particular attribute—for example, convincing consumers that bad taste is a good quality in mouthwash. Any attempt to change the values placed on product attributes must rely on prior research showing that a certain segment of the market would be receptive to such a change. For example, the packaging component of many products is rarely the most important criterion in selection. Pringles potato chips were introduced in a new cylindrical container as a means of preserving freshness. Such a strategy can be successful only if the company has done prior research to demonstrate that the importance of the package could be increased through advertising an association between the package and freshness. However, Procter & Gamble overestimated the importance of the package. Its advertising failed to increase the value consumers placed on freshness relative to taste. As a result, poor taste determined consumers' attitude, and P&G had to reformulate and reintroduce the product.

Values based on deep-seated social and cultural norms are the most difficult to change. The values consumers place on the taste of a mouthwash or the freshness of potato chips may be changed, but it is doubtful that advertising could influence a change in values related to social attractiveness, security, or status.

2. *Change beliefs.* By far, the most common strategy is one that attempts to change consumer beliefs about brands through product and advertising strategies. The important point is to ensure that the beliefs being changed will induce favorable changes in consumer brand evaluations and intention to buy. Quaker Oats is trying to change consumer beliefs about Quaker Rice Cakes.[13] Typical comments from consumers in consumer research indicated that rice cakes taste like styrofoam or cardboard. The introduction of flavored rice cakes brought back some past users. However, Quaker had to attract nonusers who generally had negative attitudes. It did so with an effective campaign showing a foam cup with a piece bitten out and with the headline "If this is what you think of rice cakes, wait till you taste them now." (See Exhibit 9.3.)

Marketers can change consumer beliefs by introducing new product attributes as well as by communicating the benefits of existing attributes. Nestle convinced consumers that the attribute large, dark granules was associated with a richer and heftier tasting instant coffee. Similarly, Procter & Gamble convinced consumers that a blue detergent is stronger and cleaner than a white one.

Features that consumers take for granted cannot be the basis for attitude change. For example, advertising good taste for a ground coffee cannot be a basis for changing beliefs about a brand because consumers expect all ground roast coffees to have good taste. On the other hand, taste could be a determining attribute for decaffeinated coffee, as consumers do not always expect a decaffeinated coffee to be good-tasting. General Foods successfully changed consumer beliefs about Sanka over a five-year period. Originally, its image was that of a medicinal brand for older people. By introducing a campaign empha-

▶**EXHIBIT 9.3**
Changing beliefs about
rice cakes

Source: Courtesy of The
Quaker Oats Co.

sizing that Sanka was 100 percent pure coffee, the company successfully changed beliefs to an image of a more flavorful coffee.[14]

   3.   *Change brand attitudes (evaluations).*   Marketers also try to influence consumer brand attitudes directly without specific reference to product attributes. This shortcut strategy may involve associating a positive feeling (affect) with product usage. Miller Lite ran a campaign showing a group of men drinking the brand after winning a hectic athletic event (or in a similar happy environment). If consumers accept the association of product use with success, a favorable brand attitude has been established with little reference to product attributes. The operating principle is conditioning, since the advertiser is trying to link the symbols and images producing positive feelings to the product. In their advertising, many cosmetic companies try to associate a feeling of mystery, romanticism, or social success with their products. This type of advertising could change brand attitudes if the feeling created is sufficient to differentiate the brand from others.

   As we noted in the last chapter, marketers are putting more emphasis on changing consumer brand evaluations through symbols and imagery to create uniqueness in increasingly standardized product categories.

4. *Change behavioral intentions or behavior.* Another change strategy is to induce consumers to purchase a brand that is not preferred—that is, to induce attitude-discrepant behavior. The assumption is that some inducement to try an unpreferred brand (possibly by lowering the price or by offering a deal or a coupon) may change consumers' brand attitude after the purchase to conform to their behavior.

For example, an individual may purchase a pain reliever with a 25-cents-off coupon. Assume there is little difference in effectiveness between the regular brand and the new brand. To justify the purchase, the consumer might decide that the new brand provides immediate relief and, therefore, decides to buy it again, even when the price returns to normal. This strategy makes use of the theory of cognitive dissonance. According to Festinger, the magnitude of such inducements to switch should not be large; otherwise, consumers could always say the only reason for a brand switch was the obvious price difference.[15] The tendency then would be to switch back to the regular brand when the price of the less-preferred brand returns to normal. However, if the difference is a relatively small price change, but one sufficient to cause a saving, consumers will have to find a reason other than price to justify the purchase.

Functional Theory and Attitude Change

Another model that has implications for strategies of consumer attitude change before a purchase is Katz's functional theory of attitudes.[16] As noted in the previous chapter, Katz believes that attitudes serve four functions: utilitarian function, value-expressive function, ego-defensive function, and knowledge function. Marketing strategies can attempt to change attitudes serving each of these functions.

Changing Attitudes Through the Utilitarian Function. One way to influence a positive change in brand attitudes is to show how the product can solve a utilitarian goal consumers may not have previously considered. For example, Arm & Hammer began advertising various utilitarian uses of baking soda in an attempt to increase sales. According to the Arm & Hammer package, the product:

- Soothes minor skin irritations (insect bites, sunburn, etc.).
- Absorbs carpet odors ("helps eliminate all types of odors in a safe, effective way").
- Is a pure, natural skin conditioner ("for a relaxing bath and soft, smooth feeling skin").
- Is an antacid (to alleviate heartburn, sour stomach, and/or acid indigestion).
- Is a bleach booster (when using liquid chlorine bleach, add baking soda).

This array of uses for a traditional cooking and baking product may induce a favorable change in consumers' attitude toward the brand. These uses satisfy a set of utilitarian functions.

Changing Attitudes Through the Value-Expressive Function.   Advertising that attempts to influence the value-expressive function deals with personal values that may be difficult to change. For example, advertising retirement communities by extolling the virtues of getting older would be a poor campaign. Rather, advertising should accept the predominant value orientation of youth and vigor by emphasizing the physical activities and facilities these communities provide to help one stay young. The clear principle is that advertising should accept deep-seated values rather than attempt to change them.

By advertising its benefits to baby boomers, Miami Beach, the epitome of retirement communities, attempted to change an image that only the elderly

---

STRATEGIC APPLICATIONS OF CONSUMER BEHAVIOR

Changing Beliefs: Can Gallo Be Seen as an Upscale Wine?

When they hear the name Gallo, most consumers think of inexpensive wines. In recent years, Ernest and Julio Gallo, founders of the winery, have been trying to change that. They have been moving upscale with the introduction of varietal wines —wines made from a specific variety of grapes. Gallo first started introducing varietals in the mid-1970s at $3 to $5 a bottle. Over time, it then introduced varietals at $5 to $7.

In 1992, they really began moving upscale, introducing a line at the $8 to $10 dollar range with plans to go higher. In 1993, the Gallo name appeared on two new ultrapremium wines, a Chardonnay at $30 a bottle and a Cabernet Sauvignon at $60.

Wait a minute. The Gallo name on a $60 bottle of wine? The move to higher-priced wines has aroused much skepticism among both consumers and the trade. Further, the Gallo brothers are defying conventional wisdom by putting their name on the wine. Most marketing experts would have advised them to use a different name and keep the Gallo label for less expensive wines.

How is Gallo moving upscale? Primarily with a $20 million advertising budget for its higher-priced varietals. One commercial showed baby boomers drinking Gallo sauvignon blanc with their grilled salmon with the theme "It's time to change the way you think about Gallo." And, in a direct application of Heider's balance theory, Gallo hooked up with Waterford crystal for a 1992 holiday ad campaign. Hopefully, consumers with a positive image of Waterford will improve their attitudes toward Gallo to create balance, making it easier to accept Gallo's higher-priced wines.

Given the marketing savvy of the Gallo brothers, they should not be counted out in fighting the odds that Gallo can move its image upscale. Some of the skeptics are starting to become believers.

Sources: "The Gallos Go for the Gold, and Away from the Jugs," *The New York Times* (November 22, 1992), p. F5; and "A Holiday with Waterford," *Brandweek* (November 30, 1992), p. 3.

and infirm live there. The campaign did not persuade baby boomers and alienated older residents. The town council would have been wiser to continue to appeal to older residents but to use youthful themes more in accord with the personal values of potential retirees, rather than targeting a new segment with ingrained beliefs about the community.

Changing Attitudes Through the Ego-Defensive Function.   Research has consistently shown that the more ego-defensive the attitude, the less subject it is to outside influence. The heavy drug user is likely to ignore information about the dangers of drug use. Avoiding painful information is an ego-defensive reaction. Advertising should accept and adapt to ego-defensive attitudes rather than try to change them. This means that rather than taking a negative approach by showing the dangers of drug use, advertising should instead show what steps the user can take to decrease usage. Such an approach would account for the user's ego-defensive reaction.

Changing Attitudes Through the Knowledge Function.   The knowledge function organizes and classifies information, facilitating consumers' information-processing task. It is important for marketers to provide a clear and unambiguous positioning for their product to ensure favorable attitudes.

A good example of a clear and unambiguous positioning is Carnation Instant Breakfast. The company clearly positioned the product as a breakfast food directed to nutritionally oriented consumers who did not have time to prepare a traditional breakfast. The company provided information on the nutritional value and caloric content of the product. Had the product tried to reach a broader market with a more ambiguous positioning, it might have failed. For instance, an alternative strategy might have been to position it as a nutritional pick-me-up at any time of the day. Although this positioning may be directed to a greater number of usage situations, it would be more likely to confuse the consumer. Consumers could have seen the product as a breakfast food, a nutritional snack, or a dietary supplement. Such an ambiguous positioning might have led to a less-favorable evaluation of the brand.

Social Judgment Theory and Attitude Change

Sherif's theory of social judgment provides direct implications for strategies of attitude change.[17] Two strategies cited earlier—to change consumer beliefs about a brand or to change their values associated with these beliefs—require that consumers accept the advertising message. Sherif's theory predicts that if the change suggested by advertising is too extreme, consumers will reject the message because it will fall into their latitude of rejection. If the message suggests moderate changes, however, consumers will accept it because it is within their latitude of acceptance. Therefore, marketers may be more successful in inducing attitude change with small changes in beliefs over a longer period of time.

More-involved consumers are less likely to accept messages proposing a change in beliefs or values. However, consumers are not highly involved with most product categories. Therefore, consumers are more likely to accept advertising suggesting moderate changes in beliefs or values.

Club Med, the worldwide vacation resort firm, attempted to change its image from a firm running resorts for swinging singles to one that also offered married couples and families a carefree environment. It opened resorts targeted to older, more conservative vacationers and advertised accordingly.[18] The target group accepted the change because a Club Med for married couples and vacationers was within their latitude of acceptance. More importantly, the appeals did not fall into the latitude of rejection for swinging singles, as Club Med still ran resorts and ads positioned to this group.

Some evidence suggests that messages attempting to change consumer beliefs and values that are extreme, but not extreme enough to bring about rejection of the message, may create curiosity and lead to product trial.[19] Introducing a high-styled refrigerator (different color and design, possibly even different shape) would represent an extreme change in beliefs for a standard product. However, the change may not be extreme enough to be rejected outright, especially as it does not threaten consumers' basic values or self-identification. An arousal of curiosity, a visit to a store to see the product, and, in some cases, a purchase may result.

Heider's Balance Theory

Heider's balance theory also provides direct implications for attitude change. Balance theory says that attitudes will change to avoid conflict between beliefs and evaluations.[20] Marketers implicitly use balance theory to create attitudinal conflicts in the hope that the resultant change in consumer brand attitudes will be positive. Thus, Gallo's link to Waterford crystal created conflict because of the luxury image of Waterford and the economy image of Gallo. Balance theory would predict that either Waterford's image will suffer because of the linkage, or Gallo's image will improve. Both Waterford and Gallo obviously believed the latter to be more likely than the former.

The implication in balance theory is that when attitudes conflict, they are easier to change because of consumers' desire for balance. For example, many consumers' attitudes toward environmental control and toward consumption of certain products are in conflict. An individual may have a positive attitude toward disposable diapers but also be strongly in favor of pollution control. According to Heider, such imbalance will produce tension and lead to a change in one or both attitudes. The consumer may realize that disposable diapers are not fully biodegradable. As a result, the consumer's attitude toward disposable diapers will become more negative. On the other hand, the consumer may maintain a positive attitude toward disposable diapers and decrease his or her emphasis on the environment. In either case, attitudes about disposable diapers and environmental protection have to be modified to achieve balance.

Processing Models and Attitude Change: The Elaboration Likelihood Model

The elaboration likelihood model (ELM) described in Chapter 5 is another theory with strategic implications for attitude change.[21] It states that involved consumers process information through a "central route" in which message cues are more likely to be processed, whereas uninvolved consumers use a more peripheral route in which nonmessage cues are more likely to be processed. As a result, in high involvement conditions, attitude change can best be accomplished through advertising that conveys product benefits and information on performance. In low involvement conditions, attitude change can best be accomplished through the use of spokespersons and symbols attached to the product. Because of his likable image that appeals to kids, Bill Cosby was an effective spokesperson for Pudding Pops (a low involvement product). He had little to say about product attributes. All he had to do was appear on TV with a Pudding Pop in his hand.

An important extension of ELM is a consideration of the thoughts consumers have when they process marketing stimuli such as advertisements or sales promotions (referred to as **cognitive responses**).[22] According to cognitive response research, when consumers are involved, they produce thoughts that are more relevant to the message. For example, a consumer who becomes aware of the advertising for Lean Strips, a new product designed by General Foods a number of years ago as a low-fat substitute for bacon, may think to herself, "This product might be good for my diet," or "This might be a good bacon substitute because it is low in fat." In both cases, these thoughts support the advertising; that is, they are **support arguments.** The consumer might also think, "I have my doubts about a bacon substitute. How can it really taste like bacon? Is it as greasy and as fatty as bacon?" This would represent a **counterargument** to the advertised claim.

The existence of both support arguments and counterarguments indicates that the consumer is actively processing the ad's information in a high involvement context. The impact of the ad on the consumer will depend not only on the information in the ad, but also on the interaction between the consumer's thoughts and the ad's message.

In low involvement situations, when consumers process information, they are likely to react with thoughts that are more related to peripheral cues than to the message itself.[23] One such peripheral cue is the source of the message. Less involved consumers might be more likely to reflect on the motives of the advertiser or on less important components of the ad such as the background or the voice of a spokesperson. For example, the consumer seeing the ad for Lean Strips might react more to the source than to the message if he or she is not involved with the product. The consumer might think, "General Foods sponsored this ad and I like their products." This is an example of **source bolstering.** On the other hand, the consumer might react by thinking, "This ad is sponsored by a company trying to sell the product, so why should I believe its claim?" This would be an example of **source derogation.**

Support arguments and counterarguments, therefore, are cognitive responses to marketing stimuli more likely to occur in high involvement situations; source bolstering and derogation are cognitive responses more likely to occur in low involvement situations.

Cognitive Responses and Attitude Change in High Involvement Processing

Consumers involved with breakfast foods and nutrition will pay more attention to and better comprehend a Lean Strip ad. Since involved consumers are more likely to introduce their own thoughts (support arguments or counterarguments) when evaluating ads, there is a greater likelihood that these message-related thoughts will influence beliefs and attitudes about the brand.

To create more positive attitudes, advertisers must discourage counterarguments and promote support arguments. One way to do this is suggested by **inoculation theory,**[24] which proposes that consumers can be "inoculated" against negative thoughts about a product when processing a marketing message with messages that anticipate these negative thoughts and refute them. Such an approach is known as *two-sided refutational advertising.* For example, a spokesperson for Lean Strips in a commercial might say, "You might think a bacon substitute cannot taste as good as bacon; and if it is anything like bacon, it is probably greasy and fatty. [This portion of the commercial anticipates negative reactions.] Well, you have a surprise coming. Just one taste will convince you that Lean Strips tastes like bacon. *And* it is healthier for you because it is less fatty and lower in cholesterol. [This portion is the refutation.]" Such an approach might be successful in changing attitudes for involving products. (Two-sided advertising will be considered further in Chapter 20 when we discuss marketing communications.)

Cognitive Response and Attitude Change in Low Involvement Processing

Marketers can also change consumer attitudes by influencing cognitive responses in low involvement conditions. Just as marketers will attempt to discourage counterarguments and encourage support arguments for involved consumers, they will seek to discourage source derogation and encourage source bolstering for uninvolved consumers.

Two strategies designed to discourage source derogation are to increase the attractiveness of the source and to increase its credibility. If consumers are not involved, an effective way to draw attention to the ad is through an attractive and likable spokesperson. Bill Cosby was used as a spokesperson for Pudding

Pops because of his attractiveness, not because of any expertise he had regarding the product. The second strategy to discourage source derogation is to increase the credibility of the source.[25] A testimonial from the American Dental Association for the cavity prevention properties of fluoride in Crest made it the leading toothpaste brand. Expert spokespersons such as Michael Jordan for Nike basketball sneakers or Ella Fitzgerald for Memorex sound tapes also enhance the credibility of the ad.

Of the two strategies, increasing source attractiveness is more likely to change attitudes for uninvolved consumers because they may consider product expertise not that important in a category for which their brand evaluation is minimal. Not surprisingly, marketers use spokespersons to increase attractiveness for less involving products like Pudding Pops, whereas they use experts for more involving products like athletic shoes and sound tapes.

◆ ATTITUDE CHANGE AFTER A PURCHASE

Marketers may seek to change consumer brand attitudes after as well as before a purchase. Such a strategy may attempt to counter competitive advertising that creates doubts in consumers' mind about the purchase, or it may attempt to counteract negative experiences with the product. Three theories provide strategy implications for attitude change after the purchase: dissonance theory, attribution theory, and the theory of passive learning. These theories are briefly reviewed here within the context of attitude change strategies.

Dissonance Theory

Dissonance theory suggests that marketers should seek to reduce dissonance by supplying consumers with positive information about the brand after the purchase. Runyon cites five strategies to provide supporting information after the purchase and, thus, to reduce dissonance:

1. Provide additional product information and suggestions for product care and maintenance through brochures or advertising.
2. Provide warranties and guaranties to reduce postpurchase doubt.
3. Ensure good service and immediate follow-up on complaints to provide postpurchase support.
4. Advertise reliable product quality and performance to reassure recent purchasers of product satisfaction.
5. Follow up after the purchase with direct contacts to make sure the customer understands how to use the product and to ensure satisfaction.[26] A study by Hunt showed that such postpurchase reassurances from a seller were effective in reducing consumer dissonance after purchase of a refrigerator.[27]

All of these strategies are relevant for high risk, high involvement product categories. They are designed to change consumer attitudes toward the product by reducing postpurchase doubts.

Attribution Theory

Attribution theory states that consumers seek to estimate causes (or attributions) for events, often after the fact.[28] Postpurchase behavioral attributions are most likely to occur when a consumer has purchased the product with little evaluation of brand alternatives. The consumer can attribute product performance to his or her choice (I made a very economical purchase) or to the product (This brand is a good value for the money). In both cases, the reason the consumer ascribed to the purchase is essentially an afterthought resulting in a change in attitudes as a result of the behavior.

If this is true, attribution theory implies that advertisers should give consumers positive reasons for the purchase after they have bought the product. For example, a consumer buys a brand of coffee on sale and attributes the purchase to the fact the brand is cheaper. Such an attribution is unlikely to win any long-term converts to the brand. However, if the manufacturer's advertising could convince the consumer that the brand makes a richer, heftier brew, the consumer is likely to buy again. The important point is that the manufacturer is trying to convince the consumer of the claim after the purchase.

Based on attribution theory, a marketing strategy for low involvement products is to demonstrate potentially significant product differences that consumers can use as a rationale for having purchased after the fact. Such differences give consumers a reason for buying again. Marketers cannot rely solely on price promotions to influence consumers to buy uninvolving products. They must use advertising to provide a nonprice rationale to buy the same brand again.

Passive Learning

Krugman's passive learning theory states that consumers learn about brands with little involvement and purchase with little evaluation of alternative brands.[29] Attitudes are more likely to be formed after, rather than before, a purchase.

Krugman's theory is most relevant for developing strategies to increase the level of consumer involvement after the purchase. Marketers seek to increase involvement with their brand because a higher level of commitment means that true, rather than spurious, brand loyalty is more likely to result. In Chapter 5, we cited the following strategies for increasing involvement:

1. Link the product to an involving issue.
2. Link the product to an involving personal situation.
3. Link the product to involving advertising.
4. Change the importance of product benefits.
5. Introduce an important characteristic in the product.

The first three strategies cited are illustrated in the Kmart ad discussed at the beginning of this chapter. Showing a working woman relishing a relaxing moment between work and family is an involving issue, an involving personal situation, and an involving ad for the target segment. Any increase in involvement with Kmart should result in a more favorable attitude toward the store. As in dissonance and attribution theories, such a favorable shift in attitude often follows behavior.

◆ TYPES OF STRATEGIES FOR ATTITUDE REINFORCEMENT AND CHANGE

Given the preceding principles of attitude change, we can now cite various types of strategies that serve either to reinforce existing attitudes or to change them. Such strategies rely on **product positioning,** that is, communicating product attributes and benefits to a defined target segment. Since product positioning is closely linked to defining market segments, we will be considering positioning alternatives in more detail when we discuss market segmentation in Chapter 12.

Strategies to Reinforce Attitudes

Marketers can use **reinforcement strategies** to attract new users or to appeal to existing users with new or existing products. These alternatives, illustrated in Figure 9.2, produce four types of reinforcement strategies:

1. Reinforcing positive attitudes among existing users of a brand.
2. Attracting new users to an existing brand by emphasizing the brand's positive benefits.
3. Positioning new products to meet the needs of existing users.
4. Positioning new products to satisfy the needs of new and emerging markets.

In each of these strategies, marketers are reinforcing existing attitudes rather than attempting to change them.

Reinforcing Existing Users

Companies use advertising to maintain users' positive attitudes toward their products. In this way, companies are ensuring the loyalty of their core users. Most advertising by Campbell's Soup is directed to increasing the amount of soup consumed by existing consumers. Because of its dominant position in the canned soup market, Campbell's most effective strategy is to reinforce attitudes of existing users rather than to try to change the attitudes of nonusers.

In the past, Campbell tried to increase soup consumption by touting the benefits of canned soup with themes such as "Soup for Lunch," and "Soup for

▶**FIGURE 9.2**
Marketing strategies to
reinforce positive
attitudes

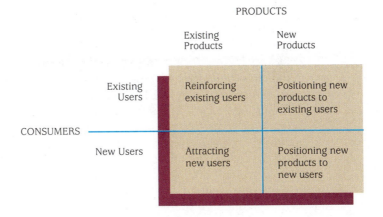

One." With a share of the canned soup market close to 80 percent, increasing canned soup consumption meant increasing Campbell's sales. However, as competition from dried soup cut into Campbell's sales and the market became more value-oriented, simple appeals to eat more soup began to wear thin. So in 1991, Campbell began advertising individual soups to specific targets, often on a regional basis—for example, nacho-cheese soup targeted to the Southwest, Creole soup to southern markets, and red bean soup to Hispanic markets.[30] The focus on existing users remains, but the emphasis has shifted from advertising the product category to advertising individual soup flavors.

Attracting New Users to Existing Products

Management will attract new users to their existing products by showing that they can better deliver desired benefits than can other alternatives. Nestlé developed an ad campaign to appeal to heavy users of iced tea. A study of attitudes toward iced tea among users found that the heaviest users were those who viewed iced tea as a way of restoring energy and as a good year-round drink.[31] This group accounts for 17 percent of the market but 36 percent of the volume of iced tea used. However, most of the heavy users bought competitive brands. Clearly, "restores energy" and "good year-round drink" were the key benefits that might convince heavy iced tea drinkers to switch to Nestea. Further, each advertising dollar directed to the heavy users has the potential to be twice as effective as a dollar spent on the total market, as this group consumes twice as much as the average iced tea drinker.

The least concentrated group is made up of consumers who rated iced tea low on "restores energy" and on "easy to prepare." Members of this group represented 30 percent of the market but only 16 percent of consumption. One may argue that changing these consumers' beliefs about iced tea to a product that "restores energy" would be a good expenditure of resources, as they then would behave more like heavy iced tea drinkers. This could be true, but it would entail more risks than a reinforcement strategy of appealing to the heavy user group. If consumers strongly hold the belief that iced tea does not restore energy, then there is little chance that advertising will change it.

Positioning New Products to Existing Users

Companies introduce new products to meet the well-defined needs of existing users of a product category. Frequently, these products represent line extensions of existing brands. The introduction of Crest in gel form was meant to appeal to a more taste-oriented segment of the toothpaste market. The original brand was not effectively positioned to this segment.

Similarly, Coca-Cola's introduction of Diet Coke was meant to meet the need for a low-calorie cola among men. Tab, the company's well-established low-calorie cola, appealed primarily to women. In its initial advertising, Diet Coke featured Phil Esposito, the sports announcer, and Judd Hirsch, the actor. The campaign was built on the positive association with Coca-Cola and was directed to an existing market—males who drink low-calorie colas. Eventually, the brand became so successful that it appealed to women and dominated Tab.

Positioning New Products to New Users

Marketers seek opportunities to meet the needs of new and emerging markets. In these cases, the intent is not so much to reinforce existing attitudes but to establish new ones. For example, Motorola's introduction of cellular telephones in the mid-1980s met the need for mobile communications in the business market. Motorola was instrumental in developing in-car and walk-around (hand-held) cellular telephones as well as the regional cells that ensure decreased interference compared to regular portable and car telephones. Motorola's link with mobile communications in customers' minds made it easy for the company to establish positive attitudes toward a new product, cellular telephones.

Let us consider how Motorola might have investigated the opportunity to introduce cellular telephones into the business communications market. Motorola first determines the benefits that businesspeople seek in business communications. It develops a vocabulary of communications benefits (precision, speed, service, walk-around communications, in-car communications, privacy, and so on) and then surveys business organizations responsible for communications. It then asks these organizations to determine their most important benefits.

On this basis, Motorola identifies three benefit segments, shown in Figure 9.3. One emphasizes interference-free communications while driving. This group is composed of customers in sales and service-related businesses. Another group emphasizes interference-free walk-around communications. This group is composed primarily of doctors and other medical professionals. A third group emphasizes the greater privacy portable communications affords. This group is composed primarily of corporate executives.

Motorola then presents a concept description of a cellular telephone to various businesspeople to get their reaction. Researchers ask the businesspeople

▶FIGURE 9.3
Benefit segments in the cellular telephone market

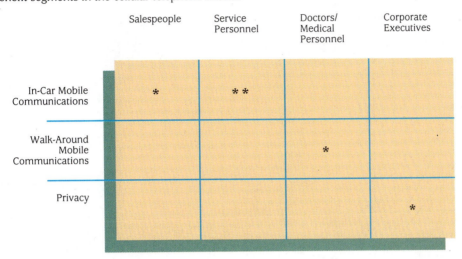

	Salespeople	Service Personnel	Doctors/ Medical Personnel	Corporate Executives
In-Car Mobile Communications	*	**		
Walk-Around Mobile Communications			*	
Privacy				*

*   = Primary market
** = Secondary market

to rate the cellular telephone concept as well as other modes of communications by the key communications attributes. The analysis in Figure 9.4 shows how businesspeople rate the various communications modes. Mail is seen as providing documentation and interference-free communications; fax transmissions, as providing speed and precision; and the telephone, as providing economy and service. The cellular telephone (shown as "cellular concept test") is seen as delivering the key benefits of both in-car and walk-around mobile communications and, to a lesser extent, privacy with no interference. Furthermore, as expected, doctors more strongly link cellular to the benefit of walk-around mobility; salespeople, to the benefit of in-car communications; and corporate executives, to the benefit of privacy (as shown by the circles in Figure 9.4).

These are the beliefs customers have of each mode of communications. The next step is to determine how these beliefs influence overall attitudes. Researchers now ask customers their preferences for each mode. They find that salespeople and service personnel have strong positive attitudes to cellular. Corporate executives have generally positive attitudes, although many are not sure that cellular provides distinct benefits over other less expensive forms of communication. Doctors are divided between cellular and beepers, but many decide that beepers are sufficient for their needs. On this basis, Motorola decides that its initial target will be customers in sales and service businesses with a possible future extension of the market to doctors and corporate executives.

The next step is to produce a few prototype cellular telephones for product testing. Motorola then asks sales and service organizations to try the prototype and then rate it in relation to other modes of communication. The ratings

▶**FIGURE 9.4**
Beliefs regarding alternative communications modes

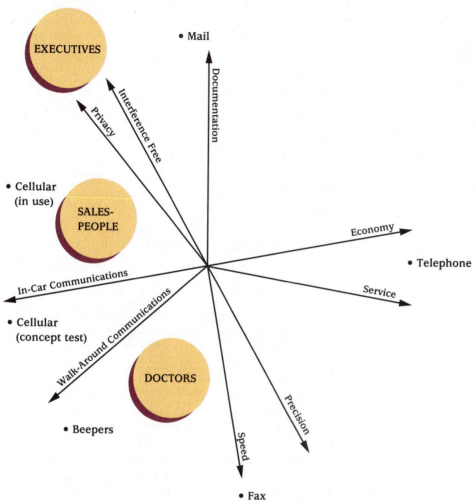

of the cellular phone in this use test (shown in Figure 9.4 as "cellular in use") are similar to those in the concept test. This means that customers received the expected benefits when they used the product.

Finally, customers are asked their intention to buy cellular telephones. Thus, Motorola's researchers have asked customers all components of the attitudinal model: beliefs, attitudes (overall evaluation), and intentions. Researchers have also confirmed that an opportunity to market cellular telephones exists based on the positive linkages among (1) beliefs and brand attitudes; (2) brand attitudes and intention to buy; and (3) beliefs, attitudes, and intentions for the product concept and the product in use.

Strategies to Change Attitudes

Strategies that attempt to change consumer attitudes generally require repositioning an existing brand; that is, changing the set of attributes and benefits communicated to consumers to influence them to buy. Marketers can direct such repositioning strategies to existing users to improve the brand's image or target them to nonusers to influence them to switch to the brand.

Changing Attitudes of Existing Users

Companies faced with declining sales often attempt to reposition their offerings to existing users. We saw that both People Express and Oldsmobile attempted to reposition themselves in a declining market and failed, largely because their images were so entrenched in consumers' minds.

Arrow Shirts has been more successful in repositioning itself. The company's image as a purveyor of conservative white shirts was restricting sales in an increasingly fashion-oriented market; so, Arrow expanded its offerings with a wider line of sports shirts and casual wear. Its innovative campaign to change its image is shown in Exhibit 9.4.

Very often, attempts at repositioning to reverse downward demand trends are undertaken on an industry-wide basis through a cooperative advertising effort. The California Milk Advisory Board's campaign in Exhibit 9.1 is an example. The industry has been successful in positioning milk as the fitness drink of the '90s because its appeals conform to the current emphasis on health and nutrition.

In the past, cooperative campaigns to reverse downward demand trends were run for men's hats and for sterling silverware. Both campaigns failed because they were swimming against, rather than with, the consumer tide. The campaign for men's hats tried to bring back a conservative look that contradicted the trend toward youth and vigor. The campaign for sterling silverware failed because it tried to bring back the custom of giving sterling silverware as a wedding present. The campaign contradicted the trend toward greater informality.

Changing Attitudes of Nonusers

In an attempt to appeal to new segments of the market, companies often attempt to change attitudes among nonusers. Often these changes are necessary for the company to assure future sales. We saw that AT&T is trying to change its image among younger consumers who are using alternative services. Similarly, Kmart is trying to change its image among more fashion-oriented, affluent working women. In both cases, younger consumers view these companies as conservative and old-fashioned.

By appealing to married couples and families, Club Med was successful in changing the attitude that the resort chain is for swinging singles. Avon is changing attitudes toward its offerings by advertising higher-priced lines for more-affluent women.

▶**EXHIBIT 9.4**
Changing attitudes to conform to an expanded product line
Source: Courtesy of The Arrow Company, a division of Cluett, Peabody & Co., Inc.

◆ SOCIETAL APPLICATIONS OF ATTITUDE CHANGE

So far, we have discussed changes in consumer attitudes regarding brands and companies. Marketing also has a role in changing consumer attitudes toward social issues. An example is the advertising campaign cited in Chapter 6 (Exhibit 6.5) to correct the many misconceptions about AIDS. The campaign, sponsored by the U.S. Department of Health, was designed to eliminate some of the fears about contracting AIDS, and in so doing, to encourage the public to become less fearful of and more tolerant toward those who have contracted the disease.

Changing attitudes toward social issues such as AIDS is a difficult task because such attitudes are almost always deep-seated. Very often people reject the message because it conflicts with strongly held beliefs. Another factor creating difficulty is that such attempts are generally public-service campaigns that rely on free media time. As such, TV time is relegated to off-peak hours and exposure is minimal.

There have been some successes in changing consumer attitudes through marketing communications. Both the American Cancer Society and the American Heart Association have used advertising to increase awareness of the risks of smoking. Such advertising has been successful over the years in a supportive role in conjunction with information from government sources (for example, the Surgeon General's Office).

One of the most successful campaigns to change attitudes toward a social issue was organized by business rather than nonprofit institutions. A group of advertising agencies and media companies formed the Partnership for a Drug-Free America to develop an advertising campaign to reduce drug use. The purpose was to create an attitude of intolerance toward drugs. The target was nonusers and occasional drug users. If attitudes toward drug use could be changed among this broad-based group, then peer group and family pressure might discourage drug use among heavier users.[32]

Unlike other social issue campaigns, this one was intensive. Some 300 ads were created for all the major media and run without charge. (See Exhibit 9.5.) Had a product been advertised, the equivalent expenditures would have been $900 million. Because of this intensive effort, the campaign has been highly successful. In markets where the ads were run most frequently, more teens said there is a greater risk in using marijuana and more preteens spoke to teachers about drugs. Further, the use of cocaine went down during this period.[33] Although these changes cannot be solely attributed to the campaign, the greater improvement in attitudes and decreased use in markets with more advertising suggest the ads were highly effective.

The efforts of the consortium of companies making up the Partnership shows that business can play a constructive role in changing consumer attitudes toward social issues. Similarly, the campaign the Department of Health ran regarding AIDS shows that government also has a role in such attitude change. Obviously, business, government, and charitable agencies can do more on a host of social issues from environmental protection to health care.

SUMMARY

This chapter has described principles of attitude reinforcement and change. Attitudes are easier to change when they are weakly held, when consumers are not involved with the product, when consumers have little confidence in evaluating the brand, and when information is ambiguous. Certain components of attitudes are easier to change: Beliefs are easier to change than desired benefits, and beliefs are easier to change than evaluations of the brand.

Various attitudinal theories were described as a basis for changing consumer attitudes before and after a purchase. The attitudinal theories most relevant for changing attitudes before a purchase are multiattribute models, Katz's functional theory of attitudes, Sherif's social judgment theory, Heider's balance theory, and the elaboration likelihood model. Multiattribute models suggest

▶**EXHIBIT 9.5**

Changing attitudes toward a social issue

Source: Courtesy of Partnership For a Drug-Free America

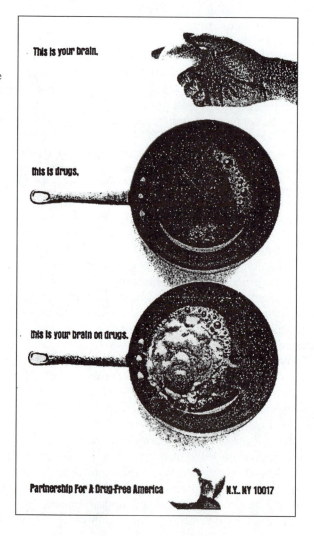

changing desired benefits, beliefs about a brand, the overall evaluation of the brand, or behavior directly without attempting to change attitudes. Functional theory provides guidelines for strategies to change utilitarian, value-expressive, and ego-defensive attitudes and to change attitudes by providing knowledge. Social judgment theory suggests that attitude change should take place within consumers' latitude of acceptance. Balance theory says that attitudes change to avoid conflict between beliefs and evaluations.

The elaboration likelihood model distinguishes attitude change in high and low involvement conditions. It suggests using message cues to influence consumer attitudes in high involvement situations and peripheral cues such as use of spokespersons or the layout of an ad to change attitudes in low involvement conditions.

Marketers may also seek to change consumer attitudes toward a brand after a purchase. Three theories provide strategic guidelines. Dissonance theory suggests that advertisers should provide consumers with positive information after they purchase it to reduce dissonance. Attribution theory suggests that marketers supply consumers with a reason for purchasing after the fact. The theory of passive learning suggests that inertia can be translated into brand loyalty by increasing consumers' commitment to the brand.

The chapter also discussed various strategies to reinforce or change consumer attitudes. Strategies to reinforce consumer attitudes are designed to:

- Reinforce positive attitudes among existing users.
- Attract new users by emphasizing benefits of existing products.
- Introduce new offerings to existing users of the product category.
- Introduce new products to new users.

Strategies to change attitudes are designed to reposition products to strengthen the brand among existing users or to attract new segments.

The chapter concluded by considering attitude change for social issues. Marketing has an important role in changing consumer attitudes toward key issues such as preventive health care, perceptions of AIDS, smoking, and environmental protection.

The last four chapters have been concerned with consumer thought variables. The next two chapters cover consumer characteristics; namely, demographics, personality, and lifestyle.

QUESTIONS

1. Why is it easier to implement strategies reinforcing rather than changing attitudes?
2. Which of the following companies might find it most difficult to change consumers' attitudes toward its products and why?
   - Manufacturer of breakfast cereals trying to attract the adult market.
   - Specialty retailer introducing a line of designer clothes.

- Low-priced, no-frills airline that decides to expand its routes, add services, and increase fares.
- Fast-food outlet that decides to open a chain of low-priced restaurants.

3. Which of the companies cited in Question 2 do you think would find it easiest to change consumer attitudes? Why?

4. What problems might the Department of Transportation face in mounting an advertising campaign to influence people to switch from automobiles to mass transit?

5. When Cadillac introduced a medium-sized car, it could have developed a reinforcement or a change strategy in communicating this basic change in its line. What focus could advertising have taken in following (a) a reinforcement strategy and (b) a change strategy?

6. A manufacturer of high-priced stereo components finds that attitudes toward the company's line of products are very positive, but many stereo purchasers are uncertain of the criteria to use in selecting components and, therefore, reduce risk by buying the lowest-priced or the best-known brand. The company would like to increase consumers' confidence in the purchase process. By doing so, it believes it will increase the likelihood consumers will buy its products. What strategies can the company use to increase consumers' self-confidence in the purchasing process?

7. Consider this statement: "Attitudes are easier to change when there is a low level of ego involvement." In view of this statement, why might it be particularly hard to change attitudes toward a consumer's regular perfume, baby food, and clothing store?

8. Values based on deep-seated social and cultural norms are the most difficult to change. Can you cite examples of advertising campaigns that have attempted to change such deep-seated norms? Were they successful? Why or why not?

9. What are the differences among (a) dissonance theory, (b) attribution theory, and (c) the theory of passive learning in explaining attitude change after a purchase?

10. A producer of ready-to-eat cereals conducts a survey and finds that consumers who rate the company's brand high on nutrition are more likely to buy it. These consumers tend to be younger and more affluent. The advertising manager decides to direct a major portion of the advertising budget to nonusers (older, less-affluent consumers) to try to convince them of the cereal's nutritional content. The manager reasons there will be a higher payoff in attempting to change attitudes of nonusers than in reinforcing attitudes of users. What are the pros and cons of this argument?

11. If Motorola found that mobile communication was a relatively unimportant attribute of cellular phones, one option would be to try to change benefit criteria by demonstrating the importance of mobile communication to businesses through an advertising campaign.
    - What are the pros and cons of such a strategy?
    - Under what circumstances is such a strategy most likely to succeed?

12. What role can marketing play in changing consumer attitudes toward social issues? Why are such attempts more difficult than changing attitudes for products and brands?

RESEARCH ASSIGNMENTS

1. Select a frequently purchased product for study (such as soft drinks, coffee, detergents). Select a sample of about 100 product users.
   a. Develop a description of a fictitious brand and give it to consumers. The description should come from a neutral source such as a government agency.
   b. Ask the consumer to rate the brand from poor to excellent.
   c. Split the sample into three groups:
      • Group 1 receives an ad reinforcing the prior brand description (a reinforcement strategy).
      • Group 2 receives an ad meant to change beliefs about the brand ("Brand X is much tastier or much more effective than previously described").
      • Group 3 receives an ad attempting to change values (for example, an ad saying brands with low sudsing ability are more effective).
   d. Ask consumers to rate the brand again after they see one of these three ads.

   If a reinforcement strategy is more effective, one would expect the first ad to produce the most positive attitudes. Furthermore, of the two change strategies, one would expect the ad attempting to change beliefs to produce more positive effects than the ad attempting to change values. Do your findings conform to these expectations?

2. Principles of attitude change suggest that attitudes are easier to change when consumers are less confident in their evaluations of a brand. Pick a product category and ask consumers to rate three of the leading brands on (a) an overall basis and (b) a vocabulary of product attributes. In addition, ask consumers to (c) rate their degree of confidence in making judgments about brands in the category and (d) rate the degree to which they think the product is important to them.

   Present consumers with ads for each of the three brands in a dummy magazine format. Have consumers rate the brands once again on an overall basis and on the vocabulary of product attributes.
   • Do overall brand ratings for those consumers who have less confidence in their brand evaluations shift more than those of consumers who have a greater degree of confidence?
   • Do ratings shift in the direction of the advertised claims?
   • Attitude theory also suggests that those who rate the product category as less important are more likely to change attitudes. Do your findings support this?

3. Marketers sometimes seek to induce a behavior change without appeals to attitudes by offering brands at a lower price. The theory of cognitive dissonance would predict that if the consumer bought a brand other than the regular brand at a much lower price, the attitude toward the brand would be more negative than if the brand were bought at a price only slightly lower than the regular brand.

- Select a heavily dealed product category such as coffee, paper towels, or detergents. Identify a sample of consumers who recently bought a brand other than their regular brand on a price deal or by coupon. Determine attitudes for the brand purchased.
- Do your data confirm the hypothesis that the greater the price differential between the regular and the dealed brand, the more negative the attitude toward the brand purchased on deal?

NOTES

1. "Will Kmart Ever Be a Silk Purse," *Business Week* (January 22, 1990), p. 46.

2. "For Big or Small, Image Is Everything," *Adweek* (March 8, 1993), pp. 28–29.

3. "Shaping Kmart's New Style," *Advertising Age* (December 7, 1992), pp. 20–21.

4. "How Polaroid Flashed Back," *Fortune* (February 16, 1987), pp. 72–76; and "Polaroid Snaps the Customer," *American Demographics* (February, 1987), pp. 21–22.

5. "Polaroid Enlarges Ad Budget," *Advertising Age* (February 7, 1987), p. 76.

6. James McCullough, Douglas MacLachlan, and Reza Moinpour, "Impact of Information on Preference and Perception," in Andrew Mitchell, ed., *Advances in Consumer Research,* Vol. 9 (Ann Arbor, MI: Association for Consumer Research, 1982), pp. 402–405.

7. S. P. Raj, "The Effects of Advertising on High and Low Loyalty Consumer Segments," *Journal of Consumer Research,* 9 (June, 1982), pp. 77–89.

8. Richard J. Lutz, "Changing Brand Attitudes Through Modification of Cognitive Structures," *Journal of Consumer Research,* 1 (March, 1975), pp. 49–59.

9. M. Sherif and C. E. Hovland, *Social Judgment* (New Haven: Yale University Press, 1964).

10. "How Lubriderm Shed Its Image as a Cream for Problem Skin," *Adweek's Marketing Week* (July 3, 1989), pp. 44–45.

11. Neil H. Borden and Martin V. Marshall, *Advertising Management: Text and Cases* (Homewood, IL: Richard D. Irwin, 1959), p. 126.

12. Benjamin Lipstein, "Anxiety, Risk and Uncertainty in Advertising Effectiveness Measurements," in Lee Adler and Irving Crespi, eds., *Attitude Research on the Rocks* (Chicago: American Marketing Association, 1968), pp. 11–27.

13. "Resorting to Blandishments to Fight Image of Blandness," *The New York Times* (August 10, 1992), p. D7.

14. Joseph W. Newman, *Marketing Management and Information* (Homewood, IL: Richard D. Irwin, 1967), pp. 211–217, Sanka Case (B).

15. Leon Festinger, *A Theory of Cognitive Dissonance* (New York: Harper & Row, 1957).

16. Daniel Katz, "The Functional Approach to the Study of Attitudes," *Public Opinion Quarterly,* 24 (Summer, 1960), pp. 163–204.

17. Sherif and Hovland, *Social Judgment, loc. cit.*

18. "The Pleasure Merchants of Club Med," *Marketing Communications* (April, 1986), pp. 21–24.

19. John C. Maloney, "Is Advertising Believability Really Important?" *Journal of Marketing,* 27 (October, 1963), pp. 1–8.

20. Fritz Heider, *The Psychology of Interpersonal Relations* (New York: John Wiley, 1958).

21. Richard E. Petty and John T. Cacioppo, *Attitudes and Persuasion: Classic and Contemporary Approaches* (Dubuque, IA: William C. Brown Co., 1981).

22. See Peter Wright, "The Cognitive Processes Mediating Acceptance of Advertising," *Journal of Marketing Research,* 10 (February, 1973), pp. 53–62.

23. Martin R. Lautman and Larry Percy, "Cognitive and Affective Responses in Attribute-Based versus End-Benefit Oriented Advertising," in Thomas C. Kinnear, ed., *Advances in Consumer Research,* Vol. 11 (Provo, UT: Association for Consumer Research, 1984), pp. 11–17.

24. George J. Szybillo and Richard Heslin, "Resistance to Persuasion: Inoculation Theory in a Marketing Context," *Journal of Marketing Research,* 10 (November, 1973), pp. 396–403.

25. See Robert B. Settle and Linda L. Golden, "Attribution Theory and Advertiser Credibility," *Journal of Marketing Research,* 11 (May, 1974), pp. 181–185.

26. Kenneth B. Runyon, *Consumer Behavior and the Practice of Marketing* (Columbus, OH: Charles E. Merrill, 1977), p. 287.

27. Shelby D. Hunt, "Post-Transaction Communications and Dissonance Reduction," *Journal of Marketing,* 34 (July, 1970), pp. 46–51.

28. D. Bem, "Attitudes as Self-Descriptions: Another Look at the Attitude-Behavior Link," in A. Greenwald, T. Brock, and T. Ostrom, eds., *Psychological Foundations of Attitudes* (New York: Academic Press, 1968). For applications of attribution theory to consumer behavior, see Bobby Calder, "When Attitudes Follow Behavior—A Self-Perception/Dissonance Interpretation of Low Involvement," in John C. Maloney and Bernard Silverman, eds., *Attitude Research Plays for High Stakes* (Chicago: American Marketing Association, 1979), pp. 25–36.

29. Herbert E. Krugman, "The Impact of Television Advertising Learning Without Involvement," *Public Opinion Quarterly,* 29 (Fall, 1965), pp. 349–356.

30. "Hail to the Chef," *Fortune* (February 11, 1991), pp. 52–54; and "M'm, M'm, Okay," *Adweek* (October 10, 1988), p. 22.

31. Henry Assael, "Segmenting Markets by Group Purchasing Behavior: An Application of the AID Technique," *Journal of Marketing Research,* 7 (May, 1970), pp. 153–158.

32. Media-Advertising Partnership for a Drug-Free America, *What We've Learned About Advertising* (New York: American Association of Advertising Agencies, 1990).

33. *It Works* (New York: American Association of Advertising Agencies, 1991), pp. 31–37.

10

Demographics and Social Class

BMW TARGETS A KEY DEMOGRAPHIC GROUP: PROFESSIONAL WOMEN

Demographic characteristics such as age, income, family size, and employment status are the objective descriptors of individual consumers and households. The markets for most products are influenced by consumer demographic characteristics. For example, marketers consider whether a family is just starting out (more likely to buy kitchen appliances), whether a consumer is middle-aged when economic stress is likely to be greatest (more likely to buy stomach remedies), or whether a consumer is in the mature market and has more disposable income (more likely to travel).

The 1980s saw major changes in the demographic composition of American consumers, and these changes have had a substantial impact on the fabric of life and purchasing patterns in American society. Consider one of the most significant changes: the increasing proportion of working women, and more particularly, rise of the professional woman. As she broke new ground and increased her earning power, the woman executive became a major economic force. The shift created opportunities for marketers who understood her needs and psychology. Cosmetics companies such as Revlon and clothing manufacturers such as Donna Karan were among them. However, not everyone was adept at targeting products to the needs and attitudes of the professional woman. The luxury auto market, for instance, stumbled terribly in its attempts to reach working women. It had spent so many decades using scantily clad models to entice men that it seemed to have no idea what the professional woman wanted.

At first, some car makers tried placing women in the same product ads they had always produced for men. However, it quickly became clear that a more dramatic approach was needed, especially when the automobile showroom remained a place where women were treated like second-class citizens. So companies such as BMW began a large-scale effort to better understand a group that spends an estimated $65 billion on cars annually.[1]

The new demographic research was revealing. BMW, for example, had thought that professional women wanted a car designed specifically for them, but focus groups showed that they share the same desires as men: They want a car that is safe, reliable, and durable. Likewise, conventional wisdom held that women tended to buy with their children in mind. However, a survey conducted recently by the Condé Nast magazine group found that women are "more likely to purchase cars for themselves" while men are "more likely to buy cars for the family."[2]

While BMW has shied away from creating a "woman's commercial," it has used this data to stress style and performance in its appeals to women. In 1993, for instance, the company invited women journalists to view video testimonials from female BMW owners discussing road feel and driving excitement. The hope was that the writers would convey the testimonials to their audience, thereby creating interest among prospective women customers. BMW also opened a driving school for women who are interested in learning advanced driving skills, such as how to take a high-speed turn. As one BMW executive noted in explaining why car companies must stop talking down to women drivers: "Women under 40 grew up driving, not sitting in the passenger seat." To reach the 25- to 50-year-old women with an active lifestyle who it believes is its ideal customer, BMW underwrites rock climbing competitions, biking events, marathons, and even triathalons.

The 1980s and 1990s have seen many other major demographic changes that have had an impact on American society. There is the aging baby boom market (the group born in the two decades after World War II), the growth of the mature market (those over 50), and the changing composition of U.S. households with later marriages, more divorces, and more single-member households.

In this chapter, we will consider each of these trends, starting with the most basic trend of all: Changes in the rate of population growth. We then consider:

- Results of past population growth on the age distribution of the American market.

- Socioeconomic changes affecting purchasing power and patterns of consumption; namely, income, education, and the increasing proportion of working women.
- Changes in household composition.

The chapter concludes by describing how marketers use demographics to formulate brand strategies.

One caution: This chapter considers demographic trends in the U.S. market. Worldwide demographic trends have also affected marketing strategies of international companies. Global aspects of consumer behavior are considered in Chapter 14. Also, there are major differences in demographic characteristics between whites, African-Americans, Hispanic-Americans, and Asian-Americans. These differences are also considered in Chapter 14 in a discussion of subcultures in the United States.

NATURE OF DEMOGRAPHIC CHARACTERISTICS

In the previous four chapters, we have been dealing with consumer thought variables—consumer perceptions and attitudes. The distinction between these thought variables and demographics is important. Perceptions and attitudes are product-specific, whereas demographics are generalized. A perception or attitude must be related to a particular brand or product (advertising the need for a pick-me-up may be relevant for coffee but not for detergents). A demographic characteristic such as age is relevant for both coffee and detergents.

Perceptions and attitudes represent cognitive processes; that is, they take place in consumers' minds. Both cognitive processes are subjective and difficult to formulate and measure. Demographics are more objective, standardized, and measurable. (Age is age; income is income.) As a result, demographics are the most widely used consumer descriptors. However, standardization is also a weakness. Perceptions and attitudes may be better related to consumer behavior because they have been defined with the product in mind. Nevertheless, demographics are important as consumer descriptors because they often define whether consumers can buy (income) and whether they want to buy (age, marital status, household composition).

Marketers are interested in both long-term demographic trends, such as the changing age profile of the U.S. market, and the more particular demographic profile of their customers. When marketers ask who their customers are, they frequently refer to the age, income, and regional makeup of customers buying their brand. For example, when AT&T asked why its share of the long-distance phone market fell by a sizable 23 percent between 1984 and 1991, it found that adults under age 40 (*young baby boomers*) found it unapproachable and stodgy. So it redesigned its media campaign to position itself as an innovative computer and communications company, reasoning that, in the words of one executive, "Younger people want to experiment more."[3]

In the next section, we consider the broadest demographic trend: changes in population growth.

◆ POPULATION GROWTH

Although the rate tapered off between 1970 and 1990, the U.S. population has increased steadily since this country was formed. In this decade, however, the United States is expected to experience its biggest population jump since the 1950s.[4]

Population growth is determined by three factors: birthrate, life span, and immigration. Immigration was instrumental in fueling growth until 1920. A high birthrate has fueled growth at various periods in our history, often tied to war and prosperity. For example, the birthrate was at a low during the Depression and World War II, and then it more than doubled after the war in what is known as the baby boom period. More recently, a rise in the birthrate, increased life expectancy, and increases in immigration have fueled population growth. Let us consider these three factors further.

Birthrate

Substantial swings have occurred in the birthrate since World War II. (See Figure 10.1.) The birthrate increased by 50 percent from 1940 to its highest point in 1957 and then decreased to a historic low in 1976. The period from 1946 to 1964 is known as the baby boom period, a term that reflects the higher birthrate at the time. From 1965 to 1976, the birthrate steadily increased. Some called this period the "baby bust" period. From 1976 to 1985, the birthrate increased slightly, largely as a result of the baby boom generation entering its childbearing years. As a result of this "echo boom," by 1991 there were 15 percent more preschoolers than there were in 1980.[5]

The rate is expected to increase through the mid-1990s, as thirty-something baby boomers, new immigrants, and professionals in their 40s who have delayed having families push the national fertility rate higher. The rate has gone from 1.825 births per woman in 1986 to approximately 2.1 births per woman in 1992.[6] However, the birthrate is expected to drop sharply again by the turn of the century as the baby boomers leave their childbearing years and the smaller baby buster group enters theirs.

Gerber illustrates the impact of variations in the birthrate on marketing strategy. Declining baby food sales in the late 1960s and 1970s led the company to seek growth elsewhere. It unsuccessfully tried to diversify into foods for the elderly, life insurance, and transportation. The current increase in the birthrate provided an opportunity for the company to revert to the business it knew best—baby products. In 1993, it introduced a microwaveable line of foods for toddlers called Gerber's Graduates after previously lending its name to

▶**FIGURE 10.1**

Birthrate in the United States: 1940 to 2000

Sources: U.S. Department of Health and Human Services, *Monthly Vital Statistics Report* (June 7, 1990), Table I-1, p. 1–7; U.S. Department of Commerce, Bureau of the Census, *Statistical Abstract of the United States, 1990* (Washington, D.C.: Government Printing Office, 1990), Table 821, p. 63; U.S. Department of Commerce, Bureau of the Census, *Statistical Abstract of the United States, 1992* (Washington, D.C.: Government Printing Office, 1992).

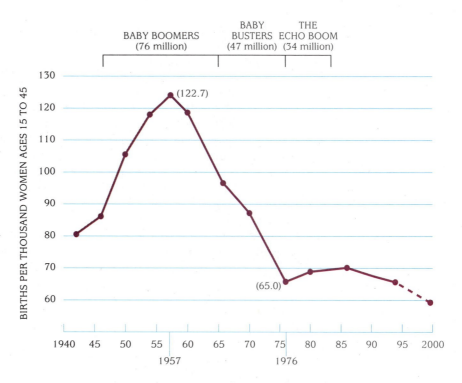

toiletries, clothing, toys, and humidifiers. It financed this growth by selling off some of its ventures into adult products.[7]

Gerber's move from food to a larger array of baby products reflects the baby boomers' willingness to spend more on their children. Since many marry and have children relatively late in life, they are willing to spend more on baby clothes and toys, thus creating a more lucrative market.

Life Expectancy

Due to medical improvements, life expectancy has been constantly increasing in recent years. Advances in combating heart disease and cancer have been instrumental in increasing longevity. Of equal importance has been the American public's awareness of how to care for themselves better. The proportion of smokers has declined steadily since the Surgeon General first linked smoking to cancer in 1965. The fact that Philip Morris makes substantially more money from cigarettes than from its ownership of General Foods, Kraft, and Miller combined is due to overseas cigarette sales. (Greater health awareness seems to be more of an American and Western European phenomenon than it is a worldwide trend.)

Americans are also more conscious of what they eat. The desire to reduce cholesterol intake has caused a shift away from red meat and dairy products. The trend was substantial enough to cause beef producers to band together and mount an educational campaign to convince consumers that beef is healthful. The trend to healthier foods has primarily affected product, rather than promotional, strategies. Producers of dairy foods are coming out with lines of low-cholesterol products, cereal companies with high-fiber products, and liquor manufacturers with lower-alcohol lines to reflect the trend away from hard liquor.

The combined effects of better medical care and greater health awareness have resulted in increased longevity in the past 20 years. From 1970 to 1992, life expectancy of the average American went from 70 to 76 years and should reach 80 by the turn of the century. The number of people age 85 and older, meanwhile, will double to 6.5 million by the year 2020 and grow to 17.7 million by 2050. By then, the number of Americans aged 100 and older will rise to 1 million, from 45,000 today.[8]

It should be noted that there are substantial differences in longevity by race and social class. Longevity for African-Americans, which averages six years less than for whites, reflects poorer health care and less access to health care facilities.

Immigration

The third factor affecting population growth is immigration. With successive waves from the English-speaking countries, Western Europe, China, and Eastern European countries up to 1920, immigration was a significant factor in creating the American "melting pot." More recently, it has had an equally significant effect on the nation's population growth. The greatest immigration has occurred from Mexico and Central America, as well as from such Asian countries as Korea and Vietnam. In fact, it is estimated that by the middle of the next century, the U.S. population will include 82 million people who arrived in this country after 1991 or who were born to parents who did. This group will account for one out of every five Americans.[9]

Given this recent pattern, marketers are asking themselves how they can best target the Hispanic-American and Asian-American markets. Gerber, for one, has responded by introducing a line of foods made from tropical fruits such as papayas and mangos for the Hispanic-American market, which buys more prepared baby food than any other ethnic group.[10] Other marketers may target these markets with the same products and promotional strategies but will use media they are more likely to see or read. We will consider marketing to these groups when we discuss subcultures in Chapter 14.

◆ CHANGING AGE COMPOSITION OF U.S. MARKET

Figure 10.1 identifies three age groups that have been the focus of marketing strategy: (1) **baby boomers,** born between 1946 and 1964 and representing about 76 million consumers; (2) **baby busters,** or the youth market, born between 1965 and 1976 and representing about 47 million consumers; and (3) **teens** and **preteens,** those born in the "echo boom" between 1976 and 1985, representing about 34 million consumers. Because they are not independent purchasers, children born after 1985 are generally not included as a segment. However, they can influence the parent's decision for items such as candy, cereals, or fast-food outlets.

A fourth group that has become increasingly important but is not shown in Figure 10.1 is the **mature market** (those born before 1944 and representing 64.3 million consumers).

Figure 10.2 shows that the two fastest-growing groups by age are the baby boom generation and the 65-plus group (representing about half of the mature market). As the baby boom generation aged, they swelled the ranks of the 30- to 49-year-old group, increasing it by 44 percent from 1975 to 1991.[11] The 65-plus group increased by about 40 percent during this period as medical care improved and life expectancies rose. On the other hand, the numbers of consumers in their 20s and 30s are likely to decrease (along with their purchasing power) as baby busters grow older.

We will consider each of these groups below and the strategic implications of marketing to them.

Baby Boomers (30 to 49)

Marketers have focused on the baby boom generation (aged 30 to 49) more than any other group. The reasons are not hard to find: They are 75.7 million strong, or 30 percent of the U.S. population. Most are in their prime spending years and have $985 billion in income.[12] As these baby boomers age, their spending power will increase. Over the next ten years, average income for all

▶**FIGURE 10.2**

The two fastest-growing age segments in the U.S. population

Sources: Estimated from U.S. Department of Commerce, Bureau of the Census, *Statistical Abstract of the United States, 1990* (Washington, D.C.: Government Printing Office, 1990), Table 13, p. 13; U.S. Department of Commerce, Bureau of the Census, *Statistical Abstract of the United States, 1992* (Washington, D.C.: Government Printing Office, 1992), Table 12, p. 14.

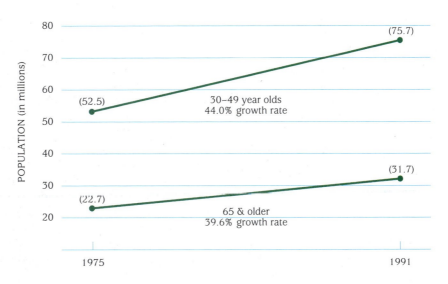

U.S. households should increase by about one-half. However, income for baby boomers should double.[13] Baby boomers will represent the largest chunk of purchasing power in the country as they begin to move into their 50s.

The greater purchasing power of baby boomers is also a result of their high level of education. They are less likely to marry; but if they do, they are more likely to be in dual-income households and to delay parenthood. These factors combine to create higher discretionary income.

Marketing Implications

The values of the baby boom generation have largely shaped marketing strategies to this group. Once rebellious as a result of the Vietnam War and Watergate, baby boomers then became more acquisitive, materialistic, and conservative. By the early 1980s, they were spending more on furniture and cars than the average American.[14] The FM rock radio stations targeted to baby boomers in the 1960s have adjusted to the changes in their needs. In addition to compact discs, acne remedies, and high-style clothing, these stations now advertise condominiums and suburban homes. The term *yuppies* (young, urban professionals) was coined to describe these acquisitive and self-indulgent boomers.

By the late 1980s, however, a subtle shift began taking place. Middle-aged introspection combined with the stock market crash in 1987 caused many to step back and question the easy affluence and acquisitiveness of the 1980s. As a result, baby boomers became less materialistic. Focusing on issues outside of themselves, they became more concerned with the environment, social issues, and personal development. In addition, they started focusing on their children and the society they would grow up in. These former free-spenders turned more serious and concerned about quality-of-life issues, earning them the nickname *grumpies* for grown-up urban mature professionals.

As a result, advertising appeals to materialism and acquisitiveness began to be less relevant. Michelob Light's campaign, asserting "You can have it all," failed because it assumed that baby boomers were, in the words of one writer, motivated by "the compulsive compilation of more and more achievement-oriented activities."[15] The theme simply did not link the product to the needs of grumpies, since most realized that you simply cannot have it all. By 1993, the beer company had shifted its strategy to appeal to the values of an older audience.

In fact, most marketers have come to believe that their products' success will depend on how they adapt to this generation's transition to middle age. That is why Lee Apparel invested $15 million to attract adults whose waistlines have expanded. The image and tag line "You're not a kid anymore" convey that Lee is sympathetic to the baby boomer's transition to middle age.[16] Similarly, Varilux began a campaign to attract aging baby boomers who need bifocals with the tag line "Erase the line between youth and middle age." (See Exhibit 10.1.)

However, pinning these adults down is far from easy. As one marketer remarked: "From the outside, the folks who made it cool to be thirty-something

▶EXHIBIT 10.1
Strategies portraying the aging baby boomer

appear fairly settled and respectable. But really they're more individualistic, hedonistic and powerful than their parents were at this age."[17] American Express has tried to navigate that chasm with ads that portray boomers in unique family situations, such as one that shows a father on the beach with his son under the slogan "You have your own view of what's important."

Changes in values will also cause baby boomers to spend more money on home improvements, travel, education, recreation, and other facets of self-development. As a result, companies developing new products and services in these areas are likely to benefit most from the growing affluence of baby boomers.

Younger Versus Older Baby Boomers

Given the size of the baby boom market, it would be misleading to treat them as one generation with homogeneous tastes and values. Broadly speaking, there are two segments of baby boomers. The older baby boomers (those born in the first half of the baby boom generation from 1946 to 1954) represent less than half of all baby boomers. However, this is the group that has caught the attention of marketers and shaped the definition of what baby boomers want and value. The ads in Exhibit 10.1 are all geared to the older group.

Younger baby boomers (those born from 1955 to 1964) represent the majority. They are not the anti-establishment generation that was molded by the Vietnam War and Watergate.[18] They tend to be more conservative than their older siblings and did not go through the change from materialism to personal development described above. Appeals to the older baby boomers do not always catch the attention of the junior group. If anything, younger baby boomers resent the older group because as 30- to 40-year-olds, they had to compete in a tight job market during the 1990–1991 recession and often found their way blocked by older boomers.

Marketers must fine-tune their ads to distinguish between the older and younger groups or develop a theme that is relevant to all. The ad in Exhibit 10.2 is geared to younger baby boomers, since they are more likely to be recently engaged (as in the De Beers ad).

Baby Busters (18 to 29)

The baby bust generation (the youth market) is composed of 47.4 million consumers born from 1965 to 1976. Since this was a period of the lowest birthrate in this century, there are fewer teenagers and young adults today than there were 10 or 15 years ago. However, consumers in their late teens and 20s are responsible for $125 billion in spending each year.[19] About a quarter of their

▶**EXHIBIT 10.2**
Strategy portraying younger baby boomers
Source: Courtesy of De Beers

annual spending comes from discretionary income, making baby busters prime customers for restaurants, alcoholic beverages, clothing, and electronics.[20]

Baby busters are a varied lot, from college juniors to young executives. However, in general terms, they can be described as more multicultural, media-savvy, and cynical about their future than baby boomers. They are coming of age in an economically depressed time (the median income for households headed by adults under 30 is $24,500—a 21 percent decline from 1973 in constant dollars), and busters blame their elders for leaving them the check after a decade of free spending. They also tend to feel neglected by a marketing establishment that has been distracted by the higher-profile boomers, leading some to dub the busters as the anonymous "Generation X."[21] All of this has made busters more conservative than their elders and more concerned with environmental issues, drugs, and the AIDS epidemic.

Marketers have tried targeting busters by appealing to their pragmatism and by creating ads that are stripped of glitz—a trend that a 1993 *Forbes* magazine article called "ostentatious self-deprecation."[22] Exhibit 10.3 shows how The Gap used this approach, playing upon busters' practical sensibilities when selling its clothing. The IBM ad in Exhibit 10.3 employs the same sentiment, using the "Get Real" theme to sell computers to college students. Its purpose was to reverse IBM's stodgy image among students who thought the company was geared exclusively to corporations.[23]

Teens (13 to 17)

There are 17 million teenagers aged 13 to 17 who were born in the echo boom. Their combined spending is over $50 billion a year on products and services.[24]

Because these teens have spent more hours outside their parents' influence than any generation before, they have taken on more family responsibilities such as food shopping. One study found teens responsible for $28 billion a year in groceries.[25] Not surprisingly, advertisers such as General Foods, Castle & Cooke, Kraft, and Lipton have begun targeting magazines such as *Seventeen,* where food advertising went up by 30 percent in 1990.[26] Fortune 500 companies such as AT&T have used a number of other teen market magazines—from *Details* to *YM* to *Sassy*—to get their messages across in the hopes that teens will be able to influence their parents' behavior.

Teens are also major consumers of other media. They watch 5.25 hours of MTV a week, see 2.5 motion pictures a month, are heavy FM radio listeners, and are the largest group of regular prime time TV viewers.[27] Because of their media consumption and the fact they are willing to experiment with new products, teens form a very attractive market for manufacturers looking to establish long-term loyalty. As the publisher of *Teen* magazine has remarked, "Teens may sample extensively as they struggle with forming their own identities, but brand loyalty sets in by age 18."[28]

Among the companies trying to build long-term loyalty is Kodak. The film company made a commitment to the teen market in 1992 after its survey data

▶**EXHIBIT 10.3**
Targeting baby busters

showed that teenagers like taking photos of one another and consider it a bonding experience. Kodak reacted by creating commercials for its Kodacolor film that show a teenage girl's room with photos of her friends strewn across it.[29] Levi Strauss & Co. is another company targeting teens by introducing its 900 Series® of "Real Jeans." The ad in Exhibit 10.4 shows the ambivalence of today's teenagers who want to demonstrate independence yet still have strong ties to the home.

The youth experience has been one of America's most successful exports, making teen demographic marketing a global phenomenon. Like their American peers, Japanese teens are ruggedly individualistic and have rebelled against the flashy advertising of the 1980s. In fact, they have come to be called the *shinjinrui*, or "new breed of man," because they are so different from their elders.[30] As a result, environmentally sensitive cosmetics that The Body Shop makes sell better in Japan than those from Chanel, and value-oriented products such as L. L. Bean are popular.[31]

The teen market should continue to be an enormously influential one here and abroad. The Census Bureau predicts the teen population will grow as the younger component of the echo boom reaches its teens.[32]

Preteens (8 to 12)

The nearly 17.5 million 8- to 12-year-olds are important to marketers as much for their potential as future consumers as for their current purchasing power.

▶**EXHIBIT 10.4**
Levi Strauss & Co.
targets teens

Source: Courtesy of Levi
Strauss & Co.

Estimates of their pocket money range from $6 billion to $30 billion.[33] However, parents are an even greater source of purchasing power for this group. Preteens are the children of baby boomers, and most are in dual-earning or single-parent households. Between 1970 and 1990, the number of dual-earning married couples with children increased by 5 million to 17.7 million.[34] The number of children living with single parents almost doubled to 16 million in the same period.[35]

Many parents feel guilty for not spending more time with their children and assuage this guilt by being more willing to buy what children want. The combination of parents' expenditures plus their own money makes preteens an area of opportunity for many product categories. One survey found that children influenced $132 billion in purchases in more than 60 categories in the early 1990s.[36] This makes kid-spending one of the fastest-growing sectors of the American economy.

In fact, as retail sales sagged during the 1991–1992 recession, manufacturers looked to the preteen market to boost profits. To keep the refrigerated yogurt category growing in double digits, for instance, General Mills rolled out Yoplait Trix Lowfat, with two colored layers and a third on top. Dannon followed suit with Sprinkl'ins—a fruit-flavored cup doused with rainbow-colored sprinkles.[37] Likewise, Procter & Gamble tried to mine the largely ignored 8- to 12-year-old shampoo set by placing the Pert name on a product for the group.[38] As a result of these types of activities, a new niche of magazines has emerged to cater to children. Two of the best known are Time Warner's *Sports Illustrated for Kids* and the Walt Disney Company's *Disney Adventures*.

Among the other nontraditional preteen areas that marketers have expanded into is consumer electronics. Polaroid introduced its Cool Cam instant camera to this group in 1988; and with a sticker price of less than $40 for the camera, it expected most purchases to be made by preteens.[39] Macintosh, meanwhile, introduced a family computer called the Performa in 1992. As Exhibit 10.5 shows, Macintosh's strategy contrasts with Polaroid's because it is targeting the parent with ads in magazines such as *Better Homes and Gardens*.

Companies market to preteens as future adults. A McDonald's spokesperson said, "You can see McDonald's appealing to kids to buy hamburgers to create brand recognition and preference so they buy hamburgers for themselves and their children later on."[40] Similarly, in referring to Banquet Kid Cuisine, the president of ConAgra has noted, "The appeal isn't simply satisfying kids' needs now, but also developing them as users of our products so that they'll buy as adults."[41]

Mature Market (50-Plus)

The 64.3 million Americans who are 50 and over are often divided into four subsegments to distinguish younger and older consumers in the mature market. The four groups are 50 to 64 (representing about half of the mature market), 65 to 74, 75 to 84, and 85-plus. As consumers age, their purchasing power

▶Exhibit 10.5
Targeting electronic products to preteens and to their parents
Source: (left) Courtesy of Apple Computer Inc.

and income decrease. However, discretionary income continues to rise, because they have fulfilled obligations like mortgages and children's education. People age 65 and older have the highest discretionary income of any group.[42]

Overall, the mature market represents the most powerful buying group in the American economy. Although they are one-fourth of the U.S. population, they control half its discretionary income and 77 percent of its assets. Despite the fact that many in this group are retired, they still earn more than $800 billion in income each year, a figure close to the earning power of baby boomers.[43] Further enhancing the desirability of marketing to this group is the fact that the mature market represents 80 percent of all expenditures for leisure travel, 50 percent of all purchases of domestic cars, and 44 percent of all expenditures for home remodeling.[44] In addition, the baby boom generation will start entering the mature market as the first baby boomers hit 50 in 1996.

Given this group's tremendous purchasing potential, it is curious that marketers target so few products and ads to this group. According to Grey Advertising, a large ad agency, only 6 or 7 percent of TV commercials target the mature market; and only a handful of products or services are tailored to their needs. Of the handful of commercials targeted to older consumers, almost all suffer from what Grey calls the Methuselah Syndrome; that is, portraying the 50-plus

Ever since Pepsi declared it was the cola of a "new generation" in the mid-1960s and took on the mantel of the "Pepsi Generation," its future has been tethered to America's youth. From one campaign to the next, the perennial second-place finisher in the cola wars has ceded mature drinkers to Coke and unapologetically gone after their kids. However, in 1992, Pepsi's planners became concerned that a decreasing birthrate would sharply cut into their core market. Census estimates indicated that the Pepsi Generation of teens and preteens would nosedive by 11 percent, taking 7.7 million of Pepsi's prime customers with it.

The demographic trend was too stark to ignore. It also came at a time when Pepsi was trying to figure out how to maintain loyalty among aging baby boomers. Had the new generation campaign become too limiting for an aging country? Pepsi's planners concluded it had; and during the Superbowl of 1992, it introduced ads that represented its first major strategy shift in a quarter century.

Commercials hawking the new tag line "Gotta Have It" featured mature celebrities from Yogi Berra to Regis Philbin swept up in what was portrayed as a national craze over the cola. Interspersed with those ads were ones featuring more youthful stars, such as the television star Shannen Doherty and MTV veejays.

Pepsi called the campaign an "evolution" of its prior efforts, with one executive explaining that "we're maintaining the Pepsi attitude for people who think young and want to celebrate life." However, critics were mystified at Pepsi's strategy, especially since it pushed the company's image closer to Coke at a time when it was doing fine on its own. The result? Pepsi's sales fell as the traditional message became diluted.

After a management shakeup, Pepsi decided that it had to contain the damage quickly. So exactly one year after "Gotta Have It" was unveiled, Superbowl watchers were treated to a new campaign: "Be young, have fun, drink Pepsi." Using fast-cuts and humorous scenes making fun of social conventions such as weddings and first kisses, the cola company went right for the teen and preteen markets. Pepsi has clearly concluded that its future growth is in the hands of the teenagers who give the drink its youthful image, and always have.

Sources: "Pepsi Bridges 'Generation' Gap in Ads," *Advertising Age* (January 20, 1992), p. 1; "The Media Business," *The New York Times* (January 22, 1993), p. D2; "Pepsi Harkens Back to Youth," *Advertising Age* (January 25, 1993), p. 3.

consumer as frail, cutesy, and prune-like.[45] As one executive quipped, "Everyone in the world of advertising seems to move straight from 32 to 75-plus."[46]

There are two probable reasons why marketers have not targeted the mature market. First, most marketers are under 50 and do not understand how to appeal to older consumers. Second, older consumers do not like to be reminded of their age. The general approach to the mature market has been to advertise a product to, say, baby boomers using youthful models in the expectation that a portion of the mature market will also buy it. There is some validity to this approach. In general, mature consumers think of themselves as 15 years younger than their actual age. One survey found that consumers aged 50 and older believe old age does not start until age 79; in 1985, they said it began at age 71.[47] As a result, mature consumers prefer to identify with younger spokespersons.

Advertisers are beginning to portray a more vital and involving mature consumer. When Quaker Oats positioned its oatmeal to older consumers, it first used the veteran character actor Wilford Brimley in scenes where he sat stolidly at the dining room table or walked slowly through a park with his grandchildren. However, the image of Brimley as an old geezer backfired in attempting to appeal to mature consumers. So Quaker re-energized the actor, presenting him as a vigorous, frenetic senior. One of the new commercials features him on horseback and another has him building a corral at his ranch. The response was overwhelmingly positive.[48]

The conclusion is that strategies to the mature market based on negative stereotypes are inappropriate. The ad for Manchester Clinic in Exhibit 10.6 is an example of a negative portrayal of mature consumers. Marketers who emphasize vitality and fun, rather than age, are more likely to be successful. The Freedent ad showing an older couple embracing in the rain and the Moisture Drops ad showing a young-looking Debbie Reynolds dancing both share a theme of vigor and youthfulness. (See Exhibit 10.6.)

This emphasis on youth is targeted primarily to consumers from 50 to 74. For those over 75, marketers must design products with their age in mind. For example, AT&T has developed phone-receiver amplifiers, automatic emergency dialing attachments, and daytime long-distance discounts for older retired consumers.[49] Choice Hotels has set aside rooms for older customers fitted with TV remote controls, telephones that have large buttons, and wall switches with faint lights so guests can find them easily at night.[50]

◆ CHANGING FAMILY COMPOSITION

The American family is becoming a smaller, less cohesive unit. Marriage rates are at an all-time low, and Americans are marrying later and having fewer children. For the first time in the country's history, there are more families without children at home than there are families with children.[51] Childless families

▶**EXHIBIT 10.6**

Negative and positive portrayals of the mature market

Source: (left) Courtesy of Wm. Wrigley Jr. Company

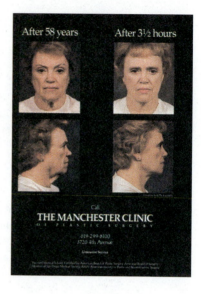

accounted for 28.4 percent of all households in 1992, while homes with children accounted for 26.7 percent.[52]

Also contributing to a change in family composition is the decline in the traditional family—that is, a working father, a nonworking mother, and at least one school-age child. In 1950, 70 percent of all households fit this description. By the early 1990s, less than a third could be classified as traditional families.[53]

An increasing divorce rate has also contributed to a splintering of the traditional family. Half of all marriages today end in divorce, triple the rate in 1970. As a result, single parents and households composed of unrelated people rose from 29 percent in 1970 to 44 percent in 1991.[54] As one might expect, single-parent homes are likely to have lower incomes. Forty-five percent of households with a female head with children at home live in poverty, as do 19 percent of households headed by a male with children. In contrast, just 8 percent of married couples with children live in poverty.[55]

Another effect of high divorce rates is the number of people living alone. According to the most recent census, 25 percent of households are single persons, and their numbers are growing 2.5 times faster than the overall population.[56] The number of single women living alone has jumped 91 percent since 1970.[57]

The marketing impact of these trends is significant. Singles and childless couples spend more on travel, leisure products, and investments. Unmarried households, for example, spend 50 percent of their food dollars dining out, compared to 37 percent for two-person households.[58] Smaller households also have led some companies to emphasize foods and toiletries in smaller sizes and to introduce kitchen appliances and furnishings in smaller models. Singles are also more willing to buy on credit and to spend more on restaurants and entertainment.

Marketers have been uneven in their understanding of this lucrative market. One example is Campbell's Soup, which decided to sell smaller-portioned cans to singles under the Soup For One label. Consumers reacted coolly, believing that the name implied loneliness. "They didn't need to be reminded that they were eating alone," a Campbell's executive later remarked. In 1990, the company removed the Soup For One label and watched sales improve. MCI, on the other hand, has tried to portray the singles market more attractively. The company's strategy plays upon the fact that because singles are not in family situations, they are more emotionally attached to their friends. So the phone company discounts calls to the people its customers call most and advertises the plan with commercials showing adults calling friends.[59]

Some marketers are looking at the changes in family composition outside the United States. With 22 million babies born in China each year (six times the number in the United States), Heinz, for instance, saw an opportunity for introducing baby products. In 1990, it began marketing an instant rice cereal for babies and almost immediately saw a profit. The cereal is precooked and instant and appeals to the 70 percent of Chinese women who work.[60]

◆ REGIONAL DIFFERENCES

One of the most common demographic characteristics marketers use in analyzing purchasing behavior is region. Differences in consumer purchasing habits and tastes by region have led many marketers to vary their marketing strategies on a regional basis. Consider the following regional differences:

- Close to one-half of new car buyers in California purchase foreign cars, compared to one-fourth of new car buyers in the rest of the country.[61]
- In the Northeast, car buyers are more concerned with fuel economy and want front-wheel drive.[62]
- Westerners buy more health foods and exercise machines than consumers in the rest of the country.[63]
- Northeasterners like chicken noodle and tomato soups; Californians like cream of mushroom; Philadelphians like pepperpot soup; and Westerners like cream of vegetable.[64]
- Easterners like darker potato chips; Westerners, lighter ones. (That is why Borden sells its darker Wise potato chips in New York and its lighter Laura Scudder brand in California.)[65]

How have marketers reacted to these differences? They vary their products and advertising themes on a regional basis. For instance, the auto industry has spent more money in the last five years on regional and local "spot" advertising than on national campaigns. Much of it has gone to California, where cars are seen as important lifestyle indicators. While Chevrolet advertises its Cavalier as a utility family vehicle in most states, it emphasizes the car's sportiness and excitement in California. Similarly, while Chrysler stresses the luxury of its LeBaron GTS in the Midwest, it hypes the car's acceleration and handling in West Coast ads.[66]

The regional strategy is particularly important to national retailers. Kmart maintains a master database at its Troy, Michigan, headquarters of all the items sold in its 2,300 stores and tailors the stock in each according to local preferences. For instance, peak interest in bowling usually occurs when the weather turns cold. However, not in Phoenix. There, it occurs in the summer, when it is too hot to go outside. So Kmart stores in Phoenix advertise bowling products in the spring, while its stores in Detroit do not do so until fall.[67]

Differences in consumer tastes and purchases can cut across regions and be identified by specific localities. Similarities in age, income, or family composition cutting across regions can translate into similarities in purchase behavior. For example, Claritas, a market research firm, is using the 1990 census to group neighborhoods across regions into 40 groups based on similar demographics. One such group, identified as "Blue Blood Estates," includes Chappaqua, New York, and Winnetka, Illinois. This group is described as "America's wealthiest socioeconomic neighborhoods, populated by established managers, professionals, and heirs to old money."

Such analysis is called **geo-demographic analysis,** and marketers can use it to identify demographic target groups. For example, Dannon Yogurt could determine average yogurt consumption in each of the 40 clusters and then distribute products to clusters such as "Blue Blood Estates" or "Shotguns and Pickups" based on the average amount of yogurt purchased. The company also could distribute coupons or mailers to those clusters that represent the heaviest consumption groups. In a variation of this, GfK Marktforschung of Germany divides European shoppers into 16 "Euro-style" categories, including "Euro-Protest" for activists who would be more likely to buy environmentally friendly products, and "Euro-Gentry" for established money types more interested in large-ticket items.[68]

◆ SOCIOECONOMIC TRENDS

A key set of demographic variables that defines consumers' current and future purchasing power is **socioeconomic factors;** that is, consumers' occupational status, income, and education. We will describe the most important occupational trend in the past 40 years, the increasing proportion of working women, and additional trends in income and educational status in the United States.

Occupational Status: Increase in the Proportion of Working Women

The first socioeconomic factor impacting on consumer choice is occupational status of household members. Changes in occupational status directly affect purchasing power. For instance, increased unemployment and underemployment (a decrease in time devoted to the job or taking a lesser job to avoid unemployment) during the 1990–1991 recession restricted purchasing power.

The farthest-reaching change in occupational status has been the increasing proportion of working women. Figure 10.3 shows that the proportion of women in the labor force went from 33 percent in 1950 to 58 percent in 1991, and it is expected to reach 63 percent by the turn of the century.

The increase in the proportion of working wives has also been dramatic, more than doubling between 1950 and 1991. Among mothers with children from ages 6 to 13, close to 70 percent are employed. However, even these figures understate the impact of working women, because many women work on a part-time basis. Among women from 18 to 49, fully 90 percent were part of the labor force at some time in the past two years.[69]

▶**FIGURE 10.3**

Percentage of women in the labor force

Sources: "Employed Person with Single and Multiple Jobs by Sex," *Monthly Labor Review* (May, 1982), Table 1, p. 48; "A Portrait of the American Worker," *American Demographics* (March, 1984), p. 19; *Handbook of Labor Statistics* (June, 1985), Tables 1, 6, and 50; *Monthly Labor Review* (February, 1986), Table 1; U.S. Department of Commerce, Bureau of the Census, *Statistical Abstract of the United States, 1990* (Washington, D.C.: Government Printing Office, 1990), Table 625, p. 378; U.S. Department of Commerce, Bureau of the Census, *Statistical Abstract of the United States, 1992* (Washington, D.C.: Government Printing Office, 1992).

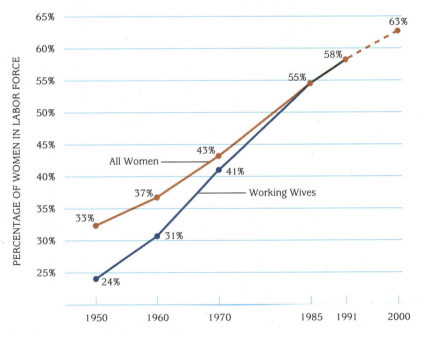

The increasing number of working women has had both economic and social consequences: economic in the greater affluence and purchasing power of dual-earning households; social in the changing family roles as a result of more women working.

An important effect of the greater proportion of working women is the increased affluence of dual-earner households. In 1990, the median income of the family with a working wife was $46,777, compared with $30,265 for families without one.[70] A Bureau of Labor Statistics' study found that differences between families with and without working wives extend beyond income. Dual-earner families are younger, better educated, and less likely to have children. They are more secure about the future and less likely to delay purchases, as evidenced by the fact that they save less.

The increasing proportion of working women has had dramatic effects on marketing strategies. Perhaps the most direct impact is the result of the time crunch working women face. In 1975, 45 percent of working women believed they had enough leisure time. By 1990, only 35 percent believed they had enough time. What is the impact of this increasing time crunch? Working women are fueling a boom in catalog shopping, telephone shopping, and direct mail because they do not have time to shop. Furthermore, household products that previously focused on the pride of a job well done (such as shinier floors) now focus on the time the product saves (faster-drying floors). One advertising executive said, "Women are no longer finding their identities and self-esteem in brighter-than-bright dishes and glasses without spots."[71]

Food companies have adapted to the time crunch working women face by emphasizing easy-to-prepare foods. Campbell's Chunky soups, for example, are advertised as the perfect light meal that even a husband can fix for his working wife.[72] Food concerns have also hedged their bets by buying fast-food outlets. General Mills, General Foods, Quaker Oats, CPC International, and Pepsi-Cola are all mindful of statistics that show working wives average 7.4 meals out per week.[73]

However, the impact on marketing strategy goes beyond household convenience and food. As we saw at the introduction of this chapter, auto makers have recognized the greater involvement of working women in car-buying decisions. Similarly, as the Sharp and Pitney Bowes ads in Exhibit 10.7 show, office electronics companies have begun to target their products to women executives based on studies that found women own 32 percent of the nation's sole proprietorships and that 75 percent of women managers have a role in buying office equipment.[74]

Income

A direct correlation exists between income level and the purchasing power of a household. As a result, marketers segment consumers by income level and frequently allocate greater effort to the more affluent segments.

▶**EXHIBIT 10.7**

Ads targeting working women

Source: (left) Courtesy of Sharp Electronics Corporation; (right) Courtesy of Pitney Bowes © Scott Goodwin

Although most Americans would like to think that their country promotes greater equality, the fact is that in economic terms, the decade of the 1980s saw greater inequality in income. Consider the following data:[75]

	Average Income 1977	Average Income 1988	Percentage Change 1977–1988
Top 10% by income	$70,459	$89,783	+27.4%
Bottom 10% by income	$ 3,528	$ 3,157	−10.5%

The data show that the rich have become richer and the poor poorer.

The social consequences of these changes are likely to be significant, particularly in urban areas. The infrastructures of some cities are decaying, with a shrinking tax base and fewer support services available. One reflection of this decay has been the decrease in retail facilities in center cities. The long-term shift of department stores and mass merchandisers to the suburbs and the development of shopping malls indicate that retailers are "moving to where the money is."

Added to the greater disparities in income are underlying disparities by race and ethnic origin. In 1992, African-Americans accounted for only 60 percent of the median income of whites and Hispanic-Americans for 71 percent.[76]

Given these disparities, it is not surprising that in recent years marketers have tended to position most products as either economy or premium brands, with fewer brands positioned in the middle. Although economy brands do appeal to lower-income consumers, it would be a mistake to assume that this is the only, or even the primary, market for economy brands. More accurately, economy brands are positioned to appeal to the *price-sensitive* consumer who is often the middle-income consumer. The deep recession in the early 1990s has made consumers even more price-sensitive, thus expanding the market for economy brands well beyond lower-income consumers.

The popularity of private (retailer-controlled) brands and generic (no brand name) products for many packaged foods categories reflects greater price sensitivity. Manufacturers also have established lower-priced alternatives in many lines. Procter & Gamble has come out with a line of lower-priced paper towels to compete with private brands for the price-sensitive segment. L&M has been able to survive in the cigarette industry by producing low-priced generic cigarettes. Perhaps the sharpest divisions in price can be seen in the car market, with a 1993 price for a Hyundai Excel below $8,000, compared to luxury-class cars for well over $30,000.

Because marketers tend to allocate resources by purchasing power, it is not surprising that they pay more attention to the affluent end of the market. The increasing proportion of working women and the greater number of single-member households have increased purchasing power for many consumers, which further spurs interest in the high-priced end. Close to 20 percent of all households are expected to earn more than $50,000 by 1995, double the number in 1980.[77] As a result, a super-premium price niche has developed in many categories from ice cream to beer.

Education

Education is directly related to purchasing power, as there is a high correlation between education and income. The educational level of Americans has been rising rapidly. In 1940, only 25 percent of American adults completed high school; by 1991, 78.4 percent had done so. The proportion of college-educated Americans also increased, from 5 percent in 1940 to 21.4 percent in 1991.[78]

As with income, significant disparities by race and ethnic origin exist. Only 66.7 percent of African-Americans and 51.3 percent of Hispanic-Americans completed high school in 1991. Restricted educational attainment of minority groups directly constrains their income and purchasing power. Still, educational levels have increased. For example, in 1940, only 1 percent of African-Americans completed college; by 1991, 11.5 percent had.[79]

Education affects the way consumers make decisions. Evidence suggests that less-educated consumers do not have the same amount of information on brand alternatives and prices as better-educated consumers. For example, in making decisions, the less educated are not as likely to use unit price information in stores. However, consumers using such information are more aware of lower-priced alternatives.[80] Furthermore, poor and less-educated consumers often do not have the means to comparison shop. As we saw in Chapter 2, the net result is that the underprivileged often pay more than necessary.

◆ USING DEMOGRAPHICS TO DEVELOP MARKETING STRATEGY

The growth of the mature market, the greater purchasing clout of baby boomers, and the increasing proportion of working women do not mean that every marketer will seek to appeal to these segments. Marketers use demographics to describe and better understand existing and potential users of their products. Marketers also use demographics to identify market segments for a brand or product, select media, and evaluate the potential for new products.

Identifying Market Segments

Marketers use demographics to identify a target group for their brand or product category. A demographic description of a brand's target group can help in media selection, advertising, and product development.

Demographic segmentation is the basis for Kodak's decision to shift from product-driven to age-driven marketing. Now, instead of selling its film to all audiences with a general campaign, the company is creating different commercials for different age groups. One of the ads, for example, aims at teenage girls by showing how photos provide a good record of one's adolescent years.[81] Similarly, demographic studies convinced Avon to segment by income group, with Giorgio perfumes positioned for more-affluent women and the traditional Avon line for middle- to lower-income women. Demographics were also the key factor in Levi Strauss & Co.'s decision to advertise its 900 Series® jeans to young women in their late teens and early 20s. (See Exhibit 10.4.) Levi Strauss & Co. found that this demographic group has an individualistic streak but has ties to home and tends to be serious about its future. Therefore, the company tailored its ads to reflect those sentiments.

Segmenting with demographic data is also critically important for international marketers. For example, one U.S. bleach firm that was interested in selling to developing countries found that women in Kenya, Bangladesh, Algeria, and Pakistan tended to have five or more children who they were unable to furnish with proper medical attention. So, it positioned its bleach as a disinfectant and because literacy rates are low, advertised its use with pictures.[82]

Selecting Media

Marketers have widely used demographics to select media that have a higher probability of reaching a defined target group. For example, in 1988, a food manufacturer wanted to determine which TV shows would be the best buys for advertising its line of frozen diet entrees. Based on a survey, it determined that the group most likely to buy frozen diet entrees were females from 18 to 49 years old. It then analyzed 23 shows to determine which programs this target group was most likely to watch.

The results for seven of the shows aired in the 1988-1989 viewing season are presented in index form in Table 10.1.[83] A show indexed below 100 meant that females aged 18 to 49 were less likely to watch it compared to the total population; more than 100 meant they were more likely to watch it. Thus, "Moonlighting" appeared to be a good buy because more of the target group watched it.

One additional piece of information was necessary to select the best TV shows: a cost-per-thousand figure; that is, the cost of reaching 1,000 viewers of the show. A show that appears to be a good pick but is very costly might not be cost-efficient for reaching the target group. The second column in Table 10.1 shows the cost index. The higher the index, the lower the cost to reach viewers. On this basis, "Wiseguy" was significantly less expensive than "Moonlighting." When we multiply the exposure index of the target group by cost, we get an index that represents the selection criterion. The best pick, according to the table, was "Wiseguy." Even though only an average number of women aged 18

▶TABLE 10.1

Selecting TV shows to reach a demographic target (Females 18 to 49)

Show	Exposure Index for Females 18 to 49		Cost Index per Show (Higher index means show is less expensive)		Selection Criterion (Column 1 times Column 2)
"Moonlighting"	120	×	65	=	78
"Alf"	115	×	92	=	106
"Growing Pains"	112	×	99	=	111
"Cheers"	111	×	68	=	75
"Wiseguy"	96	×	151	=	145
"Golden Girls"	83	×	110	=	91
"Murder, She Wrote"	66	×	124	=	82

SOURCE: Adapted from Henry Assael and David Poltrack, "Using Single Source Data to Select TV Programs Based on Purchasing Behavior," JOURNAL OF ADVERTISING RESEARCH (August-September, 1991), p. 11.

to 49 watched the show, it was highly cost-efficient. The next best pick was "Growing Pains." Here, a greater than average number of the demographic target watched the show (an index of 111), and its cost was about average.

The key to selecting the TV shows was to identify the target group as females aged 18 to 49. This allowed the company to determine exposure to TV shows among this group. Once cost of the shows was included in the analysis, the company could determine the most cost-efficient shows to reach the target.

Evaluating the Potential for New Products

Marketers frequently use demographics to identify prospective purchasers of new products. For example, a large food manufacturer interviewed 600 respondents in four markets to determine the reaction to a new product concept: low-calorie breakfast strips designed as a substitute for bacon. The basic purpose of the study was to identify the segment of the market most likely to buy based on their demographic and lifestyle characteristics. Once the respondents reacted to the concept, the company gave the product to those who had eaten bacon within the previous year and who said they would definitely or probably buy the new product.

Two demographic segments were most likely to buy: (1) older (55 years and over), less-educated respondents and (2) middle-aged respondents with one or more teenagers in the household. The older segment was more likely to emphasize cholesterol content and health concerns; the middle-aged segment, calories and nutrition. This finding suggested that the product should be positioned to the older market using a primary health appeal (easier to digest, low in cholesterol) with a secondary appeal to dieting and nutritional benefits. The appeals should be reversed for the middle-aged market.

In addition to positioning implications, the demographic analysis identified the primary target groups for media purposes. Marketers gave relative weights based on purchase potential to the two segments and established media priorities by the ability of print and TV advertising to reach potential consumers.

◆ SOCIAL CLASS INFLUENCES

Three socioeconomic factors were described in a previous section—occupation, income, and education. Marketers use these three factors to identify another important dimension of consumer behavior, social class. **Social class** defines the ranking of people in a society into a hierarchy of upper, middle, and lower classes based on their power and prestige. In American society, power and prestige are generally equated to one's occupation, income, and education. Therefore, social class is based on demographic variables.

Another indicator of social class is our possessions—the clothing we wear, the houses we live in, and the cars we drive. When Thorstein Veblen wrote of *conspicuous consumption* at the turn of the century, he was referring to the tendency of affluent consumers to demonstrate upper-class membership through their possessions. Veblen saw conspicuous consumption as a demonstration of this group's "new" wealth. Among the aristocratic "old wealth," there was a reverse tendency to take possessions for granted and downplay them as indicators of affluence.[84]

Since the basis for defining power and prestige vary from one society to another, the composition of upper, middle, and lower classes is also likely to vary. One study found that in the United States, physicians, scientists, government officials, college professors, and lawyers rated highest on the social scale.[85] These ratings are dependent on the ideals and values of American society. In Europe, college professors and lawyers probably would be rated lower than artists and writers.

Nature of Social Class

Social classes exert influence on consumers in an indirect way. A vice president of marketing for a food manufacturer who is regarded in the *upper-middle class* may be one of 30 million consumers in the same social class. Such social class status does not imply face-to-face influence. This is reserved for peer groups and family who interact on a day-to-day basis. Social class status is likely to indicate common values and similar purchasing patterns. For example, studies have shown that individuals in the upper-middle class emphasize education, are fashion-oriented, and are less likely to be brand loyal than other groups. Such similarity in norms, values, and purchasing patterns means that social classes serve as a frame of reference for the purchasing behavior of consumers in a particular social class.

Social Class Categories and Measurement

As we noted, one's position on the social hierarchy is defined by socioeconomic factors related to occupation, income, and education. These factors are combined into an index of social status that serves to define a consumer's social class.

Warner's Index of Status Characteristics

The most widely used index was W. Lloyd Warner's **Index of Status Characteristics (ISC).**[86] Warner developed his index in a study of social class lines in a Midwestern city in the early 1940s.[87] The ISC is based on the following socioeconomic indicators:

- Occupation (ranging from unskilled workers to professionals).
- Source of income (ranging from public relief to inherited wealth).
- House type (rated from very poor to excellent).
- Dwelling area (ranging from slums to "gold coast" areas).

Warner identified seven social class categories based on these four demographic characteristics.

Coleman-Rainwater Social Standing Hierarchy

The fact that Warner's index was developed right before World War II led two sociologists, Richard Coleman and Lee Rainwater, to update it in 1978. The resulting groupings, shown below in Table 10.2 and known as the **Coleman-Rainwater Social Standing Hierarchy,** are similar to Warner's, but they more directly reflect the power and prestige associated with each group.

Because it focuses on power and prestige, the Coleman-Rainwater Hierarchy draws social class lines more sharply. Whereas Warner refers to the next to lowest group as on private relief and living in semi-slum conditions, Coleman and Rainwater describe the group as portraying behavior that is judged by others as "crude" and "trashy," thus reflecting the severe judgments by upper- and middle-class Americans of the lower classes. In so doing, the Social Standing Hierarchy better reflects the tensions between social groups.

Another advantage of the Coleman-Rainwater Hierarchy over Warner's classification is that it distinguishes between a middle class and a working class. Although the middle class tends to be white-collar and the working class blue-collar, the distinction reflects the values of each group as well as occupation. For example, Coleman describes working-class Americans as "family folk,

▶**TABLE 10.2**

Categories in the Coleman-Rainwater Social Standing Hierarchy

Upper Americans
Upper-Upper (0.3%)—The "capital S society" world of inherited wealth, aristocratic names
Lower-Upper (1.2%)—The newer social elite, drawn from current professional, corporate leadership
Upper-Middle (12.5%)—the rest of college graduate managers and professionals; lifestyle centers on private clubs, causes, and the arts
Middle Americans
Middle Class (32%)—Average pay white-collar workers and their blue-collar friends; live on the "the better side of town," try to "do the proper things"
Working Class (38%)—Average pay blue-collar workers; lead "working class lifestyle" whatever the income, school background, and job
Lower Americans
"A lower group of people but not the lowest" (9%)—Working, not on welfare; living standard is just above poverty; behavior judged "crude," "trashy"
"Real Lower-Lower" (7%)—On welfare, visibly poverty-stricken, usually out of work (or have "the dirtiest jobs").

SOURCE: From SOCIAL STANDING IN AMERICA by Richard P. Coleman and Lee P. Rainwater. Copyright© 1978 by Basic Books, Inc. Reprinted by permission of Basic Books, a division of HarperCollins Publishers Inc.

depending heavily on relatives for economic and emotional support."[88] The values of working-class Americans are reflected in their preference for local rather than national news, for vacationing with relatives at local resorts, and for buying American. In contrast, middle-class Americans tend to buy based on their perception of the norms and values of the upper class. They want to do the right thing and buy what is popular. Their upward mobility distinguishes them from the working class.

Most applications combine the first two groups of the Social Standing Hierarchy in Table 10.2 because the top group is generally too small as a marketing target for anything but luxury goods. The lower two groups are also frequently combined because of their limited purchasing power. This produces the following categories:

1. Upper class (1.5 percent of the population).
2. Upper-middle class (12.5 percent).
3. Middle class (32.0 percent).
4. Working class (also called lower-middle class; 38.0 percent).
5. Lower class (16.0 percent).

A 1990 update of the distributions of these groups showed little change from the percentages produced by Rainwater and Coleman in 1978.[89] The 1990 figures do not reflect the severe recession of 1990–1991, however. A further update could show some downward social mobility, particularly among the middle and working classes as a result of unemployment and underemployment.

Profiles of the Social Classes

Research into the norms, values, and lifestyles of the five social classes just discussed makes it possible to describe a general profile of each.

Upper Class (1.5 Percent of the Population)

This group is composed of the social elite (inherited or old wealth) and the leaders in business and the professions (the new social elite). They dress conservatively and well and avoid ostentatious purchases. They emphasize self-expression, buy quality merchandise, and reflect an ideal of "spending with good taste." While not a target for the mass marketer, the upper class would make an excellent market for specialty items such as expensive clothing, jewelry, furniture, or boats.

Upper-Middle Class (12.5 Percent of the Population)

This group is also comprised of successful professional and business people, but it does not have the wealth or status of the upper class. Combined with the upper class, the upper-middle class possesses most of the wealth in the United States. The two groups own two-thirds of the securities and almost two-thirds of the real estate in this country, even though they represent only 14 percent of the population.[90] The upper-middle class is career-oriented and achievement-motivated. Members of this group emphasize education; most are college graduates. Because they are well educated, this group is more likely to appraise product alternatives critically. They emphasize quality and value and good taste, rather than status, in their purchases. Women in this group are more likely to be employed, active, and more self-expressive than women in other groups.

Appeals to the old wealth of the social elite in the upper class and the new wealth of professionals and managers primarily in the upper-middle class are likely to differ. Investment planning is a good example. The two ads in Exhibit 10.8 advertise investments directed to old wealth and to new wealth. The ad for JP Morgan cites a $15 million portfolio and the advantages of dealing with one investment service. The target is obviously a very small group of investors. The ad for the Franklin funds cites a goal of investing to ensure that retirement income is sufficient beyond social security checks. It is directed to a broader group of professionals and managers who can afford to invest independently for retirement.

Middle Class (32 Percent of the Population)

This group is represented by white-collar workers, owners of small businesses, and highly paid blue-collar workers. There is a split in this group between those who emphasize traditional norms and those who subscribe to more modern values.[91] Traditionalists are more home- and family-oriented. Women in this group pride themselves on their role of mother and homemaker. Their orientation is toward traditional, conservative benefits such as pride in meal preparation and satisfaction in the upbringing of their children.

The non-traditional consumers in this group reflect the values of the upper-middle class because they are upwardly mobile. Compared to the traditionalists, wives are more likely to work, husbands and wives are more likely to make joint decisions, and they are more likely to emphasize a college education for their children. Time-saving benefits in food preparation and appliances that are likely to appeal to the non-traditionalist middle-class families are unlikely to appeal to the traditionalists.

Because they seek the trappings of wealth of the upper-middle class, non-traditionalists are more likely to buy based on status considerations. They are more likely to own credit cards, top-of-the-line electronic equipment, and designer clothes.

Working Class (38 Percent of the Population)

The working class consists primarily of blue-collar workers. They depend on friends and relatives for emotional support and escape from uncreative jobs. The narrow dimensions of and lack of self-expression in their jobs lead to a pattern of impulse purchasing to escape from the dull routine. This group would rather buy for today than plan for tomorrow; therefore, advertising appeals to fantasy and escape are likely to be successful.

▶**EXHIBIT 10.8**

Appeals to old wealth and to new wealth for investment services

Source: (left) Courtesy of Franklin/Templeton Distributors, Inc.

Their view of life tends to reflect the "old" traditionalism. The husband is likely to be the breadwinner and the decision maker; the wife, the traditional homemaker. Whereas over one-half of middle-class women work, only about one-third of working-class women are employed.[92]

Lower Class (16 Percent of the Population)

This group represents the unskilled, poorly educated, and socially disadvantaged. They earn only one-fifth the income of the average American.[93] Lower-class consumers often live in poverty, frequently on welfare, and are more likely to have a female head of house. Lower-class families often have difficulty moving up the social hierarchy. As a result, they are frustrated and angry about their economic status and inability to share in the "American Dream."

The bulk of the lower-class consumer's income goes to rent and heat. This group also spends a disproportionate amount of their income on food and medicine, reflecting a lower income level. They often pay higher prices for goods than do other groups because they are restricted to poor, inner-city areas and do not have the means or mobility to comparison shop.[94]

Is America Becoming a Classless Society?

A key question that may inhibit the use of social class in consumer behavior studies is whether social class lines are becoming more blurred. The universal ownership of television sets means everyone is exposed to the same mass communications. The rise of mass merchandising and the standardization of consumer packaged goods means that most people buy similar brands. The universal ownership of automobiles means greater mobility. In addition, greater access to a college education and, consequently, higher job mobility have created a greater movement up the social scale for many lower-class consumers.

However, recent evidence suggests that social class lines are becoming sharper. The deep recession of 1990–1991 drove many middle-class consumers into the lower class. At the same time, opportunities for managers and professionals in high-technology and service areas have provided the means for many middle-class consumers to move into the upper class.[95] The result has been more pronounced distinctions between the upper and lower classes. One recent study found sharp differences among upper- and lower-class consumers in the way they saw individual brands of automobiles, appliances, detergents, and deodorants.[96] One writer described an erosion of the American egalitarian spirit and a re-emergence of the class system as a result of these trends.[97] Social class in America is still very much a reality and a component to be considered in explaining consumer behavior.

Applications of Social Class to Marketing Strategy

Marketers have found social class measures important because of substantial differences in behavior between classes. As a result, social class characteristics have been related to every aspect of marketing strategy.

Advertising

The most important applications of social class influences are for advertising. Social class values can give direction to advertisers. The social class to which the advertising is directed must understand the language and symbols used in advertising. For example, Levy found that working- and lower-class consumers are more receptive to "advertising that is strongly visual in character, that shows activity, ongoing work and life, impressions of energy, and solutions to practical problems in daily requirements."[98] In contrast, upper-class consumers are more open to subtle symbolism, to approaches that are more "individual in tone . . . that offer the kinds of objects and symbols that are significant of their status and self-expressive aims."[99]

An example of these distinctions is the two ads in Exhibit 10.9. The Seagram's Gin ad associates the product with style in elegant surroundings. The appeal is to status under the tag line "Those who appreciate quality enjoy it responsibly." The ad for HUD-financed homes is directed to working-class consumers who assume they cannot own their own home. It reflects the focus on a solution to a very practical problem, guaranteeing home ownership with financial security.

A frequently used symbol of social class is power. Power themes have been directed to the higher end of the social scale, based on the economic power and social status of upper-class consumers. For example, the two ads at the left

► **EXHIBIT 10.9**
Appeals to upper-class values of style and prestige and working-class values of security

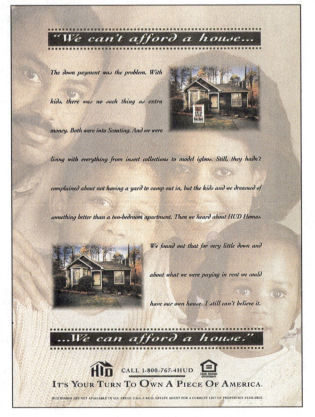

in Exhibit 10.10 refer to power in the workplace and are directed to professionals and managers (the upper-middle and upper classes). The ad for Air France, positioned to executives, cites a "*power* upgrade" to business class on its Concorde jets. The ad for Apple cites the potential for the computer to improve job performance with the tag line "The power to be your best."

The ad for Amway at the right in Exhibit 10.10 directs a power theme to working-class consumers but does so in a more subtle fashion. It cites an Amway distributorship as a means of extra income. In this context, money is a source of power through financial security.

Market Segmentation

The substantial differences among social classes in the purchases of clothing, furniture, appliances, leisure goods, financial services, and food products provide marketers with a basis for segmenting consumers. For example, upper classes are likely to emphasize style and color in purchasing appliances, whereas lower-class consumers emphasize appliances that work.[100] In each case, different product lines for different social class segments would be appropriate. Some companies are adapting to social class influences abroad. For example, Nestlé sees an emerging middle class in many less-developed countries. It has sought to establish manufacturing facilities for many of its packaged goods in countries such as Egypt, India, and Pakistan to facilitate the targeting of its goods to middle-class consumers. Former communist countries such as Poland are also on the list.[101]

▶**EXHIBIT 10.10**
Power themes directed to upper class and working class consumers
Source: (middle) Courtesy of Apple Computer Inc.; (right) Reprinted by permission of Amway Corporation

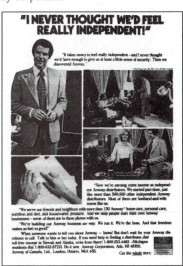

Distribution

Social classes frequently differ in store patronage. Lower-class consumers are more likely to shop in discount stores and in neighborhood stores where they feel most comfortable and can rely on friendly salespeople for information. Upper-class consumers are more likely to shop in regular department stores for products they consider risky and in discount stores for products with little risk.[102]

These findings suggest that social class characteristics can provide guidelines for distribution strategies. If the target market is more likely to be in the lower socioeconomic group, neighborhood stores should be used rather than downtown shopping centers. There should be more emphasis on sales personnel and a friendly store environment. Middle- and upper-class target groups suggest the use of regular department stores, with primary emphasis on the nature and variety of merchandise.

Product Development

Social classes may react differently to product characteristics and styles. A study by AT&T examined the style and color preferences for telephones among various social groups.[103] Lower-class consumers were not interested in a decorative or modern phone; they just wanted one that worked. The working class placed the greatest emphasis on phones of different designs and colors. These findings demonstrate that the lower-class group would be a poor target for decorative phones, but the working class is a surprisingly good target. Had AT&T assumed that higher socioeconomic groups were the best target for high-style phones, it might have missed an important target group.

SUMMARY

Consumers' demographic characteristics influence the markets for most products. Demographics influence whether consumers can buy (based on income) and whether they want to buy (based on factors such as age and household composition).

Demographic trends in the U.S. market have had a direct impact on marketing strategies. Several basic trends were considered in this chapter:

- Population growth in the post-war period, resulting in the baby boom and a long-term decline in the birthrate since 1964.
- The effect of population growth on the changing age composition of the U.S. population, in particular:
  —Increasing purchasing potential of the baby boom generation (those born between 1946 and 1964).
  —Needs and values of the baby bust generation (those born between 1965 and 1976).
  —Increasing purchasing power and influence of teens and preteens (those born in the echo boom between 1976 and 1985).

— Greater numbers and importance of the mature market (those born before 1944).

- Socioeconomic trends, particularly the increase in the proportion of working women.
- Changes in family composition such as increases in the divorce rate, decreases in family size, and increases in single-parent households.
- Regional differences in tastes and purchasing habits.

The effects of these changes on purchasing and consumption behavior were also considered. For example, the increase in the proportion of working women has resulted in changing purchasing and consumption roles within the family, less time for shopping, and greater patronage of fast-food establishments.

The chapter also considered the use of demographics in developing marketing strategy. Marketers most frequently use demographics to (1) identify market segments, (2) select media, and (3) evaluate the potential for new products.

The chapter concluded by describing social classes. Social class refers to consumers' positions on a social scale based on three key demographic factors—occupation, income, and education. Consumers are classified by these criteria into social class groupings. The most frequently used classification is a five-part designation of upper-, upper-middle, middle-, working-, and lower-class consumers.

Each of these groups has distinctive norms, values, family roles, and patterns of purchasing behavior. On this basis, social classes vary markedly in the purchase of such items as clothing, furniture, leisure goods, and even food. These differences permit marketers to use social class criteria to identify market segments, select the language and symbols used in advertising, develop in-store strategies, and indicate appropriate product characteristics and styles.

In the next chapter, we consider two key descriptors that further influence purchase behavior: consumer personality and lifestyles.

QUESTIONS

1. How have the following factors influenced marketing strategy: (a) a decrease in the birthrate; (b) an increase in life expectancy; (c) population growth due to immigration? Cite examples of the impact of each of these factors on marketing strategy.
2. What are the marketing implications of the changes in the values of many baby boomers from materialism to personal development?
3. What is the importance of the distinction between older and younger baby boomers? Are appeals to one group likely to be effective for another? Why or why not?
4. One marketer, speaking of the 8- to 12-year-old group, said, "They may be able to buy candy and soft drinks on their own, but they still need parental approval when it comes to buying clothes, cameras, or most other items. My recommendation is, when you advertise to preteens, you've got to

advertise to the parents as well." Are preteens likely to buy clothing and cameras independent of their parents? Why or why not?

5. Why are so few ads and products targeted to the mature market? Is this lack of attention to the mature market likely to change in the future? Why or why not?

6. A large food producer is considering directing a wide range of packaged food products specifically to the singles market.
   - How do the needs of single-person households differ from those of multiple-person households?
   - What are the implications for the marketer?

7. Cite examples of companies that have used regional differences in tastes and purchasing behavior as a basis for marketing strategy.

8. What is meant by geo-demographic analysis? How can marketers use it to target geographic segments?

9. What are the marketing implications of the greater emphasis working women put on time-saving conveniences?

10. How have marketers adjusted to the increasingly influential role of working women in buying decisions that men used to dominate? Provide specific examples.

11. Two companies produce different lines of furniture. One directs its line toward upper-middle class consumers; the other, to working-class consumers. What are likely to be the differences in (a) product styles and features, (b) print media used, and (c) distribution and in-store environment?

12. A magazine publisher decides there are sufficient differences in the orientation, role, and purchasing behavior of working women in different social classes to segment the magazine market by introducing three different magazines: one directed to the working woman in the upper-middle class, another to the working woman in the working class, and a third to the working woman in the lower class.
   - Do you agree with the publisher's premise?
   - Specifically, how might each magazine differ in (a) editorial content and (b) advertising?

13. A company is introducing a new line of instant baking products designed to facilitate the preparation of more complicated recipes for breads, cakes, and pies.
   - Should the company segment its line so that one set of products is directed to higher social classes and another to lower social classes?
   - How would the advertising campaigns to each group differ?

14. Some researchers believe that sports and leisure-time activities serve a different purpose for the upper and lower classes. For the upper class, sports activities may be a compensation for a more sedentary existence as most of these activities involve active movement.[104] For the lower class, sports and leisure-time activities are more of an escape from the dull routine of jobs. What are the implications of this finding for a large producer of sporting equipment such as AMF?

RESEARCH ASSIGNMENTS

1. Select a group of working women and nonworking women (approximately 30–40 women in each group). Select two food products requiring preparation (for example, cake mix, coffee). Ask respondents to rate various need criteria in selecting brands (such as importance of time saving, ease of preparation, good taste, good for the whole family) and to identify their favorite brand in each category.
   - Do the needs of working and nonworking women differ?
   - Do they prefer different brands?
   - Do the results conform to your expectations about differences between working and nonworking women? In what ways?

2. A study by a large electronics firm determined the demographic characteristics of purchasers of compact discs. These purchasers tended to be in the higher-income group ($40,000 and over) and in professional or managerial occupations.
   - Try to obtain a copy of a Simmons Report or another readership service (it is all right if the report is somewhat dated). Analyze 10 or 12 magazines to determine their relative efficiency in reaching the target group identified above. Incorporate cost-per-thousand data for each magazine if they are available. If not, analyze the magazines solely on their ability to reach the target group.
   - If data are also available for TV shows, do the same analysis for a selected number of shows as well.

3. Select 20 consumers in each of the following occupational groups:
   - Professionals/managers
   - White-collar workers
   - Blue-collar workers

   The first group is generally in the upper-middle or upper class, the second in the middle class, and the third in the working class. Ask each consumer about:

   a. Lifestyles (based on items such as those in Table 10.1).
   b. Product and brand ownership for selected durables (cars, stereos, kitchen appliances) and leisure goods (sporting equipment).
   c. Price paid for these items.
   d. Magazines read most frequently.
   e. Demographics.
      - What are the most significant differences among the three groups in relation to the above?
      - Are these differences due primarily to income level or to different norms and values between social classes?
      - What are the marketing implications of these differences?

NOTES

1. "In the Fast Lane," *Brandweek* (July 5, 1993), p. 22.

2. *Ibid.*

3. "Ma Bell Faces Up to Her Generation Gap," *Adweek's Marketing Week* (June 22, 1992), p. 19.

4. "The Population Is Taking Off Again," *American Demographics* (December 7, 1992), p. 14.

5. U.S. Department of Commerce, Bureau of the Census, *Current Population Reports,* 1991 (Washington, D.C.: U.S. Government Printing Office, 1991), Series P-25, No. 1045.

6. "Population Growth Outstrips Earlier U.S. Census Estimates," *The New York Times* (December 4, 1992), p. A1.

7. "Gerber Stumbles in a Shrinking Market," *The Wall Street Journal* (July 6, 1993), p. B1; and "Gerber: Concentrating on Babies Again for Slow, Steady Growth," *Business Week* (August 22, 1993), p. 52.

8. *The New York Times* (December 4, 1992), *loc. cit.*; and life expectancy for 1970 in *Statistical Abstract* (1990), Table 104, p. 73. Life expectancy for 1990 projected in Randolph E. Schmid, "Statistics: National Death Rate Drops to Record Low," *Associated Press Wire Service* (February 8, 1986).

9. *The New York Times* (December 4, 1992), *op. cit.,* p. D18.

10. *The Wall Street Journal* (July 6, 1993), *op. cit.,* p. B5.

11. "Secrets of the Age Pyramids," *American Demographics* (August, 1992), p. 50.

12. "The Boomer Report," *Adweek's Marketing Week* (January 22, 1990), pp. 20–27; and Andrew P. Garvin, *The Boomer Report Newsletter.*

13. "The Baby Boomers Are Richer and Older," *Business Month* (October, 1987), pp. 24–28.

14. "What the Baby Boomers Will Buy Next," *Fortune* (October 15, 1984), p. 31.

15. "Michelob Piles It On," *Advertising Age* (September 12, 1985), p. 32; and "The Going Gets Tough and Madison Avenue Dumps the Yuppies," *The Wall Street Journal* (December 9, 1987), p. 1.

16. "Lee Aims at Bigger Targets: Pudgy People," *The Wall Street Journal* (January 27, 1993), p. B7.

17. "Here Come the Grumpies," *New York Magazine* (October 5, 1992), p. 26.

18. "Peace, Love and Tie-Dye Turn Off 'Anti-Boomers,'" *Adweek's Marketing Week* (April 9, 1990), p. 17.

19. "Move Over, Boomers," *Business Week* (December 14, 1992), p. 75.

20. "How to Talk to Young Adults," *American Demographics* (April, 1993), p. 50.

21. *Business Week* (December 14, 1992), *loc. cit.*

22. "Ugly Chic," *Forbes* (September 13, 1993), p. 200.

23. "Big Blue's Hip Campaign Targets Cool Collegians," *Marketing News* (October 11, 1993), p. 6.

24. Estimated from "Irvington, 10533," *Brandweek* (August 17, 1992), p. 12.

25. "Reaching Teen-agers, Without Using a Phone," *The New York Times* (January 18, 1993), p. D6.

26. "Sex, Buys and Advertising," *NBC TV* (July 31, 1990).

27. "The Child Research, Custom, Consulting and Qualitative Divisions," *MSW Newsletter.*

28. "The Teen Dream," *Mediaweek* (July 22, 1991), p. 27.

29. "Their Generation: No More Kid Stuff," *Adweek* (June 15, 1992), p. 66.

30. "Japan's Prodigal Young Are Dippy About Imports," *Fortune* (May 11, 1987), p. 118.

31. "You Just Can't Talk to These Kids," *Business Week* (April 19, 1993), p. 104.

32. "Married with Children," *American Demographics Desk Reference* (July, 1992), p. 6.

33. *Fortune* (May 8, 1989), p. 115; and "Targeting the 'Tween' Market," *Advertising Age* (November 23, 1987), p. 51.

34. *American Demographics Desk Reference* (July, 1992), *loc. cit.*

35. "Single Parents," *American Demographics Desk Reference* (July, 1992), p. 12.

36. "They May Be Small, But They Spend Big," *Adweek* (February 10, 1992), p. 39.

37. "Yogurt Makers Sweet-Talk the Young Set," *The Wall Street Journal* (February 23, 1993), p. B1.

38. "P&G Heads Shampoo into Preteen Segment with Pert Line Extension," *Advertising Age* (April 20, 1992), p. 3.

39. "New Polaroid Cool Cam Develops Kids' Interest," *Advertising Age* (September 19, 1988), p. 90.

40. "Children Come of Age as Consumers," *Marketing News* (December 4, 1987), p. 8.
41. *Fortune* (May 8, 1988), *op. cit.*, p. 115.
42. "Boomers Bringing Buying Power," *Advertising Age* (November 16, 1992), p. S2.
43. "Older Consumers Adopt Baby-Boomer Buying Behavior," *Marketing News* (February 15, 1988), p. 8.
44. "U.S. Companies Go for the Gray," *Business Week* (April 3, 1989), p. 67.
45. "The Who and How-To of the Nifty 50–Plus Market," *Grey Matter Alert* (Grey Advertising Agency, 1988), pp. 1–6.
46. *Adweek* (July 22, 1991), *op. cit.*, p. 21.
47. "Ads for Elderly May Give Wrong Message," *The Wall Street Journal* (December 31, 1991), p. D4.
48. "Quaker Oats Spotlights Vigorous Elderly," *The New York Times* (November 13, 1992), p. D6.
49. *Business Week* (April 3, 1989), *op. cit.*, p. 65.
50. "Lodging Chain to Give Older Guests a Choice," *The Wall Street Journal* (February 19, 1993), p. B1.
51. *Statistical Abstract, 1990*, Table 61, p. 48.
52. "The Changing American Household," *American Demographics Desk Reference* (July, 1992), p. 3.
53. "Mass Marketing to Fragmented Markets," *Planning Review* (September, 1984), p. 34; and *Sales & Marketing Management* (April, 1987), p. 29.
54. "The Nine Household Markets," *American Demographics* (October, 1991), p. 38.
55. "Single Parents," *American Demographics Desk Reference* (July, 1992), p. 12.
56. "The Singles Scene," *American Demographics Desk Reference* (July, 1992), p. 19.
57. "Home Alone—with $660 Billion," *Business Week* (July 29, 1991), p. 76.
58. "Rise in Never-Marrieds Affects Social Customs and Buying Patterns," *The Wall Street Journal* (May 28, 1986), p. 1.
59. *Business Week* (July 29, 1991), *loc. cit.*
60. "Feeding China's 'Little Emperors'," *Forbes* (August 6, 1990), pp. 84–85.
61. "Detroit Strives to Reclaim Lost Generation of Buyers," *The New York Times* (April 9, 1991), p. D4; and "To Detroit," *American Demographics* (January, 1987), p. 29.
62. "Mapping Regional Marketing Differences," *Advertising Age* (June 16, 1986), p. S32.
63. *American Demographics* (January, 1987), *op. cit.*, p. 24.
64. "Different Folks, Different Strokes," *Fortune* (September 16, 1985), p. 68.
65. "Where Mallomars Don't Exist," *The New York Times* (September 20, 1989), p. C4.
66. Michael R. Solomon, *Consumer Behavior: Buying, Having and Being* (Boston: Allyn and Bacon, 1992), pp. 464–466.
67. *American Demographics* (March, 1992), *op. cit.*, p. 31.
68. "Reaching the Real Europe," *American Demographics* (October, 1990), pp. 38–43.
69. "Panel Sees Change in U.S. Family But Not in Jobs," *The New York Times* (January 17, 1986), p. 11; and "What Is a Working Woman?" *American Demographics* (July, 1988), pp. 24–27.
70. *Statistical Abstract, 1990*, Table 709, p. 452.
71. "Societal Shift," *The Wall Street Journal* (June 29, 1982), p. 1.
72. "Eating Habits Force Changes in Marketing," *Advertising Age* (October 30, 1978), p. 30.
73. *Ibid.*
74. "PC Makers, Palms Sweating, Try Talking to Women," *Business Week* (January 15, 1990), p. 48; and "Women Start Younger at Own Business," *The Wall Street Journal* (February 15, 1993), p. B1.
75. *Congressional Budget Office;* Figures reported in James F. Engel, Roger D. Blackwell, and Paul W. Miniard, *Consumer Behavior* (Hinsdale, IL: Dryden Press, 1990), p. 640.
76. *Statistical Abstract, 1992,* Table 697, p. 446. A median figure is the point at which 50 percent of the population lies above the figure and 50 percent lies below.
77. "Family Futures," *American Demographics* (May, 1984), p. 50.
78. *Statistical Abstract, 1992*, Table 221, p. 144.
79. *Ibid.*
80. Reed Moyer and Michael D. Hutt, *Macromarketing* (New York: John Wiley, 1978), pp. 123–141; Clive W. Granger and Andrew Billson, "Consumers' Attitudes Toward Package Size and Price," *Journal of Marketing Research,* 9 (August, 1972), pp. 239–248; and J. Edward Russo, Gene Dreiser, and Sally Miyashita, "An Effective Display of Unit Price Information," *Journal of Marketing,* 39 (April, 1975), pp. 11–19.

81. "Kodak Will Advertise by the Numbers," *Adweek* (April 27, 1992), p. 2; and "Their Generation: No More Kid Stuff," (June 15, 1992), *loc. cit.*

82. Del I. Hawkins, Roger J. Best, and Kenneth A. Coney, *Consumer Behavior* (Homewood, IL: Irwin, 1992), p. 33.

83. A. C. Nielsen Co., *Cost Per Thousand Report* (May and November, 1988).

84. Thorstein Veblen, *The Theory of the Leisure Class* (New York: Macmillan, 1912).

85. Robert W. Hodges, Paul M. Siegel, and Peter H. Rossi, "Occupational Prestige in the United States 1925–1963," *American Journal of Sociology,* 70 (November, 1964), pp. 290–292.

86. W. Lloyd Warner, Marcia Meeker, and Kenneth Eells, *Social Class in America: Manual of Procedure for the Measurement of Social Status* (New York: Harper & Row, 1960).

87. W. Lloyd Warner and Paul S. Lunt, *The Social Life of a Modern Community, Yankee City Series,* Vol. 1 (New Haven: Yale University Press, 1941).

88. Richard P. Coleman, "The Continuing Significance of Social Class to Marketing," *Journal of Consumer Research,* 10 (December, 1983), p. 270.

89. "Up & Down the Income Scale," *American Demographics* (July, 1990), pp. 26–27.

90. "New Boundaries of Affluence," *Marketing Communications* (February, 1986), p. 33.

91. Coleman, "The Continuing Significance of Social Class to Marketing," *op. cit.,* p. 272.

92. "Women's On-the-Job Attitudes," *Research Alert* (February 5, 1988), p. 3.

93. "Reaching Downscale Markets," *American Demographics* (November, 1991), p. 40.

94. Andre Gabor and S. W. J. Granger, "Price Sensitivity of the Consumer," *Journal of Advertising Research,* 4 (December, 1964), pp. 40–44; David Caplovitz, *The Poor Pay More* (New York: The Free Press, 1963); and Frederick E. Webster, Jr., "The Deal-Prone Consumer," *Journal of Marketing Research,* 1 (August, 1964), pp. 32–35.

95. "The Middle Class Comes Undone," *Ad Forum* (June, 1984), pp. 32–39.

96. J. Michael Munson and W. Austin Spivey, "Product and Brand User Stereotypes Among Social Classes," in Kent B. Monroe, ed., *Advances in Consumer Research,* Vol. 8 (Ann Arbor, MI: Association for Consumer Research, 1981), pp. 696–701.

97. Florence Skelly, "Prognosis 2000," Speech before New York Chapter of the American Marketing Association, December 15, 1977.

98. Sidney J. Levy, "Social Class and Consumer Behavior," in Joseph W. Newman, ed., *On Knowing the Consumer* (New York: John Wiley, 1966), pp. 146–160.

99. *Ibid.*

100. A. Marvin Roscoe, Jr., Arthur LeClaire, Jr., and Leon G. Schiffman, "Theory and Management Applications of Demographics in Buyer Behavior," in Arch G. Woodside, Jagdish N. Sheth, and Peter D. Bennett, eds., *Consumer and Industrial Buying Behavior* (New York: North-Holland, 1977), pp. 74–75.

101. "Nestlé Courts the LDC Middle Class," *The Wall Street Journal* (June 4, 1990), p. A13.

102. V. Kanti Prasad, "Socioeconomic Product Risk and Patronage Preferences of Retail Shoppers," *Journal of Marketing,* 39 (July, 1975), pp. 42–47.

103. Roscoe, LeClaire, and Schiffman, *op. cit.,* p. 74.

104. Doyle W. Bishop and Masaru Ikeda, "Status and Role Factors in the Leisure Behavior of Different Occupations," *Sociology and Social Research,* 54 (January, 1970), pp. 190–208.

11

Personality and Lifestyle Influences

CONAGRA TARGETS A HEALTHIER LIFESTYLE

The two remaining consumer characteristics we will consider, personality and lifestyles, provide marketers with a fuller understanding of consumer behavior than do demographics alone. When researchers first began to study consumer behavior, they turned to existing personality theories to explain motivations. First among these theories was Freud's psychoanalytic approach that stresses subconscious drives. However, theories designed to explain childhood conflicts, adult neuroses, and social disorders are unlikely to explain consumer behavior. As a result, researchers turned to lifestyle variables as factors that more closely reflect consumers' day-to-day interests and, therefore, are more likely to explain consumer purchases.

Lifestyles are measured by the attitudes, interests, and opinions of consumers. Marketers have viewed the lifestyle trends of the

1980s and 1990s with particular interest because these trends have affected every facet of marketing strategy.

Conagra, for instance, introduced its hugely successful Healthy Choice frozen food line because of lifestyle research that found increasing concern among consumers with salt and cholesterol in foods. The idea for Healthy Choice came from Conagra's CEO, Charles Harper. For most of his 57 years, Harper had not given a second thought to smoking two packs of cigarettes a day, routinely drinking 15 cups of coffee, or eating an artery-hardening diet of beef and fudge. However, that all changed in 1987, when Harper was felled by a massive heart attack and had to curb his diet.

While recuperating at home, Harper invited a company executive to a lunch of freshly made chili. Watching his guest rave about the healthy meal his wife had cooked, Harper realized that there had to be millions of men out there just like him, all desperate for tasty foods that suited their diets.[1] Subsequent research proved Harper's thesis. The only problem was that most consumers rejected the idea of low-salt, low-cholesterol dinners as being tasteless and associated them with "sick people's food."

Agreeing that a tasty product and a strong name would be needed to combat these impressions, Conagra began a program that eventually resulted in a method of reducing fat and salt in frozen foods while retaining the taste. Conagra then sent test samples of the new product to national health conferences while drumming up professional interest by sending direct mailings explaining the product to dieticians. By January 1989, when the first 14-item line was rolled out under the name Healthy Choice, advance word about it was widespread.[2]

Backed by ads that evoked family values (a grandfather with his kids under the tag line "Listen To Your Heart"), Healthy Choice caught on like wildfire, capturing a quarter of the $700 million frozen foods market. Soon, low-calorie, low-salt and low-cholesterol frozen hot dogs, hamburgers, fish sticks, cold cuts, pizza, and more began rolling into supermarkets, enticing not just men but women as well.[3]

Conagra quickly drew hoards of competitors with their own low-salt, low-cholesterol lines, from Kraft General Foods, which introduced a new product line, to Weight Watchers and Stouffer's, which repositioned old ones. The increased competition was a tribute to the foresight of Charles Harper who recognized an important lifestyle trend and got Conagra to target it.

In this chapter, we first discuss personality variables, despite their limited applications, because they are especially relevant when deep-seated purchasing motives are involved. We then focus on lifestyles, particularly the lifestyle trends that are changing the face of marketing in the 1990s, and the measurement of lifestyle variables. We close by considering the strategic applications of lifestyle variables.

◆ PERSONALITY

An individual's personality represents another set of characteristics that marketers can use to describe consumer segments. **Personality** is defined as patterns of behavior that are consistent and enduring. Personality variables, therefore, are more deep-seated than lifestyle variables.

Personality characteristics can be valuable guides to marketers. For example, knowing that users of a brand of headache remedies are more likely to be compulsive led one company to advertise the product in an orderly setting that described a fixed routine. Another company found that an important segment of users of artificial sweeteners tended to be compliant and to accept guidance from others, especially medical experts, in an attempt to lose weight. This finding suggested advertising these products through an authority figure.

Personality characteristics may be a basis for product positioning. One segment of the market may diet primarily because of adherence to group norms and may seek to be conspicuous in using diet products. Another segment may diet because of internalized rather than group norms. A company positioning a line of diet products to the first segment would portray group approval as a result of product use, whereas a positioning to the second segment would portray individual achievement.

Marketers have used four personality theories to describe consumers: (1) psychoanalytic theory, (2) social theory, (3) self-concept theory, and (4) trait theory. These four theories vary greatly in their approach to personality measurement. The psychoanalytic and social theories take a qualitative approach to evaluating personality variables; trait theory is the most empirical; and self-concept theory is somewhere in between qualitative and quantitative in its orientation.

We will first describe the more qualitatively oriented theories and conclude with trait theory, the most widely used approach to personality measurement in marketing.

Psychoanalytic Theory

Freud's **psychoanalytic theory** stresses the unconscious nature of personality as a result of childhood conflicts. These conflicts are derived from three components of personality: id, ego, and superego. The **id** (or the **libido**) controls the individual's most basic needs and urges such as hunger, sex, and self-preservation. The source of all innate forces that drive behavior, the id operates on one principle—directing behavior to achieve pleasure and to avoid pain. The id is entirely unconscious, with no anchor in objective reality. A newborn baby's behavior, for example, is governed totally by the id.

The **ego** is the individual's self-concept and is the manifestation of objective reality as it develops in interaction with the external world. As manager of the id, the ego seeks to attain the goals of the id in a socially acceptable manner. For example, rather than manifest a basic need to be aggressive in antisocial ways, an individual may partially satisfy this need by buying a powerful sports car.

The **superego** is the leash on the id and works against its impulses. It does not manage the id but restrains it by punishing unacceptable behavior through the creation of guilt. Like the id, it operates in the unconscious and often represses behavior that would otherwise occur based on the id. The superego represents the ideal rather than the real. It motivates us to act in a moral way.

According to Freud, the ego manages the conflicting demands of the id and the superego. The way the child manages these conflicts (particularly sexual conflicts) determines the adult personality. Conflicts that are not resolved in childhood will result in **defense mechanisms** (strategies that the ego uses to reduce tension) and will frequently influence later behavior in a manner that the adult is unaware.

Motivational Research

Psychologists applying Freud's theories to marketing believe the id and superego operate to create unconscious motives for purchasing certain products. Although these motives would be extremely hard to determine, they might be central to explaining certain purchasing behaviors. Because the focus is on developing means to uncover these unconscious motives, applications of psychoanalytic theory to marketing are known as **motivational research.**

Motivational researchers take a nonempirical approach to evaluating a consumer's personality and believe that deep-seated purchasing motives can best be determined through indirect methods by researching a small number of consumers. Two techniques derived from psychoanalytic theory and applied to marketing—depth interviews and projective techniques—have been used frequently in marketing studies.

Depth Interviews.   Depth interviews, a technique discussed in Chapters 1 and 8, are interviews with individual consumers designed to determine deep-seated or repressed motives that structured questions cannot elicit.[4] Consumers are encouraged to talk freely in an unstructured interview, and their responses are interpreted carefully to reveal motives and potential purchase inhibitions. An offshoot of the depth interview is the **focus group interview,** in which 8 to 12 consumers are brought together under the direction of a moderator to discuss issues that may reveal deep-seated needs or unconscious motives. The advantages of focus groups are that they are likely to stimulate discussion because of the group context, and they may elicit thoughts and motives that individual depth interviews will not.

The foremost proponent of depth and focus group interviews was Ernest Dichter, acknowledged as the father of motivational research. A Freudian psychologist by training, Dichter came to the United States in the late 1930s and began applying psychoanalytic theory to advertising. One of his first applications was for Procter & Gamble in 1940. The company asked Dichter if there was some way to revitalize Ivory Soap. Based on depth interviews with teenagers, he found that they considered bathing as almost a ritual, especially before a date. It was a means of "getting rid of all your bad feelings, your sins, your immorality, and cleansing yourself."[5] On this basis, Dichter developed the slogan "Be smart, get a fresh start with Ivory Soap . . . wash all your troubles away." Dichter used depth and focus group interviews in numerous studies that have provided actionable findings; for example:[6]

- Consumers want a sense of freedom and power when they get behind the wheel of a car. They look for that surge of acceleration to free themselves of the mundane aspects of everyday life. If you want to advertise gasoline, go along with this feeling and advertise the "tiger in your tank." (See Exhibit 11.1.)
- Men resist giving blood because they equate it with a loss of potency. The Red Cross would be smart to advertise to potential donors that they are lending rather than giving their blood, because blood is regenerated in a short period of time.
- Men dislike air travel because of posthumous guilt (the anticipation of making their wives into widows). The solution? Airlines should advertise how quickly they can return the businessman home to his loved ones.

▶**EXHIBIT 11.1**
An appeal to the consumer's desire for power when driving a car

Source: Courtesy of Exxon Company, U.S.A.

- Candy consumption is a source of guilt because of childhood associations with reward and punishment. Any attempt to market candy to adults should emphasize the fact that they deserve the rewards associated with candy consumption.

Projective Techniques. **Projective techniques** are the second set of methods derived from psychoanalytic theory and applied to marketing.[7] Like depth interviews, these techniques are designed to determine motives that are difficult to express or identify. Because consumers may not be aware of their motives for buying, researchers cannot ask direct questions consumers may not be able to answer. Instead, consumers are given a situation, a cartoon, or a set of words and asked to respond. They project their feelings and concerns about products to this less-threatening or involving situation.

In one famous experiment in the late 1940s, Haire used a projective technique to discover why women were reluctant to purchase instant coffee when it was first introduced.[8] He constructed two shopping lists that were identical, except that one included regular coffee and the other instant coffee. Respondents then were asked to project the type of woman most likely to have developed each shopping list. The shopper who included instant coffee in the list was characterized as lazy and a poor planner. These findings demonstrated that many women had a deep-seated fear of buying products like instant coffee or instant cake mixes because of a concern that their husbands would believe they were avoiding their traditional role as homemakers. As a result of the study, instant coffee was advertised in a family setting portraying the husband's approval. A replication of the study today would produce very different results since this traditional view of a woman's role is not as widespread. The study is a classic example of a psychoanalytically oriented approach to the determination of consumer motives.

Criticisms of Motivational Research

Motivational research has been criticized for its lack of empiricism. Some have also questioned whether advertising could or should influence deep-seated motives. The psychoanalytic approach may not be empirical, but motivational researchers were the first to argue that consumers are "complex, devious, difficult to understand and driven by mighty forces of which they are unaware."[9]

Social Theory

A number of Freud's disciples shifted from his view of personality in two respects. First, they thought that social variables, rather than biological drives, are more important in personality development. Second, they believed that conscious motives are more important than unconscious motives; that is, behavior is most frequently directed to known needs and wants. Furthermore, Freud's understanding of personality focused primarily on observations of emotionally disturbed people. Many researchers believed that insights into personality development should also rely on observations of people who function normally in the social environment.

Alfred Adler was the foremost proponent of this social orientation. Rather than focus on the importance of sexual conflicts, Adler emphasized the individual's striving for superiority in a social context. He stressed that children develop feelings of inferiority, and their primary goal as adults is to overcome these feelings.

Karen Horney was another social theorist. She believed that personality is developed as an individual learns to cope with basic anxieties stemming from parent-child relationships. She hypothesized three approaches to coping with this anxiety: compliance, a strategy of moving toward people; aggressiveness, moving against people; and detachment, moving away from people.

In one of the few studies relying on social theories of personality to explain purchase behavior, Cohen developed a **compliance-aggressiveness-detachment (CAD) scale** based on Horney's work.[10] Cohen measured CAD using a 35-item inventory. In applying the CAD scale, Cohen found that compliant types used more mouthwash, toilet soaps, and Bayer aspirin; aggressive types used more cologne and after-shave lotion and bought Old Spice deodorant and Van Heusen shirts; and detached types drank more tea and less beer. These findings suggest advertising the use of mouthwash or toilet soap as a means of social approval, advertising colognes and after-shaves as a means of social conquest, and advertising tea in a nonsocial context.

Measures such as Cohen's CAD scale are important because they were constructed for marketing applications and have a theoretical base in personality theory. In such cases, the researcher begins a study with defined hypotheses of which personality variables to measure.

Self-Concept Theory

Another personality theory applied to marketing is **self-concept** (or **self-image**) **theory.** This theory holds that individuals have a concept of self based on who they think they are (the actual self) and a concept of who they think they would like to be (the ideal self). Self-concept theory is related to psychoanalytic theory, since the actual self is similar to the ego and the ideal self is similar to the superego. It is more empirical than psychoanalytic theory: Consumers are asked to describe how they see themselves or how they would like to see themselves on various attributes such as:

happy	serious
dependable	self-controlled
modern	successful
practical	sensitive
energetic	aggressive

Self-concept theory is governed by these two principles: the desire to attain self-consistency and the desire to enhance one's self-esteem. Attaining self-consistency means that individuals will act in accordance with their concept of actual self. For example, a consumer may see himself as a practical and self-controlled individual. He buys conservative suits, drives a large four-door sedan, and spends quiet evenings at home. Deep down, however, he would like to be more carefree and reckless. If he were to act more like his ideal self, he might own a small sports car, dress in jeans and sportshirts, and go to rock clubs. Such actions would enhance his self-esteem by drawing him closer to his ideal self.

Actual Self

Applied to marketing, the concept of **actual self** says that consumers' purchases are influenced by the image they have of themselves. They attain self-consistency by buying products they perceive as similar to their self-concept. That is, there is congruence between brand image and self-image.

Several studies have confirmed that consumers buy products related to their self-concept. Dolich studied this relationship for beer, cigarettes, bar soap, and toothpaste.[11] He found that respondents tend to prefer brands they rate as similar to themselves. Several studies have shown the same relationship for automobiles.[12] An owner's perception of his or her car is consistent with self-perception. Furthermore, the consumer's self-image is similar to his or her image of others with the same automobile.

More recently, Burnkrant and Page concluded that the relationship between brand image and self-image is somewhat more complicated because consumers change their self-image with each situation.[13] For example, a consumer may have one self-image in a social situation but another one in a business situation.

Ideal Self

The concept of the **ideal self** relates to one's self-esteem. The greater the difference between the actual self and ideal self, the lower an individual's self-esteem. In a marketing context, dissatisfaction with oneself could influence purchases, particularly for products that could enhance self-esteem. Thus, a woman who would like to be more efficient, modern, and imaginative may buy a different type of perfume or deodorant or tend to shop at different stores than a woman who would like to be more warm and attractive.

A study by White illustrates research based on the discrepancy between actual and ideal self-concept. White defined three segments based on this discrepancy.[14] High discrepants are dissatisfied with their self-image and wish for great and unrealizable changes; middle discrepants are somewhat dissatisfied and want to improve themselves in a realistic way; and low discrepants have accurate and often severe notions of themselves and little tolerance for fantasy. White related these categories to ownership of compact cars and found that a significant proportion of the middle discrepants owned compact cars. Compact car ownership seems to be greater among a relatively realistic group that could be appealed to effectively with a moderate amount of fantasy interspersed with a good dose of reality concerning durability and economy.

Richins found that advertising themes and images often create greater discrepancy between the real and ideal selves.[15] Advertising that portrays beautiful models or luxurious lifestyles creates an idealized world that is unreachable. As a result, consumers are left with a sense of inadequacy based on a comparison of their real self with these idealized images. In acting to increase the disparity between the real and ideal selves, advertising tends to lower consumers' self-esteem.

The desire for both self-consistency and self-esteem could be conflicting. Consumers who buy in accordance with their actual self-concept may be achieving consistency but may not be enhancing self-esteem. We saw that the consumer who sees himself as practical and self-controlled would achieve consistency by buying conservative suits and spending quiet evenings at home, but these actions do nothing to bring him closer to his ideal self. Generally, consumers buy products that conform to their actual self-image. But if they are low in self-esteem (that is, if there is greater disparity between the actual and ideal selves), they are more likely to buy based on what they would like to be rather than on what they are.

Buying to achieve an unrealizable self-image can lead to compulsive purchasing behavior. Frequent purchasing is a means to overcome the discrepancy between the real and ideal selves and to relieve a sense of low self-esteem.[16]

Extended Self

Another dimension of self-concept theory is applicable to consumers. Not only does our self-image influence the products we choose (as suggested above), but also the products we choose frequently influence our self-image.[17] Certain products have symbolic (badge) value. They say something about us and the way we feel about ourselves. For example, when we buy a certain suit or dress, we may anticipate that it will enhance our self-esteem.

On this basis, Belk has identified an **extended self** as distinct from the actual self.[18] The extended self incorporates some of our more important possessions into our self-concept, because what we own reflects our personality. In simple terms, we are what we wear, and we are what we use.

This extension of self-concept theory has been called **symbolic interactionism** because it emphasizes the interaction between individuals and the symbols in their environment. It means that consumers buy products for their symbolic value in enhancing their self-concept. It also means that consumers tend to buy groups of products because of their symbolic association. As Solomon noted, "While the Rolex watch, Brooks Brothers suit, New Balance running shoes, Sony Walkman, and BMW automobile on the surface bear no relation to one another, many consumers would easily group these disparate products together as a symbolic whole."[19]

Research based on the concept of extended self would examine the constellation of products a consumer owns and try to equate these groups of products to the consumer's self-concept. This type of research is very different from looking at a single product and determining if it is related to a consumer's actual or ideal self-concept. It seeks to understand the symbolic role that groups of products play in shaping the consumer's self-concept.

Advertisers have understood the symbolic role of products in influencing self-image. Advertising for jewelry, cosmetics, automobiles, and clothing frequently communicates an image of the user. (See the ads for Nike and Calvin Klein in Exhibit 11.3.) As a result, it is surprising that very little research has focused on examining the role of groups of products on self-image.

Trait Theory

Trait theory has been used most widely for measuring personality because it is the most empirical. **Trait theory** states that personality is composed of a set of traits that describe general response predispositions. Trait theorists construct personality inventories and ask respondents to respond to many items, perhaps agreeing or disagreeing with certain statements or expressing likes or dislikes for certain situations or types of people. These items then are statistically analyzed and reduced to a few personality dimensions. This method does not predetermine personality traits and is unlike psychoanalytic and social theories, which have specific hypotheses about the traits that affect behavior (for example, compulsiveness, aggressiveness, and detachment in Horney's theory).

In marketing, the most frequently used inventory has been the Edwards Personal Preference Schedule (EPPS). The EPPS measures 14 personality items such as achievement (to rival and surpass others, to do one's best), compliance (to accept leadership, to follow willingly), and order (to have things arranged, to be organized).[20] Other inventories used in marketing are the Gordon Personal Profile, which measures traits such as ascendancy, responsibility, emotional stability, and sociability, and the Thurstone Temperament Schedule, which measures dominance, stability, impulsiveness, and other traits. Marketers use these inventories because they contain personality traits that are not too abstract and can be hypothesized to relate to purchasing behavior.

A number of studies have used personality traits to segment markets. A study of smoking behavior using the Edwards Personal Preference Schedule found that heavy smokers scored higher on heterosexuality, aggression, and achievement and lower on order and compliance.[21] Heavy smokers are more likely to be oriented toward power and competitiveness and may be more influenced by sexual themes and symbols. They are not as compulsive or submissive as nonsmokers. Because of this emphasis on power and competitiveness, it is not surprising that one of the most successful cigarette campaigns has been the Marlboro Cowboy.

In another study, the Thurstone Temperament Schedule was used to segment the automobile market.[22] No differences were found between owners of standard and compact cars, but convertible owners tended to be more active, vigorous, and impulsive. On this basis, advertising appeals for convertibles would be directed to active, carefree individuals.

Despite these findings, in most cases, the association between personality traits and behavior has been weak. Perhaps the most important reason for the difficulty in relating personality traits to consumer behavior is that multitrait inventories were not originally designed to discriminate consumer behavior.

When personality measures are specifically developed for consumer behavior applications, they have more strategic applications. For example, Gottleib hypothesized that compulsive and punitive consumers would be more frequent users of antacids.[23] Compulsiveness and punitiveness were measured by agreement or disagreement with a set of predetermined statements such as "I like to set up a schedule for my activities and then stick to it" (compulsiveness) and "Discipline is the single most important factor in building children's character" (punitiveness). As expected, high compulsives tended to consume more antacids; punitive respondents, less. Because of these results, the advertising for the brand under study emphasized a specific routine and regimen to appeal to the compulsive segment. The results also suggested that it was not necessary to make antacids taste bad to appeal to the punitive segment, as was originally thought.

Limitations of Personality Variables

Consumer behavior researchers have seen drawbacks in using personality characteristics to explain purchasing behavior. Personality theories are meant to describe enduring patterns of behavior. Quite often, the focus is on aberrant, rather than typical, behavior. To apply measures developed for these purposes to consumer behavior assumes that consumers are motivated to buy based on deep-seated drives. As we have seen, however, most consumer behavior is a mundane, day-to-day affair. Kassarjian summarized the limitations of personality measures:

> Instruments originally intended to measure gross personality characteristics such as sociability, emotional stability, introversion, or neuroticism have been used to make predictions of the chosen brand of toothpaste or cigarettes. The variables that lead to the assassination of a president, confinement in a mental hospital, or suicide may not be identical to those that lead to the purchase of a washing machine, a pair of shoes, or chewing gum. Clearly, if unequivocal results are to emerge, consumer behavior

researchers must develop their own definitions and design their own instruments to measure the personality variables that go into the purchase decision.[24]

The limited capability of personality theories to explain more mundane, day-to-day consumer behavior led researchers to look elsewhere for an understanding of such behavior. The investigation of consumer lifestyles was motivated by these limitations of personality variables.

◆ LIFESTYLE

A **lifestyle** is broadly defined as a mode of living that is identified by how people spend their time (activities), what they consider important in their environment (interests), and what they think of themselves and the world around them (opinions). Lifestyle variables are also known as **psychographic characteristics** because attitudes, interests, and opinions are psychologically oriented variables that can be quantified. Some activities, interests, and opinions that define lifestyles are listed here:[25]

Activities	*Interests*	*Opinions*
work	family	personal relations
hobbies	home	social issues
social events	job	politics
vacation	community	business
entertainment	recreation	economics
club membership	fashion	education
community	food	products
shopping	media	future
sports	achievements	culture

Lifestyle factors are relevant to marketers on two levels. First, broad lifestyle trends such as changing male/female purchasing roles have altered the habits, tastes, and purchasing behavior of American consumers. Second, lifestyles can be applied on a product-specific basis. For example, Snapple, a manufacturer of "New Age" juice and tea drinks that have no artificial ingredients, is gaining national attention after six years of doubling sales annually. The company might identify its target segment as health-conscious fitness types[26] and develop advertising and promotional appeals based on this lifestyle profile.

In this section, we first consider the broad lifestyle trends that are changing American consumers in the 1990s and then we turn to the more product-specific applications of lifestyle variables.

Changing Lifestyle Trends of American Consumers in the 1990s

Changes in the lifestyles of American consumers are due partially to changes in their demographic characteristics and partially to changes in their values. Six broad changes in lifestyles are occurring in the 1990s:

1. Change in male/female purchasing roles.
2. Leveling off of concerns about health and fitness.
3. More self-awareness.
4. More professionals working at home.
5. Return to traditionalism and a more frugal lifestyle.
6. Increasing emphasis on convenience.

Changes in Male Purchasing Roles

The increase in the number of working women and the decrease in family size have meant a shift away from the traditional roles of a working male and a stay-at-home female. The change in the male's purchasing role is most apparent in increased responsibilities for shopping and child care and in more involvement with cooking and housecleaning—all traditional female roles. A 1991 survey by Maritz Marketing Research found that 35 percent of men buy all the food for their homes, about 30 percent buy all the cleaning supplies and housewares, and about 67 buy all their own personal items.[27] When they do shop, men do not act that differently from women. They tend to spend the same amount of time preplanning purchases, checking prices, and redeeming coupons.[28]

The participation of males in traditional female roles goes beyond shopping. More men are involved in cooking, cleaning, laundry, and child care. A national study by the not-for-profit Families and Work Institute shows that in households where only the husband works, wives do 94 percent of the cooking and 93 percent of child care. However, in homes where both work, the man's role jumps to 20 percent of cooking and 30 percent of child care. These findings must be taken in perspective, however. The fact that men account for about one-third of all homemaking activities means that women still have by far the greatest responsibilities. Also, men are not yet comfortable talking about their role. According to the Institute, some men who depart work early to care for their kids tell co-workers that they are leaving to go to a bar.[29]

Companies such as Kraft General Foods are shifting a significant proportion of their print advertising budget away from women's magazines to general interest and male-oriented magazines. A recent issue of *Men's Health* magazine had ads for Dannon yogurt, Colgate toothbrushes, Kraft salad dressing, and Nutrasweet.[30] On television, Kmart has tried making the transition for men easier by showing Mike Starr, a notable movie bad guy, placing shampoo in his shopping cart as he wheels his son down the aisle.[31]

The changing male role is not a function of demographics only. It is also a result of changes in male values. In a study, Campbell's Soup found that the men who are most likely to shop view themselves as liberated, considerate, achievement-oriented individuals.[32] These are the types of males who do not feel the need to conform to a "macho" image. As a result, a second change has occurred in male purchasing roles: Males are beginning to buy products that at one time might have been dismissed as too feminine—jewelry, skin care products, moisturizers, and cosmetics. In marketing these products, advertisers have had to depict males in a way that is very different from the traditional strong, masculine image of the Marlboro Cowboy or in the typical beer commercial. A new concept of masculinity has emerged—the sensitive male who is as vulnerable in many ways as his female counterpart. As a result, a growing number of advertisers have begun telling males that being sensitive and caring does not conflict with masculinity.

The Calvin Klein Eternity ad in Exhibit 11.2 is a good example. The model is presented as handsome, soft, and pensive; and the presence of his son gives him the added dimension of being a family man. Another example of this trend in Exhibit 11.2 is the ad for Claiborne, a fragrance for men produced by Liz Claiborne. The man in the ad is sitting at a bar watching a woman and is uneasy

▶**EXHIBIT 11.2**
Ads depicting a changing male image

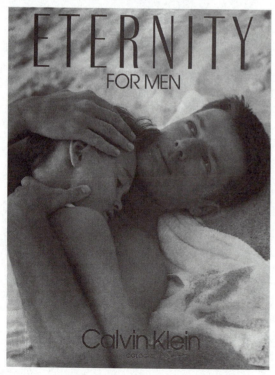

because he cannot decide if she is smiling or laughing at him. Other variations of the ad show one man wondering if his masculinity is on the wane and another admitting that the future is scary because when he looks in the mirror, he sees his father's face. As the creative director for the campaign explained, "A lot of men today don't want to be seen as strong, silent John Wayne types. Men and women have been thinking about a lot of the same things for a long time. We are only now starting to talk about it."[33]

The net result of the greater involvement of men in shopping and housekeeping activities and their willingness to shed a traditional male image has led to a merger of male and female purchasing roles. Today, it would be as shortsighted for a marketer conducting a survey of paper towels, disposable diapers, or frozen foods to restrict the sample to the "woman of the house" as it would be for a marketer of financial services or automobiles to restrict the sample to the "man of the house."

Changes in Female Purchasing Roles

Working women's greater affluence, independence, and self-confidence have created a substantial change in women's purchasing roles. As their purchasing power has increased, they have flexed more muscle in just about every product category, making almost no enclave a male-preserve anymore.[34] As we saw in Chapter 10, for instance, women spend $65 billion on cars every year.

Women's increasing independence suggests a desire for an identity beyond their traditional roles. A survey of women under 35 found that 90 percent did not aspire to being lifelong homemakers. Three-fourths of these women planned to combine job and homemaking throughout their lives.[35] As a result, most women no longer identify with ads that tell them how to clean their floors or to please their husbands. The problem is creating ads they do identify with. The advertising industry does not have an illustrious track record in this regard. The National Advertising Review Board found that until the late 1970s, women were typically portrayed as "stupid [and] too dumb to cope with familiar everyday chores unless instructed by children or a man."[36] Wisk's "ring around the collar" ad is a good example of the attitude that a woman's worth depends on the approval of her husband and on her laundering abilities. In the early 1980s, many advertisers went to the other extreme, creating a "superwoman" model, which one ad executive described derisively as:

> that disgustingly perfect specimen who serves her family a bountiful, hot breakfast, dashes off to run a corporation all day, and then glides in at 6 p.m. to create a lavish gourmet meal while at the same time changing diapers, leading Cub Scouts, and carrying on stimulating conversation with her husband.[37]

Today, the race is on to win back disgruntled women with campaigns that identify with their professionalism and reinforce their self-esteem. Both the Nike and Calvin Klein ads in Exhibit 11.3 make this point by representing a more realistic voice for today's woman.

However, advertisers must be careful not to go to extremes in depicting the independent woman. Subaru made a fundamental miscalculation when it aired a TV commercial in 1993 designed to appeal to strong-willed women. The ad began by showing a young woman complaining that "Every guy I know thinks he knows everything about cars and the '69 Mets." After she asserts that she is the one who usually explains the car's ABS brake system and all-wheel drive to her dates, she adds with a wink to the camera: "Oh ya. And the '69 Mets? The Cubs choked." While the ad made the point that women may also know more about baseball than men, it obscured Subaru's long-standing slogan, "Inexpensive. And built to stay that way." As a result, sales fell and the campaign was discontinued.[38]

Healthier Lifestyles

American consumers are more aware of the effects of dietary habits on health and are more conscious of cholesterol and salt levels, caffeine content, and food additives. According to Food and Drug Administration estimates, 40 percent of consumers are concerned about salt in their diet, while at least one-half of the U.S. adult population is trying to lose weight at any given time.[39]

This awareness has been translated into a change in consumer purchasing patterns. A 1989 study found that almost half of consumers surveyed reported

▶**EXHIBIT 11.3**
More realistic portrayals of women in advertising

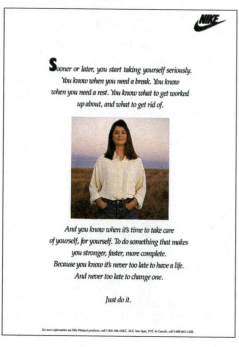

buying a food product promoting good health in the previous 30 days.[40] It is estimated that almost half of the adult population takes vitamin supplements and over one-third of adults use low-calorie foods and beverages. Consumption of certain products has also decreased. Per capita consumption of cigarettes, liquor, and coffee has steadily decreased in the past 15 years. Consumers have been switching from red meats to poultry because of cholesterol concerns, and their purchase of some dairy products has declined, with a switch to low-fat products such as skim milk and yogurt.

As a result of these concerns, health and nutritional claims have become widespread. There is hardly a food company that does not have at least one line of diet or nutritionally oriented products. Companies that repositioned existing products to health-conscious consumers were able to post strong profits. Tums saw its sales grow by 50 percent when it repositioned itself as a calcium supplement targeted to women concerned about bone disease later in life, even though calcium was always part of the product.[41] Bertolli repositioned its olive oil as a means of avoiding saturated oils; the tag line is "Eat well, live long, and be happy." Also, Motts was pleasantly surprised when it found the small six-packs of apple juice that it had introduced to adults were catching on with kids. So it repositioned the brand, recognizing that as more baby boomers age, concern about their childrens' nutrition would lead to enhanced sales.[42]

On the other side of the coin, industries faced with decreasing demand as a result of the emphasis on health have had to make adjustments. Cigarette companies have diversified into foods and beverages. Today, Philip Morris is the second-largest food company in the world because of its acquisition of Kraft and General Foods. Beer makers have jumped headlong into the marketing of nonalcoholic brews, leading to a 32 percent growth rate in the category during 1992[43]; and hard-liquor companies such as Seagram's are expanding into flavored alcohol cocktails while buying juice companies like Tropicana.[44] Finally, coffee companies have tried countering caffeine concerns by devoting more advertising dollars to decaffeinated brands.

Despite the attention devoted to healthier and more nutritious foods, increasing evidence suggests that this trend has peaked. A 1993 Louis Harris poll of 1,251 adults found that Americans gained more weight and ate less carefully than they did the year before.[45] The days of obsessive dieting seem to be fading, and marketers are more willing to appeal to an increasingly indulgent American consumer. The ad for Häagen-Dazs in Exhibit 11.4 is an example with its appeal to "Love It. Need It."

As a result, marketers are positioning fewer products to the health segment. For example, new products claiming to have no or low cholesterol dropped to 11.9 percent in 1992 from 14.1 percent the year before, and those claiming to have no- or low-saturated fat dipped to 2 percent from 3.4 percent.[46]

Also, companies introducing light versions of their products have not always fared well. Frito Lay, for example, reported "marginal to disappointing results" in 1993 after introducing light versions of Cheetos and Doritos.[47]

▶**EXHIBIT 11.4**
Appealing to a more
self-indulgent consumer

Concerns About Fitness

Just as the days of obsessive dieting are fading, so too are the days of obsessive exercising. Americans continue to be concerned about maintaining fitness, but the preoccupation with achieving perfect bodies at all costs has gone the way of the 1980s—a decade known for self-absorption. The more current surveys would seem to suggest that Americans are more willing to accept the bodies they have and resent advertisers who make them feel anxious about it. This is particularly true among women. The average female fashion model is 5-foot-9 and weighs 123 pounds; the average U.S. woman, on the other hand, is 5-foot-4 and weighs 144 pounds.[48]

The trend to fitness in the 1980s had strong marketing impact, particularly with respect to spending on exercise equipment, health clubs, and sporting goods. By the mid-1980s, an estimated 12,000 health and racquet clubs crisscrossed the country and were grossing over $6 billion. Sporting apparel grossed about $3.5 billion and exercise equipment close to $1 billion.[49]

However, as the economy soured and people had to work longer hours, the amount of time devoted to out-of-home exercising declined. Though the share of adults belonging to health clubs grew from 15 to 24 percent in the five years after 1987, the average member spent 12 percent less time there at the end of the period, according to a time-use research study Reebok did.[50] The share of adults who exercised at home, meanwhile, went from 18 to 23 percent.

Faced with that new reality, marketers adapted by catering to the home-based exercise market. Reebok, for example, marketed a home version of its popular step aerobics program in the United States and then extended it abroad as the ad for Reebok in France shows in Exhibit 11.5. Similarly, advertisers flocked to home health magazines such as *Walking,* which posted a 54 percent increase in ad pages between 1990 and 1991—the heart of the recession.[51]

In a 1992 survey of 2,500 people, Yankelovich Clancy Shulman, the research firm, recorded the sentiments of most Americans. It found most consumers are comfortable with their life choices and, therefore, do not try to impress others when they exercise; they are not attracted by novelty; they are not willing to sacrifice everything for an idealized vision of what a marketer thinks they should look like; and they do not want to give up their occasional indulgences.[52] Food and beverage companies are positioning products to appeal to this ethic. The ad for Evian in Exhibit 11.5 advocates fitness by eating right rather than through a rigorous exercise program.

Higher Level of Self-Awareness

The 1990s is seeing an increase in the demand for products and services that offer a sense of personal achievement such as sports equipment, home electronics, and educational products. Two prerequisites for a more self-aware

▶**EXHIBIT 11.5**

Appealing to fitness in the 1990s

Source: (right) Courtesy of Evian Waters of France

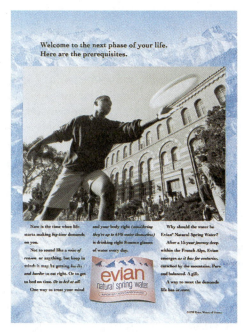

lifestyle are the money required to pursue self-satisfying activities and the time to do so. However, consumers are finding that their time is more constrained. One study estimated that leisure time decreased by about one-third in the 1980s.[53] Arthur D. Little, a large consulting firm, sees the resolution of this conflict as an "increasing emphasis on activities that can be mastered easily, can provide high rewards in a short time period, and can be accomplished at or near the home. As a result, such things as home computers, cable TV, and exercisers will be high on consumer shopping lists."[54]

In appealing to self-awareness, many marketers used to focus on high levels of personal achievement. Now, they are using a more relaxed style to focus on improving one's self-image. For example, one of Michelob's print ads depicts headlines torn from other papers admonishing women to "lose fat," "make yourself over," and "have perfect arms in 14 days." The tag line reads: "Relax. You're OK. Improve your beer."[55]

This focus on self with a minimum of anxiety parallels a broader change in the values of most Americans. As we saw in the last chapter, mature consumers, baby boomers, and even baby busters have left behind the obsessive purchasing that marked the 1980s. Consumers now concentrate instead on more pragmatic concerns—namely, family, economic security, and the environment. There is a significant increase in products trying to help people address these concerns. *The New York Times Book Review*, a leading indicator of popular reading tastes, became so filled with "How-To" books that the newspaper had to create a separate category for them. Also, late-night television has become crowded with infomercials advising consumers how they can feel better about themselves.

More Professionals Working at Home

An offshoot of the trend toward more self-awareness is the larger numbers of Americans who work at home. Electronics has made it easy for home-based entrepreneurs to operate as if they worked in a corporate office. All that is needed is a facsimile machine, a copying machine, and a personal computer.

According to federal estimates, between 10 and 13 percent of the work force is self-employed. Many have taken the freelance route as a lifestyle choice to maximize their personal time and to cut down on commuting. However, the fastest growing group in the segment are 50-something white males with managerial and administrative experience—the prime victims of the corporate layoffs of the 1990s. These highly educated, white-collar executives, whose ranks swelled to 700,000 in the past decade, often find that their skills no longer fetch the price they once did. They find their best course is to become independent operators, even though they are likely to earn less than they did in the corporate world. This was one of the main outcomes of the recession of the early 1990s and a prime reason why most of the new businesses started at home tend to involve consulting, graphic design, computer maintenance, and personnel. These are the areas that have suffered greatly from corporate downsizing, but at the same time require minimal start-up capital.[56]

Since they began advertising on television, beer companies have used provocatively clad women to titillate their male customers. So when Stroh's Brewery decided to sell its Old Milwaukee beer by showing a giggling band of blond bombshells called the Swedish Bikini Team parachuting into a campsite of sex-starved men, no one at the company figured it would cause a ripple. However, in December 1991, Stroh's female employees filed a suit against the beer maker claiming the ads were degrading and encouraged sexual harassment.

The Stroh's controversy forced the entire beer industry into a state of reexamination. Though women buy 35 percent of all domestic beer and 45 percent of light beer, few companies have seen a need to talk directly to them. By the time Stroh's pushed the envelope too far, women had become used to macho beer advertising. As a result, they either bought brands *in spite* of their advertising or chose unadvertised selections. In an attempt to turn that liability into an asset, Anheuser-Busch has tried building new bridges.

In 1991 Anheuser-Busch shot ads for Bud Dry from a woman's point of view. They featured five different nightmare date scenarios—including a nerd who talks about his mother's meatloaf and a grating yuppie who keeps interrupting conversation to talk on his cellular phone. The spoofs adopted a gender-oriented slant and used humor to diffuse old hostilities. Anheuser followed with ads for Bud Light showing two women drinking beer in a realistic social context. (See Exhibit 11.6.)

In 1992, Anheuser's Michelob brand went one step further with more serious quality-of-life spots. In one, four professional-looking women are seen drinking Michelob inside an upscale neighborhood pub. The copy begins by saying, "They used to call you the Sullivan Sisters." Then, after listing their new married names, the ad conjures a sentimental image of the four enjoying old memories by adding that once again, "Tonight, you're the Sullivan Sisters." The ad has a psychographic element; it associates Michelob with a specific lifestyle scenario—in this case, four married sisters getting together for a rare night out and choosing a special beer. With only 1.8 percent of the beer market, it was apparent that, as one analyst wrote, "Michelob certainly wasn't getting anywhere with guys, so its [approach with women was] worth a try."

Shortly after the spots appeared, Michelob's sales rose 3.3 percent. However, women's memories will be understandably long when it comes to forgetting the overboard sexism that is evident in ads like the one that landed Stroh's in court.

Sources: "Michelob Ads Feature Women—And They're Not Wearing Bikinis," *Marketing News* (March 2, 1992), p. 2; and "This Bud's for You. No, Not You—Her," *Business Week* (November 4, 1991), p. 86.

Beer advertisers target
women with more
realistic themes

Not all home-based workers are self-employed, however. Many companies now allow their employees to work from home via computer hookups to save time and to free employees from nonproductive office distractions. Baxter Health Care, American Express, Apple Computer, IBM, Sears, and J.C. Penney are just a few of the firms with work-at-home policies.

Marketers have responded by trying to serve the rapidly expanding niche of home-based workers. Computer software designers such as Lotus and Borland are leading the way with programs that enable individuals to create elaborate graphics packages and presentations. However, they are by no means alone. Apple, IBM, Canon, Fujitsu, and other companies are all appealing to the home-based entrepreneur, all through personalized versions of office machines. One of the fastest-growing segments of the copying industry involves small "bubble-jet" machines that stand upright and take up no more room than an in/out box.

The ads for Apple and Fujitsu in Exhibit 11.7 take a remarkably similar approach in advertising two key components of the home office, a personal computer and a fax machine. Both ads address the particular needs of the home office. The Apple ad claims that "you can accomplish a lot more working in your home office if you're working on a Macintosh," and the Fujitsu ad states

▶EXHIBIT 11.7

An appeal to people who work at home

Source: (bottom) Courtesy of Apple Computer Inc.

FINALLY, A LOW-COST FAX THAT MAKES BUSINESS FEEL RIGHT AT HOME.

After 50 years of creating total communication solutions for big business, Fujitsu is introducing a major innovation for small business: A fax designed to save you time, space and money—at home.

The Fujitsu dex® 80.

Without all the backup of a conventional office, your home business fax actually has to work harder. The dex 80 meets business demands at a price that's as easy to live with as its compact design.

An answer for one-liners.

The dex 80 has a built-in answering machine interface so when you're away you can receive both faxes and phone messages on your one phone line. The full-function integrated phone handset is also a space-saver. It makes the dex 80 the only phone you need in your home office.

Prime cuts.

The dex 80 automatically cuts incoming documents to the length of the originals. And with a transmission speed of 15 seconds a page, it can even help cut your phone bills (and keep your phone line free).

Right to privacy.

No more junk fax. The dex 80 lets you program up to 50 numbers for "selective rejection."

We make house calls.

So your home stays in business, the dex 80 is backed by a nationwide dedicated fax service network.

For more information on how the dex 80 is making business feel right at home contact Fujitsu Imaging Systems of America, 3 Corporate Drive, Danbury, CT 06810 or call 1-800-243-7046.

FUJITSU

The global computer & communications company.

How to succeed in business without leaving the house.

Business isn't just 9-5 anymore. Ideas come quietly on weekends. And rush projects scream for overtime.

Nor is business confined to glass and steel superstructures. Many entrepreneurs are operating out of brownstones and split-levels.

So with business obviously overcoming time and space, now seems the perfect time to consider a Macintosh™ personal computer for your space at home.

The Macintosh is so easy to use, anyone can train themselves to be more productive in no time. And there are thousands of programs available to be more productive with. Two facts not lost on the growing number of *Fortune 500* companies now employing Macintosh.

Second generation software like Word 3.0, Omnis 3 Plus and Excel give Macintosh state of the art word processing, data base and spreadsheet capabilities. Which gives you an executive secretary, chief accountant and market forecaster all under one roof. Your own.

You can add an ApplePax™ modem that lets you send hard copy to any facsimile machine in the world. And hard disks that store over 10,000 pages.

Add an ImageWriter® LQ and you can print those pages with professional quality. All this and you're only steps away from the refrigerator.

To explore the Macintosh Personal Office, call 800-538-9696, ext. 600. Then successfully compete with the Home Office from your office at home. 🍎 The power to be your best.™

that "So your home *stays* in business, the dex 80 is backed by a nationwide dedicated fax service network."

More Traditional and Frugal Lifestyle

The 1980s saw a return to traditionalism in American lives. In the youth market, greater conservatism was reflected in an increasing focus on careers and money. For baby boomers, greater conservatism was reflected in more time at home with the family. Some have referred to this trend as "cocooning"; others have referred to stay-at-home baby boomers as "couch potatoes." More traditional attitudes among teenagers and college students were also particularly evident. The youth market began placing more emphasis on materialism and financial stability as life goals. Traditional attitudes also extended to the family. Because divorce levels are so high, many teens emphasize family continuity.

When combined with the recession of the early 1990s, this return to traditionalism is creating a marked trend toward frugality among consumers. Among the signs are fewer expenditures on luxury items, renewed demands for quality, and the loosening of brand loyalties.[57] The market for luxury products has suffered because consumers are framing their lives in terms of survival and security instead of success and acquisition. As one researcher observed:

> In the 1980s, people wanted to make it big; now they just want to make it. People today are more concerned about money, less concerned about 'having it all.' Needs are more basic—less luxury, less concern with the trendy [and] less faith in their ability to fulfill the American dream.[58]

This placed luxury product marketers in the awkward position of selling high-end products with practical arguments, often using a conservative "family values" theme. Waterford, for instance, used a down-home family setting to sell its fine and expensive crystal: In one ad, a barefoot toddler pulled cherries from a pricey Waterford bowl. However, the campaign failed. As one marketing consultant said of Waterford's attempt, "Who gives two-year-old kids Waterford bowls to eat out of? It's a disaster."[59] Similarly, luxury car makers have attempted to adapt to a more practical orientation. In one campaign, Audi used the theme: "If the 90s are a time of getting more for your money, the new Audi 90 is ideally suited to the times." (See Exhibit 11.8.)

The desire for quality has gone hand in hand with the trend toward economy, creating a *value* orientation. Though consumers were buying less expensive products, they sought the same level of quality. This value orientation has resulted in a loosening of brand loyalties and an increase in the purchase of private label and lower-priced brands. According to a 1992 Yankelovich study of 2,500 consumers, shoppers are more secure with themselves and no longer need to impress others with expensive purchases. They are more interested in quality merchandise at bargain prices than they are in brand names.

▶**EXHIBIT 11.8**
Luxury products appeal to the new frugality
Source: Courtesy of Audi

Greater Emphasis on Convenience

We saw in the last chapter that the increasing proportion of working women has put a premium on time for most families. As a result, some marketers have concluded that "time has come to rival money as the commodity people crave most."[60] The focus on time-saving convenience in the 1990s has created two trends in consumption—"grazing" and "refueling."

Grazing is the need to eat on the run. People eat breakfast in the car on the way to work, munch on a sandwich while walking, or eat lunch at their desks. This trend is the result of the demise of sit-down breakfasts and lunches in most households. The need for quick food has led many marketers to repackage their products into smaller sizes and to change them to suit grazers' dietary needs. In 1993, Nestlé reformulated its entire Instant Breakfast line, increasing the vitamin and mineral levels of its Breakfast Bars while cutting the fat content. It also introduced its first granola bars and reformulated the contents of its powdered drink mixes, advertising the change with a campaign that read, "Your breakfast just got more nutritious."[61] Other companies targeting grazers are General Mills, which introduced Yoplait frozen yogurt in a squeezable paper cone, and Oscar Mayer, which sells Lunchables, packaged meat and cheese slices in plastic trays.[62]

Refueling refers to less time spent in preparing and eating dinner. The primary reflection of this trend is the growing importance of microwave ovens in people's lives. Microwaveable food increases the amount of leisure time available to the harried working woman or the single consumer because it promises independence from kitchen chores. The increase in ownership of microwave ovens during the past decade has been phenomenal. In 1980, 15 percent of homes had microwaves; today, close to 80 percent of U.S. households own them.[63] Because of this growth, shelf-stable foods now account for $4 billion in sales annually.[64] Weight Watchers sells sandwiches; Chef Boyardee has a line of Main Meals; Conagra offers Armour Dinner Classics; and Hormell has introduced Kids' Kitchen dinners, all designed for microwave cooking.

However, after investing more than $2 billion on researching how to make microwave food taste as good as stove-prepared dishes, the industry finds results uneven. For example, Campbell's Le Menu line—introduced to compete with Conagra's Healthy Choice dinners—watched as its sales dropped 36 percent in 1992.[65]

Measuring Lifestyle Characteristics

The previous section described lifestyle trends and their marketing implications. Unlike these general trends, lifestyle characteristics that are specific to certain consumers and product categories must be defined and measured if they are to be useful to marketers. For instance, it would be relevant for a food company to identify a dieter segment or a clothing company to identify a fashion-conscious segment. However, the researcher must define lifestyle characteristics, in contrast to demographics, since there are no fixed definitions such as age, income, or occupation. As a result, marketers must devise methods to measure lifestyles.

AIO Inventories

The most common method for measuring lifestyles is to develop an inventory of activities, interests, and opinions (an **AIO inventory**), which marketers use to identify lifestyle categories such as homemakers, sports enthusiasts, and fashion-conscious consumers. Marketers develop these inventories by formulating a large number of questions regarding consumer activities, interests, and opinions and then selecting a smaller number of questions that best define consumer segments. As an example, Wells and Tigert formulated 300 AIO statements and asked respondents to agree or disagree with each one on a six-point scale.[66] Typical statements were "I like to be considered a leader" and "I usually keep my home very neat and clean."

Wells and Tigert then reduced these 300 items to 22 lifestyle dimensions (see Table 11.1.) by **factor analysis,** a method for grouping items that are highly correlated. The factor analysis showed, for example, that consumers who agreed with the statement "I shop a lot for specials" also tended to agree with the statements "I find myself checking prices," "I watch advertisements for sales,"

▶**TABLE 11.1**
Sample lifestyle categories based on perceived activities, interests, and opinions

Price-Conscious
I shop a lot for specials.
I find myself checking the prices in the grocery store even for small items.
I watch the advertisements for announcements of sales.
A person can save a lot of money by shopping for bargains.

Fashion-Conscious
I usually have one or more outfits of the very latest style.
When I must choose between the two I usually dress for fashion, not comfort.
An important part of my life and activities is dressing smartly.
I often try the latest hairdo styles when they change.

Homebody
I prefer a quiet evening at home over a party.
I like parties with lots of music and talk. (Reverse scored)
I would rather go to a sporting event than a dance.
I am a homebody.

Community-Minded
I am an active member of more than one service organization.
I do volunteer work for a hospital or service organization on a fairly regular basis.
I like to work on community projects.
I have personally worked in a political campaign or for a candidate or an issue.

Child-Oriented
When my children are ill in bed,

I drop most everything else to see to their comfort.
My children are the most important things in my life.
I try to arrange my home for my children's convenience.
I take a lot of time and effort to teach my children good habits.

Compulsive Housekeeper
I don't like to see children's toys lying about.
I usually keep my house very neat and clean.
I am uncomfortable when my house is not completely clean.
Our days seem to follow a definite routine such as eating meals at a regular time, etc.

Self-Confident
I think I have more self-confidence than most people.
I am more independent than most people.
I have a lot of personal ability.
I like to be considered a leader.

Self-Designated Opinion Leader
My friends or neighbors often come to me for advice.
I sometimes influence what my friends buy.
People come to me more often than I go to them for information about brands.

Information Seeker
I often seek the advice of friends on which brand to buy.
I spend a lot of time asking friends about products and brands.

Dislikes Housekeeping
I must admit I really don't like household chores.
I find cleaning my house an unpleasant task.
I enjoy most forms of housework. (Reverse scored)
My idea of housekeeping is "once over lightly."

Sewer
I like to sew and frequently do.
I often make my own or my children's clothes.
You can save a lot of money by making your own clothes.
I would like to know how to sew like an expert.

Canned Food User
I depend on canned food for at least one meal a day.
I couldn't get along without canned foods.
Things just don't taste right if they come out of a can. (Reverse scored)

Dieter
I drink low-calorie soft drinks several times a week.
I buy more low-calorie foods than the average housewife.
I have used Metrecal or other diet foods at least one meal a day.

Financial Optimist
I will probably have more money to spend next year than I have now.
Five years from now, the family income will probably be a lot higher than it is now.

SOURCE: Adapted from William D. Wells and Douglas J. Tigert, "Activities, Interests and Opinions," JOURNAL OF ADVERTISING RESEARCH, 11 (August, 1971), p. 35. Reprinted from the JOURNAL OF ADVERTISING RESEARCH © 1971, by the Advertising Research Foundation.

and "A person can save a lot by shopping for bargains." People who agreed with these statements were called price-conscious consumers. By using responses to the 300 statements, Wells and Tigert could describe certain consumers as price-conscious, fashion-conscious, child-oriented, and so on.

Wells and Tigert then used these 22 lifestyle dimensions in the same manner as demographics to describe and segment consumers. For instance, users of eye makeup tended to agree with the items defining fashion consciousness, whereas nonusers did not. The heavy user of shortening liked housekeeping, was more child-oriented, and was more of a homebody than was the nonuser.

We must recognize that lifestyles are constantly changing. The financial optimist and the compulsive housekeeper segments in Table 11.1 are smaller today than at the time of Wells' and Tigert's study, and the price-conscious segment is larger. Furthermore, new lifestyle trends develop. For example, any AIO inventory developed today would probably identify a health-conscious segment and an environmentally aware segment.

Value and Lifestyle Survey (VALS)

Another approach to measuring lifestyles is to conduct consumer surveys to identify consumer activities, interests, and opinions, and then to develop lifestyle categories on this basis. The Value and Lifestyle survey (VALS), which the Stanford Research Institute (SRI) developed in 1978, reflects this approach.[67] VALS conducts yearly surveys of 2,500 consumers and has identified groups such as actualizers, strivers, and strugglers based on common lifestyles and values. For example, actualizers have a high level of self-esteem, are open to change, and buy the finer things in life. They would be good targets for laptop computers, adult education courses, or the latest in sound systems. They could best be targeted through upscale magazines rather than television. Such lifestyle profiles help marketers target products to specific consumer groups. That helps explain why the VALS system is the most widely used method of assessing cultural and lifestyle values. Over 150 companies subscribe to its findings on a yearly basis.

VALS 1.   There are really two VALS programs, identified as VALS 1 and VALS 2. The earlier program, VALS 1, identified three broad consumer segments based on cultural values: (1) outer directed, (2) inner directed, and (3) need driven. Outer-directed consumers are those who buy "with an eye to appearances and to what other people think." This segment, which buys in accordance with established and traditional norms, is by far the largest, constituting 68 percent of American consumers.[68] Consumers in the inner-directed segment buy to meet their own inner wants rather than respond to the cultural norms of others. These are the consumers who strive for greater self-expression and represent 21 percent of American consumers.

The need-driven segment is the group whose discretionary income is severely restricted. Its purchases are motivated by need rather than by choice. Its members are the "least psychologically free Americans and they are farthest removed from the cultural mainstream."[69] According to VALS 1, they represent 11 percent of American consumers.

VALS 2. In 1988, SRI introduced a new measure of values called VALS 2.[70] Revising the questions it used to measure cultural and lifestyle values, SRI defined different value segments of the population on this basis. The segments in VALS 1 were found to be too general. For example, two out of three Americans were identified as outer-directed consumers, a category that was too gross, despite the fact that VALS 1 did split outer-directed consumers into additional groups. In addition, the definitions in VALS 1 tended to be driven by a focus on baby boomers and ignored older and younger consumers.

The VALS 2 system identifies eight groups, as shown in Figure 11.1. The groups are split on two dimensions. The vertical dimension represents consumers' resources—not only money, but also education, self-confidence, and energy level. Actualizers have the most resources; strugglers, the least. The horizontal

▶**FIGURE 11.1**

The VALS 2 consumer segments

Source: SRI International, Menlo Park, CA, as shown in Martha Farnsworth Riche, "Psychographics for the 1990s," *American Demographics* (July, 1989), p. 26. Reprinted with permission. © American Demographics, July 1989. For subscription information, please call (800) 828-1133.

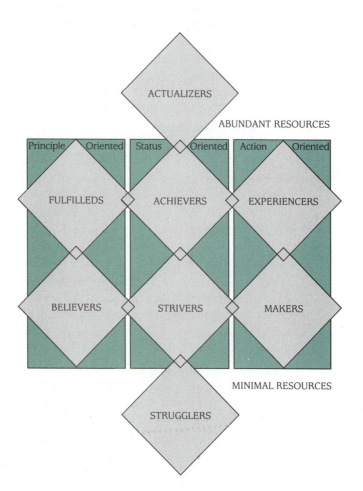

resources—not only money, but also education, self-confidence, and energy level. Actualizers have the most resources; strugglers, the least. The horizontal dimension represents three different ways consumers see the world. Principle-oriented consumers are guided by their views of how the world is or should be; status-oriented consumers, by the opinions of others; action-oriented consumers, by a desire for activity, variety, and risk taking. Each of these three orientations has two groups, one with abundant and one with minimal resources. The groups in VALS 2 are more fully defined in Table 11.2.

The classification of these groups is based on a theory of value development that subscribes to Maslow's hierarchy of needs. According to this theory, once consumers' basic needs are met (that is, they are not in the "struggler"

▶**TABLE 11.2**
Definition of value-based groups in VALS 2

- *Actualizers* have the highest income and self-esteem. They have a wide range of interests and are open to change. Their purchases are directed to the finer things in life.

- *Fulfilleds* are the wealthier of principle-oriented customers. They are mature, responsible, well-educated professionals. They are centered on the home but are open to new ideas and social change. They value education and travel and are likely to be health-conscious.

- *Believers* are the less wealthy of the principle-oriented group. They are more traditionally oriented than the fulfilleds. Their lives are centered on family, church, community, and nation. They respect rules and trust authority figures.

- *Achievers* are the more wealthy of the two status-oriented segments. They are work-oriented and get their satisfaction from their jobs and families. They like to buy products to show off their success to their peers.

- *Strivers,* the other status-oriented segment, have values similar to achievers, but they have fewer resources and lead a more isolated existence. Style is important to strivers in purchasing, as they try to emulate achievers.

- *Experiencers* are the youngest of the segments. They have a lot of energy, and they pour it into physical exercise and social activity. They spend heavily and tend to buy new products. They strive for wealth and power.

- *Makers* are more practical because of limited resources. They are focused on family, work, and physical recreation, with little interest in the broader world.

- *Strugglers* are the oldest segment with the lowest income. They have too few resources to be located in any of the three self-orientation categories. They have limited interests, and their primary concerns are safety and security. They tend to be brand-loyal.

SOURCE: Adapted from Martha Farnsworth Riche, "Psychographics for the 1990s," AMERICAN DEMOGRAPHICS (July, 1989), p. 30. Reprinted with permission. © American Demographics, July 1989. For subscription information, please call (800) 828-1113.

status-oriented consumers in the middle column in Figure 11.1) or by emphasizing individual achievement (the action- and principle-oriented consumers in Figure 11.1).[71] At the top of the hierarchy are the self-actualizers, those who have reached the highest level of attainment. These categories subscribe to Maslow's hierarchy. (See Chapter 3.)

Applications of Lifestyle Characteristics to Marketing Strategies

The most direct applications of lifestyles to marketing strategies have been through the use of the VALS groups shown in Figure 11.1. Marketers have used VALS to develop market segmentation, media, and advertising strategies.

Market Segmentation

A good example of the application of lifestyles is Timex's use of VALS 2 data to identify segments for a new line of products, a package of three digital instruments for home use (a weight scale, a thermometer, and a blood pressure monitor) under the name Healthcheck.[72] The company believed that consumer attitudes toward health maintenance and home diagnostic products were likely to be value-based and that demographic segmentation would be insufficient. Timex subscribed to VALS and ranked the VALS groups by the degree to which they used high-tech and health-related products. Two target segments were identified for Healthcheck: achievers and fulfilleds. Despite the fact that one group was status-oriented and the other was principle-oriented, both segments showed a concern with health and were better educated than other groups. This identification of the primary target segments drove all subsequent marketing strategy for the Healthcheck line.

Media Selection

Timex also used the VALS typology in media selection for Healthcheck. The data showed that achievers and fulfilleds do not watch much TV; therefore, Timex used print advertising. When these groups do watch TV, it is generally news programs. Timex scheduled its introductory campaign during early and late news programs, with no prime-time or daytime TV advertising.[73]

Advertising

The basic theme Timex used to promote Healthcheck was "Technology—where it does the most good." Models in the ads gave off "the self-satisfied vibes achievers can relate to."[74] Clothing had to appear natural looking and be in muted tones to appeal to the fulfilleds, but "statusy enough" to appeal to achievers. Models also were featured outside, often riding bicycles, playing tennis, or doing a similar activity. Both the ads and the package provided information to appeal to the factual needs of the two target groups. As a result of these strategies, the Healthcheck line moved to the top spot in its market within four months of its introduction.

Iron City Beer also used VALS 2 data to develop its advertising strategy. In the early 1990s, Iron City was well-known in Pittsburgh but was losing sales. The core drinkers—makers and believers—were aging and drinking less, while younger drinkers were not identifying with the brand. So the ad agency, Della Femina, used VALS data to show that the experiencers were the highest-volume beer drinkers, followed by strivers. Using a technique called picture sorting, the agency gave focus groups filled with experiencers and strivers decks of playing cards that depicted different types of people. The agency then asked the group to pick those most like themselves. The focus group subjects wound up portraying themselves as hard-working but fun-loving, and—much like Pittsburgh itself—gaining economic strength while rejecting a heavy industry image.

Using this data, Della Femina crafted ads mixing images of the Old Pittsburgh with ones of a new, vibrant city and depictions of young experiencers and strivers working hard and having fun. The soundtrack used the song "Working in a Coal Mine," but changed the words to "working on a cold iron." Partly as a result of this campaign, sales of Iron City increased by 26 percent.[75]

SUMMARY

Two consumer characteristics of importance to marketers are personality and lifestyle. Personality characteristics, which are enduring and deep-seated, reflect consistent patterns of response developed since childhood. Lifestyle is represented by consumers' activities, interests, and opinions. Personality and lifestyle characteristics make up a richer set of descriptors than do demographics because they represent the psychological makeup of consumers.

Marketers can use personality characteristics to describe consumer segments, guide advertising, select media, and develop new products. Personality variables, however, are more difficult to use in marketing because they are not as closely related to brand usage as are lifestyles and demographics. Because marketers continually use personality variables, several personality theories were reviewed:

- Psychoanalytic theory stresses the unconscious nature of consumer motives as determined in childhood by the conflicting demands of the id and the superego. Marketers have applied psychoanalytic theory by using depth and focus group interviews and projective techniques to uncover deep-seated purchasing motives. These applications are known as motivational research.
- Social theory emphasizes environmental variables in personality development. It goes beyond psychoanalytic theory in examining conscious, goal-directed behavior and considering individuals who function normally in a social environment.
- Self-concept theory suggests that individuals have an actual self-image based on who they think they are and an ideal self-image based on

who they would like to be. Marketers have applied this theory in the belief that there may be a congruence between consumers' self-image and their image of the brand. An extension of this theory realizes that the symbolic properties of groups of products and brands can influence people's self-image based on the assumption that we are what we use.

- Trait theory seeks to measure personality traits by the development of personality inventories. Trait theory is the most widely applied of the personality theories in marketing because specific personality variables can be measured and related to consumer usage.

The following important changes in lifestyles occurred in American society in the 1980s and are likely to continue through the 1990s:

- Change in male/female purchasing roles.
- Leveling off of concerns over health and fitness.
- Greater self-awareness.
- More professionals working at home.
- Return to traditionalism and a more frugal lifestyle.
- Greater emphasis on convenience.

Marketers have used lifestyle characteristics in studies by developing inventories to measure consumers' activities, interests, and opinions. Another approach is to conduct consumer surveys to determine lifestyles. The most widely used consumer lifestyle survey—the Value and Lifestyle survey (VALS)—identifies eight lifestyle segments based on their values and economic resources.

Marketers widely use VALS to identify market segments, develop advertising strategies, and provide guidelines for media selection.

In the next chapter, we describe the use of demographic, personality, and lifestyle variables in segmenting markets and positioning products.

QUESTIONS

1. Because it deals with deep-seated needs and motives derived from childhood conflicts, psychoanalytic theory has been criticized for having little relevance to marketing.
   - Do you agree?
   - For what types of product categories might psychoanalytic theory provide insights into consumer purchasing motives?
2. How have marketers used depth interviews and projective techniques to understand consumer behavior better? Provide specific examples of marketing applications.
3. A working woman sees herself as efficient, competitive, and achievement-oriented. Ideally, she would like to combine these traits with greater warmth and understanding. How would her behavior differ if she governed her purchases based on her actual self-image versus her ideal self-image?

Under what circumstances might she be more likely to buy based on her ideal self rather than on her actual self?

4. What are the marketing implications of a merger of male and female purchasing roles?

5. A producer of men's toiletries decides to introduce a new line by promoting a strong male image, one that portrays a dominant man who easily attracts women. What might be the problem with such a positioning? Does it conform to recent trends in male-female roles?

6. An ad for a leading detergent manufacturer depicts a woman using the product and being praised by her husband for getting his clothes clean.
   - What are the potential problems with this positioning?
   - What alternative positionings might you suggest to reflect the changing role of women in today's society?

7. An executive for a food company has said, "There has been some talk around here about repositioning some of our existing products to promote health and nutritional benefits. I see companies promoting beans as having fiber and tuna packed in spring water. I am against such repositionings because consumers are just going to see them as a ploy to get on the nutritional bandwagon. It is much better to introduce new products for health and nutritional benefits than to reposition existing products."
   - Do you agree with the executive's position? Why or why not?

8. Liquor, coffee, and cigarette companies initially viewed the trend to health and nutrition as a threat. How have some of these companies turned this threat into an opportunity?

9. What evidence is there that concerns about health and fitness are leveling off in the 1990s?

10. What are the marketing implications of a more frugal lifestyle?

11. Define "grazing" and "refueling." How are these trends reflected in consumers' behavior? What are the marketing implications of each trend?

12. What are the marketing implications in using any of the lifestyle groups cited in Table 11.1 for describing users (or prospective users) of:
    - A new detergent that advertises that it makes washing easier?
    - Personal care appliances such as curling irons or facial care appliances?
    - A new magazine designed to provide up-to-date marketing and financial information to the working woman?
    - A new breakfast cereal for the diet-conscious and active adult?

13. What is the relation of Maslow's hierarchy of needs to the development of the VALS system illustrated in Figure 11.1?

14. Based on Figure 11.1 and Table 11.2, which VALS group or groups might be the best targets in marketing the following?
    - Ecologically oriented products.
    - Weight-lifting equipment.
    - A new family-oriented magazine.

RESEARCH ASSIGNMENTS

1. Self-concept theory suggests that the disparity between a consumer's actual and ideal self-images could predict the purchase of brands or products related to the consumer's identity.

   - Select 10 or 15 adjectives like those on page 381. Submit these items to a sample of consumers and ask respondents to rate themselves on both actual and ideal selves. Ask the same respondents to identify brands they regularly purchase for products such as perfume, clothing, magazines, automobiles, or any other items that may be related to self-image.
   - Determine the disparity between actual and ideal self-images by summing across the differences for each item in the scale. Are these differences related to brand or product ownership?

2. Select a sample of consumers in the youth market (primarily teenagers and college students) and consumers in the baby boom generation (ages 26–44). Ask consumers in each group to rate the importance to them of a wide variety of products (life insurance, automobiles, jeans, banking services, do-it-yourself products, phosphate-free detergents, cameras, deodorants, cereal, and so on). Ask respondents for their (a) demographic characteristics, (b) view of their economic future, (c) political preferences, and (d) level of price consciousness. (See Table 11.1.)

   - What are the similarities and differences between the two age groups on the variables you measured? Explain these similarities and differences.
   - Can you identify a more and a less price-conscious group in each age segment? Are these differences related to demographics? To economic outlook?

3. Using lifestyle criteria, you would like to distinguish users of natural food products (granola, wheat germ, yogurt, and so on) from nonusers. You plan to use lifestyles to position a new line of natural food products and to develop guidelines for advertising.

   - Conduct a number of depth interviews with users of natural foods. On this basis, develop a lifestyle inventory designed to identify natural food users.
   - Submit the inventory to a sample equally divided between users and nonusers of natural foods. Does the lifestyle inventory discriminate between the two groups? If so, what are the distinctive lifestyle characteristics of natural food users?
   - What are the implications of these lifestyle characteristics for (a) advertising and (b) new product development?

NOTES

1. "How a Heart Attack Changed a Company," *The New York Times* (February 26, 1993), pp. C1, C6.

2. *Marketing & Media Decisions* (March, 1990), p. 36; and "One from the Heart," *Marketing & Media Decisions* (March, 1990), p. 34.

3. *The New York Times* (February 26, 1993), *op. cit.*, p. C6.

4. Sidney J. Levy, "Interpreting Consumer Mythology: A Structural Approach to Consumer Behavior," *Journal of Marketing,* 45 (Summer, 1981), pp. 49–61.

5. Rena Bartos, "Ernest Dichter: Motive Interpreter," *Journal of Advertising Research,* 26 (February-March, 1986), p. 20.

6. *Ibid.*; and "Work Motivates Psychoanalysis," *Advertising Age* (November 1, 1984), p. 45.

7. Dennis W. Rook, "The Ritual Dimension of Consumer Behavior," *Journal of Consumer Research,* 12 (December, 1985), pp. 251–264.

8. Mason Haire, "Projective Techniques in Marketing Research," *Journal of Marketing,* 14 (April, 1950), pp. 649–656.

9. William D. Wells and Arthur D. Beard, "Personality Theories," in Scott Ward and Thomas S. Robertson, eds., *Consumer Behavior: Theoretical Sources* (Englewood Cliffs, NJ: Prentice-Hall, 1973), pp. 142–199.

10. Joel B. Cohen, "An Interpersonal Orientation to the Study of Consumer Behavior," *Journal of Marketing Research,* 4 (August, 1967), pp. 270–278.

11. Ira J. Dolich, "Congruence Relationships Between Self-Images and Product Brands," *Journal of Marketing Research,* 6 (February, 1969), pp. 80–85.

12. For example, Al E. Birdwell, "Influence of Image Congruence on Consumer Choice," in *Proceedings, Winter Conference, 1964* (Chicago: American Marketing Association, 1965), pp. 290–303; and Edward L. Grubb and Gregg Hupp, "Perception of Self-Generalized Stereotypes and Brand Selection," *Journal of Marketing Research,* 5 (February, 1968), pp. 58–63.

13. Robert E. Burnkrant and Thomas J. Page, Jr., "On the Management of Self-Images in Social Situations: The Role of Public Self-Consciousness," in Andrew Mitchell, ed., *Advances in Consumer Research,* Vol. 9 (Ann Arbor, MI: Association for Consumer Research, 1982), pp. 452–455.

14. Irving S. White, "The Perception of Value in Products," in Joseph W. Newman, ed., *On Knowing the Consumer* (New York: John Wiley, 1967), pp. 90–106.

15. Marsha L. Richins, "Social Comparison and the Idealized Images of Advertising," *Journal of Consumer Research,* 18 (June, 1991), pp. 71–83.

16. See "Compulsive Buying: A Phenomenological Exploration," *Journal of Consumer Research,* 16 (September, 1989), pp. 147–157; and Alice Hanley and Mari S. Wilhelm, "Compulsive Buying: An Exploration into Self-Esteem and Money Attitudes," *Journal of Economic Psychology,* 13 (1992), pp. 5–18.

17. Michael R. Solomon, "The Role of Products as Social Stimuli: A Symbolic Interactionism Perspective," *Journal of Consumer Research,* 10 (December, 1983), pp. 319–329.

18. Russell W. Belk, "Possessions and the Extended Self," *Journal of Consumer Research,* 15 (September, 1988), pp. 139–168.

19. Michael R. Solomon and Henry Assael, "The Forest or the Trees? A Gestalt Approach to Symbolic Communication," in Jean Umiker-Sebeok and Sidney J. Levy, eds., *Marketing and Semiotics: New Directions in the Study of Signs for Sale* (Bloomington: Indiana University Press, 1988).

20. Allen L. Edwards, *Edwards Personal Preference Schedule Manual* (New York: Psychological Corp., 1957).

21. Arthur Koponen, "Personality Characteristics of Purchasers," *Journal of Advertising Research,* 1 (September, 1960), pp. 6–12.

22. Ralph Westfall, "Psychological Factors in Predicting Product Choice," *Journal of Marketing,* 26 (April, 1962), pp. 34–40.

23. Morris J. Gottlieb, "Segmentation by Personality Types," in Lynn H. Stockman, ed., *Advancing Marketing Efficiency, Proceedings of the 1959 Conference* (Chicago: American Marketing Association, 1960), pp. 148–158.

24. Harold H. Kassarjian, "Personality and Consumer Behavior: A Review," *Journal of Marketing Research,* 8 (November, 1971), pp. 409–419.

25. Joseph T. Plummer, "The Concept and Application of Life Style Segmentation," *Journal of Marketing,* 38 (January, 1974), pp. 33–37.

26. "Does Snapple Have the Juice to Go National?" *Business Week* (January 18, 1993), p. 52.

27. "The Brave New World of Men," *American Demographics* (January, 1992), p. 40.

28. "Man: Forever the Forager," *Madison Avenue* (February, 1986), pp. 88–90.

29. "For Many Fathers, Roles Are Shifting," *The New York Times* (June 20, 1993).

30. "Real Men Buy Paper Towels, Too," *Business Week* (November, 1992), p. 75.

31. *Ibid.*

32. "Do Real Men Shop?" *American Demographics* (May, 1987), p. 13.

33. "In Ads, Men's Image Becomes Softer," *The New York Times* (March 26, 1990), p. D12.

34. "Working Women Now More Attractive—Y&R," *Advertising Age* (January 11, 1982), p. 76.

35. "Working Women Task Advertisers," *Advertising Forum* (July, 1982), p. 35.

36. *Advertising Age* (July 26, 1982), p. M13.

37. *Advertising Age* (April 2, 1984), p. M10.

38. "The Message, Clever As It May Be, Is Lost in a Number of High-Profile Campaigns," *The Wall Street Journal* (July 27, 1993), p. B1.

39. "Shoppers Say 'Yes' to Less," *Progressive Grocer* (May, 1984), p. 192; and "What Americans Eat Hasn't Changed Much Despite Healthy Image," *The Wall Street Journal* (September 12, 1985), p. 1.

40. "Wary Consumers Want More Health Ad Info," *Advertising Age* (December 4, 1989), p. 12.

41. *Fortune* (May 26, 1986), p. 62.

42. "Food Companies Offer Healthful Fare to Kids Toting Lunch Boxes," *Adweek's Marketing Week* (September 5, 1988), pp. 32–34.

43. "Big Beer Makers Go After the Sober Set with Assortment of Nonalcoholic Brews," *The Wall Street Journal* (March 30, 1992), p. B1.

44. "So Far, So Good for Seagram's Beverage Shot," *Adweek's Marketing Week* (June 25, 1990), p. 54; and "Seagram Taking 'Light Whiskey' to All of U.S.," *The Wall Street Journal* (April 23, 1990), p. B1.

45. "Tempted by Taste, and Tiring of Tofu, Shoppers Are Bringing Home the Bacon," *The Wall Street Journal* (March 18, 1993), p. B1.

46. "Gimme a Double Shake and a Lard on White," *Business Week* (March 1, 1993), p. 59.

47. *Ibid.*

48. *American Demographics* (January, 1993), p. 56.

49. *Adweek's Marketing Week* (June 25, 1990), *loc. cit.*; and *The Wall Street Journal* (April 23, 1990), *loc. cit.*

50. "How Reebok Fits Shoes," *American Demographics* (March, 1993), p. 54.

51. "Everything in Moderation," *Adweek* (August 17, 1992), p. 35.

52. "Physical Fitness: It's All in the Balance," *Adweek* (August 17, 1992), pp. 36–37.

53. "Americans Devote More of Their Shrinking Leisure Time to Arts," *Ad Forum* (February, 1985), p. 10.

54. "Tomorrow's New Rich: Postwar Babies Are Grown Up," *Sales & Marketing Management* (October 6, 1981), p. 29.

55. *American Demographics* (January, 1993), *loc. cit.*

56. "Newest Corporate Refugees: Self-Employed but Low-Paid," *The New York Times* (November 15, 1993), pp. A1, D-2; and "Do Homework Before Taking the Plunge," *New York Newsday* (November 21, 1993), p. 76.

57. "The QRCA Trends Project: How Qualitative Researchers See the Consumer of the 1990s," *Marketing Review.*

58. *Ibid.*, p. 10.

59. "Marketers of Luxury Goods Are Turning from Self-Indulgence to Family Values," *The Wall Street Journal* (October 22, 1992), p. B1.

60. "Little Wishes Form the Big Dream," *The Wall Street Journal* (September 19, 1989), p. B1.

61. "Nestlé Gives Carnation Breakfast Line a Makeover," *Adweek* (September 20, 1993), p. 13.

62. "Now, Food for the Otherwise Engaged," *The New York Times* (April 15, 1987).

63. *The Wall Street Journal* (September 19, 1989), *loc. cit.*

64. "Many Food Companies Find the Prospects for Microwave Product Aren't That Hot," *The Wall Street Journal* (February 2, 1993), p. B1.

65. *Ibid.*

66. William D. Wells and Douglas J. Tigert, "Activities, Interests and Opinions," *Journal of Advertising Research,* 11 (August, 1971), pp. 27–35.

67. See Arnold Mitchell, *Changing Values and Lifestyles* (Menlo Park, CA: SRI International, 1981).

68. *Ibid.*, pp. 2-3; and personal communication from SRI International, July 30, 1986.

69. Mitchell, *Changing Values . . . , op. cit.,* p. 2.

70. Martha Farnsworth Riche, "Psychographics for the 1990s," *American Demographics* (July, 1989), pp. 24–32, 53–54.

71. See Arnold Mitchell, *The Nine American Lifestyles* (New York: Warner Books, 1983).

72. "Timex and VALS Engineer a Psychographic Product Launch," *Ad Forum* (September, 1984), p. 12.

73. *Ibid.*

74. *Ibid.,* p. 14.

75. "VALS the Second Time," *American Demographics* (July, 1991), p. 6.

12

Market Segmentation and Product Positioning

GOODYEAR TIRE SEGMENTS CONSUMERS GLOBALLY

As the American market has become more fragmented by demographics and lifestyles, marketers find it increasingly important to target specific groups. This means that most firms can better maximize profits by developing products to meet the needs of specific segments rather than by introducing a single product to a mass market.

A strategy of **market segmentation** requires identifying customers with similar needs or characteristics and targeting these segments with product offerings. The basis for such segmentation strategies has been described in this section of the text; namely, grouping consumers by similarities in what they want (benefits and attitudes) and who they are (demographics, lifestyle, and personality characteristics).

In addition to segmenting markets, marketers must position their products to meet the needs of these segments. Therefore, the identification of the needs and characteristics of target groups is a prerequisite to product positioning. In addition, the success of positioning strategies depends on how the target segments react to the marketing strategies directed to them. Because of this link between market segmentation and product positioning, these topics are treated together in this chapter.

The importance of market segmentation and product positioning was demonstrated in Chapter 1 when we described Levi Strauss & Co.'s shift from a mass-market approach to a strategy of segmenting markets by demographics. In so doing, the company positioned specific product lines to targeted demographic groups—Action Slacks to the mature segment, the Dockers line to baby boomers, and 501 buttonfly jeans to teens. We also saw the importance of market segmentation when Kellogg's revived the sagging cereal market by introducing adult cereals to diet, fitness, and nutritional segments.

Goodyear Tire implements segmentation strategies on a global basis because of differences in what consumers emphasize in tires in different parts of the world. It identifies four global segments of the tire market: quality buyers, trusting patrons, value-oriented shoppers, and bargain hunters.[1] *Quality buyers* emphasize the brand. They are upscale, brand loyal, and buy well-known brands. Consumers in Belgium and Italy are more likely to be in this segment because they are more brand loyal. *Trusting patrons* are loyal to a particular retail outlet and regard the brand of tire as unimportant. Customers in this group are downscale and are likely to live in less-developed countries. *Value-oriented shoppers* consider the brand first and price second. This group tends to buy major brands, compares brands closely, and is more involved in the purchase. A high proportion are in France and Greece. The fourth segment, *bargain hunters*, rely exclusively on price and are least involved in the purchase. They tend to be younger, are the least brand loyal, and regard buying tires as a necessary nuisance. The greatest proportion are in the United States.

Goodyear varies its positioning strategy in each country, depending on which segment is predominant. For quality buyers, the company emphasizes the latest in technology with distribution through specialty stores. Ads targeted to trusting patrons emphasize the store. Brand image advertising is used to convey quality to value buyers, with occasional price promotions. Positioning to bargain hunters is based strictly on economy, with frequent price promotions and distribution through discount stores.[2]

In this chapter, we first consider approaches to identifying market segments and the alternative strategies used to segment markets. We then consider how marketers evaluate product positioning alternatives and develop positioning strategies.

IDENTIFYING MARKET SEGMENTS

Before targeting market segments for marketing effort, marketers must first identify these segments. Once marketers determine the needs, brand attitudes, and demographic and lifestyle characteristics of a target segment, they can then develop products and marketing strategies to appeal to it.

Table 12.1 lists three bases for identifying market segments: by benefits, behavior, and consumer response elasticity. A marketer who wishes to identify opportunities for new product introductions should first identify the benefits (needs) consumers seek and then segment consumers by differences in benefits. For example, the adult cereal market could be segmented into consumers who are oriented toward nutrition, taste, and diet concerns. The company could then develop new products to meet these needs (for example, cereal with all-natural ingredients targeted to the nutrition segment). This type of segmentation is called **benefit segmentation**.

Assume a new all-natural cereal has been introduced. Who are the purchasers of the product? What are their demographic and lifestyle characteristics? What is their attitude toward the new brand? In this case, the basic distinction is a behavioral one; that is, marketers are trying to identify the characteristics of users and nonusers to determine if they are reaching their target. This segmentation approach, called **behavioral segmentation**, assists management in developing marketing strategies based on differences between user groups.

A third type of segmentation is **response elasticity.** Marketers may wish to identify consumers by their responsiveness to marketing strategy. For example,

▶**TABLE 12.1**
Three bases for market segmentation analysis

Basis for Segmentation	Strategic Objective	Criteria
Benefits (needs)	Develop new products and position existing products	• Nutrition • Health • Economy • Good taste • Performance • Prestige Etc.
Behavior	Develop marketing strategies	• Brand usage • Product category usage • Level of use (heavy or light) • Shopping behavior
Response elasticity	Target the marketing effort	• Price elasticity • Deal elasticity • Advertising elasticity

they may wish to determine which consumers are most likely to switch brands when price changes (the price-elastic segment) and which tend to be loyal to a brand without much regard for price (the price-inelastic segment). Marketers may also want to know which consumers tend to buy most frequently using price deals or coupons (the deal-prone segment) or which consumers are most likely to be influenced by such things as advertising or sales promotion (the advertising-elastic segment).

This information is essential for targeting the marketing effort. The characteristics of the price-elastic segment define those customers most likely to switch out of a marketer's brand if the price increases. The characteristics of the deal- or coupon-prone consumer provide guidelines for directing price promotions to certain segments. Marketers could send coupons by direct mail to households that best match the demographic profile of the heavy coupon redeemer. Knowledge of the characteristics of segments most responsive to advertising permits marketers to direct advertising dollars to these groups.

After segmenting a market by one of these three criteria, the marketers' next step is to determine the demographic and lifestyle characteristics of the segment. As we saw in Chapter 10, this step allows marketers to select media to reach the target segment. When Kellogg's found that the segment of adults who wanted nutritional cereal were primarily upscale baby boomers, the company could then select the TV shows and print media most likely to reach this group. Lifestyle characteristics provide a basis for the advertising setting. If many of the upscale baby boomers are also outdoor types, then a logical setting for nutritional cereals would be outdoor settings.

Benefit Segmentation

A consumer-oriented approach to marketing requires developing product strategies based on known consumer needs. Marketers use benefit (need) criteria to determine the potential for new products. A beverage company might identify a common need among many women over the age of 50 for calcium-enriched products to strengthen bones. Since they have a common need, women within this group would be a benefit segment. The company might consider introducing a calcium-fortified fruit drink to appeal to this group based on the similarity of their needs.

A snack food company (Great Snacks) used benefit segmentation to identify opportunities in the snack food market. Great Snacks conducted a study to define segments by similarity in needs for snack foods. Table 12.2 identifies six benefit segments based on the study. (See items in the second row.) Thus, nutritional snackers represent a benefit segment because consumers in this group want a snack that is nutritious, has no artificial ingredients, and is natural. The table is based on a study conducted by the company of 1,500 snack food users to investigate new product opportunities in the nut and chip-type snack category.

Great Snacks was already doing well among the party and indiscriminate snacker segments with its existing chip snack line and among economical

TABLE 12.2
Benefit segmentation of the snack food market

	Nutritional Snackers	Weight Watchers	Guilty Snackers	Party Snackers	Indiscriminate Snackers	Economical Snackers
Percentage of snackers	22	14	9	15	15	18
Benefits sought	Nutritious No artifical ingredients Natural snack	Low-calorie Quick-energy	Low-calorie Good-tasting	Good to serve guests Proud to serve Goes well with beverage	Good-tasting Satisfies hunger	Low price Best value
Demographics	Better educated Have younger children	Younger Single	Younger or older Females Lower socio-economic group	Middle-aged Nonurban	Teens	Larger families Better educated
Lifestyle and personality characteristics	Self-assured Controlled	Outdoor types Influential Venturesome	High anxiety Isolate	Sociable	Hedonistic	Self-assured Price-oriented
Consumption level of snacks	Light	Light	Heavy	Average	Heavy	Average
Types of snacks usually eaten	Fruits Vegetables Cheese	Yogurt Vegetables	Yogurt Cookies Crackers Candy	Nuts Potato chips Crackers Pretzels	Candy Ice cream Cookies Potato chips Pretzels Popcorn	No specific products

snackers due to its frequent coupon promotions. It now wanted to try to capture nutritional snackers and weight watchers. Table 12.2 shows the consumption, demographic, lifestyle, and personality characteristics of these two segments. They snack primarily on natural products (fruits and vegetables), are younger and upscale, and are self-assured and influential.

The company then formulated its marketing strategy on the basis of this profile. It developed a natural ingredients snack composed of chips, nuts, and dried fruit positioned primarily to nutritional snackers. The advertising strategy featured young, upwardly mobile consumers on the go having a nutritional snack between meals. Demographics helped the company select magazines for its print advertising and time slots for TV targeted to young, upscale consumers.

Another example of benefit segmentation for a total product line is provided by Coca-Cola. (See Figure 12.1.) When it introduced Tab in 1963 as a diet cola positioned to women, Coca-Cola was one of the first to recognize the importance of diet products. Twenty years later, it used the magic name Coke on a product other than its flagship brand for the first time by introducing Diet Coke positioned to men. In 1983, it also introduced caffeine-free versions of Coca-Cola, Diet Coke, and Tab positioned to a health-oriented segment. Cherry Coke was a further extension of the Coke name to appeal to teenagers who wanted a sweeter cola drink. The company has also positioned Sprite to those who like lemon-lime and introduced Minute Maid soda as a fruit-based drink that was leveraged from Coca-Cola-owned Minute Maid fruit juice.

Coke's most famous move was the introduction of New Coke to replace the original so as to appeal to teenagers who favored Pepsi. After the consumer outcry, Coca-Cola brought back the original brand as Coca-Cola Classic. It reinforced its benefit segmentation strategy by positioning New Coke to those who wanted a sweeter drink and Classic Coke to traditional Coke loyalists who preferred the original formula.

Overall, Figure 12.1 represents a consistent benefit segmentation strategy, particularly since 1983 when Coca-Cola started expanding its product line in earnest. Other examples of benefit segmentation are cited in studies by Calantone and Sawyer;[3] Anderson, Cox, and Fulcher;[4] and Young, Ott, and Feigin.[5]

Behavioral Segmentation

Once a product is in the marketplace, companies must determine who is buying and why. Table 12.1 lists four criteria for defining segments by consumer behavior:

1. Brand usage.
2. Product category usage.
3. Level of product use (heavy vs. light).
4. Shopping behavior.

In each case, marketers must identify the demographics, lifestyles, and brand attitudes of these user groups.

▶**FIGURE 12.1**
Benefit segmentation of Coca-Cola's product line

| | | PRODUCTS | | | |
BENEFIT SEGMENTS	Cola	Diet Cola	Caffeine-Free	Fruit-Based	Lemon-Lime
Taste-Oriented: Like sweet-tasting colas	New Coke Cherry Coke				
Taste-Oriented: Like unsweetened colas	Coca-Cola Classic				
Taste-Oriented: Like fruit juice				Minute Maid	
Taste-Oriented: Like lemon-lime					Sprite
Health/Nutrition-Conscious			Caffeine-Free Tab, Coke, and Diet Coke	Minute Maid	
Weight Watchers		Diet Coke, Tab, and Diet Cherry Coke			

By Brand Usage

The most frequently used form of behavioral segmentation is to distinguish those who purchase the company's brand from those who purchase competitive brands.

Once brand users are defined, marketers can take two approaches. The first directs resources to those segments with the highest probability of purchasing the brand. Yamaha uses this approach in choosing cities for new dealerships.[6] Yamaha assumes that prospective purchasers of its motorcycles will be similar to existing owners. As a result, it identifies the demographic characteristics of Yamaha owners. Using Census Bureau data, it then determines the demographic characteristics of areas where it is considering new dealerships. It locates dealerships in those areas whose demographic profiles most closely match the demographic profile of the Yamaha owner. The basic assumption is that nonowners with similar characteristics to owners are more likely to buy the brand.

The second approach in segmenting by brand usage is to direct new products to segments that are unlikely to buy the existing brand. The segmentation of the snack market in Table 12.2 is a good example. Great Snacks developed a chip, fruit, and nut snack product to appeal to the nutritional segment because this segment was less likely to buy the company's current snack food offerings.

By Product Category Usage

Product category usage is a common basis for behavioral segmentation. Marketers may wish to identify consumers who buy a product category rather than a brand. Purchasers of salt-free snacks, for example, may tend to be older, health-conscious consumers, regardless of what brand of snack food they buy. Their demographic characteristics reflect the need for the product. In such cases, marketers are more likely to use product, rather than brand, purchase as a guide in selecting media or determining advertising appeals.

Segmenting by product usage is particularly useful when companies band together to advertise a product—for example, the California Milk Advisory Board or the Beef Council. In such cases, the cooperative wants to determine the characteristics of nonusers to target them more effectively with advertising and other promotions.

Peters identified usage segments by product category in one study by defining segments of owners of compact, medium-sized, large-sized, and foreign cars.[7] In another study, Hisrich and Peters identified users of a wide range of entertainment services.[8]

By Level of Usage

Marketers commonly segment markets by level of product usage (heavy versus light users). A company then has two options: to position a product to the heavy users, who generate more product volume and revenues, or to position a product to the light users, who may represent an ignored niche in the marketplace.

Nestlé chose to position its iced tea to heavy users. It segmented consumers of tea by their level of usage and identified the benefits heavy and light users associated with iced tea. The company found that the heaviest usage group drank twice as much tea (47.5 glasses per month) as the average consumer (24 glasses per month) and represented over one-third of total iced tea volume. This group saw iced tea as a year-round drink that restores energy. A second segment drank an average amount of tea and saw iced tea as a low-calorie drink. This segment also represented about one-third of iced tea volume.

Nestlé had three strategic options. First, it could have targeted heavy users with a year-round energy theme and ignored the low-calorie segment. Second, it could have tried to capture the low-calorie segment with the same product by advertising year-round energy as a primary theme and low calorie as secondary. The danger would be that a low-calorie theme might alienate the primary target group if its members are not specifically looking for a low-calorie drink. A third choice would be to develop a separate product that might be even lower in calories than the current product and then position it to weight watchers. This strategy assumes differences in demographics and lifestyles between these two groups that help select media and provide guidelines for promotional appeals.

Other studies have used level of product usage as a basis for behavioral segmentation. They include one by Bass, Tigert, and Lonsdale for ten food products and toiletries[9] and Assael's studies of frequent users of long-distance telephoning for the residential[10] and business[11] markets.

By Shopping Behavior

Studies have segmented shoppers by their orientation to shopping. Lesser and Hughes reviewed many of these studies conducted in 17 communities and identified 7 types of shoppers: inactive, active, social, traditional, dedicated fringe, price-oriented, and transitional.[12] The shopping attitudes, demographic and lifestyle characteristics, and criteria used in store selection are shown for each shopper type in Table 12.3. For example, inactive shoppers are older, detached consumers who dislike shopping and emphasize service when selecting stores.

The strategic implications of these profiles are also shown. For example, retailers who want to attract the inactive shopper should provide multiple outlets in convenient locations and a variety of services to minimize shopping effort. Similarly, retailers targeting active shoppers should stress the prestige and status of affordable merchandise to appeal to this segment's achievement orientation and socioeconomic level. Retailers who want to appeal to traditional shoppers should emphasize a friendly store environment to make them feel at home.

One group that Lesser and Hughes left out of their classification are *compulsive shoppers*, a segment that relieves anxieties and feels good about themselves through shopping. One study found that 6 percent of American shoppers are in this segment. Most of these shoppers shop at least once a day, and many run up huge debts with little worry as to where the money is coming from.[13]

Moschis provided another strategic dimension to shopper profiles by relating shopping orientation to purchasing behavior.[14] He defined six types of shoppers who purchase cosmetic products:

TABLE 12.3
A profile of shopper types

Types	Inactive	Active	Social	Traditional	Dedicated Fringe	Price	Transitional
*Percentage of shoppers**	15.0%	12.8%	10.0%	14.1%	8.8%	10.4%	6.9%
Shopping attitudes	Dislike shopping	Enjoy shopping	Impatient/store loyal	Dislike shopping/insecure	Average	Comparison shoppers	No interest
Demographics and lifestyles	Inactive/older/detached	Middle class/outdoor types/achievers	Upscale/self-actualizers/professionals	Outdoor/blue-collar/family-oriented	Loners/discontent/try new products	Home-oriented	Young/try new products/followers
Shopping emphasis	Service	Quality/fashion/price	Convenience/service	Price/service	In-home shopping	Price	Variety
Strategic implications	Offer many locations/expand variety of services	Stress status and affordability	Offer more services at higher prices	Make shopper feel at home/stress bargains	Use catalogs and direct mail	Stress low prices and sales promotions	Use advertising to show variety and immediate gratification

*22.1% of respondents not classified into these seven groups.

SOURCE: Adopted from BUSINESS HORIZONS, 29. Copyright (1986) by the Foundation for the School of Business at Indiana University. Used with permission.

- Special sales.
- Brand loyal.
- Store loyal.
- Problem solvers.
- Socializers (buy cosmetics that friends use).
- Name conscious (judge cosmetics by store that sells them).

Such a profile of shopper types provides retail management with guidelines for determining the information these segments demand and for reaching them. For example, the brand-loyal and name-conscious shopper uses advertising as a source of information about cosmetics, whereas socializers rely on friends or neighbors for information. Problem solvers spend the most time watching TV. The special sales shopper should be given information on price alternatives and can best be reached by home-oriented magazines. The name-conscious shopper can best be reached by fashion magazines and should be told the brand alternatives that various stores carry.

Segmenting by Response Elasticity

The third basis for segmenting markets is by consumer sensitivity, known as response elasticity, to marketers' strategies. Some customers are more sensitive to a price increase, a change in advertising expenditures, or an increase in deal effort than are others. Response elasticity measures consumers' sensitivity to a particular marketing stimulus by associating a percentage change in the stimulus with a percentage change in quantity purchased. Underlying segmentation by response elasticities is the basic principle that marketers should increase or decrease allocations to a segment according to the response of that segment. If all segments responded equally to marketing effort, there would be no basis for differentially allocating resources.

Price Elasticity

Segmenting by response elasticity is commonly based on sensitivity to changes in price, as measured by consumers' price elasticity. **Price elasticity** is measured by the percentage change in quantity purchased compared to a percentage change in price; that is:

$$\text{Price Elasticity} = \frac{\text{Percent Change in Quantity}}{\text{Percent Change in Price}}$$

If the percentage change in quantity is more than the percentage change in price, demand is elastic. In such a case, a decrease in price will produce a more than proportionate increase in quantity, resulting in an increase in the company's revenues. If the percentage change in quantity is less than the percentage change in price, demand is inelastic. In this case, an increase in price will produce a less than proportionate decrease in quantity, resulting in an increase in revenue. Therefore, price decreases in an elastic market and price increases in an inelastic market generally increase a company's revenues.

When consumers are price elastic, they switch brands based on price. When they are inelastic, they tend to remain loyal to a brand. Price is fairly elastic for items consumers ordinarily purchase in supermarkets or drugstores and inelastic for prestige products such as designer clothes or gourmet foods. Demand can be inelastic for everyday products, however. For example, a consumer loyal to Pampers disposable diapers or to Bounty paper towels may continue to buy even if prices increase by 10 or 20 percent.

A distinction exists between **upside price elasticity** (sensitivity to price increases) and **downside price elasticity** (sensitivity to price decreases). The importance of this distinction became apparent when coffee prices increased sharply in the mid-1970s. Coffee consumption decreased because many consumers switched to tea and other beverages. When coffee prices began to decrease, some of these consumers continued to drink other products. Thus, consumption did not increase as much as expected. These consumers demonstrated upside price elasticity and downside inelasticity.

Ideally, a marketer would want things reversed; that is, upside price inelasticity (no substantial change in consumption as prices go up) and downside elasticity (increased purchases as prices go down). Marketers try to encourage upside price inelasticity by advertising products on a prestige basis and downside price elasticity by advertising low prices or price promotions. For example, the Hermes ad in Exhibit 12.1 is an attempt to create upside price inelasticity by advertising watches from $1,075 to $2,975 based on the prestige of the Hermes name. The Timex ad is appealing to downside elasticity by advertising a reliable watch with a well-known name for $50.

Studies of consumer price elasticity have focused on factors that may change such price sensitivity. For example, one study found that the consumer's price elasticity decreases when the consumer is accompanied by a friend;[15] and another study found less price elasticity when the salesperson is viewed as an expert.[16] Consumers are more likely to be price elastic when they are shopping alone and when they are confident of their own appraisal of the product.

Price elasticity is also related to involvement. Consumers who are involved with a product category on an enduring basis are less likely to be price elastic. Consumers' purchases are initiated by the emotional tie to the product rather than by price. Less involved consumers are likely to buy based on a price promotion alone, as found in a study by Inman, McAlister, and Hoyer.[17]

Segmenting by Price Elasticity

An important approach in segmenting markets is to classify consumers by their price elasticity. Marketers can direct deals, coupons, or sales strategies to price-sensitive consumers who have particular demographic or regional characteristics. For example, suppose Nestlé runs a price promotion targeted to consumers over 55 living in nonurban areas. The promotion represents a 10 percent decrease in price and results in a 15 percent increase in purchases among the targeted group. This segment would be identified as price elastic since the percentage decrease in price resulted in a greater percentage increase in

> **EXHIBIT 12.1**
Encouraging upside price inelasticity and downside price elasticity

Encouraging upside price inelasticity

Encouraging downside price elasticity

purchases. Targeting this segment with a price promotion would be profitable for Nestlé.

A good example of segmenting by response elasticity is a study AT&T conducted after an increase in long-distance rates.[18] The company identified consumers who either increased or maintained their rate of calling in the face of a price increase (the price-inelastic segment) and those who decreased their usage (the price-elastic segment). The study found that the price-inelastic segment tended to be higher-income consumers who were either young married couples or families with teenagers. These two groups are less sensitive to a price increase because of their greater dependence on the phone. Because of the price sensitivity of lower-income consumers, one implication of the study was to better inform these segments of lower rates for off-peak and direct-dial calls.

A few studies have attempted to segment markets by price elasticity. The energy crisis in the 1970s prompted some studies of the price elasticity of individual consumers for gasoline. Willenborg and Pitts studied purchase intentions for autos and gasoline among a panel of South Carolina consumers from 1973 to 1979.[19] In 1973, the majority of consumers indicated that they would begin driving less frequently when prices increased by eight to ten cents a gallon. When prices actually stabilized at these higher levels, however, consumers expressed little willingness to drive less. Overall, there was a disparity between what people said and what they did about gasoline consumption. Consumers seemed to express greater price elasticity in the face of price increases but showed more upside price inelasticity in their actual demand for gasoline than their own perceptions indicated.

Segmenting by Responses to Other Marketing Stimuli

Consumers can be segmented by their responses to marketing stimuli other than price—for example, deal, coupon, advertising, and even package-size elasticity. The value of segmenting by such response elasticities is that it provides management with a basis to:

- Direct price promotions, deals, and coupons to the most responsive consumers (an important consideration in a recessionary period).
- Identify groups most likely to respond positively to increases in advertising expenditures.

Few studies have used response elasticity to segment markets. Two, one by Massy and Frank[20] and another by McCann,[21] analyzed consumer purchases over time to estimate advertising and price elasticities. Studies of response elasticity are likely to increase with the greater availability of scanner data; that is, sales data from stores with laser scanners. In some markets, consumers buy groceries using magnetically coded cards, allowing manufacturers to determine what an individual consumer has purchased and at what price. Companies can then identify consumers who tend to switch brands frequently because of changes in price and promotions (the price-elastic segment) and consumers who stay loyal to a given brand (the price-inelastic segment). In addition, some of these households have monitors to determine their television viewing. This allows marketers to relate what consumers have viewed to what they are buying, providing a measure of advertising elasticity for individual households.

Quantitative Techniques for Market Segmentation

To segment by benefits, behavior, or response elasticities, marketers must be able to describe these segments. In the snack food markets, for example, what are the demographic, lifestyle, or personality characteristics of the nutritional segment (benefit segmentation), the heavy snackers (behavioral segmentation), and the price-sensitive snackers (response-elasticity segmentation)?

Identifying market segments requires developing a cohesive demographic and lifestyle profile of each segment to provide guidelines for selecting media and creating ads. For example, the benefit segmentation analysis of the snack food market shown in Table 12.2 identified a nutritional snacker segment as people who have children, are well educated, controlled, and self-assured. A program known as **cluster analysis** developed this profile in two steps. The first step grouped together respondents with similar needs so there would be greatest similarity among respondents in a given segment and greatest differences among segments. In this way, the respondents in the nutritional segment were identified as distinct from the other segments based on their needs. The second step determined each segment's demographic, lifestyle, and personality characteristics.

It is beyond the scope of this text to describe the quantitative techniques used in market segmentation analysis.[22] The basic purpose of such analysis is to develop guidelines for positioning new brands; repositioning existing brands; and developing advertising, media, and pricing strategies. In the rest of this chapter, we focus on product positioning as an important adjunct to market segmentation.

◆ MARKET SEGMENTATION STRATEGIES

Market segmentation strategies differ according to whether a company appeals to one or to several segments with one or several products. As shown in Figure 12.2, these two dimensions produce four types of segmentation strategies.

Concentrated segmentation involves targeting one product to one segment. When Procter & Gamble first entered the coffee market, it followed a concentrated segmentation strategy by appealing only to ground roast users with its Folgers brand. Similarly, Subaru targets one product, its four-wheel drive cars, to a particular segment, rural consumers.

Market segment expansion targets the same product to several segments. Johnson & Johnson followed a concentrated segmentation strategy for 50 years by targeting its Baby Shampoo for the obvious segment, babies. However, when the company found adults frequently using the product, it successfully expanded its appeal by advertising to adults as well. A key consideration in

▶**FIGURE 12.2**
Types of Market
Segmentation Strategies

	ONE SEGMENT	SEVERAL SEGMENTS
ONE PRODUCT	Concentrated Segmentation	Market Segment Expansion
SEVERAL PRODUCTS	Product-Line Segmentation	Differentiated Segmentation

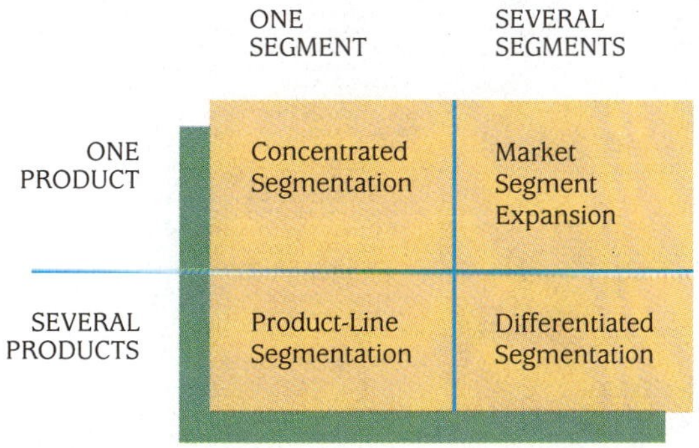

market segment expansion is to ensure that any such expansion does not alienate core users. Parents using Baby Shampoo on their children are not alienated when the product is advertised as good for adults as well. Coors faced a similar issue when it was trying to decide whether to follow a multiple segmentation strategy by advertising its flagship brand to women as well as to men. Other companies have not targeted women for fear their ads may alienate male drinkers. Coors is willing to take the risk, as women represent 17 percent of the beer market and account for $6.5 billion in sales a year.[23]

Firms can also target several products to one segment, called a *product-line segmentation strategy*, because the products are part of a product line. Toddler University is a small company that targets one segment, babies. It targets one product line, athletic shoes, by performance category; for example, a shoe for babies in the crib, another for toddlers, and another for babies who are just starting to walk. (See Exhibit 12.2.)

Many larger firms follow a *differentiated segmentation strategy* by targeting several products to several segments. American Express reached a differentiated strategy for its charge card line by first following a concentrated strategy and then a strategy of segment expansion. Until 1980, the American Express card was one product targeted to one segment, male executives. When card

▶**EXHIBIT 12.2**
A product-line segmentation strategy

Source: Courtesy of Toddler University

membership leveled off, the company followed a segment expansion strategy by marketing the green card to working women, students, and senior citizens. The next step to ensure growth was to expand its product offerings through differentiated segmentation. American Express introduced the gold card to provide additional services, then the platinum card for prestige, and most recently, the Optima card to extend credit to cardholders. (See Exhibit 12.3.) The Optima, green, gold, and platinum cards segment the market from lower- to higher-income groups.

◆ IDENTIFYING AND EVALUATING A PRODUCT'S POSITION

Market segmentation and product positioning strategies must be developed together. Marketers must identify market segments by their common needs and must position products to meet those needs.

The link between market segmentation and product positioning is illustrated by the success of Miller in establishing the light beer category. Rheingold

▶**EXHIBIT 12.3**
Differentiated segmentation: American Express introduces the Optima card

introduced the first light beer, a brand called Gablingers, and targeted it to weight-conscious consumers. The positioning of Gablingers as a diet beer caused it to fail because most beer drinkers shunned the diet connotation. Miller saw an opportunity to introduce a light beer without emphasizing low calories and defined its target as the heavier beer drinking blue-collar segment. It legitimized light beer to this group by showing athletes such as Boog Powell and Dick Butkus drinking light beer. The definition of the target segment and the positioning went hand in hand since a substantial segment of heavier beer drinkers wanted a lighter alternative to regular beer.

To position products like Miller Light, marketers must identify the benefits and attributes the target segment emphasizes. These benefits and attributes then become the basis for communicating the product's position. In this section, we consider how a product's position can be identified. Positioning a product requires (1) defining a vocabulary of attributes and benefits, (2) developing several alternative positionings to determine which is best, and (3) testing one or more positionings relative to those of the competition.

Developing a Product Vocabulary

Assume Great Snacks is first considering a more nutritious snack product and wants to determine the attributes and benefits consumers use to evaluate snacks. The most frequently used approach to derive a vocabulary of attributes and benefits is the focus group interview. **Focus group interviews** are unstructured interviews conducted by a trained moderator in which eight to twelve people are asked to discuss a topic. The purpose is to gain better insight into the consumers' needs and motives than that obtained in a predesigned, structured interview. Generally, focus groups are more productive than individual interviews because members of the group stimulate and support each other, providing a more open forum for discussion. Researchers frequently use focus groups to elicit the product attributes and benefits consumers use in selecting brands. This way, researchers can develop a vocabulary of such attributes and benefits.

Another approach in developing a product vocabulary is to ask consumers why they view certain brands as similar and to identify the attributes they use most frequently to describe brand similarities. Using this technique, Great Snacks might conduct a small test on 100 consumers and ask them to rate three existing chip-type brands for similarity: Wise, Pringles, and Lays potato chips. Consumers respond to which of the two are most similar, why, and how they differ from the third brand. The attributes they use to define similarities and differences are recorded. Another set of three brands is introduced and the process is repeated. This technique, known as the **Kelly Repertory Grid**,[24] allows the company to define five key attributes: crispiness (keeps fresh), easy-open package, low price, not oily, and natural ingredients.

Developing Alternative Positionings

Now assume Great Snacks wants to investigate the possibility of introducing a new sixth benefit, fewer calories. It must now ask what combination of benefits it should introduce. Obviously, the ideal would be to introduce all six benefits, but this may be too costly or technologically impossible. Therefore, it is necessary to test alternative product positionings representing different combinations of characteristics.

To test various positionings, researchers develop alternative *product concepts*. As we saw in Chapter 6, a product concept is a description of the bundle of attributes and benefits used to communicate the product's position. Researchers develop several descriptions of concepts and present them to consumers to get their reactions. In the snack study, one concept might be a crispy, low-calorie, chip-type snack with an easy-open package. A second might be a crispy, low-calorie, chip-type snack with natural ingredients. A third might be a low-priced, low-calorie, chip snack that is not oily. Consumers would be given these combinations of benefits and asked to choose which is most desirable. This approach is known as **trade-off analysis**[25] because consumers have an opportunity to trade off one benefit (lower price) for another (natural ingredients). On this basis, marketers can identify the concept with the optimal set of benefits.

Testing the Product's Position Relative to Competition

Assume that trade-off analysis identifies the optimal concept as a crispy, low-calorie, chip-type snack with natural ingredients. On this basis, Great Snacks decides to further examine the possible introduction of a chip, fruit, and nut snack. If such a product is technologically feasible and cost-effective, researchers would test it on consumers relative to competitive brands. Such a **product concept test** requires presenting a description of the concept and competitive brands to consumers. Consumer responses in the concept test are often presented in the form of a **perceptual map** such as that in Figure 12.3. In the concept test, consumers are asked to rate the similarity of the new snack concept to existing snack foods brands (labeled Brands A to F). These data were fed into a computer program that is known as **multidimensional scaling**.[26] The program determines the relative position of the existing brands and the test concept in a perceptual map based on consumers' similarity ratings. It is apparent from Figure 12.3 that consumers in the study saw the new product concept as similar to Brands A and B. This result suggests a danger of a positioning as a "me too" brand.

Consumers were also asked to rate each brand on a vocabulary of eight product attributes and benefits. Another computer program known as **PROFIT**

▶**FIGURE 12.3**
Perceptual mapping to evaluate a new product concept

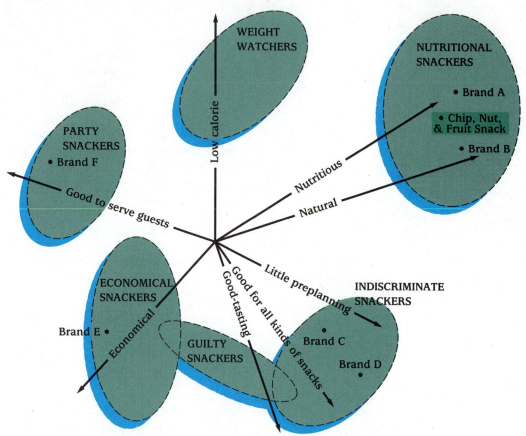

(**property fitting**) was used to determine the association of the attributes and benefits with the brands.[27] The program identifies the position of each attribute by determining the best fit between the attributes and the brands in the perceptual map. This analysis produced the eight arrows representing the attributes in Figure 12.3. It is apparent that the chip, nut, and fruit snack and Brands A and B were most closely associated with "nutritious" and "natural." Brands C and D were associated with "good for all kinds of snacks" and "little preplanning"; Brand E, with "economical"; and Brand F, with "good to serve guests."

Finally, consumers were asked to rank their preference for each brand and the test concept (Which item do you prefer most? second? third? and so on). Each consumer was positioned on the perceptual map so that he or she would be closest to the brand preferred most and farthest from the brand preferred least. Consumers preferring similar brands were grouped together by a third computer program, cluster analysis.[28] These groups are represented by circles in Figure 12.3. The cluster program identified the six segments in Table 12.2. The largest segment, nutritional snackers, preferred the chip, nut, and fruit snack. In this respect, the product was targeted correctly. Indiscriminate snackers preferred Brands C and D. Consumers who preferred a brand also tended to emphasize the benefits associated with that brand. That is, nutritional snackers emphasized "natural ingredients"; indiscriminate snackers, "good for all kinds of snacks"; and so on.

Figure 12.3 provides management with a picture of the market for the concept and for competitive brands. It permits management to evaluate the way target segments see the new product concept and whether the concept has fulfilled its intended positioning.

In summary, the steps involved in identifying and evaluating alternative product positionings are to:

1. Generate a vocabulary of evaluative attributes through application of the Kelly Repertory Grid or by conducting focus group interviews.
2. Develop and test a number of alternative product concepts by trade-off analysis and select one or two best concept positionings.
3. Conduct a product concept test and ask consumers to rate the concept(s) and competitive brands by similarity and preference.
4. Utilize statistical techniques to develop a perceptual map and position the concept relative to existing brands.

If results of the product concept test are positive, a fifth step is required— a product use test. The company produces the new product on a limited basis and asks consumers to try it. On this basis, the company decides whether to introduce the product.

Using Quantitative Techniques for Positioning

Product positioning analysis is an excellent example of the link between consumer behavior and quantitative applications in marketing. The positioning analysis described in this section demonstrates the use of **multivariate statistical techniques** (techniques capable of analyzing many variables simultaneously) for the evaluation of consumer data. Marketers can use trade-off analysis to screen a large number of concepts and identify several candidates for further testing. Multidimensional scaling can analyze results of a concept test using consumer similarity or preference ratings. In addition, marketers can use other multivariate techniques such as discriminant analysis[29] and factor analysis[30] for positioning. The PROFIT program can associate brand positions with evaluative attributes, and cluster analysis will identify consumer segments. Using these techniques sequentially, marketers can develop a planned approach to positioning analysis.

As noted, it is not within the scope of this text to discuss these techniques in detail. However, it is important for the student of consumer behavior to recognize the indispensable role of statistical analysis in evaluating brand positionings and in identifying market segments.

◆ MARKETING APPLICATIONS OF PRODUCT POSITIONING

Product positioning analyses have been applied in two key areas: (1) the normative evaluation of new products to determine where they should be positioned (as in the snack food study) and (2) the descriptive evaluation of existing products to determine whether they are positioned correctly.

A key consideration for both new and existing products is whether consumers see the brand as the company intended. When General Foods introduced an artificial bacon product, it positioned it as a leaner and more nutritious alternative to bacon. The problem was that consumers considered the product as greasy and fatty as regular bacon. General Foods had to reformulate the product to ensure that consumers' perceptions would conform to the company's positioning strategy.

Consumers might also see existing products in a manner that is inconsistent with the company's intended positioning. We saw that Oldsmobile could not change perceptions from an old and stodgy car to the intended positioning of an innovative one. Similarly, Kmart is facing a difficult road in repositioning itself from the polyester palace to a high-fashion retailer. Although difficult to implement, such repositioning strategies are often necessary to maintain a company's ability to meet consumer needs.

Positioning New Products

Marketers have used perceptual mapping in new product development for evaluating new product concepts and for evaluating shifts in the product's position once consumers have used the product.

The snack food study in Figure 12.3 is a good example of the application of positioning analysis to evaluate a new product concept. Three questions were used to evaluate the positioning of the new concept. First, is it in a distinctive position relative to that of the competition? In this case, the answer is *no* because there is the danger that the new chip, nut, and fruit snack will compete head on with Brands A and B. Second, is the positioning in line with managerial objectives? *Yes*, because the concept is perceived as having nutritional benefits and, thus, is positioned to the intended target. Third, does it appeal to a sufficiently large segment to warrant further testing? *Yes*, because nutritional snackers compose the largest segment.

Further testing is required to answer the following questions before Great Snacks can make a decision to introduce the product: Can the concept be distinguished from Brands A and B on key nutritional benefits? Will enough consumers select the new product over Brands A and B? What are the needs and characteristics of consumers who would buy the chip, nut, and fruit snack? Once the concept is translated into a product and tested, will the same positioning be maintained, or will consumers change their perceptions?

The analysis in Figure 12.3 also provides implications for additional new product possibilities by defining "gaps" in the perceptual space. The most obvious is that no segment perceives any product as a low-calorie snack. Thus, a snack product positioned to weight watchers might represent a prime marketing opportunity. In addition, there may be an opportunity to position a snack to guilty snackers since they have no strong preference for any existing snack products. If Great Snacks considers these opportunities, additional concept tests would have to be run and perceptual maps developed to position the new concepts against existing brands.

Other examples of using perceptual mapping to evaluate new product concepts can be found in approaches described by Wind[31] and Stefflre.[32]

Positioning Existing Products

It is important for management to evaluate not only where a product should be, but also where it is. Existing products have been evaluated for two purposes:

1. To determine their position relative to competitors.
2. To evaluate the effects over time of a repositioning strategy.

Evaluating a Product's Relative Position

Descriptive positioning studies have been conducted to evaluate the position of product categories and brands relative to those of the competition. However, few such studies have been reported because of their proprietary nature. One exception is Chrysler's report of a perceptual mapping analysis of the car market. The analysis was meant to determine how consumers distinguish between car makes that have become more similar over the years. According to Chrysler's manager of marketing planning, "With size less of a dominant factor, it's no longer that easy to know what any single product represents in the minds of consumers."[33]

Chrysler conducted the analysis by asking consumers to rate general makes of cars (Chrysler, Chevrolet, Buick, and so on) on criteria such as youthfulness, luxury, and practicality. Results are shown in Figure 12.4. Based on these positionings, Chrysler concluded that its cars needed a more youthful image. It also concluded that "Plymouth and Dodge needed to move up sharply on the luxury scale."[34] Similarly, General Motors might conclude that its Chevrolet division, traditionally targeted to first-time car buyers, should have a more practical and youthful image. Another problem for GM is the similarity in image between the company's Buick and Oldsmobile divisions, suggesting that "they are waging a marketing war more against each other than against competition."[35]

▶**FIGURE 12.4**

Positioning existing products in the automobile market

Source: Adapted from "Car Makers Use 'Image' Map as Tool to Position Products," *The Wall Street Journal* (March 22, 1984), p. 33. Reprinted by permission of *The Wall Street Journal*, ©Dow Jones & Company, Inc. 1984. All rights reserved worldwide.

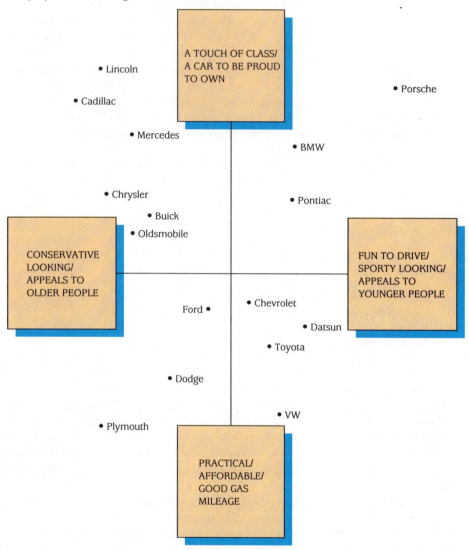

Chrysler also used perceptual mapping to test specific models. For example, it found that consumers positioned its Lancer and Commander models next to the Honda Accord, the exact positioning Chrysler desired.

Other brand positioning studies are Wilkes'[36] earlier study of the automobile market and Johnson's[37] study of the beer market.

Retailers develop positioning strategies for their stores just as manufacturers develop positioning strategies for their products. Developing the right positioning strategy carries the same requirements for a store as for a product: (1) identify shopper segments for marketing effort, (2) determine the benefits and attributes these segments seek, and (3) develop a positioning strategy to communicate these benefits and attributes.

As with products, a key question is whether shoppers see the store in line with the retailer's positioning strategy. A survey by advertising agency BBDO Worldwide among upscale women reveals the image of the leading New York City department stores. Figure 12.5 shows the psychological benefits associated with each of the eight stores in this study. The stores are positioned along two key dimensions: luxury versus thriftiness and tradition versus innovation. Specific benefits and attributes associated with these dimensions are also shown. For example, security is associated with tradition, sophistication and physical attractiveness with luxury, and creativity and being up-to-date with innovation.

Lord & Taylor is associated with security and tradition, a positioning that may be strong among older consumers but one that is likely to limit future growth among aging baby boomers. A repositioning strategy that would move the store down the vertical axis toward innovation and creativity would be desirable. Barneys is in a strong position, being associated with innovation and creativity. However, its association with a male-oriented line may limit sales to the female market. Although Bergdorf Goodman may appear to be in a strong position as the pinnacle of luxury, the positioning is inconsistent with the store's current strategy of starting to offer more lower-priced lines. Bergdorf must decide whether or not it wishes to sustain its luxury image or broaden its appeal.

One store that appears to be where it wants is Macy's, with an image of patriotism, family, wholesomeness, and variety. As one analyst said, "Macy's is the retailing equivalent of Mom, apple pie, and Chevrolet."

The perceptual map in Figure 12.5 is valuable in helping stores determine whether they are positioned where they want to be or whether a repositioning is necessary.

Source: "Image and Attitude Are Department Store's Draw," *The New York Times* (August 12, 1993), p. D1.

STRATEGIC APPLICATIONS OF CONSUMER BEHAVIOR

Product Positioning Applies to Stores As Well As Products

▶**FIGURE 12.5**

Evaluating a department store's positioning

Source: "Image and Attitude Are Department Store's Draw," *The New York Times* (August 12, 1993), p. D1.

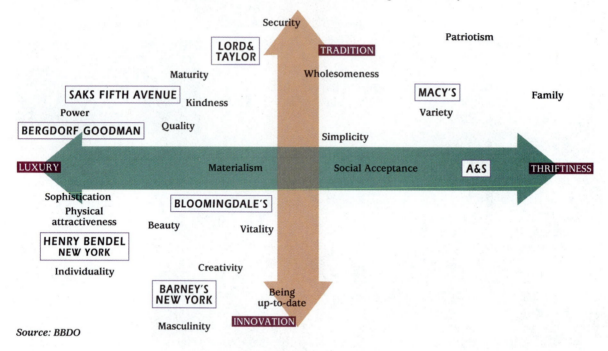

Source: BBDO

Evaluating Repositioning Strategies

The purpose of repositioning analysis is to track the results of attempts to change a brand's image. When Philip Morris bought the Seven-Up Company, it decided to reposition the company's flagship brand, 7-Up, by moving away from the Uncola campaign in an attempt to compete more directly with Pepsi and Coke. The company positioned 7-Up as a healthier alternative by advertising a lack of caffeine with the theme "Never had it, never will."[38]

Evaluating this repositioning strategy would require tracking consumer perceptions of the 7-Up brand. Figure 12.6 shows 7-Up's position in the late 1970s as the Uncola. If 7-Up's repositioning was successful, it would be perceived as a good-tasting, caffeine-free substitute for regular colas. Such a shift is illustrated by the broken arrow in Figure 12.6 and shows the positioning as of 1983. When Pepsi and Coke came out with caffeine-free offerings, Seven-Up then reverted in 1988 to its Uncola campaign, but with the addition of the no-caffeine claim. (See ad in Exhibit 12.4.)

Multidimensional scaling techniques have been used to evaluate repositioning strategies in studies by Perry, Izraeli, and Perry;[39] Moinpour, McCollough,

▶FIGURE 12.6
Evaluating the repositioning strategy of 7-Up

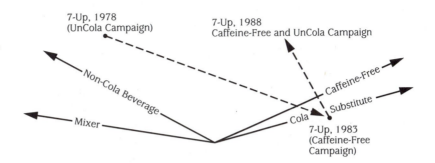

▶EXHIBIT 12.4
Seven-Up reverts back to the Uncola theme

and MacLachlan;[40] and Narayana.[41] These studies report shifts in consumer perceptions by portraying differences in perceptual maps before and after an advertising campaign or other promotional stimulus.

An interesting extension of repositioning strategy is the forced repositioning by federal regulation requiring corrective advertising. For example, the Federal Trade Commission's ruling requiring Listerine to cease further advertising of the brand as a cold remedy also required corrective advertising. Listerine had to change consumer perceptions and, in so doing, reposition the brand.

Whether repositioning is voluntary or mandatory, communications strategies designed for change must measure change; and perceptual mapping is an effective analysis for doing so.

◆ PRODUCT POSITIONING STRATEGIES

Once a specific positioning is established for a product, marketers must translate it into a strategy to communicate product attributes and benefits. Marketers have used two broad approaches in positioning products, as Figure 12.7 shows. One is to focus on the consumer; the other, on competition. In both cases, the result should be to associate the product with consumer needs. **Consumer positioning** specifically links the product to consumer benefits and product features or, more generally, associates the product with an appealing image or setting. For example, Great Snacks might logically position its new snack product on key benefits such as natural ingredients and nutrition. **Competitive positioning** communicates the product's benefits by comparing them to a competitor's brand. In this case, Great Snacks might communicate the benefits of the new snack product by comparing it to other competitive products that use artificial ingredients.

Consumer Positioning Strategies

Figure 12.7 shows that marketers can position products by consumer benefits on a continuum from informational to image. Informational positioning is specific and attempts to establish a direct product-to-benefit link by citing product features. Such a positioning can be based on detailed information, as when a car manufacturer cites performance measures and car features, or on one particular benefit, as when Crest advertises cavity prevention or Bounty paper towels advertises absorbency. In all cases, consumer benefits are linked to product features.

▶**FIGURE 12.7**
Product positioning
strategies

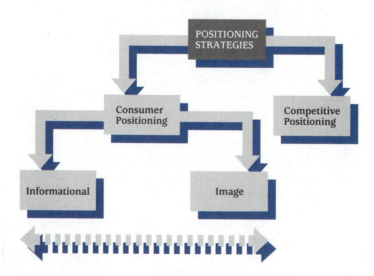

Positioning by image is a more general approach that attempts to appeal to vague and ambiguous benefits. Such a strategy allows consumers to "read in" the desired benefits. Effective advertising may be vague enough to be many things to many people, yet specific enough to create a product-to-benefit link. Godiva Chocolates, a high-priced imported chocolate line, positions itself as a prestige, luxury brand and uses the theme "Make a wish." Lenox China uses the theme "Because art is never an extravagance." These themes attempt to reflect consumers' fulfillment of their desires and fantasies by purchasing these products.

The two ads in Exhibit 12.5, both for cellular phones, demonstrate the information to image continuum. The ad for Motorola is clearly informational in citing 17 features of the Tough Talker Transportable phone. The ad for Muratec is closer to the image side of the continuum. It does not cite any product features and tries to create a warm, emotional response by showing that the phone permits a father to spend more time with his child.

These ads also show that a product category can shift along the informational to image continuum. Interestingly, the Motorola ad appeared when cellular phones were first marketed. As cellular phones became more established, companies no longer felt the need to inform consumers and could use a more image-oriented approach such as Muratec's. The shift from an informational to an image approach in positioning over a product's life cycle is true of many product categories. It reflects a greater use of symbolism and imagery as companies try to differentiate themselves in an increasingly competitive market.

There is a danger of going too far to the informational or the image side in positioning products. Informational positioning may be too specific and may restrict the brand to a narrow focus. In focusing primarily on specific performance features, Motorola may be focusing too narrowly on high-tech executives. Image-oriented ads might create excessive ambiguity that could lead to confusion especially if the ad runs the risk of creating a vague image of the product. At first glance, it is not apparent that the Muratec ad is for a cellular phone, creating some risk of confusion as to the positioning of the product.

Competitive Positioning Strategies

Another approach to positioning is to achieve a product-to-benefit link by focusing on competition. One strategy links the product to associations that are already in consumers' minds. The positioning of 7-Up as the Uncola was described as "linking the product 7-Up to what is already in the mind of their prospect. [As a result], 7-Up has established itself as an alternative to Coke and Pepsi. No product features, no customer benefits, no company image. Only the mental leverage factor of one word. The 'un-cola.'"[42]

Marketers frequently achieve competitive positioning through **comparative advertising**; that is, naming competitors in ads. Comparative advertising is a means of using the leader as the frame of reference and positioning the brand

▶**EXHIBIT 12.5**
Consumer positioning
by information versus
image

Positioning by information

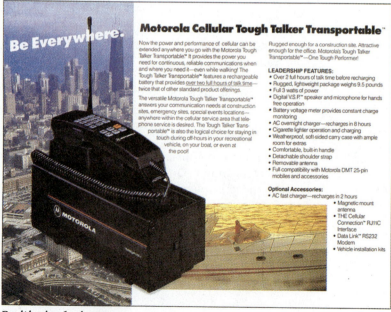

Positioning by image

by posing a direct challenge to the leader. For example, MCI claims that it provides better service than AT&T. (See Exhibit 12.6.) Burger King has advertised that McDonald's fries their hamburgers, and the Pepsi Challenge campaign advertised taste tests against Coke. The danger in such competitive positioning is that consumers may confuse the brand's position with that of competitors. One study found that comparative advertising was likely to lead to confusion and could create more awareness for the competitive brand than the advertised brand.[43]

Another risk in competitive positioning is that the market leader may retaliate. As a result of comparative advertising campaigns, Pepsi provoked Coke and Burger King provoked McDonald's to retaliate. In the latter case, both McDonald's and Wendy's filed suit challenging Burger King's claims that its hamburgers are tastier and meatier.[44]

Despite these shortcomings, competitive positioning remains a viable strategy to establish a distinctive product-to-benefit link in consumers' minds, using competition as a reference point.

▶**EXHIBIT 12.6**
A competitive
positioning strategy

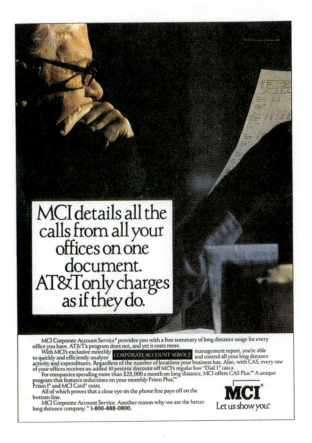

SOCIETAL IMPLICATIONS OF SEGMENTATION AND POSITIONING STRATEGIES

Targeting products to particular segments can lead to abuses, particularly when products are positioned to children or to minorities.

As we saw in Chapter 2, targeting products to children raises particular societal issues, and two issues arise most frequently. First, the limited cognitive ability of young children can lead to abuses. Marketers could take advantage of children's limited abilities to discriminate between claims and a tendency to take most advertising literally.

Second, marketers often target children without adequate concern for safety. For example, food companies have directed advertising for microwaveable entrees to preteens with little concerns for the dangers of children using microwave ovens. Marketers have found a ready market in children whose parents are not home after school and have argued that food preparation teaches the child confidence and self-reliance. There is no question that part of the responsibility for ensuring safe product usage lies with parents; however, companies do have a responsibility to ensure product safety. Similar issues arise for other potentially unsafe products targeted to children such as all-terrain vehicles.

Marketers also have a responsibility to ensure that ads for products such as cigarettes or beer do not appeal to children. The most controversial issue in this regard has been R. J. Reynolds' introduction of the Joe Camel cartoon character. Appeals by consumer groups and nonprofit agencies to Reynolds to cease using the character have been of no avail, despite the fact that Camel's share among teens increased by 32 percent since the introduction of Joe Camel.[45]

Another societal issue is targeting minorities with potentially harmful products. This issue arose when R. J. Reynolds targeted Uptown cigarettes specifically to African-Americans. Before Uptown came along, cigarette companies had devoted part of their advertising budget for their existing brands to African-Americans and Hispanics, but none had ever developed a product with the intent of targeting it to a minority segment. Reynolds' plans provoked an outcry that was successful in getting the company to withdraw the product. However, apparently the lesson did not fully sink in. Shortly after it withdrew Uptown, a Reynolds plan surfaced for a cigarette called Dakota positioned to blue-collar women under 21.[46] Although there was no evidence R. J. Reynolds planned to introduce Dakota, the company's tentative plans raised questions about a dubious segmentation strategy.

SUMMARY

This chapter has described market segmentation and product positioning from the standpoint of behavioral analysis and marketing strategy. Market segmentation and product positioning are closely linked since products generally are positioned to meet the needs of defined market segments.

In the first part of the chapter, we considered the means of identifying market segments and strategies for segmenting markets. Three approaches were described for identifying market segments. In benefit segmentation, consumers are defined by similarity in needs (for example, consumers emphasizing cavity prevention versus white teeth in the toothpaste market). New products are positioned and existing products are repositioned to meet these needs. In behavioral segmentation, marketers identify users based on several behavioral criteria such as brand usage, product usage, level of usage (heavy versus light users), or shopping behavior. Markets also can be segmented by consumer response elasticities; that is, consumer sensitivity to changes in price, advertising, or other marketing stimuli. The purpose is to identify the characteristics of consumers who may be induced to buy based on a price deal or who may be influenced by an increase in advertising expenditures.

Once segments are identified, marketers can develop strategies for reaching them. A classification of segmentation strategies was described based on whether one or many products are targeted to one or many segments.

We then considered the process of identifying and evaluating a product's position based on four steps:

1. Generate a vocabulary of product attributes and benefits.
2. Test alternative product positionings.
3. Conduct a product concept test to evaluate the proposed positioning against competitive brands.
4. Analyze the results using perceptual mapping analysis.

Applications of product positioning analysis are primarily in two areas: evaluating new products or defining the position of existing products. Such strategies can be based on positioning to consumers or to competitors. Positioning to consumers requires identification of consumer needs. Competitive positioning requires use of a competitive brand as a frame of reference and development of an appropriate product claim.

The chapter concluded by considering the societal implications of segmentation and positioning strategies, particularly issues involved in targeting products to children and to minorities.

In the next section of the text, we change our focus from the individual consumer to the consumer's environment.

QUESTIONS

1. What benefit segments may be identified for the following markets: (a) soft drinks, (b) household cleaners, (c) personal care appliances, and (d) credit cards? What are the implications of identifying these segments for (a) positioning new products or (b) repositioning existing products?
2. Under what circumstances would a marketer wish to segment by the following behavioral criteria: (a) brand users versus nonusers, (b) product users

versus nonusers, (c) heavy versus light users of the product category, and (d) shopper types?

3. Table 12.2 cited nutritional, weight watchers, and guilty segments in the snack food market. What would be the usefulness of identifying each of these segments by (a) demographics, (b) lifestyles, and (c) brand attitudes?

4. What are the implications for (a) pricing, (b) advertising, and (c) store service of appealing to the shopper segments listed in Table 12.3?

5. What are the strategic implications of segmenting the coffee market according to (a) deal or coupon sensitivity and (b) sensitivity to changes in package size? How would marketers identify the deal segments and package-sensitive segments?

6. What is meant by upside and downside price elasticity? What is the relevance of this concept to marketers? Cite an example.

7. What types of segmentation strategies did American Express use for its line of credit cards in the last 15 years based on the classification defined in Figure 12.2? What was the rationale for each strategy?

8. Assume a company wants to develop a new snack food to appeal to those consumers who would like a snack that is nutritious and can be eaten at any time (morning, afternoon, after dinner, before bedtime). How can the company use (a) the Kelly Repertory Grid and (b) trade-off analysis to develop an appropriate concept?

9. At one time, Campbell's Soup was interested in determining the position of its Chunky and regular condensed soups relative to related food and beverage products.
   - How could the company use perceptual mapping to position its Chunky soups and regular soup line relative to other products?
   - What data would be required for this analysis?

10. What are the strategic implications of the positioning of the chip, nut, and fruit snack in Figure 12.3? What other strategic implications can you formulate based on the figure?

11. How can the Federal Trade Commission use perceptual mapping techniques to determine if required corrective advertising (for example, by Listerine) has the desired effects on consumer perceptions of the brand in question?

12. What are the strategic implications for repositioning strategies of one or more of the department stores in the perceptual map in Figure 12.5?

13. What are the risks of repositioning a product? Provide an example of these risks.

14. What are the purposes of a positioning strategy based on information? On image? What are the risks of positioning products primarily by information? By image?

15. What are the advantages and disadvantages of positioning a brand relative to competition? Under what circumstances should marketers use competitive positioning?

16. What societal issues arise from segmentation strategies targeted to children and to minorities?

RESEARCH ASSIGNMENTS

1. Select a product category and identify three or four key benefits. Select a sample of product users and ask them to identify the most important benefit desired. On this basis, form three or four benefit segments (for example, consumers who emphasize "lets me sleep," "freshly brewed," or "economy" for coffee). Try to ensure that there are at least ten consumers in each benefit segment. Ask the sample for information on the following: (a) demographic characteristics, (b) brand regularly used, (c) frequency of use, and (d) a select number of lifestyle characteristics (as in Table 11.1).

   - What are some of the key differences between benefit segments based on this information?
   - What are the implications for (a) new product positioning, (b) repositioning of existing products, (c) advertising, (d) media selection, and (e) pricing strategies?

2. Use the Kelly Repertory Grid technique on a small sample of consumers to identify relevant attributes that might be introduced into a new product concept. Then use trade-off analysis to test various combinations of attributes that might be included in a new product (for example, calcium in a soft drink or a three-in-one shampoo/cream rinse/conditioner). Ask a sample of about 20 to 30 consumers to rank their preferences for the combinations of attributes (concept formulations) you have developed.

   - After examining the data, what appears to be the best prospective product formulation?
   - Can you identify one group of consumers that tends to prefer one concept and another group that prefers another? What are the differences in the demographic or brand usage characteristics of the two groups?
   - What are the implications of your findings for (a) the way the product should be positioned and (b) the target group it should be positioned to?

NOTES

1. "Attitude Research Assesses Global Market Potential," *Marketing News* (August 1, 1988), pp. 10, 13.
2. *Ibid.*
3. Roger J. Calantone and Alan G. Sawyer, "The Stability of Benefit Segments," *Journal of Marketing Research,* 15 (August, 1978), pp. 395–404.
4. W. Thomas Anderson, Jr., Eli P. Cox III, and David G. Fulcher, "Bank Decisions and Market Segmentation," *Journal of Marketing,* 40 (January, 1976), pp. 40–45.
5. Shirley Young, Leland Ott, and Barbara Feigin, "Some Practical Considerations in Market Segmentation," *Journal of Marketing Research,* 15 (August, 1978), pp. 405–412.
6. "Computer Mapping of Demographic Lifestyle Data Locates 'Pockets' of Potential Customers at Microgeographic Level," *Marketing News* (November 27, 1981), Section 2, p. 16.
7. William H. Peters, "Using MCA to Segment New Car Markets," *Journal of Marketing Research,* 7 (August, 1970), pp. 360–363.
8. Robert D. Hisrich and Michael P. Peters, "Selecting the Superior Segmentation Correlate," *Journal of Marketing,* 38 (July, 1974), pp. 60–63.
9. Frank M. Bass, Douglas J. Tigert, and Ronald T. Lonsdale, "Market Segmentation Analysis," *Journal of Marketing Research,* 5 (August, 1968), pp. 264–270.

10. Henry Assael and A. Marvin Roscoe, Jr., "Approaches to Market Segmentation Analysis," *Journal of Marketing,* 40 (October, 1976), pp. 67–76.

11. Henry Assael, "A Research Design to Predict Telephone Usage Among Bell System Customers," *European Research,* 1 (January, 1973), pp. 38–44; and (March, 1973), pp. 59–61.

12. Jack A. Lesser and Marie Adele Hughes, "Toward a Typology of Shoppers," *Business Horizons,* 29 (November-December, 1986), pp. 56–62.

13. "Fifteen Million Americans Are Shopping Addicts," *American Demographics* (March, 1992), pp. 14–15.

14. George P. Moschis, "Shopping Orientations and Consumer Uses of Information," *Journal of Retailing,* 52 (Summer, 1976), pp. 61–70.

15. Arch G. Woodside and J. Taylor Sims, "Retail Sales Transactions and Customer 'Purchase Pal' Effects on Buying Behavior," *Journal of Retailing,* 52 (Fall, 1976), pp. 57–64.

16. Arch G. Woodside and J. William Davenport, Jr., "Effects of Price and Salesman Expertise on Customer Purchasing Behavior," *Journal of Business,* 49 (January, 1976), pp. 51–59.

17. J. Jeffrey Inman, Leigh McAlister, and Wayne D. Hoyer, "Promotion Signal: Proxy for a Price Cut?" *Journal of Consumer Research,* 17 (June, 1990), pp. 74–81.

18. Assael and Roscoe, "Approaches to Market Segmentation Analysis," *op. cit.,* p. 74.

19. John F. Willenborg and Robert E. Pitts, "Gasoline Prices: Their Effect on Consumer Behavior and Attitudes," *Journal of Marketing,* 41 (January, 1977), pp. 24–30.

20. William F. Massy and Ronald E. Frank, "Short-Term Price and Dealing Effects in Selected Market Segments," *Journal of Marketing Research,* 2 (May, 1965), pp. 171–185.

21. John M. McCann, "Market Segment Response to the Marketing Decision Variables," *Journal of Marketing Research,* 11 (November, 1974), pp. 399–412.

22. For descriptions of quantitative techniques used in segmentation analysis, see Paul E. Green and Donald S. Tull, *Research for Marketing Decisions,* 3rd ed. (Englewood Cliffs, NJ: Prentice-Hall, 1975), Part IV; and Henry Assael, "Segmenting Market Segmentation Strategies and Techniques," *European Research,* 1 (September, 1973), pp. 190–194; and (November, 1973), pp. 256–258.

23. "New Print Ad for Coors Beer Targets Women," *The Wall Street Journal* (June 2, 1987), p. 33.

24. W. A. K. Foost and R. L. Braine, "The Application of the Repertory Grid Technique to Problems in Market Research," *Commentary,* 9 (July, 1967), pp. 161–175.

25. For examples of two different approaches to trade-off analysis, see Richard M. Johnson, "Trade-Off Analysis of Consumer Values," *Journal of Marketing Research,* 11 (May, 1974), pp. 121–127; and Paul E. Green and Yoram Wind, "New Ways to Measure Consumers' Judgments," *Harvard Business Review,* 53 (July–August, 1975), pp. 107–117.

26. For a full description of multidimensional-scaling applications in marketing, see Paul E. Green and Frank J. Carmone, *Multidimensional Scaling and Related Techniques in Marketing Analysis* (Boston: Allyn and Bacon, 1970).

27. For a description of the PROFIT program, see *Ibid.,* pp. 58–59.

28. For a description of clustering techniques, see Green and Tull, *Research for Marketing Decisions, op. cit.,* Chapter 15.

29. For an example of the use of discriminant analysis to position brands, see Richard M. Johnson, "Market Segmentation: A Strategic Management Tool," *Journal of Marketing Research,* 8 (February, 1971), pp. 13–19.

30. For an example of the use of factor analysis to position products, see Henry Assael, "Perceptual Mapping to Reposition Brands," *Journal of Advertising Research,* 11 (February, 1971), pp. 39–42.

31. Yoram Wind, "A New Procedure for Concept Evaluation," *Journal of Marketing,* 37 (October, 1973), pp. 2–11.

32. Volney Stefflre, "Market Structure Studies," in F. M. Bass, C. W. King, and E. A. Pessemier, eds., *Applications of the Sciences in Marketing Management* (New York: John Wiley, 1968), pp. 251–268.

33. "Car Makers Use 'Image' Map as Tool to Position Products," *The Wall Street Journal* (March 22, 1984), p. 33.

34. *Ibid.*

35. *Ibid.*

36. Robert E. Wilkes, "Product Positioning by Multidimensional Scaling," *Journal of Advertising Research,* 17 (August, 1977), pp. 15–22.

37. Johnson, "Market Segmentation: A Strategic Tool," *loc. cit.*

38. "Drive to Revive Seven-Up Co. Opening," *The New York Times* (March 29, 1982), p. D1.

39. Michael Perry, Dov Izraeli, and Arnon Perry, "Image Change as a Result of Advertising," *Journal of Advertising Research,* 16 (February, 1976), pp. 45–50.

40. Reza Moinpour, James M. McCollough, and Douglas MacLachlan, "Time Changes in Perception: A Longitudinal Application of Multidimensional Scaling," *Journal of Marketing Research,* 13 (August, 1976), pp. 245–253.

41. Chem L. Narayana, "The Stability of Perceptions," *Journal of Advertising Research,* 16 (April, 1976), pp. 45–49.

42. Jack Trout, "Marketing in the '70s: Product Positioning," *Conference Board Record* (January, 1976), p. 42.

43. Philip Levine, "Commercials That Name Competing Brands," *Journal of Advertising Research,* 16 (December, 1976), pp. 7–16.

44. "Burger King Ads Cook Up a Storm," *Business Week* (October 11, 1982), p. 39.

45. "Kids Know 'Old Joe,'" *New York Newsday* (December 11, 1991); and "Camel's Success and Controversy," *The New York Times* (December 12, 1991), pp. D1, D17.

46. "New RJR Brand Under Fire," *Advertising Age* (February 19, 1990), pp. 1, 74.

PART IV

ENVIRONMENTAL INFLUENCES ON CONSUMER BEHAVIOR

CULTURE

FACE-TO-FACE GROUPS

SITUATIONAL DETERMINANTS

THE INDIVIDUAL CONSUMER

The focus in Part Four shifts from the individual consumer to the consumer's environment, the components of which can be viewed as an inverted pyramid. The broadest based environmental influences are considered first—the consumer's culture (including subcultural and cross-cultural influences). Then, the influences of face-to-face groups on purchase behavior are discussed, with particular emphasis on reference groups and the family. Finally, the purchase and usage situations are identified as environmental conditions that directly influence purchase behavior.

The strategic and societal implications of each of these environmental influences on consumer behavior are considered.

13

Cultural Influences

The broadest environmental factor affecting consumer behavior is *culture*, as reflected by the values and norms society emphasizes. Culture affects purchasing behavior because it is reflected in the values consumers learn from society—values such as individuality, independence, achievement, and self-fulfillment. Products and services such as Levi jeans, Coca-Cola, and McDonald's fast-food outlets have come to symbolize the individuality inherent in American values. This is one reason why East Germans quickly accepted Coke after the fall of the Berlin Wall.[1]

Cultural values are more enduring and deep-seated than the lifestyle values described previously in Chapter 11. For example, describing someone as a sports enthusiast reflects a component of his or her lifestyle. A more deep-seated cultural value that might drive one's interest in sports is the desire for an exciting life or for the self-fulfillment one might feel in being involved in a challenging sports activity. Because cultural values are enduring, attempts to change them have generally failed—for example, the attempt on the part of sterling silver manufacturers to revive the use of formal dinnerware in the face of a general cultural trend to informality.

As a result, marketers almost always attempt to swim with, rather than against, the cultural tide. One company that has successfully done so is McDonald's. In the early 1980s, the company's advertising theme, "McDonald's and You," reflected a "me" orientation; that is, a desire to avoid self-sacrifice and to live for today. By the mid-1980s, there was a general shift to a "we" orientation as reflected in a more traditional focus on family values. McDonald's advertising shifted accordingly by moving from the focus on the individual consumer to family-oriented themes. Its campaign centering on the theme "It's a Good Time for the Great Taste of McDonald's" was effective in communicating food and fun in the context of family values. The creation of the Ronald McDonald character and the introduction of kiddie playgrounds in many McDonald's outlets further strengthened the family image. The success of McDonald's strategy was confirmed by a study that found that people saw the company as friendly and nurturing. In contrast, its prime rival, Burger King, was described as aggressive, masculine, and distant.[2]

The deep recession in the early 1990s produced another cultural change and a parallel shift in McDonald's strategy. Many consumers became less optimistic about the future, more insecure about the traditional American dream, and more price sensitive—a trend we will refer to later in the chapter as the *new reality*. In 1991, McDonald's began instituting a series of price cuts, introduced numerous price promotions, and began emphasizing value as the dominant theme in its advertising. McDonald's also adapted to another cultural change: the increasing emphasis consumers are placing on environmental protection. In this case, the company had come under attack from consumer advocates regarding its plastic packaging and low-nutrition menus before it instituted change. In 1990, McDonald's eliminated polystyrene packages, switched from beef tallow to vegetable oil in preparing its hamburgers, and added bran muffins and low-fat yogurt to the menu.[3]

McDonald's has not only reflected American culture, but it has also influenced it. The golden arches is a symbol of fast foods, now a staple in American society. As the fast-food craze became global, the golden arches became a worldwide symbol.

In this chapter, we consider the nature of cultural values and how they are identified. We then discuss how culture influences consumer behavior, particularly through the role of product symbols and consumption rituals. Changes in cultural values in the 1990s are discussed. The chapter closes by considering societal issues that arise from the effects of cultural values on consumers.

◆ NATURE OF CULTURE

Culture is a set of socially acquired values that society accepts as a whole and transmits to its members through language and symbols. These societal values are likely to influence its members' purchases and consumption patterns. For example, one consumer may place a high value on achievement and may demonstrate success by symbols of luxury and prestige. Another consumer may have a culturally derived desire to appear young and active, may buy cosmetics that advertise a "younger look," and may enroll in an exercise program. In either case, the marketer must define the consumer's value orientation and determine the symbols that reflect these values.

Cross-Cultural and Subcultural Influences

The increasing importance of international trade in the 1990s makes it essential for marketers to understand the value systems of other cultures as well as their own. Such **cross-cultural influences** form the basis for marketing strategies abroad. Understanding that the greater emphasis on health and nutrition was not just an American phenomenon, Kellogg's correctly saw that appeals to health could change breakfast eating habits abroad, thus increasing demand for packaged cereals. On the other hand, Gerber failed to recognize that the strong emphasis on family values in Brazil would cause many mothers to reject processed baby foods. These mothers' attitude was that only they can prepare food for their babies.[4]

The determination of such societal values is essential in applying culture to marketing strategies. For example, it would be logical for a furniture manufacturer marketing abroad to determine the value consumers place on beauty, social recognition, and comfort in each country. The manufacturer would have to develop different product lines and marketing strategies for each market. If beauty is the dominant value, consumers would desire highly styled and pleasurable furniture. Advertising symbols for this market would appeal to integrity with the environment and to pleasure. A market that emphasizes social recognition would desire furniture that demonstrates status. The furniture might be richer in design, and advertising would use symbols oriented to acceptance in a social environment. Marketing to consumers that emphasizes comfort would require demonstrating product features in an informative campaign.

Not everyone in a particular country holds cultural values to the same degree. While values of comfort and social recognition are widely held in American society, differences in these values between groups provide marketers with a basis for developing different strategies within as well as across countries. Frequently, strategies are targeted to particular **subcultures;** that is, broad groups of consumers with similar values that distinguish them from society as a whole. Subcultures can be defined by age, region, religious affiliation, or ethnic identity. Older baby boomers might be considered a subculture because many of them experienced a shift in values from acquisitiveness to personal development. Many consumers in New England might constitute a subculture because they demonstrate traditional Yankee values of stubborn individualism. In a broad sense, African-American, Hispanic-American, and Asian-American consumers are subcultures because they demonstrate certain similarities in tastes and purchasing behavior.

We will be considering subcultural and cross-cultural influences in the next chapter. In this chapter, we focus on the effects of cultural values on consumer behavior in a given culture.

Cultural Values

Rokeach defined **cultural values** as beliefs that a general state of existence is personally and socially worth striving for.[5] Rokeach considered these cultural values as **terminal values** or goals to be attained and developed an 18-item inventory of these terminal values. (See Table 13.1.) Rokeach also defined another category of values, **instrumental values,** which are the means of achieving the desired goals. Values such as ambition, friendliness, logic, and

▶**TABLE 13.1**
Cultural values, consumption, specific values, and product attributes

Cultural (Terminal) Values	Consumption-Specific (Instrumental) Values	Product Attributes
A comfortable life	Prompt service	Service quality
An exciting life	Reliable advertising claims	Reliability
A world at peace	Responsiveness to consumer needs	Performance
Equality	Accurate information	Safety
Freedom	Elimination of pollution	Ease of use
Happiness	Free repair of defective products	Durability
National security	Convenient store locations	Economy
Pleasure	No deceptive advertising	Convenience
Salvation	Courteous and helpful salespeople	Styling
Self-respect	Low prices	
Social recognition	Solutions to urban decay and unemployment	
A world of beauty	Legislation to protect the consumer	
Wisdom	No product misrepresentation	
Family security		
Mature love		
Accomplishment		
Inner harmony		

SOURCES: Cultural values from Milton J. Rokeach, "The Role of Values in Public Opinion Research," PUBLIC OPINION QUARTERLY, 32 (Winter, 1968), p. 554; Consumption-specific values from Donald E. Vinson, Jerome E. Scott, and Lawrence M. Lamont, "The Role of Personal Values in Marketing and Consumer Behavior," JOURNAL OF MARKETING, 41 (April, 1977), p. 47. Reprinted with permission from the Journal of Marketing.

independence are guideposts for action to attain desired end states. They are not goals in and of themselves.

Applying Rokeach's classification to purchasing behavior, terminal values are the ultimate purchasing goals, and instrumental values are consumption-specific guidelines to attain these goals. We can go a step beyond consumption-specific values and also cite product attributes and benefits that can attain these values. Thus, in consumer behavior terms (1) product attributes are the means for attaining (2) consumption-specific (instrumental) values which are the vehicle for attaining (3) cultural (terminal) values. (See Table 13.1.)

Because culture is such an important influence on consumer behavior, marketers should consider wider use of inventories such as Rokeach's. However, few marketing studies have utilized cultural values as descriptors of consumer behavior. One reason for their limited use is that most marketing studies operate on a brand-by-brand basis. Cultural values are more likely to influence broad purchasing patterns, but it can be argued that a better understanding of the motivation behind brand purchases can be gained by understanding culturally derived purchasing values.

Characteristics of Cultural Values

Four characteristics are common to all cultural values:

1. *Cultural values are learned.*   Children are instilled with cultural values at an early age. The process of learning the values of one's own culture from childhood is known as **enculturation.** Learning the values of another culture is known as **acculturation.** Cultural learning can occur by *informal learning* (a foreigner copying local customs), by *formal learning* (a child taught by family members how to behave), and by *technical learning* (a child taught in a school environment). Enculturation takes place through a process of instilling values from key institutions, particularly the family, schools, and religious institutions. The family is particularly important since it is the vehicle for passing values from one generation to the next. Advertising also has a role in enculturating consumers through informal learning. The use of spokespersons (Michael Jordan for Nike sneakers) encourages consumers to imitate these role models or experts and to adopt certain products or styles.

The process of acculturation is particularly important for businesspeople in foreign markets, since an understanding of the local culture is necessary before they can develop product and advertising plans.

Hair and Anderson studied the process of acculturation among immigrants to America.[6] They found that consumers from developed countries were more quickly acculturated than were those from developing countries. One explanation is that the heritages and lifestyles of consumers from developed countries are closer to those of American consumers. Hair and Anderson also found that acculturation takes place faster for consumer behavior than it does for other forms of behavior. The reason is that material objects are integrated more easily into one's behavior than are more abstract, nonmaterial characteristics.[7]

2. *Cultural values are guides to behavior.*   Cultural values guide and direct an individual's behavior through the establishment of **cultural norms.** Such norms establish standards of behavior regarding proper social relations, means of ensuring safety, eating habits, and so forth. If behavior deviates from the cultural norm, society may place sanctions or restrictions on behavior.

3. *Cultural values are both permanent and dynamic.*   Cultural values gain permanence as parents pass them on to children. Schools and religious groups also are important in maintaining the permanence of cultural values. The emphasis on values such as freedom, self-respect, and individuality has not changed substantially over time in the United States. However, culture is also dynamic; values must change as society changes. Basic changes in values have taken place in the American culture during the past 40 years. The Depression, wars, and economic dislocation have drastically changed traditional values such as the work ethic, materialism, and respect for authority figures.

A research service that tracks changes in cultural values called *The Monitor Service* found some important differences in values between the 1980s and 1990s, largely as a result of the deep recession in the early 1990s.[8] The service found the following changes:

1980s	1990s
Belief in the American dream	A new reality
Live to work	Work to live
Be a winner	Do not be a loser
Family, religion	New alternatives
Home as a cocoon	Home as a resource center
Control the environment	Manage the environment
Control technology	Adapt to technology
Conspicuous consumption	Prudent purchasing

These are important societal changes that we explore later in the chapter. They are rich in their strategic implications. For example, the greater pessimism regarding the future embodied in the "new reality" suggests that many luxury goods may be on the decline in a more austere 1990s environment. Further, the change in the perspective of the home from a focus on love and nurturing to a resource center for work and entertainment is intriguing. It reflects the extension of work from home to office with the use of cellular phones and fax machines (see the Fujitsu ad for fax machines in Exhibit 11.7), as well as an increasing proportion of consumers who work at home full-time based on this flexible technology.

4. *Cultural values are widely held.*   Each culture has certain widely held and commonly accepted values that differentiate it from other cultures. Individuality and youthfulness are widely shared values in the United States, whereas conformity to the group and respect for the aged are widely shared values in many Asian countries.

The sharing of values is facilitated by a common language. In multilingual countries such as Canada, India, and the Soviet Union, the lack of a single cultural bond through language has led to divisiveness. In the United States, the mass media have facilitated the sharing of cultural norms. When two out of three households with television sets view a particular program at the same time, they must share values. As one writer stated shortly after TV ownership became widespread, "Advertising now compares with such long-standing institutions as the schools and the church in the magnitude of its social influence."[9]

Traditional American Values

Four widely held traditional values in American society are materialism, individualism, youthfulness, and a work ethic.

Materialism

Materialism, a reflection of the accumulation of wealth and objects, is manifested in two ways. One is the attainment of goods to achieve a desired goal— for example, buying a new computer to increase storage capacity and speed or acquiring a cellular telephone to provide mobile communications. Using Rokeach's classification, this is known as *instrumental materialism* since the acquisition of such goods is instrumental in attaining cultural values. A second manifestation of materialism is owning items for their own sake. This is known as *terminal materialism* because the acquisition of such goods is directly motivated by cultural values rather than by some intermediate goal. Buying a piece of jewelry for its beauty or acquiring an automobile for its status, rather than its functional benefits, would be examples of terminal materialism. The ad for Florsheim in Exhibit 13.1 is an example of instrumental materialism—clothing as a means to gain success. The ad for Gucci is an example of terminal materialism—the ownership of a product for its own sake. The Gucci ad shows that appeals to terminal materialism are often aimed at status and luxury.

Materialism is a dominant value in most advanced economies—North America, Europe, Japan. Advertising appeals in the United States tend to focus more on instrumental materialism—products as a means of attaining goals. Appeals to terminal materialism are more frequent in Western Europe (the Gucci ad, for example) and Japan, possibly because of a greater focus on status and upward social mobility in these regions as compared to American society.

Materialism is not a dominant value worldwide. Some segments of society promote spiritual as opposed to material values, even to the extent of encouraging members to renounce worldly wealth. Communist countries tried to discourage materialism in favor of sacrifice for the state and acceptance of communal values. The current popularity of Western goods in these countries demonstrates the power of materialistic values.

▶**EXHIBIT 13.1**
Examples of instrumental and terminal materialism
Source: (left) Courtesy of Florsheim Shoe Co.; (right) Courtesy of Gucci

Instrumental values

Terminal values

Individualism

American society tends to favor individual initiative, often at the expense of conformity to group goals. Themes focusing on individualism and "standing apart from the crowd" are often seen in advertising. The Marlboro Cowboy is a typical manifestation of this individualism. The Gap ad in Exhibit 13.2 is a good example of an appeal to individualism. The person shown in the ad can express his individualism as an artist, a caring father, and through the clothes he wears.

In Japan there is a greater desire to subjugate individuality in favor of group and societal conformity. Such themes as "McDonald's and *You*" would not reflect this dominant value. But recent evidence suggests that the traditional Japanese value system is changing among the young who have a greater desire for American-made goods. For example, L.L. Bean's first retail store outside of its home base in Maine opened in Japan in 1992. Bean's outdoor look is strongly identified with American individualism.[10]

▶**EXHIBIT 13.2**
An appeal to the
American consumer's
individualism

CHARLES ARNOLDI, artist,
with son RYLAND in GapKids jeans, $26.
Photographed by Herb Ritts.

Youthfulness

Most Americans are preoccupied with trying to look and act young, regardless of their age. As we saw in Chapter 10, advertising to the mature market has tried to portray older Americans as active, vital, and younger looking than their age. Advertising to baby boomers is also focused on maintaining their youth through face creams, moisturizers, exercise machines, and health clubs.

This penchant for youthfulness is not universal. In Asian countries, the aged are more revered than they are in the United States. Whereas in the United States, youth dominates almost all ads, in Asian countries, the elderly are portrayed more frequently and with greater respect. An elderly spokesperson is more likely to be accepted in these countries as an expert or a role model.

Work Ethic

A work ethic has been a traditional value in American society as a means of personal achievement and attainment of material rewards. Advertisers often seek to promote their products as a reward for work. McDonald's former theme, "You Deserve a Break Today," is an example.

The Monitor Service suggests that the nature of the work ethic in American society may be changing. The "live to work" orientation of the 1980s meant that people saw work as its own reward, a means of personal achievement and self-gratification. However, the demise of the "booming '80s" and the severe recession in the early '90s promoted a skepticism that has been translated into people's viewing work as a means of acquiring the necessities of life ("work to live"). This means the *ethic* behind work has changed. Rather than being a terminal goal (work is rewarding), work has become an instrumental goal (work is a means of getting what I want).

Japan has also accepted a work ethic as a traditional value. Interestingly, it seems to be experiencing the same shift to a view of work as a means to an end rather than as an end in itself. One aspect of the desire for L.L. Bean clothes among younger Japanese consumers is to look more relaxed and casual as a manifestation of this trend.

Other Core Values

Other core values in the United States are progress, freedom, and activity. *Progress* is reflected in people's belief in technology and continued improvement in the standard of living. Here again, *The Monitor Survey* suggests that the belief in progress might have been partially undermined by greater skepticism in the economy. In addition, in the post-cold war period, America's role as the leader of the free world is no longer as compelling. As a result, many consumers no longer see economic progress as a necessary outgrowth of America's world leadership.

Freedom is another traditional American value that is reflected in people's ideals of equality and freedom of expression for all. In marketing terms, this value has been translated into the consumer rights described in Chapter 2: the right to choose, the right to be informed, the right to be heard, and the right to safety.

Activity—that is, the importance Americans attach to being physically active—is another traditional value probably having its genesis in the establishment of frontier farming communities in colonial times. This value seems to have been transformed in an urban setting into a hectic lifestyle that many societies regard as peculiar to American culture. The "grazing" phenomenon cited in Chapter 11 and the popularity of fast-food chains are means of facilitating an active lifestyle.

Identifying Cultural Values

The changes in American values between the 1980s and 1990s demonstrate the need to identify cultural values over time. Researchers have used several methods to track cultural values, namely (1) cultural value inventories such as Rokeach's classification, (2) research services such as *The Monitor Service*, (3) observation through field studies, and (4) content analysis of a society's literature and media.

Cultural Inventories

Researchers develop cultural value inventories by studying a particular culture, identifying its values, and then determining whether these values are widely held. The best-known inventory is the *Rokeach Value Survey*. The cultural values identified by the survey are based on a study of American culture and are in the left-hand column in Table 13.1.

Kahle, Beatty, and Homer developed another widely used cultural inventory, the *List of Values (LOV)*.[11] LOV was developed as an alternative to Rokeach's value inventory because the terminal values identified by Rokeach were too abstract and difficult to apply to marketing situations. The LOV inventory measures nine values:

1. Self-fulfillment.
2. Excitement.
3. Sense of accomplishment.
4. Self-respect.
5. Sense of belonging.
6. Being well-respected.
7. Security.
8. Fun and enjoyment.
9. Warm relationships with others.

A study by Homer and Kahle, which utilized the LOV scale, found that purchasers of natural foods are more likely to emphasize self-fulfillment, excitement, and accomplishment.[12] These values reflect a desire to control one's life as reflected in an emphasis on health and nutrition. Consumers who emphasized belonging and security were least likely to buy natural foods because they were more likely to let others control their lives.

Research Services

In an attempt to identify changes in cultural values, several research services conduct periodic surveys of consumers. *VALS 2*, discussed in Chapter 11, identifies values as well as lifestyles. Categories such as actualizers, achievers, and strivers not only reflect a particular lifestyle, but they also suggest the terminal values driving these groups.

For example, family security is most important to makers, social recognition to strivers, and accomplishment to achievers. These end state values are manifested in the lifestyles described for each group in the previous chapter.

Like VALS, *The Monitor Service* interviews 2,500 randomly selected respondents every year in order to determine changes in values measured by a series of multiple-choice questions.[13] *The Monitor Service* was one of the first to identify the "me" orientation in the early 1980s and a more conservative trend resulting in a shift to a "we" orientation in the mid-1980s. It also identified the greater concern with environmental protection starting in the 1980s.

Over 115 companies have subscribed to the service, including Kraft-General Foods, General Electric, and CBS.[14] The trends found in Monitor surveys have direct implications for these companies. For example, General Electric could cite the greater value placed on beauty in the home and concern about the environment (two trends that Monitor identified) to produce more stylish yet energy-efficient appliances. CBS could consider two other trends identified by the service—toward personal creativity and physical fitness—to justify daytime TV programming aimed at self-improvement (cooking, exercise, and art programs, for example).

Observation and Field Studies

Both research services and cultural inventories rely on surveys of consumers to determine cultural values. Marketers also rely on qualitative analysis to assess the impact of culture on consumer behavior. The most important qualitative technique—observation—is borrowed from cultural anthropology. Anthropologists determine cultural values through field studies in which they live with a group or a family in a culture and observe their customs and behavior. The study of culture by observation is known as **ethnography.** Marketing researchers are not likely to spend months living with a single group or family to study its purchasing behavior. Rather, they utilize the observational techniques of anthropologists by observing consumers in their natural environment (consuming at home or shopping in a store) on a short-term basis. The purpose is to understand the role of the product in a cultural context.

An observational study of chocolate lovers found that many keep secret stashes of chocolate around the house—in freezers, on top of china cabinets, under sofas—and are embarrassed to admit it. This discovery led to a campaign based on the theme "The true confessions of chocolaholics."[15] Similarly, a field study for the U.S. Postal Service found that consumers in rural areas see the letter carrier as a contact with society. As a result, a campaign was introduced in 1992 with the theme "We deliver for you." (See Exhibit 13.3 for a segment of the TV ad.)[16]

A more extensive application of an ethnographic field survey is illustrated in a study by Belk, Sherry, and Wallendorf of the behavior of buyers and sellers

▶**EXHIBIT 13.3**
An advertising campaign based on field studies

SPONSORED BY THE U.S. POSTAL SERVICE

at swap meets.[17] Swap meets are markets in which buyers and sellers exchange goods for other goods or for money. A swap meet is distinct from a flea market in that downscale consumers generally frequent swap meets and barter is the more prevalent mode of exchange. The researchers used both observation and open-ended qualitative interviews to try to develop an understanding of the participants' value system and the cultural underpinnings of swap meets.

In studying one swap meet, Belk *et al.* concluded that freedom is an important motivation for buyers and sellers. Participants enjoy being free from the institutional constraints of buying in retail stores, yet accept the social order inherent in swap meets such as establishing and running stalls, adhering to opening and closing times, and following certain rules such as not allowing dogs. The researchers also found that male-female roles were sharply defined, with men responsible for setting up booths and displays and women acting as clerks and salespersons. Other findings related to the mutual values participants held, the nature of bargaining, and the symbolism associated with what is bought and sold.[18]

The use of such field studies in marketing is rare. However, applications of ethnographic techniques are increasing as behavioral researchers seek broader explanations of consumer behavior tied to cultural values.

Content Analysis

Whereas the techniques described above measure cultural values consumers hold, content analysis measures these values as they are reflected in a culture's media and literature. Researchers employing content analysis review a culture's literature and mass communications to identify repetitive themes. In his famous study, McClellan identified the degree to which cultures were motivated by achievement by conducting a content analysis of the themes in children's stories.[19]

Belk applied content analysis to investigate how materialistic values are portrayed in comic books. Wealthy characters were portrayed ambivalently. On the one hand, some were portrayed as selfless and honest, while others were portrayed as spendthrifts. Overall, Belk concluded that these portrayals had a positive socializing influence on children by holding the work ethic in high esteem.[20] Content analyses have also been performed to determine whether the portrayal of African-Americans and females in advertising is an accurate reflection of their role in society.

◆ CULTURAL VALUES AND CONSUMER BEHAVIOR

As we have seen, marketing strategies generally attempt to reflect, rather than change, the core cultural values of American society. Rokeach's classification of values (Table 13.1) best illustrates the role of cultural values in influencing consumer behavior. Figure 13.1 portrays the interface between culture and consumer behavior illustrated by the Table. The figure shows that:

1. Product attributes and benefits are generally a reflection of cultural (terminal) values.
2. These product attributes and benefits are the vehicle for achieving consumption-specific goals.
3. These consumption-specific goals are instrumental in attaining cultural values.

Means-End Chain

Gutman has described the interface in Figure 13.1 as a **means-end chain** in that the means (product attributes) are the vehicle for attaining cultural values (the ends) with consumption goals as an intermediary between them.[21] Gutman's conceptualization relies on two theories. First is Rokeach's distinction between terminal and instrumental values, reflected in Gutman's cultural (terminal) values and consumption (instrumental) goals. Gutman makes Rokeach's conceptualization more applicable to marketing by adding another factor, product attributes, as a means of attaining consumption goals.

The second theory underlying the means-end chain in Figure 13.1 is Rosenberg's **expectancy-value theory.**[22] Rosenberg posits that consumers will evaluate products based on the degree to which they are instrumental in achieving cultural values. Consumers evaluate the projected consequences of their actions and will buy products that achieve the desired consequence. Thus, a consumer who values a world of beauty (a terminal value) will favor product attributes such as biodegradability because the consequence of buying a biodegradable product is to help preserve the environment. Applying Rosenberg's theory, the means-end chain leading to the purchase of the product is:

- Product attribute: Biodegradability.
- Consumption consequence: Helping to preserve the environment.
- Cultural (terminal) value: A world of beauty.

FIGURE 13.1
The Culture-Consumer
Behavior Interface

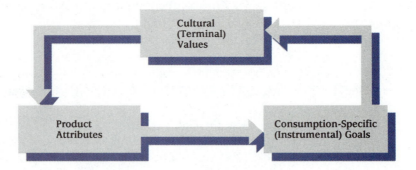

In short, the theories of Gutman, Rokeach, and Rosenberg all reflect the means-end chain in Figure 13.1, leading to the attainment of cultural (terminal) values through product attributes and consumption goals.

Laddering

Reynolds and Johnson applied the means-end chain to the development of marketing strategies through a process they called **laddering**.[23] Laddering involves a series of consumer interviews to determine the links among product attributes, consumption goals, and cultural values. Consumers are "helped up the ladder" through a series of probes that start with concrete product attributes and then uncover more abstract consumption goals and even more abstract cultural values. As an example, a consumer might state a preference for a flavored potato chip with a strong taste. Probes show that she favors these attributes because they cause her to eat less which results in her losing weight and looking better (consumption goal). This results in greater self-esteem (a terminal value).

Marketers can then use the three components of the means-end chain in the ladder to develop marketing strategy as follows:[24]

1. *Message elements:* The specific product attributes to be communicated in advertising. In the above example, advertising would focus on flavor and taste as key elements.
2. *Consumer benefits:* The positive consumption consequences of using the product. The key requirement in the above example is to link the product attributes of flavor and taste to the benefit of weight control.
3. *Leverage point:* The way advertising attempts to associate the attributes and benefits to the terminal values and to activate them. The executional requirement in the advertising is to show that weight loss as a result of product consumption creates greater self-esteem. This can be done by portraying self-confident and attractive consumers in the advertising or by showing greater peer group acceptance as a result of product usage.

Once the marketer develops advertising, it is evaluated based on its ability to climb up the means-end ladder from message element to consumer benefit to leverage point.

In the next two sections, we consider the two main cultural interfaces in Figure 13.1—the impact of culture on the product and on consumption.

◆ CULTURE AND PRODUCTS

Products and services are a reflection of our culture, and their cultural meaning is often expressed in symbolic form. As we saw in Chapter 3, consumers frequently buy products for their symbolism rather than for their utility.

Laddering was applied to the development of advertising strategies for Federal Express by generating a detailed means-end map of the value secretaries placed on overnight delivery. (See Figure 13.2.) Specific attributes such as reliability and on-time delivery were associated with positive goals resulting from the use of overnight delivery services such as to get promoted or to avoid looking bad. In turn, these goals led to terminal values such as peace of mind, in control, and self-esteem.

The three means-end chains shown in Figure 13.2 represent three segments in the overnight delivery market emphasizing different attributes, consequences, or terminal values. One segment values peace of mind and being in control of the office. The other two emphasize self-esteem and accomplishment but through different consumption benefits and product attributes. The left-hand chain suggests that these terminal values can be attained through the intermediate consumption goals of doing more and saving time and through the availability of a drop box for convenience (product attributes). The middle chain shows that self-esteem and accomplishment are attainable through the consumption goals of making more money and getting promoted and through product attributes based on reliability and on-time delivery.

Before the study was performed, Federal Express used a humorous approach that demonstrated the problems with relying on competitive services. The attributes emphasized were reliability and on-time delivery, and the consumption benefits were less worry and avoid looking bad to the boss. The message was targeted to the right-hand segment in Figure 13.2, but the message was not being translated into positive terminal values. Federal Express needed to differentiate itself from competitors by focusing on its strengths rather than on competitors' weaknesses. Further, management wanted to ensure that competition could not dominate any such point of differentiation.

Federal Express's unique point of differentiation was its satellite communications system to ensure reliability and on-time delivery. The company developed a new advertising campaign that kept the humorous execution while focusing on the satellite communication system. It emphasized the superiority of the tracking system (product attribute) in ensuring reliability and making work easier (consumption benefits). Most important, an evaluation of the campaign found that it did reach the top of the ladder by translating consumption benefits to terminal values. Secretaries saw Fedex's services as a means of being in control and attaining peace of mind.

Source: Thomas J. Reynolds and Alyce Byrd Craddock, "The Application of the Meccas Model to the Development and Assessment of Advertising Strategy: A Case Study," *Journal of Advertising Research,* 28 (April/May, 1988), pp. 43-54.

▶FIGURE 13.2

A means-end ladder for overnight delivery services

Source: Thomas J. Reynolds and Alyce Byrd Craddock, "The Application of the Meccas Model to the Development and Assessment of Advertising Strategy," *Journal of Advertising Research,* (April/May, 1988), p. 45.

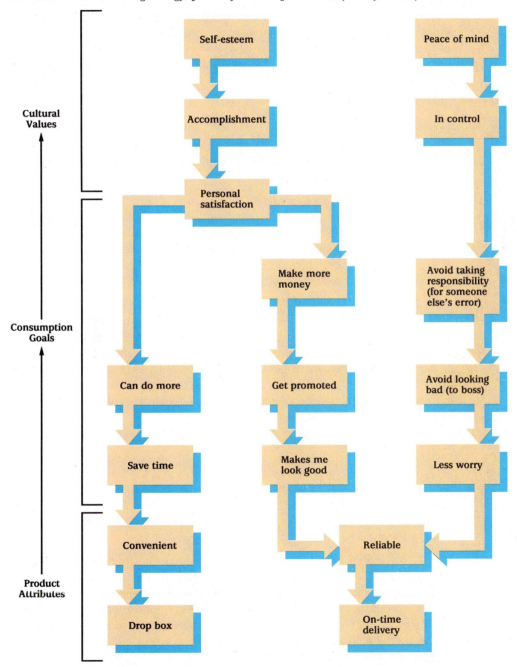

Marketers try to establish symbols that equate the product with positive cultural values. McDonald's golden arches are meant to be a reflection of fun and family values; the Marlboro Cowboy is a portrayal of rugged individualism and independence; the Mercedes emblem is meant to portray status and security.

A symbol sometimes takes on a meaning of its own beyond its association with the product and comes to represent the culture. McDonald's golden arches, Levi jeans, and the Coca-Cola logo have become symbols of Western culture. Before the fall of Communism, youths in Eastern Europe valued Levi jeans as a representation of Western culture and independence. Wearing Levis was a safe way to protest against a police state.

Role of Product Symbolism

Tharp and Scott have identified five symbolic roles of products that reflect cultural values:[25]

1. *Products are a means of communicating social status.*   As we saw in Chapter 10, "Demographics and Social Class," products often connote a consumer's status in society. Symbols of status may be a Gucci scarf, a Mercedes car, or a Rolex watch. In the inner cities, an equally important symbol of status might be a pair of Air Jordan sneakers. Marketers try to establish their products as symbols of prestige, whether aiming at affluent business executives or inner-city kids.

2. *Products are a means of self-expression.*   As such, products reflect the values that are most important to consumers. Marketers try to associate their products with symbols of achievement, individualism, or personal development. The ad in Exhibit 13.4 links Pepe Jeans to an old, folded poster of James Dean (or a current lookalike). The attempt is to associate the product with a cultural icon and, thus, to express youth, freedom, and individualism, important values for the baby busters the ad is targeted to.

3. *Products are a means of sharing experiences.*   Products often provide a basis for sharing experiences. Food and drink on social occasions, flowers for happy or sad events, and gifts are all a means of sharing social events. In this respect, products have an important symbolic role since the nature of the product defines the occasion. Serving beer or wine at a party, sending roses or carnations for a special occasion, or giving a pen or a piece of jewelry as a graduation present all have very different meanings.

4. *Products are hedonic.*   That is, they often have aesthetic or sensual qualities that give the consumer pleasure. Examples might be jewelry, perfume, foods, clothing, furniture, and works of art. The emphasis on the hedonic, as opposed to utilitarian, qualities of a product reflect consumers' values. Various cultures might tend to emphasize one or the other. The French fashion industry has traditionally placed more emphasis on the hedonic value of clothing, whereas American styles are more likely to emphasize the utilitarian.

5. *Products are experiential.* That is, they remind consumers of past experiences. On a personal level, an engagement ring is experiential as is an old photo album or a record or CD that triggers memories of past events. Marketers sometimes attempt to project the experiential value of products. The ad in Exhibit 13.5 is an example. The theme "A diamond is forever" projects the experiential value of an engagement ring far in the future.

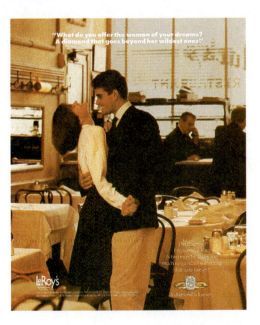

Semiotics

Semiotics is the study of the meaning of signs and symbols. To understand how people derive meaning from symbols, researchers must understand the shared meaning of various signs in a culture. For example, when Lever introduced a new fabric softener with the symbol of a huggable teddy bear named Snuggle, it used semiotics to evaluate the symbolism of a bear. It found that the bear connotes aggression, but a teddy bear is seen as a softer and nurturing side of that aggression. The teddy bear is a logical symbol of tamed aggression and a good representation of a fabric softener that tames rough clothing.[26]

Such a semiotic analysis is based on three components as seen in Figure 13.3: a sign (the symbol of a teddy bear), an object (Snuggle), and an interpretant (the consumer interpreting the symbol.)[27] This figure represents the same interface between culture and consumer behavior in Figure 13.1. Lever's analysis showed that the symbolism of the teddy bear was instrumental in attaining a terminal value (controling nature) through a consumption goal (softening rough clothes) based on Snuggle's product attributes.

Because it demonstrates the different meanings various cultures place on the same signs and symbols, semiotics is an important tool in cross-cultural analysis. For example, in American society, animals are accepted as symbols of speed (jaguar) and freedom (eagle). However, in many Asian countries, animal symbolism is rejected since animals are seen as a lower life form.

Products as Fantasies and Myths

Marketers sometimes establish product symbols in the form of fantasies and myths to better link the product to cultural values. The ad for Hermes in Exhibit 13.6 is an example of the use of fantasy. The symbolism of a woman wearing a Hermes scarf in the desert is meant to convey both luxury and fantasy.

Myths are stories or character representations in fantasy form that attempt to portray cultural values. The Maytag repairman who waits by the phone that never rings is a mythical character designed to communicate dependability. The

▶**FIGURE 13.3**

The components of semiotic analysis

Source: Adapted from David Glen Mick, "Consumer Research and Semiotics: Exploring the Morphology of Signs, Symbols, and Significance," *Journal of Consumer Research,* 13 (September, 1986), p. 198. Reprinted with permission from The University of Chicago Press.

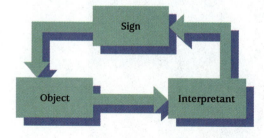

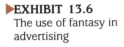

EXHIBIT 13.6
The use of fantasy in
advertising

Marlboro Cowboy is also a mythical character, a symbol of America's pioneering spirit.

Marketers also create mythologies around places. Pepperidge Farm's advertising takes us back to a time of farming communities and old-fashioned values. Similarly, advertising for Maxwell House 1892 coffee creates a mythology of a less-harried time when coffee tasted better.[28]

◆ CULTURE AND CONSUMPTION

Culture not only influences the way products are portrayed; it also influences the way they are consumed. In particular, culture is important in defining the ritualistic role of consumption for many product categories.

Consumption Rituals

A **ritual** is a series of symbolic behaviors that occur in sequence and are repeated frequently.[29] *Grooming* is a ritual for most people since it involves a series of behaviors (showering, brushing teeth, using deodorants, brushing hair) that occur in sequence and are repeated frequently. Marketers will try to link their products to these rituals—for example, brush your teeth twice a day or shampoo frequently.

Gift-giving is also a ritual that requires a sequence of events; namely, acquiring a gift, exchanging gifts, and then evaluating the receiver's reaction. The exchange of gifts, the types of gifts exchanged, and the occasions are all fairly well prescribed in our society. Some industries rely primarily on gift-giving for sales. Gift-giving at Christmas alone represents close to $40 billion in sales and is a substantial portion of yearly business for most retailers.

Holidays also involve ritual behavior in addition to gift-giving rituals. Christmas rituals prescribe the consumption of special foods and drink. Holidays may also involve vacation rituals such as going to the same vacation spot and being involved in the same activities every year.

Each of these types of ritual behavior has three things in common. First, they involve **ritual artifacts,** often in the form of consumer products. Colored lights, mistletoe, wreaths, and Santa Claus representations are all artifacts associated with Christmas rituals. Second, rituals involve a **script** that prescribes how, when, and by whom products will be used. The use of the ring, cake, and photographs at weddings is fairly well scripted by society, for example. Third, rituals require that **performance roles** be prescribed for certain individuals.[30] The roles of the bride, groom, best man, and bridesmaids are all well-defined at weddings.

Marketers try to promote their products as artifacts in the process of ritual consumption. The ad in Exhibit 13.5 portrays a diamond ring as an artifact in a pre-wedding ritual, the engagement. Marketers can also portray the sequence of behaviors in rituals. An ad for Lubriderm lotion shows a brushing, cleaning, and moisturizing sequence in portraying a grooming ritual.

Sacred and Secular Consumption

Culture also influences the way goods are consumed. An important distinction in this respect is between sacred and secular consumption.[31] **Sacred consumption** is the consumption of goods that promote beauty, the preservation of nature, and cooperation. Consumers who seek the sacred aspects of consumption are attracted to natural imagery and appeals to family ties. They favor food products with natural ingredients and fashions with simple styles.

Hirschman cites several campaigns that reflect such a sacred orientation to consumption as follows:[32]

- *Gallo wines.* Accompanied by soft music, the opening visuals show the homecomings of family members for Christmas. Imagery includes snow on evergreens, wooden porches, red plaid flannel shirts, and down jackets. The gathered, multigenerational family sits at a wooden table bedecked with a turkey, yams, bread, and bottles of wine.
- *Tropicana Orange Juice.* A young woman, dressed in jeans and a cotton shirt, stands in an orange grove. She recalls eating oranges from her father's grove as a young girl. Her hands and face would get sticky from the sweet, delicious juice; and her mother would help her wash up when she returned home. [The announcer says] "Tropicana is natural and pure, just the way the rain and sun make it . . . It comes fresh from nature, without any artificial additives."

Secular consumption is the consumption of goods that promote technology, the conquest of nature, and competition. Consumers who seek the secular aspects of consumption are attracted to products that improve control over one's life.

Hirschman also cites several campaigns that reflect such a secular orientation to consumption:[33]

- *Static Guard.* A woman enters a restaurant in an elegant dress. When she removes her coat, static cling (an undesirable natural event) causes the dress to rumple unbecomingly. She is embarrassed. A technological product (Static Guard) is sprayed upon the offending natural phenomenon and conquers it.
- *Oil of Olay.* An attractive brunette woman states, "I don't intend to grow old gracefully. I intend to fight it every step of the way. I'm going to be 40 and wonderful." The announcer states, "Oil of Olay beauty fluid helps to replenish the fluids your skin loses with time."

The two ads reflecting sacred consumption emphasize natural food, natural settings, a rural environment, and family. Implicitly, nature is viewed as nurturing and life-giving. The two ads reflecting secular consumption emphasize control over nature through the use of manufactured products—in one case, to overcome an unwanted event; in another, to conquer aging. Here, nature is viewed as potentially harmful and the focus is on controling it.

Depending on the values they wish to convey through the product or service, marketers will emphasize the sacred or the secular. Both Gallo and Tropicana use sacred imagery because they want to convey the natural aspects of their products. Static Guard and Oil of Olay use secular imagery because they want to portray their products as vehicles for controling nature.

The two Kodak ads in Exhibit 13.7 reflect the same dichotomy. The ad for Gold Ultra 400 emphasizes the sacred by showing some heartwarming and intimate pictures of a child. The ad emphasizes values of beauty, nature, and family. In contrast, the ad for Kodak copiers emphasizes the secular by focusing on performance and service. The purpose is to portray Kodak copiers as a means of gaining a competitive edge through mastery over the business environment.

◆ CHANGES IN CULTURAL VALUES IN THE 1990s

Several significant and interrelated changes occurred in the American consumer's value system from the 1980s to the 1990s. One, cited above, is a *new reality* about the limits of prosperity and the attainment of the American Dream. This change occurred largely as a result of the severe recession in the early 1990s and a decline in American economic and political leadership in the post-cold war world.

▶**EXHIBIT 13.7**
Kodak ads reflecting the sacred and secular dimensions of consumption

Three other changes started in the mid-1980s and have carried into the 1990s. They are:

1. Greater traditionalism, as reflected in a shift in focus from a "me" to a "we" orientation.
2. More emphasis on self-fulfillment.
3. Emergence of a new materialism.

New Reality

The new reality has had a profound effect on American consumers and their spending patterns. Many have come to realize that there are limits to growth in the American economy and that these limits translate into restricted future purchasing potential. As a result, consumers have become more price-conscious and value-oriented. As we have seen in previous chapters, consumers are less likely to be brand loyal and more likely to buy lower-priced private brands and to comparison shop. A major change in buying motives is from *prestige* to *value*. Purchasing based on status is out; purchasing based on quality and performance is in.

The Monitor Service identified several dimensions of the new reality. One is a decline in commitment to organizational values and a greater willingness to explore other options. Despite the risks, starting one's own business or free-lancing has gained new legitimacy as an alternate course to climbing the orga-nizational ladder. As a result, the home is increasingly viewed as a work as well as a family center. Another dimension is a more constrained view of technol-ogy and the environment. People have shifted from a strong belief in technol-ogy and science as a means of conquering the environment to a belief in tech-nology as a means of managing and preserving the environment. A manifestation of this shift is the greater emphasis consumers place on envi-ronmental protection.

This more sober consumer view is likely to continue to the turn of the cen-tury. Marketers have already adjusted by placing more focus on quality mer-chandise at lower prices. The acronym EDLP—everyday low prices—reflects a more common marketing strategy. These changes reflect not only an economic shift, but also a more basic shift in cultural values from achievement to secu-rity and from environmental control to environmental management.

Greater Traditionalism

The shift to traditionalism represents a greater emphasis on family and patri-otic values. Until the mid-1980s, a "me" orientation was fairly pervasive, espe-cially among baby boomers and the youth segment. It reflected a need to live life "my way" and a fierce desire to live for today without concern for the more restrictive values that society or family might impose. The "me" orientation was a reaction to the self-sacrifice imposed on Americans by the Vietnam War, the disillusion brought on by Watergate, and subsequent economic dislocations. It started in the early 1970s, gained momentum through the early 1980s, and then began to wane by the end of the '80s as many consumers began to de-emphasize self-gratification.

The shift to a "we" orientation is reflected in a more traditional focus on family values, patriotism, and the work ethic. As evidence of this shift, a study of baby boomers found that 69 percent said they are more family-oriented than they thought they would be when they were younger.[34] Why this greater tra-ditionalism? As we saw in Chapter 11, baby boomers have shifted away from the drive for affluence to a greater focus on personal development. An impor-tant component of personal development is the need to balance the compet-ing demands of work, home, and recreational pursuits.

Two broad groups share a greater emphasis on traditionalism. The *new tra-ditionalists* integrate family values with the new-age lifestyles reflected in the focus on personal development and self-actualization. *Old traditionalists* subscribe to traditional beliefs without acceptance of new lifestyles. Marketers have captured this old traditionalism by focusing on patriotic appeals such as Chevrolet's "Heartbeat of America," Miller's "Made the American Way," and Wal-Mart's "Buy American."

The two ads in Exhibit 13.8 reflect the new and the old traditionalism. The ad for the Ford Audio System emphasizes family togetherness, but in the context of a lifestyle that sees "life as more of an adventure than a routine." The ad for Haggar slacks epitomizes the "old" traditionalism, with a family portrayed in front of a church and the tag line "A feel for America."

Emphasis on Self-Fulfillment

A greater emphasis on self-fulfillment might seem to reflect more of an emphasis on "me" than "we," but the trend does not contradict the new traditionalism. As we noted, during the 1980s, many young people found that the self-indulgence of a "me" orientation was not sufficient. They sought a deeper satisfaction in their day-to-day lives. As a result, they redefined their priorities

▶**EXHIBIT 13.8**

Ads that appeal to new traditionalists and old traditionalists

Source: (left) Courtesy of Ford Motor Co.; (right) Courtesy of Haggar Apparel

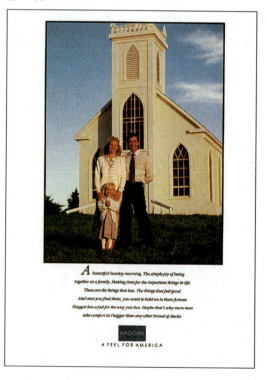

by reducing the importance of money and increasing the importance of personal self-enhancement and meaningful work. They sought several new dimensions in their lives:

- Physical fitness and well-being.
- Personal creativity as expressed through a wide variety of activities, hobbies, and other personal expressions of fulfillment.
- Cultural self-expression; that is, the wish to acquire more cultivation, knowledge, and appreciation of cultural topics.[35]

This focus on self does not mean that an individual cannot also obtain satisfaction from larger social units such as the family, community, or country. In fact, the new traditionalism suggests the desire to combine self-fulfillment with family values.

New Materialism

Greater emphasis on self-fulfillment might suggest a decrease in the traditional focus on materialism in American society, but this is not the case. The United States remains a materialistic, consumption-driven society. However, the nature of materialism has changed. In the past, affluence was desired as a means of enhancing one's social status through "conspicuous consumption." Today, the emphasis on wealth as a means of status is not as important. Wealth is seen as a means of expressing individualism rather than group conformity. As one writer noted, "[Consumers] are becoming more individualistic and are less defined by traditional social groupings. . . . For example, a consumer may drive a $40,000 luxury automobile and buy gasoline from a self-serve discounter. Another may buy designer suits from an exclusive retailer and $3 socks from a discount store."[36]

Affluence is seen not only as a means of expressing individualism, but also as a means of enhancing personal development. Booming expenditures on adult education, recreation, and travel reflect the focus on personal development. The ad for *Money* magazine in Exhibit 13.9 reflects the new materialism. The main theme is that "The rewards of Money" are the means to achieve family togetherness rather than higher social status.

◆ SOCIETAL IMPLICATIONS OF CULTURAL VALUES

Cultural values can have both positive and negative effects on society. The increasing value placed on the preservation of the environment will have positive consequences in protecting the limited natural resources of this planet for future generations. The shift in values reflected in the new reality in the 1990s is also likely to be positive in the long run. In putting more emphasis on value,

EXHIBIT 13.9

An ad depicting the new materialism

Source: Courtesy of Money Magazine

American consumers are becoming more efficient shoppers. Similarly, manu-facturers are learning to do more with less by increasing their productivity and decreasing costs. This has enabled them to deliver the value that consumers seek.

There are also negative consequences in the impact of cultural values on society. Materialism may increase our standard of living. However, it also encourages the accumulation of wealth and creation of a greater gap between the haves and have-nots. The emphasis on youthfulness may promote an active and vibrant society, but it also encourages society to ignore the needs of the aged. This problem will become magnified with the aging of the American pop-ulation into the next century. The emphasis on individualism may reflect Amer-ica's pioneering spirit, but it has also created barriers to teamwork. Such bar-riers put many American companies at a disadvantage in competing with more group-oriented Japanese corporations.

Cultural values may also produce undesirable consumption consequences. Consider addictive consumption. While drug and alcohol consumption are the most serious abuses, addictions develop for many other products. The negative consequences of addiction to cigarettes is now widely recognized, even among lifelong smokers. Addictions can also develop for more mundane products such as chocolates, diet sodas, and snack foods. Compulsive purchasing behavior can be as socially undesirable as compulsive consumption. In the previous chap-ter, we saw that one result of addictive shopping is that consumers run up large debts that they often cannot repay.

Cultural values such as materialism may also encourage antisocial behav-ior such as theft, shoplifting, or insurance fraud. Loss of merchandise due to shoplifting has increased prices by an estimated $300 per year for a family of four.[37]

Overall, cultural values have a positive impact on consumers by directing their behavior in constructive ways. However, it is also important to recognize the negative consumption consequences of some cultural values.

SUMMARY

This chapter introduced the broadest environmental influence on consumer behavior—culture. Cultural influence is transmitted through societal values, which are learned from childhood through socialization and form permanent guides to understanding consumer behavior. Cultural values are terminal values or desirable end states to be attained. Another category of values, instrumental values, are the means of achieving these end states.

Cultural values have four key characteristics: They are learned; they are guides to behavior; they are dynamic; and they are widely held by members of society. Four such widely held values in American society are materialism, individualism, youthfulness, and the work ethic.

There are various means of identifying cultural values including cultural inventories such as Rokeach's Value Survey, research services that conduct consumer surveys to determine changes in values such as *The Monitor Service*, field studies and observation, and content analysis of a society's mass media and literature.

In marketing terms, consumers seek to attain cultural values through a means-end chain in which (1) product attributes are a means for achieving (2) consumption goals that are instrumental in attaining (3) cultural values. The effect of culture on consumer behavior is reflected in its impact on the way products are portrayed and consumed. The means of portraying products in cultural terms is through symbols such as McDonald's golden arches. Marketers sometimes attempt to create myths and fantasies for products to strengthen their symbolism.

Culture is also important in defining a ritualistic role for many products. Consumers often purchase and consume products associated with grooming, gift-giving, and holidays in a series of symbolic acts that reflect cultural values. One perspective in better understanding the impact of culture on consumption is to view consumption as sacred or secular. Sacred consumption emphasizes beauty and the preservation of nature, whereas secular consumption emphasizes technology and the conquest of nature.

Several significant changes occurred in the American consumer's value system during the 1980s. The most important is a new reality that modifies the American Dream of unimpeded growth and recognizes future limits on purchasing power and spending. Other changes extending into the 1990s are a new traditionalism, reflected in a shift from a "me" to a "we" orientation; greater emphasis on self-fulfillment; and the emergence of a new materialism that views wealth as a means of enhancing self-fulfillment rather than social status.

Cultural values can have both positive and negative effects on consumers and society. Some of the negative effects are addictive consumption, compulsive purchasing behavior, and antisocial behavior such as shoplifting or insurance fraud. Overall, cultural values have a positive impact on consumers by directing their behavior into constructive channels.

In the next chapter, we will focus on more specific components of culture—subcultural and cross-cultural influences.

QUESTIONS

1. Why is it rare for a marketing strategy to try to change cultural values?
2. What is the distinction between terminal and instrumental values? What terminal and instrumental values might influence the purchase of a designer suit? A sports car?
3. What are the strategic implications of the changes in values between the 1980s and 1990s (labeled the new reality) for (a) advertising fax machines, (b) marketing disposable diapers, and (c) selling luxury goods?
4. What is the difference in the value placed on individualism in American and Japanese societies?
5. What changes have occurred in the work ethic in American society between the 1980s and 1990s? What are the strategic implications of these changes?
6. What are the theoretical underpinnings for Gutman's concept of a means-end chain as reflected in Figure 13.1?
7. What is the relationship between laddering and the means-end chain? How can marketers use laddering to develop advertising strategies?
8. Why is semiotics useful in analyzing cultural influences on consumer behavior? Why is it particularly important to marketers in evaluating cross-cultural influences?
9. What do all consumption rituals have in common? How can marketers use these components in developing marketing strategy?
10. A manufacturer of plastic wrap is considering using the sacred dimensions of consumption to advertise the company's brand. A competitor decides to use the secular dimensions of consumption. How would each advertising campaign differ on this basis?
11. How have marketers reacted to changes in consumer values reflected in a "new reality"?
12. Assume a manufacturer of personal hair care appliances (hair dryers, setters, and so on) wants to introduce two different lines: one directed to new traditionalists; the other, to old traditionalists. What type of appeals could the manufacturer use to appeal to each segment?
13. What are the implications of the emphasis on self-fulfillment for positioning (a) a new line of perfumes directed to the working woman and (b) a line of exercise machines?

14. What do we mean by the "new materialism"? In what way does the ad in Exhibit 13.9 reflect the new materialism?

RESEARCH ASSIGNMENTS

A study of automobile purchase preferences identified two segments based on cultural values: a self-enhancement segment and a social-recognition segment.[38] The two segments had very different need criteria for automobiles, different purchasing patterns, and different emphases on social issues. The self-enhancement group placed more emphasis on durability, environmental controls, and ease of repair. The social-recognition segment put more emphasis on luxury, prestige, and spaciousness. Regarding social attitudes, the self-enhancement group put more emphasis on equality, logic, and intellect; the social-recognition segment, on national security and law and order.

- Use the attitudes toward the following five items to identify these two segments: (1) law and order, (2) national security, (3) religion, (4) individual freedom, and (5) logic. (The self-enhancement segment would place less emphasis on the first three items and more emphasis on the last two; the social-recognition segment would do the reverse.)
- Select a sample of respondents and place them into one of the two segments based on their responses. (You may wish to form a third segment composed of those who do not clearly fit into one of the two segments.) Ask the respondents the criteria they emphasize in purchasing a particular durable good (a car, a stereo set, furniture, and so on). Determine particular brands or models owned.
- What are the differences in (1) need criteria emphasized and (2) brand ownership between the self-enhancement and the social-recognition segments?

NOTES

1. "We Got the Achtung Baby!" *Brandweek* (January 18, 1993), p. 25.
2. "Advertisers Put Consumers on the Couch," *The Wall Street Journal* (May 13, 1988), p. 21.
3. "McDonald's Isn't Looking Quite So Juicy Anymore," *Business Week* (August 6, 1990), p. 30.
4. "Culture Shocks," *Advertising Age* (May 17, 1982), p. M9.
5. Milton J. Rokeach, "The Role of Values in Public Opinion Research," *Public Opinion Quarterly,* 32 (Winter, 1968), pp. 547–549; and Milton J. Rokeach, "A Theory of Organization and Change Within Value-Attitude Systems," *Journal of Social Issues* (January, 1968), pp. 13–33.
6. Joseph F. Hair, Jr., and Rolph E. Anderson, "Culture, Acculturation and Consumer Behavior: An Empirical Study," in Boris W. Becker and Helmut Becker, eds., *Combined Proceedings of the American Marketing Association,* Series No. 34 (1972), pp. 423–428.
7. Bernard Berelson and Gary A. Steiner, *Human Behavior: An Inventory of Scientific Findings* (New York: Harcourt Brace & World, 1964), p. 652.

8. Adapted from "Rewriting the Book on Buying and Selling—Angry and Anxious Americans Seek Out New Values," *Adweek* (November 30, 1992), pp. 20–23.

9. David M. Potter, *People of Plenty* (Chicago: University of Chicago Press, 1954).

10. "Japan to Get L. L. Bean's Outdoor Chic," *The New York Times* (March 5, 1992), p. D3.

11. Lynn R. Kahle, Sharon Beatty, and Pamela Homer, "Alternative Measurement Approaches to Consumer Values: The List Values (LOV) and Values and Life Style (VALS)," *Journal of Consumer Research,* 13 (December, 1986), pp. 405–409.

12. Pamela Homer and Lynn R. Kahle, "A Structural Equation Test of the Value-Attitude-Behavior Hierarchy," *Journal of Personality and Social Psychology,* 54 (April, 1988), pp. 638–646.

13. Daniel Yankelovich, *The Yankelovich Monitor* (New York: Daniel Yankelovich, 1974).

14. "Lifestyle's Monitor," *American Demographics* (May, 1981), p. 22.

15. "Socks, Ties, and Videotape," *American Demographics* (September, 1991), p. 6; and "You Are What You Buy," *Newsweek* (June 4, 1990), pp. 59–60.

16. "Anthropologists in Adland," *Advertising Age* (February 24, 1992), pp. 3, 49.

17. Russell W. Belk, John F. Sherry, Jr., and Melanie Wallendorf, "A Naturalistic Inquiry into Buyer and Seller Behavior at a Swap Meet," *Journal of Consumer Research,* 14 (March, 1988), pp. 449–470.

18. *Ibid.*

19. David C. McClellan, *The Achieving Society* (Princeton, NJ: Van Nostrand, 1961).

20. Russell W. Belk, "Material Values in the Comics," *Journal of Consumer Research,* 14 (June, 1987), pp. 26–42.

21. Jonathan Gutman, "A Means-End Chain Model Based on Consumer Categorization Processes," *Journal of Marketing,* 46 (1982), pp. 60–72.

22. Milton J. Rosenberg, "Cognitive Structure and Attitudinal Affect," *Journal of Abnormal and Social Psychology,* 53 (1956), pp. 367–372.

23. Thomas J. Reynolds and Jonathan Gutman, "Laddering Theory, Method, Analysis, and Interpretation," *Journal of Advertising Research,* 28 (February/March, 1988), pp. 11–31.

24. Thomas J. Reynolds and Alyce Byrd Craddock, "The Application of the Meccas Model to the Development and Assessment of Advertising Strategy: A Case Study," *Journal of Advertising Research,* 28 (April/May, 1988), pp. 43–59.

25. Mary Tharp and Linda M. Scott, "The Role of Marketing Processes in Creating Cultural Meaning," *Journal of Macromarketing* (Fall, 1990), pp. 7–60.

26. "Agencies Scrutinize Their Ads for Psychological Symbolism," *The Wall Street Journal* (June 11, 1987), p. 25.

27. Charles Sanders Pierce, (*Collected Papers*), Charles Hartshorne, Paul Weiss, and Arthur W. Burks, eds. (Cambridge MA: Harvard University Press, 1931–1958); and David Glen Mick, "Consumer Research and Semiotics: Exploring the Morphology of Signs, Symbols, and Significance," *Journal of Consumer Research,* 15 (September, 1986), pp. 196–213.

28. These examples are from "The Power of Mythology Helps Brands to Endure," *Marketing News* (September 28, 1992), p. 16.

29. Dennis W. Rook, "The Ritual Dimensions of Consumer Behavior," *Journal of Consumer Research,* 12 (December, 1985), pp. 251–264.

30. *Ibid.,* p. 253.

31. Elizabeth C. Hirschman, "The Ideology of Consumption: A Structural-Syntactical Analysis of 'Dallas' and 'Dynasty'," *Journal of Consumer Research,* 15 (December, 1988), pp. 344–359.

32. Elizabeth C. Hirschman, "Point of View: Sacred, Secular, and Mediating Consumption Imagery In Television Commercials," *Journal of Advertising Research,* 31 (December, 1990/January, 1991), pp. 38–43.

33. *Ibid.*

34. "Double Standards of Post-War Adults," *Research Alert* (June 24, 1988), p. 1.

35. Daniel Yankelovich, Florence Skelly, and Arthur White, "Social Trends Measured in *Monitor No. 3,*" *The Yankelovich Monitor* (New York: Daniel Yankelovich, 1981).

36. "Marketers Must Consider Component Life Styles," *Marketing News* (August 29, 1988), p. 9.

37. "Shoplifting: Bess Myerson's Arrest Highlights a Multibillion Dollar Problem That Many Stores Won't Talk About," *Life* (August, 1988), p. 32.

38. Donald E. Vinson, Jerome E. Scott, and Lawrence M. Lamont, "The Role of Personal Values in Marketing and Consumer Behavior," *Journal of Marketing,* 41 (April, 1977), pp. 44–50.

14

Cross-Cultural and Subcultural Influences

LEVI STRAUSS & CO. THINKS GLOBALLY BUT ACTS LOCALLY

The previous chapter focused on the ways cultural values influence consumer purchasing behavior in the United States. There are two variations to the theme of cultural influences in a particular country. One is differences in values across countries, referred to as **cross-cultural influences.** The other is differences in values among groups within a country, referred to as **subcultural influences.**

Because many U.S. firms have operations in countries where values are very different from the values of American consumers, cross-cultural influences are increasing in importance. Unfortunately, firms often assume that marketing strategies that work in this country will work abroad. As the scope of international operations increases, more and more domestic firms are finding it necessary to gain a better understanding of cross-cultural influences.

As tastes in music, fashion, and technology become more common across the world in the 1990s, a countervailing force to cross-cultural influences is the increasing globalization of values. The global reach of MTV is an example. This trend has led to the development of world brands; that is, brands that are advertised on a universal basis but with variations to meet local tastes. As a result, many firms have accepted the strategic advice to *think globally but act locally* (an approach we will later refer to as *flexible globalization*).

Levi Strauss & Co. follows such a strategy. Levi jeans are the only U.S. apparel label that can be called a world brand. The company has achieved its world brand status by marketing Levi's as an enshrined piece of Americana. Teenagers wearing Levi jeans portray common values whether in Bangkok, Leningrad, Paris, or Rio.

Levi's American roots are adapted to each country by local managers. (See Exhibit 14.1.) In Indonesia, managers selected a TV commercial showing Levi clad teenagers cruising around Dubuque, Iowa, in a 1960 convertible. In Japan, local managers use past movie stars such as Marilyn Monroe because of the obsession for American movie icons among Japanese youth.[1] The company is now entering Eastern Europe and the countries of the former Soviet Union. It is finding fertile ground since consumers in these countries hunger for any symbol of Americana, from McDonald's arches in Moscow to Coca-Cola cans in Warsaw.

Many companies also target subcultures within their domestic markets. **Subcultures** are broad groups of consumers who have similar values that distinguish them from society as a whole. Subcultures can be identified by age, geography, or ethnic identity. Baby boomers might be considered a subculture

▶**EXHIBIT 14.1**
Levi Strauss & Co.'s global perspective
Source: Courtesy of Levi Strauss & Co.

because many of them experienced a similar shift in values from acquisitiveness to personal development. Consumers in New England might constitute a subculture because many demonstrate traditional Yankee values of stubborn individualism.

In a broad sense, those consumers who are African-American, Hispanic-American, and Asian-American are also subcultures because they demonstrate certain similarities in tastes and purchasing behavior. These three ethnic subcultures are important to marketers because together they represent nearly one-fourth of the United States' population and account for over $400 billion in expenditures yearly. In terms of purchasing power, they are the ninth most powerful economic entity in the world, surpassing Canada or Sweden.[2] Levi Strauss & Co. targets these three subcultures in much the same way as it targets markets cross-culturally—by using common themes but varying the message in selected media targeted to these groups. For example, when the company advertises its products to Hispanic-Americans, it shows warm scenes in a family setting to appeal to this group's strong sense of family values.

In this chapter, we first consider cross-cultural and global influences. We describe marketing strategies that adapt to local differences versus those that are more global. We then turn to subcultural influences by focusing on the three key ethnic subcultures in the American market: African-Americans, Hispanic-Americans, and Asian-Americans. The marketing implications of appealing to segments within these subcultures are considered.

◆ CROSS-CULTURAL INFLUENCES

Marketing abroad has become an increasingly important part of American business. Today, three out of four manufacturing jobs are linked to products sold abroad, directly or indirectly.[3] American companies such as Procter & Gamble, Colgate-Palmolive, Kellogg's, Coca-Cola, IBM, Gillette, and Johnson & Johnson earn more of their revenue abroad than here. Many foreign-owned companies, such as Nestlé, Lever, and Shell Oil, which are often mistaken for American companies, earn a significant percentage of their revenues in the United States.

As foreign markets emerge and offer opportunities for growth, marketing abroad is likely to increase in importance. With the end of communism, free-market systems have begun to develop in the nations of Eastern Europe and the former Soviet Union, and American firms are finding opportunities in these countries. For example, Procter & Gamble has "spent millions of dollars researching the Russian consumer's mind and blitzing the airwaves with commercials that offer almost comic contrast to the dismal hardships of everyday life."[4] It is introducing Russian consumers to brands that offer unheard of benefits such as dandruff control and skin moisturizing creams. On gift-giving occasions, Russian consumers wrap bars of Camay soap and Bottles of Pert Plus shampoo to give to loved ones. Before Camay was introduced (at a cost eight times that of Russian soaps), the only soaps available were coarse bars wrapped in brown paper.

Even China, the world's largest market is becoming quite consumption-oriented despite the crackdown on the democracy movement in 1989. Chinese consumers are becoming brand-oriented as ads for Coca-Cola, Contac cold capsules, and Head and Shoulders shampoo regularly appear on Chinese TV.[5] Coca-Cola figures that if the Chinese drink half as much Coke as Americans, the additional income would far exceed the company's total revenues.

The other side of the coin is the opportunity for foreign companies to market in the United States. Cross-cultural considerations apply equally in this case, as foreign companies have to become aware of the differing needs of American consumers and the nature of business customs here. Japanese marketers have been particularly successful in challenging the leadership of American companies in autos, computers, and electronics. They have done so by adapting their products to the needs of American consumers—for example, by recognizing the need for compact, well-designed electronics products at reasonable prices.

Companies have generally been successful in marketing abroad by recognizing local differences in consumer needs and customs. To do so, such companies have had to *acculturate* themselves by learning local consumers' needs and values. Thus, McDonald's varies its offerings by selling beer in Germany, wine in France, mango milk shakes in Hong Kong, mutton pie in Australia, and McSpaghetti in the Philippines to compete with local noodle houses.[6] However, there is the danger that companies will assume what works at home will work abroad. Such companies take an **ethnocentric** view of foreign consumers; that is, they assume foreign consumers have the same norms and values as domestic consumers.

Such an ethnocentric view is bound to fail. For example, P&G assumed that a 1990 campaign for Camay soap in Europe would also be successful in Japan. The campaign depicted a Japanese husband who walked in on his wife as she sat in a bathtub and complimented her on her complexion. Although the basic premise of the campaign—that women want to be attractive to men—is universally correct, the campaign flopped. Unlike most Europeans who considered the campaign sexy, the Japanese regarded it as bad manners to intrude on a woman's privacy.[7]

Cultural Variations Influencing Consumer Behavior

International marketers subscribing to an acculturated view of foreign markets have been affected by two cross-currents. First, they recognize differences in customs and values between countries and a need to adapt marketing strategies to these differences. Second, they also recognize a greater commonality between countries in cultural values as the result of global communications through TV and more frequent travel.

Cross-cultural differences require companies to develop localized strategies on a country-by-country basis, whereas global influences provide them an opportunity to standardize strategies. In this section, we consider cross-cultural variations that influence consumer behavior. In the next section, we consider global influences.

There are at least four cross-cultural factors that influence marketing strategies abroad: differences between countries in (1) consumer customs and values, (2) language, (3) symbols, and (4) the economic environment.

Consumer Customs and Values

American businesspeople often take an ethnocentric view by assuming the values of American consumers are universal. However, as we saw in the previous chapter, traditional American values placed on achievement, materialism, individualism, and youthfulness are not nearly as strong in other parts of the world. In many Asian countries, acceptance of one's place in society is more important than individual initiative in influencing behavior. Differences in the perspective of time also exist. Americans structure their day into times for work and pleasure based on business, family, and individual needs. In many South American and European countries, however, people are more likely to mix business with pleasure; and being late for an appointment may be the norm.

Such differences in cultural values affect consumers' purchasing behavior. A failure to account for these differences is likely to spell trouble for the foreign marketer. For example, P&G failed in Russia when it introduced Wash & Go, a combination shampoo and conditioner. Shampoo was a relatively new concept to Russians who still washed their hair with soap, and a hair conditioner was completely foreign. In fact, many Russian consumers mistook the claim as "air conditioner." Wash & Go was quickly popularized into a euphemism for washing down a vodka before heading out.[8]

When American companies have accounted for foreign consumers' norms and values, they have been effective. Ford recognized a growing independence among Japanese women. In a traditionally male-dominated society, many more women were working full-time. In 1990, Ford began targeting its Festiva car to single, young Japanese working women. In the past, Japanese carmakers had assumed Japanese women would have deferred to fathers, husbands, or brothers in the purchase decision for a car. (See Exhibit 14.2.)

Differences in cultural values among countries are likely to result in differences in product preferences, and product usage.

Product Preferences. Product preferences are likely to differ sharply across countries, as shown by the listing in Table 14.1 of the ten brands with the strongest images in the United States, Europe, and Japan. Businesspeople operating abroad must be aware of differences in product preferences that are culturally based. For example, when Campbell introduced its line of condensed

▶**EXHIBIT 14.2**

Automakers target the Japanese working woman

Source: Courtesy of Ford Motor Co.

▶**TABLE 14.1**

Brands with the strongest images in the United States, Europe, and Japan

United States	Europe	Japan
1. Coca-Cola	Coca-Cola	Sony
2. Campbell's	Sony	National
3. Disney	Mercedes-Benz	Mercedes-Benz
4. Pepsi-Cola	BMW	Toyota
5. Kodak	Philips	Takashimaya
6. NBC	Volkswagen	Rolls-Royce
7. Black & Decker	Adidas	Seiko
8. Kellogg	Kodak	Matsushita
9. McDonald's	Nivea	Hitachi
10. Hershey	Porsche	Suntory

SOURCE: "Consumers Know Native Brands Best," *ADWEEK* (September 17, 1990), p. 31.

soups in Britain, it was not sensitive to the fact that English consumers preferred ready-to-eat soups and were unaware of the condensed soup concept. Campbell's cans were at a disadvantage in the store because English consumers considered them small. Initially, the company did not adequately explain the necessity of adding water. In addition, the variety of flavors was not tailored to English tastes. It took several years of low sales to make the company aware of the difficulties and the required adjustments.

Product Usage.   When operating abroad, American executives must consider differences in product usage. Consider the following:

- Venezuelan women wash their laundry by using slivers of bar soap they knead together to form a paste. After Colgate researchers observed this process, they decided to put the paste in a plastic bowl and market it. The result was Axion soap paste, the leading laundry cleaner in Latin America.[9]
- The Singer Company found that its predominant form of promotion—demonstration classes for women—had to be altered in Moslem countries.[10] Women were not allowed to leave the home to attend sewing lessons at Singer centers. One Singer representative in the Sudan was jailed for attempting to encourage women to attend classes. Once the men in those countries began to attend classes, however, they were convinced that sewing lessons would be of value to their wives, whom they then ordered to take lessons.
- Pepsodent tried to sell its toothpaste in Southeast Asia by using the same basic appeal as it did in the United States—getting teeth whiter. However, the campaign was ineffective in some regions because of the custom of chewing betel nuts to achieve the social prestige of darkly stained teeth.[11]

Physiological differences between consumers in various countries also affect product usage. People in Peru and Bolivia use the powdered milk the United States gives them to whitewash houses. Why? They cannot drink milk because they do not retain an enzyme enabling them to digest it.[12]

Language

Language provides the means of communicating the customs and beliefs of a culture. Marketers must be aware of the meaning and subtleties of languages and dialects when selling in foreign markets. Many marketing blunders have resulted because of a lack of awareness of language. For example:

- When Coca-Cola was introduced in China, shopkeepers made their own signs in calligraphy with the words *ke kou ke lu*, which translated into "bite the wax tadpole," an association that would not be likely to encourage sales. When the company discovered this, it researched 40,000 Chinese characters and came up with *ko kou ko le*, which not only sounds more like the real thing, but also means "may the mouth rejoice."[13]

- PepsiCo had to change its slogan "Come alive with Pepsi" in certain Asian countries because the theme translated into "Bring your ancestors back from the dead."[14]

- General Motors discovered it could not use the name *Nova* on its models worldwide because in Spanish-speaking markets the name translated into "won't go" (*No va*).[15]

- Gillette had to change the name of its Trac II razor in many foreign markets when research showed that *trac* in some Romance languages means "fragile."[16]

- Kellogg had to rename Bran Buds cereal in Sweden when it discovered that the name translated into "burned farmer."[17]

Symbols

Symbols in a culture also influence purchasing behavior. Companies must be particularly sensitive to the use of color in advertising. Pink is associated with femininity in the United States, but yellow is considered the most feminine color in much of the rest of the world.[18] Many Latin American countries disapprove of purple because it is associated with death; brown and gray are disapproved of in Nicaragua.[19]

Symbols other than color also influence behavior. Two elephants are a symbol of bad luck in many parts of Africa. This forced Carlsberg to add a third elephant to its label for Elephant Beer. A moon appears frequently in Chinese ads because it is a traditional symbol of good luck in that country.

Amoco Oil Company provides a good example of cultural awareness in its corporate advertising campaign in China. The purpose was to reach decision makers in Chinese ministries who are responsible for petroleum exploration. One of Amoco's biggest challenges was finding the working and visual images to convey in magazine advertisements. The result was advertising that used colorful and large illustrations and the theme "Share a new world of opportunities." The company used red and purple in the ads because red stands for life and purple for quality in Chinese culture.[20]

Economic Environment

A country's economic environment influences consumer behavior. Three factors are particularly important: a country's standard of living, its economic infrastructure, and its economic policies.

With one of the most advanced industrial nations in the world, the United States' high *standard of living* allows for widespread ownership of electronics, appliances, and automobiles. Underdeveloped countries do not approach the level of ownership of TVs and telephones in the United States (over 95 percent). When Kellogg introduced its cereals into Southeast Asia, it knew it would have to try to change breakfast eating habits to influence Asian consumers to accept cereals. It also knew that a TV campaign would not be an effective way to do so because of limited TV ownership. Similarly, marketing researchers investigating consumer attitudes and behavior abroad cannot rely on collecting information by telephone in many countries because only upscale households own phones.

The facilities a country uses to conduct business—media, telecommunications, transportation, and power—are known as the country's *economic infrastructure*. Media, telecommunications, and distribution facilities in many underdeveloped countries are primitive. For example, although consumers in Russia and Eastern Europe crave American goods, difficulties abound in marketing them because of archaic distribution networks and limited facilities for advertising. Marketers cannot take for granted basic requirements such as good road networks and warehousing facilities. Companies targeting less-developed countries face similar limitations in implementing marketing strategies.

A country's economic policies also influence consumer behavior. Many countries have instituted tariff barriers against imports to protect domestic industries, thus limiting their consumers' access to foreign goods. While tariffs have been reduced substantially in the post-World War II period, they still remain as barriers to consumer choice in many countries.

Global Influences on Behavior

Supporters of global strategies in international marketing cite increased similarity in tastes and values across countries. Improvements in transportation and communication have resulted in distribution of products and transmission of advertising messages on a worldwide basis. As a result of worldwide communications and common tastes, brands such as Coca-Cola and Levi jeans and fast-food outlets such as McDonald's and Pizza Hut can be regarded as world brands.

Certain values such as materialism, desire for beauty, nurturing of children, and security exist in most countries. If consumers can associate these values with a product category, a standardized marketing strategy across countries may be possible. For example, Polaroid developed a single global campaign based on the theme of pictures as a universal language. The campaign was successful because a theme of communicating through pictures was relevant to most cultures.[21]

Several factors have increased global influences on consumer behavior, including the availability of common TV programs from global cable networks, common values among teenagers worldwide, a general decrease in trade barriers, and the Americanization of values on a global basis.

Worldwide Communications

Because of the advent of worldwide cable networks, television has become a global medium. Propelling this phenomenon is the global influence of MTV, the rock video channel, and CNN, the worldwide news channel. MTV estimates its audience at 210 million in 78 countries and expects to come close to tripling its audience by the turn of the century. CNN reaches 78 million households in more than 100 countries.[22] Because of these networks, marketers can more easily create world brands by advertising them across many countries with a single theme. In Europe, MTV's 200 advertisers almost all run unified, English-language campaigns across its 28-nation broadcast area.[23]

One communications theory proposes that individuals tend to see the world around them largely based on information from the mass media. Therefore, heavy viewers of TV will develop similar perceptions of reality because they are exposed to similar stimuli. This effect, known as **mainstreaming,**[24] means that global TV networks such as MTV and CNN are promoting similar norms and values on a global basis. As a result, mainstreaming has encouraged the development of a global teenager; that is, teens with similar values across countries. MTV aired its first global show in 1989 because it "bet that teen tastes and attitudes are now sufficiently similar to warrant a global assault."[25]

Global Teenager

MTV is not the only factor that has encouraged the development of the global teenager. Greater travel and the demise of communism have also spurred the development of common norms and values among teens worldwide. As the director of MTV in Europe said, "Eighteen-year-olds in Paris have more in common with 18-year-olds in New York than with their own parents. They buy the same products, go to the same movies, listen to the same music, sip the same colas."[26] As a result, a Russian rock band could be mistaken for an American group. Thai, French, and Brazilian teenagers are wearing the same brand of jeans; and teenagers in Asia, Western Europe, and Latin America are using the Sony Walkman.

A growing number of marketers have begun targeting the global teenager. Swatch has a worldwide campaign for the simple reason that it sells 60 percent of its watches to teenagers. The company advertises the same image around the world, but varies the copy in its print ads to adapt to different languages. Examples of an American print ad portraying global teenagers is in Exhibit 14.3.

Universal Demographic Trends

In Chapter 10, we described key demographic trends in the United States such as the increasing proportion of working women, the greater proportion of single-member households, increasing divorce rates, later marriages, and fewer children per household. These trends are not restricted to the United States; they apply to most of the developed countries of the world, from France to Taiwan.

These common trends encourage global marketing strategies. For example, the increasing divorce rate in France, Japan, Sweden, Russia, and the United States was one factor behind the global success of Toys "R" Us. The company realized that parents who separate are more likely to give toys to their children.[27] Similarly, the increasing proportion of working women in Thailand, Malaysia, and Hong Kong led Jusco, a Japanese supermarket chain, to open

▶**EXHIBIT 14.3**
Targeting the global teenager

stores in these countries. Although most women in these countries shop in open-air markets and small grocery stores, Jusco recognized that working women no longer have the time to shop in traditional ways and would want the time-saving convenience of supermarkets.[28]

Decrease in Trade Barriers

Trade barriers are decreasing worldwide, facilitating the flow of goods among nations and the consequent emergence of common tastes and values. The North American Free Trade Agreement will facilitate the flow of goods between the United States, Canada, and Mexico; and the demise of communism has opened markets previously closed to many Western goods.

The elimination of trade barriers in 1992 among the 12 nations of the European Community is likely to lead to a Euroconsumer, one who has many shared values with consumers in neighboring countries. As one European manager for Lever said, "Europeans share yearnings for odor-free underarms; fresh-smelling breath; and soft, easy-to-wash clothing."[29] As a result, companies are trying to sell products the same way across Europe, leading to the development of a **Eurobrand;** that is, a brand with several languages on the same package under the same brand name. Sara Lee has selected the Dim name as its Eurobrand for socks, underwear, and lingerie. Using a common strategy, Sara Lee can sell these items to all European Community countries.

Americanization of Consumption Values

The globalization of communications, decreasing trade barriers, and the demise of communism have spurred the acceptance of American consumption values across the globe. Consumers in all parts of the world crave American goods as status symbols. Consider the following:

- In Russia, youthful consumers have turned to Western goods to maintain their traditionally disheveled look. They wear Chicago Bears and L.A. Lakers T-shirts, knock-off high top basketball sneakers, and baseball caps. The taste for fast foods has caught on like wildfire, with an *Amerikanski gamburgeri* and a Budweiser being on the top of the list for chic.[30]

- In Japan, the Americanization of consumption values goes beyond a craving for American movie icons in commercials. Japanese consumers are equally in the throes of the fast-food craze with a fierce loyalty to *Bi-gu Ma-kus*. Japan now accounts for close to 10 percent of McDonald's sales worldwide. Japanese consumers also insist on American labels. For example, the L. L. Bean label is associated with a ruggedly functional American look that is now regarded as a status symbol, if not an icon, in Japan.[31]

- In Brazil, one executive attributed the failure of the Jack-in-the-Box chain to the fact that "There was nothing in them, like in McDonald's, to evoke for Brazilians 'the American way of life.'"[32]

- In Holland, an Amsterdam taxi driver points out a pedestrian dressed in a New York Yankee jersey, bluejeans, and green-striped Air Jordans. "I can smell an American anywhere," he says, "but that's a Dutchman." ("Why?" asks his passenger.) "Because he looks too much like an American."[33]

American companies are taking advantage of this trend by using American themes in their advertising, American celebrities, and English slogans. However, this does *not* mean that American companies are being ethnocentric. These companies are actually following the desires of foreign consumers rather than assuming American values can be imposed on them. Further, companies do adjust American-oriented ads to local needs and tastes. When Reebok advertised in France, it deleted a boxing theme from Planet Reebok commercials because of French consumers' aversion to any depiction of violence.[34]

Limits of Global Influences

The focus on global influences might suggest that a company can market one standardized product with a uniform, worldwide advertising campaign. This is rarely the case. No matter how universal the product is, some adaptation to local customs and language is necessary. Even the most universal of brands, Coca-Cola, does not follow a strictly global approach. It makes variations in the brand's formula in certain countries; and while Coca-Cola uses a global theme, it creates variations in its advertising for each country. When the company launched its General Assembly campaign in 1987, showing children of the world singing the Coke jingle in one big assembly, each country's ads focused on a closeup of a local youngster. Thus, a unifying theme was adapted to different countries.

There are also limits to global communications. For example, despite the increasingly global reach of MTV, in Australia all commercials have to be reshot with Australian film crews.[35]

When a company follows a strictly global approach with little adaptation to local needs, it runs into trouble. Parker Pen tried to standardize every component of its marketing strategy in 154 countries but failed because of inadequate attention to local differences. Its global advertising campaign overlooked the fact that Scandinavia is a ballpoint pen market, whereas consumers in France and Italy want fancier pens.[36]

Applications of Cross-Cultural and Global Influences

Whether to sell on a localized basis, a global basis, or somewhere in between is perhaps the most important decision a marketer selling abroad must make. Such a decision must be based on the extent of cultural differences across countries and on the degree to which common norms, tastes, and values justify a more global approach. At one extreme, a company could follow a completely localized strategy by adapting product characteristics, advertising, and distribution requirements to the particular needs of each country it serves. Such a strategy may be unfeasible because of the costs of running a separate campaign in every country.

At the other extreme, a company could follow a completely global campaign. Coca-Cola has achieved world-brand status through its objective of "one look, one sight, one sound," meaning that its advertising message is being constantly reinforced, whether consumers see it at home or abroad. Although such an approach may achieve a universal image and important economies of scale, some adjustment to local conditions is almost always necessary.

As a result, companies rarely follow a completely global strategy. Some degree of adaptation to local consumer needs is required. Such an approach reflects the "think globally but act locally" strategy employed by Levi Strauss & Co. We will refer to this strategy as **flexible globalization;** that is, an attempt to standardize marketing strategies across countries but to be flexible enough to adapt components of the strategy to local conditions. Such strategies are becoming the norm due to the shortcomings of a strictly local or global approach.

Since some companies follow a more localized approach and others more global strategies, we will consider these two approaches first. We then will describe the increasingly common strategy of flexible globalization designed to achieve the advantages of both local and global strategies.

Localized Strategies

Because of substantial differences between countries in tastes, customs, and product usage, many companies opt to localize their marketing strategies abroad. For example, Heinz alters its ketchup to reflect local tastes. Americans like a relatively sweet ketchup, whereas Europeans prefer a spicier variety. In central Europe and Sweden, Heinz is selling a Mexican variety and a curry flavored ketchup. In contrast to many companies that emphasize their American roots, Heinz plays down the fact ketchup is a typically American product, preferring to let consumers think it is of more local origins.[37]

Domino's Pizza also follows a localized strategy by varying its pizzas with what it calls "cultural toppings." For example, pizzas are topped with sweet corn in the United Kingdom, salami in Germany, and prawns in Australia. In Japan, Domino's offers a chicken teriyaki gourmet pizza for $15.[38]

Many companies also take a localized approach to advertising because of differences in needs or customs between countries. Renault advertised its Clio differently to various European countries because of differences in the features consumers consider most important in a car. The company emphasized road performance and features in Portugal, security and safety in France, self-image in Spain, style in Italy, and "new" in Belgium. (See Exhibit 14.4.)

Globalized Strategies

The cross-cultural differences cited above suggest that companies should vary their strategy for a product from country to country. However, in some cases, a company could use the same promotional campaign and positioning in each country if the product has a more global appeal. There may be compelling reasons for following a more global strategy. The resulting standardization in marketing strategies across countries results in important economies of scale. Coca-Cola saves about $8 million a year from economies in producing similar ads across countries.[39]

Companies like PepsiCo, Coca-Cola, Black & Decker, Singer, Levi Strauss & Co., and Goodyear have followed a global approach because they believe their products have universal appeal. By reinforcing the same theme in their advertising, companies can build a world image and a competitive advantage in their product category. Pepsi, whose strength has always been teenagers, uses this tag line in its Russian commercials, "The new generation chooses Pepsi," which is a variation on its universal theme of "The choice of a new generation."[40] (See Exhibit 14.5.) Its red, white, and blue can is a universal symbol, regardless of language.

Generally, it is easier to implement a global strategy for the product than it is for advertising. Product formulations may not need to change across countries, but advertising generally must accommodate variations in language, symbols, and images to conform to local conditions. Many companies sell fairly standardized products across countries. Black & Decker power tools look exactly the same everywhere. The only variation is to accommodate different voltages and circuits among countries. McDonald's has been working with farmers in

▶**EXHIBIT 14.4**
Examples of localized
strategies for one
product

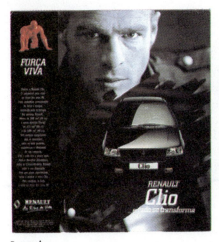

▶**EXHIBIT 14.5**
Pepsi's global strategy
Source: Courtesy of Pepsi-Cola Co.

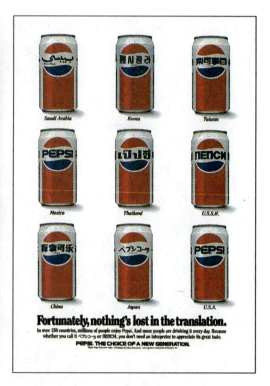

Hong Kong to grow exactly the right potato for processing into french fries. Why? Because McDonald's fries must look and taste the same at each of its 11,600 stores worldwide.[41]

Companies also have followed fairly standardized advertising approaches. One of the most standardized was VISA's campaign, which ran identical ads for its card in various countries with language the only change. (See Exhibit 14.6.) Similarly, Gillette introduced its new Sensor razor in 1990 with a standardized campaign in North America and Europe because the company believes that "men around the globe relate to shaving in very much the same ways."[42] The VISA and Gillette campaigns are the exception rather than the rule, however. Most standardized campaigns require more adjustments to local customs and a more flexible approach to globalized strategies.

Flexible Globalization

The trend in international marketing has been to move toward a compromise between global and local strategies, which we have referred to as *flexible glob-*

▶**EXHIBIT 14.6**
A standardized advertising campaign for VISA

alization. This compromise requires the company to establish an overall marketing strategy but to leave implementation to local executives who are aware of national traits and customs.

For example, until 1992, Harley Davidson insisted that local markets use its U.S. print advertising campaign. It then decided to customize its domestic strategy to account for different cultures. In Japan, Harley's local manager recognized that the American campaign featuring desolate scenes and the tag line "One steady constant in an increasingly screwed-up world" would not win over Japanese riders. So, he got permission to run a separate campaign juxtaposing American and Japanese images: American riders passing a geisha in a rickshaw or Japanese ponies nibbling at a Harley motorcycle.[43]

Similarly, Philip Morris uses the Marlboro Cowboy ads on a universal basis but creates significant local differences in implementation. In Hong Kong, urban residents do not identify with horseback riding in the country; so, the Marlboro Cowboy is better dressed and shown in a pickup truck.[44] In Brazil, the Cowboy becomes a rancher. In many countries, the Cowboy cannot be shown at all; so, the company uses western accoutrements like a saddle horn, spurs, and cowboy boots to evoke the Marlboro image.

◆ SUBCULTURAL INFLUENCES

In a society, individuals do not all have the same cultural values. Certain segments may be identified as subcultures because they have homogeneous values and customs that distinguish them from society as a whole. The individual who identifies closely with a certain religious, ethnic, or national subculture will accept the norms and values of that group. As a result, members of a subculture frequently buy the same brands and products, read the same magazines and newspapers, and shop in the same types of stores. Because American society is so diverse, it is important that marketers identify subcultures and determine whether to direct specific strategies to them.

Characteristics of Subcultures

The influence of a subculture on consumer behavior depends on several factors:

- *Subcultural distinctiveness.* The more a subculture seeks to maintain a separate identity, the greater is its potential influence. The Hispanic subculture is distinctive because many of its members have maintained their language as a means of cultural identification.
- *Subcultural homogeneity.* A subculture with homogeneous values is more likely to exert influence on its members. Hispanics appear to be a diverse subculture composed of Mexicans, Cubans, Puerto Ricans, and individuals from South American countries. Some might consider each of these groups separate subcultures. However, in general, it is appropriate to talk of a Hispanic subculture because of common threads among all of these groups; namely, strong family and religious ties, conservatism, male dominance, and a common language.
- *Subcultural exclusion.* At times, subcultures have sought exclusion from society or have been excluded by society. The Amish communities in Pennsylvania, Ohio, and Indiana have purposefully sought exclusion to maintain and protect their beliefs. African-Americans have at times been excluded from a white dominant society through the denial of educational and occupation opportunities. Exclusion tends to strengthen the influence of subcultures by isolating them from society and, thus, encouraging the maintenance of subcultural norms and values.

United States: Melting Pot or Salad Bowl?

Distinctiveness, homogeneity, and exclusion interact to maintain subcultural identity separate from the general culture. In many subcultures, an individual is torn between maintaining a distinctive subcultural identity and integrating into the general society. The traditional path of immigrants in this country has been integration into the American "melting pot."

More recently, pressures to acculturate by accepting traditional, American middle-class values have lessened. For example, many Hispanic and Asian immigrants have a strong desire to maintain their language and heritage. This desire to maintain subcultural values has led one writer to refer to America in the 1990s not as a melting pot but as a salad bowl "brimming with a polyglot, multi-hued potpourri of people who mix but don't blend. These immigrant groups have a need to maintain their separate identities rather than to meld into a cultural mainstream."[45] The challenge for marketers is to appeal to the separate identities of these subcultural groups while also appealing to the broader market.

Types of Subcultures

Subcultures in the United States can be defined by age, geography, religion, and, most important, ethnic identification. A key question is whether marketers should appeal to these groups with the same strategy they use for the general market or whether they should design specific campaigns targeted to particular segments of the African-American, Hispanic-American, or Asian-American market.

Metropolitan Life's strategy has been to target particular ethnic groups with specific campaigns geared to their language and their customs. In appealing to Hispanic-Americans, the company dispensed with Snoopy, the cartoon character, in its English-language ads and developed themes geared specifically to this segment for the Spanish-language media.[46] Metropolitan has also developed specific ads targeted to Chinese-Americans and Korean-Americans. In each case, the company recognized that themes directed to the broad American market had to be adapted to the differing values and tastes of particular subcultures. Metropolitan is a trailblazer in this respect because many companies consider the 6 million Asian-Americans too small a target.[47]

Age

While some may debate whether age groups have sufficiently homogeneous and distinctive values to constitute a subculture, marketers have tended to identify as subcultures the three groups that were introduced in Chapter 10: baby busters (the youth market), baby boomers, and the elderly. They cite the consumption orientation of baby busters, the evolution from self-indulgence to self-enhancement of baby boomers, and the greater focus on fitness, vitality, and a full life of the elderly as examples of homogeneous values warranting designation as subcultures.

However, these age groups may be too broad to be defined as subcultures. More specific designations, such as younger versus older baby boomers or the "young" old versus the elderly, do a better job of defining age groups with homogeneous norms and values.

Geography

Geographic groups could also be identified as subcultures because of differences in their tastes and behavior. As with age groups, however, geographic designations may be too diverse to be labeled subcultures unless marketers can identify specific areas with homogeneous needs and values. One popular approach, cited in Chapter 10 as geo-demographic analysis, involves identifying areas with common demographic characteristics across the United States. For example, residents of retirement communities, whether in Florida, Arizona, or New Jersey, might be identified as a subculture because of common values regarding housing, medical care, and retirement benefits.

Differences in tastes, lifestyles, and values are often distinct enough to define broader regional subcultures. For example, Easterners prefer to watch TV, read, and go to the movies, while consumers in the West prefer eating out, dancing, and visiting with friends. Consumers in the South prefer to stay at home, work around the house, and avoid organized entertainment.[48]

Religion

Religious groups can also be regarded as subcultures. Catholics, Protestants, Jews, Mormons, and followers of other religions practice traditions and customs tied to their beliefs and passed on from one generation to the next. These traditions and customs are likely to be reflected in purchasing behavior. Jews are less likely to eat pork and shellfish, Mormons are less likely to smoke tobacco and drink liquor, and Catholics are more likely to eat fish on Friday. The non-materialistic values of born-again Christians make them poor targets for credit cards but good targets for fast foods and do-it-yourself products.[49]

Religious affiliation can also influence the way consumers evaluate brands. For example, Hirschman found that Jewish consumers are more likely to seek information in the process of brand evaluation and to transfer that information on consumption experiences to others.[50]

Nontraditional Subcultures

Subcultures can also be grouped around lifestyle choices—for example, the gay community. As this subculture grew more politically and economically visible through the 1980s, advertisers began actively courting it, mindful that gay couples tend to have more discretionary income than the average American, high-end tastes, and fierce brand loyalty. Cigarette companies, clothing manufacturers, and car makers began targeting their products to homosexual consumers; and magazines designed for that audience debuted. Though the gay community is also diverse, its members—like those in other lifestyle subcultures—share common needs and aspirations that are outgrowths of their common beliefs.

Ethnic Subcultures

The most important subcultural entities in the United States are defined by ethnic origin, particularly by race and/or national origin. Consumers in a particular racial or national group are considered part of a subculture when they have a common heritage or environment that influences values and purchasing behavior.

As with age, geographic, or religious groups, we might consider African-, Hispanic-, and Asian-Americans to be too diverse to constitute subcultures. For example, the diversity that exists among lower-, middle-, and higher-income African-Americans is probably as great as that for white consumers. However, as one writer noted, "Regardless of income brackets, African-Americans have a unique culture, and the African-American community has a distinct personality."[51] We will devote the remainder of this chapter to the three key ethnic subcultures: African-Americans, Hispanic-Americans, and Asian-Americans.

African-American Subculture

More African-Americans tend to identify with their ethnic group than whites do with theirs. About twice as many African-Americans say that ethnic identity is more important than national identity.[52] This ethnic identity, plus the fact that African-Americans differ in many ways from whites in their tastes and purchases, justifies characterizing them as a subculture. In this section, we first review differences in characteristics and purchasing behavior and then consider how companies direct marketing strategies to the African-American market.

Distinctiveness of Characteristics and Behavior

African-American consumers differ from whites by demographic characteristics. There are also marked differences in products and brands purchased, shopping behavior, prices paid, and media selected.

Demographic Characteristics. The 30 million African-Americans make up 12 percent of the total population in the United States and account for $270 billion in purchasing power.[53] The median income of African-American households is less than two-thirds that of whites. Although African-Americans represent 12 percent of the population, they own less than 1 percent of all stocks and bonds held by individuals in the United States.[54] Disparities in educational level parallel those in income. Only 10 percent of African-American adults have college degrees, compared to 20 percent of whites; and 63 percent have high school degrees, compared to 76 percent for whites.[55]

Lower income and educational levels among African-Americans are the result of decades of discrimination. As barriers to equality have decreased, income and educational levels of African-Americans have improved, resulting in a growing middle class. In the past 20 years, the aggregate annual income for African-Americans has risen sixfold; and now an average of one in ten African-American families has an income that exceeds $50,000.[56]

Educational levels have improved as well. Since 1940, the proportion of whites finishing high school tripled, while that of African-Americans increased nine times, making them the fastest growing group to earn high school diplomas in the country.[57] Still, despite these positive trends, this country has a long way to go to ensure income and educational equality.

Another demographic factor that indicates increasing purchasing potential for African-Americans is age. The average African-American consumer is six years younger than the average white consumer. More than half of African-Americans are 18 to 34 years old, compared to 37 percent of whites,[58] which means that a larger proportion have entered their prime spending years in the 1990s as compared to whites.

Some people might conclude that as the African-American middle class grows, it will lose its cultural identity. This is not the case. One study found that the greatest cultural affiliation occurs among affluent African-Americans rather than among the underprivileged. Among college-educated African-Americans earning more than $30,000 a year, 55 percent said ethnic identity was more important than national identity. This percentage is a much larger proportion than African-Americans in general.[59]

Purchasing Patterns.   Differences exist in purchasing patterns between African-Americans and whites. African-Americans spend proportionately more than whites for cosmetics, toiletries, and clothing; and whites spend more on medical care, entertainment, and insurance. These differences are largely the result of lower-income levels among African-Americans, since lower-income households spend proportionately more of their dollars on necessities.

Since African-Americans spend a greater proportion of money on necessities, marketers might believe they spend substantially less on luxuries. This assumption ignores the growing African-American middle class. As Figure 14.1 shows, in 1991, a larger proportion of African-Americans owned CDs and telephone answering machines than did whites; and the same proportion of African-Americans and whites owned VCRs. Even more striking, when we look at planned purchases, African-Americans were more likely to make purchases in every category except vacation and travel.

That is not to say, however, that African-Americans are disinterested in tourism. They comprise the fastest-growing segment of the industry, spending $30 billion a year.[60] However, they have different travel patterns compared to those of whites. They are 50 percent less likely to travel outside the United States; and when they do, they prefer destinations that are "color comfortable" such as the Caribbean, according to one 1993 survey.[61]

Figure 14.1 puts to rest a misconception that the African-American market is a poor economic target. As a result, companies producing major appliances and electronics are increasingly targeting African-American consumers.

Marketing to African-American Consumers

Viewing African-American consumers as a homogeneous subculture can lead to oversimplified marketing strategies. Marketers can use most of the same demographic, lifestyle, and value criteria to segment the African-American market as they use to segment the white market. As a result, specific segmenta-

▶**FIGURE 14.1**

Ownership and planned purchases of luxury goods among African-Americans and whites

Source: "6 Myths About Black Consumers," *Adweek's Marketing Week* (May 6, 1991), p. 18. Reprinted with permission of *Adweek's Marketing Week*. Data from studies by Deloitte & Touche and Information Resources, Inc.

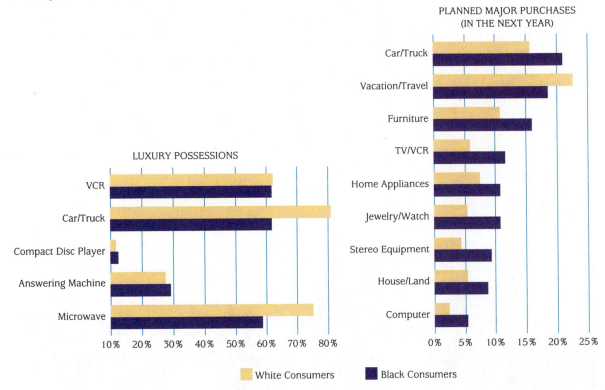

tion, product development, advertising, media, and distribution strategies are required when selling to the African-American market.

Market Segmentation. Marketers frequently position products to African-Americans; but in doing so, they fail to recognize the nuances and diversity of the African-American market. For years, Pillsbury could not understand why African-Americans were not buying as much of its Hungry Jack pancake syrup as the rest of the population. Only when the company conducted surveys did it find that African-Americans did not relate to the white lumber jack on the product's label. So, it replaced the character in 1992 with a more street-savvy slogan directed to African-Americans—"You look hungry, Jack." Sales soared.[62]

Changes such as these reflect the growing attention being paid to marketing to African-Americans. Between 1980 and 1990, advertising spending in African-American media tripled to 3 percent of the national total. However, this spending still remains low when one considers that African-Americans account for 12 percent of the population.[63] Part of the change has been a slow but steady recognition that separate African-American consumer segments exist and can be targeted, each providing a source of great incremental profits.

For instance, car manufacturers have been able to draw a line between the luxury and economy segments of the African-American market. As Exhibit 14.7 shows, Chrysler developed an ad for its luxury Eagle Vision that used an African-American jazz musician to convey an image of individuality. Chrysler also targeted the segment interested in economy and practicality with its campaigns for the Dodge Caravan and Plymouth Voyager. This luxury/economy segmentation parallels the same strategy automakers have used for years with whites.

Segmenting the African-American market by income is only one criterion. Marketers should consider other segments such as the same age groups identified in Chapter 10 (baby busters, baby boomers, and so on), lifestyle factors such as nutritionally oriented African-Americans, and cultural factors such as African-American consumers who are new versus old traditionalists.

▶**EXHIBIT 14.7**
Targeting the luxury and economy segments of African-Americans

Product Development.   Cultural factors also play a large part in the design of new products. As African-American women emerged as a force in the workplace, they looked for cosmetics that suited their skin tones. A handful of African-American-run companies such as Fashion Fair filled the void until the major cosmetics companies estimated that the ethnic cosmetics market was worth at least $100 million. As a result, Maybelline developed a line called Shades of You; Revlon, a line called Color Style.[64]

Product development is also required to meet the needs of the African-American community at large. J. C. Penney met this need in 1992 by opening boutiques in 20 markets that carry African-style fashions such as caftans, housewares, and art.[65]

Advertising.   Companies have used two approaches in advertising to African-Americans: (1) using African-Americans to foster ethnic identification and (2) using the same advertising to African-Americans as to whites but placing the ads in African-American media. Exhibit 14.8 shows an ad for Creme of Nature that takes an ethnically aware approach by emphasizing the distinctive hairstyles of African-Americans and fostering Afro identity. The ad for Maybelline duplicates the style the company uses in other markets. It shows an African-American model with a more general hairstyle.

African-Americans are likely to reject advertising symbols and imagery they cannot relate to. Greyhound discovered this when it bought time on African-American radio stations and aired a commercial with a country music soundtrack that few of the hoped-for customers could relate to.[66] At the same time, advertisers using African-American models must be careful to avoid portraying them in a stereotyped way such as dancing to rap music in ghetto street scenes.

To prevent such gaffes but to take advantage of the African-American middle class's economic clout, Fortune 500 companies are hiring African-American-owned ad agencies to get it right. Kmart and Toys "R" Us are among them. In 1992, Kmart introduced a campaign focusing on clothing that ran ads in magazines such as *Ebony* and *Essence* and on radio stations targeted to African-Americans. The ads used the slogan "Looking Good" to appeal to the greater clothes-consciousness of many African-American consumers. (Kmart's campaign directed to Hispanic-Americans used Spanish-speaking TV channels rather than radio and showed a husband, wife, and children shopping in the store to emphasize family values.)[67]

Advertisers have an expanding range of broadcast and print media for reaching African-Americans. There are hundreds of radio stations directed to African-Americans across the country, over 200 African-American newspapers, and 22 national magazines.[68] Radio is particularly effective, because African-Americans listen to radio 20 percent more than the general public.[69] The one weak spot is television. There are few African-American TV stations in the United States, despite the fact that African-Americans spend 44 percent more time than whites watching TV. An exception is the Black Entertainment Network, the nation's only African-American cable TV network, which reaches 53 percent of African-American households.[70]

▶**EXHIBIT 14.8**

Hair care products positioned to appeal to Afro identity versus the general market

Source: (bottom) Courtesy of Maybelline, Inc.

Media

The dominant issue in selling to African-Americans is whether general or specialized media are more effective. The evidence is not clear-cut. African-Americans can identify more closely with products if ads appear in African-American magazines or radio. However, for nationally advertised products, mass media will reach both African-Americans and whites. The best strategy for products with a broad appeal is to use specialized media vehicles to reach African-Americans and more general media to reach the mass audience.

Distribution

Marketers must gear distribution policies to the purchasing behavior of African-Americans. For example, in the early 1980s, Zayre Discount Stores began locating many of its branches in lower-income, inner-city minority areas. According to its president, the company made a "significant commitment to become very good at something that [other retailers] were running away from."[71] The inventory of its inner-city stores was tailored to the special needs and tastes of its predominantly African-American customers. The stores stocked a wide variety of items because customers had fewer places to shop. The stores featured African-American models in their in-store promotional materials and had primarily African-American employees.

Manufacturers also try to find creative ways to inject their products into African-American communities. For instance, Procter & Gamble and Coca-Cola distribute samples in gift bags handed out after Sunday service to parishioners at African-American churches.[72]

Hispanic-American Subculture

Because they have largely resisted assimilation of their language and customs into American society, Hispanic-Americans are a distinct subculture. A 1990 survey found that almost 90 percent of Hispanics say that the Spanish language is the most important aspect of their culture. More than two-thirds of Hispanic-Americans prefer to speak Spanish at home, and one-fifth do not even speak English.[73]

In this section, we will see the challenges and opportunities posed by the strong cultural identity of this fast-growing subculture.

Demographic Characteristics

Hispanic-Americans make up the second largest minority group in the United States. In 1990, there were 22 million Hispanics in the United States, representing nearly 9 percent of the population and over $130 billion in purchasing power.[74] Because of a growth rate four times faster than that of the general population, Hispanics will number 39 million in the United States by the turn of the century.[75]

Among Hispanics, Mexicans represent more than 60 percent of the total, with the remainder being people of Puerto Rican and Cuban origin. Many are immigrants (one-third have come to the United States since 1981), and all are united by a common language and family bonds that make them nurture their heritage.

Hispanics tend to be younger, with a median age of 23, as compared to 32 for the rest of the population.[76] Their median income is about two-thirds that of the average American, and educational levels are well below average. However, both income and education are rising rapidly.[77] Hispanic family size is also larger, with about 3.5 persons per household, as compared to 2.7 for the general population.[78] Hispanics are also more likely than whites or African-Americans to live in metropolitan areas. Over 60 percent live in the top ten urban areas in the United States.[79]

Hispanics have traditional and conservative values, which are reflected in the respect they give their elders and a strong commitment to family. These values are reflected in the fact that, as one writer said, "Machismo is still strong and women's lib has a long way to go in Hispanic communities."[80] As a result of these values, one Hispanic marketer concluded, "The Spanish market will cling to its language, customs, and cultural background and will not, like other ethnic groups, be absorbed into the melting pot tradition of the U.S."[81]

These differences in values and customs justify defining the Hispanic market as a separate subculture, despite differences among Mexicans, Cubans, and Puerto Ricans.

Purchasing Patterns

Hispanic-Americans are a highly brand-loyal segment of the market. One 1993 survey found that 62 percent of Hispanics buy the same food, beverage, and household items on a regular basis.[82] Hispanics demonstrate faith in the quality of well-advertised national brands and are less likely to buy private brands and generic products. This is at least partly the result of their behavior in their native countries and explains why Colgate, which has a strong South American presence, holds a 70 percent market share among recent immigrants.[83]

Because of their large family sizes, Hispanics also spend twice as much money per week as non-Hispanics on soft drinks, coffee, canned goods, household cleaners, and beauty aids.[84] The brands they are loyal to also differ. For example, market share of the following brands among Hispanics is at least 20 percent higher than that for whites:

- Dove and Zest bar soaps.
- Coors and Budweiser beers.
- Avon and English Leather colognes.
- Alberto and Head & Shoulders shampoos.[85]

Marketing to Hispanic-American Consumers

Overall, the commitment of consumer goods companies to the Hispanic-American market in the form of advertising and new products is limited. Many of them believe that the Hispanic market needs no special marketing effort. This view is changing, however, and more companies are directing segmentation, advertising, and product strategies to Hispanic-Americans.

Market Segmentation.   Marketers have generally avoided segmenting the Hispanic market because the small budgets allocated to Hispanics preclude preparation of separate campaigns for individual segments. Frito Lay is among them, treating Hispanic-Americans as a single market because, in the words of one executive, the company tries to project a "consistent national image."[86]

However, differences in customs and language among various Hispanic groups warrant separate strategies for Mexicans, Cubans, and Puerto Ricans. Donnelley Marketing Information Services recently introduced a model that splits the market into 18 components. An illustration of the use of the model is as finely tuned as a segment described as "Higher income, younger Puerto Ricans living in single family homes."[87]

One company that recognizes such differences is Anheuser-Busch. It follows a segmentation approach for Budweiser, the leading beer among Hispanics, by using different advertising for Mexican, Cuban, and Puerto Rican consumers. The purpose is to ensure that "each campaign should pick up on the regional nuances of [these] groups."[88] Thus, the Puerto Rican commercial is set in a disco and features salsa rhythms; the Mexican commercial is set in a rodeo to mariachi music; and the Cuban commercial takes place on a private boat because Cubans are the most affluent Hispanic group.

Another possible basis companies could use for segmentation is distinguishing those who are steeped in their Hispanic heritage versus those who are becoming more assimilated into the American cultural mainstream. Such a segmentation would parallel that used to identify consumers with and without a strong sense of African-American identity.

Product Development.   In the product development area, there are parallels between Hispanics and African-Americans. Estée Lauder designs makeup shades for Hispanic- as well as African-Americans. Fabergé has also developed shampoos and conditioners specifically designed for the Hispanic woman's typically long and thick hair.[89]

In foods, Frito-Lay introduced Plantanitos in the East because plantain chips are popular with Puerto Ricans and Cubans. Gerber Products Co. has added a 16-item tropical fruit line to appeal to Hispanics, while rice maker Riviana is testing new products for the Latino market in Los Angeles.[90]

Advertising.   Marketers must be aware of the norms, values, and language nuances of the Hispanic market. In failing to recognize these factors, some companies have made classic blunders. For example, Coors was left red-faced when its slogan "Get loose with Coors," translated into Spanish as "Get the runs with Coors."[91]

Companies use two basic approaches to advertise to Hispanics. One uses the same ads as those in English, but with Spanish copy or personalities. The other adapts the campaign to the specific values of the Hispanic market. Exhibit 14.9 shows both sides. If not for the Spanish copy, the Jack Daniels ad could appear anywhere. The danger with such an approach that merely translates a general campaign into Spanish is that it may not reflect Hispanics' specific needs and values. Advertising approaches to the Hispanic market should reflect its conservative values and emphasis on family and children. This is better illustrated in Exhibit 14.9 by the Polaroid ad for its Spectra instant camera. The ad shows the picture a father took of his wife and newborn baby. Hispanic marketer Marcelo Salup noted that ads like these "appeal to everything that unites us—heritage, tradition, family—without being heavy handed or a tear jerker."[92] When Polaroid advertises to the general market, it focuses more on the camera and its features.

Companies seeking to reach Hispanics are turning to advertising companies Latinos run. Pizza Hut was able to boost sales by hiring a Latino ad agency that created a TV spot with a twist. Because the English slogan "Make It Great" did not quite work among Hispanics, the agency came up with the slogan *Un*

▶**EXHIBIT 14.9**
Taking a general approach versus targeting Hispanic identity
Source: (left) Courtesy of Jack Daniel's Distillery

mundo de sabor, or "A world of taste," and set it to a salsa beat. Pizza Hut's sales improved in Chicago, Los Angeles, New York, Miami, San Antonio, and Albuquerque.[93] One reason for this response is that Hispanics are "significantly more likely to believe that advertising represents an honest and helpful portrayal of products."[94]

Media.   Because a network of Spanish-speaking television stations exists, the Hispanic-American market is easier to target than the African-American market. There are 112 local Spanish TV stations plus two national Spanish networks, Univision and Telemundo. Radio is almost as effective as TV in reaching Hispanics, with about 125 Spanish-language stations nationwide.

Television and radio are effective in this market because Hispanics are more likely to tune into these media, and half of the time they tune into Spanish-speaking stations. While Hispanics are less likely to read magazines and newspapers than the average consumer, Spanish-language magazines and newspapers are becoming more important. *Vista*, a Sunday magazine newspaper supplement, reaches 1.2 million Hispanic households.[95] *Vanidades* magazine is aimed at Hispanic women in their late teens and early twenties, while *Cosmopolitan en Espanol* is targeted to the younger, more modern Hispanic woman. *Miami Mensual* is designed to reach affluent Hispanic audiences.

Distribution.   Many Hispanics shop in *bodegas*, small grocery stores that specialize in Hispanic foods and also serve as a place for socializing. Hispanics value the personal interaction with friends and shopowners in the *bodegas*. One reason Goya Foods has been a successful marketer of Hispanic products is that it has cultivated strong relationships with *bodega* owners, who account for 45 percent of Goya's sales.[96] Similarly, by establishing strong distribution through *bodegas*, P&G has been successful as the largest marketer of Hispanic products. The company has a bilingual sales and distribution force that caters to *bodegas* in key metropolitan areas such as New York and Miami. Hispanics are also known to favor large supermarkets and department stores.[97]

Asian-American Subculture

Asian-Americans are the third largest minority group, with 7.3 million people representing about 3 percent of the U.S. population.[98] The reason for identifying Asian-Americans as a subculture is the same as that for African-Americans and Hispanic-Americans: strong ethnic identity. Most are recent immigrants; 70 percent have arrived in this country during the past 20 years.[99] Furthermore, 68 percent speak their native language at home.[100]

Demographic Characteristics
Asian-Americans are the most highly educated and affluent minority group. About 42 percent have college degrees, compared to 28 percent for the general population, and their median income is about 20 percent higher than that of other Americans. The average age of this group is almost a decade younger than that of the general population.[101]

By the year 2000, California will become the first state in the United States where African-, Hispanic-, and Asian-Americans constitute a majority of the population. In anticipation of that benchmark, marketers are pulling out all the stops to woo ethnic customers whom they largely ignored just a decade ago. In the process, they are learning that selling to ethnic shoppers requires considerably more effort than putting an Asian or a Latino actor in an English commercial.

These efforts are being felt most in the Hispanic community, which grew 70 percent between 1980 and 1990 and now accounts for a quarter of the state's population, and the Asian community, which doubled in the 1980s to become 10 percent of the state's total. Banks, phone companies, TV stations, and super-market chains are all quickly learning about the diversity, nuances, and perceptions of these communities so they can apply a strategy that one consultant calls "international marketing within your own borders." This means that just as American strategies may not work abroad, marketers cannot assume that strategies designed for a homogeneous U.S. market will work in ethnic enclaves. New immigrants are often mystified by American norms, and those who have assimilated frequently retain their cultural identity.

In contrast, Bank of America showed more ethnic sensitivity in dealing with the fact that most of the new Latino residents from Mexico and Central America had never set foot in a bank. It embarked on a massive education campaign, including a slick soap-opera video that followed a Latino couple through marriage, having children, and buying their first home—with explanations at each juncture about how a bank can help. The Bank gives these videos to various outreach groups that socialize new Americans.

Some of the worst blunders have occurred because California marketers have not been sensitive to ethnic cultures. For instance, Met Life once tried appealing to Korean customers by running an ad picturing a family in traditional dress; the only problem was it was Chinese dress. Similarly, Coors was roundly criticized for sexual stereotyping during the 1988 Chinese New Year when it erotically portrayed a Chinese woman in the folds of a silk dragon. Marketers must also be sensitive to the nuances of a subculture's language. When Pepsi tried aiming its "Choice of a New Generation" campaign at Chinese-Americans, it suffered a major embarrassment when the slogan was unintentionally translated into "Come and wake up your dead ancestors."

Asians pose more difficulties than Hispanics for California marketers because of the variety of languages they speak—Vietnamese, Cantonese, Mandarin, Korean, Tagalog (spoken by Filipinos), or Cambodian. One strategy for bridging the gap is to rely less on mass-market tools

STRATEGIC APPLICATIONS OF CONSUMER BEHAVIOR

California: On the Cutting Edge of Catering to Ethnic Identity

such as television and use the growing list of ethnic newspapers. Companies such as the Bank of America follow this strategy. Still others appeal to shared characteristics. Thirty-six percent of Asians in the San Francisco area named Macy's their favorite store because, among other things, it caters to Asian women with petite sizes.

It is often said that California leads the rest of the United States. As minorities become the majority in state after state, California's ethnic marketers will surely have much to teach the rest of the nation.

Sources: "Catering to Consumers' Ethnic Needs," *The New York Times* (January 23, 1992), pp. D1, D8; "Solutions: Making a Connection," *Adweek* (October 7, 1991), p. 46; "California's Asian Market," *American Demographics* (October, 1990), pp. 34-37.

Asian-Americans are more varied than Hispanic- and African-Americans, accounting for 29 distinct ethnic groups.[102] Chinese represent the largest group, followed closely by Filipinos and then by Japanese, Vietnamese, and Koreans. The Asian-American segment is growing 14 times faster than the general population, primarily because of a high rate of immigration. About 93 percent live in highly urbanized areas, and most of those areas are in the West. Thirty-nine percent of Asian Americans live in California alone, while 18 percent live in the Northeast, 14 percent in the South, 12' percent in the Midwest, and 11 percent in Hawaii.[103]

Given the importance of the Asian-American market, it is surprising that more key demographic information on this market is not available. The U.S. Bureau of the Census separates basic income and educational information by whites, African-Americans, and Hispanics. However, it does not group Asian-Americans as a separate category.

Marketing Strategy to Asian-American Consumers

Because the Asian-American market is small, few marketers direct advertising strategies to it. Their philosophy is that Asian-Americans need no special marketing effort and that general advertising campaigns will also attract this segment. These marketers also find targeted marketing difficult because of the community's diversity and range of native tongues. A recent survey discovered that most Asian-Americans speak their native language at home, particularly Koreans (94 percent) and Chinese (90 percent.)[104]

As a result, Asian-Americans are poor consumers of American media. On average, they watch only about 12 hours of English-language television a week and listen to only 80 hours of American radio, well below the national average. One survey found that about half those polled did not read English-language magazines.[105] In addition, there is no national Asian cable TV network.

However, some companies are beginning to target Asian-Americans because their youth and greater affluence make them an attractive market. Exhibit 14.10 shows how two companies have targeted Asian-Americans. To emphasize its long-distance service and bilingual operators, MCI appeals to the close ties many Asian-Americans have to their native country. Metropolitan Life focuses on the emphasis that Asian-Americans place on education and stresses the role of insurance in planning for their future. These attempts to target the broad Asian-American market are the exception, however. For most companies, it is difficult to implement such campaigns due to the diversity of the Asian-American market.

Specific Asian nationalities can be targeted because they tend to live in the same areas. For example, the heavy concentration of Chinese-Americans in California made it possible for Bank of America to target this market selectively. The Bank took English-language spots, dubbed them or added subtitles in Cantonese, and ran them on local Chinese-language cable TV stations. The Bank also targeted immigrants in the central valley of California who were primarily from Southeast Asia by advertising in newspapers in Vietnamese, Cambodian, and Laotian. The ads urged readers to "come see us" as these recent immigrants mistrusted banks.[106] Bank of America's campaign is one of the few examples of marketing to specific segments of Asian-Americans. Given the diversity of this market, such a segmented approach is essential.

◆ SOCIETAL IMPLICATIONS OF CROSS-CULTURAL AND SUBCULTURAL INFLUENCES

The nature of cross-cultural and subcultural influences creates a number of societal issues that bear on consumer rights in the marketplace.

Cross-Cultural Issues

Consumers in foreign markets should have the same rights as those outlined in Chapter 2—the right to safe products, to full information, to adequate choice, and to redress of grievances. This should be true whether consumers live in developed or in Third World countries. One of the most contentious issues in international marketing is that consumers in Third World countries do not have adequate protection when it comes to product safety and full disclosure of product contents and performance. Some companies have even been charged with selling products that have misled and harmed consumers in underdeveloped countries.

The most widely publicized case in this regard was Nestlé's infant formula products. Many infants died in Third World countries because the formula was often mixed with contaminated water from local sources. A worldwide boycott of Nestlé products ensued in the late 1970s. The company attempted to resolve

▶**EXHIBIT 14.10**
Targeting Asian-
American consumers

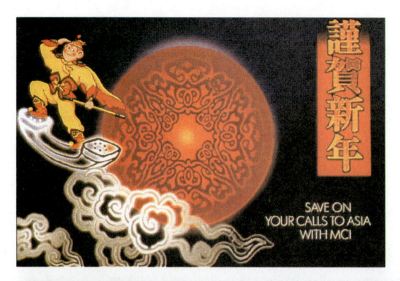

the issue by following guidelines the United Nations set for promotion and distribution of infant formula. As a result, the boycott was lifted. The issue arose again in 1989 when Nestlé was again charged with distribution of infant formula that did not conform to the spirit of the UN guidelines.[107] The issue has still not been fully resolved.

Another issue drawing increasing attention is American cigarette companies targeting brands to consumers in less-developed countries. Consumer advocates believe that it is unethical to encourage smoking in countries where famine and disease are prevalent. A World Health Organization study found that marketing campaigns by U.S. cigarette companies have "caused immediate jumps in consumption among women and teens, traditionally non-smoking groups in less-developed economies."[108]

Consumer activists in Asian countries are accusing American companies of manipulating Asian youth. They charge that American companies are taking advantage of the globalization of American consumption values by linking cigarettes to such themes as the Marlboro Cowboy or Joe Camel. One activist states that youth in underdeveloped countries are "smoking the American dream."[109] In Taiwan, one consumer group was successful in stopping a rock concert sponsored by R.J. Reynolds. Admission was by empty packs of Winston.

Subcultural Issues

Many of these same issues arise regarding consumer rights of minority groups. We noted in Chapter 2 that minority consumers should have the same rights as others without being at a disadvantage. However, this is not always the case. Minority consumers in lower socioeconomic groups are often at a disadvantage when it comes to adequate brand alternatives, fair prices, and the assurance of product safety.

Another issue, as we saw in Chapter 12, has been the attempt by one cigarette manufacturer to target minority consumers with a specific brand of cigarette—Uptown. Although the brand was eventually withdrawn, the issue remains—attempting to target underprivileged consumers with potentially unsafe products.

SUMMARY

Differing cultural norms and values result in different patterns of purchasing behavior in various countries. These cross-cultural influences require companies to adapt their marketing strategies to the local conditions of various countries. Four important cross-cultural factors influence marketing strategy: consumer customs and values, language, symbols, and the economic environment.

These cross-cultural factors encourage companies to adapt to local conditions. However, several factors are creating common tastes and purchasing preferences on a global basis. These include (1) global communications, (2) demographic trends across countries such as the greater proportion of working women, (3) a reduction in trade barriers worldwide, and (4) the Americanization of consumption values, particularly in Europe and Russia.

Based on these influences, three types of international marketing strategies were discussed. A localized strategy is important in adjusting to differences in norms and customs in various countries. A globalized strategy achieves economies of scale and a universal image but may fail to adapt to differences in needs and purchasing habits across countries. A company following flexible globalization thinks globally but acts locally by establishing a standard strategy but allowing countries to vary details to meet local needs and customs.

Subcultures are important to marketers because they represent groups with distinct values, customs, and purchasing habits. The more distinctive and homogeneous a subculture, the greater will be its influence on consumer purchases.

Subcultures in the United States can be identified on the basis of five things: age, geography, race, religion, or national origin. The three most important subcultures for marketers are African-Americans, Hispanic-Americans, and Asian-Americans, who together represent close to one-fourth of the U.S. population. These subcultures also represent significant purchasing power—over $400 billion a year—and are profitable markets because they tend to be more brand loyal.

Marketers have increasingly directed strategies to these groups. The African-American consumer market has seen more cosmetic and toiletry products directed to its specific needs. In addition, marketers have directed ads to African-Americans through African-American magazines and radio; and ad campaigns have frequently attempted to foster Afro identity. Targeting marketing strategies to Hispanics is facilitated by some homogeneity in values. Companies such as Anheuser-Busch and Polaroid have developed Spanish-speaking ad campaigns for their national brands. However, companies find targeting ad campaigns to Asian-Americans difficult because of the diversity of nationalities and languages within this broad segment. Overall, marketers have a long way to go in recognizing the potential of the African-, Hispanic-, and Asian-American markets and adequately targeting marketing efforts to these groups.

The chapter concluded by considering some societal implications of cross-cultural and subcultural influences; namely, the need to protect consumer rights abroad, particularly in Third World countries, and the need to protect the rights of underprivileged consumers at home.

In the next chapter, we consider another environmental factor: the influence of reference groups on consumer behavior.

QUESTIONS

1. What are the dangers of an ethnocentric view in marketing abroad? Provide some examples of these dangers.
2. What is meant by "mainstreaming"? How has mainstreaming contributed to the development of a global teenager? How does it facilitate the establishment of world brands?

3. What is the evidence that there is a global teenage market? How might a producer of designer jeans target the global teenager?

4. The chapter noted that many demographic trends have occurred in the United States, such as an increasing proportion of working women, higher divorce rates, smaller families, and later marriages. These trends have also occurred in most of the developed nations of the world. What are the strategic implications of these trends for a:
   - Car manufacturer in Japan considering a marketing campaign directed to women?
   - Large toy manufacturer in the United States considering exporting its products?
   - Manufacturer of household cleaning products considering a worldwide advertising campaign for its line?

5. What are the advantages and disadvantages of a globalized marketing strategy? What are the limits of implementing a truly standardized marketing strategy worldwide? When are such strategies most likely to work?

6. Localization of marketing strategies was suggested as a way to adjust to conditions in specific countries. What are the pros and cons of using a localized strategy?

7. What is meant by "flexible globalization"? Why is it becoming a more common strategy in international markets? Cite examples of (a) product strategies and (b) advertising strategies that have followed this approach.

8. What are the characteristics that identify a subculture? Would you identify residents of retirement communities as a subculture? Why or why not?

9. What are the marketing implications if America becomes more of a "salad bowl" than a melting pot in the 1990s?

10. On what basis could you support identification of the African-American consumer market as a subculture? On what basis could you argue against such an identification? What are the marketing implications of each position?

11. A company is considering three alternative strategies in marketing a hair care line to African-American consumers:
    a. Introduce two lines: one positioned to those who seek Afro identity; the other, to those who identify with white middle-class values.
    b. Introduce one line to appeal to both segments.
    c. Introduce one line to appeal only to those seeking Afro identity.
    What are the pros and cons of each strategy? Which would you select? Why?

12. The Creme of Nature ad in Exhibit 14.8 fosters Afro identity, while the Maybelline ad does not. What is the rationale for introducing an advertising campaign to African-Americans that does foster Afro identity? That does not?

13. Hispanic-Americans have been described as a more homogeneous ethnic subculture than African-Americans. Why? What are the marketing implications of a greater level of homogeneity?

14. An ad for a household cleanser targeted to Hispanic women uses an appeal showing the husband's approval when entering a sparkling clean home. Do you think such an appeal would be successful among Hispanic women? Among the general population? Why or why not?
15. What are the pros and cons of targeting Asian-American consumers?
16. What ethical issues might arise in marketing to foreign consumers, especially in less-developed countries? To subcultures in a domestic market, especially to underprivileged consumers?

RESEARCH ASSIGNMENTS

1. A lively debate has ensued in the marketing community regarding the viability of a global strategy. As the chapter suggests, some marketers believe in the convergence of tastes and values and see globalization increasing in the future as a result of more travel and more universal communication facilities. Others believe that local differences between countries will dominate marketing strategies, regardless of the so-called trend to universal values.

   To familiarize yourself with this issue, read the following:
   - Theodore Levitt, "The Globalization of Markets," *Harvard Business Review* (May–June, 1983), pp. 92–102. (This article supports the notion that markets are becoming more global and that the trend should be toward more standardized strategies.)
   - "Marketers Turn Sour on Global Sales Pitch Harvard Guru Makes," *The Wall Street Journal* (May 12, 1988), p. 1. (The article debates Levitt's position.)
   - Teresa Domzal and Lynette Unger, "Emerging Positioning Strategies in Global Markets," *Journal of Consumer Marketing*, 4 (Fall, 1987).
   - "Goodby Global Ads," *Advertising Age* (November 16, 1987), pp. 22–24. (This article argues against globalized strategies.)

   Interview at least ten marketing executives in multinational companies. The companies can be large or small, manufacturers or distributors, product or service companies. The important objective is to talk to managers with experience in marketing abroad. Ask these managers to comment on the following:
   - Do they think tastes and values are becoming more similar worldwide? If so, is this trend likely to facilitate globalized marketing strategies in the future?
   - Will decreasing trade barriers affect the company's operations? If so, in what ways? If not, what general opportunities do they think these events will create for American businesses?
   - Under what circumstances do they believe globalized strategies are more effective? When are localized strategies more effective? For what types of product categories or services?
   - What products or services have they been involved with abroad? What types of strategies did they use?

- Did they adapt strategies to the customs and values of specific countries? How?

Once you have collected this information, summarize the views of the executives you have interviewed. Consider the following:

  a. What differences in views emerged regarding the issues you investigated?
  b. Were there differences in views by type of company (for example, product versus service companies, producers of packaged goods versus durable goods)? If so, why do you believe these differences in views emerged?

2. Identify an ethnic group that can be regarded as a subculture (whether by race, religion, or national origin). Interview 30 people in this group and 30 people in the general population.

  a. Ask respondents to:
  - Rate their agreement with lifestyle items such as those in Table 11.1.
  - Indicate how frequently they purchase products such as cosmetics, household cleaners, and soft drinks.
  b. Do your findings justify identifying the group you selected as a subculture? Specifically:
  - What are the differences in values, lifestyles, and purchases between the subcultural group and the general group?
  - Is the subcultural group more homogeneous in lifestyles and values than the general group?
  c. What are the implications of your findings for developing (a) products and (b) advertising strategies for the subcultural group?

NOTES

1. "For Levi's, a Flattering Fit Overseas," *Business Week* (November 5, 1990), pp. 76–77.
2. "Reaching the New Immigrants," *Adweek's Marketing Week* (September 11, 1989), p. 24.
3. Teresa Domzal and Lynette Unger, "Emerging Positioning Strategies in Global Markets," *Journal of Consumer Marketing*, 4 (Fall, 1987), p. 24.
4. "P&G Uses Skills It Has Honed at Home to Introduce Its Brands to the Russians," *The Wall Street Journal* (April 14, 1993), p. B1.
5. "The Awakening Chinese Consumer," *The New York Times* (October 11, 1992), p. F1.
6. "Ad Fads: Global Sales Pitch by Harvard Guru Appears Much Easier in Theory, Marketers Find," *The Wall Street Journal* (May 12, 1988), p. 4.
7. "Global Ad Campaigns After Many Missteps, Finally Pay Dividends," *The Wall Street Journal* (August 27, 1992), pp. A1, A8.
8. "Arise Comrades, Cast Off Your Chains and Go Get a Coke," *Brandweek* (July 20, 1992), pp. 23–24.
9. "Seeing Is Believing," *Marketing & Media Decisions* (February, 1988), p. 52.
10. J. Douglas McConnell, "The Economics of Behavioral Factors on the Multi-National Corporation," in Fred C. Allvine, ed., *Combined Proceedings of the American Marketing Association,* Series No. 33 (1971), p. 265.
11. David A. Ricks, *Big Business Blunders* (Homewood, IL: Dow Jones-Irwin, 1983), p. 65.
12. Albert Stridsberg, "U.S. Advertisers Win Some, Lose Some in Foreign Markets," *Advertising Age* (May 6, 1974), p. 42.
13. *Business Marketing* (July, 1984), p. 112.
14. Ricks, *Big Business Blunders, op. cit.,* p. 84.
15. "Maintaining a Balance of Planning," *Advertising Age* (May 17, 1982), p. M21.

16. "America's International Winners," *Fortune* (April 14, 1986), p. 44.

17. *Ibid.*

18. Ricks, *Big Business Blunders, op. cit.*, p. 33.

19. Charles Winick, "Anthropology's Contribution to Marketing," *Journal of Marketing,* 25 (July, 1961), p. 59.

20. Theodore J. Gage, "Pipelining Image Ads to China," *Advertising Age* (May 17, 1982), p. M20.

21. Domzal and Unger, "Emerging Positioning Strategies in Global Markets," *op. cit.*, p. 29.

22. *The Wall Street Journal* (August 27, 1992), *loc. cit.*

23. *Ibid.*

24. Thomas C. O'Guinn, *et al.,* "The Cultivation of Consumer Norms," in Thomas K. Srull, ed., *Advances in Consumer Research,* Vol. 16 (Provo, UT: Association for Consumer Research, 1989), pp. 779–785.

25. "The First Global Generation," *Adweek's Marketing Week* (February 6, 1989), p. 18.

26. *The Wall Street Journal* (August 27, 1992), *loc. cit.*

27. "A New Mass Market Emerges," *Fortune* (Fall, 1990 Special Issue), p. 51.

28. *Ibid.,* p. 56.

29. "In Pursuit of the Elusive Euroconsumer," *The New York Times* (April 23, 1992), p. B1.

30. *Brandweek* (July 20, 1992), *op. cit.,* pp. 22–24; and "Pepsi Takes a Seat on Moscow Fast-Food Express," *The New York Times* (June 11, 1993), p. D1.

31. "Den Fujita, Japan's Mr. Joint-Venture," *The New York Times* (March 22, 1992), pp. F1, F6; and "Moose-Hunting in Japan?" *The New York Times* (February 28, 1993), Section 9, p. 4.

32. "Fast-Food Franchises Fight for Brazilian Aficionados," *Brandweek* (June 7, 1993), p. 20.

33. "Pushing U.S. Style, Nike and Reebok Sell Sneakers to Europe," *The Wall Street Journal* (July 22, 1993), pp. A1, A8.

34. *Ibid.*

35. *The Wall Street Journal* (August 27, 1992), *loc. cit.*

36. "Parker Pen," *Advertising Age* (June 2, 1986), p. 60.

37. "Heinz Aims to Export Taste for Ketchup," *The Wall Street Journal.*

38. "Pizza in Japan is Adapted to Local Tastes," *The Wall Street Journal* (June 4, 1993), p. B1.

39. Domzal and Unger, "Emerging Positioning Strategies in Global Markets," *op. cit.,* p. 26.

40. *Brandweek* (July 20, 1992), *loc. cit.*

41. *Fortune* (Fall, 1990 Special Issue), *op. cit.,* p. 66.

42. "Global Lather," *Forbes* (February 5, 1990), p. 146.

43. "The Rumble Heard Round the World: Harleys," *Business Week* (May 24, 1993), pp. 58–60.

44. Ricks, *Big Business Blunders, op. cit.,* p. 52.

45. "Reaching the New Immigrants," *Adweek's Marketing Week* (September 11, 1989), p. 24.

46. "If You Want a Big, New Market," *Fortune* (November 21, 1989), p. 181.

47. "Firms Translate Sales Pitches to Appeal to Asian-Americans," *The Wall Street Journal* (April 10, 1986), p. 35.

48. Michael Solomon, *Consumer Behavior* (Boston: Allyn and Bacon, 1992), pp. 464–465.

49. "Bringing in the Sheaves," *American Demographics* (August, 1988), pp. 28–32.

50. Elizabeth Hirschman, "American Jewish Ethnicity: Its Relationship to Some Selected Aspects of Consumer Behavior," *Journal of Marketing,* 45 (Summer, 1981), pp. 102–105.

51. "Madison Avenue Blindly Ignores the Black Consumer," *Business and Society Review* (Winter, 1987), p. 11.

52. "6 Myths About Black Consumers," *Adweek's Marketing Week* (May 6, 1991), p. 17.

53. "Marketing to African Americans," *B&E Review* (April–June, 1993), p. 3.

54. "The Black Middle Class," *Business Week* (March 14, 1988), p. 64.

55. U.S. Department of Commerce, Bureau of the Census, *Statistical Abstract of the United States, 1990* (Washington, D.C.: Government Printing Office), Table No. 215, p. 133.

56. *B&E Review* (April–June, 1993), *loc. cit.*

57. "Many Marketers Still Consider Blacks 'Dark Skinned Whites'," *Marketing News* (January 18, 1993), p. 1.

58. "Afro-American Market Opportunities," *Merchandise Discount* (May, 1990), p. 121.

59. *Adweek's Marketing Week* (May 6, 1991), *loc. cit.*

60. "Myths Discourage Marketing to African Americans," *Marketing Week* (January 20, 1992), p. 4.

61. "The Difference in Black and White," *American Demographics* (January, 1993), p. 49.

62. *Ibid.*

63. *Mediaweek* (January 21, 1991), p. 18.

64. "Mining the Non-White Markets," *Brandweek* (April 12, 1993), p. 29.

65. "Buying Black," *Time* (August 31, 1992), p. 52; and "J. C. Penney Finds Profit in Africa," *American Demographics* (November, 1992), p. 12.

66. *American Demographics* (January, 1993), *loc. cit.*

67. "2 Big Retailers Reach Out to Minorities," *The New York Times* (December 31, 1991), p. D16.

68. "Minority Marketing Looks to the 80s," *Advertising Age* (April 7, 1980), p. S19; and *Advertising Age* (October 19, 1981), p. S52.

69. "Arbitron Radio Survey," *The New York Times* (June 14, 1984), p. D21.

70. *Marketing News* (January 18, 1993), *op. cit.*, p. 13.

71. "Zayre's Strategy of Ethnic Merchandising Proves to Be Successful in Inner-City Stores," *The Wall Street Journal* (September 25, 1984), p. 31.

72. *Time* (August 31, 1992), *loc. cit.*

73. "Do All Hispanics Speak a Common Cultural Language?" *Ad Forum* (December, 1984), p. 16.

74. "Help Wanted," *Adweek's Marketing Week* (July 9, 1990), p. 28; and "Death of the Frito Bandito," *American Demographics* (March, 1980), p. 28.

75. "The Largest Minority," *American Demographics* (February, 1993), p. 59; *Adweek's Marketing Week* (July 9, 1990), *loc. cit.;* "Hispanic Supermarkets Are Blossoming," *The Wall Street Journal* (January 23, 1989), p. B1; and *American Demographics* (March, 1980), *loc. cit.*

76. "Hispanics in the Eighties," *American Demographics* (January, 1988), p. 45.

77. "No habla espanol," *Forbes* (December 23, 1991), p. 142; and "Despite Some Gains by Hispanics, Report Finds Their Income Lags," *The New York Times* (April 11, 1991), p. A14.

78. "Hispanic Market Profile: Resisting the Winds of Change," *Marketing Communications* (July, 1983), p. 27.

79. "Marketing to Hispanics," *Advertising Age* (March 21, 1985), p. 13.

80. "Cultural Differences Offer Rewards," *Advertising Age* (April 7, 1980), p. S20.

81. *Ibid.*

82. "Poll: Hispanics Stick to Brands," *Advertising Age* (February 16, 1993), p. 6.

83. "What Does Hispanic Mean?" *American Demographics* (June, 1993), p. 50.

84. "The Effects of Hispanic Subcultural Identification on Information Search Behavior," *Journal of Advertising Research* (September/October, 1992), p. 6.

85. "Familiarity Breeds Success," *Adweek's Marketing Week Supplement* (September 25, 1989), p. 10; and "Competition Heats Up for Hispanic Consumer's Dollar," *Ad Forum* (July, 1983), p. 29.

86. *American Demographics* (June, 1993), *loc. cit.*

87. *Ibid.*, p. 48.

88. *Marketing Communications* (July, 1983), *op. cit.*, p. 37.

89. *Ad Forum* (July, 1983), *op. cit.*, p. 30.

90. "Ethnics Gain Market Clout," *Advertising Age* (August 5, 1991), p. 12.

91. "Minority Markets," *Credit Magazine* (January/February, 1992), p. 9.

92. "Versatility, Values—And Hold the Cliches," *Adweek's Marketing Week* (July 9, 1990), p. 38.

93. "The United States of Miami," *Adweek's Marketing Week* (July 15, 1991), p. 19.

94. *Listening Post* (June, 1984), p. 1.

95. *Business Week* (June 6, 1988), p. 64.

96. *Advertising Age* (February 13, 1989), p. S12.

97. *Journal of Advertising Research* (September/October, 1992), *op. cit.*, p. 56.

98. "The Asian American Market for Personal Products, *DCI* (November, 1992), p. 32.

99. *Ibid.*

100. "Asians in U.S. Get Attention of Marketers," *The New York Times* (January 11, 1990), p. D19.

101. *DCI* (November, 1992), *loc. cit.;* "Asian Americans: Consumer Oriented," *Research Alert* (December 16, 1988); and "Easing Into the Ethnic Market," *Best's Review* (December, 1988), pp. 50–56.

102. "'Hot' Asian-American Market Not Starting Much of a Fire Yet."

103. "A New Look at Asian Americans," *American Demographics* (October, 1990), p. 30.

104. "Taking the Pulse of Asian-Americans," *Adweek's Marketing Week* (August 12, 1991), p. 32.

105. *Advertising Age* (February 16, 1993), *loc. cit.*

106. "The Art of Reaching Asian Immigrants," *Adweek's Marketing Week* (January 1, 1990), p. 23.

107. Carol-Linnea Salmon, "Milking Deadly Dollars from the Third World," *Business & Society Review* (Winter, 1989), pp. 43–48.

108. "Even Overseas, Tobacco Has Nowhere to Hide," *Adweek's Marketing Week* (April 1, 1991), p. 4.

109. *Ibid.*, p. 5.

15

Reference Group Influences

FROM PUDDING POPS TO NIKES: ADVERTISERS USE CELEBRITIES TO MIRROR GROUP INFLUENCES

One of the most important environmental influences on consumer behavior is the face-to-face group. A consideration of the influence of groups is based on the **reference group;** that is, a group that serves as a reference point for the individual in the formation of his or her beliefs, attitudes, and behavior. Marketers frequently advertise their products in a group setting—the family eating breakfast cereals, the neighbor admiring a sparkling floor. In each of these cases, the purpose is to demonstrate the influence that friends and relatives have on consumers.

To implement such a strategy, marketers commonly use "typical" consumers as spokespersons for the product. The typical consumer reflects the purchaser's norms and values and acts as a representative of the consumer's reference group. For example, in a print ad campaign for Dove soap, six women cite the benefits of the product under the tag line "Women from Scranton to Sacramento will tell you Dove is better."

Using celebrities is another advertising approach that tries to mirror group influence. In this case, the celebrity represents a member of a group the consumer might aspire to rather than an actual member of the consumer's reference group. The assumption is that consumers are likely to be influenced by these individuals because they want to identify with the celebrity. Nike, for example, has used sports stars such as Michael Jordan and Andre Agassiz in its advertising to attract purchasers who identify with these stars.

Bill Cosby, a well-known celebrity, has promoted products ranging from Jell-O Pudding Pops to the brokerage house, E.F. Hutton. Cosby was an effective celebrity endorser for Pudding Pops (see Exhibit 15.1) because the ads were directed to fans of his TV show who saw him as a likable family role model. However, when he intoned E.F. Hutton's tag line "When E.F. Hutton talks, everybody listens," he fell flat. E.F. Hutton hoped Cosby's good guy image would help repair the firm's reputation after it was rocked by a Wall Street scandal. However, consumers did not perceive Cosby's loveable TV character as having any special financial know-how. As one wag said, "When Cosby talked, nobody listened," meaning that celebrities can serve to reflect group influence only when they are relevant as role models for the product.

This chapter describes various types of reference groups, considers the roles they play, and explores the ways they influence the individual consumer. In

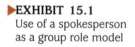

EXHIBIT 15.1
Use of a spokesperson as a group role model

introducing the topic of group influence, this chapter sets the stage for a consideration of family decision making and group communications.

◆ WHEN DO REFERENCE GROUPS EXERT INFLUENCE?

Reference groups provide us with roles and standards of conduct that directly influence our needs and purchasing behavior. The family influences what the child eats for breakfast; the peer group, what the teenager listens to on the radio and watches on TV; and the organizational group, what the adult wears to work. In each case, the group provides the individual with information on how to act and often pressures the individual to conform to group norms.

In adapting to group norms, we not only subscribe to the values established by the family, peer group, or organization, but we also define ourselves.[1] In fact, one essential element of self-concept is how we think others see us. This influence, referred to as the "looking glass self," means that reference groups provide the points of comparison by which we evaluate our own attitudes and behavior.

The influence a group exerts on an individual's purchasing behavior depends on three factors: (1) the individual's attitude toward the group, (2) the nature of the group, and (3) the nature of the product.

Regarding the first factor, a study by Bearden and Rose found wide variations in an individual's susceptibility to group influence.[2] An individual's purchasing behavior is more likely to be influenced by the group if he or she:

- Views the group as a credible source of information about the product or service.[3]
- Values the views and reactions of group members regarding purchasing decisions.[4]
- Accepts the rewards and sanctions meted out by groups for appropriate or inappropriate behavior.[5]

As for the second factor, the nature of the group, reference groups are more likely to influence a member's behavior[6] if they are:

- Homogeneous in that members have similar norms and values.
- Frequently interacting, thus creating more opportunities to influence members.
- Distinctive and exclusive in that membership in the group is highly valued.

The third factor that determines the degree of influence a group has on an individual is the nature of the product. Groups are more likely to be influential for (1) visible products such as clothing, cosmetics, and furniture, and for (2) exclusive products that might connote status.[7]

Before we consider the nature of these group influences in more detail, we will discuss the types of reference groups consumers can belong to.

Types of Reference Groups

Reference groups provide points of comparison by which to evaluate attitudes and behavior. A consumer can either be a member of a reference group, such as the family, or aspire to belong to a group (for example a tennis buff might aspire to associate with tennis pros). In the first case, the individual is part of a **membership group;** in the second, the individual is part of an **aspiration group.**

Reference groups can also be viewed negatively. For example, an individual may belong to or join a group and then reject the group's values. This type of group would be a **disclaimant group** for the individual.[8] Moreover, an individual may regard membership in a particular group as something to be avoided. Such a group is a **dissociative group.**

These four types of reference groups are shown at the top of Figure 15.1. Advertisers rarely appeal to the desire to avoid or disclaim a group, but they do appeal to the desire to be part of a group. Even appeals to nonconformity are made on the positive note of being different from everyone else, not on the negative note of dissociating oneself from certain groups. Marketers, therefore, tend to focus on positive reference groups.

Membership Groups

Because positive reference groups are important, Figure 15.1 further breaks down membership and aspiration groups. In the middle of Figure 15.1, positive membership groups are classified as primary or secondary and informal or formal. If a person has regular contact with certain individuals, such as family, friends, and business associates, those individuals are a primary group. Shopping groups, political clubs, and fellow skiers or joggers constitute a person's secondary groups because he or she has less frequent contact with them. Primary groups are more important to the consumer in developing product beliefs, tastes, and preferences and have a more direct influence on purchasing behavior. Reingen and his colleagues found that members of groups with the greatest contact in a variety of situations (that is, primary groups) were more likely to buy the same brands.[9] Because of their influence, these groups are more interesting to the marketer.

Groups also can be divided by whether they have a formal structure (a president, secretary, and treasurer) with specific roles (fund-raising, teaching, transmitting information) or an informal structure. The structures and roles of informal groups are implicit.

This classification produces four types of membership groups as shown in Figure 15.1. The family and peer groups represent **primary informal groups,** which are by far the most important groupings because of the frequency of contact and the closeness between the individual and group members. As a

▶FIGURE 15.1
Types of reference groups

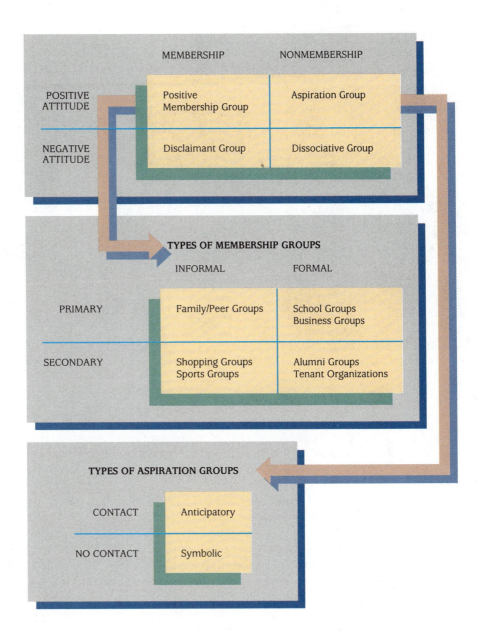

result, advertisers frequently portray consumption among friends and family. For example, by showing Mr. Redmond's extended family, the Redmond ad in Exhibit 15.2 tries to associate the company's hair care products with family usage.

Primary formal groups, which have a more formal structure than do family and friends, are groups with which the consumer frequently comes into contact. Examples are school class groups assigned to a project or business groups

▶**EXHIBIT 15.2**
Ads portraying primary and secondary group influences
Source: (middle) Courtesy of Omega Watch Corp.; (right) Courtesy of Oliver Peoples Inc.

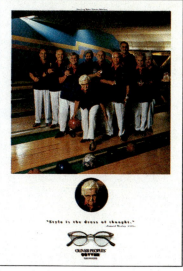

Primary informal group   *Primary formal group*   *Secondary group*

working together on a daily basis. Advertisers portray membership in such groups as a means of winning product approval. For example, Omega associates its watch with positive moments for a business group. The indirect message is that Omega is associated with a successful group effort. (See Exhibit 15.2.)

Secondary informal groups have no formal structure and meet infrequently. Examples are shopping groups or sports groups that get together once in a while. Such groups may directly influence purchases. In his study of shopping groups, Granbois examined the influence of secondary informal groups.[10] He found that when an individual shops in a group of three or more persons, compared to a smaller group, there is twice as much chance that he or she will purchase more than originally planned. Exhibit 15.2 also shows the use of secondary informal groups in advertising. The ad for Oliver Peoples eyeglass frames shows a member of a bowling group wearing the company's product.

Secondary formal groups are the least important to the consumer and, therefore, to the marketer, as they meet infrequently, are structured, and are not closely knit. Examples include alumni groups, business clubs, and tenant organizations. While marketers of specialized products (such as travel agents or developers of executive programs) may have some interest in these groups, marketers of national brands generally do not portray or appeal to these groups.

Aspiration Groups

Two types of aspiration groups, anticipatory and symbolic, are classified at the bottom of Figure 15.1. **Anticipatory aspiration groups** are those an individual anticipates joining at a future time and, in most cases, with which he or she has direct contact. The best example is a group higher in the organizational hierarchy that an individual wishes to join. This desire is based on the rewards that have been generally accepted to be most important in Western culture: power, status, prestige, and money. Marketers appeal to the desire to enhance one's position by climbing to a higher aspiration group. Clothing and cosmetics are frequently advertised within the context of business success and prestige.

Manufacturers of men's clothing and fragrances traditionally have used such themes; and women's products increasingly rely on appeals to organizational aspirations because of the growing number of women in the work force. A good example of a direct appeal to aspiration group norms within the organization is the ad for Johnnie Walker Black Label. (See Exhibit 15.7 on page 549.) The ad appeals to the anticipation of eventually arriving at the top in the business organization. The purchase of the product represents an acceptance of aspirational group norms.

Symbolic aspiration groups are those to which an individual is not likely to belong, despite acceptance of the group's beliefs and attitudes. Fisher and Price found that purchasing a product linked to the aspiration group is a means of establishing a vicarious connection with this group[11]—for example, a football fan buying a sports jacket or a jersey with the team's logo prominently displayed. An important condition for such influence is that the product is visually obvious, such as team-sponsored clothing.

Marketers appeal to symbolic aspirations by using celebrities to advertise certain products. The ad for the Sharp Camcorder showing Wayne Gretzky and his daughter (see Exhibit 15.3) is an example. Gretzky's appearance in the ad is based on his fame as a hockey star, not on his expertise in the product category. Anyone who associates with sports stars like Gretzky might be influenced to buy a Sharp Camcorder.

◆ NATURE OF REFERENCE GROUPS

Reference groups have certain characteristics that affect their influence on consumers. They establish norms, roles, status, socialization, and power. These characteristics are described in the following section.

Norms

Norms are the (generally undefined) rules and standards of conduct the group establishes. Group members are expected to conform to these norms, which may relate to the appropriateness of clothes, eating habits, makes of cars, or

brands of cosmetics. A few years ago, when Rossignol skis became the norm among a number of ski clubs, there was general conformity in ownership of this brand.

Roles

Roles are functions that the individual assumes or that the group assigns to the individual to attain group objectives. In group purchasing behavior, marketers can identify specific roles in an attempt to offer the best available brand or product category. The following roles have been identified in family decision making: the influencer, the gatekeeper (the individual who has the most control over the flow of information into the group), the decision maker, the purchasing agent, and the consumer.

Status

Status refers to the position the individual occupies within the group. High status implies greater power and influence. A chairperson of the board has the highest status within an organization but may be the weakest member of a weekly bridge club. Symbols of dress or ownership are frequently associated with both high and low status. For example, the chairperson's oak-paneled office symbolizes status, but so does the janitor's uniform.

Consumers sometimes purchase products to demonstrate status in a broader societal sense so that the message is one of wealth and implied superiority. The elegant dress and expensive car may be status symbols; but in some groups, symbolism operates in exact reversal to one's wealth and position. Jeans and small cars may be the norm among wealthy suburbanites, and large cars and more expensive clothes may be status symbols among lower socioeconomic groups.

Socialization

The process by which an individual learns the group's norms and role expectations is called **socialization.** The individual moving from one job to another must learn the informal rules and expectations from primary work groups along with the organization's formal rules and expectations.

Consumer socialization is the process by which consumers acquire the knowledge and skills necessary to operate in the marketplace. The two most important types are the socialization of children and the socialization of new residents in a community. (We will consider the socialization of children in more detail in Chapter 16 on family decision making.)

Power

The influence that a group has on an individual is closely related to the group's power. Various sources of group influence have been identified,[12] but three are particularly relevant for marketing strategy: expert power, referent power, and reward power.

Expert Power

To have **expert power,** an individual or group must have experience and knowledge. A consumer may accept a friend's purchase recommendation if the friend is regarded as more knowledgeable or experienced with the product. A sales representative also may be regarded as an expert source as long as the salesperson has established credibility with the consumer.

Referent Power

The basis for **referent power** is the individual's identification with members of the group. The greater the similarity between the individual's beliefs and attitudes and those of group members, the greater the referent power of the group. The individual either is a member of a group or may aspire to belong to a group because of common norms and values.

Reward Power

Reward power is based on the group's ability to reward the individual. The business organization can reward an employee with money and status. The family can reward the child with praise and approval. Social groups can also provide rewards in purchasing behavior. Compliments on clothes or looks provided by a relevant group member reinforce the consumer's choice.

Groups that have reward power may also have **coercive power** over the individual. That is, the group "giveth and taketh away." The greater the importance of the group, the greater is its power to express disapproval and even punishment. The organization has the power to fire an individual, parents to punish a child, and social groups to exclude individuals for deviant behavior.

Reference Group Influences on Consumers

The three types of group power suggest the ways reference groups influence consumer choice.[13] First, expert power suggests **informational influence.** The testimonial of an expert in an advertisement or the experiences of a knowledgeable friend are informative communications. Second, referent power suggests that groups have **comparative influence** in permitting a comparison of the individual's beliefs, attitudes, and behavior to those of the group. As referents, groups provide the consumer with the basis for evaluating one's self-image. Third, reward power suggests that reference groups have **normative influence** by directly influencing attitudes and behavior based on group norms and encouraging compliance with these norms.

Table 15.1 shows each type of influence within the context of consumer behavior by citing the type of influence exerted on the consumer, the objectives for the consumer, the basis for group influence, and the effects on behavior.[14]

▶**TABLE 15.1**
Types of influence exerted by reference groups

Nature of Influence	Objectives	Perceived Characteristics of Source	Type of Power	Behavior
Informational	Knowledge	Credibility	Expert	Acceptance
Comparative	Self-maintenance and enrichment	Similarity	Referent	Identification
Normative	Reward	Power	Reward or coercion	Conformity

SOURCE: Based on Robert E. Burnkrant and Alain Cousineau, "Informational and Normative Social Influence in Buyer Behavior," JOURNAL OF CONSUMER RESEARCH, 2 (December, 1975), p. 207. Reprinted with permission from The University of Chicago Press.

Informational Influence

A consumer will accept information from a group if he or she considers the group a credible source of information and expertise and if he or she believes the information will enhance knowledge about product choices.[15] Information can be obtained directly from group members the consumer regards as knowledgeable or by observing the behavior of group members.

Consumers are more likely to seek expert advice from personal sources such as friends and neighbors than from commercial sources such as advertising because they regard personal sources as more trustworthy. Consumers may regard a manufacturer's advertising claim with suspicion because of the company's vested interest in promoting the product.

Table 15.1 illustrates the nature of informational influence by describing the consumer's objectives as obtaining knowledge, the condition for accepting information as credibility, the source of power as expertise, and the final behavior as acceptance of influence. Table 15.2 lists various types of statements that illustrate informational, comparative, and normative influences. Park and Lessig used the statements in a study to determine the relative importance of these three influences in the selection of twenty products.[16] Statements 1-5 all reflect the objective of seeking information from expert sources or friends and neighbors with reliable information. In addition, observation (Statement 5) is regarded as an important source of information.

There are two conditions when informational influence is likely to be most important. First, according to Friedman and Churchill, is when there is social, financial, or performance risk in buying the product.[17] A consumer buying a car will seek information from knowledgeable friends, relatives, or salespeople because of the social visibility of a car, the costs of buying, and possible mechanical failures. In this case, the advice of an expert is probably more important than that of a referent. Second, if the individual has limited knowledge or experience regarding the product, informational influence is likely to be most important. A consumer with little knowledge of technical products such as computers, cellular phones, or fax machines is likely to seek expert advice.

Marketing studies provide evidence of the importance of personal sources of information. A study by Robertson found that personal sources were more important than commercial sources for purchases of small appliances and were somewhat more important for food items.[18] This study suggests that expert power may be based on usage and experience by friends and neighbors as well as on professional expertise.

Comparative Influence

Consumers constantly compare their attitudes to those of members of important groups. In so doing, they seek to support their own attitudes and behavior

▶**TABLE 15.2**
Conditions reflecting informational, comparative, and normative influences

Informational Influence

1. The individual seeks information about various brands of the product from an association of professionals or independent group of experts.
2. The individual seeks information from those who work with the product as a profession.
3. The individual seeks brand-related knowledge and experience (such as how Brand A's perfume compares to Brand B's) from those friends, neighbors, relatives, or work associates who have reliable information about the brands.
4. The brand that the individual selects is influenced by observing a seal of approval of an independent testing agency (such as *Good Housekeeping*'s).
5. The individual's observation of what experts do influences his or her choice of a brand (such as observing the type of car that police drive or the brand of TV that repair people buy).

Comparative Influence

6. The individual feels that the purchase or use of a particular brand will enhance the image that others have of him or her.
7. The individual feels that the purchase of a particular brand helps show others what he or she is or would like to be (such as an athlete, successful businessperson, etc).
8. The individual feels that those who purchase or use a particular brand possesses the characteristics thast he or she would like to have.
9. The individual sometimes feels that it would be nice to be like the type of person advertisements show using a particular brand.

Normative Influence

10. The individual's decision to purchase a particular brand is influenced by the preferences of people with whom he or she has social interaction.
11. The individual's decision to purchase a particular brand is influenced by the preferences of family members.
12. The desire to satisfy the expectations that others have of him or her has an impact on the individual's brand choice.

SOURCE: Adapted from C. Whan Park and V. Parker Lessig, "Students and Housewives: Differences in Susceptibility to Reference Group Influence," JOURNAL OF CONSUMER RESEARCH, 4 (September, 1977), p. 105. Reprinted with permission from The University of Chicago Press.

by associating themselves with groups with which they agree and by dissociating themselves from groups with which they disagree. As a result, the basis for comparative influence is in the process of comparing oneself to other members of the group and of judging whether the group would be supportive.

For example, if a family moves into a new home and meets new neighbors, the parents might compare the neighbors' attitudes toward political issues, education, and child rearing with their own. The parents also identify brands and products the neighbors purchase. New residents naturally will be attracted to neighbors who are similar to themselves because those neighbors reinforce existing attitudes and behavior. This is the main reason why neighborhoods are made up of people with similar social and economic characteristics.

Table 15.1 on page 536 shows that comparative influence is a process of self-maintenance and enrichment. The individual's objective is to enhance his or her self-concept by associating with groups that will provide reinforcement and ego gratification. The source of power is referent power, and the individual's behavior toward the group is one of identification. Table 15.2 shows that the conditions relating to comparative influence deal with the enhancement of an individual's self-image through membership in a group (Statements 6 and 7) or identification with other people who are liked and admired as members of an aspiration group (Statements 8 and 9).

Comparative influence implies that those being influenced should have characteristics similar to those doing the influencing. A study by Moschis found that consumers are likely to seek information from friends viewed as similar to themselves and to regard such sources as credible.[19] The study concluded that advertisers should try to use spokespersons whom consumers perceive as being similar to themselves (that is, "typical consumers"). The notion of similarity between influencer and influencee also extends to customer-salesperson interactions. Several studies have found that when a customer sees the salesperson as similar in terms of tastes, attitudes, and even religion, the salesperson is likely to be effective.[20]

Comparative influence may also be due to proximity. Several studies have shown that influencers and influencees tend to live close to each other.[21] One study of elderly residents of a retirement community found that 81 percent of the exchange of information and advice about a new product occurred between persons who live on the same floor.[22]

Normative Influence

Normative influence refers to the influence a group exerts to conform to its norms and expectations. According to Park and Lessig, a consumer is motivated to conform to the norms and behavior of the group if (1) the group provides significant rewards for compliance and punishment for lack of compliance and (2) the individual's behavior in conforming is visible to members of the group.[23]

The primary reward for *compliance* with group norms is acceptance. One study found that consumers used friends and relatives as sources of information for products because they provided positive social interaction.[24] Such rewards are more likely if the behavior is visible. A group can exert normative influence in the purchase of clothes, furniture, and appliances because these items are visible. Normative influence may also occur for items such as mouthwash and denture adhesive, even though the items themselves are not visible, because of fear that lack of use may be visible (bad breath, loose dentures). Visibility is less important in exerting informational and comparative influence because, in these cases, the objective is not conformity but knowledge and self-enhancement. The consumer could obtain information from the group and gain satisfaction in identifying with the group without any overt action.

Whyte demonstrated the importance of visibility in his study of a Philadelphia suburb's purchase of air conditioners.[25] Research indicated the direct influence of friends and neighbors in purchasing the product, but the most apparent influence was *seeing* an air conditioner in a neighbor's window.

According to Table 15.1, normative influence is based on the individual's desire to receive the rewards of the group. The basis for power is reward or coercion; the resulting behavior toward the group is conformity and compliance. Table 15.2 indicates that conditions reflecting normative influence deal with a desire to conform to group preferences (Statements 10 and 11) and to satisfy the expectations of group members (Statement 12).

Conformity in Consumer Behavior

Conformity to group norms is the ultimate goal of normative influence, as it means that consumers will buy the brands and product categories the group approves. Marketers are interested in such imitative behavior because it implies a snowball effect once the most influential members of a group accept products. The idea of "keeping up with the Joneses" reflects imitative behavior.

Various studies have confirmed that individuals do imitate group behavior. These studies have been largely experimental and were inspired by social psychology studies demonstrating individual conformity to group norms. One of the most famous of these experiments brought groups of seven to nine college students together to judge the length of lines drawn on a card.[26] All group members but one were instructed to give the same incorrect response. The subject, who was not aware of the experiment, was confronted with the obviously incorrect choice of a unanimous group. In 37 percent of the cases, the subject went along with the group, even though the choice appeared to contradict his or her senses.

In an experiment by Venkatesan, three identical men's suits labeled "A," "B," and "C" were described to respondents as being of different quality and manufacture.[27] Three of four students in each group were told to pick Suit B. In the majority of cases, the fourth student also picked Suit B. When pressure was put on the individual to go along with the other three, however, the chances of conforming went down; students reacted negatively to such pressure. This situation, known as **reactance,** suggests that consumers will conform to group pressures only to a certain point. When group pressures become too intense, consumers will reject group norms and demonstrate independence.

Group pressure may also be rejected if an individual tries to attribute the group's actions to certain causes. Rose, Bearden, and Teel found that when an individual attributed reasons for a group's use of drugs and alcohol such as saying "they just want to get high" or "they don't think they will get caught," such attributions encouraged the individual to dissent from the group's actions.[28]

Social Multiplier Effect

The desire to emulate the behavior of a group often leads an individual to buy the same brand or product. Such imitative behavior reflects a demonstration principle. First formulated by economist James Duesenberry,[29] the **demonstration principle** states that with the American consumer's increased mobility and purchasing power, consumers increasingly will come into contact with new products and will have the purchasing power to buy them. For example, when compact disc players were first marketed, once one family bought one, friends and neighbors came into contact with the product. Since these people were likely to have the same level of purchasing power, they also bought CDs. In turn, other individuals came into contact with the recently acquired product, and the pattern of ownership spread within the group and to other groups. The demonstration principle is similar to the idea of "keeping up with the Joneses" because of the element of social pressure to own new products. We will refer to it as the **social multiplier effect** because ownership increases in multiples as a function of group influence and product visibility.

One of the best examples of the social multiplier effect is a 1928 ad for Victrola (Exhibit 15.4). The headline "Keeping Up With the Joneses" was the main appeal for buying the new phonograph player. The copy illustrates the

▶**EXHIBIT 15.4**

A 1928 example of the social multiplier effect

Reproduction of 1928 RCA Corporation ad

Source: Reprinted by permission of RCA Corporation

social multiplier in action: "The day it came, we celebrated by having the neighbors come over."

The social multiplier effect illustrates the volatility of group influence in the American economy. Certain brands or product categories may be highly visible today and representative of group norms; but five or ten years from now, such influence may become minimal. Because of the social multiplier effect, products that once were considered a luxury (record players, refrigerators, automobiles, air conditioners) are now considered a necessity. To a large degree, the social multiplier effect has powered the American economy to higher standards of living.

Information, Comparison, or Conformity?

Is group influence on consumer purchasing behavior due primarily to the information supplied by groups, the identification with groups, or the pressure that groups bring to bear on individuals? The obvious answer is that all three components influence consumers. The type of influence that is most important, however, may be a function of the type of product being evaluated.

Influence by Product Type

Park and Lessig measured the relative effects of informational, comparative, and normative influence in the purchase of 20 products.[30] They asked a sample of college students to rate the 20 products by the statements listed in Table 15.2. The types of products most likely to be subject to informational influences are those that are technologically complex (autos, color TVs, air conditioners) or require objective informational criteria for selection (insurance, physicians, headache remedies). The products most subject to comparative influence are those that serve as a means of self-expression and identity (autos, clothing, furniture). Automobiles and clothing are also subject to normative influence because they are visible and are, therefore, a means of conforming to group norms. The fact that automobiles and clothing were subject to more than one type of group influence illustrates the importance of these products to college students.

Is Information the Most Important Component?

Information is probably the most important component of group influence. However, the evidence is conflicting. The studies of comparative and normative influence suggest that consumers use groups as a means of identification and reward, but they may well use groups more for the information supplied.

Hansen believed that many of the studies purporting to find conformity to group norms actually may represent the processing of information supplied by groups.[31] A consumer's tendency to buy the products and brands the group purchases can be interpreted in two ways: (1) conformity to group norms or (2) an assertion of quality (the uniformity of purchasing behavior within the group shows that the brand is in fact highest in quality). The latter case does not represent conformity; it represents action based on credible information.

Burnkrant and Cousineau supported the notion that groups are more important in supplying information than in influencing compliance to group norms.[32] They found that the consumer's belief in the credibility of information provided by peers influenced the ratings of brands of coffee more than any pressure to conform to group norms. Similarly, Park and Lessig found that informational influence was more important to college students than comparative or normative influence for most of the products studied.[33] Ward and Reingen also supported the importance of groups as sources of information rather than of conformity. They found that group members moved toward the group's position not because of pressures to conform to group norms, but because of discussions and "shared knowledge that leads to a change in beliefs."[34]

Summarizing these studies, Kaplan and Miller conclude that "in general, informational influence produces more frequent and stronger shifts (in beliefs) than does normative influence."[35]

These findings suggest that marketers should place more emphasis on the group as a source of information than as a source of compliance. Ads should picture typical consumers citing their experiences and providing information on relevant product attributes. Rather than picture a woman marveling at a sparkling floor (compliance to group norms of cleanliness), ads might be more relevant if they show the woman transmitting information on a new and improved version of the same product. Such an approach shifts the emphasis from conformity to information. Ads using "typical consumers" may be effective in supplying information because consumers may identify with them and accept their judgments, even if the manufacturer sponsors the ad. The use of typical consumers who are presumably unaware they are being filmed is an example of this approach.

Group Influence Versus Product Evaluation

If group influence is such an important source of information, does it supplant objective product evaluation? That is, do many consumers say, "Since most of my friends recommend it, I may as well use it because it must be good," and as a result forego a process of brand evaluation? In many cases, yes; reference group influence is a substitute for brand evaluation.

Rosen's and Olshavsky's study supports the likelihood that group recommendations often supplant brand evaluation.[36] They studied brand selection for two disparate product categories, pizza and stereos. They considered three possibilities: that consumers will (1) go along with the group's recommendations without evaluating brand alternatives, (2) evaluate alternative brands, or (3) rely on group recommendations to narrow the choice to a few brands and then evaluate these brands.

They found that group recommendations outweighed brand attribute evaluations for both product categories. That is, in most cases, consumers either totally rely on the group's recommendations or use these recommendations to narrow the choice to a few brand alternatives. Surprisingly, this was as true for a high-risk product like stereos as for a low-risk product like pizza. Based on such evidence, Moschis concluded that as a result of relying on peers for information, "consumers often choose products without evaluating them on the basis of objective attributes."[37]

◆ GROUP INFLUENCE BY TYPE OF PRODUCT

Group influence may be greater for certain types of products than it is for others. As noted in the beginning of the chapter, pressures to conform to group norms is more likely for products that are (1) exclusive and (2) visible. Exclusive products are those that convey luxury and are owned by only a few people. Visible products are those that are consumed in public view.

After examining various studies of group influence, Bourne hypothesized that groups would be more likely to influence the *product decision* for exclusive products because owning such a product (a yacht, for example) would in itself make a statement. Groups would be more likely to influence the *brand decision* for visible products because the brand owned (a Rolex watch, for example) would be apparent, even if the product itself was not exclusive.[38] Thus, groups could influence the purchase of a product, the purchase of a brand, or both. On this basis, Bourne developed the typology of reference group influences shown in Figure 15.2.

In the late 1940s, Bourne classified various products based on his typology. Three of his classifications, automobiles, refrigerators, and black-and-white TV sets, are in parentheses in Figure 15.2 because their original placement is now outdated. Bourne determined that both product and brand decisions for automobiles are subject to group influence. Today, the automobile is not as exclusive a product as it was 40 years ago. Groups probably influence the make of car that consumers will purchase (upper right in Figure 15.2), not their decision to buy.

Bourne classified refrigerators as subject to brand but not product influence because of their visibility but lack of exclusivity. In the late 1940s, the more traditional norms among consumers probably made the kitchen a more central focus. As a result, the refrigerator might have been a more visible kitchen appliance. Today, refrigerators are so commonplace that it is even questionable they are subject to any group influence. Similarly, Bourne also determined that groups influence the decision to buy black-and-white TV sets. Since few people owned TVs then, they were exclusive products. There is no doubt that black-and-white TV sets are not subject to group influence today for the simple reason that they are obsolete.

Bearden and Etzel's 1983 study both updated and largely confirmed Bourne's typology: Groups influence product decisions for exclusive products

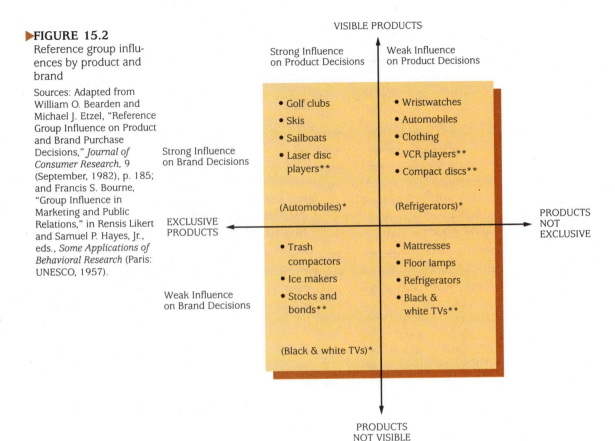

▶**FIGURE 15.2**
Reference group influences by product and brand

Sources: Adapted from William O. Bearden and Michael J. Etzel, "Reference Group Influence on Product and Brand Purchase Decisions," *Journal of Consumer Research,* 9 (September, 1982), p. 185; and Francis S. Bourne, "Group Influence in Marketing and Public Relations," in Rensis Likert and Samuel P. Hayes, Jr., eds., *Some Applications of Behavioral Research* (Paris: UNESCO, 1957).

VISIBLE PRODUCTS

Strong Influence on Product Decisions | Weak Influence on Product Decisions

Strong Influence on Brand Decisions

- Golf clubs
- Skis
- Sailboats
- Laser disc players**

- Wristwatches
- Automobiles
- Clothing
- VCR players**
- Compact discs**

(Automobiles)* | (Refrigerators)*

EXCLUSIVE PRODUCTS | PRODUCTS NOT EXCLUSIVE

- Trash compactors
- Ice makers
- Stocks and bonds**

- Mattresses
- Floor lamps
- Refrigerators
- Black & white TVs**

Weak Influence on Brand Decisions

(Black & white TVs)*

PRODUCTS NOT VISIBLE

* Products categorized by Bourne in the late 1940s
** Products added by the author
All other products are from Bearden and Etzel

and brand decisions for visible products.[39] The products listed in Figure 15.2 are based on this later study.

1. *Influence on product and brand.* Products in the upper left in Figure 15.2 are both exclusive and visible (golf clubs, skis, and sailboats). A new product such as interactive TV will be subject to both product and brand influence by groups once it is introduced since the item is exclusive and is used in a visible setting. Once such an item begins to gain acceptance and lose its distinctiveness, it most likely will be subject to brand but not product influence. This was the case with products such as VCRs and compact disc players. When they were first introduced, ownership was subject to group influence. However, as ownership became more widespread, groups primarily influenced the brand rather than the product decision.

2. *Influence on brand only.*   Products in the upper right are visible but no longer exclusive. Items include wristwatches, automobiles, and clothing. Strong brand influences may occur, particularly if certain brands have luxury connotations. Groups are unlikely to influence the decision to buy a watch or a car, but they certainly might influence a decision to buy a Rolex watch or a BMW car.

3. *Influence on product only.*   Certain products may be exclusive enough to be representative of group norms, but they are not particularly visible (lower left in Figure 15.2). Thus, a consumer in a suburban household may be influenced to buy an ice maker even though the product is not used in a visible way. Similarly, ownership of stocks and bonds may connote prestige and socioeconomic status and may be subject to group influence. In these cases, groups influence consumers' decision to own the product, not the brand purchased.

4. *No group influence.*   Products not subject to group influence are neither exclusive nor visible (lower right in Figure 15.2). Bearden and Etzel list products such as mattresses, floor lamps, and refrigerators in this category. Interestingly, they categorize refrigerators as products that are not subject to group influence, whereas Bourne saw group influence in the brand of refrigerator purchased.

For products lacking in group influence, consumers will make a purchase decision based on product attributes. The refrigerator's energy efficiency or size is more likely to influence their choice than a neighbor's comments.

◆ STRATEGIC APPLICATIONS OF REFERENCE GROUP INFLUENCES

Marketers have used the three types of group influence—informational, comparative, and normative—to develop both advertising and personal selling strategies.

Advertising Strategies

Advertising strategies have portrayed informational influence through expert spokespersons, comparative influence by portraying typical consumers, and normative influence by showing the rewards of using a product or the risks of not using it.

Use of Expert Spokespersons

Marketers have tried to convey informational influence through advertising as a counterweight to the dominant influence of friends and relatives. They have attempted to exert informational influence by using expert spokespersons to communicate product features and performance.

Marketers have two approaches to portraying expert spokespersons. One is to portray the role the expert plays—a doctor for a medical product, an engineer for a technical product. A second approach is to show a celebrity who has expertise in the product area—a tennis star's testimonial for a tennis racket, for example. Exhibit 15.5 shows both approaches. The ad for Benadryl is a tongue-in-cheek portrayal of expert medical roles. Even though children are portrayed, the message is clear—the medical profession stands behind Benadryl as a safe and effective allergy medication for children.

The second approach uses celebrities to provide product testimonials. Such testimonials are accepted only to the degree that consumers view the spokesperson as being an expert on the product. Exhibit 15.5 shows André Agassiz in an ad for Nike tennis apparel. Consumers are likely to view a testimonial from Agassiz for the product category as credible.

Advertisers also create their own experts. General Motors has established Mr. Goodwrench as an expert in car maintenance. General Mills created Betty Crocker in 1921, and she has become "a sort of 'First Lady of Food,' the most

▶**EXHIBIT 15.5**
Conveying informational influence
Source: (left) Courtesy of Benadryl

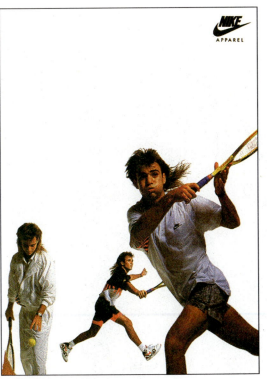

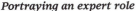

Portraying an expert role   *Using an expert spokesperson*

highly esteemed home service authority in the nation."[40] Also, Reuben H. Donnelley, the leading source of direct-mail coupons, has established Carol Wright as the expert spokesperson on how to achieve value through coupon redemptions.

Using Referent Spokespersons

Advertisers attempt to portray comparative influence by using a "typical consumer" approach to persuade consumers that people like themselves have chosen the advertised product. The typical consumer is a referent because, by citing common needs and problems, he or she is portrayed as similar to the prospective purchaser. The Ford ad in Exhibit 15.6 is an example. The individuals pictured are typical consumers whom Ford asked to brainstorm regarding what they want in a car. A consumer in the market for a car could easily identify with these individuals.

Another way advertisers convey comparative influence is to use a celebrity as a referent. This approach is effective if a segment of consumers wants to identify with the referent because he or she is likable and/or attractive. Wayne Gretzky is an effective referent in the ad for the Sharp Camcorder in Exhibit 15.3. As a sports superstar, he is portrayed in a likable situation playing with

►**EXHIBIT 15.6**
Using referent spokespersons to convey comparative influence
Source: Courtesy of Ford Motor Co.

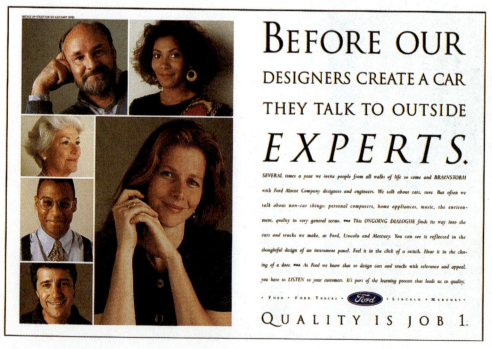

his daughter. Whereas the Ford ad depicts referents as part of a consumer's membership group, the Sharp ad shows a referent as part of the consumer's aspiration group. In the case of Ford, consumers consider themselves similar to the referent; in the case of Sharp, consumers would like to be similar to the referent. Since most consumers realize they will not become sports superstars by using a Sharp Camcorder, Gretzky is portrayed as a symbolic referent.

The role of Wayne Gretzky can be contrasted with that of André Agassiz. While both are sports celebrities, Agassiz is an expert spokesperson based on his profession, and Gretzky is a referent spokesperson based on his image.

Conveying Normative Influence

Marketers have tried to convey normative influence by showing group approval in advertising. Praise for a good cup of coffee, a shiny floor, glorious hair, good sherry, and a quiet and comfortable ride are all examples of advertising's simulation of social approval. In each case, an individual who is important to the consumer (spouse, neighbor, friend, business associate) has expressed approval of the consumer's choice. The Johnnie Walker ad in Exhibit 15.7 shows reward power by associating the product with the rewards for achievement in the business organization.

▶**EXHIBIT 15.7**
Ads conveying normative influence through reward and punishment
Source: (left) Courtesy of Johnnie Walker Black Label

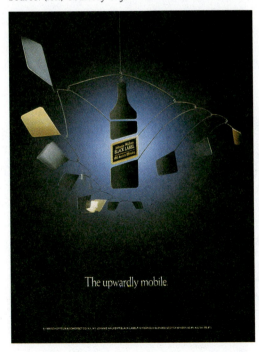

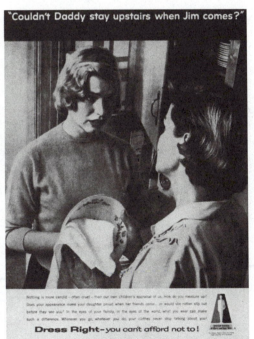

Celebrities are best used as experts in advertising when consumers see them as being knowledgeable about the product category and conveying legitimacy in their message. Arnold Palmer is an effective spokesperson for golf balls; Ella Fitzgerald, for sound tapes; and Mario Andretti, for motor oil. Expert spokespersons do not necessarily have to represent products associated with their professions. Consumers see Jimmy Connors and Nolan Ryan as expert spokespersons for analgesics because consumers believe these aging sports stars must know what they are talking about when it comes to relieving aches and pains.

STRATEGIC APPLICATIONS OF CONSUMER BEHAVIOR

When Should Advertisers Use Celebrities as Experts or Referents?

Celebrities have been used as referents when they come across as likable and attractive; that is, someone with whom many consumers would like to identify. The product has to be one that lends itself to identification with the celebrity as a referent, however. Elizabeth Taylor is a very effective spokesperson for Passion perfume because she evokes empathy as a result of her "struggles with weight control, substance abuse, and men . . . Women figured if Liz can get control of her life, why can't I? That forged a very strong bond." The same degree of empathy would be unlikely if she were used as a spokesperson for pain relievers or investment services because these products do not evoke the intimacy of perfume.

When advertisers stray from the principles that experts must communicate knowledge and legitimacy and that referents must communicate likability and attractiveness, they get into trouble. We saw that Bill Cosby was an effective referent for Pudding Pops because he is one of the most likable personalities on TV, but he bombed as a referent for a brokerage house because his good guy image did not convey any special expertise or credibility for financial services.

Of even more concern, the use of referent spokespersons could backfire if they lose their relevance. The Beef Industry Council experienced a double whammy when it used Cybil Shepherd as a spokesperson who subsequently announced she never eats meat, and then used James Garner who had a heart attack soon after. Referents could also run the risk of losing their likability. When Calvin Klein used Marky Mark as a spokesperson for its apparel, it discovered that he had made a series of racial slurs in his younger days.

The same risks apply to the use of expert spokespersons. However, since expertise dominates likability, the risks are less. For example, Michael Jordan's endorsement of Air Jordan sneakers for Nike did not seem to be affected by disclosures of gambling involvement.

The risks involved in associating a valuable brand name to a celebrity have caused some companies to stop using celebrities altogether. Others such as Diet Coke, Hershey, and Levi Strauss & Co. have come up with the ultimate solution by using legendary celebrities such as Humphrey Bogart, Marilyn Monroe, and James Dean as referent spokespersons. They are sure to remain likable and to stay out of trouble.

Sources: "New Tactics on Celebrity Endorsement," *The New York Times,* (April 3, 1992), p. D5; "Even Without HIV Issue, Using Celebs Can Be Risky," *Marketing News* (December 9, 1991), p. 2; and "Doesn't Everyone Want to Smell Like . . . ," *Forbes* (April 2, 1990), p. 144.

Marketers have also used normative influence to show the potential results of not using the product. Poligrip uses the fear of social disapproval due to loose dentures, and Dial demonstrates the fear of group ostracism due to body odor. In each case, use of the product changes disapproval to approval—which demonstrates the fact that coercive power and reward power are linked. Such appeals use the fear of a group's coercive power to gain compliance to group norms. An ad campaign for the Men's & Boy's Wear Institute that ran in the early 1950s is an example. It shows a daughter who does not want her father to meet her boyfriend because she is ashamed of the way he dresses. The tag line, "Dress right, you can't afford not to," implies that poor clothes can lead to failure. Although dated, the ad is a clear use of normative influence through punishment.

Personal Selling Strategies

Marketers also use the three types of reference group influences to develop sales strategies to influence customers. Informational influence is used when the salesperson is considered to be knowledgeable about the product category and a legitimate source of information. Such influence reflects *expert power*. Comparative influence applies when a consumer perceives the salesperson as someone with similar needs and characteristics. Under such circumstances, the salesperson is likely to exert influence through *referent power*. Normative influence applies to the relative *bargaining power* of the buyer and seller to achieve favorable terms of sale. Such influence reflects *reward or coercive power*.

Sales Strategy Implications of Informational and Comparative Influence

Applications of informational and comparative influence suggest two general approaches to customer-salesperson interactions:

1. The salesperson can be an objective source of information (expert influence).
2. The salesperson can attempt to reinforce the customer's ego and social needs by demonstrating similar needs, concerns, and predispositions (referent influence).

Weitz has attempted to determine the conditions in which salespersons should establish expertise rather than similarity.[41] Expertise should be established if (1) the salesperson has the knowledge and credentials to be seen as an expert, (2) the customer is engaged in a high-risk, complex buying task requiring expertise, and (3) the salesperson does not regularly sell to the buyer, which therefore creates a need to impress the buyer. Conversely, similarity is best established when the salesperson is in fact similar, the buying task is simple and low risk, and the salesperson regularly sells to the buyer.

Based on findings such as these, expertise appears to be more important in a problem-solving approach, particularly for complex goods such a personal computers or music systems due to their greater complexity and variety. In addition, many consumer services fall into this category. For example, the variety of financial offerings available to consumers requires more expertise on the part of insurance agents, stockbrokers, and financial advisers. Whether the emphasis is on expertise or similarity, the burden falls on the salesperson to develop a proper impression of the customer and to formulate a sales strategy accordingly.

Sales Strategy Implications of Bargaining Power

Normative sales influence rests on **bargaining power;** that is, the degree of influence the buyer and seller have on each other to achieve favorable terms of sale. Bargaining is most likely to occur when there is a need to negotiate price, delivery, and product specifications. On this basis, bargaining is likely for products such as cars, appliances, furniture, real estate, and second-hand items. In such cases, the consumer's willingness and ability to bargain may directly influence the sales outcome. One study found that the major reason certain customers can obtain items for lower prices is because of their bargaining strength and knowledge.[42]

Not only does the process of bargaining heighten the complexity of the customer-salesperson interaction, but it also gives rise to conflicts over economic goals. Research has focused on the types of bargaining strategies buyers and sellers develop to resolve conflicts and reach agreement over terms of sale. Two broad strategies are competitive and coordinative bargaining behavior. In **competitive bargaining behavior,** the party with stronger bargaining power exerts that power to force concessions from the weaker party. In **coordinative bargaining behavior,** the parties approach bargaining in a problem-solving manner to achieve these goals. Bargaining power is less likely to be exerted in an arbitrary manner.[43]

Several studies have confirmed that satisfactory sales agreements are most likely to occur when coordinative strategies are used. Competitive bargaining power results in sales agreements under some conditions. According to Schurr and Ozanne, the factor most likely to lead to agreement in competitive bargaining is trust in the seller. Even though a buyer expects tough bargaining, if the buyer trusts the seller, agreement on the terms of sale is likely.[44]

◆ SOCIETAL IMPLICATIONS OF
REFERENCE GROUP INFLUENCES

The portrayals of membership or aspiration group influences in this chapter have been generally positive—membership group influence for hair products, watches, and automobiles; aspiration group influence for tennis apparel and electronics.

More difficult issues arise for products such as cigarettes and liquor. Marketers frequently portray peer groups in social situations in print ads for these product categories, implying that the product is "in" with the group. In most cases, the groups portrayed are young adults. A key issue is whether such advertising is socially responsible. In fostering group identity with their brands, marketers are encouraging liquor and cigarette consumption among young adults. However, it could be argued that young adults are subject to group influence for a wide variety of products and should be free to choose the brands and products they want to consume.

Overall, marketers of cigarettes, liquor, and beer must be sensitive in portraying group acceptance of their products, especially among younger consumers.

SUMMARY

This chapter focused on reference group influences on consumer behavior. Reference groups can be classified into membership groups and aspiration groups. Membership groups can be classified further into formal and informal groups and primary and secondary groups. By far, the most influential groups are informal primary groups, represented by family and peer groups. Aspiration groups can also be divided into groups in which the consumer anticipates membership (anticipatory groups) and groups that the consumer admires at a distance (symbolic groups).

These group designations are important, as advertisers frequently portray group influences directly (for example, one friend advising the other) or employ spokespersons to influence consumer aspirations.

Reference groups serve a number of important functions. They provide norms of conduct, assign roles within the group to individuals, designate status positions within the group, and are a vehicle for consumer socialization. They also influence individuals by exerting three types of power: expert, referent, and reward.

These three types of power correspond to three types of influence. Groups exert informational (expert) influence, comparative (referent) influence, and normative (reward) influence. Informational influence depends on the credibility of the source of information, comparative influence on the degree of similarity between the consumer and influencer, and normative influence on the levels of reward or punishment meted out by the group.

Marketers have emphasized normative influence most, since it results in conformity to group norms. Conformity is most likely when products are visible and related to group norms. Such conformity may produce a social multiplier effect: one consumer buys a product, and others come into contact with the consumer and are influenced to buy. Their purchase in turn results in a spread of ownership throughout the group and, eventually, to other groups.

Marketers have used informational, comparative, and normative influence in establishing advertising and personal selling strategies. In advertising, informational influence is portrayed through expert spokespersons, comparative influence through typical consumers, and normative influence by showing the rewards of using a product or risks of not using it. In personal selling, informational influence is established by the expertise of the salesperson, comparative influence by the similarity of the salesperson to the customer, and normative influence by the relative bargaining power of the salesperson and the customer.

In the next chapter, we will consider one of the key sources of group influence: the family.

QUESTIONS

1. What is meant by the "looking glass self"? How does this concept affect consumer behavior?

2. What is the distinction between aspiration groups and membership groups? Are both types of groups relevant for marketers? In what ways?

3. What is the distinction between anticipatory and symbolic aspiration groups? How do the Sharp ad in Exhibit 15.3 and the Johnny Walker Black Label ad in Exhibit 15.7 depict one or the other of these group influences?

4. How are expert, referent, and reward power translated into informational, comparative, and normative influences?

5. What do we mean by "reactance"? Cite some examples. Is a marketer likely to illustrate reactance in advertising? Why or why not?

6. How would you classify the following products based on the typology in Figure 15.2?
   • Laptop computers.
   • Cable television.
   • Air conditioners.
   • Cigarettes.
   In each case, state the rationale for your classification.

7. What do we mean by the "social multiplier effect"? What conditions are required for the social multiplier to take effect? Cite some examples of the workings of the social multiplier.

8. Products such as air conditioners, cars, and record players were once distinctive and then lost their distinctiveness, partly as a result of the social

multiplier effect. What implications would this loss of distinctiveness have for a marketer's (a) pricing strategy and (b) advertising strategy?

9. What types of products are most likely to be subject to informational influence, comparative influence, and normative influence? Why?

10. In this chapter, it was suggested that there may be too much emphasis on normative group influences in advertising. Why?

11. Under what conditions should an advertiser use a spokesperson as a referent? As an expert? What are the risks of each strategy?

12. Under what conditions are a salesperson's (a) referent power or (b) expert power likely to be more important in influencing the customer?

RESEARCH ASSIGNMENTS

1. Ask a group of students to evaluate four identical unlabeled cans of soda. Four students should do the evaluation at the same time. Have three students act as "ringers" and ask them to state a preference for the same can of soda. The fourth student will be an actual respondent. Conduct about 20 such tests so that there are 20 actual respondents. In one-half of the cases, the ringers should express a preference in a low-keyed manner. In the other half, they should be adamant about their preference (for example "Wow, this soda is much better!"). One would expect that on a random basis, the fourth student would agree with the other three 25 percent of the time.
   - Is the proportion who conform significantly greater than the 25 percent chance expectation?
   - Is there a difference in acceptance between those who were subjected to a low-keyed preference and those who were subjected to a more definite preference?

   Once the taste test is completed, ask the actual respondents to rate themselves on (a) self-confidence and (b) predisposition to take risk (for example, "I like to try new and different things"). Do those who conformed differ from those who did not on these two characteristics?

2. Identify a salesperson who is willing to cooperate in an experiment. The salesperson could be a local merchant or a student with a job in sales. Develop a scenario in which the salesperson attempts to influence customers by (a) expressing similar interests and opinions (referent appeals), (b) acting knowledgeable (expert appeals), and (c) a combination of both. Determine the influence on the customers, using sales results or likelihood of a purchase. Which appeals were most successful? Why?

   If possible, replicate the above experiment in another type of store.
   - Were the same results obtained?
   - If not, why were there differences between the two types of stores? To what extent did differences in the product categories influence the results of the experiment?

NOTES

1. William O. Bearden, Richard G. Netemeyer, and Jesse E. Teel, "Measurement of Consumer Susceptibility to Interpersonal Influence," *Journal of Consumer Research,* 15 (March, 1989), pp. 473–481.

2. William O. Bearden and Randall L. Rose, "Attention to Social Comparison Information: An Individual Difference Factor Affecting Consumer Conformity," *Journal of Consumer Research,* 16 (March, 1990), pp. 461–471.

3. Paul W. Miniard and Joel B. Cohen, "Modeling Personal and Normative Influences on Behavior," *Journal of Consumer Research,* 10 (September, 1983), pp. 169–180.

4. Bobby J. Calder and Robert E. Burnkrant, "Interpersonal Influences on Consumer Behavior: An Attribution Theory Approach," *Journal of Consumer Research,* 4 (June, 1977), pp. 29–38.

5. Vernon L. Allen, "Situational Factors in Conformity," in Leonard Berkowitz, ed., *Advances in Experimental Social Psychology,* Vol. 2 (New York: Academic Press, 1965), pp. 133–175.

6. James H. Leigh and Terrance G. Gabel, "Symbolic Interactionism: Its Effects on Consumer Behavior and Implications for Marketing Strategy," *The Journal of Consumer Marketing,* 9 (Winter, 1992), p. 30.

7. Francis S. Bourne, "Group Influence in Marketing and Public Relations," in Rensis Likert and Samuel P. Hayes, Jr., eds., *Some Applications of Behavioral Research* (Paris: UNESCO, 1957).

8. Leon G. Schiffman and Leslie L. Kanuk, *Consumer Behavior* (Englewood Cliffs, NJ: Prentice-Hall, 1978), p. 214.

9. Peter H. Reingen *et al.,* "Brand Congruence in Interpersonal Relations: A Social Network Analysis," *Journal of Consumer Research,* 11 (December, 1984), pp. 771–783.

10. Donald H. Granbois, "Improving the Study of Customer In-Store Behavior," *Journal of Marketing,* 32 (October, 1968), pp. 28–33.

11. Robert J. Fisher and Linda L. Price, "An Investigation into the Social Context of Early Adoption Behavior," *Journal of Consumer Research,* 19 (December, 1992), pp. 477–486.

12. John R. French and Bertram Raven, "The Bases of Social Power," in D. Cartwright, ed., *Studies in Social Power* (Ann Arbor, MI: Institute for Social Research, 1959), pp. 150–167.

13. H. C. Kelman, "Processes of Opinion Change," *Public Opinion Quarterly,* 25 (Spring, 1961), pp. 57–78.

14. Robert E. Burnkrant and Alain Cousineau, "Informational and Normative Social Influence in Buyer Behavior," *Journal of Consumer Research,* 2 (December, 1975), pp. 206–215.

15. *Ibid.,* p. 207.

16. C. Whan Park and V. Parker Lessig, "Students and Housewives: Differences in Susceptibility to Reference Group Influence," *Journal of Consumer Research,* 4 (September, 1977), pp. 102–110.

17. Margaret L. Friedman and Gilbert A. Churchill, Jr., "Using Consumer Perceptions and a Contingency Approach to Improve Health Care Delivery," *Journal of Consumer Research,* 13 (March, 1987), p. 503.

18. Thomas S. Robertson, *Innovative Behavior and Communications* (New York: Holt, Rinehart and Winston, 1971).

19. George P. Moschis, "Social Comparisons and Informal Group Influence," *Journal of Marketing Research,* 13 (August, 1976), pp. 237–244.

20. F. B. Evans, "Selling as a Dyadic Relationship—A New Approach," *American Behavioral Scientist,* 6 (May, 1963), pp. 76–79; and Timothy C. Brock, "Communicator-Recipient Similarity and Decision Change," *Journal of Personality and Social Psychology,* 1 (June, 1965), pp. 650–654.

21. See William H. Whyte, "The Web of Word of Mouth," *Fortune* (November, 1954), pp.140–143; and Sidney P. Feldman, "Some Dyadic Relationships Associated with Consumer Choice," in Raymond M. Haas, ed., *Proceedings of the American Marketing Association,* Series No. 24 (1966), pp. 758–775.

22. Leon G. Schiffman, "Social Interaction Patterns of the Elderly Consumer," in Boris W. Becker and Helmut Becker, eds., *Combined Proceedings of the American Marketing Association,* Series No. 34 (1972), p. 451.

23. Park and Lessig, "Students and Housewives . . . ," *loc. cit.*

24. Henry Assael, Michael Etgar, and Michael Henry, "The Dimensions of Evaluating and Utilizing Alternative Information Sources," Working paper, New York University, March, 1983.

25. Whyte, "The Web of Word of Mouth . . . ," *loc. cit.*

26. S. E. Asch, "Effects of Group Pressure upon the Modification and Distortion of Judgments," in Harold Geutzkow, ed., *Groups, Leadership and Men* (Pittsburgh, PA: Carnegie Press, 1951).

27. M. Venkatesan, "Experimental Study of Consumer Behavior Conformity and Independence," *Journal of Marketing Research,* 3 (November, 1966), pp. 384–387.

28. Randall L. Rose, William O. Bearden, and Jesse E. Teel, "An Attributional Analysis of Resistance to Group Pressure Regarding Illicit Drug and Alcohol Consumption," *Journal of Consumer Research,* 19 (June, 1992), pp. 1–13.

29. James Duesenberry, *Income, Savings and the Theory of Consumer Behavior* (Cambridge, MA: Harvard University Press, 1949).

30. Park and Lessig, "Students and Housewives . . . ," *loc. cit.*

31. Flemming Hansen, "Primary Group Influence and Consumer Conformity," in Philip R. McDonald, ed., *Proceedings of the American Marketing Association's Educators Conference,* Series No. 30 (1969), pp. 300–305.

32. Burnkrant and Cousineau, "Informational and Normative Social Influence . . . ," *loc. cit.*

33. Park and Lessig, "Students and Housewives . . . ," *loc. cit.*

34. James C. Ward and Peter H. Reingen, "Sociocognitive Analysis of Group Decision Making Among Consumers," *Journal of Consumer Research,* 17 (December, 1990), pp. 245–262.

35. Martin Kaplan and Charles Miller, "Group Decision Making and Normative Versus Informational Influence: Effects of Type of Issue and Assigned Decision Role," *Journal of Personality and Social Psychology,* 53 (1987), pp. 306–313.

36. Dennis L. Rosen and Richard W. Olshavsky, "The Dual Role of Informational Social Influence: Implications for Marketing Management," *Journal of Business Research,* 15 (1987), pp. 123–144.

37. Moschis, "Social Comparisons . . . ," *op. cit.,* p. 240.

38. Bourne, "Group Influence In Marketing and Public Relations," *loc. cit.*

39. William O. Bearden and Michael J. Etzel, "Reference Group Influence on Product and Brand Purchase Decisions," *Journal of Consumer Research,* 9 (September, 1982), pp. 183–194.

40. Julian L. Watkins, *The 100 Greatest Advertisements* (New York: Dover Publications, 1959), p. 205.

41. Barton A. Weitz, "Effectiveness in Sales Interactions: A Contingency Framework," *Journal of Marketing,* 45 (Winter, 1981), pp. 85–103.

42. G. David Hughes, Joseph B. Juhasz, and Bruno Contini, "The Influence of Personality on the Bargaining Process," *Journal of Business,* 46 (October, 1973), pp. 593–603.

43. Dean G. Pruitt, *Negotiation Behavior* (New York: Academic Press, 1981).

44. Paul H. Schurr and Julie L. Ozanne, "Influences on Exchange Processes: Buyer's Preconceptions of a Seller's Trustworthiness and Bargaining Toughness," *Journal of Consumer Research,* 11 (March, 1985), pp. 939–953.

16

Family Influences

TYSON TARGETS BOTH KIDS AND THEIR PARENTS

The last chapter focused on the importance of reference groups in influencing a consumer's purchase behavior. By far the most important reference group is the family. Not only do family members influence one another's purchasing decisions, but they are also frequently involved in making joint decisions. Parts One and Two of this text have been devoted almost exclusively to the individual consumer. The realization that many purchasing decisions are made jointly by several members of a family suggests the importance of studying the family as a decision unit.

The strategic importance of joint decisions within the family is apparent when auto manufacturers advertise in women's magazines, in recognition of the wife's increasing influence over a traditionally male-dominant purchasing decision, or when manufacturers of food and household products advertise to men, in recognition of their greater involvement in shopping tasks.

In addition, marketers have been paying more attention to children's influences on family decisions. With the great majority of mothers in the work force, three out of four American children now have no full-time parent at home.[1] These "latchkey kids" (that is, children with no parent at home after school) have been buying and preparing food for themselves and their families. As a result, children are the prime purchase influencers for a wide array of products, even though parents are the ultimate decision makers.

Tyson Foods is targeting its Looney Tunes microwaveable meals to latchkey kids because these meals are easy to prepare, and over 80 percent of 6- to 14-year-olds use microwave ovens.[2] Tyson realizes that children under 14 are unlikely to be the decision makers for packaged foods, but they can certainly exert influence on their parents. So, its strategy is to try to encourage children to request their parents to buy the products. In licensing Warner Brothers' Looney Tunes characters for use on its packages, Tyson features the characters trying to upstage each other in TV commercials to kids. Tyson also advertises to parents to try to gain approval for children's requests. In this case, print ads are used emphasizing the nutritional value of the meals through the same Looney Tune characters. The product manager for Looney Tunes Meals explained that "When you're talking to two diverse audiences like parents and kids, different vehicles are required."[3]

Tyson's strategy recognizes the dynamics of parent-child influences in its advertising to children. Parents are more likely to be influenced by children for a wide range of products; and even if they are not the prime decision makers, children are increasingly targeted for these products. The unresolved issues are whether such advertising to children is responsible and whether children should be encouraged to use products such as microwaveable meals.

This chapter focuses on both joint and individual decision making within the family. In the first part of the chapter, a model of family decision making is described. Next, we consider the relative influence of the husband and wife as well as the parent-child interaction in the purchasing process. The strategic implications of family influences are illustrated. The chapter closes by picking up a theme from Chapter 2—the broader societal issues involved in advertising to children.

◆ HOUSEHOLDS AND FAMILIES

Our focus in this chapter is family influences. However, in a broader sense, we also talk about household influences. A **household** is composed of any individuals living singly or together with others in a residential unit. A **family** is two or more people living together who are related by blood or marriage. A family is, therefore, a category of a household.

The 95 million households in the United States in 1993 were composed of the following categories:[4]

1. Married couples with children under 18 (about 27 percent of all households).
2. Married couples with children 18 and over (about 15 percent of households).
3. Married couples without children (15 percent).
4. Single parents living with children (8 percent).
5. Unmarried couples (both heterosexual and gay; 6 percent).
6. People living alone (24 percent).
7. Other nonfamily households (for example, roommates, college students; 5 percent).

Families represent about 71 percent of all households. These can be divided into traditional and nontraditional families. *Traditional families* are represented by the first two categories, married couples with children, representing 42 percent of all households. A substantial number of households are in the *nontraditional* category, 29 percent, representing married couples without children, single-parent households, and unmarried couples.

The proportion of traditional families has been decreasing steadily, from 70 percent of all households in 1950 to the current 42 percent.[5] A number of factors cited in Chapter 10 explain this decrease—higher divorce rates, later marriages, and a decreasing birthrate.

Traditional families can further be categorized as nuclear or extended. **Nuclear families** are married couples with one or more children, and **extended families** are nuclear families with at least one grandparent living at home. At the turn of the century, this three-generational unit (often including aunts and uncles) was the norm. A government study found that in 1900, half of all households in Boston were extended families. Today, mobility, geographic dispersion, changing patterns of immigration, and a decrease in trans-generational ties have made the extended family almost extinct. By 1976, only 4 percent of households were extended families.[6] Today, the figure is probably lower. The virtual extinction of the extended family means that nuclear and traditional families are synonymous.

◆ A MODEL OF FAMILY DECISION MAKING

Figure 16.1 presents a model of family decision making. As the model shows, family decision making is different from individual decision making because of three factors: (1) the likelihood of joint decisions, (2) different role specifications for family members in the process of decision making, and (3) the need to resolve conflicts among family members when making purchasing decisions. These three areas are highlighted in Figure 16.1.

Let's assume an upper middle-class family with two children is considering its vacation plans for the year. For the past five years, the family has vacationed

▶**FIGURE 16.1**

A model of family decision making

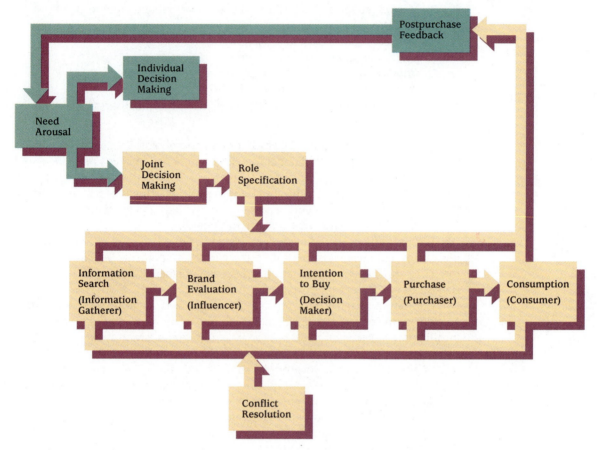

at the same resort area about 200 miles from their home. This year, the children approach their parents and ask if they can take a trip instead. The parents consult about budget and alternative expenditures and decide to explore the possibilities of a two-week trip requiring air travel. Need arousal has occurred because the family members all tended to agree that a change in vacation plans is warranted.

At this point, the family could decide to delegate all authority to one of the parents because of expertise or a high level of involvement with the decision. However, a joint decision is more likely for three reasons. First, the decision is *important to the family*. Second, the *perceived risks* of the decision (the expense, the fact that the family will be close together, and the importance of having a good time) are fairly high. Third, there is *no time pressure* as it is March and the family plans an August vacation.

Once the need for a joint decision has been established, specification of roles will occur, as shown in Figure 16.1. Such specification may be explicit or assumed. Before the children made the suggestion to change vacation plans, they had collected information about alternative areas. One collected information on Mexico; the other, on several Caribbean islands. Although the children initiated the process of information search, the whole family may be regarded as *information gatherers* since the husband and wife will now begin to be aware of travel information.

The prime *influencers* in the decision are the children who initiated the decision process and specified two primary alternatives—Mexico and the Caribbean. The *decision makers* will be the husband and wife since they make the budgetary decisions. The *purchasing agent* will be the wife since she is a part-time travel agent and can easily make the arrangements. The *consumers* will of course be the whole family.

In the process of collecting information and evaluating alternative vacation spots, a *conflict* arises between the two children. The son would like to go to one of the Caribbean islands because he is interested in snorkeling. The daughter would like to go to Mexico because she is interested in Mayan ruins. The parents prefer Mexico to the Caribbean and decide to resolve the conflict by telling their son that if they take a trip again next year, his choice will prevail over his sister's. In any case, they will spend a few days at a beach area in Mexico to allow for snorkeling.

By summertime the family finds it can afford the trip to Mexico. They make the purchase; they all enjoy the vacation (postpurchase evaluation); and they agree that if they can afford it, they will consider returning to Mexico.

In this section, we will consider the three components that distinguish family from individual decisions: (1) joint decision making, (2) role specification, and (3) conflict resolution.

Joint Decision Making

Under what conditions are purchasing decisions likely to be made jointly by the family, and under what conditions are they likely to be made by an individual family member? Sheth found that joint decision making is more likely in the following situations:[7]

1. *When the level of perceived risk in buying is high.* Because a wrong decision will affect the whole family, a joint decision is likely to occur to reduce risk and uncertainty. A decision regarding the purchase of a new home is invariably a joint decision because of the financial risks, the social risks involved in neighborhood interaction, and the psychological risks.

Some evidence suggests that joint decision making may encourage the group to make riskier decisions because all members of the group can share the blame for a wrong decision. This so-called **risky shift phenomenon** would mean that a decision the husband and wife make may result in the purchase of a more expensive house than if either spouse make a decision alone. Wood-side studied whether a risky shift occurs in consumer decisions and found that wives were more willing to make riskier decisions for a variety of products after group discussion.[8]

2. *When the purchasing decision is important to the family.*   Importance is closely related to risk. However, in some cases, the decision may be impor-tant and the risk low—for example, deciding whether to return to the same vacation resort the family has gone to for the past five years. Decisions to buy major appliances and automobiles are generally joint decisions because of their importance. Decisions for low involvement products are more likely to be made individually because it may not be worth the time and effort to engage in joint decisions for such products.

3. *When there are few time pressures.*   Time pressures will encourage one member of the family to make the purchase decision. The greater number of working wives has created greater time pressures within the family, a situation that encourages individual decision making for many products that ordinarily might be purchased on a joint basis.

4. *For certain demographic groups.*   Several demographic factors are likely to encourage joint decision making:

- Joint decision making is less likely among upper and lower socioeco-nomic groups. Lower-income households are more wife-dominant; higher-income households are more husband-dominant. The middle-income groups are most likely to engage in joint decision making.[9]
- Younger families (those under age 24) show a higher frequency of joint decision making.[10] One study found the greatest amount of shared decisions in the first year of marriage.[11] As the family gets older, joint decisions tend to decrease. Family members learn to make decisions that are acceptable to each other, and there is less need for shared decisions.[12]
- Joint decision making is more likely if there are no children in the family.[13] As a family adds children, roles become more clearly defined, and husband and wife are more willing to delegate authority to each other. Thus, the need for joint decision making is reduced.[14]
- Joint decision making is more likely if only one of the parents is work-ing, as time pressures are less.

Role Specification

Family members can play any of five roles in decision making. In any given situation, the same member may take on several or even all five roles:

1. The *information gatherer* (sometimes called the *gatekeeper*) influences the family's processing of information by controlling the level and type of stimuli the family is exposed to. The information gatherer has the greatest expertise in acquiring and evaluating information from various sources and is most aware of alternative sources of information.

2. The *influencer* is most likely to influence the manner in which alternative brands are evaluated. That is, the influencer establishes the decision criteria by which brands are compared (cost, durability, and so on) and influences the other family members' evaluation of alternative brands. In so doing, the influencer determines the brands that best fit the family's needs. The influencer may or may not be the same person as the information gatherer.

3. The *decision maker* decides which brand to purchase, probably because he or she has budgetary power and, therefore, final approval. Again, this could be the same person as the information gatherer or influencer, but not necessarily.

4. The *purchasing agent* carries out the decision by purchasing the product for the family. The purchasing agent may or may not have discretion regarding the brand to buy because the decision may have already been made. He or she may have discretion only regarding the store. However, when an in-store decision is made, the purchasing agent and decision maker are the same.

5. The *consumer* uses the product and evaluates it, giving some feedback to other family members regarding satisfaction with the chosen brand and desirability of purchasing the same brand again. The consumer could be the whole family or an individual family member.

From the marketer's standpoint, one of the most important distinctions is that between the purchaser and consumer. Many strategic decisions are made without recognizing this important distinction. In many cases, the purchasing agent may have little importance since the consumer is making the postpurchase evaluation and will decide on future brand purchases. In other cases, the purchaser may decide the brand for others in the family. A study by *McCall's* magazine found that almost one-third of beer consumers delegated the brand decision to the purchasing agent (in most cases the wife) and that the purchasing agent was aware of the consumer's beer preferences 90 percent of the time.[15]

Conflict Resolution

Whenever two or more people are involved in decision making, some conflict is likely in purchasing objectives, attitudes toward alternative brands, and the selection of the most desirable alternative. The family is no exception. One writer believes that because of close interdependence of family members, joint decisions are likely to lead to conflict.[16] Another states that since families are small and involuntary groups, conflict is the norm.[17] These writers refer to family decisions in general rather than to purchasing decisions.

Are purchasing decisions likely to create conflict in the family? Davis believes so. He states, "Families quite often bargain, compromise, and coerce rather than problem-solve in arriving at decisions."[18] Davis cites studies of husband-wife decision making for housing,[19] automobiles,[20] and family planning[21] that show substantial differences in choice criteria, perceptions, and attitudes. In family planning, for example, husbands emphasized the positive effects of small family size on living costs, whereas wives viewed small families as an advantage in giving them more time. Davis also found conflict regarding the roles husbands and wives are to play in the decision in terms of who should make various purchase decisions and who should implement them.

The marketer must be aware of such conflicts and adjust marketing strategies accordingly. For example, salespersons should be aware of any potential conflict in joint decisions. Families frequently visit automobile showrooms together and talk to dealers jointly. The husband may emphasize roominess and style to impress business associates, and the wife may be concerned with gas economy and service costs—or the husband may emphasize cost; the wife, style. In any case, differences are likely to occur, and the sales representative must appeal to both parties.

Family Strategies to Resolve Conflict

The existence of conflict in family decisions raises the important question of how families resolve such conflicts. Families use various strategies to try to resolve conflicts to the satisfaction of all family members. Conflicts may arise over (1) the reasons for buying an item or (2) the evaluation of alternative choices. Conflict over buying motives is more serious and requires *accommodation* among family members. Most purchase-related conflicts in the family are over product alternatives, rather than goals, and usually are resolved by *consensus*. This is because the family is a cooperative group; that is, one whose members' goals are compatible.[22]

Davis studied various strategies to resolve conflicts by consensus (that is, when family members agree about goals) and by accommodation (when they disagree).[23] Table 16.1 shows three strategies to reach consensus: problem solving, role delegation, and budgetary allocation. In problem solving, three means of decision making are likely to lead to consensus among family members. First, family discussion may lead to a better solution than that proposed by any one member of the family. Second, one family member is recognized as having expertise and can be relied on to make a recommendation. The family then makes a decision based on this recommendation. Third, the family may decide to satisfy conflicting desires by making multiple purchases as a way to avoid conflict.

Consensus does not always mean the family will come together and mutually arrive at a decision. The family could opt for individual rather than joint decision making as a means of avoiding conflict, by delegating responsibility for the decision to one member of the family (the specialist). Another alterna-

▶**TABLE 16.1**

Alternative strategies in family decision making

Goals	Strategy	Ways of Implementing
Consensus (family members agree about goals)	Problem solving	The expert
		The better solution
		The multiple purchase
	Role delegation	The specialist
	Budgetary allocation	The controller
Accommodation (family members disagree about goals)	Bargaining	The next purchase
	Politicking	The irresponsible critic
		Coercion
		Coalitions

SOURCE: Adapted from Harry L. Davis, "Decision Making Within the Household," JOURNAL OF CONSUMER RESEARCH, 2 (March, 1976), p. 255. Reprinted with permission from The University of Chicago Press.

tive is to assign responsibility for the budget to one family member (the controller). In this case, there will still be room for joint decision making. The husband or wife may have decided how much to spend for a vacation, but the family may jointly decide where to go.

When family members disagree about goals, they use two strategies: bargaining and politicking. *Bargaining* involves some give and take. *Politicking* is a means of influencing someone to agree to a decision he or she would not otherwise make.

An example of a bargaining strategy is to allow one member of the family to buy the desired item on this purchase if the other member will be able to have his or her way on the next purchase. This was the method used in our example of family decision making: The daughter was allowed to determine the vacation spot this year as long as the son got his preference next year.

Methods of politicking are also listed in Table 16.1. The *irresponsible critic* criticizes the decision of the family by dissociating himself or herself from it. If the decision is right, he or she has nothing to lose; if it is wrong, the irresponsible critic can always say, "I told you so." *Coercion* involves direct threat. For example, the parent may threaten to reduce an allowance if the child uses most of it to purchase candy, or one spouse may threaten another ("Since you bought that suit, I have a right to buy the winter coat I saw"). *Coalitions* may be formed within the family, as when children support one parent in a conflict. Coalitions may also be formed to bring dissenters into line. Everyone in the family wants to buy a stereo console except the teenage son, who wants to buy components. The weight of family opinion forces the teenage son to comply.

Sheth regards coercion and coalitions as the least desirable forms of conflict resolution.[24] Such politicking is most likely to occur when family members disagree not only about buying goals, but also about lifestyles and fundamental attitudes. It is more difficult to resolve a conflict when a husband and wife disagree over whether a teenage daughter needs a car than when they disagree over the relative emphasis to place on the price and style of a car.

Several studies have examined the use of conflict resolution strategies such as those illustrated in Table 16.1. Park studied couples buying a home and found that if one spouse had expertise in a particular area (e.g., kitchen appliances), he or she assumed responsibility for evaluating that aspect.[25] If expertise did not exist, the spouse who felt most strongly about a point won out (for example, "If you really want a two-car garage, it's OK with me"). Since there was little preplanning involved in the purchase of a home, Park described the way husbands and wives resolve conflicts as a process of "muddling through" the decision.

Corfman and Lehmann also found that couples often resolve conflicts by choosing the alternative of the spouse with the strongest preference.[26] If neither spouse has a strong preference, the spouse who has had his or her way less often in the past makes the selection. In other words, if no one has a strong preference, couples "take turns" in getting their way. Spiro studied conflict in the context of husband-wife relationships and found that more contemporary families (families with greater equality between husband and wife) tended to use problem-solving strategies, particularly reliance on a spouse's expertise. By contrast, traditional (husband-dominant) families were more likely to use politicking strategies.[27]

When Are Conflicts Most Easily Resolved?

There are three situations in which family conflicts are most easily resolved. The first occurs when the family recognizes one person as the legitimate authority. Conflict is simply resolved by delegating decision making to this individual. The second occurs when one family member is more involved in the decision than the others. The family may agree that the highly involved individual will make the decision. The third situation is when one family member may be more empathetic to another's needs.

Burns and Granbois studied the influence of husbands and wives in automobile decisions to determine if these three factors—recognized legitimacy, involvement, and empathy—reduce conflict.[28] They found that each factor facilitated conflict resolution. Conflict was less likely if the husband and wife agreed that the decision should be made jointly or by one of them alone. Even if the couple failed to agree on authority, conflict was less likely if one of them was more involved in the purchase. Finally, conflict was less likely if one of the spouses was more empathetic. For autos, the husband was more involved and less empathetic to the wife's needs. Therefore, the wife was more likely to cede decision authority to the husband. Menasco and Curry's study of husband-wife choices of investment options supported these findings. Spouses gravitated to one or the other's preferences as a result of empathy.[29]

◆ HUSBAND-WIFE INFLUENCES

The husband and wife are clearly the dominant influences in family decision making. Most studies have focused on their roles in decision making and the dominance of one or the other. The relative influence of the husband and the wife is likely to vary according to four things: (1) type of product considered, (2) the stage in decision making, (3) the nature of purchase influence, and (4) family characteristics.

Type of Product Considered

Traditionally, husbands have been regarded as the dominant decision makers for products such as automobiles, financial services, and liquor. Wives have been viewed as the prime decision makers for foods, toiletries, and small appliances. However, as we saw in Chapter 11, many of these roles have merged and even been reversed due to the greater proportion of working wives and changes in family norms.

In 1974, Davis and Rigaux undertook one of the most detailed studies of husband-wife influences by product category.[30] They studied family decision making for 25 products and classified them into one of four categories:

1. Products for which the husband tends to be the dominant influence.
2. Products for which the wife tends to be the dominant influence.
3. Products for which decisions are made by either the husband or the wife, with either person equally likely to be dominant (**autonomous decisions**).
4. Products for which decisions are made jointly by husband and wife.

Putnam's and Davidson's 1987 update of their study for U.S. households is shown in Figure 16.2.[31] The higher the product is on the vertical axis, the more likely it is that the wife will be the dominant influence. The farther to the right it is on the horizontal axis, the more likely the decision is to be a joint one. Therefore, products in the upper left are wife-dominant, products in the middle left are based on individual decisions by either husband or wife (autonomous), and products in the lower left are husband-dominant. Products to the right are joint decisions and involve both husband and wife as equal influences. Products to the left are individual decisions.

Some of the product classifications in Figure 16.2 confirm previous studies. Husbands are more dominant in decisions for lawn mowers, sports equipment, and hardware items. Wives dominate decisions for food, clothing, and kitchenware. Either the husband or the wife will make decisions for cameras and for the husband's clothing on an individual basis. They will most likely make joint decisions for vacations, furniture, and refrigerators.

A number of items changed their position between the original study in 1974 and the 1987 study. Cars, TV sets, and financial planning moved from a

▶**FIGURE 16.2**

Husband-wife rules in family decisions by product category

Sources: Original study in Harry L. Davis and Benny P. Rigaux, "Perception of Marital Roles in Decision Processes," *Journal of Consumer Research*, 1 (June, 1974), p. 54. Figures based on Mandy Putnam and William R. Davidson, *Family Purchasing Behavior: II, Family Roles by Product Category* (Columbus, OH: Management Horizons, Inc., a division of Price Waterhouse, 1987).

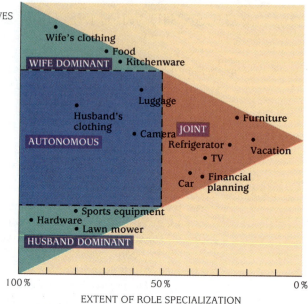

RELATIVE INFLUENCE OF HUSBANDS AND WIVES

EXTENT OF ROLE SPECIALIZATION

husband-dominant position to joint decision making, reflecting the greater influence of working wives.

The classifications in Figure 16.2 have important implications for marketers. If a product is in the husband- or wife-dominant category, marketers must tailor messages to one spouse or the other and must select media that are male- or female-dominant. If the product is in the joint decision category, marketers must tailor the message for the couple and must purchase media that are likely to reach both spouses. If the product is in the autonomous category, either spouse could make the decision. In some cases, the husband is dominant; in others, the wife. Therefore, there are two audiences, and marketers may need two campaigns. An advertiser of men's clothing might recognize the wife's influence by introducing two campaigns, one directed to the wife and the other to the husband, using different appeals. Trying to develop one campaign to appeal to both spouses may not be as effective.

Stage in Decision Making

The influence of the husband or wife may vary according to the stage in decision making. One spouse may initiate a decision, another may dominate in gathering information, and both may make the final decision. In the family planning area, both husband and wife are likely to initiate decision making, but the wife is more involved than the husband in searching for information.[32] One study of the adoption of IUDs in India found that in 44 percent of the cases, the husband made the final decision.[33]

In the Davis and Rigaux study, husband-wife influences were studied in three phases of the decision: (1) problem recognition, (2) information search, and (3) the final decision.[34] Davis and Rigaux traced the pattern of influence for the 25 products they studied across these three decision phases. They found that in going from problem recognition to information search, the husband became a more dominant influence for most products. On the other hand, when moving from information search to the final decision, the pattern of influence became more equal. Information search was likely to be an individual process, whereas the final decision was more likely to be made jointly.

Nature of Purchase Influence

The nature of the purchase influence may specify husband-wife roles. The most important classification by purchase influence defines instrumental versus expressive roles in family purchasing.[35] **Instrumental roles** are related to performing tasks that help the group make the final purchasing decision. Decisions on budgets, timing, and product specifications would be task oriented. **Expressive roles** facilitate expression of group norms and provide the group with social and emotional support. Decisions about color, style, and design are expressive since they reflect group norms.

Historically, the husband has been associated with the instrumental role and the wife with the expressive role.[36] However, we saw in Chapter 11 that as more wives enter the work force, husbands are more likely to assume household roles and wives budgetary and planning roles. As a result, instrumental and expressive roles are becoming more intermingled between husband and wife.

Several studies found that working wives are less likely to accept traditional homemaking tasks associated with expressive roles.[37] In their study, Ferber and Lee suggested that the wife may be just as likely to fulfill certain instrumental roles as the husband.[38] They identified the role of the financial officer in the family; that is, the person who pays the bills, keeps track of expenditures, and determines the use of leftover money. Clearly, this is an instrumental, rather than an expressive, role because it is budgetary. Ferber and Lee found that in the first year of marriage, the husband and wife were equally likely to assume this role. In the second year of marriage, however, the wife was more likely to be the financial officer.

Family Characteristics

Even though husbands tend to dominate decisions for certain product categories and wives for others, these roles may vary in the degree of dominance within each family. In some families, the husband may be more dominant, regardless of the product being considered (patriarchal families); in others, the wife may be more dominant (matriarchal families).

Various studies show that a husband will generally be more influential in the purchase decision than his wife when:

1. His level of education is higher.
2. His income and occupational status are higher.
3. His wife is not employed.
4. The couple is at an earlier stage in the family life cycle (young parents).
5. The couple has a greater than average number of children.[39]

The opposite is true for a wife-dominant family: The wife is employed, has a higher level of education than the husband, and so forth. One study by Skinner and Dubinsky confirmed this profile. Wives who were more involved than husbands in forming insurance decisions tended to be employed and better educated than their husbands.[40]

The profile of the husband-dominant family suggests a family with traditional values and attitudes toward marital roles. The husband's higher income provides him with financial power within the family. A nonworking wife with a lower level of education usually means that more traditional values prevail. A survey of 257 married women supported the more traditional orientation of the husband-dominant family.[41] Wives were classified as conservative, moderate, or liberal with regard to female roles. Women who had liberal views of their role were much more likely to make purchase decisions than were conservative women. They were also more than twice as likely to make decisions about family savings, vacation plans, and major appliances than were conservative women. Conversely, Qualls' study of husbands found that those with conservative perceptions of their marital role believed they had more influence on decisions for vacations, insurance, and savings than did husbands with more liberal views.[42]

Both studies indicate that traditional (conservative) views of marital roles encourage greater male influence and contemporary (liberal) views encourage greater female influence.

Changing Patterns of Husband-Wife Influences

As we saw in Chapter 11, changes in marital roles have led to the husband's greater influence in decisions the wife has traditionally assumed (see Exhibit 16.1) and the wife's greater influence in areas traditionally assumed to be the husband's domain. Men bought 25 percent of the groceries in 1992, up from 17 percent in 1987. Further, they made more than half the household decisions for soaps, cereals, soft drinks, and snack foods.[43] One advertising agency reached the following conclusion: "Nontraditional advertising media for household products will become more of a factor in the marketing mix. Recipe ads, for example, may very well appear in magazines like *Esquire* and *Playboy*. Commercials for dishwashing detergents might, hopefully, interrupt . . . 'Monday Night Football.' " [44]

Other studies have cited women's increasing role in decisions about insurance, automobiles, and financial services as a result of the greater economic

▶**EXHIBIT 16.1**
Changes in husband's purchasing roles
Source: (left) Courtesy of Gerber Products Co.; (right) Courtesy of Whirlpool Corp.

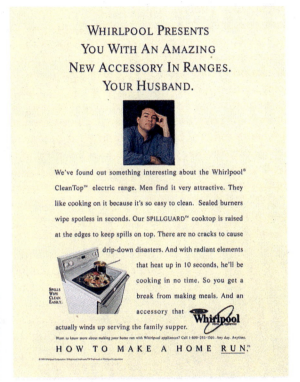

power of working wives.[45] As one researcher noted, an employed wife results in a more equal distribution of family power between husband and wife and will, therefore, lead to more joint decisions.[46]

The changes in husband-wife purchasing roles are illustrated by these facts. In 1955, only 25 percent of all auto decisions were made jointly by husband and wife, whereas by 1982, 57 percent of auto decisions were made jointly.[47] Similarly, in 1973, 30 percent of all life insurance decisions were made jointly. By 1982, 57 percent of insurance decisions were made jointly.[48] For both cars and insurance, the primary mode of decision making shifted from husband-dominant to joint.

The implications for marketing are direct. Marketers for a wide range of products can no longer rely on traditional buying patterns. Producers of food products and household items should direct more effort toward husbands. Marketers of a wide range of "big-ticket" products and services should direct more effort toward wives.

◆ PARENT-CHILD INFLUENCES

Children are playing a more important part in family decision making for several reasons. First, almost 70 percent of all households with children are dual-earning households. Working couples foster greater self-reliance among children, often requiring them to shop and prepare meals. Second, the rapid increase of single-parent families has also increased the number of children involved in shopping and meal preparation. Third, as family size has steadily decreased, the influence of each child has increased. Fourth, women are having children later and have more to spend on their children because of greater earning capacity.[49]

As a result of these trends, children are likely to influence decisions for products the whole family consumes. One study estimates that children influence $132 billion in family expenditures over 62 product categories. The bulk of this influence is in food and beverage products.[50]

Studies of parent-child influences in purchasing have been divided between research on children 12 or under and on adolescents (13 to 17 years old). Research on younger children has focused on how they learn about purchasing and consumption tasks (the child's socialization in the marketplace) and on the mother-child interaction in the purchasing process. Research on adolescents has been directed toward the relative influence of parents and peer groups in teenage purchasing decisions. This focus is due to the general belief that children rely more on parents for norms and values when they are younger and more on their peer groups as they grow older. In the following sections, we first consider the consumer socialization of children, then the mother-child interaction, and finally the peer group-adolescent interaction.

Consumer Socialization of Children

Consumer socialization is the process by which "young people acquire skills, knowledge, and attitudes relevant to their functioning in the marketplace."[51] Children learn about purchasing and consumption primarily from their parents. While television may have a persuasive influence on what children see and how they react to certain brands, "the family is instrumental in teaching young people rational aspects of consumption, including basic consumer needs."[52] The role of parents in trying to teach their children to be more effective consumers is illustrated by the following findings:

- Parents teach price-quality relations to their children, including experiences with the use of money and ways to shop for quality products.[53]
- Parents teach their children how to be effective comparison shoppers[54] and how to buy products on sale.[55]
- Parents influence children's brand preferences.[56]
- Parents have influenced children's ability to distinguish fact from exaggeration in advertising.[57]

Methods of Socialization

How do children learn these various facets of purchase and consumption behavior from their parents? One method they use is *observation*. Children watch and imitate parental behavior because parents serve as role models. Another method of learning is through *co-shopping* with the parent. Grossbart, Carlson, and Walsh found that mothers who co-shop have more explicit consumer socialization goals for their children. They seek to expose children to the experiences associated with visiting stores and use these occasions to teach children consumer skills.[58]

A third method of socialization is through *direct experience*. The increase in dual-earning and one-parent households has resulted in children often shopping on their own. As a result, the process of consumer socialization is occurring much earlier and much faster than it used to. Also, socialization is occurring through direct experience because the child is often the purchasing agent for the family.

Parents are not the only source of consumer socialization. Television and the school environment are also important influences. Children learn to make associations from TV ads and programs. According to **cultivation theory,** children learn about a culture's norms and values from the media. The greater the children's exposure to TV, the greater the likelihood that they will accept the images and associations seen. Thus, young children may learn that using a deodorant is a must in social situations, and many begin to use the product even though body odor does not occur until adolescence.

Schools are becoming a more controversial source of consumer socialization. Whittle Communication's Channel One gives schools TV equipment for the right to broadcast 2 minutes of commercials and 10 minutes of programming a day. Similarly, Scholastic Inc. creates school magazines and posters for corporations to sponsor. These ventures have provoked charges of excessive commercialism in the schools. However, some of the efforts may be constructive. Sears Roebuck's Discover Card division supports Scholastic's *Extra Credit* magazine, which teaches kids about personal finances and economics.[59]

One additional source of socialization is other children. Younger children may emulate older children's behavior and, in so doing, develop consumption skills. The child's peer group can also affect consumer socialization by influencing brand preferences and purchases.

Stages in Consumer Socialization

Children go through various stages of consumer socialization that reflects their cognitive development. The Swiss psychologist, Jean Piaget, identifies three phases.[60] Children from 3 to 7 are in a *preoperational stage* when cognitive structure is poorly organized and language skills are developing. In this stage, parents may permit some limited purchase choices—for example, in the flavors of ice cream or beverages.

From 8 to 11 years of age, children are in a *concrete operational* stage in which they are developing more complex abilities to apply logical thought to concrete problems. In this second phase of socialization, children start developing persuasive techniques learned from their peers to influence their parents to buy them what they want (e.g. "Everyone's got one except me"). In the third stage (12 to 15 years old), children enter a *formal operational stage* in which their ability to think abstractly and to associate concepts and ideas is more fully developed. In this third stage, children have greater financial resources and cognitive capabilities to make decisions on a wider range of products. Many of them will influence parental purchases for adult items such as cars, computers, and electronics.

Role of Parents in Consumer Socialization

A number of studies have investigated the pattern of family influence on children's purchasing and consumption behavior.

Moschis studied the parent's role in the child's socialization by focusing on two types of communication from parent to child: socially oriented communication designed to produce obedience from the child and to foster harmony at home and conceptually oriented communication designed to encourage openness and to foster a more independent outlook.[61]

Moschis found that children from families characterized by the more open conceptual style of communication had more knowledge about consumer-related matters. They were "better able to filter puffery in advertising and to manage a typical family budget, and they had more information about products and their characteristics."[62] These children showed a higher regard for their parents' opinions and had a higher preference for functionally oriented sources of product information such as *Consumer Reports*. Children from families characterized by the more socially oriented communication style tended to rely more on information from peer groups and the mass media than from their parents. These findings suggest that parents are the main source of consumer socialization when they encourage communication and independence. The peer group and television are stronger sources of socialization when parents encourage obedience and deference in their children.

Carlson and Grossbart studied the role of parents in children's socialization as consumers.[63] They identified four types of families:

1. *Authoritarian parents* seek a high level of control over their children and expect unquestioned obedience. They try to shield children from outside influences and are more likely to engage in socially oriented communications.

2. *Neglecting parents* are distant from their children and do not exert much control over them. They do little to maintain or encourage their children's capabilities.

3. *Democratic parents* foster a balance between parents' and children's rights. They encourage children's self-expression and value autonomy. They are warm and supportive, but they also expect mature behavior from children. If they regard children as "out of bounds," they use

Marketers have attempted to influence children's consumer socialization by getting them to recognize company and brand names early even if their companies do not sell children's products. Yogurt, a decidedly adult, health-oriented category, is an example. Children generally tell their moms that they hate the taste. However, as baby boomer parents began to extend their nutritional orientation to their children, yogurt marketers saw an opening. In 1993, Dannon introduced Sprinkl'ins, with a thicker consistency that children like, and Yoplait introduced Trix with fruit flavors layered into the cup. Advertising targets children with fun themes, while targeting moms with nutritionally oriented benefits. The president of Yoplait explains the consumer socialization strategy for children in saying, "If you can get kids hooked on yogurt, you can develop a habit that hopefully will continue through their entire life."

Another producer of adult products, Black & Decker, has engaged in a similar strategy. The company manufactures power tools and appliances. It licensed its name to a line of toys that are miniature versions of its small appliance line. One company executive reasoned, "Youngsters don't buy Black & Decker drills. But they might someday if they start out on toy Dustbusters." Similarly, Sony introduced "My First Sony," a new line of portable audio equipment for children to try to establish brand awareness early and "make kids Sony purchasers for life."

Socialization strategies have also been educationally motivated. First National Bank of Tennessee introduced a savings club for children under 12 to teach them fiscal responsibility with a marketing campaign featuring Moola-Moola, a fuzzy monster who visits schools. One executive says, "If they have an account here when they're young, where are they going to keep it when they do get more money?" Similarly, Burpee Seeds introduced a Little Gardener promotion by offering plastic gardening tools and packets of seeds through McDonald's stores. A company executive said, "Our business depends on the continuing success of developing new gardeners [and] it's never too early to start name awareness."

Children learn to be consumers primarily from their parents, but they seem to be getting a lot of help from marketers as well.

Sources: "Yogurts Sprinkle in Fun to Stir Kids," *Advertising Age* (February 8, 1993), p. S22; "Growing Up in the Market," *American Demographics* (October, 1992), pp. 47–48; "What's Up, Kids," *Marketing & Media Decisions* (May, 1990), pp. 49-52; "Burpee Plants Its Name in Kids' Minds," *Adweek's Marketing Week* (September 11, 1989), p. 17; "As Kids Gain Power of Purse, Marketing Takes Aim at Them," *The Wall Street Journal* (January 19, 1988), p. 15; and "Children Come of Age as Consumers," *Marketing News* (December 4, 1987).

discipline. Democratic parents are more likely to engage in conceptually oriented communications.

4. *Permissive parents* seek to remove as many restraints from children as possible without endangering them. They believe children have adult rights but few responsibilities.

Although these categories are not all encompassing, Carlson and Grossbart used them to study parent-child interactions. They found that democratic and, to a lesser extent, permissive parents had the most active role in children's socialization as consumers. These parents shop with their children and are more likely to seek their advice compared to authoritarian and neglecting parents. Democratic parents also are more likely to view TV with their children, but they express more concern about advertising to their children and try to control their TV viewing. As expected, authoritarian households place the most restrictions on children's consumption behavior.

One implication of the study is that families most involved in children as consumers are also most concerned about the legitimacy of advertising to children. Marketers should try to increase the value of advertising in the eyes of these parents by providing more information on nutrition or product safety, for example. In so doing, they would allay some of the concerns of democratic parents by showing the positive role that advertising can play in the socialization process.

Intergenerational Influences

The process of consumer socialization is **intergenerational;** that is, influences are passed on from one generation to the next. Such influences are most apparent when researchers study brand preferences of parents and children. One study found that 93 percent of college freshmen patronize the same bank as do their parents.[64] State Farm Insurance's study found that about 40 percent of married couples held auto policies with the same company as the husband's parents.[65]

Such influences tend to decrease with consumers' age. The State Farm study found that 65 percent of husbands in their 20s had the same auto policy as their parents. However, by the time they were in their 50s, only 25 percent had a policy with the same company.[66]

Intergenerational influences are not one-directional. That is, they also pass from children to parents. (See Exhibit 16.2 for an example.) Adolescents are likely to influence parents' preferences for products involving new technologies. For example, a survey by a leading research firm found that 57 percent of teens influenced the choice of a personal computer.[67]

Intergenerational influences are likely to be stronger in many foreign countries that have a greater proportion of extended families. Childers and Rao compared family influences in Thai and U.S. families and found that the greater number of extended families in Thailand resulted in stronger intergenerational

influences.[68] Because of a close-knit traditional family structure, brands that parents and grandparents purchase exert a stronger influence than they do in U.S. families.

Children's Influence in the Purchasing Process

Figure 16.3 shows the products that children 12 and under buy and influence their parents to buy. The extent of children's influence varies sharply by product category. Children are most likely to buy product categories one would expect—candy, gum, toys, soft drinks, and snack foods. A significant proportion use their own money to buy presents, books, fast foods, and even clothing and sports equipment. In addition, a large proportion of children also influence their parents' purchases of these same items, particularly clothing. Figure 16.3 also shows that a significant number influence the purchase of such adult-oriented items as cars and electronic products.

Children's involvement may go beyond influencing parents. In some cases, parents and children make joint decisions, particularly when the child is highly involved in the decision. For example, many parents will decide jointly with the child on the choice of a summer camp, private school, or a family vacation.

▶**FIGURE 16.3**

Products purchased and influenced by children

Sources: Influence data reprinted with permission © *American Demographics*. February, 1992. For subscription information, please call (800) 828-1133. Purchase data from "Young Consumers, Perils and Power," *The New York Times* (February 11, 1990); based on a study by Yankelovich, Clancy, and Shulman (Copyright 1990 by The New York Times Co. Reprinted by permission.)

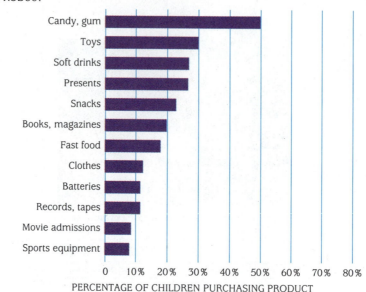

PERCENTAGE OF CHILDREN PURCHASING PRODUCT

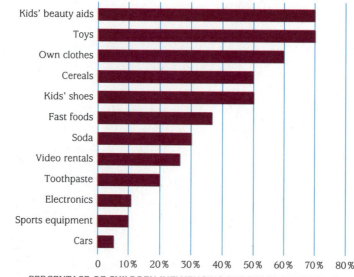

PERCENTAGE OF CHILDREN INFLUENCING PURCHASE OF PRODUCT

Exhibit 16.3 implies such a joint decision-making process in deciding on the Greenbrier resort for a vacation.

Children's influence varies by age.[69] Ward and Wackman found that only 21 percent of the mothers yielded to clothing requests from 5- to 7-year-old children, but 57 percent yielded to requests from 11- to 12-year-old children. Record albums were another category in which children's influence increased markedly with their age.[70]

Greater affluence and earlier consumer socialization of children may be resulting in a greater likelihood that children will get their way. Another reason that children are more likely to get their way is that parents feel guilty for leaving children at home and are more permissive in letting them buy what they want. As a result, marketers have begun to treat children as influentials for adult-oriented products. Although the Sansui advertisement in Exhibit 16.4 is directed to adults, it suggests that children can influence parents to buy models that kids can program easily.

Mother-Child Interaction

The focus in research on parent-child influences in purchasing has been on the interaction between mother and child. Several researchers have considered mothers' responses to children's request to purchase various products.

▶**EXHIBIT 16.3**
An ad implying joint parent-child decision making

Source: Courtesy of The Greenbriar, America's Resort

It's no wonder children keep bringing their parents back...

▶**EXHIBIT 16.4**
An ad depicting children's influence on the purchase of adult products

Ward and Wackman found that the older children were, the more likely mothers were to yield to their request.[71] However, older children made fewer purchase requests for several reasons. As children become older, they may be able to make decisions independently because they get more money from the parents or because they begin to look to the peer group and disregard parents as sources of information. Mothers are more likely to go along with children's requests because they may regard older children as more competent in making purchasing judgments. Finally, older children are less likely to accompany their mothers to the store; and as a result, they simply are not available to make purchase requests.[72]

An interesting cross-cultural study of children's influence found that American children made the most requests (19 over a two-week period), and Japanese children made the fewest requests (9 in two weeks). However, Japanese parents were more likely to accede to children's requests when made. American parents were more likely to negotiate and discuss purchase requests with their children. The authors concluded, "Japanese children are encouraged to be respectful and harmonious in the family and purchase requests may be viewed as 'pushy'; however, since Japanese parents are highly indulgent of their children, they most often agree to buy requested items."[73]

Parent Versus Peer Group Influence Among Adolescents

The purchasing influence of teenagers has increased as working parents have shifted more responsibilities to them for shopping and other chores. One survey found that, on average, teenage girls spend over an hour a week shopping for the family and that over 80 percent do some cooking at home. One marketing expert concluded that the influence of teens in food shopping is almost on a par with their mothers. Another survey found that from 40 to 60 percent of teenagers have a say in family decisions for personal computers, cars, and TV sets; and about 70 percent influenced family vacation decisions.[74]

The traditional view is that as children enter adolescence, they shift their allegiance from parents to the peer group, and parental purchase influence declines. However, various studies suggest that children continue to rely on parents for information and influence into adolescence. One study found that high school students were just as concerned with parents' approval as were elementary school students.[75] Another found that 16- to 19-year-olds were more likely to be influenced by parents than by friends in the purchase of sports equipment and small appliances.[76] When products are expensive and complex, teenagers tend to rely more on parental than on peer influence.[77]

These findings are supported by a comprehensive study of parent and peer group purchasing influences among adolescents. Moschis and Moore conducted a study of purchase influences for eight product categories among 734 adolescents.[78] They found that adolescents preferred parents to friends as a source of influence. The fact that a parent liked the product was a more important criterion than the fact that a friend liked the product. Also, adolescents were almost three times as likely to buy these products with a family member along than with a friend. Parents' influences were particularly important for more expensive products such as wristwatches, dress shoes, and pocket calculators. Friends were more important than parents as sources of information and influence for only one product, sunglasses.

The importance of parents in purchasing decisions does not diminish the importance of the peer group. In the same study, Moschis and Moore found that as teenagers get older, they rely on more information sources, and peer groups become increasingly influential in purchase decisions.[79]

◆ FAMILY LIFE CYCLE

An important dimension of family influence is the **family life cycle;** that is, the progression of a family from formation to child-rearing, middle age, and finally retirement. This progression is not only a function of age, but it also reflects income and changes in family situation. As parents move from being newly married, to having younger children, to seeing them grow and leave the house, and to retirement, changes occur in age, disposable income, and family responsibilities that affect every facet of purchasing behavior.

Traditional Family Life Cycle

In the mid-1960s, two researchers, William Wells and George Gubar, proposed eight stages to describe the family life cycle.[80] The stages described in the top of Table 16.2 reflect the progression of a *traditional family* from marriage to retirement. The categories in Table 16.2 affect both what is bought and the decision process by which it is purchased. This scheme was based on an analysis of demographic and spending data and, until recently, was a very useful framework for classifying families. Demographic changes since 1980 have made it necessary to consider other life cycle categories, but the various stages are still relevant in suggesting changes in spending patterns.

Nature of Purchases

Income constraints and family responsibilities define many of the purchase decisions of families along the traditional life cycle. For example, both young singles and newly married couples have significant discretionary income, the latter because husband and wife are likely to be employed. Whereas young singles spend more on clothing, entertainment, vacations, and other leisure pursuits, newly marrieds spend more on the required trappings of a new household. One study found that they account for 41 percent of all stereo sales and 25 percent of sales of bedroom furniture.[81]

When children arrive (Full Nest I), the couple is likely to move into a new home, purchase baby-related products, and buy home appliances. Discretionary income declines. As the children grow older (Full Nest II and III), the family buys more food and household items. Parents are likely to allocate money to home improvements and to replacement of old cars and appliances. They also begin to spend more on children and teen-related items such as clothing, electronic toys, and recreational products. In the later stages of the full nest, educational costs increase.

In the empty nest stage, discretionary income increases; and parents can afford to spend more money on themselves. Spending for travel and luxury items increases. In the later stages of the empty nest and in the solitary survivor stage, parents generally retire from work. Their income begins to decrease, and they spend more on medical expenses.

Nature of Family Decision Process

The family life cycle operates in influencing the nature of decision making. As we saw, joint decision making is most likely early in the family life cycle. As husband and wife gain experience, they are willing to delegate responsibilities for decisions to each other. The arrival of children further decreases joint

▶**TABLE 16.2**
Traditional and nontraditional life cycle categories

Traditional Family Life Cycle Categories

1. *Young Singles*
Single people under the age of 35. Incomes are low since they are starting a career, but they have few financial burdens and a high level of discretionary income.

2. *Newly Married*
Newly married couples without children. High level of discretionary income because the wife is usually working.

3. *Full Nest I*
Married couples with the youngest child under 6. Greater squeeze on income because of increased expenses for child care.

4. *Full Nest II*
Married couples with children from 6 to 12. Better financial position since parents' income is rising. Most children are "latchkey kids" because both parents are working.

5. *Full Nest III*
Married couples with teenage children living at home. Family's financial position continues to improve. Some children work part-time. Increasing educational costs.

6. *Empty Nest I*
Children have left home and are not dependent on parental support. Parents are still working. Reduced expenses result in greatest level of savings and highest discretionary income.

7. *Empty Nest II*
Household head has retired, so couple experiences sharp drop in income. Couple relies on fixed income from retirement plans.

8. *Solitary Survivor*
Widow or widower with lower income and increasing medical needs.

Nontraditional Family Life Cycle Categories

1. *Married Couples Without Children*
Married couples of all ages who have remained childless. Have high level of discretionary income.

2. *Unmarried Couples*
Include both heterosexual and gay couples. Usually dual-earner and childless. Have high level of discretionary income.

3. *Young Single Parents*
Parent under 35 with one or more children at home. Over three out of four headed by female. Restricted income. Many near poverty level.

4. *Middle-Aged Single Parents*
35 and over with one or more children at home. Restricted income. Severe time pressure.

SOURCE: William D. Wells and George Gubar, "Life Cycle Concept in Marketing Research," JOURNAL OF MARKETING RESEARCH, 3 (November, 1966), pp. 355-363. (Top of Table.)

decisions as time becomes more constrained and husband and wife assume specific roles.

Regarding patterns of family influence, husbands tend to be more influential in families in the early stages of the life cycle. Over time, the wife becomes more assertive in decision making, particularly if she is employed and has some financial leverage over decisions. The arrival of children affects family influences for the simple reason that an additional person often must be considered in the decision process. Children not only act as influencers over a wide range of decisions, but they also serve as occasional mediators in any disagreements between husband and wife. One study of vacation decisions found that children "may have the potential to influence family decisions by forming alliances with either husband or wife to produce a 'majority' position."[82]

Nontraditional Family Life Cycle Categories

The traditional life cycle sequence does not represent a substantial proportion of households. It has no provision for nontraditional categories, and, thus, its applications are limited. As a result, researchers have suggested more modernized family life cycle categories. For example, Gilly and Enis remove marriage as a requirement for a life cycle category to account for unmarried couples and children born out of wedlock.[83] Murphy and Staples suggest five new categories to account for divorced couples and married couples without children.[84]

The bottom of Table 16.2 lists four nontraditional categories that should be included in a more complete family life cycle. These expanded categories provide a more complete profile of American families in the 1990s.

- *Married couples without children.* About 15 percent of households are married couples without children. This sizeable group has substantially more discretionary income than couples with children, particularly in their younger and middle-aged years. After about 45 years of age, empty nesters start to catch up with this group in the amount of discretionary income.
- *Unmarried couples.* Unmarried couples represent about 6 percent of households and are increasing in numbers. They include both heterosexual and gay partners. They also tend to have more discretionary income, primarily because most are childless.
- *Young single parents.* The proportion of young single parents has been increasing because of higher rates of divorce. From 3 to 4 percent of households are young single parents, and 20 percent of children live in single-parent households.[85] Over three-fourths of single-parent households are headed by a female. As we saw in Chapter 10, single-parent households have lower income and many live in poverty. Adding to the financial burden is the limited time a working parent has to spend with his or her child.

- *Middle-aged single parents.* Middle-aged single parents face even greater financial and time pressures than do young single parents. Expenditures on children increase as they grow older, especially if they are college-bound; and the parent's income may not keep pace. Children in this segment assume the greatest responsibility for shopping and household chores.

◆ FAMILY DECISION MAKING AND MARKETING STRATEGIES

Family decision making influences every phase of marketing strategy—the advertising message, the media selected, product development, pricing strategies, and distribution.

Advertising Messages

The nature of family decision making influences the content of advertising messages. If the wife or husband is dominant in making the decision, marketers must direct the advertising message to the needs of the dominant party. A more difficult strategic issue arises when spouses make decisions jointly. Should marketers direct separate messages to husband and wife, or should they design one campaign to appeal to both? In car advertising, some manufacturers have used separate campaigns on the assumption that husband and wife emphasize different benefits. Chevrolet, for example, began targeting 30 percent of its ad budget to women, gearing its themes to fashion and style. However, one study found that 65 percent of women felt misrepresented by such advertising because it implied they were not very interested in performance.[86] Increasingly, automakers are targeting their campaigns to both husband and wife, with performance as the primary benefit and style as a secondary theme. (See Exhibit 16.5.)

Another strategic issue is whether to target the child alone or to target both child and parent for children's products. Hawaiian Punch targets kids with themes like "The only 'Punch' that won't get you sent to the principal's office," and "If you tried blending 7 Natural Fruits, you'd make a mess and Mom would have a cow."[87] However, when parental approval is required, marketers target parents as well. We saw that for microwaveable meals, producers such as Tyson target both parents and kids.

Media

The selection of media is based on who is involved in the decision. Husband- or wife-dominant decisions require the selection of magazines and TV programs

▶**EXHIBIT 16.5**
An auto campaign that
targets both husband
and wife

Source: Courtesy of Nissan
Motor Corporation U.S.A.

that are male- or female-oriented. If the decision is autonomous—that is, the decision is made by husband or wife and either one is equally likely to make it—the marketer is faced with a difficult choice. Should the advertising budget be split equally between male- and female-oriented media, or should the marketer appeal to one or the other?

Men's clothing is a good example. The marketer could advertise men's clothing in women's magazines, in men's magazines, or in both. If both are used, marketers need two separate campaigns. The danger of this approach is that the media budget may be spread too thin. A joint decision poses a different problem. Should the marketer attempt to reach both husband and wife together, using the same media vehicles, or should there be an attempt to reach each separately through male- and female-oriented media? In joint parent-child decisions, marketers generally reach the parent and child separately to emphasize different benefits. Banquet's Kid Cuisine follows a strategy similar to Tyson's. Banquet advertises its microwaveable product to children on the Nickelodeon cable channel and on TV shows such as "Cosby" and "Growing Pains," while it targets nutritionally oriented print ads to mothers in magazines such as *Good Housekeeping* and *Parents*.

Product Development

A key strategic question is whether products involving family influence should be designed for one family member or for more than one member. Children's clothing, for example, is designed primarily to the mother's specifications. Until recently, life insurance was designed primarily to the husband's specifications, but companies now are developing policies geared specifically to the working wife.

Marketers are also increasingly willing to change the characteristics of adult products to suit the needs of children. We saw that Dannon introduced Trix yogurt with a sweeter taste and thicker consistency to appeal to children. Similarly, Procter & Gamble launched Pert Plus for Kids in a tear-free formulation.[88] The company also introduced a sparkle-filled version of Crest toothpaste to get children to brush.[89]

Pricing

The identity of the decision maker may also influence price strategies. The marketer no longer can assume that the coupon redeemer and price-sensitive consumer is necessarily the wife. Husbands are increasingly involved in making pricing decisions in food stores. Conversely, marketers can no longer assume that husbands determine how much to spend for automobiles and must direct price advertising for automobiles to women.

Children exert some pricing influence. One study found that mothers were more willing to yield to children's requests when the explanation was that the brand was economical or was being sold at a premium.[90] That is, parents were willing to accept arguments when economy was the rationale.

Distribution

The nature of family decision making may also influence distribution strategies. If spouses make decisions jointly, stores may be required to stay open longer to accommodate both the husband and the wife. The orientation of a product to each member of the family means separate merchandising displays.

In-store promotional displays must reflect purchase influence. Wackman found that children are more likely to get their preferred brand when they make a request in the store rather than at home.[91] This implies that marketers should direct in-store promotions for cereals, snacks, candy, or toothpaste toward the child as well as the adult.

◆ MEASUREMENT OF FAMILY INFLUENCE

Studies of family decision making rely on measures of family influence that are assumed to be valid. Two questions arise: Who should be interviewed to determine relative influence, and how should influence be measured?

Whom to Interview

Three approaches have been used in determining husband-wife influences: (1) interview both together, (2) interview each separately, (3) interview the wife to determine her influence and the husband's.

Most studies that have interviewed husbands and wives separately have found a moderate level of agreement between them as to their respective influence.[92] One study found that 68 percent of husbands and wives agree about their roles across 25 product categories.[93] Disagreement over influence is usually about who makes the decision. Another study found that 90 percent of husbands say they make the primary decision to buy auto accessories, whereas only 55 percent of wives say husbands control these purchases. Conversely, 44 percent of wives say they make the decision for major appliances, buy only 25 percent of husbands agree that the wife makes the decision.[94]

These studies suggest that interviewing one spouse to determine the influence of another may not be a reliable means of determining family influence. Interviewing both spouses together to obtain some consensus may be more effective.

Another issue is who should be interviewed in parent-child studies. In most cases, parents are interviewed to estimate the children's influence, even though the validity of the parents' response as a reflection of their children's influence has not been tested. Recently, children have begun to be studied to determine their perceptions of family decision making.[95] Such studies generally have been with adolescents, rather than with younger children, because adolescents are easier to interview. In one of the few studies to interview parents and children, Foxman and her colleagues evaluated the purchase influence of husbands, wives, and adolescent children.[96] They found that compared to parents' ratings, children overestimated their influence.

How to Measure Influence

Most measures of the relative influence of the husband and wife have been on a scale from husband-dominant to wife-dominant. The simplest is a three-point scale: (1) husband decides, (2) equal influence, and (3) wife decides. These measures do indicate relative influence, but they do not indicate the nature of the influence. If the wife decided about a piece of furniture, was it because the husband was not interested, a decision was made to delegate authority to the wife for the purchase, or the husband and wife engaged in negotiations? Determining the nature of influence requires more complex measures and in-depth interviews involving both spouses.

Measures of children's purchase influence are even more questionable. Studies generally have relied on mothers' reports of children's purchase requests with little attempt to gauge the nature of children's purchase influence beyond determining their reaction to their mothers' purchase decision. Here, also, better measures of parent-child influence are required.

◆ SOCIETAL IMPLICATIONS OF FAMILY INFLUENCE

The primary societal issue in family decision making is the effect of advertising on children. We saw in Chapter 2 that the primary concern is the inability of children to process advertising information adequately because of undeveloped cognitive capacities.

Armstrong and Brucks cite two issues regarding the effects of children's advertising in the context of family influence:[97] First, does children's advertising increase parent-child conflict? Second, does such advertising create undesirable consumer socialization by teaching children poor consumption and social values?

Increased Parent-Child Conflict

Critics of children's advertising suggest that advertising may undermine parental control. Seeing ads makes children badger their parents for products they cannot afford or do not want to give to their children. As one Federal Trade Commission critique says, the effect is to turn the child unwittingly into an "assistant salesperson."[98]

Advertisers retort by saying that children's requests of parents are a natural part of the parent-child relationship. They also cite polls showing little support from parents for increased advertising regulation.

Undesirable Consumer Socialization

Critics claim that children's advertising teaches children materialism, impulsiveness, and immediate gratification. As a result, it creates poor consumption values. Further, in fostering impulsive choices, advertising encourages children to buy inappropriate products such as expensive or unneeded toys, sugared cereals, and junk food.[99] It may also create favorable attitudes toward harmful products such as cigarettes. As we saw in Chapter 2, R.J. Reynold's Joe Camel campaign has been faulted on this score.

Defenders claim that advertising provides information that helps children make more informed decisions. They cite consumer socialization as a parental, rather than an advertising, responsibility. Further, they note that **advertisers have been instrumental** in promoting positive socialization by funding such high-quality children's programs as *CBS Schoolbreak Specials* and *ABC After-school Breaks*.

Alternative Solutions

We saw in Chapter 2 that stricter regulations have limited the amount of commercial time on children's programs and required clearer division between programs and commercials. Further, an industry-sponsored organization, the Children's Advertising Review Unit, monitors TV ads on children's programs to determine their suitability and issues complaints against advertisers who violate their guidelines.

These efforts do not address how to prepare children to process and evaluate advertising better. Advertisers might try to develop commercials that children can process more easily, assuming such commercials are responsible. For example, Peracchio found that when ideas and events were repeated visually and were put in a relevant context, younger children were as effective as older children in processing information.[100] Advertisers using repetitive themes in a salient context might improve children's processing of the message, but the question remains whether the message is responsible and improves children's consumer socialization skills.

Ultimately, the primary role for improving children's skills in evaluating advertising rests with the parents. As Armstrong and Brucks note, "Parents can [best] monitor their children's television viewing, get children to think about advertising claims, evaluate children's purchase requests, and help children compare advertising claims against product performance."[101] However, such consumer socialization requires active and involved parents. In this respect, little can be done in protecting children from undue advertising influence if parents simply do not care.

SUMMARY

This chapter focused on the most important reference group—the family. A model of family decision making identified three distinguishing factors. First, decisions within families are likely to be made jointly. Joint decisions are more likely when perceived risk is high, the purchase decision is important to the family, and there are minimal time pressures.

Second, family members have prescribed roles in the decision process. Family members can perform the roles of information gatherer, influencer, decision maker, purchasing agent, and consumer. Third, joint decisions invariably produce some conflict in purchase objectives. As a result, families develop strategies to resolve purchase conflicts through persuasion, problem solving, or bargaining.

Husband-wife influences dominate the family purchasing process. Four types of decision processes were defined: (1) husband-dominant, (2) wife-dominant, (3) autonomous (either husband or wife is equally likely to make an individual decision), and (4) joint decision making. Traditionally, husbands dominate decisions for cars and insurance; wives, for food and toiletries. However, these traditional domains have become blurred as working wives have gained more influence in household decisions for automobiles and financial services.

Parent-child influences were also considered. Children have exerted more influence over family purchase decisions, especially in single-parent and dual-earning households. An important aspect of parent-child interaction is children's consumer socialization. Parents teach children how to be effective consumers and influence their brand preferences. Purchase influences and consumer learning are intergenerational in that they are passed from one generation to another.

The chapter also considered the strategic implications of family decision making and the measurement of family influence. The nature of family decision making influences all facets of marketing strategy, especially since family decision making defines the nature of information seeking, purchase influence, and brand evaluation.

In the last section, we considered the societal implications of advertising to children, particularly in the context of family influences. Advertising may have two negative consequences in regard to parent-child relation; first, it may create parent-child conflict by encouraging children's purchase requests; second, it may instill poor consumption values. Both government and industry have a role in regulating children's advertising. However, ultimately, it is the parents' responsibility to try to counter any negative effects of advertising by trying to improve their children's capacity to process and evaluate advertising messages.

In the next chapter, we consider another environmental influence on consumers: situational influences.

QUESTIONS

1. Are families likely to make the following product decisions on a joint basis or on an individual basis? Why?
   - Life insurance.
   - Hair shampoo.
   - Toothpaste.
   - Compact disc players.
2. Using the categories in Table 16.1, cite two or three strategies for resolving family conflicts that marketers could use in the following cases:
   - The wife wants a smaller house than the husband does because it is easier to maintain. The husband wants a larger house to impress friends and business associates.
   - The daughter wants a TV set in her room to have freedom of choice in program selection. The parents resist the idea for fear the daughter will give less attention to homework.

- The teenage son wants a car. The teenage daughter wants to go on a summer vacation with friends. Parents cannot afford both.

3. Advertising campaigns for products in which spouses make decisions on an autonomic basis are more difficult to formulate because either spouse could make an individual decision. The advertiser could try to develop (a) separate campaigns for each spouse, (b) a joint campaign for both, and (c) a campaign aimed at one or the other. Under what conditions will each of the above strategies be most effective?

4. What may be the effect of a contemporary versus a traditional view of the woman's role in the family on (a) the purchase of convenience foods, (b) family shopping behavior, and (c) the criteria used in selecting food products?

5. Instrumental roles traditionally have been associated with the husband; expressive roles, with the wife. What changes have taken place in American society that have caused a blurring of these traditional roles?

6. There has been a greater shift toward joint decision making for many product categories that have been within the husband's traditional domain (autos, financial planning) and the wife's (appliances, furniture). What are the implications of this shift for (a) new product development, (b) product-line strategies, and (c) advertising?

7. Why has the influence of children in family purchase decisions increased substantially?

8. What are the implications for children's consumer socialization in each of Piaget's three phases of child development?

9. How have marketers attempted to influence children's socialization as consumers?

10. Mothers are more likely to yield to children's requests that are made in the store rather than in the home. Why do you suppose this is true? What are the strategic implications of this finding for (a) advertising and (b) in-store promotional policy?

11. How do stages of the traditional family life cycle affect family decision making? What might be the impact on decision making of being in one of the four nontraditional life cycle categories?

12. How have marketers of children's products that generally require parental approval tried to gain such approval? Cite examples.

13. What are some of the problems in measuring family influence in purchase decisions?

14. What may be the potential negative effects of advertising on the consumer socialization of children? How can children's consumer socialization skills be improved?

RESEARCH ASSIGNMENTS

1. Trace a family decision for two families: one fairly high on the socioeconomic scale and one fairly low. Make sure the product or service involves joint decisions by parents and children (for example, a family vacation, selec-

tion of a college, purchase of an automobile). Identify each family member's (a) specific roles, (b) perceptions and attitudes of the alternatives being considered, (c) conflicts in decision making, (d) modes of conflict resolution, and (e) postpurchase evaluation.

- Does the decision process conform to the model in Figure 16.1?
- What are the differences in the decision processes between the two families?
- What are the implications of decision making for (a) advertising, (b) product-line development, (c) product positioning, and (d) pricing?

2. Conduct separate interviews with third- or fourth-grade children and their mothers to determine perceptions of each child's influence. A good way to do this is to make contact with an elementary school class. Interviews with children should be conducted in class with the teacher's cooperation. Mothers can be interviewed at home.

- Ask mothers about the influence of their children and ask children about their influence relative to their mothers' for products such as cereal, toothpaste, candy, and fast-food restaurants. Use a simple scale that children can understand, such as "I make the decision," "My mother makes the decision," and "We both make the decision." Ask both mothers and children what brand they last purchased and to rate the brand from excellent to poor.
- Is there agreement between mother and child on (a) degree of influence, (b) brand purchased, and (c) brand ratings?

3. Replicate Assignment 2 for 12- to 13-year-old girls buying clothes. In this case, ask children and mothers to divide up ten points based on purchase influence. Determine degree of agreement on (a) purchase influence, (b) evaluation of store in which purchased, and (c) evaluation of clothing purchased.

NOTES

1. " 'Parental Guidance' Lost on This Crop," *Advertising Age* (July 30, 1990), p. 26.

2. "What's Up, Kids," *Marketing & Media Decisions* (May, 1990), p. 50.

3. *Ibid.,* p. 52.

4. Percentages in categories estimated from "The Future of Households," *American Demographics* (December, 1993), p. 29; and "American Families Aren't What They Used To Be," *Adweek's Marketing Week* (April 24, 1989), p. 60.

5. "Mass Marketing to Fragmented Markets," *Planning Review* (September, 1984), p. 34.

6. Joseph A. Califano, Jr., *American Families: Trends, Pressures and Recommendations.* Preliminary report to Gov. Jimmy Carter September 17, 1976 (mimeographed).

7. J. N. Sheth, "A Theory of Family Buying Decisions," in Jagdish N. Sheth, ed., *Models of Buyer Behavior* (New York: Harper & Row, 1974), pp. 17–33.

8. Arch G. Woodside, "Informal Group Influence on Risk Taking," *Journal of Marketing Research,* 9 (May, 1972), pp. 223–225.

9. Mira Komarovsky, "Class Differences in Family Decision-Making on Expenditures," in Nelson Foote, ed., *Household Decision-Making* (New York: New York University Press, 1961), pp. 225–265.

10. Elizabeth H. Wolgast, "Do Husbands or Wives Make the Purchasing Decisions?" *Journal of Marketing,* 22 (October, 1958), pp. 151–158.

11. Robert Ferber and Lucy Chao Lee, "Husband-Wife Influence in Family Purchasing Behavior," *Journal of Consumer Research,* 1 (June, 1974), pp. 43–50.

12. Donald H. Granbois, "The Role of Communication in the Family Decision-Making Process," in Stephen A. Greyser, ed., *Proceedings of the American Marketing Association Educators' Conference* (1963), pp. 44–57.

13. Pierre Filiatrault and J. R. Brent Ritchie, "Joint Purchasing Decisions: A Comparison of Influence Structure in Family and Couple Decision-Making Units," *Journal of Consumer Research,* 7 (September, 1980), p. 139.

14. William F. Kenkel, "Family Interaction in Decision-Making on Spending," in Foote, *Household Decision-Making, loc. cit.*

15. John S. Coulson, "Buying Decisions Within the Family and the Consumer-Brand Relationship," in Joseph W. Newman, ed., *On Knowing the Consumer* (New York: John Wiley, 1967), p. 60.

16. J. Sprey, "The Family as a System in Conflicts," *Journal of Marriage and Family,* 31 (November, 1969), pp. 699–706.

17. R. O. Blood, Jr., "Resolving Family Conflicts," *Journal of Conflict Resolution,* 4 (June, 1960), pp. 209–219.

18. Harry L. Davis, "Decision Making Within the Household," *Journal of Consumer Research,* 2 (March, 1976), p. 252.

19. Raymond Loewy/William Snaith, Inc., *Project Home: The Motivations Towards Homes and Housing.* Report prepared for the Project Home Committee, 1967.

20. P. Doyle and P. Hutchinson, "Individual Differences in Family Decision Making," *Journal of the Market Research Society,* 15 (October, 1973), pp. 193–206.

21. T. Poffenberger, *Husband-Wife Communication and Motivational Aspects of Population Control in an Indian Village* (Green Park, New Delhi: Central Family Planning Institute, 1969).

22. Kim P. Corfman and Donald R. Lehmann, "Models of Cooperative Group Decision-Making and Relative Influence: An Experimental Investigation of Family Purchase Decisions," *Journal of Consumer Research,* 14 (June, 1987), p. 2.

23. Davis, "Decision Making Within the Household," *loc. cit.*

24. Sheth, "A Theory of Family Buying Decisions," *op. cit.,* p. 33.

25. C. Whan Park, "Joint Decisions in Home Purchasing: A Muddling Through Process," *Journal of Consumer Research,* 9 (September, 1982), pp. 151–162.

26. Corfman and Lehmann, "Models of Cooperative Group Decision-Making," *op. cit.,* pp. 1–13.

27. Rosann L. Spiro, "Persuasion in Family Decision Making," *Journal of Consumer Research,* 9 (March, 1983), pp. 393–402. See also William J. Qualls, "Household Decision Behavior: The Impact of Husbands' and Wives' Sex Role Orientation," *Journal of Consumer Research,* 14 (September, 1987), pp. 264–279.

28. Alvin C. Burns and Donald H. Granbois, "Factors Moderating the Resolution of Preference Conflict in Family Automobile Purchasing," *Journal of Marketing Research,* 14 (February, 1977), pp. 77–86.

29. Michael B. Menasco and David J. Curry, "Utility and Choice: An Empirical Study of Wife/Husband Decision Making," *Journal of Consumer Research,* 16 (June, 1989), p. 95.

30. H. L. Davis and Benny P. Rigaux, "Perceptions of Marital Roles in Decision Processes," *Journal of Consumer Research,* 1 (June, 1974), pp. 51–62.

31. Mandy Putnam and William R. Davidson, *Family Purchasing Behavior: II, Family Roles by Product Category* (Columbus, OH: Management Horizons, Inc., a division of Price Waterhouse, 1987).

32. J. Palmore, "The Chicago Snowball: A Study of the Flow and Diffusion of Family Planning Information," in D. J. Bogue, ed., *Sociological Contributions to Family Planning Research* (Chicago: Community and Family Planning Center, University of Chicago, 1967), pp. 272–363.

33. D. C. Dubey and H. M. Choldin, "Communication and Diffusion of the IUD: A Case Study in Urban India," *Demography,* 4 (1967), pp. 601–614.

34. Davis and Rigaux, "Perception of Marital Roles . . . ," *loc. cit.*

35. Bernard Berelson and Gary A. Steiner, *Human Behavior: An Inventory of Scientific Findings* (New York: Harcourt, Brace & World, 1964), p. 314.

36. William F. Kenkel, "Family Interaction in Decision-Making and Decisions Choices," *Journal of Social Psychology,* 54 (1961), p. 260; and Davis

37. Kenkel, "Family Interaction in Decision-Making . . . ," *op. cit.,* p. 152; and Mary Lou Roberts and Lawrence H. Wortzel, "Role Transferral in the Household," in Andrew Mitchell, ed., *Advances in Consumer Research,* Vol. 6 (Ann Arbor, MI: Association for Consumer Research, 1982), p. 264.

38. Ferber and Lee, "Husband-Wife Influence in Family Purchasing Behavior," *loc. cit.*

39. Benny Rigaux-Bricmont, "Explaining the Marital Influences in Family Economic Decision-Making," in Subhash C. Jain, ed., *Proceedings of the American Marketing Association Educators' Conference,* Series No. 43 (1978), pp. 126–129.

40. Steven J. Skinner and Alan J. Dubinsky, "Purchase Insurance: Predictors of Family Decision-Making Responsibility," *Journal of Risk and Insurance,* 51 (September, 1984), p. 521.

41. Robert T. Green and Isabella C. M. Cunningham, "Feminine Role Perception and Family Purchasing Decisions," *Journal of Marketing Research,* 12 (August, 1975), pp. 325–332.

42. William J. Qualls, "Changing Sex Roles: Its Impact upon Family Decision Making," in Andrew Mitchell, ed., *Advances in Consumer Research,* Vol. 9 (Ann Arbor, MI: Association for Consumer Research, 1982), p. 269.

43. "Real Men Buy Paper Towels Too," *Business Week* (November 9, 1992), p. 75; and "Study Boosts Men's Buying Role," *Advertising Age,* (December 4, 1989).

44. "Large Numbers of Husbands Buy Household Products, Do Housework," *Marketing News* (October 3, 1980), p. 3.

45. See "Working Women Now More Attractive—Y & R," *Advertising Age* (January 11, 1982), p. 76; and "A Long Drive for Recognition," *Advertising Age* (June 22, 1981), p. S24.

46. Harriet Holter, "Sex Roles and Social Change," *Acta Sociological,* 14 (Winter, 1971), pp. 2–12.

47. Isabella C. M. Cunningham and Robert T. Green, "Purchasing Roles in the U.S. Family, 1955 and 1973," *Journal of Marketing,* 38 (October, 1974), p. 63; and Qualls, "Changing Sex Roles . . . ," *op. cit.,* pp. 267–270.

48. *Ibid.*

49. "The Littlest Shoppers," *American Demographics* (February, 1992), pp. 48, 50.

50. *Ibid.,* p. 53.

51. Scott Ward, "Consumer Socialization," in Harold H. Kassarjian and Thomas S. Robertson, eds., *Perspectives in Consumer Behavior* (Glencoe, IL: Scott, Foresman, 1980).

52. George P. Moschis, "The Role of Family Communication in Consumer Socialization of Children and Adolescents," *Journal of Consumer Research,* 11 (March, 1985), pp. 898–913, at p. 902.

53. Scott Ward, Daniel B. Wackman, and Ellen Wartella, *How Children Learn to Buy: The Development of Consumer Information Processing Skills* (Beverly Hills, CA: Sage, 1977).

54. George P. Moschis, "Acquisition of the Consumer Role by Adolescents," Ph.D. diss., Graduate School of Business, University of Wisconsin, Madison, 1977.

55. George P. Moschis and Roy L. Moore, "Purchasing Behavior of Adolescent Consumers," in Richard P. Bagozzi *et al.,* eds., *Proceedings of the American Marketing Association Educators' Conference,* Series No. 45 (1980), pp. 89–92.

56. Joseph N. Fry *et al.,* "Customer Loyalty to Banks: A Longitudinal Study," *Journal of Business,* 46 (October, 1973), pp. 517–525.

57. George P. Moschis, "A Longitudinal Study of Consumer Socialization," in Michael Ryan, ed., *Proceedings of the American Marketing Association Theory Conference* (1984).

58. Sanford Grossbart, Les Carlson, and Ann Walsh, "Consumer Socialization and Frequency of Shopping with Children," *Journal of the Academy of Marketing Science,* 19 (Summer, 1991), pp. 155–162.

59. "Getting 'Em While They're Young," *Business Week.*

60. B. J. Wadsworth, *Piaget's Theory of Cognitive Development* (New York: David McKay, 1971).

61. Moschis, "The Role of Family Communication," *op. cit.,* p. 899.

62. *Ibid.*

63. Les Carlson and Sanford Grossbart, "Parental Style and Consumer Socialization of Children," *Journal of Consumer Research,* 15 (June, 1988), pp. 77–94.

64. Fry *et al.,* "Customer Loyalty to Banks . . . ," *loc. cit.*

65. Larry G. Woodson, Terry L. Childers, and Paul R. Winn, "Intergenerational Influences in the Purchase of Auto Insurance," in W. Locander, ed.,

Marketing Look Outward: 1976 Business Proceedings (Chicago: American Marketing Association, 1976), pp. 43–49.

66. *Ibid.*

67. *Advertising Age* (July 30, 1990), *loc. cit.*

68. Terry L. Childers and Aksay R. Rao, "The Influence of Familial and Peer-Based Reference Groups on Consumer Decisions," *Journal of Consumer Research,* 19 (September, 1992), pp. 198–211.

69. Leslie Isler, Edward T. Popper, and Scott Ward, "Children's Purchase Requests and Parental Responses: Results from a Diary Study," *Journal of Advertising Research,* 27 (October–November, 1987), p. 34.

70. Scott Ward and Daniel B. Wackman, "Children's Purchase Influence Attempts and Parental Yielding," *Journal of Marketing Research,* 9 (August, 1972), pp. 316–319.

71. *Ibid.*

72. Isler, Popper, and Ward, "Children's Purchase Requests . . . ," *loc. cit.*

73. "Children's Requests: When Do Parents Yield?" *Wharton Alumni Magazine* (Fall, 1987), p. 19.

74. *Advertising Age* (July 30, 1990), *loc. cit.*

75. David C. Epperson, "Reassessment of Indices of Parental Influence in the American Society," *American Sociological Review,* 29 (February, 1964).

76. Paul Gilkison, "What Influences the Buying Decisions of Teenagers?" *Journal of Retailing,* 41 (Fall, 1965), pp. 36–41.

77. Russell L. Langworthy, "Community Status and Influence in a High School," *American Sociological Review,* 24 (August, 1959), pp. 537–539.

78. George P. Moschis and Roy L. Moore, "Decision Making Among the Young: A Socialization Perspective," *Journal of Consumer Research,* 6 (September, 1979), pp. 101–112. See also Ellen R. Foxman, Patriya S. Tansuhaj, and Karin M. Ekstrom, "Family Members' Perceptions of Adolescents' Influence in Family Decision Making," *Journal of Consumer Research,* 15 (March, 1989), pp. 482–491.

79. George P. Moschis and Roy L. Moore, "Purchasing Behavior of Adolescent Consumers," in Richard P. Bagozzi *et al.,* eds., *Proceedings of the American Marketing Association Educators' Conference,* Series No. 46 (1980), p. 93.

80. William D. Wells and George Gubar, "Life Cycle Concept in Marketing Research," *Journal of Marketing Research,* 3 (November, 1966), pp. 355–363.

81. Ben J. Wattenberg, "The Forming Families: The Spark in the Tinder," *Combined Proceedings of the American Marketing Association* (Chicago: American Marketing Association, 1975), p. 52.

82. Filiatrault and Ritchie, "Joint Purchasing Decisions," *loc. cit.*

83. Mary C. Gilly and Ben J. Enis, "Recycling the Family Life Cycle: A Proposed Redefinition," *Advances in Consumer Research,* 9 (Provo, UT: Association for Consumer Research, 1982), pp. 271–276.

84. Patrick E. Murphy and William S. Staples, "A Modernized Family Life Cycle," *Journal of Consumer Research,* 6 (June, 1979), pp. 12–22.

85. "Life Without Father," *American Demographics* (December, 1986), pp. 42–47.

86. "Auto Makers Set New Ad Strategy to Reach Women," *Advertising Age* (September 23, 1985), p. 80.

87. "Growing Up in the Market," *American Demographics* (October, 1992), p. 49.

88. "Makers of Personal-Care Products Hope to Clean Up with Brands for Children," *The Wall Street Journal* (January 28, 1993), p. B1.

89. "The ABC's of Marketing to Kids," *Fortune* (May 8, 1989), p. 120.

90. Pat L. Burr and Richard M. Burr, "Parental Responses to Child Marketing," *Journal of Advertising Research,* 17 (December, 1977), pp. 17–20.

91. Daniel B. Wackman, "Family Processes in Children's Consumption," in Neil Beckwith *et al.,* eds., *Proceedings of the American Marketing Association Educators' Conference,* Series No. 11 (1979), pp. 645–652.

92. C. Whan Park and Easwar Iyer, "An Examination of the Response Pattern in Family Decision Making," in Kenneth Bernhardt *et al., Proceedings of the American Marketing Association Educators' Conference,* Series No. 47 (1981), p. 148.

93. Davis and Rigaux, "Perception of Marital Roles . . . ," *loc. cit.*

94. "Who Buys the Pants in the Family?" *American Demographics* (January, 1992), p. 12.

95. Michael A. Belch, George E. Belch, and Donald Sciglimpaglia, "Conflict in Family Decision Making: An Exploratory Investigation," in Jerry C.

Olson, ed., *Advances in Consumer Research,* 7 (Ann Arbor, MI: Association for Consumer Research, 1980), p. 475.

96. Foxman, Tansuhaj, and Ekstrom, "Family Members' Perceptions of Adolescents' Influence in Family Decision Making," *loc. cit.*

97. Gary M. Armstrong and Merrie Brucks, "Dealing with Children's Advertising: Public Policy Issues and Alternatives," *Journal of Public Policy and Marketing,* 7 (1988), pp. 98–113.

98. *Ibid.,* p. 102.

99. *Ibid.,* p. 101.

100. Laura A. Peracchio, "How Do Young Children Learn to Be Consumers? A Script-Processing Approach," *Journal of Consumer Research,* 18 (March, 1992), pp. 425–440.

101. Armstrong and Brucks, "Dealing with Children's Advertising . . . ," *op. cit.,* p. 104.

17

Situational Influences

TIMEX POSITIONS ITS WATCHES BY USAGE SITUATIONS

One essential environmental factor that we have not explored is the situation in which consumers purchase and use brands. In asking consumers to rate preferences for brands of paper towels or makes of automobiles, a consumer could reasonably say, "The brand I select depends on how, when, where, and why I'm going to use it." A consumer may prefer one brand of paper towels for heavy-duty cleaning and another for wiping, one brand of coffee to have alone and another to serve guests, and one make of automobile for long business trips and another for local shopping trips. Therefore, the usage situation directly affects consumers' perceptions of brands, preferences for brands, and purchasing behavior.

At times, the situation is the basis for introducing and positioning a product. Timex has positioned its watches based on the usage situation in appealing to the fitness segment. It switched from plain, low-priced watches to more stylish models positioned to younger, sports-oriented consumers and geared to specific situations. One watch, the Ironman, is designed for joggers and has features such as a stopwatch to count time and laps. Another, the Skiathlom, can fit over a parka and gloves and records temperature as well as time. (See Exhibit 17.1.) As a result of Timex's repositioning to focus on particular sports situations, sales soared.[1]

Purchase situations can also be central to marketing strategies. For example, the gift-giving situation is often the basis for advertising products such as watches, electronics, and toys. Manufacturers frequently advertise products for Father's or Mother's Day and for holidays, particularly Christmas. In many retail businesses, 50 percent of sales occur between Thanksgiving and Christmas and most are for gift-giving occasions.

This chapter focuses on situational variables as determinants of consumer behavior. Three types of situations are discussed—consumption, purchase, and communication. A model of consumer behavior centered on situational effects is described next. Third, recent studies are presented that take account of the consumption and purchase situation to better explain and predict consumer attitudes and behavior. Finally, the use of situational variables in developing marketing strategies is described.

◆ NATURE OF SITUATIONAL INFLUENCES

Situational influences are temporary conditions or settings that occur in the environment at a specific time and place. They occur independently of the products or the consumers. Activities such as shopping for a gift, going skiing, or jogging fit this definition.

If marketers consider the situation in developing their marketing strategy, they must understand the nature of situational variables. To gain such an understanding, we will consider the:

- Types of situations that influence consumers.
- Characteristics of these situations.
- Development of an inventory of situations to measure how they influence consumer attitudes, preferences, and purchasing behavior.

Types of Situations

Three types of situations are relevant to marketers: consumption situation, purchase situation, and communication situation.[2]

Consumption Situation

The consumption situation is the one in which consumers use the brand. A consumer may use a particular brand of perfume or cologne for special occasions and another brand for everyday use. Another consumer may consider different brands of personal computers for home versus business use. A consumer might use regular coffee to serve to guests but instant when drinking coffee alone. Each of these consumption situations affects brand choice.

Marketers must identify consumption situations relevant to the product category. Bearden and Woodside identified the following consumption situations for beer:

- Entertaining close friends at home.
- Going to a restaurant or lounge on Friday or Saturday night.
- Watching a sports event or a favorite TV show.
- Engaging in a sports activity or hobby.
- Taking a weekend trip.
- Working at home on the yard, house, or car.
- Relaxing at home.[3]

▶**EXHIBIT 17.1**
Positioning Timex watches by sports situations

Consumers can anticipate situations like these. That is, most of the time, consumers know in advance that they will be entertaining friends or going to a restaurant. Some situations are unanticipated, however—for example, having friends drop in unexpectedly or deciding to go away for the weekend on the spur of the moment. These situations may prompt consumers to buy certain items quickly and to pay more than they ordinarily would because of a lack of time to shop around for lower prices.

The consumption situation is also likely to affect consumers' choice of services. Gehrt and Pinto identified the following consumption situations for health care services:[4]

- Whether the health problem is major or minor.
- Whether the health problem affects the consumer or another member of the family.
- Whether the health problem occurs at home or away from home.

These situations directly affect the type of health care consumers choose. For example, going to a hospital's emergency room for a major health problem is more likely when consumers are away from home than it is when they are at home.

Purchase Situation

Most of the studies cited in this chapter involve the consumption situation, but the purchase situation may also affect marketing strategy. Three factors are particularly important in affecting marketing strategy based on the purchasing situation: (1) the in-store purchase situation; (2) whether the purchase situation is for a gift-giving occasion; and (3) whether the purchase situation is unanticipated.

In-Store Situations.   We saw the importance of store influences on shopping behavior when we discussed store choice in Chapters 3 and 4. In-store stimuli such as product availability, shelf position, pricing promotions, displays, and ease of shopping are important in influencing consumer purchasing decisions, especially for unplanned purchases.

The importance of the purchase situation is documented in many studies that have demonstrated the effects of price changes, displays, and salesperson influences on consumer behavior as a result of the in-store environment.[5] One such study of beauty aids found that the following situational factors were instrumental in influencing unplanned purchases:[6]

- *Price promotions.* Fifty-six percent of respondents bought more unplanned items because of these in-store stimuli.
- *Free samples.* Thirty-five percent of respondents bought more unplanned items because of free samples.
- *Displays.* Twenty-seven percent of respondents bought more unplanned items because of displays.

The importance of in-store stimuli is further demonstrated by the fact that expenditures on sales promotions have risen more rapidly than those on advertising. In 1988, total expenditures on sales promotions exceeded those for advertising for the first time; and they have continued to increase at a more rapid rate.[7]

Because of these influences, it is important for marketers to identify various in-store situations and ask consumers how they would respond. For example, assume a manufacturer of a leading line of cereals conducts a survey and asks a sample of consumers how the following purchase-related situations may affect brand choice:

- You are in the store and find your favorite brand of cereal is not in stock. (Do you go to another store, buy a substitute brand, or delay the purchase?)
- Your favorite brand of cereal is five cents more than it was last time.
- A brand of cereal that you have used occasionally has a price deal.
- You need cereal, but there is a long line at the checkout counter as you come into the store.
- You have some difficulty finding your favorite brand of cereal. (Do you ask a clerk for help or buy a competitive brand?)

Responses to these in-store situations may affect brand strategies. One essential indicator of brand loyalty, for example, is whether consumers will stick to their favorite brand, regardless of in-store stimuli, or whether such stimuli may influence them to try a competitive brand.

Gift-Giving Situations.   A second purchase-related situation is whether consumers buy the product as a gift or for themselves. Marketers target a wide range of products from candy to clothing to electronics for holidays and other gift-giving occasions. The first ad in Exhibit 17.2 shows a product advertised for holiday occasions. The second, "Significant Moments," targets Omega watches for a more personal occasion for gift-giving—in this case, a successful dance performance.

Purchasing a gift is likely to be more involving for consumers than purchasing a product for themselves. As Belk notes, when consumers give gifts, they are giving not only the physical product, but also a symbolic message with it.[8] They want to ensure that they are sending the right message in terms of the type of gift, its price, and the brand name. As a result, they frequently spend more time selecting products for gifts than when selecting products for their own use. Consumers will use different criteria in evaluating brands and are likely to select a different brand than if the purchase were for themselves.

Even if the products themselves are uninvolving, when placed in a gift-giving context, consumers are likely to be more involved. Clarke and Belk found that when buying uninvolving products such as bubble bath or blankets, consumers visited more stores and spent more time in information search when the purchase was for a gift.[9]

▶**EXHIBIT 17.2**
Advertising for gift-
giving situations

Source: (left) © 1990. Used
courtesy of Nintendo.
(right) Courtesy of Omega
Watch Corp.

One result of this greater involvement in gift-giving is that consumers are likely to see more risk in the selection. Consumers are more likely to buy brand names and to shop in well-known stores. A study by Ryan found that consumers are more likely to purchase small appliances for gifts from stores with a high-quality image.[10]

The gift-giving situation has been described as a cultural ritual. As we saw in Chapter 13, gift-giving requires a sequence of events that often entails symbolic behavior. The consumer acquires a gift, removes the price tag, wraps the item, delivers it, awaits a reaction, receives a gift in return in some circumstances, and conveys a reaction. This process of exchanging gifts creates bonds of trust and dependence between the parties.

Sherry describes the gift-giving ritual in more detail by dividing it into three stages.[11] In the first stage, the consumer identifies a gift-giving situation. The situation might be identified by society, as in a holiday, or might be more personal, as when a parent rewards a child for some achievement. The donor determines an appropriate price and product category for a gift and makes a selection. The second stage is the process of gift-giving and possibly exchanging gifts. The donor determines the time, place, and mode of giving the gift and assesses the recipient's response. In the third stage, the gift is disposed of by being consumed, displayed, stored away, or returned. The nature of disposition will strengthen the bond between donor and receiver (as when the gift is displayed) or weaken it (as when the gift is returned).

The nature of the gift-giving ritual is culturally bound. In Japan, for instance, gift-giving rituals are more prescribed than they are in the United States. The Japanese view gifts as part of the process of bonding in a highly group-oriented society, and they define more gift-giving occasions and give gifts to a much wider network of friends, acquaintances, and family.

Unanticipated Purchase Situations. Purchase situations can sometimes be unanticipated. For example, if unexpected guests arrive, consumers may have to make a special shopping trip and may be willing to pay higher prices to obtain needed items quickly. Cote, McCullough, and Reilly studied several unanticipated purchase situations such as an unexpected price change, shopping with others who might influence choice, and being short of time.[12] Among the products studied, unanticipated situations were particularly important in explaining the purchase of hamburgers, beer, and potato chips, items that typically can serve as last-minute fill-ins for unexpected situations. The study also found that consumer behavior for most of the food items studied could be better predicted when unexpected situations were included as variables.

Two unanticipated situations—out-of-stock products and product failures—are particularly important because they precipitate the need for a purchase. Consumers finding a food item out of stock may have to make special purchase trips if the item is important enough. Product failures for durable goods like appliances and automobiles require consumers to make decisions to repair or replace the item. One study found that 60 percent of purchases of major home appliances resulted from breakdowns or the need for repairs.[13]

Communication Situation

The communication situation is the setting in which consumers are exposed to information. It can be person-to-person (word-of-mouth communications between friends and neighbors or information from a salesperson) or impersonal (advertising, in-store displays). The communication situation could determine whether consumers will notice, comprehend, and retain the information. Three types of situations may affect consumer response—the exposure situation, the context of the communication, and the consumers' mood state while receiving the communication.

Regarding the first factor, the following define various situations for advertising exposure:

- Did consumers hear a radio commercial while riding in the car or while sitting in the living room?
- Did consumers read a magazine inside or outside the home?
- Did consumers read the magazine as a pass-on issue?
- Did consumers see a TV commercial alone or with a group of people?
- Did consumers see the TV commercial in the middle of an involving program?

All of these situations are likely to influence the effectiveness of the advertisement, independent of its content.

A second situational variable that is likely to affect reaction to the communication is the context in which it appears—for example, the type of programming in which a TV commercial appears. One study found that "happy" programming, in contrast to "sad" programming, led consumers to have more positive thoughts during exposure to the commercial and a higher level of recall.[14] Program content led a number of advertisers to withdraw from the TV miniseries "The Day After." The program dealt with the aftermath of a Soviet-American nuclear war, and advertisers did not want to be associated with the program's depressing content.

A third situational variable is the consumers' mood state when receiving the communication. Research has shown that whether consumers are happy or sad affects the processing and recall of brand information.[15] As a result, consumers' mood state is also likely to affect comprehension and retention of the advertising message.[16]

Characteristics of Consumption and Purchase Situations

It is necessary to identify not only specific types of consumption or purchase situations, but also to consider the more general characteristics of such situations. Belk identified five characteristics:[17]

1. *Physical surroundings.*   For example, a store's decor and shelf layout, being indoors or outside when using a product, being in a noisy room when watching TV.

2. *Social surroundings.*   Whether guests are present, the social occasion, the importance of friends and neighbors who are present when purchasing or consuming a product.

3. *Time.*   Breakfast, lunchtime, between meals; seasonal factors such as winter versus summer relative to clothing; the time that has passed since the product was last consumed.

4. *Task definition.*   Shopping for oneself or for the family; shopping for a gift; cooking for oneself, for the family, or for guests.

5. *Antecedent states.*   Momentary conditions such as shopping when tired or anxious, buying a product on impulse, using a product when in an excited state. The consumer's mood when buying or using a product would be an antecedent state. Antecedent states such as people's moods are internal to consumers because they are determined by the consumer's state of mind.[18] The four other situational characteristics are determined by the environment and are, therefore, external to consumers.

Situations are likely to be made up of several of these characteristics. For example, the purchase situation "shopping for a snack that the family can eat while watching television in the evening" is made up of the physical surroundings (at home), the social surroundings (family), time (evening), and task definition (consumer is doing the shopping and family will do the eating).

One study of attitudes toward do-it-yourself auto maintenance examined situations that might influence these attitudes such as physical surroundings (convenient area to work, tools available), time availability, and antecedent states (knowledge of maintenance procedures before starting work). These characteristics were found to affect willingness to engage in auto maintenance.[19]

Development of Situational Inventories

To determine the influence of situations on behavior, marketers must develop an inventory of purchase and consumption situations. Such inventories must be product-specific because the situations that affect the choice of a snack food, for example, differ from those that affect the choice of a cosmetic.

The procedures for developing a situational inventory are similar to those for developing a lifestyle inventory. Consumers are brought together for an open-ended discussion of the purchase and usage of a certain product category. From these discussions, marketers identify a large number of purchase and consumption situations. They can then reduce the number of situations by eliminating any redundancy between situations (for example, a between-meal snack and an afternoon snack frequently represent the same situation) and by selecting those situations that seem to be most closely related to brand choice.

Once the situational inventory is developed, consumers can be asked the frequency with which the situation arises and how likely they are to buy a particular product or brand in that situation. Table 17.1 presents a situational inventory used in a snack food study.[20] Ten situations were identified based on preliminary in-depth interviews with consumers. The ten situations were factor-analyzed to reduce them to four situational dimensions:

1. Informal serving situations (represented by Items 5, 7, and 8 in Table 17.1).
2. Nutritive situations (Items 4, 9, and 10).
3. Impulsive consumption situations (Items 3 and 6).
4. Planned purchasing situations (Items 1 and 2).

These situations were related to the purchase of three types of snack foods: substantial snacks (sandwiches, cheese, crackers), light/salty snacks, and sweet snacks. Consumers were not homogeneous in the types of snack foods they purchased for the four situations. One segment bought substantial snacks for all occasions, except unplanned purchases. For unplanned purchases, they tended to buy light/salty snacks. A second segment bought light/salty snacks primarily for informal serving situations. A third segment bought sweet snacks primarily for impulsive situations.[21]

The study has important implications for marketing strategy. Marketers of light/salty snacks such as potato chips and pretzels would do best to portray these products in informal or party situations. The ad for Frito-Lay's line of salty

▶**TABLE 17.1**

Examples of situational inventories for snack foods and for beer

Snack Food Inventory

1. You are shopping for a snack that you or your family can eat while watching television in the evenings.
2. You are planning a party for a few close friends and are wondering what to have around to snack on.
3. Snacks at your house have become a little dull lately and you are wondering what you might pick up that would be better.
4. You are going on a long automobile trip and are thinking that you should bring along some snacks to eat on the way.
5. You suddenly realize that you have invited a couple of friends over for the evening and you have nothing for them to snack on,.
6. You are at the grocery store when you get an urge for a between-meal snack.
7. You are at the supermarket and notice the many available snack products; you wonder if you should pick something up in case friends come by.
8. You are thinking about what type of snack to buy to keep around the house this weekend.
9. You are at the store to pick up some things for a picnic you are planning with friends and are trying to decide what kind of snack to buy.
10. You are thinking about a snack to have with lunch at noon.

SOURCE: Russell W. Belk, "An Exploratory Assessment of Situational Effects in Buyer Behavior," JOURNAL OF MARKETING RESEARCH, 11 (May, 1974), p. 160. Reprinted with permission from JOURNAL OF MARKETING RESEARCH.

snacks in Exhibit 17.3 is an example. Marketers of sweet snacks such as cookies could emphasize the impulsive nature of consumption—the urge to buy and to liven up a snacking occasion. Marketers could link such a situation to the pleasure of eating sweets.

Limited Use of Situational Variables

Because the usage situation is so important in affecting brand choice, it is surprising that most marketing studies do not account for the situation. Consumers are asked to rate brands on nutrition, taste, convenience, and other variables without reference to the usage situation. Most of the attitudinal studies that you read about in Chapter 8 failed to take account of the usage situation. The assumption seems to be that attitudes toward a brand are the same regardless of the situation.

It is clear that if marketing strategy is to be geared to consumer needs and preferences, marketers must measure these needs and preferences for a particular usage situation.

▶**EXHIBIT 17.3**
Advertising salty snacks
for informal situations

Source: Courtesy of Frito-
Lay, Inc.

◆ A MODEL OF SITUATIONAL INFLUENCES

The simple model of consumer behavior in Chapter 1 described three possible
influences on purchasing behavior: (1) the consumer, (2) environmental influences, and (3) marketing strategy. A model of situational determinants on consumer behavior would describe behavior as a function of the same three basic
forces, except that the consumers' environment would be represented by the
consumption, purchase, or communications situation and marketing strategy
would be represented by the product being consumed.

This model of situational influences is presented in Figure 17.1. The two
outside forces acting on consumers are the product and the situation. Consumers react to the product and the situation and decide on the brand to be
purchased. The interaction among the consumer, the situation, and the product results in a process of choice leading to behavior. The situation and the
product can also be viewed in terms of the cognitive principles of context, with
the product as the figure and the situation as the ground. This distinction is
clear in viewing almost any print advertisement. The product generally appears
in the foreground and the situation in the background. The ads in Exhibit 17.4
are examples. The ad for Johnson's Baby Shampoo shows the product in the
foreground with a consumption situation as background, while the ad for Lionel
shows the product in the foreground with a gift-giving situation as the setting.

Although the situational model may seem simple compared to the descriptions of decision making in Chapters 3 to 5, it is not as simple as it appears.
Several issues require attention. First, do consumers attribute behavior to the
situation, to the product, or to both? Attributing behavior to the product implies
that behavior will be consistent across situations and that brand loyalty exists.
Attributing behavior to the situation implies variation in behavior across brands
since consumers will purchase different brands for different situations. As we

▶**FIGURE 17.1**

A model of situational determinants of consumer behavior

Source: Adapted from Russell W. Belk, "Situational Variables and Consumer Behavior," *Journal of Consumer Research*, 2 (December, 1975), p. 158. Reprinted with permission from The University of Chicago Press.

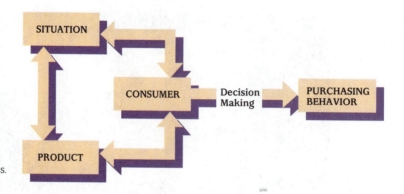

▶**EXHIBIT 17.4**

Advertising with the situation as background

Source: (left) Johnson & Johnson

will see, attribution theory sheds light on the roles of situations and products in influencing behavior.

A second and related issue is the relationship among the product, the situation, and the consumer. Behavior may be due primarily to loyalty to the product regardless of the situation, or to the situation regardless of the product, but it is more likely that behavior is due to some interaction among product, situation, and consumer. (The possibility of such interactions is represented in the model by the two-way arrows between situation, product, and consumer.)

A third issue is the contiguity of the situation to behavior. If the consumption situation is close to behavior in time, it is likely to be the determining factor in influencing behavior (for example, buying soft drinks at the last minute for a party, regardless of price or brand). If the consumption situation is not close to the purchase, it is less likely to be an influence.

These three issues will be explored in turn.

Situation Versus Product

A key consideration in the situational model is whether consumers attribute their behavior to the product's characteristics or to the situation. Attribution theory suggests that people examine their prior behavior and attribute a cause to the behavior.[22] If consumers attribute behavior to the product rather than to the situation, attitudes toward the product will be more positive, increasing the likelihood that consumers will purchase the product again.[23] Thus, if consumers attribute the purchase of a cereal to its nutritional content (a product attribute), rather than to the fact that it was on sale (a situational determinant), their attitudes toward the cereal are likely to be positive and they are likely to repurchase it. On the other hand, if attribution is to the situation ("I purchased because it was on sale"), their attitudes toward the product are not likely to be as positive.

Several principles can be stated in determining whether the product or the situation is a more important influence on consumer behavior. First, *the greater the degree of brand loyalty, the less important are situational influences.* For example, the loyal Michelob beer drinker makes no distinction between drinking Michelob when alone, with guests, while watching TV, with meals, between meals, or at any other time. This consumer happens to like Michelob, and the consumption situation will not influence purchasing behavior. The product, not the situation, is paramount in determining this consumer's behavior.

Conversely, when loyalties are not strong, the consumption situation may be the determining factor in brand choice. A consumer may prefer a certain brand of beer because it is adequate and less expensive than most beers. For social occasions, this consumer may purchase a higher-priced beer. The price sensitivity of this consumer causes him or her to consider the consumption situation in buying different brands.

A second principle relates to the distinction between enduring and situational involvement cited in Chapter 3. Enduring involvement is an ongoing interest in the product, whereas situational involvement is interest in the product triggered by a need to purchase it. By definition, *the higher the level of enduring product involvement, the less likely it is that situational factors will determine behavior*. In cases of high enduring involvement, consumers' interest in the product itself influences behavior. In cases of low enduring involvement, consumers' need to purchase the product is the motivator for their brand evaluation. Clarke and Belk studied situational and enduring involvement for four product categories.[24] They found that when enduring involvement in the product is low, the situation tends to determine behavior. When enduring involvement is high, the situation is not as important.

A third principle is that *when a product has multiple uses, situational factors will be less important in determining brand choice*. Products that consumers purchase for single-use consumption situations are most likely to be packaged goods. Studies of soft drinks,[25] snack foods,[26] beer,[27] meat products,[28] and breath fresheners[29] all have shown that the consumption situation directly affects behavior. Consumers tend to purchase these products for particular meal, between-meal, or social occasions. Products that consumers purchase for multiple uses are more likely to be durable goods. It is unlikely that consumers will own different television sets for different viewing occasions or different stereo sets for different listening occasions. In some cases, however, situational effects may be important. For example, many two-car families use one car primarily for work purposes and another for local shopping or evening entertainment. Some camera buffs may have several cameras for different types of situations. Belk concluded that even though situational effects are less likely to be important for durable goods, "there are few if any product and service purchases which are devoid of potential consumption situation influences."[30]

In summary, situational factors tend to be less important when consumers are loyal to a brand, when the consumers are involved with the product category on an ongoing basis, and when the product has multiple uses.

Interaction of Situation, Product, and Consumer

Several studies have considered the influence of the situation, the product, and the consumer on purchasing behavior. Results of studies for seven categories ranging from beverages to financial services are presented in Table 17.2. The table shows the influence of three key variables (situation, product, and consumer) on consumer behavior. The percentages in the table are the amount of variation in behavior explained by each of the variables listed on the left. For example, a consumer's choice of a beverage (first column in Table 17.2) is best explained by the type of product (P) and the situation in which it is used (S). These two factors in combination (S × P in the fourth row of the table) account for 39.8 percent of the variation in the purchases of beverages.

▶**TABLE 17.2**
Effects of situation, product, and consumer on behavior for seven product categories

	Response Category (%)[a]							
Source	*Beverage products*	*Meat products*	*Snack products*	*Fast foods*	*Leisure activities*	*Motion pictures*	*Financial services*	*Health care services*
Consumers (*C*)	0.5	4.6	6.7	8.1	4.5	0.9	12.5	10.8
Situations (*S*)	2.7	5.2	0.4	2.2	2.0	0.5	0.4	0.1
Products or Services (*P*)	14.6	15.0	6.7	13.4	8.8	16.6	14.5	44.9
S × *P*	39.8	26.2	18.7	15.3	13.4	7.0	16.5	8.1
S × *C*	2.7	2.9	6.1	2.2	4.0	1.9	2.9	1.1
P × *C*	11.8	9.7	22.4	20.1	21.2	33.7	17.7	16.2
S × *P* × *C*[b]	27.8	36.4	39.0	38.7	46.1	39.4	35.4	18.8
Total	100.0	100.0	100.0	100.0	100.0	100.0	100.0	100.0

[a]Percent of variance in behavior explained by each of the seven variables or combinations listed down the side of the table.

[b]The S × P × C term represents the three-way interaction between situation, product, and consumer, and the residual (error) variance in the analysis.

SOURCE: Adapted from Russell W. Belk, "Situational Variables and Consumer Behavior," JOURNAL OF CONSUMER RESEARCH, 2 (December, 1975), p. 160. Reprinted with permission from the The University of Chicago Press. Data for financial services from Rajendra K. Srivastava, Mark I. Alpert, and Allan D. Schocker, "A Customer-Oriented Approach for Determining Market Structures," JOURNAL OF MARKETING, 48 (Spring, 1984), pp. 32–45. Data for health care services from Kenneth C. Gehrt and Mary Beth Pinto, "The Impact of Situational Factors on Health Care Preferences," JOURNAL OF HEALTH CARE MARKETING, 11 (June, 1991), p. 47.

There are seven possibilities in Table 17.2. The first three represent the possibility that the situation, the product, or the consumer is the primary influence on behavior for the product category. These influences are known as **main effects,** as only one variable is the main influence on behavior. For example, if a cross-section of consumers like Coca-Cola for most situations, the influence on behavior would be the result of the product independent of consumer characteristics and situations (*P* in Table 17.2). If consumers have little brand loyalty and purchase beverages depending on whether they are for parties, between meals, or with meals, the influence on behavior would be the result of the situation independent of the product and consumer characteristics (*S* in Table 17.2).

The data in Table 17.2 show that very little of the variation in behavior is explained by the main effects of product, situation, or consumer only (the top three rows in Table 17.2). Rather, behavior is generally influenced by the interaction of these three factors. An **interaction effect** is the influence of a variable that is contingent on the category of another variable. Suppose most consumers drink Coca-Cola only at parties. This would be a situation-by-product interaction (*S* × *P* in Table 17.2) because the primary influence on behavior is a product (Coca-Cola) given a certain category of situation (a party). Table 17.2 shows that the *S* × *P* interactions were one of the most important across categories in explaining behavior, meaning that most consumers often buy products for specific situations.

If young consumers rather than most consumers buy Coca-Cola for parties, the interaction would be by situation, product, and consumer ($S \times P \times C$ in Table 17.2). The table shows that this type of interaction also explains a large amount of the variance in behavior, meaning that frequently only certain types of consumers buy products for certain situations.

Another important influence on behavior, the product in interaction with the consumer ($P \times C$ in Table 17.2), does not involve situational influences. That is, certain consumers purchase certain types of products regardless of the situation. This product-by-consumer interaction demonstrates the importance of brand or product loyalty since certain consumer segments buy a particular product across most situations (for example, younger consumers may drink Coke for parties, between meals, with snacks, and so on). Thus, the table shows that (1) situational influences frequently determine the product or brand purchased and (2) where this does not occur, brand or product loyalty tends to be operating.

The studies cited in Table 17.2 are instructive in showing differences among product categories. For example, the situation-by-product interaction was important for beverage and meat products, meaning that these products are particularly prone to situational influences: Certain types of beverages and meats are likely to be served for certain occasions. The product-by-consumer interaction was important for all product categories, but especially for motion pictures and less so for snack and beverage products. This means that certain types of people are loyal to certain types of motion pictures regardless of the situation. For example, some people may see every Michelle Pfeiffer or Tom Hanks movie that is released. Motion pictures may be less subject to situational influences because they may be more involving. For beverage and meat products, loyalty to a certain product regardless of the situation is much less likely.

Health care is the only category where the main effects are more important than the interactions. The key factor in health care is the service. Individuals generally select health care options independent of the situation. For example, an individual selecting emergency room care would do so whether at home or away from home and whether it was for oneself or another member of the family.

With the exception of health care, the studies cited strongly support the situational model in Figure 17.1. Consumers tend to purchase products and services for specific consumption situations.

Contiguity Between Situation and Behavior

Another issue relevant to the situational model in Figure 17.1 is the contiguity between the situation and behavior. If the purchase and the situation are close in time, then the situation is likely to influence brand choice.[31] A consumer who is shopping for food for a big dinner party that evening may buy items not ordinarily purchased. A consumer who sees a sharp reduction in price for a particular brand (a purchase situation) may buy it even though it is not among those brands regularly purchased. In both cases, behavior is situation-specific.

On the other hand, the consumer buying food items for normal usage may just be "stocking up" for the future. Situational requirements are not apparent, and the consumer will purchase preferred brands. Under such conditions, behavior is due to preferences for the product rather than to the urgency of any situation.

◆ SITUATIONAL INFLUENCES ON CONSUMER BEHAVIOR

The research cited in the previous section has shown that consumers frequently purchase products for particular situations. Research on situational influences has tended to focus on three areas: the influence of situations on (1) product attitudes (Shake 'n' Bake chicken may be rated as convenient to prepare for lunch but not for dinner), (2) product choice (Coca-Cola may be purchased for parties rather than for meal occasions), and (3) the consumer's decision process (more product attributes are considered when selecting a hair dryer as a gift than when selecting it for oneself).

Influence of Situation on Product Attitudes

A number of studies have shown that consumers' attitudes toward products vary depending on the situation.[32] These studies have tended to take a multiattribute approach by having consumers rate product attributes for various situations. The basic multiattribute model that was described in Chapter 8 is used on a situation-specific basis so that:

Attitudes toward a brand (A_o) =

| Beliefs about the brand (b) on various attributes (i) in various situations (s); for example, rating Brand X on convenience for snack occasions, meals, etc. | $\times$ | Evaluation (e) of each attribute (i) in each situation (s); for example, the value of convenience in preparing snacks, meals, etc. |

or $A_o = \Sigma b_{is} \times e_{is}$

The inclusion of the situation in the basic multiattribute model has several advantages. First, it allows the researcher to determine whether consumers vary their beliefs about brands depending on the situation. For example, a consumer may rate Budweiser as "refreshing" for "when I'm thirsty" but not for "at mealtime." The consumer may also rate the brand high on taste for "when I am drinking beer alone" but not for "when I serve beer to guests."

Second, the model can determine if consumers value certain attributes more than others in certain situations. Thus, "convenience" may be more important for lunch or snack occasions than for dinner, and "good for the family" may be more important for dinner occasions than for lunch or snacks. One study of transportation alternatives found that the value consumers placed on certain attributes varied by situation.[33] For example, individuals who avoided riding buses put more emphasis on shorter travel time and comfort when going to work than did bus riders. Such differences in needs and attitudes by situation have important implications for marketing strategy. Encouraging more people to use buses than cars to get to work would require convincing them that the bus can be as fast and as comfortable as a car.

A third advantage of the situational model is that it allows for the likelihood that certain attributes are relevant only for certain situations. For example, the belief that a certain brand of coffee has "full-bodied taste" (a b_i component) might be more relevant (the e_i component) when serving guests.

A fourth advantage of the model is that differences in attitudes by situation might also indicate strengths and weaknesses of brands. If consumers rate a certain snack food particularly low on taste for parties and social occasions, the marketer would want to correct this potential weakness: Is it a problem with the product formulation or with the brand's image? Furthermore, if a brand is stronger in a particular situation, this strength should be exploited. For example, if consumers regard Budweiser as a good beer to have alone, rather than on social occasions, perhaps marketers should emphasize taste benefits for situations when beer drinkers are alone.

Miller and Ginter undertook one of the most comprehensive studies of the situational determinants of product attitudes.[34] They asked consumers to rate eight fast-food restaurants on attributes such as speed of service, variety, cleanliness, and convenience for four situations:

1. Lunch on a weekday.
2. Snack during a shopping trip.
3. Evening meal when rushed for time.
4. Evening meal with the family when not rushed for time.

Consumers were asked to rate the importance of each restaurant attribute for each of the four situations. Convenience and speed of service were considered most important for lunch on a weekday and for evening meals when rushed. Variety of menu and popularity with children were most important for evening meals with the family when not rushed for time. Thus, consumers do differentiate product benefits by situation.

Consumers' ratings of the various fast-food outlets by situation were substantially different. They saw Arby's and Burger King as more convenient for snack occasions during a shopping trip; Burger Chef and McDonald's, as more convenient for evening meal occasions.

Influence of Situation on Product Choice

The final element in Miller's and Ginter's analysis was to evaluate the ability of the four situations in the study to predict consumers' restaurant choices. The results are in Table 17.3. In each case, the situational model correctly predicted

▶**TABLE 17.3**
Prediction of choice of fast-food outlets using a nonsituational model versus a situational model

Situation	Sample size[a]	% Correct Predictions	
		Nonsituational model	Situational model
Lunch on a weekday	210	30.5	41.3
Evening meal when rushed for time	159	38.6	44.0
Evening meal with family when not rushed for time	128	45.9	49.5
Snack during a shopping trip	94	31.6	34.7

[a]Sample size is number of respondents who purchased on each occasion during the course of the study.

SOURCE: Kenneth E. Miller and James L. Ginter, "An Investigation of Situational Variation in Brand Choice Behavior and Attitudes," JOURNAL OF MARKETING RESEARCH, 16 (February, 1979), p. 121. Reprinted with permission from the JOURNAL OF MARKETING RESEARCH.

a greater proportion of consumers' restaurant choices than a model that did not take account of the situation. For example, the situational model predicted the right choice for lunchtime occasions 41.3 percent of the time, compared to 30.5 percent of the time for the nonsituational model. This result shows the importance of situation in explaining consumer behavior.

Other studies have also found that situational variables better predict product choice. Stanton and Bonner found that situational variables outperformed demographics and attitudes in predicting the choice of a food item.[35] Similarly, Umesh and Cote found that they could better predict choice of soft drinks by including situational variables.[36]

Influence of Situations on Decision Making

Few studies have focused on the effects of different situations on decision making. However, it is likely that the number of brands considered, the amount of search, the type of information sought, and the sources of information will vary by the consumption and purchase situation. For example, one study found that when a shopper is with friends, he or she visits more stores and makes more unplanned purchases than when shopping alone.[37]

Several studies have examined differences in decision making when consumers buy a product as a gift or for themselves. We saw that consumers' purchase decisions for gifts tend to be more involving than when buying for themselves. As a result, as Clarke and Belk note, shopping for a gift "increases the overall level of arousal and causes more effort to be expended."[38] As a result, consumers' information search is more extensive when purchasing a gift than when purchasing for themselves.

Studies have found other factors that characterize decision-making for gifts:

- Consumers are more likely to use in-store information sources (such as salespeople) than out-of-store sources (such as advertising).[39]
- Consumers are likely to set a price limit beforehand.[40]
- Consumers are likely to shop in higher-quality stores and to buy prestige brands.[41]
- Consumers consider stores' policies on return merchandise to be more important.[42]

The studies that have been cited evaluated differences in decision making for purchasing situations. Ptacek and Shanteau focused on differences in decision making for consumption situations. They defined four situations in the use of paper towels:[43]

1. Heavy-duty jobs.
2. Lighter jobs.
3. As napkins and for cleaning up at a barbecue.
4. Just to have on hand.

They divided decisions into simple strategies in which consumers evaluated brands by one or two criteria and more complex strategies in which consumers used more criteria that varied by brand. When consumers purchased paper towels for light-duty, their decision strategies were more complex. When they purchased towels for heavy-duty jobs, consumers used simpler strategies based on one or two criteria, probably because the selection of a towel for heavy-duty use rests on a simpler evaluation based on strength and durability. For light-duty work, consumers probably needed more attributes to evaluate the towels, thus requiring a more complex decision strategy. The findings suggest that consumers are likely to vary their method of selecting brands depending on the consumption as well as the purchase situation.

◆ USE OF SITUATIONAL VARIABLES IN MARKETING STRATEGY

The usage situation directly influences marketing strategy because it affects the manner in which (1) markets are segmented, (2) new products are developed, (3) products are positioned, (4) brands are advertised, and (5) brands are distributed. Several studies illustrate the use of situational factors for these strategic applications.

Market Segmentation

Market segmentation often depends on consumers' use situation. The snack food study conducted by Great Snacks in Chapter 12 is an example. It identified six segments: nutritional snackers, weight watchers, guilty snackers, party snackers, and indiscriminate snackers.

The consumption situation was important in defining five of the six segments. Both nutritional snackers and weight watchers were less likely to eat snacks between meals. Guilty snackers tended to eat snack foods between meals. Party snackers obviously ate and served snacks primarily at social occasions. Price-oriented snackers bought based on the purchase situation rather than the consumption situation, buying snacks primarily when they were promoted by price deals and coupons. The only segment for which situational factors were not important was the indiscriminate snackers who tended to eat snacks in most usage occasions.

The importance of the situation was evident when Great Snacks considered introducing a new chip-type snack made of only natural ingredients. The fact that the target market—nutritional snackers—was unlikely to consume the product during the prime time for snacking (between meals) caused the company to reevaluate the viability of targeting the product to this segment.

New Product Development

Companies can develop new products for specific situations. Dickson distinguished between product benefits geared to consumer types and benefits aimed at specific situations.[44] He suggested developing a matrix of consumers by situations, as in Table 17.4. This hypothetical example for suntan lotions shows four consumer categories and four situations. Situation-specific benefits are shown at the end of each row (for example, windburn protection for beach/boat sunbathing). Consumer-specific benefits are at the bottom of each column (for example, a desirable scent for adult women). The intersection of situations and consumers defines a set of benefits that might be the basis for a new product.

A set of situation-specific products is presented for adult women to illustrate the application for a particular segment. For example, a new summer perfume for a particular situation, sunbathing on a beach or boat, might provide the situation-specific benefit of wind protection and heat resistance and the consumer-specific benefit of a desirable scent. Obviously, a company would not try to exploit every opportunity in Table 17.4, but a matrix of this kind can provide guidance for new product development.

Product Positioning

A large food manufacturer undertook a study to determine consumers' association of a broad range of food products to four types of occasions:

1. Special meal occasions.
2. Family meals.
3. Regular day-to-day meals.
4. Snacks and quick meals.

▶**TABLE 17.4**
Hypothetical matrix of consumers by situation benefits for suntan lotion

Situations	Consumer Groups				
	Young children	Teenagers	Adult women	Adult men	Situation-Specific Benefits
Beach/boat sunbathing			Summer perfume		a. Windburn protection b. Formula and container can stand heat c. Container floats and is distinctive (not easily lost)
Home-poolside sunbathing			Combined moisturizer		a. Large pump dispenser b. Won't stain wood, concrete, or furnishings
Sunlamp bathing			Combined moisturizer and massage oil		a. Designed specifically for type of lamp b. Artifical tanning ingredient
Snow skiing			Winter perfume		a. Special protection from special light rays and weather b. Antifreeze formula
Consumer-specific benefits	Special protection a. Protection critical b. Nonpoisonous	Special protection a. Fit in jean pocket b. Used by opinion leaders	Special protection Desirable scent for women	Special protection Desirable scent for men	

SOURCE: Adapted from Peter R. Dickson, "Person-Situation: Segmentation's Missing Link," *JOURNAL OF MARKETING,* 46 (Fall, 1982), p. 62. Used by permission of the American Marketing Association.

The purpose of the study was to determine whether consumers link products or groups of products to these meal occasions. For example, do consumers associate a roast with special meals, family meals, or day-to-day meals? If it is a special meal, do they associate potatoes or vegetables with the roast?

A sample of consumers was asked to associate 16 products with these occasions. Results of the analysis are shown in Figure 17.2. Each quadrant in the figure represents one of the four mealtime occasions.[45] For example, cold cuts, grilled cheese, and English muffins are associated with snacks and quick meals; hamburgers and hot sandwiches, with regular meals; and roasts and fresh

---

STRATEGIC APPLICATIONS OF CONSUMER BEHAVIOR

Lunch Bucket—A Product Developed for a Situation

In September 1987, Jewel Food Stores set up microwave ovens at its 135 outlets in the Midwest. Employees spent the next two days giving out samples of a new microwaveable product called Lunch Bucket. The result? Within two days, the chain sold 420,000 containers of the new product.

The product was introduced after seven years of product development by Dial Corp., the $870 million Phoenix-based packaged goods company. Dial Corp. saw several developments that spelled opportunity. First was the increasing proportion of working women. Second was the greater number of microwave ovens in the workplace. (About two-thirds of workers now have access to a microwave at work, and four out of five of these workers use it.) Third was the trend among younger career-conscious workers to work longer hours and eat at their desks to save time. The company put these trends together and saw an opportunity to develop a product for a specific situation: a line of microwaveable food products designed for the workplace. In the process, Dial developed a brand new food category, shelf-stable microwaveable meals.

On introduction, the line included 15 varieties of foods, including 9 entrees ranging from beef stew to scalloped potatoes flavored with ham chunks. The line is positioned to upscale working women ages 25 to 54.

Surprisingly, Lunch Bucket is not advertised on a situational basis. According to the line's advertising director, "We've found that people don't need to be told where to use it." Rather, the main theme of the campaign is convenience.

Success breeds competition; Hormel, Chef Boy-Ar-Dee, and Campbell have also introduced shelf-stable microwaveable food lines aimed at the workplace. However, Dial, being the first one in, has the edge. Dial Corp. has shown that a new product can be developed for a particular situation.

Sources: "Dial's Hearty Office Meal," *Adweek* (June 27, 1988), pp. 20–23; and "Canned Goods," *Supermarket Business* (September, 1991), p. 129.

▶**FIGURE 17.2**
Positioning products by four meal situations

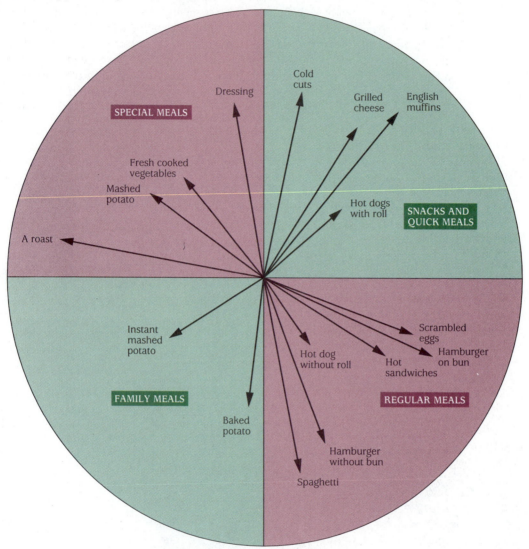

cooked vegetables, with special meals. The study provides guidelines for advertising in a situational context. For example, a marketer may have assumed that hamburgers are associated with quick meals; but the study showed that hamburgers and accessory products should be advertised in a regular meal situation. The findings also provide a rational basis for grouping products in a situational context. A logical product grouping could be cold cuts and cheeses for snacks.

The study of paper towel usage cited on page 620 also shows the importance of situational variables in positioning products. Heavy-duty uses included cleaning ovens, washing windows, cleaning cars; light-duty uses involved wiping hands, wiping kitchen counters, wiping dishes; and decorative uses were for napkins or placemats.[46] Positioning a paper towel requires recognition of the usage situation. A positioning toward heavy-duty usage should dictate the product's characteristics (multi-ply), the target segment to which the product should be positioned (the heavy-duty user), the promotional appeals (strength and durability), and possibly the media to be used (based on the demographic characteristics of the heavy-duty segment).

American Can identified a segment of heavy-duty paper towel users on this basis. It then introduced Bolt, a multi-ply towel, and positioned it as a strong product suitable for heavy-duty uses.

Advertising

The usage situation can also dictate promotional appeals. If consumers purchase a soft drink primarily for social occasions, then marketers should advertise it in this context. Similarly, if a certain segment purchases a food processor primarily for cooking for guests, marketers should advertise it in the context of meal preparations for guests rather than for the family. Deighton, Henderson, and Neslin referred to the practice of advertising products in the context of the usage situation as **framing**.[47] That is, the usage situation frames the product in a relevant context for consumers. On this basis, the ad "tells the consumer what to look for in the product-usage experience."[48]

The two ads in Exhibit 17.5 frame products in usage situations. Advil is shown as a product that provides relief for a headache, an obvious frame. NYNEX's cellular phone is framed in a business context that requires mobile communications.

Two other bases for advertising products by situation are gift-giving and seasonal usage. Exhibit 17.2 showed products advertised in a gift-giving context. An advertising campaign may also reflect seasonal usage—for example, iced tea during the summer and hot soup in the winter. While consumption of Gatorade is heavier in the summer, the company tries to smooth out demand by advertising Gatorade not only as a summer thirst quencher during active sports activities, but also as a winter fluid replacement for consumers with colds and the flu. General Foods follows a similar strategy for Sanka coffee, but with reversed seasons. Since coffee consumption is heavier in the winter, the company advertises iced Sanka for the summer.

Advertising on a situational basis requires not only a portrayal of the situation, but also a link between product benefits and the situation. The ad for Advil in Exhibit 17.5 emphasizes safe and gentle relief for headaches. NYNEX's ad for cellular phones promotes an effective service network to ensure reliable communications for business purposes.

▶**EXHIBIT 17.5**
Ads that frame products
in usage situations

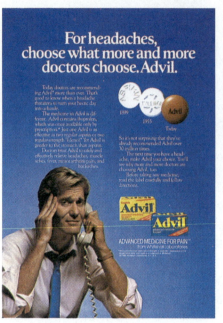

Distribution

The situation may also influence distribution strategies. One of the competitive advantages of 7-Eleven, the largest chain of convenience food stores in the country, is that it stays open late to cater to unanticipated situations food shoppers face when most supermarkets are closed.

Perrier's distribution strategy is also a function of situational influences. As a carbonated mineral water, Perrier tends to be taken at mealtimes. As a result, more than a third of its bottles are shipped to restaurants, hotels, and bars.[49]

SUMMARY

The usage situation is an important environmental factor that directly influences consumers' brand choice. However, marketers have largely overlooked this factor. It should influence marketing strategy by affecting the manner in which markets are segmented, products are positioned, and brands are advertised and distributed.

Three types of situations have important implications for marketing: the consumption situation, the purchase situation, and the communication situation. The consumption situation refers to the circumstances in which consumers use the product. The purchase situation refers to the conditions under which consumers make a decision (for example, whether purchasing as a gift or for themselves) and the in-store conditions at the time of the purchase. The communication situation refers to the conditions in which advertising exposure occurs (for example, a radio commercial heard in a car or at home, or TV watched alone or with friends).

Gift-giving was cited as a particularly important purchase situation since gifts represent a substantial portion of retail sales. Consumers buying gifts tend to be more involved with the purchase and, as a result, are more likely to see the purchase as risky.

An important part of using situational variables to explain consumer behavior is the development of a situational inventory. Situational inventories require the identification of relevant usage, consumption, or communication situations specific to the product category.

The chapter described a simple model of the decision process incorporating situational factors. The model recognizes that a consumer's decision can be a function of the brand, the situation, the consumer's own predispositions, or, more likely, some combination of these factors. Various studies were cited demonstrating that for many products, the most important factor in explaining behavior is the interaction between situation and product. That is, choice of brands is likely to vary by situation. However, the situation will not be important in all cases. When a high level of brand loyalty exists or there is enduring involvement with the product, consumers may buy a particular brand regardless of the situation.

Studies have examined the effects of situational influences on product attitudes, product choice, and the nature of consumer decision making. In most cases, situational variables led to a better understanding of consumer attitudes and a better prediction of consumer choices. The chapter concluded by describing applications of situational variables to market segmentation, product positioning, new products, advertising, and distribution strategies.

The next chapter introduces the final section of the book, communication. We first consider the nature of word-of-mouth communication between groups. Subsequent chapters deal with the diffusion of innovations across groups and with the role of marketing communication.

QUESTIONS

1. A manufacturer of instant coffee considers introducing a new line of continental flavors to be advertised for special occasions. The objective is to gear marketing strategy to the situations that warrant distinctive coffee that can be conveniently prepared.
   - For what types of situations should the coffee be positioned?
   - What are the implications for (a) defining a target segment and (b) developing an advertising strategy?

2. A product manager for a leading brand of paper towels notices substantial variation in sales performance for the brand among stores in the same trading area. The manager hypothesizes that marked differences in the in-store purchase situation may be causing variation in sales. What differences in in-store purchase situations could be causing differences in sales?

3. A manufacturer of hair dryers identifies two types of purchase situations that lead to differences in brand evaluation: (a) purchase for self and (b) purchase as a gift.
   - What are the marketing implications for positioning a product to appeal to each of these purchasing situations?
   - What may be the differences in brand evaluation in each condition?

4. Develop a list of communication situations that may affect a consumer's awareness and comprehension of (a) print advertising and (b) television advertising.

5. Under what conditions is brand choice more likely to be influenced by the situation than by product characteristics? Under what conditions is the reverse likely to be true?

6. What is an interaction effect? Provide an example of the interaction of (1) situation and product and (2) situation, product, and consumer in influencing the purchase of: (a) soda, (b) records, and (c) clothing. What are the strategic implications of these interactions?

7. What are some marketing implications of the interaction effects shown in Table 17.2? Why were situational influences less important for motion pictures than for the other product categories in the table?

8. A company marketing a leading brand of yogurt has always focused on yogurt's nutritional benefits without considering the possibility of varying its appeal to depend on the usage situation.
   - Could the product benefits consumers see in yogurt vary by the usage situation? Specify.
   - What are the marketing implications of variations in perceived benefits by usage situation?

9. Why are situational influences more important when they are contiguous to behavior? Cite some examples.

10. Market segments can be defined by usage situation for snack foods; for example, there are between-meal snackers and party snackers. What market segments could be identified by usage situation for (a) deodorants and (b) paper towels?

11. What marketing opportunities led Dial Corp. to introduce Lunch Bucket? How were these opportunities situation-specific?

12. What marketing implications other than those stated in the text are provided by Figure 17.2?

13. What do we mean by the framing effect in advertising? Cite two examples of the framing effect other than those shown in Exhibit 17.5.

14. What are some purchase and consumption situations that might influence distribution strategies?

RESEARCH ASSIGNMENTS

1. Select two product categories that are frequently given as gifts: one that is higher in price (for example, hair dryers or watches) and one that is lower

priced (compact discs or books). Select a sample of about 50 respondents and ask them (1) how much time they would spend and (2) what information sources they would consult in choosing a particular alternative for:

a. Themselves.

b. A birthday gift for a close friend.

c. A wedding gift for a close friend.

d. A thank you gift to repay someone for watching their home or apartment while they were away.

e. A birthday gift for a casual friend.[50]

- Did respondents spend more time in selecting a product for themselves (a) or as a gift (b-e)?
- Did respondents spend more time in selecting a gift in a high involvement gift-giving situation (b and c) or in a low involvement gift-giving situation (d and e)?
- How did sources of information differ for buying for themselves versus buying as a gift? For giving a gift in a high versus a low involvement situation?
- Were there any differences in the amount of time respondents spent in searching for a high-priced gift versus a low-priced gift? In the sources of information used in evaluating the higher- versus the lower-priced gift?

2. Select a product category that you believe is likely to be affected by the usage situation (soft drinks, paper towels, coffee, snacks, and so on). Conduct several depth interviews with consumers to define:

a. The most frequent usage situations for the category.

b. A vocabulary of evaluative product attributes.

- Develop a questionnaire in which consumers are asked to rate:

   a. The importance of each of the attributes by the four most important situations you defined in the depth interviews (for example, How important is a soft drink that is refreshing when drinking it alone? When drinking it at a party?)

   b. The three leading brands by the vocabulary of product attributes for the four most important situations (for example, rate Pepsi on "refreshing" when drinking it alone, drinking it at a party, and so on).

   - What is the variation in importance ratings by situation?
   - What is the variation in brand ratings by situation?
   - What are the implications of variations in importance ratings and brand image by situation for (a) positioning a new product, (b) repositioning an existing product, (c) advertising strategy, and (d) definition of a target group?

3. Do a series of depth interviews with consumers to develop a comprehensive situational inventory for snack products. Make sure the inventory contains the five elements Belk defined: physical surroundings, social surroundings, time, task definition, and antecedent states. (See Table 17.1 as an example.)

Submit the inventory to a small sample of consumers (10 to 20) and determine the frequency with which various snack foods (potato chips, pretzels, cheese, crackers, fruit, cookies) are considered for each usage occasion. What are the implications of your findings for (a) product line strategy, (b) new product development, and (c) advertising?

NOTES

1. "Sweat Chic," *Forbes* (September 5, 1988), p. 96.

2. Flemming Hansen, *Consumer Choice Behavior* (New York: The Free Press, 1972).

3. William O. Bearden and Arch G. Woodside, "Consumption Occasion Influence on Consumer Brand Choice," *Decision Sciences,* 9 (April, 1978), pp. 273–284.

4. Kenneth C. Gehrt and Mary Beth Pinto, "The Impact of Situational Factors on Health Care Preferences: Exploring the Prospect of Situationally Based Segmentation," *Journal of Health Care Marketing,* 11 (June, 1991), pp. 41–52.

5. See, for example, C. Whan Park, Easwar S. Iyer, and Daniel C. Smith, "The Effects of Situational Factors on In-Store Grocery Shopping Behavior: The Role of Store Environment and Time Available for Shopping," *Journal of Consumer Research,* 15 (March, 1989), pp. 422–433.

6. "The Teen Market," *Product Marketing* (Spring, 1982), p. S26.

7. "Sales Promotion: The Year in Review," *Marketing & Media Decisions* (July, 1989), pp. 124–126; and "Ad Spending Outlook Brightens," *Advertising Age* (May 15, 1989).

8. Russell Belk, "Gift-Giving Behavior," in J. Sheth ed., *Research in Marketing,* Vol. 2 (Greenwich, CT: JAI Press, 1979), pp. 95–126.

9. Keith Clarke and Russell Belk, "The Effects of Product Involvement and Task Definition on Anticipated Consumer Effort," in William Wilkie, ed., *Advances in Consumer Research,* Vol. 6 (Ann Arbor, MI: Association for Consumer Research, 1979), pp. 313–317.

10. A. Ryan, "Consumer Gift-Giving Behavior: An Exploratory Analysis," in D. Bellinger and B. Greenberg, eds., *Contemporary Marketing Thought* (Chicago: American Marketing Association, 1977), pp. 100–104.

11. John F. Sherry, Jr., "Gift Giving in Anthropological Perspective," *Journal of Consumer Research,* 10 (September, 1983), pp. 157–168.

12. Joseph A. Cote, James McCullough, and Michael Reilly, "Effects of Unexpected Situations on Behavior-Intention Differences: A Garbology Analysis," *Journal of Consumer Research,* 12 (September, 1985), pp. 188–194.

13. William L. Wilkie and Peter R. Dickson, "Patterns of Consumer Information Search and Shopping Behavior for Household Durables," *Working Paper Series* (Cambridge, MA: Marketing Science Institute, 1985).

14. Marvin E. Goldberg and Gerald J. Gorn, "Happy and Sad TV Programs: How They Affect Reactions to Commercials," *Journal of Consumer Research,* 14 (December, 1987), pp. 387–403.

15. Margaret S. Clark, Sandra Milberg, and John Ross, "Arousal Cues Arousal-Related Material in Memory: Implications for Understanding Effects of Mood on Memory," *Journal of Verbal Learning and Verbal Behavior,* 22 (1983), pp. 633–649.

16. Meryl P. Gardner, "The Consumer's Mood: An Important Situational Variable," in Thomas C. Kinnear, ed., *Advances in Consumer Research,* Vol. 11 (Ann Arbor, MI: Association for Consumer Research, 1984), pp. 525–529.

17. Russell W. Belk, "Situational Variables and Consumer Behavior," *Journal of Consumer Research,* 2 (December, 1975), pp. 159.

18. Sigurd Villads Troye, "Situationist Theory and Consumer Behavior," *Research in Consumer Behavior* (Greenwich, CN: JAI Press, 1985), p. 296.

19. S. Tamer Cavusgil and Catherine A. Cole, "An Empirical Investigation of Situational, Attitudinal and Personal Influences on Behavioral Intentions," in Kenneth Bernhardt *et al.*, eds., *Proceedings of the American Marketing Association Educators' Conference,* Series No. 47 (1981), p. 161.

20. Russell W. Belk, "An Exploratory Assessment of Situational Effects in Buyer Behavior," *Journal of Marketing Research,* 11 (May, 1974), p. 160.

21. *Ibid.*

22. D. Bem, "Self-Perception Theory," in L. Berkowitz, ed., *Advances in Experimental Social Psychology* (New York: Academic Press, 1972), pp. 1–62.

23. Brian Sternthal and Gerald Zaltman, "The Broadened Concept: Toward a Taxonomy of Consumption Situation," in Gerald Zaltman and Brian Sternthal, eds., *Broadening the Concept of Consumer Behavior* (Ann Arbor, MI: Association for Consumer Research, 1975), p. 144.

24. Keith Clarke and Russell W. Belk, "The Effects of Product Involvement and Task Definition on Anticipated Consumer Effort," in William L. Wilkie, ed., *Advances in Consumer Research, loc. cit.*

25. William O. Bearden and Arch G. Woodside, "Interactions of Consumption Situations and Brand Attitudes," *Journal of Applied Psychology,* 61 (1976), pp. 764–769.

26. Belk, "An Exploratory Assessment," *op. cit.,* p. 160; and Louis K. Sharpe and Kent L. Granzin, "Market Segmentation by Consumer Usage Context: An Exploratory Analysis," *Journal of Economics and Business,* 26 (1974), pp. 225–228.

27. Bearden and Woodside, "Consumption Occasion Influence . . . ," *loc. cit.*

28. Belk, "An Exploratory Assessment . . . ," *loc. cit.*

29. Rajendra K. Srivastava, Allan D. Shocker, and George S. Day, "An Exploratory Study of the Influences of Usage Situation on Perceptions of Product Markets," in H. Keith Hunt, ed., *Advances in Consumer Research,* Vol. 5 (Ann Arbor, MI: Association for Consumer Research, 1978), pp. 32–38.

30. Russell W. Belk, "A Free Response Approach to Developing Product-Specific Consumption Situation Taxonomies," in Allan D. Shocker, ed., *Analytic Approaches to Product and Market Planning* (Cambridge, MA: Marketing Science Institute, 1979), p. 178.

31. Sternthal and Zaltman, "The Broadened Concept . . . ," *op. cit.,* p. 146.

32. See Eric N. Berkowitz, James L. Ginter, and W. Wayne Talarzyk, "An Investigation of the Effects of Specific Usage Situations on the Prediction of Consumer Choice Behavior," in Barnett A. Greenberg and Danny N. Bellenger, eds., *Proceedings of the American Marketing Association Educators' Conference,* Series No. 41 (1977), pp. 90–94; and William O. Bearden and Arch G. Woodside, "Situational Influence on Consumer Purchase Intentions," in Arch G. Woodside, Jagdish N. Sheth, and Peter D. Bennett, *Consumer and Industrial Buying Behavior* (New York: North-Holland, 1977), pp. 167–177.

33. James M. Daley and James H. Martin, "Situational Analysis of Bus Riders and Non-Riders for Different Transportation Methods," *Logistics and Transportation Review,* 24 (June, 1988), pp. 185–199.

34. Kenneth E. Miller and James L. Ginter, "An Investigation of Situational Variation in Brand Choice Behavior and Attitude," *Journal of Marketing Research,* 16 (February, 1979), pp. 111–123.

35. John L. Stanton and P. Greg Bonner, "An Investigation of the Differential Impact of Purchase Situation on Levels of Consumer Choice Behavior," *Advances in Consumer Research,* Vol. 8 (Ann Arbor, MI: Association for Consumer Research, 1980), pp. 639–643.

36. U. N. Umesh and Joseph A. Cote, "Influence of Situational Variables on Brand-Choice Models," *Journal of Business Research,* 16 (1988), pp. 91–99.

37. Donald H. Granbois, "Improving the Study of Customer In-Store Behavior," *Journal of Marketing,* 32 (October, 1968), pp. 28–33.

38. Clarke and Belk, "The Effects of Product Involvement and Task Definition . . . ," *op. cit.,* p. 314.

39. Adrian B. Ryans, "Consumer Gift Buying Behavior: An Exploratory Analysis," in Barnett A. Greenberg and Danny N. Bellenger, eds., *Proceedings of the American Marketing Association Educators' Conference,* Series No. 41 (1977), pp. 99–104.

40. *Ibid.*

41. Bruce E. Mattson, "Situation Influences on Store Choice," *Journal of Retailing,* 58 (Fall, 1982), pp. 46–58.

42. *Ibid.*

43. Charles H. Ptacek and James Shanteau, "Situation Determinants of Consumer Decision Making," Working paper, 1980.

44. Peter R. Dickson, "Person-Situation: Segmentation's Missing Link," *Journal of Marketing,* 46 (Fall, 1982), pp. 56–64.

45. For an analytical method to position products by situations, see "CATALYST Measurement Mapping Method Identifies Competition, Defines Markets," *Marketing News* (May 14, 1982), Section 1, p. 3.

46. Ptacek and Shanteau, "Situation Determinants of Consumer Decision Making . . . ," *loc. cit.*

47. John Deighton, Caroline Henderson, and Scott Neslin, "Scanners and the Framing Effect," *Marketing & Media Decisions* (October, 1989), p. 112.

48. *Ibid.*

49. "Perrier Rival Talks of Serendipity," *The New York Times,* p. 35.

50. Situational items taken from Russell W. Belk, "Effects of Gift-Giving Involvement on Gift Selection Strategies," in Andrew Mitchell, ed., *Advances in Consumer Research,* Vol. 9 (Ann Arbor, MI: Association for Consumer Research, 1982), pp. 408–412.

PART
V

COMMUNICATIONS PROCESSES

In this last section we consider communications processes. Since they provide information that influences consumer purchases, communications are central to consumer decision making. Communications can be from groups or from marketing organizations. Group communications occur within and across groups. Chapter 18 describes communications within groups in the form of word-of-mouth influence, the most influential type of communication since it comes from family, friends, and neighbors—all highly credible sources of information.

In Chapter 19, we consider communications across groups through a process of diffusion of information and influence. Such a process of diffusion is likely to occur for new products, as information on and adoption of new products spreads across groups. Marketers must trace such diffusion processes since new products are a primary source of profits.

We consider communication from marketing organizations in Chapter 20. We focus primarily on communication through advertising and personal selling since these are the primary means marketing organizations use to influence consumers.

18

Word-of-Mouth Communication and Opinion Leadership

CORONA SUCCEEDS BASED ON WORD-OF-MOUTH

Word-of-mouth is interpersonal communication between two or more individuals such as members of a reference group or a customer and a salesperson. All of these people exert purchase influence through such communication. The adage "a satisfied customer is your best salesperson" illustrates the importance of word-of-mouth to the marketer: Satisfied customers influence friends and relatives to buy; dissatisfied customers inhibit sales.

Word-of-mouth can be the primary factor in the product's success. A good example is Corona beer. Before the beer was imported to the United States, many residents of the Southwest would bring it back while on vacation in Mexico. This led Corona to import the beer, first to Austin, Texas, where it began to appear in bars, chili parlors, and Mexican restaurants. The beer's popularity quickly spread by word-of-mouth. The next market was San Diego, where surfers and beach people adopted the brand. From there word spread up and down the California coast. The brand began moving east and won acceptance in Chicago, where it was most popular among yuppies. By 1984, sales had grown from 300,000 to 1.7 million cases on the strength of word-of-mouth alone. All of this growth occurred on the basis of on-premises sales in bars and restaurants.[1]

In 1987, as the brand began appearing in supermarkets, sales hit 13.7 million cases, making Corona the second largest-selling imported beer after Heineken. Limited advertising in select magazines began, but Corona planned no television advertising. By that time, Corona was being distributed on the Eastern Seaboard, where it once again relied on word-of-mouth, rather than advertising, for sales. Although sales of Corona dipped in the early 1990s due to more intense competition from foreign beers, the power of word-of-mouth communication suggests that Corona is probably here to stay.

Corona reaped the benefits of word-of-mouth without any overt attempt to stimulate it. Some marketers try to encourage word-of-mouth more directly. At one time, Canada Dry set up an advisory board of socially prominent women in major markets across the country to "serve Canada Dry club soda at their elegant dinner parties, talk it up to their socially prominent friends, and maneuver it into such upscale—and much publicized—events as the Boston marathon."[2] The company was seeking ways to compete with Perrier's sparkling water and came up with the idea of getting Canada Dry in the hands of local opinion leaders "in the hope of sparking a word-of-mouth campaign that would spread to a broader market."[3]

In this chapter, we consider word-of-mouth communication among individuals within a group. Studies have shown that such communication is a major influence on consumer behavior. We also consider a salesperson's word-of-mouth influence on a customer. A central concept in direct communication among individuals in a group is **opinion leadership;** that is, the influence that individuals interested and involved in a product exert over the attitudes and behavior of others.

The importance of word-of-mouth communication and the process by which it occurs are considered first. Communications both within groups and between salespersons and customers are considered. Key issues regarding opinion leadership are explored next. The final sections show how marketers measure word-of-mouth and opinion leadership and how they try to use these concepts to influence consumers.

◆ IMPORTANCE OF WORD-OF-MOUTH COMMUNICATION

Friends and relatives are more likely to influence consumer choice than any other source of information. Personal influence is most powerful because consumers generally regard friends and relatives as more credible and trustworthy than commercial sources of information. Moreover, information from reference and family groups is a means of reducing the risk in a purchase decision. Consumers who consider purchasing an expensive item such as a car or socially visible items such as clothing or furniture are likely to obtain the opinion of "relevant others." Such opinions not only provide information to reduce financial and performance risk, but they also serve as a means of group sanction to reduce social risk.

Katz and Lazarsfeld conducted one of the first studies establishing the importance of word-of-mouth communication in a small Midwestern community shortly after World War II. They found that word-of-mouth communication was the most important form of influence in the purchase of food products and household goods. In influencing consumers to switch brands, word-of-mouth was twice as effective as radio advertising, four times as effective as personal selling, and seven times as effective as newspapers and magazines.[4] Similarly, Whyte's study of the transmission of influence in the purchase of air conditioners in a Philadelphia suburb also concluded that word-of-mouth communication was the determining factor.[5] He found that ownership clustered in certain locations and tended to group on one side of the street but did not cross the street. He concluded that the pattern of ownership reflected the pattern of typical word-of-mouth communication between neighbors such as conversations "over the fence" and "on the back porch."

Although both studies were conducted before television became a major medium, more recent studies have confirmed the dominance of personal influence in choice decisions. Ernest Dichter, a well-known behavioral researcher, summarized 6,000 case studies and concluded that nearly 80 percent of all purchases can be traced to word-of-mouth influence.[6] Similarly, Arndt found that respondents who received positive word-of-mouth communications about a new product were three times as likely to purchase it as were those who received negative communication.[7] Engel, Blackwell, and Kegerreis found that 60 percent of consumers cited word-of-mouth as the most influential factor in their use of a new auto diagnostic center.[8] In a 1990 study of personal computers, Herr, Kardes, and Kim found that word-of-mouth communication had a much stronger impact on brand evaluations than detailed brand information from a neutral source, *Consumer Reports* magazine.[9]

The importance of word-of-mouth is related to cultural values. In cultures dominated by group cohesion and adherence to group norms, communications from group members will have more influence. In Chinese and Japanese cultures, adherence to group norms is ingrained since childhood. As a result, word-of-mouth is an even more important influence than it is in the United States.

◆ NATURE OF WORD-OF-MOUTH COMMUNICATION

If marketers are to encourage positive word-of-mouth communication about their products, they must understand the:

- Types of word-of-mouth communication that occur.
- Process by which word-of-mouth communication occurs.
- Conditions for word-of-mouth communication.
- Consumers' motives for engaging in word-of-mouth communication.

Types of Word-of-Mouth Communication

A study by Richins and Root-Shaffer of personal influence in buying autos identified three types of word-of-mouth communications: product news, advice giving, and personal experience.[10] *Product news* is information about the product such as features of car models, new advances in car technology, or performance attributes. *Advice giving* involves expressions of opinions about the car or advice about which model to buy. *Personal experience* relates to comments about the performance of the consumer's car or why the consumer bought it. Product news is fairly straightforward, but the advice and personal experience dimensions of word-of-mouth communication could be either positive or negative.

These categories suggest that word-of-mouth serves two functions: to inform and to influence. Product news informs consumers; advice and personal experience are likely to influence consumer decisions. As a result, each type of communication is probably most important at different stages in the purchasing decision. Product news is important as a means of creating awareness about product features or about a new product. Once awareness is established, hearing about product experiences from a friend or relative gives consumers the ability to judge the relative merits of one brand or another. Finally, advice is most important in making the final decision, as the opinion of a "relevant other" regarding a purchase is likely to be influential.

Process of Word-of-Mouth Communication

The process of word-of-mouth communication has been described as a communication flow between opinion leaders and followers. Of key importance in this flow is whether the information being communicated is positive or negative.

Two-Step Flow of Communication

Katz and Lazarsfeld were among the first to identify the process of word-of-mouth communication. They described it as a two-step flow from the mass media to opinion leaders and from opinion leaders to followers.[11] (See top of Figure 18.1.) They believed that opinion leaders are more exposed to the mass media than are those whom they influence.[12] As a result, opinion leaders are viewed as intermediaries between the mass media and other consumers. The majority of consumers—the followers—are viewed as passive recipients of information.

The principal contribution of the two-step flow theory is that it rejected the long-standing notion that the mass media were the principal means of influencing consumers and the principal sources of information. While the importance

▶FIGURE 18.1
Two models of word-of-mouth communication

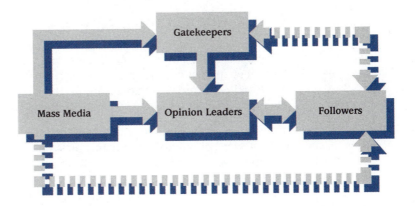

of personal influence relative to commercial influence is evident today, it was not as clear after World War II. Advertising was considered the dominant force. It was in the 1950s and, paradoxically, after the advent of television that advertising began to be viewed as a weaker force that was unlikely to change group-influenced purchasing choices. Advertising could reinforce existing product preferences, but it could not change negative opinions, particularly when consumers strongly held them.[13] The two-step flow theory encouraged the view that personal influence, not advertising, was the principal means of communication and influence.

Multistep Flow of Communication

Although the two-step flow was important in understanding the process of personal influence, it was not an accurate representation of the flow of information and influence for three reasons:

1. Followers are not passive. They may initiate requests for information as well as listen to the unsolicited opinions of others.
2. Those who transmit information are also likely to receive it; that is, opinion leaders are also influenced by followers. Conversely, those who seek information are likely to give it. Word-of-mouth influence is frequently a two-directional flow between transmitters and receivers.

3. Opinion leaders are not the only ones to receive information from the mass media. Followers are also influenced by advertising. Moreover, opinion leaders may not control the flow of information from the mass media to the group. Katz and Lazarsfeld realized that there may be "gatekeepers" or "information gatherers" who serve this function.[14] **Gatekeepers** may be distinct from opinion leaders; they introduce ideas and information to the group but may not influence it. For example, a consumer may be an avid reader of fashion magazines and may introduce certain information on the latest styles, but this consumer may not influence the adoption of these styles within the group.

Researchers have also described *market mavens;* that is, individuals who are gatekeepers across many product categories because of their general expertise about places to shop, product characteristics, prices, and other marketing information.[15] Market mavens like helping others by providing information about the marketplace; but like gatekeepers, they may not necessarily be opinion leaders.

Because of the limitations in the concept of a two-step flow, a more realistic model of word-of-mouth communication would be a multistep flow, represented at the bottom of Figure 18.1. In this model, the mass media can reach gatekeepers, opinion leaders, or followers directly but are less likely to reach the followers (as indicated by the dotted line). Gatekeepers, although represented as a source of information to both opinion leaders and followers, are more likely to disseminate information to opinion leaders. Furthermore, word-of-mouth communication between opinion leaders and followers is represented as a two-directional flow: Opinion leaders may seek information from followers, and followers may solicit information from opinion leaders.

A study by Still, Barnes, and Kooyman of the role of word-of-mouth communication and advertising in influencing moviegoers to see *Superman II* found support for the multistep flow model. The study found that followers cited both word-of-mouth and advertising as equally likely to influence them to see the movie. Thus, the pattern of influence can go from mass media to followers without opinion leaders serving as intermediaries.[16] Moreover, the study found that the same individual could serve as both information provider and seeker, a pattern that supports the two-sided arrow between opinion leaders and followers in the multistep model in Figure 18.1.

Classification of Consumers by Word-of-Mouth Communication

The recognition in the multistep model that opinion leaders and followers both may transmit and receive information leads to four possibilities. (See Figure 18.2.) The **socially integrated consumer** is one who is both an opinion leader and an information seeker. This consumer is the most socially active in encouraging word-of-mouth communication. The **socially independent consumer** scores high on opinion leadership but low on information seeking. This

▶FIGURE 18.2

A categorization of consumers by opinion leadership and information seeking for clothing decisions

Source: Adapted from Fred D. Reynolds and William R. Darden, "Mutually Adaptive Effects of Interpersonal Communication," *Journal of Marketing Research*, 8 (November, 1971), p. 451. Reprinted with permission from the *Journal of Marketing Research*.

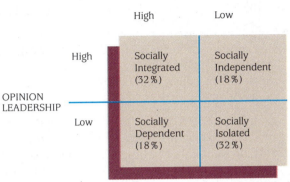

consumer represents the traditional view of opinion leadership in the two-step model: a consumer who transmits information and influence but does not solicit them. The **socially dependent consumer** is low on opinion leadership but high on information seeking. This consumer represents the traditional view of a follower: an individual who is socially active in soliciting word-of-mouth communication but is not an influencer. The **socially isolated consumer** scores low on opinion leadership *and* information seeking. This consumer, a passive individual who does not seek or transmit information, is not socially active and may avoid personal influence.

Reynolds and Darden classified women into one of these four groups on the basis of their transfer of information and influence about women's clothing fashions.[17] They classified one-third of the women as socially integrated and one-third as socially isolated; and they split the remainder equally between socially independent and socially dependent consumers. Therefore, only one-third of the sample conformed to the traditional definitions of opinion leader and follower.

Reynolds and Darden then determined the fashion interest and media behavior of each group. Socially integrated consumers were twice as likely as socially independent consumers to express a high level of interest in fashion. A high level of interest, therefore, encourages both the giving and the receiving of information and influence. That is, opinion leadership for a given area such as fashion is likely to be the result of interest and involvement in the subject.

Negative Word-of-Mouth Communication

Word-of-mouth communication can be negative as well as positive. Consumers convey information on poor product performance, lack of service, high prices, or rude sales personnel.

Negative word-of-mouth information tends to be more powerful than positive information. When consumers are dissatisfied, they complain to approximately three times as many friends and relatives as when they are satisfied. Richins' study of dissatisfied purchasers of clothing and appliances found that over half engaged in negative word-of-mouth communication about their experiences.[18] Such negative communication was most likely when:

- Consumers viewed the problem as serious.
- Consumers placed the blame for dissatisfaction directly on the manufacturer or retailer.
- Consumers believed that complaining directly to the source would not do any good.

In addition, Mizerski found that consumers are more likely to pay attention to negative than to positive information.[19] The power of negative word-of-mouth communication is illustrated by the fact that it killed the movie *Heaven's Gate* almost overnight, resulting in a $50 million loss for United Artists and the sale of the company by its conglomerate owner.[20]

Consumer Complaint Behavior.   If dissatisfied with a product, consumers have several options. One is to complain to the manufacturer; a second is to complain to a third party such as the Better Business Bureau; a third is to engage in negative word-of-mouth; and a fourth is to stop buying without communicating to anyone.[21]

As we saw in Chapter 2, most dissatisfied consumers do not complain about products to manufacturers or seek satisfaction by returning them. Deiner and Greyser found that only one out of five consumers dissatisfied with a cosmetic product either complained about it to the manufacturer or returned it.[22] Another study of several product categories found only 10 percent of dissatisfied consumers voiced complaints.[23] Even fewer dissatisfied consumers complain to third parties. Why do so few consumers complain? Because first, they believe it will do little good; and, second, they believe it is not worth the time and effort.

This lack of complaint behavior has led many companies to ignore the damaging effects of negative word-of-mouth behavior. They conclude that their consumers are generally satisfied and that negative word-of-mouth is unlikely. Other companies recognize that silence does not necessarily mean satisfaction. Companies such as Procter & Gamble, General Electric, and Whirlpool have encouraged consumers to provide product feedback through toll-free telephone numbers.

Rumors.   A type of negative word-of-mouth communication is false rumors about a company or product. Occasionally, false rumors have proved harmful to sales. One of the most pervasive was the rumor that Procter & Gamble was "in league with Satan," based on the company's 108-year-old logo—a man in the moon with thirteen stars. The problem was that the man in the moon's curly hair looked like an inverted 666. That number has long been associated with Satan. The company withdrew the logo after a five-year effort, numerous court cases against rumor generators, and hundreds of thousands of dollars spent to dispel the rumor.[24] In the late 1980s, P&G brought the logo back on four products only to have the rumors start afresh. By 1990, the company was reporting an average of 150 calls a day from consumers who wanted to know if the company had pledged its profits to the devil.[25] In 1991, the company revised the logo by giving the man in the moon straighter hair.

Sometimes, advertisers try to combat rumors with advertising campaigns that attempt to set the record straight. Consumers may have misconceptions about a product or company, and marketers use advertising to combat this negative information. A good example is the ad in Exhibit 18.1. The misperception existed among consumers that Hunt-Wesson was owned by a rich Texas magnate called Hunt. The ad dispels the false rumor by identifying the true owner, the Norton Simon company, and the true company location, California.

There have been other rumors that have harmed companies. For example:

- Gillette hair dryers were rumored to be made with asbestos, a carcinogen.[26]
- Poprocks, a General Foods candy, was rumored to cause children to explode.[27]
- McDonald's was rumored to use red worms in its hamburgers and suffered a 30-percent decrease in sales in areas where the rumors circulated.[28]
- Bubble Yum, a chewing gum positioned for children, was rumored to contain spider eggs.[29]

▶**EXHIBIT 18.1**
Using word-of-mouth communication to set the record straight

- Entenmann's, the world's largest baker of fresh cake products, was rumored to be owned by the Reverend Sun Myung Moon's Unification Church.[30]
- Tropical Fantasy, a low-priced soft drink that competes with Coke and Pepsi in downscale inner-city areas, was rumored to have been manufactured by the Ku Klux Klan.[31]

In each case, these rumors hurt company sales. Tropical Fantasy's sales plunged by 70 percent in a three-month period in 1991 because of the rumors.

In most of these cases, rumors eventually die. However, as we saw in the case of the P&G logo, they can be persistent. Entenmann's (actually owned by Warner-Lambert, the pharmaceutical conglomerate) fought the rumors of the association with Moon's Unification Church with advertising, press conferences, and letters of denial.[32] The Tropical Fantasy rumors prompted an investigation by a state district attorney's office to determine if competitors were behind the rumors.[33]

Conditions for Word-of-Mouth Communication

Word-of-mouth communication is not the dominant factor in every situation. For instance, Herr, Kardes, and Kim found that word-of-mouth is not as important in the evaluation of an automobile if (1) consumers already have a strong impression of the product, and/or (2) negative information regarding the product is available.[34] This means that word-of-mouth communication is unlikely to change the attitudes of consumers who have strong brand loyalties. A third condition in which word-of-mouth is unlikely to change attitudes is when consumers have doubts about a product because of credible negative information.

Word-of-mouth is also not dominant for every product category. It is most important when reference groups are likely to be sources of information and influence. This means that word-of-mouth is most important when:

- The product is visible and, therefore, behavior is apparent.
- The product is distinctive and can more easily be identified with style, taste, and other personal norms.
- The product has just been introduced.
- The product is important to the reference group's norms and belief system (for example, teenagers' reactions to a new rock album or older consumers' reactions to a new salt-free breakfast product).
- Consumer are involved in the purchase decision.
- Consumers see the purchase of the product as risky and, thus, are encouraged to search for additional information.

The last two conditions, involvement and risk in the purchase decision, are particularly important in influencing word-of-mouth.

Word-of-Mouth and Consumer Involvement

Consumers who are involved with a product are more likely to communicate about it and influence others, particularly if they are involved on an ongoing basis (enduring involvement). In their study of car purchasing decisions, Richins and Root-Shaffer found that individuals with enduring involvement are most likely to be opinion leaders. (See Figure 18.3.) These individuals are more likely to engage in all types of word-of-mouth by communicating product news, advice, and personal experiences.[35] Individuals who get involved in cars only when they buy (that is, those who are involved on a situational basis) tend to

---

STRATEGIC APPLICATIONS OF CONSUMER BEHAVIOR

Rumors Sink P&G's Wash n' Go in Poland

As Poland has moved to a free market economy, it has begun to experience some of the advantages of capitalism—new Western laundry detergents, yogurt, candy bars, and products Poles never knew they needed like pet food. However, companies entering the Polish market have begun to experience some of the land mines more typically associated with advanced capitalistic markets. One land mine is a jaundiced view of television advertising; another, being a rampant rumor mill.

One of the first Western products to be heavily advertised was Procter & Gamble's Wash n' Go combination shampoo and hair conditioner. The product became the country's best-selling shampoo in a matter of weeks, but then sales plunged. Why? A pervasive rumor that the Polish version of Wash n' Go was adulterated and made one's hair fall out.

The company felt helpless to dispel the rumors. Any dermatologist could verify that shampoo has no effect on hair loss, and the company could not find one single person who would admit to hair loss as a result of using the product. If P&G tried to dispel the rumors, it would merely be fueling them further by communicating them to the total market. So, it chose to try to "ride it out" and hoped they would just go away.

Where did the rumors come from? No one knows. Typically, the response is "I heard it from a friend who heard it from a friend." Ironically, P&G's effective advertising campaign helped fuel the rumors. Under the old Communist regime, television was a propaganda tool. Wash n' Go was heavily advertised. To most consumers, heavy advertising spelled suspicion. The more something was advertised, the worse it had to be. Thus, the rumors were spread in a receptive environment.

P&G's experience shows it can be hurt as badly by rumors in Poland as in the United States. Rumors are a universal phenomenon.

Source: "Poland Goes Ad-Crazy, Sometimes Beyond Belief," *International Herald Tribune* (May 27, 1992), pp. 9, 14.

▶**FIGURE 18.3**
Word-of-mouth and
consumer involvement

Source: Adapted from
Marsha L. Richins and Teri
Root-Shaffer, "The Role of
Involvement and Opinion
Leadership in Consumer
Word-of-Mouth: An Implicit
Model Made Explicit," in
Michael J. Houston, ed.,
*Advances in Consumer
Research*, Vol. 15 (Provo,
UT: Association for
Consumer Research, 1987),
pp. 32-36.

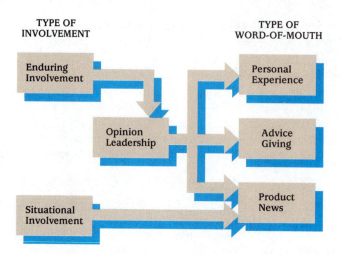

communicate product news only. They are unlikely to influence others by advising them or by communicating personal experiences, although they could inform friends and relatives about new models or performance characteristics.

Figure 18.3 suggests that if word-of-mouth is to influence rather than merely inform a consumer, it must be transmitted by someone who is involved with a product category on an enduring basis; that is, an opinion leader.

Word-of-Mouth and Perceived Risk

Consumers who see risk in the purchase are more likely to initiate product-related conversations and to request information from friends and relatives.[36] Woodside and DeLozier described a number of possible outcomes when consumers seek information from a group to reduce risk.[37] (See Figure 18.4.) For example, a consumer who considers purchasing a laptop computer decides to ask a group of friends for their advice. It is possible the group does not know very much about the product. If so, the consumer will probably explain to the group the nature of the product and its benefits and then ask their advice (right-hand branch at top of Figure 18.4).

If group members are familiar with the laptop computer (left-hand branch), the question is whether communication with the group has reduced the consumer's uncertainty about buying. If so, the consumer is likely to buy the product. If not, the next question is whether the group believes the benefits gained by purchasing are greater than the risk. If so, the consumer will probably purchase. If group members believe that the cost and the uncertainty about performance outweigh product benefits, this opinion may dissuade the consumer from buying a laptop computer. However, if the purchase is very important, the consumer may look for other sources to support the purchase. For more product information, the consumer may review *Consumer Reports* magazine or consult other groups such as business associates.

▶**FIGURE 18.4**

A model of consumer risk handling and word-of-mouth communication

Source: Adapted from Arch G. Woodside and M. Wayne DeLozier, "Effects of Word-of-Mouth Advertising on Consumer Risk-Taking," *Journal of Advertising*, 5 (Fall, 1976), p. 17. Reprinted with permission from the *Journal of Advertising*.

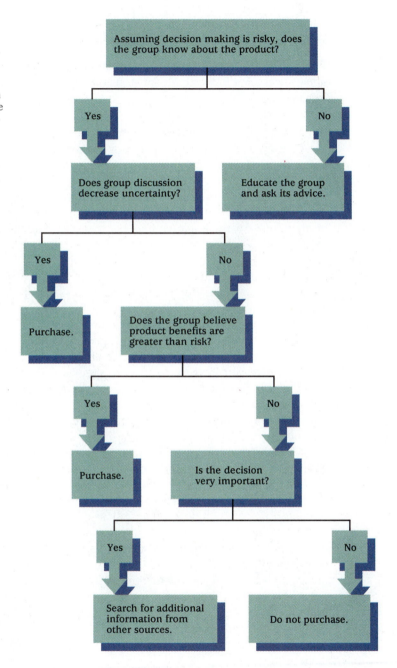

Motives for Engaging in Word-of-Mouth Communication

Why do consumers engage in word-of-mouth communication? The question applies to their motives both for transmitting and for seeking information and influence.

Motives for Transmitting Word-of-Mouth Information

Consumers have several motives for talking about brands or products. First, being involved in a decision is likely to encourage consumers to transmit information and influence. Katz and Lazarsfeld found that those most likely to transmit information are not those with experience but those who are experiencing product decisions.[38] The opinion leader for children's vitamins is not likely to be the mother with six grown children and past purchasing experience but the mother with younger children who has direct interest in the product category. Summers found that 86 percent of all transmitters of word-of-mouth information owned the product before discussing it.[39] Therefore, involvement in the product decision (situational involvement) is one important ingredient in personal communications.

Another motive for transmitting information is the inherent interest in the product (enduring involvement). Individuals who have an ongoing interest in a product category enjoy communicating about it.

A third reason for communicating about a product is to erase any doubts about product choice. A consumer may attempt to reduce dissonance by describing the positive qualities of a recently purchased car to friends and relatives. A friend's purchase of the same make confirms the consumer's original judgment.

A fourth reason for word-of-mouth communication is involvement with the group. The greater the importance of the group, the greater the likelihood consumers will seek to transmit information to it. New residents in a leisure community may want to become more involved with their neighbors and will transmit information on new products of interest to elderly consumers. Dichter suggested that such communication is a means of ensuring involvement with the group by various strategies such as gaining attention, suggesting expertise, or showing inside information.[40] Certain people may talk about products simply as a means of social interaction.

Dichter cites a fifth reason for word-of-mouth communication. Consumers like to be influential; it gives them personal satisfaction. In Dichter's words, "We like to be recommenders. A buyer likes to take credit for having discovered something. He doesn't say, 'Look at this good product put out by P&G.' He says, 'Look what I got.'"[41]

Motives for Seeking Word-of-Mouth Information

Consumers also have several motives for seeking word-of-mouth information. One is that friends and relatives are credible sources of product information.

Consumers are more likely to trust information from friends and relatives than from commercial sources such as advertisements or salespeople who have a vested interest in making a sale.

A second motive for seeking word-of-mouth communication is that information from personal sources facilitates the purchase task. A consumer might find out from a relative that a store does not have the desired item, that it is priced too high, or that it is not made of the desired material. Shopping time has thereby been reduced.

A third motive for seeking word-of-mouth information is to reduce purchase risk. Figure 18.4 shows that consumers engage in various strategies to seek the opinions of group members to reduce risk before the purchase. Another motive for obtaining word-of-mouth information is to reduce dissonance after the purchase. We saw that consumers sometimes reduce dissonance by talking about the product to assure themselves they made the right decision. Conversely, consumers also seek the opinions of friends and relatives to reassure themselves that they made the right choice.

◆ WORD-OF-MOUTH AND THE CUSTOMER-SALESPERSON INTERACTION

Word-of-mouth communication is an essential component of the interaction between a salesperson and a customer. American firms spend over $200 billion annually on personal selling, twice as much as on advertising. Most personal selling activity occurs for industrial goods (that is, products and services used in the production of other goods). In these cases, buyers and sellers frequently negotiate price, product specifications, delivery, and maintenance in a two-way process of communication. Personal selling is important for consumer goods as well, particularly in the sale of durable goods such as automobiles, electronics, and appliances.

A model of customer-salesperson communication is presented in Figure 18.5. The key factor is the third step, communicating a sales strategy to the customer. To do so, the salesperson must first determine customer needs and then formulate a sales strategy based on these needs. Once the sales strategy is communicated, the salesperson evaluates it based on the customer's response and then adjusts the strategy to better meet customer's needs.

Determining Customer Needs

In Chapter 3, we cited the example of a business school student in the market for a laptop computer. Having narrowed her choice to a Toshiba, NEC, and AST, she begins to visit computer stores to make a choice. Here, we will look at her experiences with salespeople in the decision process.

▶**FIGURE 18.5**
A model of customer-salesperson communication

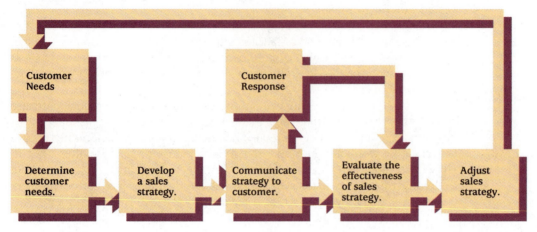

In her first visit, after she cites the three laptops she is interested in, the salesperson says they have only one model in stock (not one of her choices) and tries to generate interest in the store's model. After five minutes of listening politely, she says she is not interested and leaves. In the second store, the salesperson says he has all three makes our consumer is interested in. She asks several questions on options and cites a price limit of $2,000. The salesperson then focuses on the limitations of a laptop in that price range—less storage capacity, lack of a color screen, and so forth. She thanks him for the information and leaves. In both these cases, one-sided word-of-mouth communication occurred from salesperson to customer and discouraged further communication.

In the third store, the salesperson asks her for what purposes she will be using the computer and the features she needs for those purposes. After responding, she cites her concerns about a smaller screen and keyboard compared to those of desktops. The salesperson is now in a position to estimate the customer's needs and, on this basis, to formulate a sales approach. In this case, an interchange is developing between salesperson and customer based on the customer's needs.

Weitz studied salespeople's estimation of a customer's needs and product perceptions compared to the customer's own estimation.[42] The more accurate the salesperson was in estimating the customer's needs for particular product attributes and perceptions of the product, the greater was the likelihood of a sale. This finding confirms a consumer-oriented approach to evaluating sales performance: Sales success can best be predicted by accuracy in defining customer needs rather than by any general characteristics of the salesperson such as personality attributes.

Developing the Sales Strategy

The salesperson's strategy should depend on his or her assessment of customer needs. In our example, the salesperson decides to invite the customer to try several laptops in an in-store demonstration to display the screen and keyboard. During the demonstration, the salesperson points out that the three models the consumer is interested in have the same screen size and keyboards. He then asks what additional criteria are important to her. She states storage capacity on the hard disk, memory, and speed. The salesperson then mentions a particular model that has one-third more storage capacity and memory but a shorter warranty than the three makes being considered. The consumer expresses concern about the shorter warranty and the fact that she knows little about the company producing the suggested model. The salesperson tries to reassure her by citing the near-perfect reliability of the suggested machine and then demonstrates expertise by giving the buyer some data on the laptop's technical performance.

Generally, a salesperson can use one or a combination of four types of strategies to influence the customer:

1. Communicate information on new products (for example, make the consumer aware of new computers with CD ROM capabilities).
2. Attempt to change the importance of existing evaluative criteria (for example, the importance of speed and memory relative to screen size).
3. Attempt to change customer perceptions (for example, the perception that a shorter warranty is a definite disadvantage).
4. Introduce an unknown brand or model to the customer (the model the salesperson introduced as an alternative to the Toshiba, NEC, and AST).

Our salesperson used elements of the last three strategies in his sales approach. The effectiveness of each of these strategies depends on the salesperson's accuracy in estimating customer needs. Attempting to change brand perceptions of an attribute that is relatively unimportant to the customer obviously would be an ineffective strategy. Furthermore, changing customer needs is harder than changing brand perceptions.

Communicating the Sales Strategy

In our example, once our salesperson communicated his sales strategy to the customer, a two-way process of communication took place. He tried to convince her of the capabilities of the suggested model. When the customer expressed misgivings about the warranty, the salesperson reassured her and then communicated particular product specifications on performance.

This two-way flow of communication is characteristic of a problem-solving approach to selling, which is reflected in the model in Figure 18.5. It requires an understanding of customer needs and an attempt to fulfill these needs through two-way communication as shown in Figure 18.6. This figure shows two other possibilities, both representing one-way communication. An order-taking approach involves one-way communication from buyer to seller, as when a shopper orders an item by phone or asks a store clerk for a particular product. The seller's only required response is confirmation of the order. A canned sales approach involves one-way communication from seller to buyer. In this communication, the salesperson does not attempt to identify and meet customer needs but communicates a standard presentation and expects the buyer to act based on this information. The first two salespeople our buyer encountered used such approaches.

As companies have become more customer-oriented, they have shifted from an order-taking and a canned sales approach to more of a problem-solving approach. The main reason for this shift is that product lines have become more varied and complex for both industrial and consumer goods. In consumer goods, automobile, appliance, electronics, and computer dealers have had to become aware of a larger number of models and options available to the customer. As a result, most producers of durables have instituted sales programs to encourage their salespeople to become more knowledgeable of product options and services and to translate this knowledge into satisfying customer needs.

The shift from order taking to problem solving has occurred for more standardized items as well as for durable goods. Willamette Industries' lumber and plywood division, for example, has instituted a customer-oriented approach for a standard line of lumber and plywood products. (See Exhibit 18.2.) In the past, Willamette's salespeople might have used a canned approach to sell the line, but the ad describes a salesperson who is now required to know the market and the customer's needs before formulating a sales approach.

▶**FIGURE 18.6**

Customer-salesperson communications

Source: *Marketing: Principles and Strategy* by Henry Assael, copyright © 1990 by The Dryden Press, reprinted by permission of the publisher.

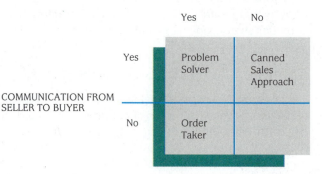

COMMUNICATION FROM BUYER TO SELLER

▶**EXHIBIT 18.2**

An illustration of the shift from an order-taking approach in sales

Source: Courtesy of Willamette Industries Inc.

We don't just take orders.

Evaluating the Sales Approach

The last step in Figure 18.5 is the salesperson's evaluation of the effectiveness of the sales approach. As the salesperson communicates the message, he or she evaluates the effects on the customer and makes adjustments. The salesperson can change his or her evaluation of customer needs, change the message, or alter the style of communicating the message.[43]

In our example, the salesperson knew he was successful in generating the buyer's interest in the suggested model because the buyer asked about price and availability. There was no need to reassess the customer's needs; but in an attempt to influence the consumer further, the salesperson decreased the price by 10 percent. The buyer said she appreciated the salesperson's efforts and wanted more time to make a choice.

When the buyer left the store, she was leaning toward the new model but was not totally convinced. She wanted to ask several friends about the suggested model and to evaluate it by looking at ratings in *Consumer Reports* magazine. She was impressed with the salesperson's candor and expertise and felt he was not trying to push an unwanted product on her. On this basis, the salesperson's approach was effective.

Weitz concluded that the best salesperson was the one who could develop the appropriate change in communication strategy, based on customer needs. This conclusion is reflected in Figure 18.5. Once a salesperson evaluates the effectiveness of his or her sales strategy, he or she makes adjustments based on customer needs. (Thus, the feedback loop from "Adjust sales strategy" to "Determine customer needs.") Once the salesperson makes the adjustment, the interchange between buyer and seller can continue; or the buyer can accept or reject the seller's offerings.

◆ OPINION LEADERSHIP

The influence of word-of-mouth communication in consumer behavior is tied closely to the concept of opinion leadership. As we saw earlier, individuals most likely to influence others through word-of-mouth are opinion leaders; and individuals most likely to be influenced are followers.

Nature of Opinion Leadership

The marketer must answer three questions before directing appeals to opinion leaders or attempting to stimulate positive word-of-mouth communication:

1. Is there a general opinion leader, or is opinion leadership specific to particular product categories?
2. Is opinion leadership really leadership?
3. Is opinion leadership dependent on the purchase situation?

Is There a General Opinion Leader?

Most studies have found that there is no general opinion leader. Instead, opinion leadership is product-specific. That is, an opinion leader for one category is not likely to be influential across unrelated categories. Personal influence in one category carries over only to closely related categories. For example, King and Summers found that opinion leaders for small appliances were also likely to be opinion leaders for large appliances. Similarly, those who were influential for packaged foods were also likely to be influential for household cleansers and detergents.[44] Another study by Myers and Robertson found that opinion leaders for household furnishings were likely to be opinion leaders for household appliances.[45]

Although most studies suggest that a general opinion leader does not exist, three categories of consumers do suggest generalized influence across product categories: influentials, market mavins, and surrogate consumers.

Influentials.   The Roper Organization, a well-known market research firm, has conducted yearly surveys since World War II to identify influentials.[46] Influentials are defined as those individuals who are active in community and public affairs. Specifically, influentials are identified as individuals who take part in three or more of the activities listed in Figure 18.7. On this basis, 10 to 12 percent of American adults are defined as influentials. Figure 18.7 shows the

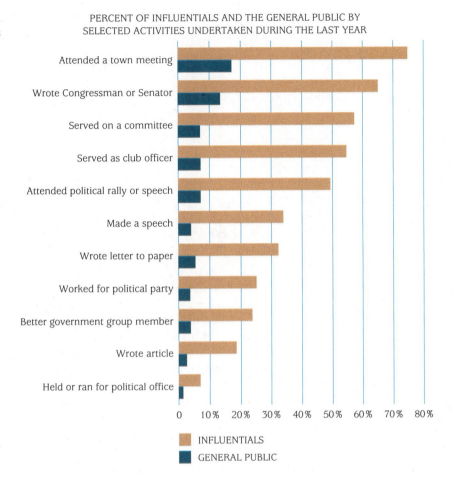

▶**FIGURE 18.7**
Defining the influentials

Source: "The Influentials,"
American Demographics
(October, 1992), p. 32.

PERCENT OF INFLUENTIALS AND THE GENERAL PUBLIC BY
SELECTED ACTIVITIES UNDERTAKEN DURING THE LAST YEAR

proportion of influentials who take part in each of the activities listed compared
to the general population. For example, three-fourths have attended town meet-
ings compared to less than 20 percent of the general population, one-half have
attended a political rally, and one-third have made a speech compared to less
than 10 percent of the general population.

Influentials tend to be upscale, and the majority are baby boomers. Well
educated and well read, they are much more likely to be asked their opinions
about government, handling children, insurance, computers, art, cooking, and
car makes. However, they are less likely to be asked about car problems, hairstyles, and rock music. Their influence tends to be most important for products and services that depend on word-of-mouth recommendations such as
restaurants, books, movies, and financial services.

Influentials also tend to buy new products when they are first marketed. They were among the first to buy a VCR and health foods, and among the first to have started jogging. They will probably be among the first to adopt interactive communications and digital audiotape players. Overall, it is clear that influentials come close to being general opinion leaders. However, as we saw, they are not influential in every product category.

Market Mavens.   Market mavens come closer to being general gatekeepers than opinion leaders. Feick and Price found that a market maven has "information on many kinds of products, places to shop, and other facets of markets, and initiates discussions with consumers and responds to requests from consumers for market information."[47]

Although market mavens are not necessarily opinion leaders, they are more likely to influence as well as to inform. According to Feick and Price, market mavens are good targets for product information—messages about product changes, prices, and new products—because they are likely to pass on this information.

Surrogate Consumers.   A surrogate consumer is "an agent retained by a consumer to guide, direct, and/or transact marketplace activities."[48] Surrogates can play a wide range of roles such as tax consultants, wine stewards, interior decorators, or financial managers. Their degree of influence varies; but in many cases, they are asked to assume the decision role for consumers. As such, they are not general opinion leaders but are clearly opinion leaders in their surrogate role.

Consumers use surrogates because they may not have the time, inclination, or expertise to go through information search and decision making. Consumers may also dislike certain tasks such as shopping and use surrogates to perform them. Also, consumers can use surrogates to narrow their choices, to collect information, or to make the actual purchase decision.

Is Opinion Leadership Really Leadership?

A number of studies have consistently found that individuals who transmit information to others are also more likely to receive information from others. That is, a consumer who frequently expresses opinions about sports equipment will also be more likely to listen to others' opinions about such equipment. A study of the adopters of stainless steel razor blades when they were first introduced found that 75 percent of opinion leaders were also influenced by others.[49] A study of women's influence in four product categories found that 80 percent of the influencers also received information from others.[50]

These findings suggest that the key element in face-to-face influence is not leadership but social communication. Those who are most likely to do the influencing are also most likely to be influenced. Therefore, individuals who transmit information and influence about a product do not have to be group leaders. Opinion leaders do not dominate others or communicate in a one-sided way. Communication occurs both ways between transmitter and receiver. As a result, better terms for the two-way exchange in word-of-mouth communications are opinion giver and receiver, rather than opinion leader and follower.

Is Opinion Leadership Situational?

Consumers do not generally meet and launch into a discussion of product experiences. Product-related conversations occur in a casual setting that generally involves a relevant situational cue, such as the use of the product, to stimulate a product discussion.

Belk did one of the few studies that examined the situations in which word-of-mouth communication is likely to take place.[51] He interviewed women in the Minneapolis-St. Paul area when Maxim coffee was first introduced. Respondents were asked, "How was it that the subject of Maxim happened to come up?" Almost 80 percent of all word-of-mouth communication about Maxim—both received and sent—took place in a situation relevant to food. In over one-third of the situations, drinking Maxim prompted discussion of the product. It is apparent that word-of-mouth communication takes place within a context relevant to the product.

Belk also concluded that a leader-follower role in word-of-mouth communication does not seem to occur. Word-of-mouth communication is more dependent on the situation than on the parties involved. Therefore, product discussion is more likely to be generated by the fact that two people are drinking coffee together than by the fact that one of them can be regarded as more influential than the other.

This finding suggests that the marketer should be concerned with identifying relevant situations that may stimulate product discussion rather than spending time and money trying to identify a group of opinion leaders.

Characteristics of the Opinion Leader

Marketers are interested in identifying opinion leaders, since these consumers may be very influential within a product category. Identification of the demographic characteristics that distinguish opinion leaders from other purchasers in a product category would permit marketers to select media most likely to reach this influential group. In identifying the attitudes or lifestyles of opinion leaders, marketers can develop promotional themes to appeal to this group.

However, reaching opinion leaders with advertising is difficult because they tend to communicate with consumers similar to themselves. Studies have found little difference between the demographic and lifestyle characteristics of opinion leaders and followers.[52] As a result, media to reach opinion leaders have not been identified. In addition, developing a profile of the opinion leader is difficult because such a profile has to be product-specific. The characteristics of the fashion opinion leader may be totally different from those of the food opinion leader. Few generalizations can be made across product categories.

Despite the difficulties of identifying opinion leaders, some general traits have been identified.

Product-Related Characteristics

Opinion leaders have been found to display certain product-related characteristics. They usually are:

- More knowledgeable about the product category.
- More involved in the product category.
- More active in receiving communications about the product from personal sources.
- More likely to read magazines and other print media relevant to their area of product interest.

In addition, opinion leaders consistently have expressed greater interest in new products in the particular product category. A study of personal care appliances such as hair dryers and curlers found that opinion leaders for these categories express a greater willingness to buy new products.[53]

Media Usage

A study of opinion leaders across product categories found that they are more exposed to the mass media. They read more newspapers, magazines, and books, watch more TV news, and listen to more radio news.[54] These findings support the notion in the two-step flow process that opinion leaders are more likely to obtain information from mass media and then transmit it to followers.

Demographic Characteristics

Few generalizations can be made about opinion leaders' demographic characteristics. Katz and Lazarsfeld found that women with more children were more likely to be opinion leaders for household products, possibly because they are likely to buy a wide range of products and, therefore, have a lot of purchasing experience. Also, Katz and Lazarsfeld found that young women in a high socioeconomic bracket were likely to be opinion leaders. They speculated that high-income consumers have more time to obtain product information and have more status in their associations with other consumers.[55] A study of clothing also found that fashion opinion leaders were likely to be younger and upscale.[56] Most marketing studies, however, have found few demographic differences between opinion leaders and followers.

Personality Characteristics

Two generalizations can be made about opinion leaders' personality characteristics across product categories: Opinion leaders are likely to be self-confident in their appraisal of the product category,[57] and they are likely to be more socially active.[58] While their self-confidence is probably a function of greater knowledge of product characteristics and interest in the product, opinion leaders' social activity is probably a function of their willingness to communicate with others in a group setting. Settle, Belch, and Alreck found that opinion leaders are also likely to be somewhat structured in their day-to-day activities.[59] In other respects, personality variables have not discriminated between opinion leaders and followers. Robertson and Myers related a large number of personality variables to opinion leadership for three product categories and concluded that "a marketer trying to reach innovative or influential individuals will find little help by identifying these people in terms of basic personality variables."[60]

Lifestyle Characteristics

Few studies have identified the opinion leaders' lifestyle characteristics. A Canadian study by Tigert and Arnold of opinion leadership across many product categories found that opinion leaders were more involved with clubs and community affairs and were more independent, more price-conscious, and more style-conscious.[61] If these findings are replicated, they may suggest that lifestyle is a more likely basis for identifying opinion leaders than is either personality or demographics.

In summary, there is little evidence overall to suggest that a generalized opinion leader can be described. Furthermore, marketers are unlikely to identify any distinctive demographic or psychographic traits of opinion leaders even on a product-specific basis. As a result, a strategy of trying to pinpoint opinion leaders and reaching them through specific media is likely to fail. These findings do not mean that the study of word-of-mouth communication provides the marketer with few strategic applications. Rather, they suggest that strategic applications are best directed to stimulating word-of-mouth communication through advertising or through some direct identification of opinion leaders.

◆ METHODS TO IDENTIFY OPINION LEADERS

Marketers have used three methods to identify opinion leaders: sociometric technique, key informant method, and self-designating technique.

Sociometric Technique

In the **sociometric technique,** group members are asked with whom they communicate about a product or idea. Specific individuals are identified and can, in turn, be interviewed to trace the network of communication. In his study, Coleman traced word-of-mouth communication between doctors.[62] Figure 18.8 shows the pattern of communication among nine doctors in a community. This network is known as a **sociogram.** Obviously Doctor 5 is an opinion leader since the eight other doctors seek his advice. Doctor 5 also adopted a new drug sooner than the other eight doctors. Doctor 6 appears to be the second most influential person in the network as indicated by the two-way flow of communication between him and Doctor 5 and the fact that two other doctors seek his advice.

▶**FIGURE 18.8**

A sociogram of word-of-mouth communication among doctors

Source: James Coleman, "Social Processes in Physicians' Adoption of a New Drug," *Journal of Chronic Diseases*, 9 (1959), pp. 1-19. Reprinted with permission.

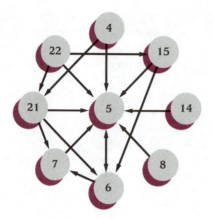

In another marketing study that used the sociometric technique, Arndt asked 332 women in an apartment complex about adoption of a new brand.[63] Women were asked the names of three others from whom they seek advice or who offer advice about new products. Responses then were cross-checked by comparing names that both parties gave.

In both studies cited, members of a particular social group (doctors in a community, residents of an apartment complex, associates in an industry) could be identified and the patterns of communication traced. Marketers can use the sociometric technique only when such a specific social group is being studied. Most brand and product studies involve influence extending beyond a single social group.

Key Informant Method

Key informants in a social group are asked to identify opinion leaders. Key informants are individuals who engage in frequent word-of-mouth communication within a group, but they are not necessarily opinion leaders. Using this technique, key informants would be asked to rate the prestige or leadership of members of their group. The method is limited because it seeks to study only opinion leaders. Furthermore, like sociometric analysis, it is restricted to a particular social group and cannot be used for the large number of marketing studies that require a sample from a population of consumers that includes many diverse groups.

Self-Designating Technique

Marketers most often use the **self-designating technique** because it attempts to identify opinion leaders beyond a single social group. As the name implies, this technique asks consumers a series of questions to determine the degree to which they perceive themselves as opinion leaders. The questions usually pertain to a particular product category and ask consumers to rate themselves on the following characteristics:[64]

- Whether they are more or less likely to be asked advice about the product compared to their friends.
- Whether they are more likely to tell their friends about the product, or whether their friends are more likely to tell them.
- Whether friends and neighbors regard them as a good source of advice about the product.

On the basis of answers to these questions, the researcher develops a single score to permit categorization of the individual as an opinion leader, a follower, or some middle category.

Most of the marketing studies cited in this chapter have used the self-designating technique. These studies are surveys of brand and product influence that extend beyond a single social group; therefore, a self-designating method is necessary.

◆ STRATEGIC APPLICATIONS OF WORD-OF-MOUTH COMMUNICATION

Marketers try to influence word-of-mouth communication among consumers in various ways. They can try to:

1. Stimulate word-of-mouth communication through free product trials.
2. Stimulate word-of-mouth communication in advertising by suggesting that consumers tell friends about the product or service.
3. Simulate word-of-mouth communication through advertising showing typical consumers saying positive things about the product.
4. Portray communications from opinion leaders.

In this section, we consider each of these strategies.

Stimulating Word-of-Mouth Communication Through Product Trial

Companies can try to stimulate word-of-mouth communication by offering products for trial. Such strategies are generally targeted to opinion leaders. If successful, product trial should stimulate a social multiplier effect, since these individuals would disseminate information and exert a disproportionate amount of influence on friends and relatives.

When Chrysler introduced its luxury LH models in 1992, Chrysler dealers in 25 areas of the country offered the cars for a test drive over a weekend to influential community leaders and businesspeople. From October 1992 to January 1993, more than 6,000 individuals took Chrysler up on the offer. A subsequent survey found strong evidence of a social multiplier effect since Chrysler estimates approximately 32,000 people were involved in the test drive when one includes secondary drivers and passengers. The survey also found that 98 percent of respondents said they would recommend the car to a friend. The promotion was so successful that Chrysler then placed the cars at 19 luxury resorts for free use by guests.[65]

How can marketers identify such opinion leaders? Two approaches have frequently been used. First, because of the close relationship between opinion leadership and new product adoption, it is possible to identify consumers who are among the first to adopt a new appliance or other product with a purchase record and assume that these individuals are opinion leaders. A second approach is to identify influentials in a community based on the activities identified by the Roper Organization in Figure 18.7. Presumably, this is the method Chrysler used.

Another example of influencing opinion leaders through product trial was an attempt to transform unknown pop records into hits in several cities. Opinion leaders in high school were identified such as class presidents, class secretaries, sports captains, and cheerleaders.[66] These individuals were invited to join a panel to evaluate rock records. Panel members were told they would receive free records in appreciation for their participation and were encouraged to discuss their choice with friends. Several of the records provided to the group reached the top ten in the trial cities without making the top ten in other cities largely on the strength of the word-of-mouth the opinion leaders generated.

Stimulating Word-of-Mouth Communication Through Advertising

Advertisers can try to encourage consumers to talk about the product. One approach is to encourage consumers to "tell your friends" or to "ask your friends." The Acme Supermarket Chain advertises, "Tell a friend. Save at Acme." Commercials for Fabergé Organics shampoo urged users to tell two friends so they will tell two friends and so on as the faces on the screen multiply to show the spread of word-of-mouth.[67] For such strategies to work, the product must be in a strong position and word-of-mouth communication must be positive. Another approach is to organize social situations in which consumers will communicate about products. The sale of Tupperware through parties is an example of capitalizing on consumers' desire to communicate about products.

Simulating Word-of-Mouth Communication

By portraying recommendations from typical consumers, advertising can simulate word-of-mouth communication. In portraying personal influence, these ads seek to simulate direct contact by consumers with friends and relatives. The assumption is that the typical person in the ad is credible enough to convince consumers to believe the information this individual provides.

General Motors built its first advertising campaign for Saturn cars around word-of-mouth communication. When it introduced Saturn in 1991, GM received unsolicited letters from satisfied customers. These letters were then routed to the company's advertising agency and used in print ads. An example, showing one such customer, is in Exhibit 18.3. Saturn's president provided the rational for simulating word-of-mouth as follows: "We want the actual owners to tell their stories...The ads are just like listening to other people, like your neighbors, tell you about their new car."[68]

TV commercials have also attempted to simulate word-of-mouth. The most frequent approach is the "slice of life" in which a real-life situation is portrayed. For example, one consumer tells another about the virtues of a brand of coffee while making it. Another approach is the hidden camera showing people in TV commercials making unsolicited recommendations for the product. A campaign for toilet tissue used an unsolicited recommendation for the product by the husband. The wife is then shown the videotape and is amazed the husband is aware of the brand differences. For such ads to succeed, consumers must believe the testimonial is spontaneous.

Portraying Communications from Opinion Leaders

A strategy that is related to simulating word-of-mouth is to portray communications from opinion leaders that influence followers. The Advil ad in Exhibit 18.4 shows two opinion leaders for pharmaceuticals, a doctor and a pharmacist, expressing their approval for the product.

▶**EXHIBIT 18.3**
Saturn simulates word-of-mouth by portraying actual consumers

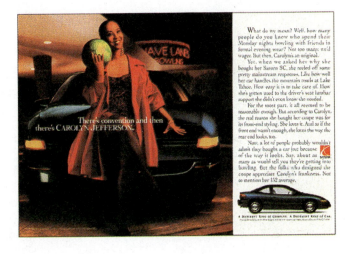

Companies will occasionally attempt to discourage and discredit certain types of word-of-mouth communication. Schering has used advertising to encourage consumers to rely on pharmacists, rather than on friends or neighbors, for information about medication. By depicting inaccurate sources of information, Schering's ad in Exhibit 18.4 attempts to discredit nonexpert medical advice.

◆ SOCIETAL IMPLICATIONS OF WORD-OF-MOUTH COMMUNICATIONS

The primary societal concerns regarding word-of-mouth influence relate to unethical sales practices. The vast majority of salespeople conduct themselves in a responsible manner, especially in light of today's greater emphasis on a problem-solving approach.

The greatest problems in selling occur with door-to-door and telephone sales. Although companies such as Avon and Mary Kay have established sound reputations based on a professional door-to-door staff, other companies have abused door-to-door selling. In one disturbing example, agents of the American National Insurance Company were found to have scanned Los Angeles newspapers for articles that chronicled bloody gang violence in low-income neighborhoods. They would then travel to the neighborhood, knock on doors, and wave the articles in front of residents as they tried to sell $10,000 policies as hedges against the possibility of violence.[69]

Telephone sales practices are also prone to unethical behavior. In one approach, customers are led to believe they have won prizes only to be told of various conditions involved requiring the purchase of products. In another, callers claim to be conducting a survey but then attempt to induce customers to buy products. Such practices undermine legitimate sales and marketing research efforts by phone.

Government has restricted powers in attempting to protect consumer rights against abusive sales practices. Most of the abuses are in the grey area of questionable persuasion rather than outright fraud. If fraud has occurred, consumers have recourse in the courts. However, as we saw, few consumers avail themselves of their right to complain to the manufacturer, let alone take the company to court.

In general, consumers must rely on a company's ability to regulate itself. Fortunately, companies have become more sensitive to the need to maintain high standards in selling. The greater complexity of many products, the greater amount of information available to salespeople, and a greater focus on meeting customer needs have encouraged a problem-solving approach that creates higher standards of personal selling.

SUMMARY

Word-of-mouth communication among consumers is the most important source of information and influence in consumer behavior. Individuals who influence the purchasing behavior of other consumers are the opinion leaders; the consumers being influenced are the followers.

Several studies have documented the greater importance of word-of-mouth communication compared to commercial information sources. Word-of-mouth influence is more likely to be important when the product is visible, distinctive, and important to the group's belief system and when consumers are involved with the purchase decision and see it as risky.

The process of word-of-mouth communication can best be described as a transmission of information between opinion leaders and followers. The mass media often serve as the source of information, with gatekeepers (those most sensitive to product information) serving as intermediaries in the information flow. Marketers try to encourage positive word-of-mouth communications, but negative word-of-mouth may occur; and it tends to be a more powerful influence on consumers than positive word-of-mouth.

Word-of-mouth also occurs between customers and salespeople. Two-way communications between buyer and seller assume a problem-solving approach in which the salesperson tries to assess customer needs and help customers meet these needs. An alternative is an order-taking approach in which salespeople just fill orders or a canned approach in which they communicate through a standardized presentation.

A model of customer-salesperson interactions demonstrated the communication process by which the salesperson evaluates customer needs, develops a sales strategy to meet those needs, communicates the sales strategy, and evaluates the sales strategy's effectiveness. An important aspect of the model is the salesperson's ability to adjust sales strategies to better meet customer needs based on two-way communications.

The influence of word-of-mouth communication is tied closely to the concept of opinion leadership. Opinion leaders are likely to exert influence for specific product categories rather than on a general basis. Furthermore, opinion leaders are likely to both transmit and receive information to and from others. The transmission of influence through word-of-mouth is most likely to occur in specific situational and social settings. Several methods to identify opinion leaders were described, including the sociometric technique, key informant method, and self-designating technique.

Marketers have several strategic options in trying to encourage positive word-of-mouth communications about their product. They can (1) stimulate word-of-mouth through product trial, generally targeting opinion leaders, (2) stimulate word-of-mouth through advertising by encouraging consumers to transmit positive experiences with the product, (3) simulate word-of-mouth by portraying communications from typical consumers, and (4) portray communications from opinion leaders to followers.

The chapter concluded by considering the societal implications of word-of-mouth communications regarding unethical sales strategies.

In the next chapter, we consider how communications spread ideas and products across groups through a process of diffusion.

QUESTIONS

1. What were the conditions that made it possible for Corona beer to be successful based on word-of-mouth alone? What are the limitations of relying solely on word-of-mouth communications to market a product on a national basis?

2. It was stated that word-of-mouth communication is the most important influence on consumer behavior. Why? Under what circumstances are other types of communication (advertising, personal selling, information from government sources) likely to be more influential than word-of-mouth?

3. Two of the major studies documenting the importance of word-of-mouth communication—Whyte's study of air conditioner ownership and Katz and Lazarsfeld's study of influence in a Midwestern town—were conducted before the advent of television. Some have argued that TV provides a basis for simulating word-of-mouth communication and, thereby, reduces the importance of word-of-mouth influence.
   - Do you agree?
   - Is it possible that TV is a more important force than word-of-mouth influence for certain groups (for example, children)?

4. What are the likely roles of the three types of word-of-mouth communication—product news, product experiences, and advice—in the consumer's decision process?

5. What are the limitations of the two-step flow model of word-of-mouth communications? What evidence supports the multistep model of communications in Figure 18.1?

6. Assume you are studying group influence in the purchase of men's cosmetics and fragrances. You hypothesize that the group members are likely to be socially independent, dependent, integrated, or isolated consumers depending on their degree of opinion leadership and communication. (See Figure 18.2.)
   • To test your hypothesis, what questions would you ask consumers?
   • Assume these four groups could be identified. What would be the strategic implications for the marketing of men's cosmetics and fragrances?

7. Why is negative word-of-mouth communication likely to be a more potent influence on consumer behavior than positive word-of-mouth?

8. Why is it more likely that rumors would arise about heavily advertised products in Poland than in the United States?

9. Weitz's study, cited in the text, suggests that salespeople can develop four strategies to influence customers. They can:
   a. Introduce a new product or product attributes.
   b. Attempt to change the priority of customer needs.
   c. Attempt to change brand perceptions.
   d. Introduce a new brand.
   Under what circumstances is each strategy likely to be effective?

10. What are the limitations of the concept of opinion leadership?

11. Studies suggest that the situation is more important than the opinion leader's role in generating word-of-mouth communication. If this is true, what would be the implications for using advertising to attempt to generate word-of-mouth communication?

12. Marketing studies have not identified any distinctive characteristics of opinion leaders. Since it is so difficult to identify opinion leaders, can the concept of opinion leadership be used in developing marketing strategies? If so, in what ways?

13. A manufacturer of designer jeans believes that word-of-mouth communication is a key element in the successful marketing of its brand and would like to document this fact by studying the nature of word-of-mouth communication within groups.
   • Develop a study design to trace word-of-mouth influence in the purchase of designer jeans.
   • What measurement technique would you use and why?

14. Would you recommend a sociometric technique to measure opinion leadership in evaluating patterns of influence in the (a) adoption of a new product in a retirement community, and (b) purchase of a new line of high-styled jeans? Why or why not?

15. What is the distinction between a marketing strategy of stimulating versus simulating word-of-mouth communication?

RESEARCH ASSIGNMENTS

1. Use a sociometric technique to trace conversations among a group of eight or nine teenagers or college students regarding opinions of rock albums. Make sure the people you interview know each other. Try to develop a network to show who talks to whom. Ask these individuals to rate themselves on opinion leadership.

- Do the sociometric and self-designating techniques agree regarding the identity of opinion leaders?
- Ask the sample to rate themselves on their (a) interest in albums, (b) self-confidence in buying and evaluating albums, and (c) level of social activity compared to that of friends and acquaintances.
- Opinion leaders would be expected to score high on these three criteria. Do your findings confirm this hypothesis?

2. Select about five or six diverse product categories such as jeans, casual wear, compact discs or tapes, stereo equipment, books for leisure reading, camera equipment, and so on. Make sure some of the products are interrelated (for example, compact discs or tapes and stereo equipment; jeans and casual wear). Ask a sample of 20 to 30 respondents to rate themselves on opinion leadership for each category. In addition, ask them to rate themselves on a lifestyle inventory (select items from Table 11.1) and to determine their demographic characteristics.

- Is there a general opinion leader who rates high on opinion leadership on most categories? If so, does the general opinion leader differ from others on demographic and lifestyle characteristics?
- Do consumers who rate high on one product also rate high on a related product category? (That is, do those who rate high on jeans also rate high on casual wear?) What are the demographic and lifestyle characteristics of the product-specific opinion leaders?
- What are the marketing implications of defining the demographic and lifestyle characteristics of the general opinion leader (if there is one)? Of the product-specific opinion leader?

NOTES

1. "Ole," *Marketing & Media Decisions* (June, 1987), pp. 95–98.

2. "Reaching Moneyed Markets," *The New York Times* (August 18, 1981), p. D19.

3. *Ibid.;* and "The Shifting Power of Influentials in Purchase Decisions," *Ad Forum* (July, 1983), p. 55.

4. Elihu Katz and Paul F. Lazarsfeld, *Personal Influence* (Glencoe, IL: The Free Press, 1955).

5. William H. Whyte, Jr., "The Web of Word of Mouth," *Fortune* (November, 1954), pp. 140–143.

6. *Ad Forum* (July, 1983), *loc. cit.*

7. Johan Arndt, "Role of Product-Related Conversations in the Diffusion of a New Product," *Journal of Marketing Research*, 4 (August, 1967), pp. 291–295.

8. James E. Engel, Roger D. Blackwell, and Robert J. Kegerreis, "How Information Is Used to Adopt an Innovation," *Journal of Advertising Research*, 9 (December, 1969), pp. 3–8.

9. Paul M. Herr, Frank R. Kardes, and John Kim, "Effects of Word-of-Mouth and Product-Attribute Information on Persuasion: An Accessibility-Diagnosticity Perspective," *Journal of Consumer Research*, 17 (March, 1991), pp. 454–462.

10. Marsha L. Richins and Teri Root-Shaffer, "The Role of Involvement and Opinion Leadership in Consumer Word-of-Mouth: An Implicit Model Made Explicit," in Michael J. Houston, ed., *Advances in Consumer Research*, Vol. 15 (Provo, UT: Association for Consumer Research, 1987), pp. 32–36.

11. Katz and Lazarsfeld, *Personal Influence, loc. cit.*

12. *Ibid.*, pp. 309–312.

13. R. A. Bauer, "The Obstinate Audience," *American Psychologist*, 19 (May, 1964), pp. 319–328.

14. Katz and Lazarsfeld, *Personal Influence, op. cit.*, pp. 118–119.

15. Lawrence Feick and Linda Price, "The Market Maven: A Diffuser of Marketplace Information," *Journal of Marketing*, 51 (January, 1987), pp. 83–87.

16. Richard R. Still, James H. Barnes, Jr., and Mark E. Kooyman, "Word-of-Mouth Communication in Low-Risk Product Decisions," *International Journal of Advertising*, 3 (1984), pp. 335–345.

17. Fred D. Reynolds and William R. Darden, "Mutually Adaptive Effects of Interpersonal Communication," *Journal of Marketing Research*, 8 (November, 1971), pp. 449–454.

18. Marsha L. Richins, "Negative Word-of-Mouth by Dissatisfied Consumers: A Pilot Study," *Journal of Marketing*, 47 (Winter, 1983), pp. 68–78.

19. Richard W. Mizerski, "An Attribution Explanation of the Disproportionate Influence of Unfavorable Information," *Journal of Consumer Research*, 9 (December, 1982), pp. 301–310.

20. "Status Shifts to Peer Influence," *Advertising Age* (May 17, 1984), p. M10.

21. Jagdip Singh, "A Typology of Consumer Dissatisfaction Response Styles," *Journal of Retailing*, 66 (Spring, 1990), pp. 57–99.

22. Betty J. Deiner and Stephen A. Greyser, "Consumer View of Redress Needs," *Journal of Marketing*, 42 (October, 1978), p. 23.

23. A. Best and Alan Andreasen, "Consumer Responses to Unsatisfactory Purchases: A Survey of Perceiving Defects, Voicing Complaints and Obtaining Redress," *Law and Society Review*, 11 (Spring, 1977), pp. 701–742.

24. "P&G Drops Logo; Cites Satan Rumors," *The New York Times* (April 25, 1985), p. D1.

25. "P&G Once Again Has Devil of a Time with Rumors About Moon, Stars Logo," *The Wall Street Journal* (March 26, 1990), p. B3.

26. Alice M. Tybout, Bobby J. Calder, and Brian Sternthal, "Using Information Processing Theory to Design Marketing Strategies," *Journal of Marketing Research*, 18 (February, 1981), p. 74.

27. *Ibid.*

28. *Ibid.*, pp. 73–74.

29. "Bubble Gum Maker Wants to Know How the Rumors Started," *The Wall Street Journal* (March 24, 1977), p. 1.

30. "A Puzzlement over a Bakery Rumor," *The New York Times* (September 10, 1981), p. A16.

31. "Rumor Turns Fantasy into Bad Dream," *The Wall Street Journal* (May 19, 1991), pp. B1, B5.

32. "Entenmann's Fights Moonie Link," *Advertising Age* (November 23, 1981), p. 33.

33. *The Wall Street Journal* (May 19, 1991), *loc. cit.*

34. Herr, Kardes, and Kim, "Effects of Word-of-Mouth . . . ," *loc. cit.*

35. Richins and Root-Shaffer, "The Role of Involvement and Opinion Leadership . . . ," *loc. cit.*

36. Scott M. Cunningham, "Perceived Risk as a Factor in the Diffusion of New Product Information," in Raymond M. Haas, ed., *Proceedings of the American Marketing Association Fall Conference*, Series No. 28 (1966), pp. 698–721.

37. Arch G. Woodside and M. Wayne DeLozier, "Effects of Word-of-Mouth Advertising on Consumer Risk-Taking," *Journal of Advertising*, 5 (Fall, 1976), pp. 12–19.

38. Katz and Lazarsfeld, *Personal Influence, op. cit.*, Chapter 10.

39. John O. Summers, "New Product Interpersonal Communications," in Fred C. Allvine, ed., *Combined Proceedings of the American Marketing Association*, Series No. 33 (1971), p. 430.

40. Ernest Dichter, "How Word-of-Mouth Advertising Works," *Harvard Business Review,* 44 (November-December, 1966), pp. 148–152.

41. *Ad Forum* (July, 1983), *loc. cit.*

42. Barton A. Weitz, "The Relationship Between Salesperson Performance and Understanding of Customer Decision Making," *Journal of Marketing Research,* 15 (November, 1978), pp. 501–516.

43. *Ibid.*

44. Charles W. King and John O. Summers, "Overlap of Opinion Leadership Across Consumer Product Categories," *Journal of Marketing Research,* 7 (February, 1970), pp. 43–50.

45. James H. Myers and Thomas S. Robertson, "Dimensions of Opinion Leadership," *Journal of Marketing Research,* 9 (February, 1972), pp. 41–46.

46. "The Influentials," *American Demographics* (October, 1992), pp. 30–38.

47. Lawrence F. Feick and Linda L. Price, "The Market Maven . . . ," *loc. cit.*

48. Michael R. Solomon, "The Missing Link: Surrogate Consumers in the Marketing Chain," *Journal of Marketing,* 50 (October, 1986), pp. 208–218.

49. Jagdish N. Sheth, "Word-of-Mouth in Low-Risk Innovations," *Journal of Advertising Research,* 11 (June, 1971), pp. 15–18.

50. Summers and King, "New Product Interpersonal Communication . . . ," *loc. cit.*

51. Russell W. Belk, "Occurrence of Word-of-Mouth Buyer Behavior as a Function of Situation and Advertising Stimuli," in Fred C. Allvine, ed., *Combined Proceedings of the American Marketing Association,* Series No. 33 (1971), pp. 419–422.

52. Katz and Lazarsfeld, *Personal Influence, loc. cit.;* and Myers and Robertson, "Dimensions of Opinion Leadership," *loc. cit.*

53. Proprietary study by a large appliance manufacturer.

54. "The Influentials," *Research Alert* (December 2, 1988), p. 1; and Rogin A. Higie, Lawrence F. Feick, and Linda L. Price, "Types and Amount of Word-of-Mouth Communications About Retailers," *Journal of Retailing,* 63 (Fall, 1987), pp. 260–277.

55. Katz and Lazarsfeld, *Personal Influence, op. cit.,* Chapter 10.

56. John O. Summers, "The Identity of Women's Clothing Fashion Opinion Leaders," *Journal of Marketing Research,* 7 (May, 1970), pp. 178–185.

57. Reynolds and Darden, "Mutually Adaptive Effects," *loc. cit.;* Summers, "The Identity of Women's Clothing Fashion Opinion Leaders," *Ibid.*

58. Reynolds and Darden, "Mutually Adaptive Effects," *loc. cit.;* Summers, "The Identity of Women's Clothing Fashion Opinion Leaders," *loc. cit.;* and Still, Barnes, and Kooyman, "Word-of-Mouth Communication . . . ," *op. cit.,* p. 341.

59. Robert B. Settle, Michael A. Belch, and Pamela L. Alreck, "Temporic Effects on Opinion Leadership, Brand Loyalty and Perceived Risk," in Kenneth Bernhardt et al., eds., *Proceedings of the American Marketing Association Educators' Conference,* Series No. 47 (1981), pp. 221–224.

60. Thomas S. Robertson and James H. Myers, "Personality Correlates of Opinion Leadership and Innovative Buying Behavior," *Journal of Marketing Research,* 6 (May, 1969), p. 168.

61. Douglas J. Tigert and Stephen J. Arnold, *Profiling Self-Designated Opinion Leaders and Self-Designated Innovators Through Life Style Research* (Toronto: School of Business, University of Toronto, 1971).

62. James Coleman, "Social Processes in Physicians' Adoption of a New Drug," *Journal of Chronic Diseases,* 9 (1959), pp. 1–9.

63. Arndt, "Role of Product-Related Conversations . . . ," *loc. cit.*

64. Everett M. Rogers and F. Floyd Shoemaker, *Communication in Innovations* (New York: Free Press, 1971).

65. "Put People Behind Wheel," *Advertising Age* (March 22, 1993), p. S28.

66. Joseph R. Mancuso, "Why Not Create Opinion Leaders for New Product Introductions?" *Journal of Marketing,* 33 (July, 1969), pp. 20–25.

67. *Ad Forum* (July, 1983), *loc. cit.*

68. "Marketer of the Year: Donald Hudler," *Brandweek* (November 16, 1992), p. 21.

69. "Bang!Bang! Selling Life Insurance When Bullets Fly," *National Underwriter* (October 22, 1990), p. 14.

19

The Diffusion of Innovations

POST-IT NOTES: AN EXAMPLE OF DIFFUSION

Two streams of research have focused on personal influence and communications. The first has been on communication within groups, which we considered in the previous chapter. The second deals with communication across groups through the diffusion of information and influence over a wider segment of society. Research on word-of-mouth communication and opinion leadership views communications on a *micro* level since communications are among a small number of individuals. In contrast, research on the process of diffusion views communications on a *macro* level since communications and product ownership are traced across a large number of individuals over time.

From the marketer's standpoint, the most relevant area of study is the diffusion of new products, particularly those that can be classified as innovations. The process of diffusion is shown in the American consumers' acceptance of VCRs and their rejection of videodiscs.

Video-cassette recorders won quick acceptance because they provided an important benefit, recording capability. Furthermore, consumers could observe VCRs in use; and VCRs were compatible with frequent TV viewing. Diffusion theory would predict that innovations with these characteristics would be successful. Although videodiscs were observable and compatible with current TV usage, they did not produce any obvious benefit compared to VCRs because of their lack of recording capabilities. As a result, RCA lost hundreds of millions of dollars when its videodisc entry, SelectaVision, failed.

The VCR was a major innovation because it changed people's behavior in a significant way by creating a new dimension in in-home entertainment. Less significant innovations are also subject to a process of diffusion. 3M's Post-it Notes is an example. A 3M scientist who was experimenting with adhesives accidentally discovered the product. He unintentionally put an adhesive on the back of notepaper and found he could easily stick the paper to surfaces and remove it. Others at 3M saw the potential for a new product as a replacement for loose paper, paper clips, and notepads. (See Exhibit 19.1.) 3M test marketed the product in Boise, Idaho, where it mailed free samples to every office in the city. Because the samples were free, many employees took the product home, and other family members began asking for it.[1] The diffusion process took over as usage spread from one group to another.

▶**EXHIBIT 19.1**
Post-it Notes: A product that encouraged rapid diffusion

Source: Courtesy of Minnesota Mining and Manufacturing Co.

The quick diffusion of Post-it Notes throughout America is due to the same characteristics that won quick acceptance for VCRs—an obvious product benefit, observability in use, and compatibility since it conforms to consumers' usage habits of writing and attaching notes. Another factor that spurred product diffusion was Post-it Notes' amenability to trial through free samples. Without heavy sampling by 3M through direct-mail giveaways, adoption and diffusion probably would have taken much longer.

This chapter describes the process of diffusion—how new products are adopted, how quickly adoption takes place, and how information and influence are communicated to other groups. Consumers are categorized according to the time they take to adopt new products. These categories—innovators, early adopters, the majority, and laggards—are described, with particular emphasis on early adopters. The chapter concludes with a consideration of the strategic applications of diffusion research and a description of methods to identify adopter categories.

◆ IMPORTANCE OF NEW PRODUCTS

Most research on diffusion has been concerned with the spread of new products, particularly innovations, across markets. The adoption of new products is a critical question to marketers because new product success is linked to profitability. Companies such as 3M and Johnson & Johnson have a policy of ensuring that at least one-fourth of company sales should come from products introduced during the previous five years.[2] In areas with rapid technological change such as computers and consumer electronics, the majority of sales are likely to come from products introduced in the last two or three years.

Overall, new products are more likely to fail than to succeed. On average, only one out of five products that a company develops and tests is successful. That represents a failure rate of about 80 percent.[3] Therefore, when we talk about the diffusion of new products, we must remember that the majority of products are not adopted by consumers and diffused across groups.

Why is corporate America willing to incur the tremendous costs of new product failures? Because it has little choice. Unless companies are successful in introducing new products over time, they will not be able to remain competitive. Quaker ran into trouble in the 1970s because it chose to pursue an acquisition strategy at the expense of new product development. In the process, the company lost market share for its mainstay grocery products. Until recently, Campbell Soup was in trouble because its new product successes, Le Menu frozen foods and Prego spaghetti sauce, have not balanced a string of product failures.

Profitability and the Product Life Cycle

The link between new products and profitability is shown in the product life cycle, depicted in Figure 19.1. New products go through stages of introduction,

The product life cycle

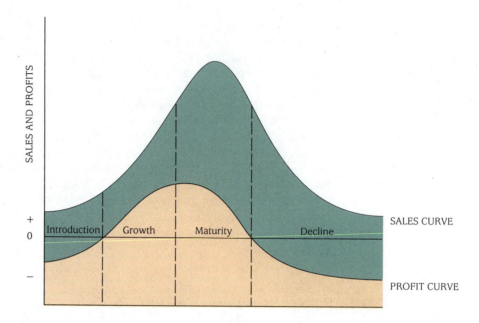

growth, maturity, and decline. As the sales and profit curves in Figure 19.1 show, profits begin to decline before sales reach their peak because competition becomes more intense. As a result, prices decrease, while promotional costs increase. Forward-looking firms must ensure that new products are introduced while the firms' current offerings are still in the growth stage. In this way, the firms' profits are maintained rather than going through cycles, and their profit positions are not overly sensitive to the life cycle of one or several products. In other words, firms try to ensure that they are not dependent on mature product lines only.

The link between new products and profitability depends on the successful diffusion of new products. Therefore, an understanding of the process of diffusion is critical.

Diffusion Research and Marketing Strategy

Diffusion research traces the spread of product acceptance and, therefore, reflects the product life cycle. It attempts to identify innovators in the introductory period of the life cycle, early adopters during growth, and later adopters during maturity and decline. These phases of adoption are important because they are linked to different marketing strategies during the product life cycle. In the introductory phase, the firm tries to establish distribution, build brand awareness, and encourage trial to begin the diffusion process. As the product takes hold, the firm can define its primary target, the early adopters. It is now trying to reinforce the toehold it has in the market by moving from an objective of creating awareness to one of broadening product appeals and product availability.

As the brand matures, competition intensifies and sales begin to level off. The firm starts to emphasize price appeals and sales promotions and begins to consider some product modifications to gain a competitive advantage. At this stage, later adopters enter the market, based largely on the influence of earlier adopters. Since others have already gone through an adoption process, later adopters do not need to rely as much on the mass media for information.

Because diffusion research traces the rate of acceptance of new products and identifies adopter categories by stages in the product's life cycle, it is directly tied to these strategic shifts.

◆ WHAT IS AN INNOVATION?

Because of the focus on the adoption of innovations, it would be relevant to ask: "What is an innovation?" **Innovations** can be technological advances that create new or improved products, or they can be symbolic representations that change the meaning of products.

Technological Innovations

Robertson defined three types of innovations based on the degree to which they represent technological advances and changes in consumer behavior:[4]

1. A **discontinuous innovation** is a major technological advance involving the establishment of a new product and new behavior patterns. Examples are the past introduction of automobiles, television, and air conditioners and the more recent introduction of personal computers, fax machines, and cellular telephones.
2. A **dynamically continuous innovation** is a new product representing major technological advances that do not basically change existing consumer behavior patterns. Examples are electric toothbrushes, color copiers, touch-tone telephones, and compact disc players.
3. A **continuous innovation** is a minor technological advance that results in an extension or modification of existing products. Examples are self-focusing cameras, liquid soap dispensers, gel toothpaste, and nonalcoholic beer.

Exhibit 19.2 shows ads for each type of innovation. Oki's pocket-sized cellular telephone is a discontinuous innovation because it allows walk-around portability in telecommunications. As such, it is a major technological advance that is likely to change behavior patterns based on the consumers' ability to carry a telephone around. Hewlett Packard's color copier is a dynamically continuous innovation because it is extending the existing technology of copying

▶**EXHIBIT 19.2**

Ads representing three types of technological innovations

Source: (top left) Courtesy of OKI telecom; (top right) Courtesy of Hewlett-Packard Co.; (bottom) Courtesy of Sony Electronics Inc.

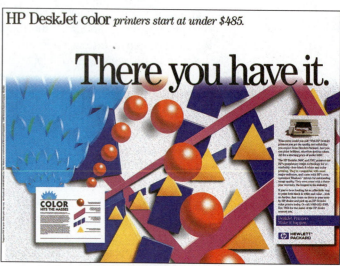

Dynamically continuous innovation

Discontinuous innovation

Continuous innovation

machines. However, it is unlikely to change existing patterns of usage. Sony's Handycam Pro camcorder is a continuous innovation because its clear image freeze-frame capability and small size represents an improvement over existing camcorders.

Most marketing studies do not deal with discontinuous innovations but with more limited, continuous innovations because such innovations are more frequent. Patterns of diffusion for continuous innovations are not as striking and well defined as are those for discontinuous innovations. For example, consumers did not talk about electric toothbrushes as widely as air conditioners, nor was the pattern of personal influence as marked.

Symbolic Innovations

Hirschman defines a symbolic innovation as one that conveys new social meaning.[5] Designer jeans were a symbolic innovation because they made purchasers view jeans in a new, fashion-oriented context. Similarly, the introduction of skin care products for men and life insurance designed specifically for women can be considered symbolic innovations because they gave each product category new social meaning. When Lee targeted jeans to women, it created a symbolic innovation by changing the meaning of the product category from a traditional male-oriented product to one that could fit the lifestyle of younger women. (See Exhibit 19.3.)

▶**EXHIBIT 19.3**
A symbolic innovation: Jeans targeted to women

Our jeans fit your genes.

Lee Relaxed Rider™ jeans are designed to fit the natural curves of a woman's body. But most importantly, they're designed to fit the natural curves of a woman's life. Dress them up. Or dress them down. Nobody fits your body...or the way you live... better than Lee.

R E L A X E D · R I D E R™

Lee
The brand that fits.

Some innovations can be both symbolic and technological. For example, the video-cassette recorder is a discontinuous technological innovation with symbolic meaning since it has changed social patterns by encouraging more in-home entertainment. Most symbolic innovations are continuous and represent little technological change. For example, fashion-oriented innovations are tied to a rapid product life cycle of adoption, diffusion, and subsequent replacement. Consumers can more easily comprehend these innovations and, therefore, are more likely to adopt them quickly.

◆ DIFFUSION PROCESS

Diffusion is the process by which the *adoption* of an innovation is spread *over time* to members of a *target market* by *communication*. Suppose a consumer buys a compact disc player soon after it is introduced. Through word-of-mouth, the consumer tells friends and relatives that the disc player provides finer sound and is easier to use than a record player. Others in the consumer's reference group buy. These individuals are regarded as early adopters. Over time, they begin to communicate positive experiences with disc players not only to members of their reference group, but also to other groups as well—casual acquaintances, sports clubs, and business associates with whom they have infrequent contact. At this point, diffusion begins to spread rapidly. The characteristics of these later adopters differ from those of earlier adopters, which means that the target for CDs differed in the earlier stages of adoption than it does now.

Based on this description, an understanding of the diffusion process in marketing requires an understanding of (1) the nature of *adoption,* (2) the element of *time,* (3) the *target market,* and (4) *communication* within and across groups. Most of the rest of this chapter is devoted to the four elements of diffusion.

Adoption Decision

The adoption of an innovation requires an individual or a group of consumers to make a decision regarding a new product. If adopters influence others to buy, both within their reference group and across groups, a diffusion process starts. Therefore, it is logical to think of adoption as the first step in the diffusion process.

The adoption of an innovation is likely to be an involving decision. The steps of the adoption process are shown on the left in Figure 19.2 and reflect a high involvement hierarchy of effects. These steps parallel those in the process of complex decision making shown on the right in Figure 19-2. The consumer recognizes a need for the product (awareness), searches for information (knowledge acquisition), evaluates the alternatives, makes a decision whether to adopt or not, and evaluates the product after the purchase. One element in the adoption decision makes it distinct from complex decision making: the importance of product trial. Product trial is likely to be more important because the product is new and risk is likely to be higher.

We will review each of the phases in the adoption decision in Figure 19.2:

1. *Awareness.* Consumers receive information from the mass media or through word-of-mouth that creates awareness of the product. The ads for a cellular telephone, a color copier, and the Sony camcorder in Exhibit 19.2 are all designed to make consumers aware of these innovations.

2. *Knowledge.* At this point, consumers are aware of the product but have not made a judgment about whether it will fulfill a need. As a result, consumers will collect information on price, product features, performance, service, and availability.

3. *Evaluation.* Using this information, consumers will evaluate the innovation more closely on a range of factors such as price, product features, frequency of use, and substitutability for existing products. On this basis, consumers will form a favorable or unfavorable attitude toward it. If consumers

▶**FIGURE 19.2**
Steps in the adoption process

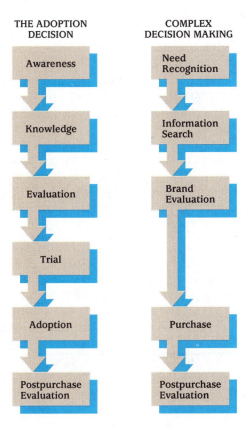

form a favorable attitude toward the product, they may decide to try it. For example, a consumer evaluating a cellular telephone might have concluded that the unit is not worth the price just to gain the benefit of taking a phone anywhere. In this case, the consumer has rejected the innovation at the evaluation stage. If the consumer decides that the price may be worth the benefits, he or she will consider the product for trial.

4.   *Trial.*   At this point, outright adoption may be too risky. Therefore, consumers will try out the product. In the case of discontinuous innovations such as cellular telephones, trial is difficult, as the manufacturer cannot give out free samples. Prospective adopters could rent the item, try one in the store, or use one that friends own. In each case, prospective adopters use the innovation for a short period to evaluate performance.

5.   *Adoption.*   If product performance is satisfactory during trial, consumers may decide to adopt the innovation. However, rejection could occur at any of the earlier stages if consumers believe the innovation is not relevant, does not meet their needs, or does not perform adequately in trial.

6.   *Postpurchase assessment.*   Once they adopt the innovation, consumers will assess satisfaction with the product and decide whether to continue using it. The primary factor in the success of most continuous innovations is not so much the level of adoption as it is the rate of repurchase. When Procter & Gamble introduced Pringles potato chips, it attracted many adopters because the chips were neatly stacked in a unique cylindrical container. However, P&G had to reformulate Pringles and reintroduce it because the repurchase rate was so low. The product's poor taste could not make up for its innovative packaging.

Initial adoption is more important in defining the success of a discontinuous innovation, since the first purchase of a product like a cellular telephone or a personal computer is significant. However, even here, postpurchase assessment is critical because, as technology changes, repurchases will occur. Many personal computer owners already have discarded their original machines to obtain second- and third-generation technologies. If many of these adopters had discontinued the use of PCs because of dissatisfaction with their first purchase, the PC market would be shrinking instead of expanding.

These stages in adoption are important to the marketer because they indicate the acceptance of the product and the effect of the promotional campaign based on answers to the following questions: To what degree is the public aware of the new innovation? Is the public's information accurate? What are consumers' attitudes toward the innovation? What is the likelihood of trial and subsequent adoption? Are consumers satisfied after adopting the innovation?

Characteristics That Encourage Adoption
The likelihood of adoption and subsequent diffusion of a new product depend on the product's nature. If marketers can anticipate a product's likelihood

of adoption, they can adjust strategies accordingly. For example, marketers can overcome resistance to adoption by offering free samples and lowering prices during an introductory period. Rogers and Shoemaker identified the following five characteristics that increase the rate of acceptance and diffusion of a new product.[6]

1. **Relative advantage** is the degree to which consumers perceive a new product as superior to existing substitutes—for example, the relative advantage of a microwave oven in cooking time or of a food processor in versatility. Michelin has a relative advantage in marketing radial tires because consumers associate the brand with safety, and the company tries to reinforce this association. (See Exhibit 19.4.) On the other hand, Polaroid's introduction of an instant movie camera failed because consumers could not see its relative advantages compared to the same capability of a VCR camcorder that has the added advantage of playback on a TV set.

2. **Compatibility** is the degree to which the product is consistent with consumers' needs, attitudes, and past experiences. An aspirin product that could be taken without water when consumers are on the run

▶**EXHIBIT 19.4**
Relative advantage: Michelin's association with safety

failed in its test market because consumers were simply unaccustomed to taking pills without water. The product was not compatible with their past experiences and habits.

3. **Simplicity** is the ease in understanding and using a new product. Products such as electric toothbrushes, instant food products, and cook-in-the-bag vegetables are easy to understand and use. Computer companies such as Apple and IBM have tried to overcome the initial complexity of using personal computers by advertising their machines as user-friendly. Apple developed software to facilitate learning and used the apple as a symbol of simplicity. When it first introduced PCs, IBM used a Charlie Chaplin figure as a friendly symbol that communicated simplicity in use in the least threatening way possible: in mime.

4. **Observability** is the ease with which the product can be observed and communicated to potential consumers. Products that are highly visible are more easily diffused. Fashion items and cars are good examples. Whyte's study of air conditioners suggested that an important element of diffusion was the high visibility of the products.[7] Fisher and Price found that when early adopters purchase a new product that is observable, it allows them to associate themselves with desirable groups. They interviewed college students and found that adoption of new stereo headphones was higher when the product was associated with acceptance by the U.S. Ski Team, a desirable referent for many of the respondents.[8]

5. **Trialability** is the degree to which a product can be tried before adoption. Discontinuous innovations generally have little trialability. Limited trial is possible by demonstrations in showrooms or by using items such as fax machines or personal computers at work and determining if adoption for home use is desirable. One element that is related to trialability is *divisibility*. If consumers can purchase a product in small quantities, then trial is relatively easy. Shoemaker and Shoaf studied five packaged goods and found that almost two-thirds of consumers made trial purchases of new brands in smaller quantities than they usually purchased.[9]

Studies of these five factors generally agree that relative advantage and compatibility are most important in influencing adoption of an innovation. For example, LaBay and Kinnear found that adopters of solar energy systems rated these systems significantly higher than nonadopters did on relative advantage and compatibility as well as simplicity.[10] Ostlund found that adopters of six new food products rated them higher than nonadopters did on all five characteristics, but particularly on relative advantage and compatibility.[11] Holak and Lehmann came up with similar findings for durable innovation categories.[12] Ostlund also found that consumers' perceptions of the product's characteristics were much more important than the consumers' demographic and personality characteristics in predicting adoption.[13] This finding suggests that individuals are more likely to be innovators because of advantages that they perceive in the product than because of any innate personal characteristics.

Characteristics That Encourage Rejection

Each of the five factors cited in the previous section—namely, lack of relative advantage, incompatibility with previous habits and experiences, complexity, lack of observability, and inability to try the product—could cause consumers to reject an innovation. Ram and Sheth considered these factors in citing three major barriers to adopting an innovation: value barrier, usage barrier, and risk barrier.[14]

Value Barrier.   The **value barrier** is a product's lack of performance relative to price as compared with substitute products. When first introduced, cellular telephones cost about $2,000 per unit. They were accepted in business markets because the advantage of mobile communications was worth the cost. However, the cost was too high for most consumers relative to the value they could get from regular telephones.

Manufacturers can overcome the value barrier in two ways. First, reduce the price through technological advances. Costs of personal computers have decreased to bring value into line for the home computer market; the same is happening for cellular telephones. Second, convey information to consumers through advertising to convince them of the product's value. Through the Charlie Chaplin campaign, IBM was able to convey the value of PCs to small business owners who doubted the worth of PCs relative to their cost.

Usage Barrier.   A **usage barrier** occurs when an item is not compatible with consumers' existing practices or habits.[15] Videotex systems, which offer in-home shopping and banking services through interactive TV, have encountered stiff resistance from consumers. Sears has poured millions of dollars into its Prodigy system (see Exhibit 19.5) in an effort to convince a doubting public to accept the innovation. The problem is that consumers like to interact with store personnel and to see the merchandise when they shop. Furthermore, shopping is a social occasion for many consumers who shop with friends. For most consumers, Videotex is not compatible with their desire for the visual and social stimuli of shopping.

Marketers have difficulty overcoming usage barriers because the innovation may be contrary to ingrained needs and usage habits. Advertising is unlikely to change consumers' needs and habits. As a result, a system like Videotex may be doomed. One option that marketers have is to try to employ change agents to overcome usage resistance. **Change agents** are opinion leaders who have more influence and credibility than commercially sponsored means such as personal selling and advertising in convincing consumers to change their needs and habits. Companies producing farm seed and equipment use change agents by first targeting farm innovations to university agricultural extension people,

▶**EXHIBIT 19.5**
Prodigy: A product
subject to a usage
barrier

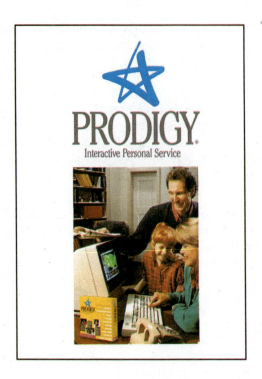

the U.S. Department of Agriculture, and larger farmers who are receptive to modernization. Once these industry leaders adopt the innovation, it is more likely to be diffused to smaller farmers.

Risk Barrier.   A **risk barrier** represents consumers' physical, economic, performance, or social risk of adopting an innovation. When microwave ovens were first introduced, consumers expressed worries about physical risk from radiation. Technological improvements and consumer education overcame this perceived risk. Adopters of home computers had fears of economic and performance risks, which were largely overcome by decreasing prices and improved software. Dickeson and Gentry found that risk was further reduced because many consumers had experience with computer-related products such as programmable calculators.[16] Consumers' social risk of adopting designer jeans was also overcome when opinion leaders in consumers' peer groups accepted these products and when they were more generally accepted across groups.

One of the most effective ways to reduce consumer risk in adopting an innovation is through trial. Free samples are an effective tool for continuous innovations such as tartar control toothpaste. Car manufacturers offer a form of trial with test rides for new models. Some marketers can offer trial even for high-priced discontinuous innovations. For example, when Sony introduced its ProMavica electronic photography system, it distributed 150 prototypes of the product to its primary target, large newspaper publishers.[17] Distribution of the prototype permitted publishers to experience the product and encouraged diffusion from these opinion leaders to other newspaper and magazine publishers.

Time

Time is a key component of diffusion theory based on two measures: first, the *time of adoption* by consumers (whether consumers are earlier or later adopters of the innovation) and second, the *rate of diffusion* (the speed and extent with which adoption has taken place across groups).

Time of Adoption

One essential element that is missing in the six-step description of the adoption process in Figure 19.2 is the time of adoption. Time of adoption is important because identification of the early adopters allows the marketer to target price, promotional, and media strategies to this group. Identification of the later adopters permits adjustments in the marketing plan to account for diffusion of the product to a larger group.

Categories of Adopters.   Rogers developed a classification of adopters by time of adoption. Examining over 500 studies of diffusion, he concluded that there are five categories of adopters: (1) innovators, (2) early adopters, (3) the early majority, (4) the late majority, and (5) laggards.[18] Using past research, Rogers determined that these categories follow a normal distribution. The distribution of adopter categories in Figure 19.3 reflects the product life cycle in Figure 19.1. As Figure 19.3 shows, innovators adopt in the introductory phase, early adopters in the growth phase, the early and late majority in the maturity

▶**FIGURE 19.3**
Distribution of adopter categories

Source: Reprinted with the permission of The Free Press, a division of Macmillan, Inc. from *Diffusion of Innovations,* 3/e by Everett M. Rogers. Copyright ©1962, 1971, 1983 by The Free Press.

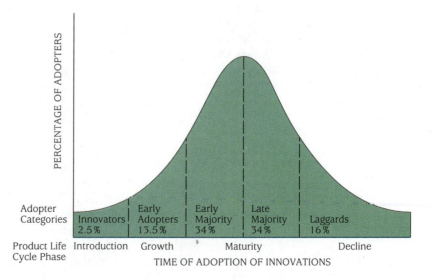

phase, and laggards in the decline phase of the product life cycle. The difference between the product life cycle curve in Figure 19.1 and the adoption curve in Figure 19.3 is that the former depicts sales levels on the vertical axis and the latter depicts the percent of adopters for a given time period. Both curves plot time on the horizontal axis. Rogers described each adopter category as follows:

1. **Innovators** represent on average the first 2.5 percent of all those who adopt. (The proportion of innovators can vary from 2 to 5 percent, depending on the product.) They are eager to try new ideas and products almost as an obsession. They have higher incomes, are better educated, are more cosmopolitan, and are more active outside of their community than noninnovators. In addition, they are less reliant on group norms, more self-confident, and more likely to obtain their information from scientific sources and experts.

2. **Early adopters** represent on average the next 13.5 percent to adopt the product, with a range from 10 to 15 percent, depending on the product. While they are not the very first, they adopt early in the product's life cycle. More reliant on group norms and values than innovators, they are also more oriented to the local community, in contrast to the innovators' cosmopolitan outlook. Early adopters are most likely to be opinion leaders because of their closer affiliation to groups. Since they are more likely to transmit word-of-mouth influence, early adopters are probably the most important group in determining whether the new product will be successful.

3. The **early majority** (next 34 percent to adopt, with a range of 30 to 40 percent) deliberate carefully before adopting a new product. They are likely to collect more information and evaluate more brands than early adopters do; therefore, the process of adoption takes longer. They are likely to be the friends and neighbors of opinion leaders. The early majority are an important link in the process of diffusing new ideas, as they are positioned between earlier and later adopters.

4. The **late majority** (next 34 percent to adopt, also with a range from 30 to 40 percent) are described by Rogers as skeptical. They adopt because most of their friends have already done so. Since they also rely on group norms, adoption is the result of pressure to conform. This group tends to be older and below average in income and education. They rely primarily on word-of-mouth communication rather than on the mass media.

5. **Laggards** are the final 16 percent to adopt and can range from 5 to 20 percent depending on the product. They are similar to innovators in not relying on the group's norms. Independent because they are tradition bound, laggards make decisions in terms of the past. By the time laggards adopt an innovation, it has probably been superseded by something else. For example, they purchased their first television set when color television was already widely owned, and many still

do not own a VCR. Laggards have the lowest socioeconomic status. They tend to be suspicious of new products and alienated from a rapidly advancing society.[19]

Figure 19.4 shows product life cycles for record albums, cassettes, and compact discs from 1973 to 1989 that reflect time of adoption. Record albums are in the declining phase of the life cycle because of new technologies. By 1989, less than 40 million records were sold, compared to ten times that number in 1977. Cassettes are entering the mature phase of their life cycle, with sales leveling off for the first time in 1988. People first buying cassette recorders in 1990 were in the late majority category. Compact discs are in the growth stage of the life cycle, with sales growing at an increasing rate. Most innovators and early adopters have probably already purchased compact disc players, and the majority are now starting to enter the market. Sales will continue to rise and will probably level off by the late 1990s as new technologies with even finer audio clarity such as digital audio tapes enter the market.

Adoption Curve. Both the product life cycle and adoption curves are shown as normal, bell-shaped curves in Figures 19.1 and 19.3. However, both may vary, depending on the type of product. Figure 19.5 illustrates some of the more common variations from the normal curve. The first curve shows a product that

▶**FIGURE 19.4**
The life cycle for three product categories

Source: "Recording Enters a New Era, and You Can't Find It on LP," *The New York Times* (April 1, 1990), pp. 1, 24. Copyright ©1990 by The New York Times Company. Reprinted with permission.

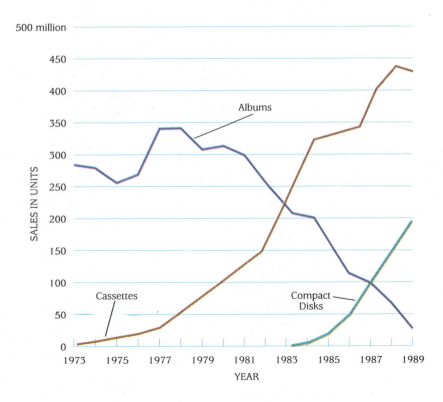

▶**FIGURE 19.5**

Variations from the normal adoption curve

Source: *Marketing: Principles & Strategy*. Second Edition by Henry Assael, copyright ©1993 by The Dryden Press, reproduced by permission of the publisher.

A. Product with Slow Adoption (Record players, Microwave ovens)	B. Product with Fast Adoption (Compact discs)	C. A Fad Product (Teenage Mutant Ninja Turtle Dolls)	D. Product with Frequent Revitalization (Personal computers)

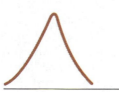
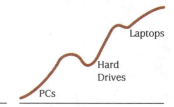

has a long introduction stage, because consumers adopt it slowly. This is typical of a major innovation. In this case, fewer individuals will adopt early but more will in the late majority and laggard categories. The life cycle for record albums was gradual because their adoption was tied to ownership of a record player; and it took at least 20 years for record players to achieve widespread adoption. Adoption of cassettes and compact discs is more rapid in a more technologically sophisticated and affluent society.

The second curve is an innovation with a fast adoption rate and a short introductory stage. The rate of adoption for compact discs from 1983 to 1989 was fairly rapid, as shown in Figure 19.4. The third curve in Figure 19.5 is a fad product with a rapid rise and a rapid decline. Movie spinoff products, such as Teenage Mutant Ninja Turtle dolls, follow such a curve. Sales for such a fad are likely to rise and fall sharply, so that the product life cycle looks more like a pinnacle than a bell. In such cases, the proportion of early adopters and those in the early majority are likely to be larger because once innovators initiate the fad, it catches on quickly. The adoption of the Cabbage Patch Doll in the 1980s is an example.

The fourth curve shows a product that has been frequently revitalized, going through periods of decline and subsequent growth. Such products go through phases of technological improvements, requiring adoption of new technology at each phase. Personal computers are an example. The curve shows adoption in three phases, the first PCs introduced, then the introduction of hard drives, and then laptops.

Adopters Versus Nonadopters.   Rogers' classification deals with adopter categories; it does not account for nonadopters. However, not all families own compact disc players, electric toothbrushes, food processors, or VCRs. As we saw, many consumers reject innovations.

To account for such nonadopters, many marketing studies have used a simple three-part classification: early adopters, later adopters, and nonadopters.[20] The early adopter group includes Rogers' innovators. In most studies of the diffusion of new products, such a classification is used because it simply is not feasible for management to direct marketing resources to the 2.5 percent of adopters represented by the true innovator. The later adopters combine the early and late majority and laggards. The nonadopter group provides for the possibility that a sizable part of the market simply may decide not to buy the new product.

Rate of Diffusion

The **rate of diffusion** is the second key time-oriented measure. It is the *cumulative* level of adoption of a new product over time *across groups*. An example of a diffusion curve for television is shown in Figure 19.6. The adoption of black-and-white television increased rapidly from 1950 to 1962; and by 1962, most households in the United States had adopted it. Color television had a slower rate of adoption from its introduction in 1955 to 1964. Initially, it lacked relative advantage because of a high price, a lack of widespread programming in color, and a high level of perceived risk.[21] After 1964, prices decreased, programming increased, and more households began to adopt. The result was a

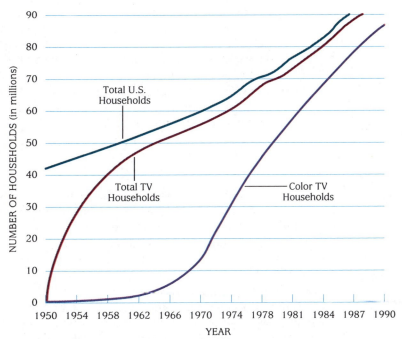

▶**FIGURE 19.6**
Diffusion curve for black-and-white and color television: 1950–1990

Sources: Figures for 1950–1974 from *Advertising Age* (April 19, 1976), p. 112. Figures for 1975–1978 from A. C. Nielsen; data for 1981 from *Standard Rates and Data* (March 15, 1982) and Simmons Market Research Bureau, *1981 Study of Media and Markets*; data for 1984 from TV Bureau of Advertising, *Trends in Television, 1950 to Date* (April, 1985), p. 3. Figures for 1985 on from *Media Week's Guide to Media,* 14

rapid diffusion curve paralleling that of black-and-white sets. By 1990, adoption was close to the point of saturation with over 90 percent of households owning a color TV set.

Figure 19.6 shows that it took approximately 10 years for close to 90 percent of American households to adopt television. Similarly, ownership of VCRs grew to 50 percent in just 6 years. Adoption for some other innovations is much slower. For example, it has taken telephone answering machines 26 years to be accepted by 12 percent of American households. The use of automatic teller machines grew to about 9 percent of consumers in 14 years.[22] In general, the speed of adoption of innovations seems to be increasing. In a study of 25 appliances, Olshavsky found that consumers are adopting new products more quickly than they used to.[23] A more rapid rate of adoption and diffusion reflects more disposable income among U.S. households, more rapid technological advances, and less time spent on decision making.

Why is the rate of diffusion faster for some products than others? Gatignon and Robertson reviewed a variety of diffusion studies and concluded that the rate of diffusion is faster if:[24]

- **There is a high level of competitive intensity.** In highly competitive markets, new products will be marketed more aggressively, leading to higher awareness of the product, lower prices, and wider availability.
- **Technology is standardized.** Such standardization reduces consumers' risk of adopting a new product. When videocassette recorders were first introduced, consumers were reluctant to buy because two competing technologies were being marketed, Betamax and VHS. Eventually, the latter won out, creating a standardized product. Similarly, the rate of diffusion for PCs was fairly rapid because of acceptance of DOS as the industry-wide standard operating system.
- **Information is communicated quickly.** The more rapidly people learn about a new product through advertising and the mass media, the more rapid is word-of-mouth communication within and across groups.

Target Market

The third component that is part of the definition of the diffusion process is the market to which the innovation is targeted. Home computers were first targeted to high-income, well-educated consumers who are more likely to work at home and are willing to take the risk of adoption (the early adopters). As adoption increased and prices were lowered, the target market definition broadened to include later adopters. Therefore, the target market changes during the diffusion process.

Diffusion studies sometimes have focused on very specific target markets. For example, one of the first diffusion studies involved farmers' adoption of hybrid seed in two Iowa communities.[25] Other studies have involved doctors' adoption of a new drug in several cities;[26] community antenna television by residents of a Wisconsin town;[27] and a new diet product by residents of a geriatric community.[28]

In each of these cases, the target market defines a **social system**, which is a set of people with a shared set of norms who tend to interact over time.[29] Farmers in Iowa communities, doctors in particular cities, and residents of a geriatric community are social systems. Social systems are much broader than reference groups because they are not restricted to face-to-face contact. It is important to define such a broader entity as the target for an innovation for two reasons: First, the social system defines the common needs of the consumers within it; second, the social system encourages the diffusion of innovations across the groups within it.

The norms and values of the social system influence the rate of diffusion. Rogers and Shoemaker defined markets that are modern versus traditional.[30] Members of a "modern" target market are more likely to accept change, have a greater respect for education and science, and are more cosmopolitan. They are more apt to be innovators or early adopters of new products. Those with a traditional orientation are more likely to be in the late majority or laggards.

Marketers must determine attitudes toward change and toward risk among members of the target market. A conservative and traditional target would suggest difficulty in introducing a new product, particularly a discontinuous innovation.

Communication in the Diffusion Process

Communication is the last key element in the definition of diffusion. When a product is first introduced, communication from the marketer to the consumer is meant to create awareness of the innovation and to provide information.[31] A study of early users of a new automobile diagnostic center in a Midwestern city found that early adopters of the service relied primarily on magazines and radio for information.[32] A study of early adopters of stainless steel blades found that their principal source of information was the mass media.[33] Also, a study of the adoption of self-diagnostic medical devices among elderly consumers found that early adopters relied more on the mass media for information.[34]

Once awareness is created, early adopters will rely more on friends and relatives to help them evaluate new products. As Figure 19.7 shows, early adopters first rely on mass media for information. Word-of-mouth influence then increases in importance as early adopters move from awareness to evaluation, trial, and adoption. However, for later adopters, word-of-mouth is likely to be the dominant influence throughout the adoption process. Later adopters first learn of innovations from friends and neighbors rather than from the mass media. On this basis, advertisers can best encourage diffusion by using an informational campaign to create awareness among early adopters and by trying to stimulate favorable word-of-mouth communication among late adopters.

Importance of mass media versus word-of-mouth in the adoption process

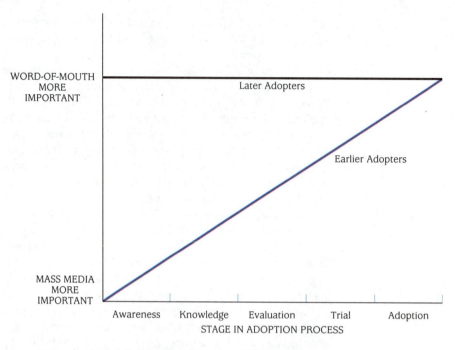

Word-of-Mouth Communication Within Groups

The studies cited above show that if diffusion is to occur across groups, favorable word-of-mouth communication must first occur within groups.

The last chapter showed that opinion leaders are more likely to communicate and receive product information. Early adopters are more likely to be opinion leaders and demonstrate more interest in and knowledge about the product category. Opinion leaders share these characteristics. Several studies have shown that there is better than a 50-percent chance that an opinion leader is also an early adopter.[35] It is not surprising, then, that many of the findings that apply to opinion leadership also apply to diffusion research.

Lambert studied the adoption of seven new products ranging from cook-in-the-bag vegetables to water spray devices for cleaning teeth.[36] He found that early adopters were more likely to tell friends and acquaintances about the products purchased. Baumgarten characterized the early adopter who is most likely to engage in word-of-mouth communication as the **innovative communicator.** He found that close to 50 percent of all early adopters of fashion innovations also communicated frequently about fashion and influenced others.[37] These and other studies demonstrate the importance of word-of-mouth communication within groups as the first step before information and influence about new products can be disseminated across groups.[38]

Figure 19.8 shows the relationship between early adopters and opinion leaders. As we noted, early adopters who are also opinion leaders are the innovative communicators. Consumers who are neither early adopters nor opinion leaders are classified as *noninfluentials* (lower right in Figure 19.8).

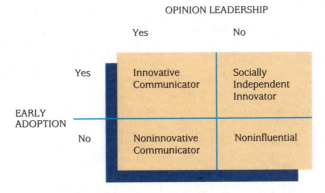

▶FIGURE 19.8
The relationship between early adoption and opinion leadership

The other two boxes show that no one-to-one correspondence occurs between an early adopter and an opinion leader. Early adopters who are not opinion leaders are called *socially independent innovators* (top right in Figure 19.8). These individuals rely on their own norms and values rather than those of the group. They tend to be the true innovators; that is, the first 2.5 percent to adopt a new product. As a result, they exert little influence on others. Opinion leaders who are not early adopters are called *noninnovative communicators*. While they communicate information and exert influence on others, they are not among the first to buy new products.

Figure 19.8 shows that despite their similarity, opinion leadership and diffusion are separate communication processes and have different implications for marketing strategy. The implications from opinion leadership tend to be applied to promotional strategies; the implications from diffusion, to new product development.

Word-of-Mouth Communication Across Groups

Diffusion requires the spread of information across different groups.[39] How is this process to occur if personal influence takes place primarily within a consumer's own peer group? It happens because consumers spread the word by interacting with individuals outside their personal networks.

Strength of Weak Ties. Groups outside an individual's personal network are known as **heterophilous**; peer and family groups are **homophilous**.[40] Individuals within heterophilous groups are dissimilar, and ties holding them together are weak; individuals within homophilous groups tend to be similar and are bonded by stronger reference group ties. Associates at higher or lower levels in an organization or individuals with whom the consumer has occasional contact, such as tennis partners or carpool riders, are examples of members of heterophilous groups.

Consumers often spread the word about new products and ideas to passing acquaintances in heterophilous groups. The fact that the weak ties of heterophilous groups are strong enough to fuel this process of diffusion is what we mean by the "strength of weak ties."

This process is shown in Figure 19.9 The purple lines show close interpersonal ties; the arrows show communication about a new product. Figure 19.9 shows that Consumers A, B, and C form one close-knit group and Consumers E, F, and G form another. Consumer D is not a member of either group. Assume that Consumer A has adopted a new product. She communicates about the product to B and D. If it were not for the strength of weak ties, the process of diffusion would stop here. Consumer B communicates about the product to Consumer C and also to Consumer E, who then communicates to F and G. The link between B and E is a weak tie since both belong to different reference groups. However, this link permits word-of-mouth communication to go *across* groups. Such contacts are essential in fueling the diffusion process, because without them word-of-mouth would be restricted to communication within groups only.

The importance of communication to weaker groups was shown in Brown and Reingen's study about adoption of a personal service. They found that most word-of-mouth occurred among friends and relatives in homophilous groups. Weak ties of the sort from B to E in Figure 19.9 occurred in only 18 percent of communications among people.[41] However, when these weak ties did occur, they were very likely to be bridges across groups in communicating about the service.

Trickle Down and Trickle Up.   One of the basic questions in analyzing communications across groups is how information and influence travel from one socioeconomic group to another.

In Chapter 10, we described the transmission of influence between socioeconomic groups as a *trickle-down* process from higher to lower groups (as with the diffusion of fashion items such as Izod alligator shirts) and a *trickle-up* process from lower to higher groups (as with the diffusion of jeans and rock music). Traditionally, the view has been that diffusion occurs from higher to lower social classes (trickle down). Two famous sociologists, Thorstein Veblen[42] and George Simmel, stated this view.[43] Both believed that the upper classes

▶**FIGURE 19.9**
The strength of weak ties

Source: Jacqueline Johnson Brown and Peter H. Reingen, "Social Ties and Word-of-Mouth Referral Behavior," *Journal of Consumer Research*, 14 (December, 1987), pp. 350–362. Reprinted with permission from The University of Chicago Press.

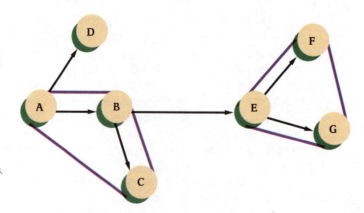

bought primarily for status and ostentation (conspicuous consumption) and that lower-quality duplicates of these products were then made for the lower classes (for example, knockoffs of Rolex watches or Gucci handbags and scarfs). Communication and influence moved from one class down to the next in the social hierarchy.

This view is reinforced by a description of innovators and early adopters as being in the highest and laggards as being in the lowest socioeconomic class. Thus, the transmission of influence from innovators and early adopters to laggards is a transmission from upper to lower socioeconomic classes.

However, as we saw in Chapter 10, the transmission of influence is occasionally from lower to upper socioeconomic groups. Innovators and early adopters of jeans and of bluegrass and rock music were those in lower socioeconomic classes who did not feel the need to conform to the norms of the dominant culture. They were free to innovate in clothing and music. Known as **grassroots innovators**, these individuals then disseminated their tastes to higher social classes. For example, African-American mule drivers working the coal mines of Appalachia created bluegrass music by fusing their instrumentation with white Appalachian music.[44] As the lower socioeconomic groups adopted bluegrass, it also began to be disseminated to a wider public through concerts, radio, and finally TV. The innovators and early adopters clearly were not the cosmopolitan, upscale consumers associated with early adopters. They were the lower-class African-Americans and whites of Appalachia. We will be reporting studies in the next section that describe early adopters of many innovations as upscale. However, it is important to recognize that early adopters can be in any segment of society, depending on the innovation.

Trickle Across. The trickle-up process shows that early adoption of an innovation can go in either direction on the social scale. Another issue is whether social status is as relevant as it used to be in defining the transmission of influence, up or down. The views of Veblen and Simmel espousing a trickle-down effect were expressed at the turn of the century, a time when class distinctions were much sharper than today. The post-World War II period produced a leveling effect in socioeconomic status, making trickle-down and trickle-up effects less relevant. Moreover, the mass media rapidly communicate information on innovations to all classes. A more likely process of diffusion is one that occurs across groups, regardless of socioeconomic status, known as a **trickle-across effect.**

King's study of fashion adoption in the Boston area illustrates this leveling effect. King found that early buyers of new fashions were not the upper-crust elite. Almost two-thirds were middle class or lower. Moreover, there was no evidence that communications went from individuals of a higher social class to those of a lower class. Four-fifths of respondents were influenced by members of their own social class. Explaining these results, King stated, "The traditional upper-class fashion leader directing the lower levels is largely short-circuited in the communication process. Within hours after the exclusive Paris and American designers' showings, the season's styles have been passed to the mass audiences via newspaper and television." [45]

King's study tends to confirm a trickle-across, rather than a trickle-down, effect in the diffusion of fashion styles. King's ideas closely conform to the social multiplier effect. That is, individuals are more likely to come into contact with new products and ideas because of the leveling of social status in American society; and as a result, influence travels in a lateral fashion across markets. A trickle-down effect is much more marked in countries with sharp social class distinctions. In the United States, it is more likely that a trickle of information and influence *across* groups will result in the diffusion of new products.

◆ CULTURAL CONTEXT OF DIFFUSION

Cultural norms often determine the acceptance of new products and the rate of diffusion. As we saw in Chapter 14, consumers reject many new product innovations because they contradict cultural norms. This was the reason that prepared baby foods were rejected in Brazil and that condensed soups had a hard time winning acceptance in England. Brazilian mothers insisted on giving their babies homemade, rather than prepared, foods; and English consumers equated quality in canned soups with hefty soups in larger cans.

Two concepts that help us understand the diffusion of innovations in different cultures are **cultural context** and **cultural homogeneity.** Hall introduced the concept of cultural context by dividing cultures into two groups: those that rely primarily on verbal and written communication to transmit meaning (low context cultures) and those that rely primarily on nonverbal communication (high context cultures.)[46] Rogers introduced the concept of group homogeneity in the diffusion process by distinguishing between homophilous and heterophilous groups.[47] The concept can also be extended to cultures by identifying uniform cultures with little difference in norms, values, and socioeconomic status among groups (homophilous), versus more disparate cultures with wider differences among groups (heterophilous).

High context cultures tend to be more homophilous. The emphasis on nonverbal communication means that such cultures will place more value on interpersonal contacts and associations. They put more value on the group, rather than on the individual, and they emphasize subscribing to the norms and longstanding rituals of society. Low context cultures place more value on individual initiative and rely more on the mass media for communication. Most Far-Eastern countries would be described as high context/homophilous, whereas the United States and Western Europe would be described as low context/heterophilous.

The rate of diffusion would be expected to be faster in high context/homophilous cultures because of their uniformity. The barrier in transmitting information from one dissimilar group to another is much lower. Further, the credibility of information on innovations is higher because the source is more likely to be friends and relatives rather than the mass media.

Takada and Jain compared the rate of adoption for three products—air conditioners, washing machines, and calculators—in high context cultures (Japan, Taiwan, South Korea) versus a low context culture (United States). In most cases, the rate of diffusion was more rapid in the three high context cultures than it was in the United States for all three categories.[48]

STRATEGIC APPLICATIONS OF CONSUMER BEHAVIOR

As Hip-Hop Music Trickles Up, Marketers Sign On

Hip-hop music, a derivative of rap, has become the darling of marketing strategists targeting the trendy and aware younger set. Established brands are tying in with hip-hop stars in ads on MTV and other cable music channels. Coca-Cola was one of the first, with ads in 1989 starring Curtis Blow, Kid'N Play, and Heavy D, all hip-hop stars. Two of the best-known stars, Hammer and Queen Latifah, have appeared in ads for Taco Bell, KFC, and The Gap.

Tapping into the hip-hop movement made sense for marketers once the music's popularity began trickling up. Hip-hop originated among African-American youths in inner-city areas. Hip-hop music began to be diffused on a broader basis as disc jockeys began to pick up and popularize it. When MTV established a specific program for rap music, "Yo! MTV Raps," the diffusion of hip-hop was well on its way. Hip-hop dance moves were also more broadly accepted along with the music. As a result, whites are now estimated to compose at least half of all hip-hop listeners.

Ken Smikle, president of the African-American Marketing and Media Association, believes that marketers who use hip-hop are not targeting just African-Americans. "Remember" he says, "if hip-hop culture had not broken out of the black domain, most companies wouldn't consider using it at all."

Hip-hop in marketing has gone beyond the use of rap stars in commercials. The music has spawned entire lines of products, including a line of potato chips by Chumpies Home Boys. Reebok also introduced a workout based on hip-hop dance moves of rappers like Hammer and Bobby Brown, called the Reebok City Jam. Also, as a further sign that hip-hop is becoming mainstream, establishment department stores are carrying whole lines of hip-hop clothes. Cross Colours, a line of hip-hop clothing, is sold in Macy's and Dayton Hudson and promoted as clothing "made by true brothers from the hood."

As hip-hop has trickled up, marketers have signed on in increasing numbers.

Source: "Marketers Tap into Rap as Hip-Hop Becomes 'Safe,'" *Marketing News,* pp. 10 and 15.

INNOVATIVENESS AND THE DIFFUSION PROCESS

In this section, we ask some key questions about the nature of **innovativeness.** By innovativeness we mean the predisposition of a consumer to adopt a product earlier than most others. We will look at the characteristics of those who adopt earlier and refer to them as *innovators*, recognizing that they represent Rogers' classification of both the true innovator group (the first 2.5 percent to adopt) and the early adopter group (the next 13.5 percent to adopt). Therefore, the general designation of innovator refers to both true innovators and early adopters.

Nature of Innovativeness

Two key questions asked about opinion leaders can also be asked about innovators. First, is innovativeness general or product-specific? The answer will help marketers determine whether marketing strategy can be directed to a general group of innovators or whether specific target segments of early buyers have to be defined on a product-by-product basis. Second, is there a negative as well as a positive innovator? That is, can one trace a negative diffusion process leading to rejection of an innovation?

Is Innovativeness Product-Specific?

It is likely that a general innovator exists for true (discontinuous) innovations. That is, the innovator who is among the first to consider buying an electric car will also be among the first to consider trying solar energy. One study found that owners of home computers are more likely to use automatic bill paying services, cable TV services, and automatic teller machines. They also are more likely to own programmable pocket calculators and video TV games.[49]

Various studies have shown that across product categories, innovators tend to be:

- Opinion leaders.
- Risk takers.
- Inner directed and independent of group norms.
- More likely to obtain information from mass media than through word-of-mouth.
- Open to new ideas and change.
- Relatively young.

Also, most studies have identified innovators as cosmopolitan and in higher socioeconomic groups (although as we noted, grassroots innovators are in lower socioeconomic groups and often from rural areas).

Most findings suggest that for less-innovative products, a general innovator does not exist. That is, the individual who is one of the first to have adopted touch-tone telephone service will not necessarily be one of the first to have tried cook-in-the-bag vegetables. As with opinion leadership, innovativeness is likely to extend across related product categories, but an innovator in one category is not likely to be an innovator in an unrelated category. For most new products, marketers must define the target market on a product-by-product basis.

Some companies have sought to portray general innovators as users of their products or services. For example, the ad in Exhibit 19.6 refers to readers of Condé Nast magazines as those who are the first to adopt new ideas, new foods, and new services.

Are There Positive and Negative Innovators?

We are assuming that the general innovator reacts positively to most discontinuous innovations. The same individual might reject an innovation, however. The consumer who was one of the first to accept VCRs, personal computers, and compact disc players might have been one of the first to reject videodiscs. Midgley proposed three categories of adopters:[50]

1. **Active adopters** are those who have adopted the product and give favorable information about it.
2. **Active rejectors** are those who have tried the product, found it deficient, and give unfavorable information about it.

▶**EXHIBIT 19.6**
Portraying a generalized innovator

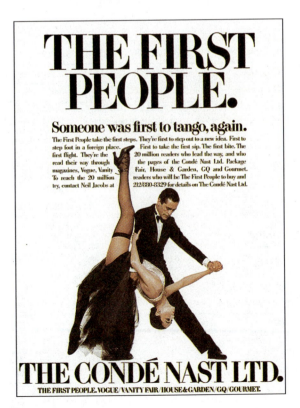

3. **Passives** are those who have adopted the product but do not give information or exert influence. They are the socially independent innovators in Figure 19.8.

Leonard-Barton conducted one of the few marketing studies that distinguished between active adopters and rejectors. She found that rejectors frequently sought experts who evaluated the innovation negatively, possibly to justify discontinuing the use of the innovation.[51] In general, little documentation of a negative diffusion process is available. It may be that marketers are reluctant to provide evidence of failures, even though studies of negative diffusion could provide insights on ways to avoid future market failures.

Characteristics of the Innovator

Marketers want to identify the segment of the market that is most likely to adopt a new product when it is first introduced. In most cases, a profile of the innovator must be product-specific. However, as we saw, a general innovator is likely to exist. Table 19.1 summarizes the personality, demographics, and media characteristics of the generalized innovator.

▶**TABLE 19.1**
Characteristics of innovators versus noninnovators

Characteristics	Innovators	Noninnovators
Personality		
Dogmatism	Open-minded	Closed-minded
Social Character	Inner-directed	Outer-directed
Self-confidence	More	Less
Demographics		
Age	Younger	Older
Income	More	Less
Education	More	Less
Mobility	More	Less
Occupational status	Higher	Lower
Media		
Magazine readership	More	Less
Newspaper readership	More	Less
Television viewing	Less	More
Other characteristics		
Opinion leadership	Higher	Lower
Perceived risk	Less	More
Involvement	Enduring	Situational

Personality Characteristics

A number of personality characteristics have been related to innovativeness. Reisman, Glazer, and Denney found innovators to be *inner directed*. Inner-directed people rely on their internal standards and values to guide behavior; other-directed people rely on the values of friends and associates.[52]

Innovators are more likely to be *self-confident* in evaluating new products. One study found that those who refinanced mortgages earliest as interest rates went down were more self-confident in evaluating financial services.[53]

Innovators also have been found to be *less dogmatic* than noninnovators. Dogmatism, which is related to perceived threat and anxiety, is reflected in a closed mind toward change. Less-dogmatic individuals are more likely to accept change and innovations requiring changes in behavior.[54]

Lifestyle Characteristics

A study by a manufacturer of personal care products demonstrates the use of lifestyle characteristics in identifying the innovator. The manufacturer asked a sample of women to rate themselves on the lifestyle characteristics listed in Table 19.2. It then classified the women by their willingness to buy new personal care products when they first come on the market. About 14 percent of the women were classified as innovators; the other 86 percent, as noninnovators. Personal care innovators were more likely than noninnovators to:

- Be style- and appearance-conscious.
- Be socially oriented and self-confident.
- Communicate about new products.
- Look for time-saving products.
- Rely on the brand name.

They were less likely to be socially isolate.

▶**TABLE 19.2**

Lifestyle characteristics of innovators of personal care products

Lifestyle Characteristics	Innovators (14% of sample)	Noninnovators (86% of sample)
Style- and appearance-conscious/ self-indulgent	39%	28%
Isolate/conservative	25%	32%
Social/self-confident	44%	27%
Bargain seekers	28%	30%
Outdoor types	31%	32%
New product/social communicators	39%	26%
Look for time-saving products	39%	25%
Rely on manufacturer's name	26%	20%

Advertising appeals to personal care innovators, therefore, should involve portrayal of a self-confident and socially aware woman who is concerned with her appearance and who emphasizes time-saving conveniences.

Demographic Characteristics

Innovators tend to be young and to have high income, educational level, and occupational status. In addition, innovators are likely to be mobile. This profile has been found to be true for innovators of solar energy systems,[55] a new automotive diagnostic service,[56] community antenna television,[57] and new personal care products. However, the demographic profile of the innovator is not always consistent. For instance, Darden and Reynolds found that the fashion and grooming innovator is less educated and in a lower-income group.[58] This inconsistency suggests differences between innovators of symbolic versus technological products and indicates the need to develop specific adopter profiles for each product category.

Media Characteristics

Marketers attempt to select mass media that are most likely to reach adopters of their products. Evidence suggests that innovators are more likely than noninnovators to read newspapers and magazines.[59] However, marketers cannot select any magazine. Summers' study of six broad product categories found that innovators tended to read magazines with editorial content relevant to the product category.[60] For example, female fashion innovators were likely to read *Glamour, Vogue,* and *Harper's Bazaar;*[61] male fashion innovators, *Playboy, Esquire,* and the *New Yorker.*[62] Appliance innovators were likely to read *Consumer Reports.*[63] These findings suggest that marketers should select media on a product-specific basis by utilizing specialty magazines.

Findings for print media do not seem to apply to radio and television. Innovators are not more likely to be exposed to broadcast media.[64] Because innovators tend to watch less TV than the general population, it is an ineffective medium for reaching adopter groups.

Perceived Risk and Product Involvement

Two additional characteristics related to innovativeness in Table 19.1 are risk and involvement. Innovators tend to perceive less risk in product adoption than do noninnovators. Lambert found that innovators of eight fairly diverse products were less likely to see uncertainty in buying the product.[65] They also were less likely to be concerned with negative consequences such as disapproval of the purchase by friends and relatives.

Innovators also are more likely to be involved with the product category on an enduring basis. Bloch, Sherrell, and Ridgeway found that consumers who are involved on an ongoing basis with clothing and personal computers are more likely to be innovators in these categories.[66] In contrast, noninnovators are more likely to be involved on a situational basis related to specific product decisions.

◆ MEASURING INNOVATIVENESS

Innovativeness is a behavioral variable, measured by the early adoption of new products. In contrast, opinion leadership is measured by consumers' perceptions regarding their interpersonal communications with others.

Innovativeness has been measured by three criteria. First, and most frequently, it has been measured by adoption over time. For example, Donnelly and Ivancevich identified early adopters of the Maverick as those who purchased the car in the first three months after it was introduced, middle adopters as those who purchased in the second and third model year, and later adopters as those who purchased thereafter.[67] Anderson and Ortinau identified personal computer innovators as those who purchased PCs prior to 1985.[68] Such a measure of innovativeness accounts for the time of adoption of the product.

A second criterion used to identify innovators is the number of new products adopted. Summers categorized consumers by number of new products adopted (from zero to six).[69] Such a criterion is useful in distinguishing between the product-specific and the general innovator. Any consumer who adopts innovations in all six product areas under study is likely to be a general innovator.

A third criterion used to measure innovativeness is how consumers view themselves. Such self-designating measures are used when the researcher wants to determine consumers' orientation to new products rather than measure specific adoption. Innovativeness could be determined by a two-question sequence:

1. How do you see yourself with regard to buying new products?
   - As one of the first to buy.
   - Purchasing after a few others have tried the product.
   - Purchasing after many people have bought the product.
   - Will not purchase.

2. If you intend to buy the product, how soon after its appearance are you likely to buy?
   - Immediately.
   - Within a week.
   - Within a month.
   - Within a year.
   - Longer.[70]

Self-designating questions were used to define the prospective innovators of new personal care products in the study illustrated in Table 19.2.

STRATEGIC APPLICATIONS OF DIFFUSION THEORY

Companies have attempted to influence both the likelihood of adoption and the rate of diffusion of innovations through marketing strategies.

Adoption

Companies have used various strategies to influence consumers to adopt innovations. In the case of continuous innovations, companies have tried to encourage trial through free samples and price promotions. We saw that sampling was a key strategy in the introduction of Post-it Notes. Encouraging adoption for discontinuous innovations is more difficult because consumers cannot purchase the product on a trial basis. Companies have used advertising to create product awareness and to communicate product features. The ads for cellular telephones and color printers in Exhibit 19.2 are examples. Companies also have tried to portray innovative behavior in advertising by showing astute buyers purchasing the most advanced products. The ads for Hewlett Packard in Exhibit 19.7 portray innovative behavior by showing previous innovators for calculators buying personal computers, both Hewlett Packard products.

In addition, marketers can attempt to overcome resistance to adoption by employing change agents. Pharmaceutical companies seek early adoption of medical innovations by respected hospitals, clinics, and physicians who have reputations as opinion leaders in the hope that these individuals and institutions will encourage others to adopt.

Rate of Diffusion

Diffusion theory can provide marketers with guidelines for adjusting strategies according to the projected rate of diffusion. Marketers have two strategic options in influencing the rate of diffusion, as shown in Table 19.3. In a **skimming policy,** marketers project a slow rate of diffusion. As a result, prices have to be set higher initially to sustain the costs of introduction. The policy aims at "skimming the cream off the market" by strategically aiming at the small, price-insensitive segment.

Such a segment is likely to be well defined by demographic and lifestyle characteristics. Advertising will probably be informationally oriented to create awareness and to supply necessary technical information. Distribution of the product will be selective. A skimming policy is most likely for discontinuous innovations. There may be barriers to widespread acceptance because the product is not likely to be simple and may not be compatible with existing products or systems. Therefore, it is logical to establish a small and specific target for adoption.

The alternative to a skimming policy is a **penetration strategy.** In this case, marketers encourage rapid and widespread diffusion by introducing the product

▶**EXHIBIT 19.7**

Ads portraying adoption of an innovation

Source: Courtesy of Hewlett-Packard

at a low price. The intention is to try to sell to a general market through an intensive campaign that uses imagery and symbolism. Distribution is widespread. Because the market is so general, identifying the characteristics of early adopters may be difficult. A penetration strategy is likely for continuous innovations such as diet soda or freeze-dried coffee since closely competitive product

▶TABLE 19.3

Strategic alternatives based on the diffusion curve

Rate of Diffusion	Slow	Fast
Marketing Strategy	*Skimming*	*Penetration*
Initial price	High	Low
Market segmentation	Target market is • Small • Well specified by demographics and lifestyle	Target market is • Larger • Harder to specify by demographics and lifestyle
Advertising	Informational approach	Use of symbols and imagery
Distribution	Selective	Intensive
Product characteristics	Discontinuous innovation	Continuous innovation

substitutes exist. Both diet soda and freeze-dried coffee were introduced at competitive prices on a widespread basis with intensive advertising campaigns using symbolism and imagery.

Once an initial strategy is established, diffusion theory can give marketers guidelines for changing marketing strategy, depending on where the product is on the diffusion curve. A product introduced by a skimming strategy eventually will move toward a penetration strategy. For example, personal computers were first introduced into the market at very high prices with little advertising and limited distribution. As technological improvements lowered prices, diffusion became more rapid. As adoption increased, distribution became more intense. Knowledge of the diffusion curve could have helped marketers of personal computers define the proper time to begin to shift from a skimming to a penetration strategy.

Similarly, marketers introducing a penetration strategy may find that a slow increase in prices is warranted when there is widespread acceptance of the product. Advertising and distribution will remain intensive, but the proper time for a change in pricing policy may be defined by the diffusion curve.

SUMMARY

This chapter described a process of diffusion that leads to the dissemination of products and services across consumers. Diffusion research provides marketers with insights into the process of new product acceptance. Such insights are particularly important because of the close link between the success of new product introductions and the firm's profit position.

The diffusion process involves the consumers' adoption of an innovation and communication to other groups over time. Adoption of a new product requires awareness, knowledge, evaluation, and trial. Consumers are more likely to adopt a product if it has a relative advantage, is compatible with their needs and past experiences, is visible, is simple to understand, and is easily tried. Consumers' rejection of an innovation can occur because of lack of perceived value, lack of compatibility with current habits and usage, and perceived risk in buying the innovation.

Time is a crucial part of the diffusion process because it determines the rate of diffusion. Time is also important in defining adoption. Adopter categories—innovators, early adopters, the majority, and laggards—are defined according to time of adoption. In communication among groups, information is likely to trickle up or down from one socioeconomic group to another or to trickle across similar groups, regardless of economic status. Because of the great mobility and lack of sharp socioeconomic distinctions in the United States, diffusion is likely to be based on a trickle-across effect.

Innovativeness was defined as a consumer's predisposition to buy a new product early. Innovators (that is, the true innovator group plus early adopters) are usually product-specific; that is, an innovator for one product may not be an innovator for another. Discontinuous innovations—that is, innovations that represent a marked change in product specifications and consumer behavior—are exceptions. In such cases, an individual may be generally predisposed to adopt innovations. General innovators tend to be better educated, more self-confident, more willing to take risks and accept change, and more socially active than other adopters. In addition, innovators are more likely to be opinion leaders.

Despite the fact that most findings are product-specific, diffusion research does provide important strategic implications. It helps marketers define those consumers who are first to adopt. Furthermore, it provides some basis for predicting the diffusion process and suggests guidelines for changes in strategy as marketers proceed on the diffusion curve.

In the next chapter, we will shift our attention from interpersonal communication to marketing communication, particularly advertising.

QUESTIONS

1. Diffusion research provides marketers with implications for the introductory phase in marketing a new product and for changes in strategy along the diffusion curve. What are the implications for changes in marketing strategy after fax machines begin to be accepted, particularly for changes in (a) definition of new target groups, (b) pricing, (c) advertising strategy, (d) product specifications, and (e) distribution?

2. In Exhibit 19.2, why is the cellular telephone cited as a discontinuous innovation, the color printer as a dynamically continuous innovation, and the Sony camcorder as a continuous innovation?

3. What are the differences in the strategic implications of diffusion research for a symbolic innovation such as skin care products compared to the implications for a technological innovation such as fax machines?

4. Evaluate the three product categories shown in Exhibit 19.2 on the five characteristics that encourage adoption: relative advantage, compatibility, simplicity, observability, and trialability. On this basis, is product adoption likely to be rapid or slow? Why?

5. Cite an example of a value barrier, a usage barrier, and a risk barrier to adoption of an innovation. How can marketers overcome each barrier?

6. The adoption curve in Figure 19.3 has the same shape as the product life cycle curve in Figure 19.1.
   • Is the adoption curve in fact the same as the product life cycle curve?
   • What are the marketing implications of your answer?

7. What do we mean by the "strength of weak ties"? Provide an example. Why is this concept important in the diffusion process?

8. The chapter cites two theories of communication between groups: a trickle-down and a trickle-across effect.
   • In what types of societies is a trickle-down flow of communication more likely?
   • Are there any groups or regions in the United States where a trickle-down flow is more likely to occur?
   • Is a trickle-up flow also possible? Cite examples.

9. What are the strategic implications of introducing a new product to a high context/homophilous culture versus a low context/heterophilous culture?

10. A study of adoption of six consumer packaged goods found that a general innovator does not exist. Consumers' perceptions of the product were more important than personal characteristics such as demographics or personality in identifying innovators. Why was it unlikely that the same consumers would buy new products across the six packaged goods categories studied?

11. The chapter cites an important gap in diffusion research—the lack of any study of a negative diffusion process. The fact that marketing managers do not like to advertise failures may explain the lack of research on negative diffusion. Such studies, however, could provide insights on how to avoid product failures.
   • Cite an example of negative diffusion for a product.
   • What insights might a marketing manager gain from studying negative diffusion to better understand (a) word-of-mouth communication and (b) product positioning?

12. How could a company introducing a new facial care appliance best appeal to the target market based on the profile of the personal care innovator in Table 19.2?

RESEARCH ASSIGNMENTS

1. Use the following questions to identify innovators for men's cosmetics. "How do you see yourself with regard to buying a new facial care preparation for men? As one of the first to buy? As one who purchases after a few others have tried it? As one who purchases after many people have bought it? As

a nonpurchaser?" Identify the innovators as those who say they would be one of the first to buy. In addition to the innovativeness question, ask the sample of males: (a) lifestyle questions based on the statements listed in Table 11.1, (b) an opinion leadership question, (c) self-confidence questions in selecting cosmetics and toiletry items, and (d) questions about demographic characteristics.

- What are the differences between the innovators and noninnovators on each of the items listed? (If your sample is large enough, split it into three groups—innovators, those tending to be innovators, and noninnovators—and determine differences among these groups.)
- What are the implications of these differences for a marketing strategy for men's cosmetics in regard to (a) market segmentation, (b) advertising and product positioning, (c) pricing, (d) product development, and (e) distribution?

2. One of the hypotheses in the chapter is that there may be a general innovator for discontinuous innovations. Determine ownership of discontinuous innovations by asking a sample of 40 to 50 consumers about ownership of items such as home computers, compact disc players, VCRs, fax machines, and so on. Determine (a) lifestyles, (b) opinion leadership, and (c) demographics as well.

- Do consumers who own one discontinuous innovation tend to own others?
- Split the sample between those who do and those who do not own two or more discontinuous innovations. What are the differences in characteristics between the two groups?

NOTES

1. "Post-it Notes Click Thanks to Entrepreneurial Spirit," *Marketing News* (August 31, 1984), p. 21.

2. "Masters of Innovation," *Business Week* (April 10, 1989), p. 58; and "At Johnson & Johnson, a Mistake Can Be a Badge of Honor," *Business Week* (September 26, 1988), p. 126.

3. *New Product Management for the 1980s* (New York: Booz Allen & Hamilton, 1982), pp. 8–10.

4. Thomas S. Robertson, "The Process of Innovation and the Diffusion of Innovation," *Journal of Marketing*, 31 (January, 1967), pp. 14–19.

5. Elizabeth C. Hirschman, "Symbolism and Technology as Sources for the Generation of Innovations," in Andrew Mitchell, ed., *Advances in Consumer Research*, Vol. 9 (Ann Arbor, MI: Association for Consumer Research, 1982), pp. 537–541.

6. Everett M. Rogers and F. Floyd Shoemaker, *Communication of Innovations*, 2nd ed. (New York: The Free Press, 1971).

7. William H. Whyte, "The Web of Word-of-Mouth," *Fortune* (November, 1954), pp. 140–143.

8. Robert J. Fisher and Linda L. Price, "An Investigation into the Social Context of Early Adoption Behavior," *Journal of Consumer Research*, 19 (December, 1992), pp. 477–486.

9. Robert W. Shoemaker and F. Robert Shoaf, "Behavioral Changes in the Trial of New Products," *Journal of Consumer Research*, 2 (September, 1975), pp. 104–109.

10. Duncan G. LaBay and Thomas C. Kinnear, "Exploring the Consumer Decision Process in the Adoption of Solar Energy Systems," *Journal of Consumer Research*, 8 (December, 1981), pp. 271–278.

11. Lymand Ostlund, "Perceived Innovation Attributes as Predictors of Innovativeness," *Journal of Consumer Research,* 1 (September, 1974), pp. 23–29.

12. Susan L. Holak and Donald R. Lehmann, "The Relationship Among Primary and Secondary Attributes of Innovative Consumer Durables," Working paper, University of Texas at Dallas, 1986.

13. Ostlund, "Perceived Innovation Attributes . . . ," *loc. cit.*

14. S. Ram and Jagdish Sheth, "Consumer Resistance to Innovations: The Marketing Problem and Its Solutions," *Journal of Consumer Marketing,* 6 (Spring, 1989), pp. 5–14.

15. See also Hubert Gatignon and Thomas S. Robertson, "A Propositional Inventory for New Diffusion Research," *Journal of Consumer Research,* 11 (March, 1985), pp. 849–867.

16. Mary Dee Dickenson and James W. Gentry, "Characteristics of Adopters and Non-Adopters of Home Computers," *Journal of Consumer Research,* 10 (September, 1983), pp. 225–235.

17. "Sony: Sorting Out the Sales Suspects," *Business Marketing* (August, 1988), pp. 44–48.

18. Everett M. Rogers, *Diffusion of Innovations* (New York: The Free Press, 1962).

19. *Ibid.,* pp. 168–171.

20. Robert L. Anderson and David J. Ortinau, "Exploring Consumers' Postadoption Attitudes and Use Behaviors in Monitoring the Diffusion of a Technology-Based Discontinuous Innovation," *Journal of Business Research,* 17 (1988), pp. 283–298.

21. Leon G. Schiffman and Leslie L. Kanuk, *Consumer Behavior* (Englewood Cliffs, NJ: Prentice-Hall, 1978), pp. 412–413.

22. Anderson and Ortinau, "Exploring Consumers' Postadoption Attitudes . . . ," *loc. cit.*

23. Richard W. Olshavsky, "Time and the Rate of Adoption of Innovations," *Journal of Consumer Research,* 6 (March, 1980), pp. 425–428.

24. Gatignon and Robertson, "A Propositional Inventory," *loc. cit.;* and Thomas S. Robertson and Hubert Gatignon, "Competitive Effects on Technology Diffusion," *Journal of Marketing,* 50 (July, 1986), pp. 1–12.

25. B. Ryan and N.C. Gross, "The Diffusion of Hybrid Seed Corn in Two Iowa Communities," *Rural Sociology,* 8 (March, 1943), pp. 15–24.

26. James Coleman, Elihu Katz, and Herbert Menzel, "The Diffusion of an Innovation Among Physi-

cians," *Sociometry,* 20 (December, 1957), pp. 253–270.

27. Ronald B. Marks and R. Eugene Hughes, "The Consumer Innovator: Identifying the Profile of the Earliest Adopters of Community Antenna Television," in Kenneth L. Bernhardt, ed., *Proceedings of the American Marketing Association Educators' Conference,* Series No. 39 (1976), pp. 568–571.

28. Leon G. Schiffman, "Perceived Risk in New Product Trial by Elderly Consumers," *Journal of Marketing Research,* 9 (February, 1972), pp. 106–108.

29. Hubert Gatignon and Thomas S. Robertson, "Innovative Decision Processes," *loc. cit.*

30. Rogers and Shoemaker, *Communication of Innovations, loc. cit.*

31. Gatignon and Robertson, "A Propositional Inventory . . . ," *loc. cit.*

32. James F. Engel, Robert J. Kegerreis, and Roger D. Blackwell, "Word-of-Mouth Communication by the Innovator," *Journal of Marketing,* 33 (July, 1969), pp. 15–19.

33. Jagdish N. Sheth, "Word-of-Mouth in Low-Risk Innovations," *Journal of Advertising Research,* 11 (June, 1971), pp. 15–18.

34. H. David Strutton and James R. Lumpkin, "Information Sources Used by Elderly Health Care Product Adopters," *Journal of Advertising Research,* 32 (July-August, 1992), pp. 20–30.

35. Thomas S. Robertson, "Determinants of Innovative Behavior," in Reed Moyer, ed., *Winter Conference of the American Marketing Association,* Series No. 26 (1967), pp. 328–332; and Engel, Kegerreis, and Blackwell, "Word-of Mouth Communication by the Innovator," *op. cit.,* p. 26.

36. Zarrel V. Lambert, "Perceptual Patterns, Information Handling, and Innovativeness," *Journal of Marketing Research,* 9 (November, 1972), pp. 427–431.

37. Steven A. Baumgarten, "The Innovative Communicator in the Diffusion Process," *Journal of Marketing Research,* 12 (February, 1975), pp. 12–18. See also David F. Midgley and Grahame R. Dowling, "A Longitudinal Study of Product Form Innovation: The Interaction Between Predispositions and Social Messages," *Journal of Consumer Behavior,* 19 (March, 1993), pp. 611–625.

38. See Johan Arndt, "Role of Product-Related Conversations in the Diffusion of a New Product," *Journal of Marketing Research,* 4 (August, 1967), pp. 291–295; and John O. Summers and Charles W.

King, "Interpersonal Communication and New Product Attitudes," in Philip R. McDonald, ed., *Proceedings of the American Marketing Association Educators' Conference,* Series No. 30 (1969), pp. 292–299.

39. Everett M. Rogers, "New Product Adoption and Diffusion," *Journal of Consumer Research,* 2 (March, 1976), pp. 290–301.

40. Gatignon and Robertson, "A Propositional Inventory . . . ," *op. cit.,* p. 857.

41. Jacqueline Johnson Brown and Peter H. Reingen, "Social Ties and Word-of-Mouth Referral Behavior," *Journal of Consumer Research,* 14 (December, 1987), pp. 350–362.

42. Thorstein Veblen, *The Theory of the Leisure Class* (New York: Macmillan, 1912).

43. George Simmel, "Fashion," *International Quarterly,* 10 (October, 1904), pp. 130–155.

44. "Grassroots Innovation," *Marketing Insights* (Summer, 1991), pp. 44–50.

45. Charles W. King, "Fashion Adoption: A Rebuttal to the 'Trickle Down' Theory," in James U. McNeal, ed., *Dimensions of Consumer Behavior* (New York: Appleton-Century-Crofts, 1969), p. 172.

46. Edward T. Hall, *Hidden Differences* (New York: Doubleday, 1987).

47. Rogers, *Diffusion of Innovations, loc. cit.*

48. Hirokazu Takada and Dipak Jain, "Cross-National Analysis of Diffusion of Consumer Durable Goods in Pacific Rim Countries," *Journal of Marketing,* 55 (April, 1991), pp. 48–54.

49. Dickenson and Gentry, "Characteristics of Adopters and Non-Adopters," *loc. cit.*

50. David F. Midgley, "A Simple Mathematical Theory of Innovative Behavior," *Journal of Consumer Research,* 3 (June, 1976), pp. 31–41.

51. Dorothy Leonard-Barton, "Experts as Negative Opinion Leaders in the Diffusion of a Technological Innovation," *Journal of Consumer Research,* 11 (March, 1985), pp. 914–926.

52. David Riesman, N. Glazer, and R. Denney, *The Lonely Crowd* (New Haven, CT: Yale University Press, 1950).

53. Robert L. Brittingham, Brent G. Goff, and Robert C. Haring, "Refinancers and Non-Refinancers: A Comparative Analysis," *Journal of Retail Banking,* 11 (Spring, 1989), pp. 27–34.

54. Howard J. Ehrlich and Dorothy Lee, "Dogmatism, Learning and Resistance to Change: A Review and a New Paradigm," *Psychological Bulletin,* 71 (April, 1969), pp. 249–260. See also Hubert Gatignon and Thomas S. Robertson, "Technology Diffusion: An Empirical Test of Competitive Effects," *Journal of Marketing,* 53 (January, 1989), pp. 35–49.

55. LaBay and Kinnear, "Exploring the Consumer Decision Process . . . ," *loc. cit.*

56. Engel, Kegerreis, and Blackwell, "Word-of-Mouth Communication by the Innovator," *loc. cit.*

57. Marks and Hughes, "The Consumer Innovator . . . ," *loc. cit.*

58. William R. Darden and Fred D. Reynolds, "Backward Profiling of Male Innovators," *Journal of Marketing Research,* 11 (February, 1974), pp. 79–85.

59. Charles W. King, "Communicating with the Innovator in the Fashion Adoption Process," in Peter D. Bennett, ed., *Proceedings of the Fall Conference of the American Marketing Association* (1965), p. 430; and Lambert, "Perceptual Patterns, Information Handling, and Innovativeness," *loc. cit.*

60. John O. Summers, "Media Exposure Patterns of Consumer Innovators," *Journal of Marketing,* 36 (January, 1972), pp. 43–49.

61. *Ibid.,* p. 46.

62. Baumgarten, "The Innovative Communicator . . . ," *op. cit.,* p. 16.

63. Summers, "Media Exposure Patterns . . . ," *op. cit.,* p. 46.

64. *Ibid.;* and King, "Communicating with the Innovator . . . ," *loc. cit.*

65. Lambert, "Perceptual Patterns, Information Handling, and Innnovativeness," *loc. cit.*

66. Peter H. Bloch, Daniel L. Sherrell, and Nancy M. Ridgeway, "Consumer Search: An Extended Framework," *Journal of Consumer Research,* 13 (June, 1986), pp. 119–126.

67. James H. Donnelly, Jr., and John M. Ivancevich, "A Methodology for Identifying Innovator Characteristics of New Brand Purchasers," *Journal of Marketing Research,* 11 (August, 1974), pp. 331–334.

68. Anderson and Ortinau, "Exploring Consumers' Postadoption Attitudes . . . ," *loc. cit.*

69. John O. Summers, "Generalized Change Agents and Innovativeness," *Journal of Marketing Research,* 8 (August, 1971), p. 314.

70. Philip Kotler and Gerald Zaltman, "Targeting Prospects for a New Product," *Journal of Advertising Research,* 16 (February, 1976), pp. 7–18.

20

Marketing Communications

In the last two chapters, we have described how interpersonal communications affect consumer behavior. Here, we focus on marketing communications. Consumers are more likely to be influenced by interpersonal, rather than marketing, communications because they generally regard friends and relatives as more credible and trustworthy sources than marketers. However, marketing communications play a key part in informing consumers of new products and product features and often influence consumers to buy. Without information, consumers cannot act. Through marketing communications, consumers learn about new products, the prices and availability of existing products, and the characteristics of alternative brands. As a result, the marketers' *communication* of information and influence and consumers' receipt of marketing information are key elements in the study of consumer behavior.

To be effective, marketing communications must convey how products and services can meet consumer needs. Product benefits can be communicated through words, symbols, and imagery; but regardless of the technique, the one constant in effective communication is conveying product benefits.

A good example is McDonald's promotional strategy. Consumers have associated McDonald's symbols such as the golden arches and the Ronald McDonald character with food, fun, and family values. Past campaigns such as "You deserve a break today" showing a family enjoying a Big Mac have reinforced this image. McDonald's communication prowess is partly a function of a $1 billion promotional budget that eclipses its competitors.[1] However, it is also a function of McDonald's ability to change its message to avoid it becoming stale. In the mid-1980s, the company quickly shifted from a lackluster "McDonald's and You" advertising campaign to a more effective and upbeat "It's a good time for the great taste of McDonald's." With the advent of a recession in 1990, the company began emphasizing economy with a "Good Food, Good Value" theme.

McDonald's communications strategy does not rely solely on advertising. Sales promotions such as sweepstakes, contests, and coupons support the benefits that advertising conveys. For example, McDonald's used a Monopoly game promotion that gave away $40 million in prizes based on "deeds" to Monopoly board locations. It was advertising, however, that established McDonald's image and ensures that 17 million Americans are served each day in one of its 10,000 fast-food outlets.[2]

In contrast to McDonald's, Burger King has had trouble staying on track and communicating product benefits. The company floundered in the mid-1980s with a "Search for Herb" campaign, a $40 million fiasco based on a search for a mythical figure called Herb who had never tasted a Whopper. The focus on Herb as a balding eccentric in glasses, white socks, and gaudy plaids did not get any particular message across regarding the benefits of visiting a Burger King. It then changed its slogan to "Sometimes you've got to break the rules." Again, customers could not understand what benefits the slogan was trying to convey. One Burger King franchisee asked "Are we telling kids to go out and buy drugs?"[3]

Having gone through eight campaigns since 1976, Burger King finally hit on a campaign in 1991 that communicated a consistent benefits-oriented message, "Your way. Right away." The slogan communicated satisfaction and quick service at Burger King outlets. To reinforce the message, the company began touting value-oriented sales promotions in a "Your Way" in-store campaign.

In this chapter, we focus on the key components of marketing communication, namely the marketers' influence on consumers (the source), the message, and the media used to transmit the message. The role of consumers in evaluating these components of marketing communication is also emphasized, as well as the need for feedback from consumers to permit marketers to evaluate the effectiveness of their communication.

◆ MARKETING COMMUNICATIONS PROCESS

The marketing communications process involves advertising, personal selling, and in-store promotions. We will be focusing primarily on advertising in this chapter. Previous chapters have considered personal selling (Chapters 15 and 18) and in-store effects (Chapters 3, 5, and 12).

Advertising is one of the most important forms of marketing communications. Yearly advertising expenditures in the United States are over $200 billion and are expected to be close to $500 billion by the turn of the century.

A detailed model of marketing communications and, more specifically, the advertising communications process is presented in Figure 20.1. The top of the figure cites the five components of communications described in Chapter 9: a source, a message, a means of transmitting the message, a receiver, and feedback from receiver to communicator to assess the message. The model is translated into an advertising process. The results of the marketing communications process are also shown, including possible barriers to effective communication from advertiser to consumer.

Figure 20.1 forms the basis for this chapter. We will first discuss the advertising process in the communications model and barriers to communication. We will then focus on the five key elements in the communications process and how they influence consumer behavior.

Advertising Process

Figure 20.1 shows how advertising is developed in the context of the five-step marketing communications model. In the first step, the source (the marketer) defines communications objectives. For example, when Ralston Purina bought Eveready in 1986, it found Duracell closing in on Eveready's 52 percent share of the $2.5 billion U.S. battery market.[4] Duracell's campaign showing battery-powered toys outlasting competitors in endurance contests was effective in conveying product benefits, while Eveready's spokesperson, Robert Conrad, was lackluster. Eveready's management realized it would have to do a more effective job in communicating key benefits—durability and a steady power source.

Next, the advertising agency encodes messages to *communicate product benefits*. A good example is the Eveready Bunny campaign cited in Chapter 7. By parodying Duracell's endurance toys, the ads were meant to convey the same benefits that Duracell was communicating—durability and reliability in a power source—but in a humorous way that was also meant to undercut Duracell.

The third step in the communications model, *transmitting the message to a target segment,* requires a media plan that is cost-effective. An effective media plan achieves a delicate balance between several potentially conflicting objectives. One possible conflict occurs between trying to reach as many people as

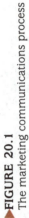

▶**FIGURE 20.1**
The marketing communications process

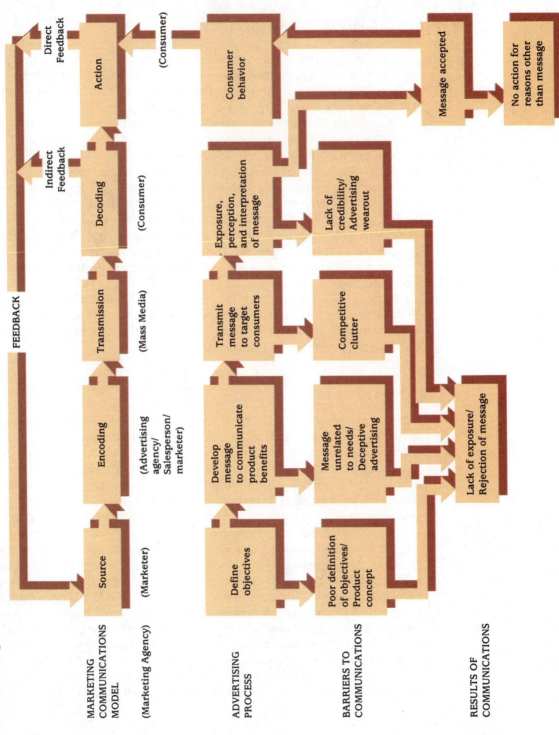

possible versus reaching them as frequently as possible. Given a limited budget, advertisers cannot maximize both **reach** (the number of people exposed to the message) and **frequency** (the number of times an individual consumer or household is exposed). Reaching as many people as possible is more important for broadly targeted products such as Crest toothpaste or Coca-Cola. Frequency is more important when trying to influence a particular target group such as young, upscale car buyers. In this case, the objective is to reach a limited market segment as often as possible within budgetary constraints.

In the Eveready Bunny campaign, the media plan involved a balance between reach and frequency. Initially, Ralston Purina used network television to reach as broad an audience as possible. By 1990, print ads began appearing in magazines such as *Newsweek*, *People*, and *Sports Illustrated* to ensure greater frequency of exposure among battery purchasers. (See Exhibit 20.1.)

The next steps involve consumers—*exposure to the message, decoding it (perception and interpretation) and possible action* based on the message. When the Eveready Bunny campaign was first introduced, many consumers remembered a *Duracell*, rather than an Eveready, campaign. Why? Because the Bunny's theme, "Still going," was a spinoff of Duracell's earlier endurance theme. Consumers simply did not decode the message correctly. There was evidence that the campaign was boosting Duracell's sales.[5] However, Ralston Purina's management was not deterred. They had faith in the campaign; and eventually, most consumers associated the Bunny correctly with Eveready.

The last step, *feedback,* is designed to determine whether consumers have decoded the message as intended and whether they are likely to translate perceptions of the message into purchasing actions. Such feedback should help advertisers determine whether to continue, change, or cancel the campaign. By 1991, Eveready claimed that brand awareness rose 33 percent from the year before and recall of the advertising message was up 50 percent.[6] The most difficult question to answer is whether such improvements in brand awareness and recall are translated into brand purchases. Apparently they were; because by 1991, Eveready stopped the hemorrhaging of its market and maintained its market position relative to Duracell.

▶**EXHIBIT 20.1**
Eveready uses the Bunny to communicate product benefits

Barriers to Communications

In evaluating the advertising communications process, marketers must ask four questions:

1. Have communications objectives been defined to reflect consumer needs?
2. Have marketers adequately encoded product benefits?
3. Has the message been transmitted to the target segment by utilizing the right media?
4. Did consumers decode the message in the manner the advertiser intended?

A negative answer to any of these questions can lead to barriers in the communications process at the source, in encoding, in transmission, or with the receiver in decoding or in action. A fifth question, whether the communication leads to a purchase, bears on the results of the communications process.

Barriers at the Source

The barrier to communication at the source is an inadequate definition of objectives. In many cases, this means a poor focus on product benefits. Such a failure is most likely to lead to an advertising message that is unrelated to consumer needs. For example, a large pharmaceutical company once developed an aspirin that consumers could take without water. The company believed consumers would want quick relief when water was not available, and initial tests of the product were encouraging. In developing the advertising campaign, the company used the key benefits of instant relief anywhere at any time. However, the product was a failure because it did not meet consumer needs: Consumers wanted the soothing effects of water when taking aspirin. As a result, the campaign was doomed to failure. No matter how creative the advertising or how well conceived the media plan, communications will not result in sales if the product does not meet consumer needs.

Barriers in Encoding

Failures in marketing communications can also be attributable to the process of encoding. At times, copywriters and artists may be more interested in developing creative, original advertising than in conveying product benefits. The result may be a message that gains attention but does not communicate benefits to the consumer. When Eveready first tried to take on Duracell, it borrowed an Australian campaign for Eveready that used an eccentric square-jawed soccer star named Jacko Jackson who said "Oy" and demanded that viewers "Get Energizer." Eveready's CEO decided that with a little grooming, Jacko could be exported to the United States. Eveready sank $30 million into a campaign doomed to failure.[7] Why? Because Jacko simply did not communicate product benefits. Americans grew to loath Jacko as a loud-mouthed irritant. The ads were as much of a debacle as Burger King's "Where's Herb?" campaign.[8] Both of the campaigns created barriers in communicating by poorly encoding product benefits.

Barriers in Transmission

Barriers to communication can occur in the process of transmission. Perhaps the greatest barrier in transmission is *competitive clutter*. The number of commercials and print advertisements has been increasing for several reasons. First, the proliferation of new products demands more commercial time. Second, competitive intensity has caused advertising budgets to rise proportionately faster than sales. Third, TV commercials are getting shorter with a shift from 30- to 15-second spot commercials. As a result, from 1967 to 1986, the number of TV commercials increased by almost four times. By 1991, *Business Week* estimated that U.S. adults are "bombarded with 3,000 marketing messages a day."[9] Because of such clutter, it is estimated that in the last 20 years, the consumer's ability to remember the last commercial seen on TV declined from 18 percent to 7 percent.[10] Clearly, the increase in the number of commercials has inhibited consumers' decoding process. (An illustration of the problem of competitive clutter is shown in Exhibit 20.2.)

Several studies have documented the fact that more frequent advertising has resulted in less consumer attention to messages. Webb found that attention and recall dropped off as the number of ads increased.[11] Burke and Srull found that more exposure to competing ads inhibits consumers' ability to remember the advertised brand.[12] They concluded that greater similarity between brands and between advertising themes creates confusion and makes

▶**EXHIBIT 20.2**
An illustration of the problem of competitive clutter

Source: From *The Wall Street Journal*. Permission, Cartoon Features Syndicate.

"We'll return to our commercials in a moment, but first this program . . ."

retrieval of specific brand information from memory more difficult. As a result, consumers are more likely to confuse ad themes for Pepsi and Coke, for Crest and Colgate, and as we saw, for Eveready and Duracell.

What can marketers do to combat the confusion competitive clutter creates? An easy answer is to increase the frequency of advertising to make a more lasting impression on consumers. However, this can be a solution only if the message is closely tied to consumer benefits (that is, the message has no source or encoding barriers). Increased frequency rescued the Eveready Bunny campaign because greater exposure caused consumers to identify correctly the source as Eveready rather than Duracell. However, success depended on the Bunny commercials' ability to convey the key benefits of durability and dependability.

Barriers in Decoding

Barriers can also occur in the decoding process. A failure to develop a product concept or to create an advertising message related to consumer needs is likely to lead to such barriers. Consumers will selectively ignore messages of no interest to them, as they did with Burger King's "Where's Herb?" and Eveready's Jacko campaigns because of their failure to communicate benefits. Furthermore, if consumers find that the source of the message is not credible, they will reject the message. For example, consumers may reject an advertisement from a large utility company justifying higher prices to finance nuclear energy for lack of credibility. However, consumers are more likely to accept a similar message from the Environmental Protection Agency.

Barriers to decoding may occur because of lack of attention to the message. Competitive clutter is a barrier not only in transmission, but also in the decoding process because it encourages inattention. The continued use of an ad for a long period of time is another cause of inattention. **Advertising wearout** may occur; that is, advertising effectiveness may decrease because of consumer boredom and familiarity with the campaign.

Results of Communications

Figure 20.1 shows that consumers may avoid exposure to a message or, if exposed, may accept or reject it. *Message acceptance* is due to an effective process of communicating product benefits that are important to a target segment. *Message rejection* may be due to lack of message credibility or believability, or it may be independent of message content and reflect consumers' attitudes, past experiences, and beliefs. For example, a consumer who has had consistently poor performance from a certain automobile make is unlikely to accept the validity of a claim that the car is well engineered and durable and provides maximum performance on the road.

From the advertiser's standpoint, the most desirable result of the communication process is a purchase as a result of message acceptance. Figure 20.1 shows that message acceptance may lead to a purchase or that consumers may decide not to purchase for reasons other than the information in the communication. Price and availability are obvious restrictions to purchase. Another is lack of an immediate need. Consumers may be attracted to a car because of the advertising but may not be in the market for one.

Regardless of the outcome, marketers would like to assess the effect of the marketing communication on the purchase. Evaluation of the communication by marketing and advertising research provides marketers with feedback. **Direct feedback** is provided when a marketing communication can be linked to sales results. Marketers can judge retail advertising announcing a sale on a given day by the number of shoppers, and they can evaluate the effects of in-store displays by comparing sales with and without displays. Also, marketers can relate coupon returns to the advertising source. However, the sales effectiveness of an advertising message in the mass media is harder to judge. Marketers have difficulty determining the degree to which an advertising campaign is instrumental in brand choice because so many other factors enter into the purchase decision. As a result, indirect feedback assumes more importance in evaluating ad campaigns. **Indirect feedback** is provided when the marketing communication is evaluated on the basis of the consumers' process of decoding the message. Indirect criteria of effectiveness relate to the advertisement's ability to produce exposure, awareness, comprehension, and retention of the advertising message.

In the rest of this chapter, the primary components of the advertising communications process are considered in detail: (1) source, (2) message (encoding), (3) media (transmission), (4) consumer (decoding), and (5) feedback.

 ## SOURCE EFFECTS IN MARKETING COMMUNICATIONS

The source of information (advertisers, salespersons, friends) directly influences consumers' acceptance and interpretation of a message. It is important to consider the *credibility* and *attractiveness* of the source to consumers to understand the effects the source has on consumer behavior.

Source Credibility

Source credibility is the level of expertise and trustworthiness consumers attribute to the source of the message.[13] *Expertise* is the ability of the source to make valid statements about the product's characteristics and performance. Few would question the ability of a Boris Becker or a Martina Navratilova to make valid assessments of tennis equipment. *Trustworthiness* is the perception that a source has made a valid statement about the product. Some spokespersons may be regarded as experts in their field, but consumers may question the trustworthiness of their product endorsements because the advertiser is paying them.

Consumers frequently question the trustworthiness of ad claims because advertisers have a vested interest in selling the brand. The use of puffery (inflated claims in advertising) reinforces this view. When nearly all toothpastes claim to do the best job of eliminating cavities or controlling tartar and when nearly all detergents claim to do the best job of getting clothes cleaner, consumers naturally wonder what they can believe.

Consumers regard neutral sources such as *Consumer Reports* magazine as trustworthy because they have no vested interest in the brand and they make no attempt to change attitudes or influence behavior. Newscasters and editorial sources also have a high degree of credibility. Walter Cronkite, the former newscaster, has been cited in polls as the most credible individual in the eyes of the American public. In addition, consumers are likely to accept the brand judgments of family and friends, particularly those viewed as opinion leaders for the product category.[14]

Some researchers have used attribution theory to explain why consumers view advertising as less credible than personal and neutral sources. Attribution theory states that receivers attribute certain motives to a communication source. When all ads consumers see are making uniformly positive claims (the best-tasting coffee, the most reliable airline, the best performing car, and so on), consumers begin to doubt the advertiser's motives. Uniformly positive claims lead consumers to attribute the message to the advertiser's desire to sell the product rather than to a desire to transmit valid information about product performance.

On the other hand, if a message provides some variation in the claim (for example, headache remedy A is stronger and provides quick relief, but it is more likely to upset the stomach), consumers are more likely to accept the source as credible. As we will see, consumers are more likely to attribute such two-sided advertising appeals to the product's actual characteristics than to the advertiser's desire to sell.

Credibility and Message Acceptance

Studies have concluded that the greater the perceived credibility of the source, the greater is the likelihood receivers will accept the message.[15] For example, Craig and McCann studied the effects of messages from Con Edison and from the New York State Public Service Commission asking consumers to save money by reducing the consumption of electricity used for air conditioning.[16] The message was enclosed in the monthly utility bill. The group receiving the message from the Public Service Commission—perceived as a more credible source—consumed substantially less electricity than the group receiving the message from Con Edison. The authors concluded that "the effectiveness of a communication advocating energy conservation can be enhanced by using a source of greater credibility."[17]

Source credibility in itself does not ensure message acceptance. Source credibility is not likely to increase message acceptance if, for example, consumers rely on their past experiences rather than on the ad in evaluating a brand.[18] Similarly, increasing the source's credibility will not increase message acceptance if the message is threatening[19] or conflicts with consumers' best interests.[20] An ad on the risks of smoking from a credible source like the American Cancer Society will not increase message acceptance by many confirmed smokers because they see the message as a threat and want to avoid it.

Increasing the Credibility of the Source

Because a lack of credibility is a major limitation to consumers' acceptance of advertising messages, advertisers should consider how they can increase their credibility. The implication from attribution theory is to vary the claim so that it is not uniformly positive. If advertisers present both positive and negative information about the product (a two-sided message), consumers are more likely to attribute the claim to the product's actual characteristics rather than to the advertiser's desire to sell. However, marketers have rarely used such two-sided advertising because they are reluctant to present negative information about their product, even on relatively unimportant attributes. Research has demonstrated, however, that consumers have more confidence in claims that cite the pros and cons of a brand.[21]

There are two other strategies to enhance the advertiser's credibility. First, utilize expertise. Salespeople who are viewed as experts seem more credible in sales situations than do nonexpert salespeople. Advertising that uses spokespersons who consumers accept as experts (for example, Ella Fitzgerald for Memorex tapes) increases credibility. In evaluating the impact of celebrity spokespersons on consumers, Ohanion found that the expertise of the spokesperson is a more important influence than his or her trustworthiness or attractiveness.[22]

A second strategy to enhance credibility is to increase trustworthiness. Marketers often utilize neutral sources to encourage trustworthiness. Ads that cite neutral sources such as ratings from *Consumer Reports* or *Good Housekeeping* Seal of Approval are more likely to gain trustworthiness.

Source Attractiveness

Another basis by which consumers evaluate the source is its attractiveness, which is determined by its likability and its similarity to consumers.[23] Research has shown that when consumers see salespeople as similar to themselves, consumers are more likely to accept and be influenced by the sales messages.[24]

Since source attractiveness increases message acceptance, marketers try to emphasize similarity and enhance likability to increase attractiveness. Advertisers have emphasized the similarity between the source and the consumer by portraying "typical consumers" using and endorsing products. When consumers see others similar to themselves using the product, they are more likely to react positively to it. Brands as diverse as Subaru cars and Tylenol analgesics have used this approach. Salespeople often emphasize similarity with consumers because a salesperson who is seen as a peer becomes more attractive as a source of information.

Marketers can use spokespersons in advertising to increase credibility and/or attractiveness. Chapter 15 cited the use of expert spokespersons to increase credibility and referent spokespersons (those to whom consumers can easily relate) as a means of increasing source attractiveness. For example, James Garner was successful as a referent spokesperson for Polaroid's regular line of instant cameras; he was likeable but had no particular credibility as an expert in photography. Conversely, the late John Houseman was effective in conveying expertise as a spokesman for the brokerage house, Smith Barney, based on his role as a law professor in the TV series "The Paper Chase." However, he was not particularly likeable as he intoned "Smith Barney makes money the old-fashioned way. They earn it!"

When should advertisers emphasize attractiveness or expertise? Mazursky and Schul found that if consumers are involved in the purchase, expertise should be emphasized; if consumers are not involved, attractiveness should be emphasized.[25] In the high involvement case, consumers will focus on the message, and an expert best presents credible information. In the low involvement case, consumers are not that focused on the message, and the source will have more of an impact. As a result, the attractiveness of the spokesperson may be effective in gaining attention. Thus, Lee Iacocca may be effective as an expert spokesperson for an involving product like cars, in his role as former CEO of Chrysler (see Exhibit 20.3), while Bill Cosby is effective as a likeable spokesperson for an uninvolving product like Jell-O.

Source Versus Message Effects

Source credibility does not always operate to increase message acceptance. As the research by Mazursky and Schul showed, involved consumers are likely to focus primarily on the message's content rather than its source. This finding conforms to the Elaboration Likelihood Model (ELM) discussed in Chapter 5. According to ELM, involved consumers process messages through a central route that focuses on message content, while less involved consumers process messages through a peripheral route that focuses on factors extraneous to the message (peripheral cues). The source of the message is a peripheral cue. Therefore, according to ELM, source credibility is most important in influencing message acceptance in low involvement conditions. Message effects are most important in high involvement conditions.

Research supports this contention. Petty, Cacioppo, and Schumann found that use of celebrity spokespersons in ads had little influence when consumers were involved. However, such spokespersons exerted a strong influence on less involved consumers.[26] Similarly, Ratneshwar and Chaiken found that consumers who processed information more fully (and were, therefore, more involved with the situation) were less likely to be influenced by the source of the message.[27] They also found that source credibility was more important if consumers had little knowledge of the brand or product category. In such cases, it would be natural for consumers to rely on an expert spokesperson.

▶**EXHIBIT 20.3**
Lee Iacocca: An effective expert spokesperson for Chrysler

Miniard and his colleagues found that source credibility may be important even when consumers are involved with the product.[28] Consumers evaluating alternative brands with similar claims may have difficulty distinguishing one claim from another. In such cases, the credibility of the source may be a deciding factor. For example, consumers evaluating advertising claims among three or four analgesic brands may find they are making similar claims regarding safety and efficacy. In such cases, use of a credible spokesperson may be decisive for an involving product category. Miniard *et al.* also found that source credibility may be important when brands make conflicting claims. If one analgesic says aspirin can irritate the stomach and another says it does not, consumers may throw up their hands and decide to believe the claim an expert spokesperson backs.

In summary, source credibility is likely to be most influential when:

- Consumers are not involved.
- Consumers have little knowledge of the appropriate characteristics to evaluate brands.
- Brands with similar claims are being evaluated.
- Brand claims are conflicting.

◆ EFFECTS OF THE MESSAGE

The advertising message is meant to inform and persuade. Informational objectives may be directed toward announcing new products or changes in existing products, informing consumers of product characteristics, or providing information on price and availability. Persuasive objectives may be directed toward convincing consumers of product benefits, trying to induce trial, or reducing uncertainty about buying the product. The methods of developing and presenting advertising messages are beyond the scope of this text, but certain aspects of message content bear directly on the likelihood that consumers will accept and act on the message. Consumer researchers have considered four questions:

1. Should the message be one-sided or two-sided?
2. Is comparative advertising (naming a competitor in the ad) an effective means of communicating product benefits?
3. What are the advantages of using fear appeals?
4. What is the appropriate role of humor in advertising?

One-Sided Versus Two-Sided Appeals

Two-sided messages are those that provide both positive and negative information about a product. The negative information is usually relatively unimportant compared to the positive information. Such messages are effective because they increase source credibility and reduce resistance to the message among skeptics.

Refuting Negative Information

Two-sided ads can be refutational (the negative information is presented and then refuted) or nonrefutational. A two-sided refutational ad might say that a car is relatively small; but for the young professional just starting out, economy is more important than comfort, and this car is the most economical on the market. A nonrefutational ad would simply present the pros and cons of the car in a straightforward fashion.

Presenting negative information about the company's product is an infrequent strategy in advertising. Advertisers are fearful that it could point out product deficiencies and discourage consumers from buying, even if the negative information is refuted. However, such a strategy can be quite effective if refuting a negative factor actually reinforces the benefits of the product. For example, for years Avis used a two-sided refutational strategy by first stating that it was not the largest company and then discounting that by saying, "We try harder." (See Exhibit 20.4.) The Avis campaign actually turned an unimportant negative into a positive benefit by convincing many consumers that being number two prompted the company to pay more attention to its customers.

▶**EXHIBIT 20.4**
Example of a two-sided message

Source: Courtesy of Avis Inc.

Avis is only No. 2. But we don't want your sympathy.

Have we been crying too much? Have we overplayed the underdog?

We didn't think so till David Biener, 11 years old, sent us 35¢, saying, "It may help you buy another Plymouth."

That was an eye-opener.

So now we'd like to correct the false impression we've made.

We don't want you to reserve Avis cars for your clients because you feel sorry for us. Give us a chance to prove that a No. 2 can be just as good as a No. 1. Or even better. Because we have to try harder.

Maybe we ought to eliminate the negative and accentuate the positive.

Instead of saying "We're only No. 2 in rent a cars," we could say "We're the second largest in the world."

Avis Fund
It hasn't come to this.

Defusing Objections to the Product

Another reason for favoring two-sided appeals is that they may defuse nonusers' objections to a product. Consider the consumer who believes that food cooked in microwave ovens is tasteless. The consumer sees a one-sided ad for a microwave oven claiming that it not only cooks food faster, but also actually enhances the taste of certain foods. We saw in Chapter 9 that when consumers obtain information that is discrepant with their beliefs, they often develop counterarguments (thoughts that counter information in the ad). The consumer develops counterarguments to the claims in the ad (How can a microwave oven cook better-tasting food than a regular oven?) and rejects the message.

Counterarguing is most likely to occur in high involvement situations when consumers see discrepant information as a threat.[29] If a two-sided ad is presented, one in which possible arguments against the brand are presented first and then refuted, the objections of consumers with discrepant beliefs are defused, as the ad has already stated the counterarguments. The consumer seeing a two-sided ad for microwave ovens may be told that microwaves improve taste in certain kinds of cooking situations but not in others and that the company's brand is most effective in retaining taste for these types of foods. The consumer is more likely to accept this type of refutational ad.

Research has shown that two-sided appeals lead to less counterarguing and greater message acceptance by consumers because their concerns have already been stated in the ad. Kamins and Assael found that two-sided appeals produced significantly less counterarguing than one-sided appeals in advertising a new product and led to higher intentions to buy.[30] Similarly, Szybillo and Heslin found that when messages were presented to consumers supporting the use of air bags (one-sided) and both supporting and rejecting their use (two-sided), the two-sided ads were more effective in convincing consumers of the air bags' merits.[31] They used *inoculation theory* (see Chapter 9) to posit that the two-sided ad "inoculated" consumers against counterarguing by preempting any of their negative thoughts. The conclusion in both studies is that two-sided advertisements are more effective in introducing a new product that must overcome some consumer objections.

Two-sided ads are less effective when consumers are not involved with the product because less-involved consumers are not as attentive to the pros and cons stated in two-sided advertising.[32] Evidence also suggests that one-sided ads produce greater message acceptance when consumers are less educated,[33] when there is agreement with the advertiser's position, and when consumers are loyal to the advertiser's brand.[34] In today's competitive environment, however, brand loyalty is less likely to occur. Advertisers, therefore, should increase their use of two-sided advertising in an attempt to provide consumers with a more realistic presentation of product benefits.

Comparative Advertising

Another type of advertising that has experienced increased usage is comparative advertising; that is, naming a competitor in the ad. The use of comparative advertising has increased since the networks removed a ban on its use in 1976. One network, NBC, reported that half of the commercials it screened in 1986 were comparative ads, compared to about one-third in 1980.[35]

Most comparative advertising is one-sided; that is, it presents the strengths of the advertised product and the weaknesses of the competitive product. For example, MCI names AT&T in its ads and claims it provides better service, Nissan compares its price to that of the Toyota Camry (see Exhibit 20.5), and Pontiac claims that its Bonneville can give car drivers the same features as a BMW or Lexus, but for $10,000 to $20,000 less. At times, the use of comparative ads can get heated. In 1992, Coors introduced a TV campaign claiming that its Extra Gold tasted more like the "real beers" of the past than Budweiser. A few months later, Anheuser-Busch (makers of Budweiser) retaliated by claiming that Coors dilutes the vaunted Rocky Mountain spring water it uses for its beers with water from one of its Virginia breweries. Coors then sued Anheuser for false advertising.[36]

Despite this potential for undermining other brands and being undermined in turn, evidence suggests that comparative ads can be highly effective in influ-

▶**EXHIBIT 20.5**
An example of
comparative advertising

Source: Courtesy of Nissan
Motor Corporation U.S.A.

encing consumers. The arguments in favor of comparative advertising are that
(1) users of competing brands are more likely to notice the ad and are, therefore, more likely to consider the advertiser's brand,[37] and (2) claims made in
comparative ads provide consumers with more information and a more rational basis for choice (an advantage cited by the Federal Trade Commission).[38]

However, studies have questioned the effectiveness of comparative advertising. Swinyard found that when it is one-sided, comparative advertising loses
credibility and generates sympathy for the brand being attacked.[39] A study by
Ogilvy-Mather, a large ad agency, found that consumers frequently confuse the
sponsor for the competitor in many comparative ads. Furthermore, there was
no difference in the persuasiveness of comparative and noncomparative ads.[40]

However, other studies have found that if the source is credible, comparative advertising is effective. Gotleib and Sarel found that credible, comparative
ads were more likely to be noticed and were more likely to influence intentions
to buy the advertised brand compared to noncomparative ads.[41] They also
found that credible comparative ads were particularly effective for new products.[42] Swinyard found that credibility can best be achieved by making a comparative ad two-sided—that is, a comparative ad that names a competitor, cites
some of the advantages of the competitive brand, and then points out the

arguments for the advertised brand.[43] Although they may be effective, these types of ads are rare because advertisers are reluctant to cite the advantages of a competitive brand, even in the context of comparative advertising.

Another study by Pechmann and Stewart went further in exploring the effectiveness of comparative advertising by showing it is best used for brands with lower market share.[44] When a low-share brand compares itself to a high-share brand, it attracts attention to itself, yet does not encourage consumers to misidentify the sponsor as the high-share brand. The implication is that low-share brands have less to lose than high-share brands in using comparative advertising campaigns. A comparison to the market leader may elevate the low-share brand to the same level of quality and popularity in the consumers' eyes. Conversely, if a market leader compares itself to a lower-share brand, it may lower itself. That is probably why MCI compares itself to AT&T and why Nissan compares itself to Toyota rather than the other way around.

Fear Appeals

Most marketing communications attempt to inform consumers of the benefits of using a product. Fear appeals do the opposite: They inform consumers of the risks of using a product (such as cigarettes) or of not using one (such as deodorants). The importance of fear appeals is reflected in the finding that an estimated 17 percent of all TV commercials are fear-oriented.[45]

Fear appeals are likely to be ineffective if they are too threatening. In the past, the American Cancer Society demonstrated the harmful effects of smoking with appeals from terminal cancer patients. The messages were so stark that consumers ignored or dismissed them because of a natural process of perceptual defense to reduce dissonance. Acceptance of these messages meant facing the possibility of death because of the individual's action (or inaction). A Federal Trade Commission report illustrated people's avoidance of such anxiety-producing information; it found that the average number of cigarettes consumed did not change after health warnings became public.[46]

At the other extreme, fear appeals are likely to be ineffective when consumers associate little or no anxiety with the message. A fear appeal for floor cleaners picturing neighbors commenting on a dirty floor is not likely to work these days because homemakers are just not very concerned. Fear appeals, therefore, are most likely to influence consumers when anxiety is moderate.[47] Research has confirmed the effectiveness of moderate fear appeals. One study tested the effects of high, moderate, and low-level fear appeals on attitudes toward drinking. Moderate-level warnings, which consumers considered most truthful, were most effective in changing attitudes towards drinking.[48]

When are fear appeals most likely to succeed? Tanner, Hunt, and Eppright investigated the effectiveness of fear appeals in changing behavior toward socially transmitted diseases (for example, the effectiveness of fear appeals in getting individuals to practice safe sex to prevent AIDS).[49] They found that fear appeals were most effective when:

- Consumers recognized the severity of the threat (AIDS can kill).
- Consumers recognize they can be affected by the threat (I could be exposed to AIDS).
- The ad shows how to deal with the problem (the threat of AIDS can be reduced by using condoms).
- The proposed course of action is easily implemented (one can just walk into a drugstore to buy condoms).

The most important finding is that fear appeals must show consumers how to deal with the problem. The antismoking ad in Exhibit 20.6 may be effective in convincing nonsmokers not to try cigarettes or occasional smokers to stop. However, its lack of specific action recommendations for heavy smokers means that it will probably be ineffective in getting them to change their behavior.

Humor in Advertising

Marketers use humorous messages because they attract attention and because advertisers believe that humor can be persuasive. One source estimates that up to 25 percent of all television commercials contain some element of humor.[50]

There are pros and cons for the use of humor in advertising. On the positive side, humor is likely to increase attention[51] and memorability.[52] It is also likely to enhance the advertiser's credibility.[53] Humor may create a positive feeling toward the advertiser and, thus, increase the persuasiveness of the message. It also may distract consumers who use competitive products from developing arguments against the advertiser's brand and may lead them to accept the message.[54]

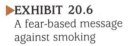
▶**EXHIBIT 20.6**
A fear-based message against smoking

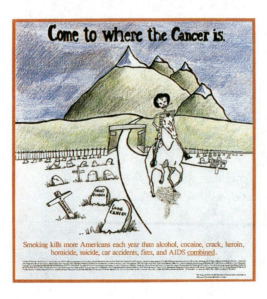

Come to where the Cancer is.

Smoking kills more Americans each year than alcohol, cocaine, crack, heroin, homicide, suicide, car accidents, fires, and AIDS combined.

In 1986, a group of advertising agencies and media companies formed the Partnership for a Drug-Free America. The purpose of the partnership was to develop a communications campaign to reduce drug use by encouraging an attitude of intolerance toward drugs.

The Partnership realized it would have to wage a campaign to make the public aware of the risk of drugs. Although the campaign was more educationally oriented, the Partnership utilized some of the key behavioral principles that apply to fear-oriented campaigns.

First, it realized that its target group would have to be those who could do something about their behavior. As a result, it directed its messages to nonusers and occasional users of drugs to convince them that "any perceived usage benefits are far outweighed by negatives."

Second, the Partnership recognized that it was dealing with an area of potentially high anxiety. Younger individuals had a genuine fear that they might be influenced by peer pressure to try drugs, and occasional users feared that they might grow dependent on drugs. The Partnership may have been tempted to show the stark results of excessive drug use (scarred arms, bodies in a morgue, convulsive addicts), but it avoided this approach, recognizing that it might just lead to avoidance based on perceptual defense.

The campaign relied on themes such as the problems with increasing drug use in small-town America and the potential health hazards of drug use, but not in a way to encourage avoidance. To date, some 300 ads have been created for all major media and are being run without charge. Had the campaign been advertising a product, the equivalent expenditures would have amounted to $900 million through 1990.

Has the campaign been effective? To answer this question, the Partnership determined markets where the ads were run frequently and infrequently. In markets such as Minneapolis, Rochester, and Miami, ads have been run very frequently (high media markets). In other markets such as Chicago and Los Angeles, air time has been infrequent (low media markets). The difference is due to the amount of time TV and radio stations in these areas have volunteered to the campaign.

Attitudes toward drugs changed more significantly in the markets with greater advertising frequency. For example, 10 percent more teens in the high media markets said there is a great risk in taking marijuana. Furthermore, usage changed along with attitudes. Use of marijuana went down 38 percent more in the high media markets as compared to the low.

It is not certain to what degree changes in advertising and usage could be attributed to the advertising campaign. It is safe to assume,

STRATEGIC APPLICATIONS OF CONSUMER BEHAVIOR

Creating Awareness of the Risks of Drug Use: The Partnership for a Drug-Free America

however, that the campaign was effective in influencing those individuals who had control over their behavior to stay away from drugs.

Source: The Media-Advertising Partnership for a Drug-Free America, *What We've Learned About Advertising* (New York: American Association of Advertising Agencies, 1990).

To be effective, humor must convey product benefits. An example is the Kohler ad in Exhibit 20.7. At best, bathroom fixtures are difficult to advertise. The picture of two dogs straddling a toilet seat is an incongruous and attention-getting device that also conveys the key benefits—sturdiness and a seat-actuated flusher.

However, there is a risk in using humor. If humor is too dominating, it may have a negative effect on message comprehension and may fail to communicate product benefits.[55] A good example of the ineffective use of humor was the "Where's Herb?" campaign for Burger King, cited earlier. The focus on Herb was attention getting but did not convey any particular message regarding the

▶**EXHIBIT 20.7**
The use of humor to communicate benefits

benefits of visiting a Burger King. If humor is to work, it must have a natural association with the product.[56]

When is the use of humor most effective? Researchers have found four conditions that make humor effective. First, humor is more effective in gaining message acceptance when consumers are not involved.[57] Since humor is peripheral to the message, it is more likely to influence consumers who are not involved with the product. Second, humor is more effective for existing products.[58] Advertising new products requires conveying information. Humor is more effective in establishing a mood than in conveying information. Third, humor is more effective when consumers have a positive attitude toward the brand to begin with.[59] Humor can reinforce positive feelings toward a brand, but it is unlikely to reverse negative feelings.

Fourth, humor is most effective when it is incongruous. Alden, Hoyer, and Lee studied the use of humorous ads in four countries—the United States, Korea, Thailand, and Germany.[60] They found that in all four cultures, a majority of humorous ads had incongruous themes. The ad in Exhibit 20.7 is certainly incongruous in showing two dogs standing on a toilet seat.

◆ MEDIA EFFECTS

The third component in the communications model is message transmission. Advertisers must ensure that the message reaches the intended target. To do so, advertisers must identify the characteristics of the target segment by demographic and lifestyle criteria and then select media that can best reach this segment. The selection of media according to consumer characteristics was described in Chapter 10. In this section, we will consider the communication effects of utilizing different types of media.

Marshall McLuhan's statement, "The medium is the message," implies that the medium communicates an image independent of any single message that is being transmitted.[61] The media environment influences consumers' reaction to a communication in two ways. First, particular types of media such as magazines may influence message evaluation. Magazines like the *New Yorker, Reader's Digest,* and *Playboy* have different images based on different editorial content, reputation, and subscribers. Second, different types of media (magazines versus television, for example) influence consumers' reaction to the message.

Differences Within Media

The role of a particular medium in communications is illustrated by the fact that the same advertisement results in different communications effects when run in different magazines or when aired on different TV shows. In their study, Aaker and Brown placed identical ads in two contrasting magazines, the *New Yorker* (a prestige magazine) and *Tennis World* (a specialty magazine).[62] The

New Yorker was more effective in persuading nonusers to consider a product when the ad stressed product quality. *Tennis World* was more effective when the ad stressed reasons for usage. The findings suggest that the medium's environment conveys a message. Specialty media were more effective as vehicles for conveying information, and prestige media were more effective as vehicles for conveying image.

Differences Between Media

Different media types also influence reaction to a communication. The most important distinction between media types is broadcast (TV and radio) and print (newspapers and magazines). Broadcast media are better at communicating imagery and symbolism, but they are not as effective as print in communicating detailed information. As a result, TV is more suitable for developing a mood or establishing a good feeling about the product, whereas print is more effective in communicating information.

Broadcast media, particularly television, have been described as low involvement media because the rate of viewing and understanding is out of the viewer's control. That is, the viewer has little opportunity to dwell on a point in television advertising. In contrast, magazines allow the reader to set the pace.[63] The reader has more opportunity for making connections and dwelling on points of interest. The result is that the print media allow for a more traditional learning environment in which information can be absorbed and integrated.

Other environmental factors also distinguish media categories. Television is a good medium for products that require a demonstration of usage or action (such as automobiles or children's toys). Radio is an effective medium for products requiring sounds: records, theater productions, and political candidates. Magazines are important as sources of information on product performance because of the ability to present messages in print. Newspapers are a particularly effective source of information on local sales and merchandise and permit consumers to preshop and to carry them around as sources of shopping information. Product samples are another type of medium that marketers can use to communicate. In this case, the message is direct product experience rather than the symbolism and imagery provided in advertising. Product samples are particularly useful in introducing a new product since they provide immediate experience in an attempt to encourage further trial.

◆ CONSUMER PROCESSING OF MARKETING COMMUNICATIONS

The fourth step in the communications model in Figure 20.1 is consumer decoding of marketing communications. Decoding requires consumers to acquire and process marketing information. The acquisition and processing of information were described in Chapter 7. Here, we are concerned with the process of decoding in the context of marketing communications.

The communications model in Figure 20.1 assumes there is one source of marketing information. Actually, consumers are exposed to many sources of information: advertising, sales promotions, salespeople, friends, and neutral sources. Figure 20.2 shows that when consumers process information, they are evaluating the *source,* the *message*, and *media* from multiple sources rather than from a single source. In this section, we consider consumers' evaluation of the source, the message, and the media.

Source Evaluation

When consumers receive a marketing communication, they evaluate the source of information. In Chapter 9, we saw that consumers develop cognitive responses (thoughts developed by consumers in response to a communication) to the source. For example, a consumer viewing an ad for E. F. Hutton featuring Bill Cosby as a spokesperson might think, "Why should I accept an actor's advice on investments?" *(source derogation).* Or the consumer might think, "If Bill Cosby is willing to sponsor E. F. Hutton, it must be reliable" *(source bolstering).* These source-oriented responses are important to marketers because they indicate the acceptability of the source.

▶**EXHIBIT 20.2**
Consumer processing of multiple messages

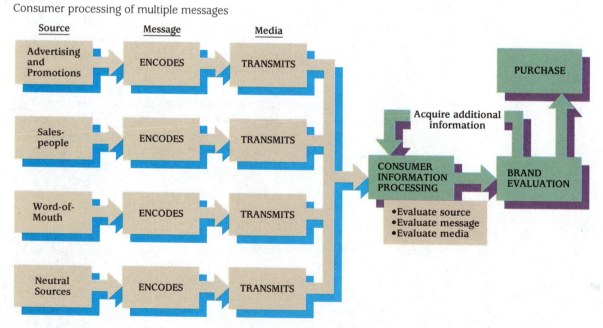

Advertisers try to avoid source derogation by enhancing their trustworthiness and credibility. As we saw, one strategy to do so is to link the product to a spokesperson with expertise regarding product performance. A second strategy is to use two-sided nonrefutational advertising as evidence that the advertiser is presenting a balanced view of the product. A third strategy is to cite an impartial source, for example, findings from *Consumer Reports* magazine or an established medical organization. Crest became the leading toothpaste because its claim that fluoride in the brand helps fight cavities was endorsed by the American Dental Association. Another strategy to reduce source derogation is to moderate claims to avoid any attribution that the advertiser is biased. Claims such as "gets clothes whiter than new," or "best gas mileage of any car on the road," encourage source derogation because consumers have doubts about the veracity of the claim.

Message Evaluation

Consumers can evaluate the message in relation to or independent of the source. In either case, they arrive at a judgment regarding the relevance, believability, and likability of the message. These responses can be divided into two types of general reactions: cognitive and affective. Cognitive responses evaluate acceptability of the claims (supportive of or counter to prior beliefs). Affective responses reflect consumers' attitude toward the message from positive to negative.

Cognitive Response

In Chapter 9, we saw that when consumers evaluate messages, they develop thoughts that support or counter the claims made in ads or other communications. These *cognitive responses* are formed based on consumers' prior beliefs.[64] For example, a consumer viewing an ad making a claim for gas economy and low service costs might think, "This claim is consistent with what some of my friends have told me. The car is one of the most economical on the market" (a *support argument*). Or the consumer might think, "In the long run, the car is not going to be very economical because I hear it has a lot of mechanical problems" (a *counterargument*). Cognitive responses are important to marketers because support and counterarguments indicate consumers' acceptance or rejection of the advertised claim.

Message-oriented cognitive responses (support and counterarguments) are more likely to occur for high involvement products, and source-oriented responses (source enhancement and derogation) are more prevalent for low involvement products.[65] Involved consumers are more likely to process messages related to product performance, and less-involved consumers are more likely to focus on ad content that is peripheral to the message such as the source or background scenery. The strategic implication for high involvement products is that advertisers should focus on gaining acceptance of the message by generating support arguments. For low involvement products, communication strategies should increase credibility and acceptance of the source.

Affective Response: Attitude Toward the Ad

Cognitive responses are the way consumers think about an advertisement; attitudes toward the ad (that is, affect) are the way consumers feel about it. **Attitude toward the ad** is the consumer's predisposition to respond favorably or unfavorably to a particular ad.[66] Positive cognitive responses (support arguments and source bolstering) are likely to produce positive consumer attitudes toward an ad; negative cognitive responses (counterarguments and source derogation) are likely to produce negative attitudes.

Cognitive and affective responses to an ad have different strategic implications. Cognitive responses are reactions to message content. Consumers' attitudes toward an ad are influenced by a wider range of peripheral factors such as color, music, symbols, and imagery. The key question is how consumers' attitudes toward an ad affect their evaluation of the advertised brand.

Effects of Positive Attitudes.   Studies have found that positive attitudes toward an ad create two desirable effects. First, positive attitudes are likely to increase attention directed to the ad. Olney, Holbrook, and Batra found that positive feelings about a TV ad increase viewing time of the ad and, by implication, increase attention to and comprehension of the ad.[67] Second, most studies have found that when consumers have a positive attitude toward an ad, they are more likely to have a positive attitude toward the advertised brand.[68] These findings suggest the desirability of creating a positive mood or feeling so that a positive attitude toward the ad will carry over to the brand.[69]

If the attitude toward the ad carries over to the brand, it can create a **transformational effect** in which the experience of using the brand becomes even more positive due to the positive feelings the ad evokes.[70] The transformational effect explains in part why consumers who cannot tell the difference between soft drinks when the cans are unlabeled nevertheless still have strong brand preferences. Consumers link the advertising to the usage experience so that even though they cannot tell the difference in taste between brands, they remain loyal to a particular brand.

Effects of Negative Attitudes.   The studies cited in this section suggest that advertisers should try to create positive consumer attitudes toward the advertising. Some of the most successful ad campaigns, however, have been the most disliked—for example, Wisk's "Ring around the collar," Ajax's "White Tornado," and "Don't squeeze the Charmin." As a result, several researchers have suggested a more complicated relationship between consumers' attitudes toward the ad and the brand; namely, that the most successful ads are those that produce either very positive or very negative attitudes.[71] Thus, a disliked ad can produce a positive consumer response because it creates attention and retention. Even though consumers disliked the Wisk ad, it created greater brand awareness. Thus, the key to influencing consumers is to create *arousal* (a direct positive *or* negative response to the ad), which results in brand familiarity and recognition once consumers are in the store.[72]

The problem with this conclusion is that it could lead advertisers to create purposefully irritating ads and negative attitudes toward the ad to gain attention and brand recognition. Irritating ads may be effective in creating arousal for certain products, but advertisers run the risk of creating negative brand evaluations. Furthermore, the American public does not particularly like advertising. A study by a large advertising agency found that 73 percent of consumers considered advertising to be exaggerated, 64 percent thought it was misleading at times, and 51 percent viewed it as not believable.[73] Given a general negative attitude toward advertising, it would be dangerous to encourage a negative attitude toward a specific campaign as a means of gaining attention and recognition.

Consumer Mood States. An important determination of consumers' attitudes toward the ad is their mood state at the time of exposure.[74] **Moods** refer to passing feelings that occur at a point in time (feeling happy, sad, silly, anxious, sexy, and so forth). Studies have shown that positive moods can create positive reactions to the ad; negative moods, negative reactions.[75]

Studies have also shown that program and advertising content can influence consumers' moods. Goldberg and Gorn found that "happy" TV programs induced happier moods when consumers were exposed to ads; unhappy programs, sadder moods.[76] Holbrook and Batra found that TV ads have evoked feelings of pleasure, arousal, and domination, and that these feelings influence attitudes toward the ad and toward the brand.[77]

There are two strategic implications of this research. First, advertisers should try to create a desired mood state. In most cases, advertisers try to create happy moods by showing the benefits of product use or by portraying the product in a positive context. The Omega watch campaign titled "Significant Moments" (see Exhibit 17.2) is an example of establishing a link between the product and a positive mood. Advertisers can also try to create anxious moods through fear campaigns. The antismoking ad in Exhibit 20.5 is an example. In both cases, the advertiser is trying to create the desired mood state.

The second implication of mood research is that advertisers can influence a desired mood state through program or readership content. This requires placing advertising with happy themes on "happy" TV shows. However, the converse does not necessarily apply. Burnkrant, Unnava, and Lord found that if the advertising has a sad theme, program content does not affect reactions to the ad.[78] The conclusion is that ads with sad themes (an insurance ad showing a family that lost its home) should not necessarily be linked to sad programs.

Media Evaluation

Consumers evaluate an advertising message in the context of the medium in which it is transmitted. They develop images of media that influence message acceptance.

Programs or editorial content may vary in a given medium; therefore, advertisers must consider whether the specific environment in which a print ad or commercial is placed may influence message acceptance. One study by Kennedy found that the effectiveness of TV commercials varies, depending on the type of show (for example, situation comedies versus suspense thrillers).[79] Another by Soldow and Principe found that when consumers are involved in a TV program, commercial effectiveness is likely to be lower because consumers focused on the program rather than the commercial. Frequently, consumers see the commercial as an irritant. When consumers are not involved in the program, they are likely to see the commercial as part of the programmatic material and are more likely to accept the message.[80]

The effects of the program environment can be applied to print ads as well as to TV commercials. The nature of the story in which a print ad is placed may influence message acceptance. One study found that for most products, placing an ad next to an upbeat story has a positive effect on message acceptance. An exception was advertising for cookies, candy, or other products that may be used to cope with anxieties. Placing ads for these types of products next to anxiety-producing stories may be more likely to promote message acceptance.[81]

◆ COMMUNICATIONS FEEDBACK

The final step in the communication process is feedback to the marketer to evaluate the effectiveness of the marketing communication. Figure 20.1 shows that marketers can obtain direct feedback by establishing a link between message effectiveness and purchase behavior or indirect feedback by evaluating the way consumers decode the message. As we saw, it is difficult to determine the effect of advertising on consumers' purchasing behavior, so advertisers have relied on indirect feedback in evaluating advertising. That is, they determine whether the ad results in consumer exposure, attention, comprehension, and retention.

McGuire summarized the types of feedback provided in each of these steps.[82] (See Figure 20.3.) In addition to exposure, attention, comprehension, and retention, McGuire added message acceptance to measure the effect of the ad on changes in brand attitudes. These steps reflect a hierarchy of effects leading to a purchase. The assumption is that as consumers move from exposure to attention, comprehension, message acceptance, and retention, the probability consumers will buy the advertised brand increases with each step. We consider the measurement of each of these steps in the decoding process that follows:

1. *Exposure* can be measured for print media by circulation and for broadcast media by reach. Circulation figures are generally available for magazines and newspapers and are usually broken out by demographic characteristics to allow advertisers to determine the best

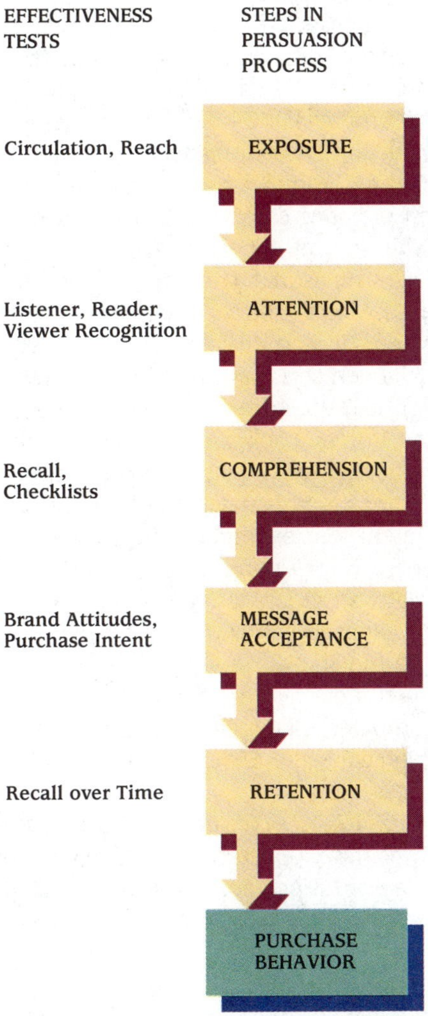

▶**FIGURE 20.3**
Methods of obtaining
feedback in the
decoding process

Source: Adapted from
William J. McGuire, "An
Information-Processing
Model of Advertising
Effectiveness," in H. L.
David and A. J. Silk, eds.,
*Behavioral and Management
Sciences in Marketing* (New
York: Ronald/Wiley, 1978),
p. 161. Reprinted with
permission from J. Wiley &
Sons and William J.
McGuire.

EFFECTIVENESS TESTS	STEPS IN PERSUASION PROCESS
Circulation, Reach	EXPOSURE
Listener, Reader, Viewer Recognition	ATTENTION
Recall, Checklists	COMPREHENSION
Brand Attitudes, Purchase Intent	MESSAGE ACCEPTANCE
Recall over Time	RETENTION
	PURCHASE BEHAVIOR

media to reach their target audience. Determining consumers' exposure to TV is more difficult. In the past, research companies such as
A. C. Nielsen have determined TV exposure through electronic meters
attached to a sample of TV sets to record the programs consumers
watch. These devices, however, could not determine who was watching the set. Recently, "People Meters" have been installed in TV sets
in a sample of households. These devices, which require viewers to
"punch in" when they are watching TV, record who is watching as
well as what is being watched.

2. *Attention* can best be measured by recognition of an advertisement.
   The Starch service computes a "seen-associated" measure for print ads
   in which consumers are asked whether they have seen the ad and

whether they can associate it with a brand or manufacturer. Advertising agencies have developed a similar measure for TV ads in which households are called the day after a TV commercial appears and are asked what commercials they remember seeing ("day-after recall" measures). With this measure, advertisers can determine whether consumers recalled a commercial and associated it with the brand. Such an association provides some assurance that consumers were attentive to the ad at the time of exposure.

3. *Comprehension* is measured primarily by tests of recall of specific points in the ad. The Gallup and Robinson readership service asks respondents to recall and describe sales messages of specific print ads. Similarly, advertisers can use "day-after recall" tests to measure comprehension of TV commercials by probing consumers who recalled the ad to play back specific points in the commercial. In this manner, advertisers can evaluate comprehension of the ad's theme.

4. *Message acceptance* is best measured by its impact on brand attitudes or purchase intent. For example, consumer attitudes toward the brand can be measured prior to and after exposure to print or TV ads. Comparisons of matched groups of consumers exposed to the message and those not exposed can show the effect of the message on attitude change. The Partnership for a Drug-Free America measured message acceptance by comparing attitudes in areas with heavy and light exposure to the campaign. Significantly greater shifts in attitudes against drug use in high-exposure areas indicated acceptance of the campaign's message.

5. *Retention* is measured by consumers' recall of the advertising message after a period of time. Consumers are likely to forget messages over time unless they are repeated. The most effective messages are those that are likely to be retained longest.

The measures in Figure 20.3 assume indirect feedback; that is, no direct link among the five steps involved in the decoding process and purchase behavior. In other words, when marketers obtain sales results, they do not know if consumers who purchased were exposed to the advertising campaign, comprehended it, or retained its messages. Recently, technology has created the possibility of establishing a link between consumers' exposure to advertising and subsequent behavior. The link is **scanner data;** that is, recording sales at checkout counters through electronic scanners. Research companies have identified households who shop in scanner stores and have installed TV meters in these households to record television exposure. In this way, researchers know if consumers who bought, for example, Diet Coke watched a Diet Coke commercial during the previous week. Such direct feedback is promising in trying to evaluate the impact of advertising on consumers' purchasing behavior.

Despite these advances, advertisers are a long way from determining with any precision the effects of marketing communications on purchasing behavior.

Advertisers still have difficulty separating their communications strategies from the many other variables that influence consumers' purchasing behavior. The problem remains much as John Wanamaker, the famous Philadelphia retailer, described it over a century ago: "I know half my advertising is working, but I don't know which half."

◆ SOCIETAL IMPLICATIONS OF MARKETING COMMUNICATIONS

Most marketing communication is socially responsible. Unfortunately, however, some strategies violate the public trust. Two types of communication are of concern: deceptive advertising and irresponsible advertising.

Deceptive Advertising

Deceptive advertising is advertising that gives false information or that willfully misleads consumers about the brand's benefits. Deception occurs when consumers acquire false beliefs because of exposure to advertising. For example, in 1990, Volvo ran an ad showing one of its station wagons being run over by a "Monster Truck." The Volvo survived, but the competing cars were crushed. The problem was that the Volvo had been reinforced with metal and wooden struts before the test, and the other cars had been weakened by having their roof supports cut. Volvo then withdrew the ad, blaming its advertising agency for the deception, and ran letters of apology in *The Wall Street Journal* and *USA Today*.[83]

As we saw in Chapter 2, the Federal Trade Commission monitors deceptive advertising by either ordering a company to cease its campaign or by ordering corrective advertising to correct deceptive claims through new advertising. The Food and Drug Administration also has a role in controlling deceptive advertising. It can order manufacturers of foods and drugs to change claims in advertising or on packages. For example, the FDA ordered several marketers of fiber cereals to stop claiming that they reduce the risk of heart disease.

Irresponsible Advertising

An advertising claim does not have to be deceptive to violate the public trust; it can be irresponsible. **Irresponsible advertising** depicts or encourages irresponsible behavior or portrays groups in an irresponsible manner.

An example of encouraging irresponsible behavior was an ad for Reebok sneakers in which two bungee-cord jumpers are shown diving from a bridge. The final shot shows only the Reebok jumper connected to his bungee cord; the other cord has a pair of empty Nike's attached to it. The campaign was meant to combine comparative advertising and humor, but it gave the unfortunate impression that the Nike wearer plunged to his death. *Adweek* magazine editorialized that "This is the sort of [advertising] that gives bad taste a bad name."[84]

Advertising has also been irresponsible at times in its portrayal of women and of minorities. Women have often been portrayed as stupid or dominated by men. African-Americans have often been stereotyped in roles as athletes, musicians, or recipients of charity. Fortunately, these depictions are becoming rare. Advertisers are now more sophisticated in dealing with female target audiences and are portraying women in more realistic roles. Subaru, for example, has changed the traditional image of women as being interested only in style by focusing on specific characteristics to attract upscale working women. Portrayals of African-Americans have also improved so that in most cases, there is little difference in role-portrayals of whites and African-Americans.

Deceptive and irresponsible advertising is unlikely to disappear. The FTC and FDA will continue an important monitoring role. However, ultimately, marketers must regulate themselves. A positive sign is the greater awareness that marketers have of their responsibility to society. An example is advertising by some beer companies to discourage underage persons from drinking. (See Exhibit 20.8 for an example.)

Socially responsible advertisers have a vested interest in providing accurate information to consumers in the interest of gaining consumer trust and loyalty. The advertising slogan of a discount retailer sums up the common interest in responsible marketing: "An educated consumer is our best customer."

▶**EXHIBIT 20.8**
An example of socially responsible advertising
Source: Courtesy of Miller Brewing Co.

SUMMARY

The chapter first presented a model of the marketing communications process in five steps: development of an idea to be communicated by the marketer, encoding the idea by the advertiser, transmission by the mass media, decoding the message and action by the consumer, and feedback to the advertiser to evaluate the effectiveness of the campaign. Marketers must consider the following questions in evaluating the effectiveness of advertising and other marketing communications:

1. Have communications objectives been formulated to reflect consumer needs?
2. Have marketers adequately encoded product benefits?
3. Has the message been transmitted to the target segment by utilizing the right media?
4. Did consumers decode the message in the manner the advertiser intended?
5. Does exposure to and acceptance of the message lead to a purchase?

The remainder of the chapter discussed the primary components of communications: source, message, media, receiver (consumer), and feedback.

Source effects focus on the credibility and acceptance of the source of the message. The greater the credibility of the source, the greater the likelihood consumers will accept the message. Source credibility is most important when consumers are not involved with the purchase. Involved consumers are more likely to focus on the message than on the source. Consumers regard reference groups, family, and impartial sources such as *Consumer Reports* and government agencies as more credible than commercial sources of information. Methods by which marketers could increase their credibility were considered.

The main issues considered in evaluating message effects were the merits of (1) one-sided versus two-sided appeals, (2) comparative advertising, (3) fear appeals, and (4) humor in advertising.

Studies of media effects demonstrate the importance of the media environment in affecting consumers' perception of an ad and acceptance of the message.

Consumers' role in the communication process was also considered. Consumers evaluate the source of a communication, the message, and the media in which the message is transmitted. In evaluating the message, consumers develop cognitive responses that determine message acceptance. They also develop attitudes toward ads that might influence their attitudes toward the advertised brand.

In the last step of the communications process, we considered certain key issues in feedback: the measurement of indirect feedback through consumer thought variables and the desirability yet difficulty of evaluating advertising based on direct consumer purchase response.

The chapter concluded by considering societal issues in marketing communications; namely, the need to monitor and control deceptive and irresponsible advertising.

QUESTIONS

1. Cite an example of an advertising campaign by describing:
   - Advertising objectives and product concept established by the source.
   - How these objectives were encoded into an advertising campaign.
   - Media plan used to transmit the message to the target group.
   - Criteria the company will use in evaluating consumers' process of decoding the message.

2. Using the model of advertising communications shown in Figure 20.1, describe the problems marketers face in (a) developing effective marketing communications and (b) evaluating marketing communications.

3. What criteria could Eveready use in evaluating the effectiveness of the Eveready Bunny campaign?

4. Use attribution theory to explain why consumers are more likely to consider advertising less credible than personal or neutral sources of information.

5. Why are source effects more important in gaining message acceptance for low involvement compared to high involvement consumers?

6. Assume Exxon initiates a campaign to convince the public that high gas prices are justified as a means of encouraging domestic exploration for oil. What principles could Exxon use to increase its credibility?

7. What strategies can companies use to increase their attractiveness as sources of marketing communications? Provide examples.

8. Two-sided advertisements were described as means of increasing both credibility and message acceptance.
   - What are the advantages of using two-sided ads?
   - Why are so few advertisements two-sided?

9. Assume state and local agencies in California wish to undertake an educational campaign to alert the public to the dangers of earthquakes. They use several ads to show the severe devastation that earthquakes can produce to convince the public of the importance of the educational campaign. What factors are likely to encourage and discourage the acceptance of the message?

10. What behavioral principles did the Partnership for a Drug-Free America use to wage an effective campaign against drug use? What evidence is there that attitude and behavioral change resulted from the campaign?

11. What are the risks of relying on an advertising campaign based on (a) comparative advertising and (b) humor?

12. How can advertisers discourage counterarguments when consumers are viewing an ad?

13. Given the difficulties in evaluating the effects of an advertising message on consumers' purchase decision, advertisers have used measures of consumer attention, comprehension, and retention of advertising as criteria of effectiveness.
    - What are some of the limitations of using these measures as criteria of advertising effectiveness?

- What approaches to advertising evaluation hold promise for providing direct feedback to establish the link between the advertising message and consumer behavior?

14. Provide examples of deceptive and irresponsible advertising. Who should be responsible for monitoring and controlling such advertising?

RESEARCH ASSIGNMENTS

1. Show consumers an ad for a high involvement product (such as a car or investment service) and a low involvement product (toothpaste, paper towels). As consumers are looking at each ad, ask them to express their thoughts. Classify their comments into those that are related to message content versus those that are related to nonmessage (peripheral) elements in the ad (the use of a spokesperson, scenery, and so on).

   Based on research cited in the text, we would expect consumers to express more message-related thoughts when viewing high involvement ads and more nonmessage thoughts expressed when viewing low involvement ads. Did your study confirm this hypothesis?

2. Develop three advertising messages:
   a. One-sided ad (for example, "Avis is great").
   b. Two-sided refutational ad ("Avis is number 2, but we try harder [than Hertz]").
   c. Two-sided nonrefutational ad ("Avis may be smaller and may not have as many locations, but Avis is best in terms of price, the reliability of their cars, and service").

   Ask 50 consumers to rate all three ads on (a) believability, (b) trustworthiness, and (c) expertise of the source. Ask consumers how likely they would be to buy the product or service after seeing each ad.
   - Do the results conform to the findings on credibility and the effects of two-sided and comparative advertising cited in the text?
   - What are the strategic implications of the findings?

NOTES

1. "Meet Mike Quinlan, Big Mac's Attack CEO," *Business Week* (May 9, 1988), pp. 92–97.
2. "Big Mac Strikes Back," *Time* (April 13, 1987).
3. "Burger King Hypes Herb Ads, but Many People Are Fed Up," *The Wall Street Journal* (January 23, 1986), p. 33.
4. "How the Bunny Charged Eveready," *Advertising Age* (April 9, 1991), p. 20; and "Eveready Loses Power in Market," *Advertising Age* (July 11, 1988), p. 4.
5. "Too Many Think the Bunny Is Duracell's, Not Eveready's," *The Wall Street Journal* (July 31, 1991), p. B1.
6. *Advertising Age* (April 9, 1991), *loc. cit.*
7. *Advertising Age* (July 11, 1988), *loc. cit.*
8. *The Wall Street Journal* (January 23, 1986), *loc. cit.*
9. "What Happened to Advertising?" *Business Week* (September 23, 1991), p. 68.
10. Herbert E. Krugman, "Point of View: Limits of Attention to Advertising," *Journal of Advertising*

Research, 28 (October-November, 1988), pp. 47–50.

11. Peter H. Webb, "Consumer Initial Processing in a Difficult Media Environment," *Journal of Consumer Research,* 6 (December, 1979), pp. 225–236.

12. Raymond R. Burke and Thomas K. Srull, "Competitive Interference and Consumer Memory for Advertising," *Journal of Consumer Research,* 15 (June, 1988), pp. 55–68.

13. Carl I. Hovland, Irving L. Janis, and Harold H. Kelley, *Communication and Persuasion* (New Haven, CT: Yale University Press, 1953). See also Grant McCracken, "Who Is the Celebrity Endorser? Cultural Foundations of the Endorsement Process," *Journal of Consumer Research,* 16 (December, 1989), pp. 310–321.

14. Henry Assael, Michael Etgar, and Michael Henry, "The Dimensions of Evaluating and Utilizing Alternative Information Sources," Working paper, New York University, March, 1983.

15. See W. Watts and William McGuire, "Persistence of Induced Opinion Change and Retention of the Inducing Message Contents," *Journal of Abnormal and Social Psychology,* 68 (1964), pp. 233–241; and G. Miller and J. Basehart, "Source Trustworthiness, Opinionated Statements and Response to Persuasive Communication," *Speech Monographs,* 36 (1969), pp. 1–7.

16. C. Samuel Craig and John M. McCann, "Assessing Communication Effects on Energy Conservation," *Journal of Consumer Research,* 5 (September, 1978), pp. 82–88.

17. *Ibid.,* p. 87.

18. Ruby Roy Dholakia and Brian Sternthal, "Highly Credible Sources: Persuasive Facilitators or Persuasive Liabilities?" *Journal of Consumer Research,* 3 (March, 1977), pp. 223–232.

19. H. Sigall and R. Helmreich, "Opinion Change as a Function of Stress and Communicator Credibility," *Journal of Experimental Social Psychology,* 5 (1969), pp. 70–78.

20. A. Eagly and S. Chaiken, "An Attribution Analysis of the Effect of Communicator Characteristics on Opinion Change: The Case of Communicator Attractiveness," *Journal of Personality and Social Psychology,* 32 (1975), pp. 136–144.

21. Michael A. Kamins and Henry Assael, "Two-Sided Versus One-Sided Appeals: A Cognitive Perspective on Argumentation, Source Derogation, and the Effect of Disconfirming Trial on Belief Change," *Journal of Marketing Research,* 24 (February, 1987), pp. 29–39; and Robert B. Settle and Linda L. Golden, "Attribution Theory and Advertiser Credibility," *Journal of Marketing Research,* 11 (May, 1974), pp. 181–185.

22. Roobina Ohanian, "The Impact of Celebrity Spokespersons' Perceived Image on Consumers' Intention to Purchase," *Journal of Advertising Research,* 31 (February/March, 1991), pp. 46–53.

23. William J. McGuire, "Attitudes and Attitude Change," in Gardner Lindzey and Elliot Aronson, eds., *Handbook of Social Psychology* (New York: Random House, 1985), pp. 233–346.

24. Timothy C. Brock, "Communication-Recipient Similarity and Decision Change," *Journal of Personality and Social Psychology,* 1 (June, 1965), pp. 650–654; and Arch J. Woodside and J. William Davenport, "The Effect of Salesman Similarity and Expertise on Consumer Purchasing Behavior," *Journal of Marketing Research,* 11 (May, 1974), pp. 198–202.

25. David Mazursky and Yaacov Schul, "Learning from the Ad or Relying on Related Attitudes: The Moderating Role of Involvement," *Journal of Business Research,* 25 (1992), pp. 81–93.

26. Richard E. Petty, John T. Cacioppo, and David Schumann, "Central and Peripheral Routes to Advertising Effectiveness: The Moderating Role of Involvement," *Journal of Consumer Research,* 10 (September, 1983), pp. 135–146.

27. S. Ratneshwar and Shelly Chaiken, "Comprehension's Role in Persuasion: The Case of Its Moderating Effect on the Persuasive Impact of Source Cues," *Journal of Consumer Research,* 18 (June, 1991), pp. 52–62.

28. Paul W. Miniard, Deepak Sirdeshmukh, and Daniel E. Innis, "Peripheral Persuasion and Brand Choice," *Journal of Consumer Research,* 19 (September, 1992), pp. 226–239.

29. R. E. Smith and S. Hunt, "Attribution Processes and Effects in Promotional Situations," *Journal of Consumer Research,* 5 (December, 1978), pp. 149–158; Daniel R. Toy, "Monitoring Communication Effects: A Cognitive Structure/Cognitive Response Approach," *Journal of Consumer Research,* 9 (June, 1982), pp. 66–76; and Lauren A. Swanson, "The Persuasive Effect of Volunteering Negative Information in Advertising," *Interna-*

tional Journal of Advertising, 6 (1987), pp. 237–248.

30. Kamins and Assael, "Two-Sided Versus One-Sided Appeals . . . ," *loc. cit.*

31. George J. Szybillo and Richard Heslin, "Resistance to Persuasion: Inoculation Theory in a Marketing Context," *Journal of Marketing Research,* 10 (November, 1973), pp. 396–403; and Kamins and Assael, "Two-Sided Versus One-Sided Appeals . . . ," *loc. cit.*

32. Smith and Hunt, "Attribution Processes and Effects . . . ," *loc. cit.;* Toy, "Monitoring Communication Effects . . . ," *loc. cit.;* and Swanson, "The Persuasive Effect of Volunteering Negative Information . . . ," *loc. cit.*

33. Mark I. Alpert and Linda L. Golden, "The Impact of Education on the Relative Effectiveness of One-Sided Communications," in Bruce J. Walker *et al., Proceedings of the American Marketing Association Educators' Conference,* Series No. 48 (1982), pp. 30–33.

34. Carl I. Hovland, Arthur A. Lumsdaine, and Fred D. Sheffield, *Experiences on Mass Communication* (New York: John Wiley, 1949), pp. 182–200; and W. E. Faison, "Effectiveness of One-Sided and Two-Sided Mass Communications in Advertising," *Public Opinion Quarterly,* 25 (1961), pp. 468–469.

35. "Big Resurgence in Comparative Ads," *Dun's Business Month* (February, 1987), pp. 56–58.

36. "Coors' Bud-Bashing Stays Regional," *Advertising Age* (March 23, 1992), p. 10; and "Coors Says Anheuser Pours Water on Reputation," *The New York Times* (August 14, 1992), pp. D1, D3.

37. William L. Wilkie and Paul W. Farris, "Comparative Advertising: Problems and Potential," *Journal of Marketing,* 39 (October, 1975), pp. 7–15.

38. "Comparative Ads," *Advertising Age* (September 22, 1980), p. 59.

39. William R. Swinyard, "The Interaction Between Comparative Advertising and Copy Claim Variation," *Journal of Marketing Research,* 18 (May, 1981), pp. 175–186.

40. "The Effects of Comparative Television Advertising that Names Competing Brands," Private report by Ogilvy and Mather Research, New York.

41. Jerry B. Gotlieb and Dan Sarel, "Comparative Advertising Effectiveness: The Role of Involvement and Source Credibility," *Journal of Advertising,* 20 (1991), pp. 38–45.

42. Jerry B. Gotlieb and Dan Sarel, "The Influence of Type of Advertisement, Price, and Source Credibility on Perceived Quality," *Journal of the Academy of Marketing Science,* 20 (1992), pp. 253–260.

43. Swinyard, "The Interaction Between Comparative Advertising and Copy Claim Variation," *loc. cit.*

44. Cornelia Pechmann and David W. Stewart, "The Effects of Comparative Advertising on Attention, Memory, and Purchase Intentions," *Journal of Consumer Research,* 17 (September, 1990), pp. 180–191. See also: Cornelia Pechmann and S. Ratneshwar, "The Use of Comparative Advertising for Brand Positioning: Association Versus Differentiation," *Journal of Consumer Research,* 18 (September, 1991), pp. 145–160.

45. Lynette S. Unger and James M. Stearns, "The Use of Fear and Guilt Messages in Television Advertising: Issues and Evidence," in Patrick E. Murphy *et al.,* eds., *Proceedings of the American Marketing Association Educators' Conference,* Series No. 49 (1983), pp. 16–20.

46. "Study Finds Nonsmokers Living 2 Years More by Heeding Alerts," *The New York Times* (September 22, 1979), p. 6.

47. William J. McGuire, *Effectiveness of Appeals in Advertising* (New York: Advertising Research Foundation, 1963).

48. Mark A. deTuck, Gerald M. Goldhaber, Gary M. Richetto, and Melissa J. Young, "Effects of Fear-Arousing Warning Messages," *Journal of Products Liability,* 14 (1992), pp. 217–223.

49. John F. Tanner, Jr., James B. Hunt, and David R. Eppright, "The Protection Motivation Model: A Normative Model of Fear Appeals," *Journal of Marketing,* 55 (July, 1991), pp. 36–45.

50. Marc G. Weinberger and Harlan E. Spotts, "Differences in British/American Television and Magazine Advertising: Myth or Reality," in Gary J. Bamossy and W. Fred van Raaij, eds., *Proceedings of the Association for Consumer Research,* European Summer Conference, 1992.

51. Calvin P. Duncan, James E. Nelson, and Nancy T. Frontczak, "The Effect of Humor on Advertising Comprehension," in Thomas C. Kinnear, ed., *Advances in Consumer Research,* Vol. 11 (Provo, UT: Association for Consumer Research, 1984), pp. 432–437; and Calvin P. Duncan and James E. Nelson, "Effects of Humor in a Radio Advertising

Experiment," *Journal of Advertising,* 14 (1985), pp. 33–40.

52. "After Serious 70s, Advertisers Are Going for Laughs Again," *The Wall Street Journal* (February 23, 1984), p. 31.

53. Brian Sternthal and C. Samuel Craig, "Humor in Advertising," *Journal of Marketing,* 37 (October, 1973), pp. 12–18.

54. Duncan, Nelson, and Frontczak, "The Effect of Humor . . . ," *loc. cit.*

55. Sternthal and Craig, "Humor in Advertising," *loc. cit.*

56. Cliff Scott, David M. Klein, and Jennings Bryant, "Consumer Response to Humor in Advertising: A Series of Field Studies Using Behavioral Observation," *Journal of Consumer Research,* 16 (March, 1990), pp. 498–501.

57. Marc G. Weinberger and Leland Campbell, "The Use and Impact of Humor in Radio Advertising," *Journal of Advertising Research,* 31 (December/January, 1991), pp. 44–52.

58. David M. Stewart and David H. Furse, *Effective Television Advertising* (Lexington, MA: D.C. Heath and Co., 1986).

59. Amitava Chattopadhyay and Kunal Basu, "Humor in Advertising: The Moderating Role of Prior Brand Evaluation," *Journal of Marketing Research,* 27 (November, 1990), pp. 466–476.

60. Dana L. Alden, Wayne D. Hoyer, and Chol Lee, "Identifying Global and Culture-Specific Dimensions of Humor in Advertising: A Multinational Analysis," *Journal of Marketing,* 57 (April, 1993), pp. 64–75.

61. Marshall McLuhan, *The Medium Is the Message* (New York: Random House, 1967).

62. David A. Aaker and Phillip K. Brown, "Evaluating Vehicle Source Effects," *Journal of Advertising Research,* 12 (August, 1972), pp. 11–16.

63. Herbert E. Krugman, "The Impact of Television Advertising: Learning Without Involvement," *Public Opinion Quarterly,* 29 (Fall, 1965), pp. 349–356; and Herbert E. Krugman, "The Measurement of Advertising Involvement," *Public Opinion Quarterly,* 30 (Winter, 1966–1967), pp. 583–596.

64. Peter L. Wright, "The Cognitive Processes Mediating Acceptance of Advertising," *Journal of Marketing Research,* 10 (February, 1973), pp. 53–62.

65. Martin R. Lautman and Larry Percy, "Cognitive and Affective Responses in Attribute-Based Versus End-Benefit Oriented Advertising," in Thomas C. Kinnear, ed., *Advances in Consumer Research,* Vol. 11 (Provo, UT: Association for Consumer Research, 1984), pp. 11–17.

66. Scott B. MacKenzie and Richard J. Lutz, "An Empirical Examination of the Structural Antecedents of Attitude Toward the Ad in an Advertising Pretesting Context," *Journal of Marketing,* 53 (April, 1989), pp. 48–61.

67. Thomas J. Olney, Morris B. Holbrook, and Rajeev Batra, "Consumer Responses to Advertising: The Effects of Ad Content, Emotions, and Attitude Toward the Ad on Viewing Time," *Journal of Consumer Research,* 17 (March, 1991), pp. 440–453.

68. *Ibid.;* and Meryl Paula Gardner, "Does Attitude Toward the Ad Affect Brand Attitude Under a Brand Evaluation Set?" *Journal of Marketing Research,* 22 (May, 1985), pp. 192–198. See also Paul W. Miniard, Sunil Bhatla, and Randall L. Rose, "On the Formation and Relationship of Ad and Brand Attitudes: An Experimental and Causal Analysis," *Journal of Marketing Research,* 27 (August, 1990), pp. 290–303.

69. Andrew A. Mitchell and Jerry C. Olson, "Are Product Attribute Beliefs the Only Mediator of Advertising Effects on Brand Attitude?" *Journal of Marketing Research,* 18 (August, 1981), pp. 318–332.

70. Christopher P. Puto and William D. Wells, "Informational and Transformational Advertising: The Differential Effects of Time," in Thomas C. Kinnear, ed., *Advances in Consumer Research,* Vol. 11 (Provo, UT: Association for Consumer Research, 1984), pp. 572–576. See also Julie A. Edell and Marian Chapman Burke, "The Power of Feelings in Understanding Advertising Effects," *Journal of Consumer Research,* 14 (December, 1987), pp. 421–433.

71. See Silk and Vavra, "The Influence of Advertising's Affective Qualities," *loc. cit.;* and Danny L. Moore and J. Wesley Hutchinson, "The Effects of Ad Affect on Advertising Effectiveness," in Richard P. Bagozzi and Alice M. Tybout, eds., *Advances in Consumer Research,* Vol. 10 (Ann Arbor, MI: Association for Consumer Research, 1983), pp. 526–531.

72. Silk and Vavra, "The Influence of Advertising's Affective Qualities," *loc. cit.*

73. "Naming the Competition in Advertising," *Listening Post* (New York: Ogilvy and Mather, 1984).

74. See Meryl Paula Gardner, "Mood States and Consumer Research: A Critical Review," *Journal of Consumer Research,* 12 (December, 1985), pp. 281–300.

75. Thomas R. Srull, "Memory, Mood, and Consumer Judgment," in Melanie Wallendorf and Paul Anderson, eds., *Advances in Consumer Research,* 14 (Provo, UT: Association for Consumer Research, 1987), pp. 404–407.

76. Marvin E. Goldberg and Gerald J. Gorn, "Happy and Sad TV Programs: How They Affect Reactions to Commercials," *Journal of Consumer Research,* 14 (December, 1987), pp. 387–403.

77. Morris B. Holbrook and Rajeev Batra, "Assessing the Role of Emotions as Mediators of Consumer Responses to Advertising," *Journal of Consumer Research,* 14 (December, 1987), pp. 404–420. See also, Julie A. Edell and Marian Chapman Burke, "The Power of Feelings in Understanding Advertising Effects," *Journal of Consumer Research,* 14 (December, 1987), pp. 421–433.

78. Robert E. Burnkrant, H. Rao Unnava, and Kenneth R. Lord, "The Effects of Programming Induced Mood States on Memory for Commercial Information," (Working Paper Series, The Ohio State University, October, 1987).

79. J. R. Kennedy, "How Program Environment Affects TV Commercials," *Journal of Advertising Research,* 11 (February, 1971), pp. 33–38.

80. Gary F. Soldow and Victor Principe, "Response to Commercials as a Function of Program Context," *Journal of Advertising Research,* 21 (April, 1981), pp. 59–65.

81. "For Some Ads, Glum People Make the Best Sales Prospects," *The Wall Street Journal* (July 25, 1985), p. 23.

82. William J. McGuire, "An Information-Processing Model of Advertising Effectiveness," in H. L. David and A. J. Silk, eds., *Behavioral and Management Sciences in Marketing* (New York: Ronald/Wiley, 1978), pp. 156–180.

83. "Candid Camera: Volvo and the Art of Deception," *Adweek's Marketing Week* (November 12, 1990), pp. 4–5.

84. "Reebok: If the Shoe Fits," *Adweek* (January 7, 1991), p. 23.

G L O S S A R Y

absolute threshold Level below which the consumer cannot detect a stimulus. Minimal stimulus values capable of being sensed.

acceptable price range A price range the consumer views as realistic. If the product is priced below this range, quality is suspect. If the product is priced above, the consumer refuses to buy.

acculturation The process of learning a culture different from the one in which a person was raised. Learning the values of another culture (e.g., a businessperson going abroad, immigrants moving to another country, foreign students).

activation One of the three factors required for retrieval of information from long-term memory. The linkages between nodes must be activated before retrieval can take place.

actual self The concept individuals have of themselves based on who they think they are.

adaptation level Point at which the consumer adjusts to a frequently repeated stimulus so that it is no longer noticed. Defined as the stimulus value (e.g., brightness, loudness) to which the consumer is indifferent and with respect to which stimuli above or below it are relatively judged.

advertising wearout Adaptation to a campaign over time that results in the consumer's boredom and fatigue; the consumer then "tunes out" the message.

affective component of attitudes The favorable or unfavorable disposition toward an object. Consumers' evaluation of a brand on a positive to negative dimension represents the affective component of attitudes.

AIO inventories A list of consumer activities, interests, and opinions constructed to measure empirically lifestyle components.

anticipatory aspiration group Group that an individual aspires to belong to and anticipates joining at some future time.

aspiration group Group to which a consumer aspires to be associated with, but one of which he or she is not a member.

assimilation/contrast theories Combines the two views of assimilation and contrast theories in the belief that assimilation is more likely to occur if the disparity between experience and effect is likely. States that when consumers are only slightly disappointed, attitudes are likely to change in the direction of expectations and remain positive. When consumers are very disappointed, a negative change in attitude is likely to occur after the purchase and may be exaggerated.

assimilation effect Theory in social psychology that focuses on a desire to maintain balance between experiences and expectations by selectively accepting information consistent with expectations. The tendency in perception for the highly similar parts of a whole to look alike as much as possible; that is, to assimilate. Assimilation occurs when the stimulus differences among the parts are sufficiently small; if the differences are sufficiently large, the opposite phenomenon of contrast tends to occur.

attention The selective process of noticing a stimulus or certain portions of it. The momentary focusing of a consumer's cognitive capacity on a specific stimulus.

attitude toward the ad Consumers' predisposition to respond favorably or unfavorably to an ad.

autonomous decisions Product decisions made by either the husband or wife, either one of whom is equally likely to make the decision.

baby boomers People born between 1946 and 1964, representing 76 million consumers.

baby busters The youths born between 1965 and 1976, representing 47 million consumers.

bait-and-switch pricing A form of deception in pricing practices that involves a low-price offer intended to lure customers into a store where a salesperson tries to influence them to buy higher-priced items.

balance theory A theory that asserts that unbalanced cognitive systems tend to shift toward a state of balance. Evaluation of an object is a function of consistently held beliefs about the object. When information about an object conflicts with consumers' beliefs, they will achieve balance by either changing their opinion about the object, about their source of information, or a combination of both. The result is a balance in beliefs about the information and the object.

bargaining power The extent of influence the buyer and seller have on each other to achieve favorable terms of sale.

behavioral segmentation Identification of consumer groups by differences in behavior (e.g., users versus nonusers or heavy versus light users).

benefit criteria The factors that consumers consider important in deciding on one brand or another based on the benefits they seek.

benefit segmentation Identification of a group of consumers based on similarity in needs. Often marketing opportunities are discovered by analysis of consumers' benefit preferences. Frequently, one or more segments are identified that are not being adequately served by existing alternatives.

benefit segments Identification of a group of consumers based on similarity in needs. Often marketing opportunities are discovered by analysis of consumers' benefit preferences. Frequently, one or more segments are identified that are not being adequately served by existing alternatives.

brand leveraging A company will use a successful brand name on a product line extension, thus creating stimulus generalization.

categorization Tendency of consumers to place marketing information into logical categories to process information quickly and efficiently and to classify new information.

change agents Opinion leaders who have more influence and credibility than commercially sponsored means, such as personal selling and advertising, in getting consumers to change their needs and habits.

chunking/grouping information Organizing stimuli that summarize a wide range of information about a brand. A brand image is formed by information chunking, meaning the consumer is processing information by brand rather than by attribute.

closure A principle of perceptual integration describing a perceiver's tendency to fill in the missing elements when a stimulus is incomplete. Experience tends to be organized into whole, continuous figures. If the stimulus pattern is incomplete, the perceiver fills in missing elements.

cluster analysis A computer program that groups respondents together by similarity so there is greatest similarity in ratings within groups and greatest differences between groups. (Statistically, the program minimizes within group variance and maximizes between group variance.)

coercive power The power of groups to express oneself to other members of the group, providing a basis for comparing one's attitudes and behavior to those of the group.

cognitive component of attitudes The tendency to act based on favorable or unfavorable predispositions toward the object; generally measured by an intention to buy scale. Beliefs link a brand to a set of characteristics and specify the extent to which the brand possesses each characteristic.

cognitive consistency A basic behavioral principle to which balance theory conforms. This principle states that consumers value harmony between their beliefs and evaluations. If one is inconsistent with the other, consumers will change their attitudes to create harmony in their cognitive structure.

cognitive responses Thoughts consumers develop that support or counter claims made in marketing communication.

Coleman-Rainwater Social Standing Hierarchy Often preferred to Warner's Index of Status Characteristics, this classification of social classes more directly reflects the power and prestige associated with each class and draws social class lines more sharply. The Social Standing Hierarchy also distinguishes between a middle class and a working class.

comparative advertising The naming of a comparative product in the marketer's ad. Used to point out weaknesses and to create a less favorable attitude toward the competitive brand, thus increasing the likelihood of buying the marketer's brand. An important means of competitive positioning.

comparative influence The process of comparing oneself to other members of the group, providing a basis for comparing one's attitudes and behavior to those of the group.

compensatory method When a consumer uses a compensatory model, perceived strength of a given alternative on one or more evaluative criteria can compensate for weaknesses on other attributes. Generally requires consumers to evaluate a brand by a number of criteria.

competitive bargaining power The party with the stronger bargaining power exerts that power to force concessions from the weaker party.

competitive positioning Communicates product benefits by establishing a distinctive position for the product compared to that of the competition (e.g., 7Up's positioning as the Uncola). Provides a clear frame of reference for consumers by relating claims to other brands.

complex decision making Making decisions through a process of active search for information. Based on this information, alternative brands are evaluated on specific criteria. The cognitive process of evaluation involves consumer perceptions of brand characteristics and development of favorable or unfavorable attitudes toward a brand. The assumption is that consumer perceptions and attitudes will precede and influence behavior.

compliance-aggressiveness-detachment (CAD) scale Relying on social theories of personality to explain purchase behavior, this scale organizes traits into categories descriptive of people's consistent means of relating to and coping with others. There are three basic types: compliant (moving toward people), aggressive (moving against people), or detached (moving away from people).

comprehension A selective process of understanding and interpreting message.

conative component of attitudes The tendency to act based on favorable or unfavorable predispositions toward the object; generally measured by an intention to buy scale.

conformity The acceptance of group norms and values. Conformity reflected by purchasing those brands and product categories the group leader's purchase. Marketers are interested in such imitative behavior because it implies a snowball effect once the most influential members of a group accept products. "Keeping up with the Joneses" is an example of conformity.

conjunctive strategy A consumer accepts a brand only if it is acceptable on key attributes. The consumer would eliminate a brand seen as negative on one or two of the most important attributes, even if it is positive on all other attributes.

constant sum scale A scale in which values assigned to objects always add up to the same amount. (E.g., assume you could select ten free bottles of soft drink in a store, how many bottles of the following brands would you select?)

consumer information processing The nature of the consumer's search for and reactions to marketing communications. The process by which consumers perceive information in four steps—exposure to information, attention, comprehension, and retention of information.

consumerism The set of activities of independent consumer organizations and consumer activists designed to protect the consumer. Concerned activists designed to protect the consumer. Concerned primarily with ensuring that the consumer's rights in the process of exchange are protected. As social movement seeking to augment the rights and power of buyers in relation to sellers.

consumer movement The activities that are generally encompassed under the heading of *consumerism* (see previous definition). Somewhat misleading term because there is no actual organization of consumers but, instead, a conglomeration of groups with separate concerns.

consumer positioning Positioning products based on the consumers' needs. In positioning analysis, consumers are positioned on a perceptual map to identify target groups for product concepts. Consumers are positioned closest to the concepts they prefer most and farthest from those they prefer least.

consumer socialization The process by which consumers acquire the knowledge and skills necessary to operate in the marketplace. The two most important types of consumer socialization are the socialization of children and the socialization of new residents in a community.

continuity Principles of grouping that emerged from Gestalt psychology and that suggest that the basic flow of stimuli should be continuous and lead to a logical conclusion (e.g., the flow of a sales message).

continuous innovation An extension or modification of an existing product (e.g., fluoridated toothpaste, law-tar cigarettes, cook-in-the-bag vegetables). Has the least disrupting influence on established purchasing patterns.

contrast The opposite of adaptation. A change from the constant conditions a consumer is used to. Advertisers try to achieve contrast by using new, attention-getting stimuli.

contrast effect States that a disparity between expectations and experiences may lead the consumer to magnify the disparity. Implies that advertisers should moderate their claims so as not to increase consumer expectations to the point there dissatisfaction (e.g., a disparity between expectation and experience) is likely to result.

coordinative bargaining power The parties approach bargaining in a problem-solving manner to achieve their goals. Bargaining power is less likely to be exerted in an arbitrary manner.

counterargument Thoughts consumers develop that are designed to counter existing information (e.g., a loyal RC Cola drinker develops thoughts to reject benefit claims Pepsi or Coca-Cola make).

cross-cultural influences Norms and values of consumers in foreign countries that influence strategies of multinational firms marketing abroad.

cultivation theory According to this theory, children learn about a culture's norms and values from the media. The greater children's exposure to TV, the greater the likelihood that they will accept the images and associations seen.

cultural context The concept of cultural context divide cultures into two groups: those that rely primarily on verbal and written communication to transmit meaning (low context cultures) and those that rely primarily on nonverbal communication (high context cultures).

cultural homogeneity Identifies uniform cultures with little difference in norms, values, and socioeconomic status among groups (homophilous) versus more disparate cultures with wider difference among groups (heterophilous).

cultural norms Those standards of behavior that govern proper social relations, means of ensuring safety, eating habits, and so forth. If behavior deviates from the cultural norm, society may place sanctions or restrictions on behavior.

cultural values An especially important class of beliefs shared by the members of a society as to what is desirable or undesirable. Beliefs that some general state of existence is personally and socially worth striving for. Cultural values in the United States include achievement, independence, and youthfulness.

culture The implicit beliefs, norms, values, and customs that underlie and govern conduct in a society. The norms, beliefs, and customs learned from society. Culture leads to common patterns of behavior.

deceptive advertising Advertising that gives false information or that willfully misleads consumers about the brand's benefits.

decoding The sequence of steps in consumer information processing from exposure to attention to comprehension of a message. Consumers translate the message so it is understood and possibly retained in memory.

defense mechanism A strategy the ego uses to reduce tension. Conflicts that are not resolved in childhood influence later behavior in a manner of which the adult is unaware.

demonstration principle Formulated by James Duesenberry, a Harvard economist, states that due to increased mobility and purchasing power in America, consumers will come into increasing contact with new products and will be more likely to buy them. Referred to as a social multiplier because ownership increases in multiples as a function of group influence and product visibility.

depth interview An unstructured, personal interview in which the interviewer attempts to get subjects to talk freely and to express their true feelings. Can be conducted individually or in groups (focused group interviews). The latter have the advantage of eliciting more information because of group interaction.

diffusion The process by which the adoption of an innovation is spread over time by communication to members of a target market.

direct feedback Marketing communications that can be linked to sales results (e.g., retail advertising announcing a sale can be related to the number of shoppers coming into the store).

disclaimant group A group to which an individual belongs although rejecting its values.

disconfirmation of expectations Negative product evaluation resulting from consumption because expectations of product performance are not met. In such cases, consumers may develop more negative attitudes toward the product after the purchase.

discontinuous innovation A major technological advance involving the establishment of a new product and new behavior patterns (e.g., solar energy, electric cars, and the videodisc). Such an innovation will significantly alter purchasing patterns.

dissociative group A group to which an individual may regard membership as something to be avoided.

downside price elasticity Sensitivity to price decreases. If consumers will buy more if prices decrease but will not buy substantially less if prices increase, consumers are elastic on the downside.

dynamically continuous innovation A new product but not a major technological advance that does not alter existing consumer behavior patterns (e.g., electric toothbrushes, touch-tone telephones).

ego Part of Freud's psychoanalytic theory—the individual's self-concept and the manifestation of objective reality as it develops in interaction with the external world.

elaboration likelihood model (ELM) An information processing model that postulates that the degree to which a consumer elaborates on a message depends on its relevance. The more relevant the message, the more elaborate or central processing takes place. The less relevant the message, the more nonelaborate or peripheral processing takes place.

encoding The process of developing the marketing stimulus. The good advertising campaign is one in which the encoding process uses symbols and imagery that successfully communicate the product benefits to consumers.

enculturation The process of learning the values of one's own culture from early childhood.

enduring involvement Continuous, more permanent involvement with a product; interest in product category on an ongoing basis.

Environmental Protection Agency (EPA) A government agency that sets controls on industry emissions, toxic, wastes, and automobile pollution.

episodic memory Images in long-term memory that reflect our memory of past events.

equal interval scale A metric scale, meaning that a rating of "2" is equidistant from "1" and "3."

ethnocentric Assuming that foreign consumers have the same norms and values as domestic consumers.

ethnography The study of culture by observation. Anthropologists determine cultural values through field studies in which they live with a group or family and observe its customs and behavior.

Eurobrand A brand marketed in Europe with several languages on the same package under the same brand name.

evaluative strategies Processing strategies for brand evaluation that require the organization of information about alternative brands. Most likely to be used when involvement with a product is high.

expectancy-value theory Developed by Milton Rosenberg, the expectancy-value theory posits that consumers will evaluate products based on the degree to which they are instrumental in achieving personal values. Consumers evaluate the projected consequences of their actions and will buy products that achieve the desired consequence.

expected price range The range of prices the consumer expects to find in the marketplace, which tends to be a wider range than the consumer's acceptable price range.

expert power Power based on the expertise of the individual or group derived from experience and knowledge. (E.g., a salesperson has expert power if the consumer regards him or her as knowledgeable.)

exposure Occurs when consumers' senses (sight, hearing, touch, smell) are activated by a stimulus.

expressive roles Family purchase roles related to the need for social and emotional support (e.g., decisions regarding style, color, or design).

extended family A nuclear family with at least one grandparent living at home.

extended self Extends our concept of self to what we own, wear, and use. Incorporates some of our more important possessions into our self-concept.

extinction Elimination of the link between stimulus and expected reward. If a consumer is no longer satisfied with a product, a process of extinction takes place. Extinction leads to a rapid decrease in the probability that the consumer will repurchase the same brand.

factor analysis A mathematical procedure for determining the intercorrelation between items and reducing the items into independent components or factors to eliminate redundancy. Typically, used to reduce a great amount of data into its more basic structure. An analytical technique that reduces purchasing motives to a smaller number of independent need criteria.

family Two or more people living together who are related by blood or marriage.

family life cycle The progression of a family from formation to child rearing, middle age, and finally retirement. Also reflects changes in income and family situation.

Federal Communications Commission (FCC) A government agency that regulates communications media and practices. Among other things, it oversees advertising directed to children.

Federal Trade Commission (FTC) A government agency established in 1914 to curb the monopoly powers of big business and unfair trade practices. It is also a watchdog over deceptive advertising.

feedback of communication Information that marketers collect to evaluate the effectiveness of the communication that was sent.

figure and ground Gestalt psychologists state that in organizing stimuli into wholes, individuals identify those stimuli that are prominent (the figure) and those stimuli that are less prominent (the ground or background). The figure appears well defined, at a definite location, solid, and in front of the ground. In contrast, the ground appears amorphous, indefinite, and continuous behind the figure. A principle of advertising is that the product should appear as the figure rather than as the ground.

flexible globalization An attempt to standardize marketing strategies across countries but to be flexible enough to adapt components of the strategy to local conditions.

focus group interview An unstructured, personal interview in which the interviewer attempts to get groups to talk freely and to express their true feelings. Has the advantage of eliciting more information because of group interaction.

Food and Drug Administration (FDA) A government agency created in 1906 to set product standards; it also requires disclosure of product contents.

forgetting Forgetting occurs when information stored in memory is lost or when new information interferes with retrieval or stored information. Occurs when the stimulus is no longer repeated or perceived. Lack of use of a product or elimination of an advertising campaign can cause forgetting.

fraudulent advertising A straightforward lie. A form of deceptive advertising.

frequency The number of times an individual consumer or household is exposed to a message marketers send.

functions of attitudes There are four functions served by attitudes: a utilitarian function, a knowledge function, a value-expressive function, and an ego-defensive function. Marketing strategies can attempt to influence attitudes serving each of these functions.

gatekeeper Information gatherer who controls the level and type of stimuli flowing from the mass media to the group. Has the greatest expertise in acquiring and evaluating information from various sources and is most aware of alternative sources of information but does not necessarily disseminate them.

geo-demographic analysis Demographic data analyzed by geographic area, generally based on census data.

Gestalt psychology A German school of psychology that focuses on total configurations or whole patterns.

Stimuli, such as advertising messages, are seen as an integrated whole. In short, the whole is greater than the sum of the parts.

grassroots innovator An innovator in a lower socioeconomic groups (generally from a rural area) who disseminates tastes and influence to higher socioeconomic groups.

heterophilous groups Groups outside of an individual's primary social network or personal network. Secondary groups.

hierarchy of effects Stipulates the sequence of cognitive states the consumer goes through in reaching a tendency to act. Needs are formulated, beliefs are formed about the brand, attitudes develop toward the brand, and the consumer then forms an action predisposition.

homophilous groups Groups that are part of an individual's personal network. Primary groups.

household Any individual living singly or together with others in a residential unit.

ideal self The concept that individuals have of themselves based on who they think they would like to be.

id/libido Part of Freud's psychoanalytic theory. The component of personality that controls the individual's most basic needs such as hunger, sex, and self-preservation.

image A total perception of an object formed by processing information from various sources over time.

impulse buying A tendency to buy on whim with little preplanning.

Index of Status Characteristics (ISC) A multi-item index combining several socioeconomic variables into one index of social class. The ISC measures four variables: occupation, source of income, house type, and dwelling area.

indirect feedback When marketing communications cannot be directly related to sales results, marketers use indirect measures to evaluate the effectiveness of communications. Indirect criteria include exposure to, awareness, comprehension, and retention of the marketing communication.

inertia A passive process of information processing, brand evaluation, and brand choice. The consumer frequently purchases the same brand by inertia to save time and energy.

inference Involves the development of an association between two stimuli; for instance, consumers may associate high price with quality.

informational influence The influence of experts or experienced friends or relatives on consumer brand evaluations.

information overload Consumers' ability to process information has been surpassed because of excessive information; as a result, decision making becomes less effective.

innovations Technological advances that create new or improved products or symbolic representations that change the meaning of products.

innovative communicator The innovator who is most likely to engage in word-of-mouth communication about an adopted innovation.

innovativeness The early adoption of a new product. Innovativeness is distinct from opinion leadership in that it is a behavioral variable (e.g., adoption). In contrast, opinion leadership is measured by the consumers' perception regarding their interpersonal influence on others.

inoculation theory A theory proposing that consumers can be "inoculated" against negative thoughts about a product when processing a marketing message with messages that anticipate these negative thoughts and refute them.

instrumental actions Actions necessary to complete the purchase of a brand (e.g., obtaining financing for a car).

instrumental roles Family purchasing roles related to task-oriented functions meant to provide direction to the group. Decisions on budgets, timing, and product specifications are task-oriented.

instrumental values As defined by Rokeach, instrumental values are the means to attain cultural goals. As applied to consumers, instrumental values are consumption-specific guidelines.

integration The tendency to perceive stimuli as an integrated whole; for example, a brand image.

interference Occurs when a related information node blocks the recall of the relevant information. Competitive advertising often causes consumers to be unable to recall advertising for a related brand; or consumers may sometimes confuse one brand with another.

intergenerational influences In the context of consumer socialization, those influences that are passed from one generation to the next.

irresponsible advertising Advertising that depicts or encourages irresponsible behavior or portrays groups in an irresponsible manner.

just-noticeable difference (j.n.d.) The minimal difference that can be detected between stimuli. The consumer will not be able to detect any difference between stimuli below his or her differential threshold. The j.n.d. varies not only with (a) the sensitivity of the receptor and (b) the type of stimuli, but also with (c) the absolute intensity of the stimuli being compared. (*See also* differential threshold.)

Kelly Repertory Grid A technique used to determine the relevant attributes consumers use to evaluate products by asking consumers to verbalize why they see pairs of brands as similar or different.

key informant method Involves the use of informed individuals (key informants) in a social system to identify opinion leaders in a given situation.

key informants Individuals who engage in frequent word-of-mouth communication within a group, but are not necessarily opinion leaders.

laddering As applied to the means-end chain, laddering involves a series of consumer interviews to determine the links among product attributes, consumption goals, and cultural values.

lexicographic strategy Requires consumers to rank product attributes from most important to least important. Consumers will choose the brand that dominates on the most important criterion. If two or more brands tie, then consumers will examine brands on the second attribute and so on until the tie is broken. A lexicographic rule follows a sequential approach.

lifestyle An individual's mode of living as identified by his or her activities, interests, and opinions. Lifestyle variables have been measured by identifying a consumer's day-to-day activities and interests.

limen The threshold level at which perceptions occur. Perceptions below the conscious level are subliminal. (*See also* subliminal perception.)

long-term memory The place where the consumer stores and retains information on a long-term basis.

low involvement purchases Purchases that are less important to the consumer. Identity with the product is low. Because it may not be worth the consumer's time and effort to search for information about brands and to consider a wide range of alternatives, low involvement purchases are associated with a more limited process of decision making.

mainstreaming The theory proposing that individuals tend to see the world around them largely based on information from the mass media. Therefore, heavy viewers of TV will develop similar perceptions of reality because they are exposed to similar stimuli.

marketing stimuli Any component of a product's marketing plan (e.g., price package, advertising, the store that sells the brand, and the brand itself). Most marketing stimuli are symbolic in nature; that is, representations of the product, not the product itself.

market segmentation analysis Involves identifying consumer groups by similarity in needs, usage, or characteristics to direct marketing strategies to these groups.

mature market Consumers over 50 years old, representing 64.3 million consumers.

means-end chain Gutman describes the interface between culture and consumer-behavior as a means-end chain. That is, the means (product attributes) are the vehicle for attaining personal values (the ends) with the consumption goals as an intermediary between them.

membership group A group to which an individual belongs and in which he or she has face-to-face communication with other members. Groups to which a person is recognized by others as belonging.

memory Represents information that the consumer retains and stores and that the consumer can recall for future use.

misleading advertising A form of deceptive advertising that involves a claim-belief interaction. The advertisement interacts with a consumer's beliefs and results in a misleading claim.

model of consumer behavior Sequence of factors that lead to purchase behavior and hypothesizes the relationship of these factors to behavior and hypothesizes the relationship of these factors to behavior and to each other.

moods Passing feelings that occur at a point in time (e.g., feeling happy, sad, silly, anxious, sexy, and so forth).

motivational research Research into consumer motives, particularly unconscious motives. These are determined through indirect assessment methods that include projective techniques and depth interviews. On this basis, hypotheses are developed regarding the motivations for consumer behavior.

multiattribute models Models that measure attitudes on a multidimensional basis by determining how consumers evaluate brands across product attributes. The sum of these ratings weighted by the value placed on each attribute represents consumers' attitude toward the brand.

multidimensional scaling A set of computer programs that determines the relative position of brands and concepts in *n*-dimensional space based on consumer similarity or preference ratings of these brands.

multivarite statistical techniques Statistical techniques capable of analyzing many variables simultaneously. For examples, see *cluster analysis* and *factor analysis*.

node Each word or image in long-term memory. Each node is linked to other words or images. (E.g., good food and fast service are nodes that a consumer may link to the McDonald's node.)

noncompensatory method A model of attitude structure in which brands are evaluated on a few of the most important attributes. Weakness of a product or brand on one attribute cannot be compensated by its strength on another. As a result, the brand can be eliminated from consideration based on one or two attributes. Requires consumers to process information by attribute across brands.

nonevaluative strategies Strategies for brand evaluation that involves the use of a simple decision rule to avoid the necessity to evaluate brands. (E.g., some consumers simply buy the cheapest brand.)

normative influence The influence exerted on an individual to conform to group norms and expectations.

norms Rules of behavior in particular circumstances that specify actions that are proper and those that are improper. Beliefs held by a consensus of a group concerning the rules of behavior to which group members are expected to conform to these norms. Rules and standards of conduct (generally undefined) that the group establishes.

nuclear family Married couple who have one or more children.

opinion leadership The influence that individuals interested and involved in a product exert over the attitudes and behavior of others.

passive learning Occurs when consumers learn about brands with little involvement and purchase with little evaluation of alternative brands. Consumers are more likely to form attitudes after, rather than before, a purchase.

penetration strategy A strategic option establishing a competitive price for a new product entry. A mass marketing approach would be used. Most relevant for continuous innovation.

perceived risk Degree of risk consumers perceive in a purchase. Composed of two elements: (1) uncertainty about the decision and (2) potential consequences of the decision.

perception The process by which people select, organize, and interpret sensory stimuli into a meaningful and coherent picture. The way consumers view an object (e.g., their mental picture of a brand or the traits they attribute to a brand).

perceptual defense Consumers' distortion of information so that it conforms to their beliefs and attitudes. This function operates to protect the individual from threatening or contradictory stimuli.

perceptual equilibrium/disequilibrium Consumers seek to maintain equilibrium in their psychological set by screening out information that does not conform to their predispositions. When consumers choose information consistent with prior beliefs or interpret information to conform to these beliefs, they are processing information to ensure perceptual equilibrium. Acceptance of contradictory information means consumers are in a state of perceptual disequilibrium.

perceptual mapping A group of quantitative techniques that seeks to position various brands on a "map" based on the way consumers perceive them. The closer one brand is to another on the map, the more similar it is to the other brand. The basic assumption is that if consumers see two brands as being similar, they will behave similarly toward the two brands.

perceptual organization The organization of disparate information so that it can be comprehended and retained.

perceptual vigilance A form of selective perception whereby the consumers' needs determine the information perceived. The tendency of consumers to select the information that helps them in evaluating brands to meet their needs. (E.g., words that connote important values are often perceived more readily. As a result, consumers will recognize preferred brand names more quickly than they will nonpreferred brand names.)

performance roles The roles prescribed for individuals who participate in rituals—e.g., the roles of bride, groom, best man, and bridesmaids in weddings.

personality A person's consistent and enduring patterns of behavior. Represents a set of consumer characteristics used to describe target segments.

placement The second of three factors required for retrieval of information from long-term memory. Placement determines which other nodes consumers will connect the activated node to.

postpurchase dissonance Perceptual disequilibrium whereby the consumer perceives conflicting information after the decision and seeks to change the information to conform to prior behavior.

preteens Consumers who are between the ages of 8 to 12 and who were born in the later part of the "echo boom" between 1976 and 1985; together with teens, this market represents nearly 34 million consumers.

price elasticity A measure of price sensitivity measured by the percentage of change in quantity compared to a percentage change in price. (See also *response elasticity*.)

primary formal group Group the consumer frequently comes in contact with that has some formal structure (e.g., school or business groups).

primary informal group Group the consumer frequently comes in contact with that has no formal structure (e.g., the family and peer groups). These groups have the greatest influence on the consumer.

primary/intrinsic stimuli Unconditioned stimulus; that is, the initial stimulus (e.g., cowboy) that another stimulus is linked to (e.g., Marlboro cigarettes) to produce a conditioned response. In marketing, the product and its components (package, contents, physical properties) are primary stimuli.

product concept A bundle of product benefits that can be directed to the needs of a defined group of consumers through symbolism and imagery. The product concept represents the organization of marketing stimuli into a coordinated product position that can be more easily directed to consumers.

product concept test Obtaining consumer reactions to a verbal description of the product generally before the product is manufactured. Usually tested against several alternative concepts.

product positioning Communication of the set of benefits the product is designed to meet. Such benefits are communicated through advertising and other marketing strategies.

PROFIT (profit fitting) program A computer program used to associate a brand's position with evaluative attributes. The program identifies the position of each attribute by determining a vector that provides the best fit between the attribute and the brands in a perceptual map.

projective techniques Techniques used for detecting and measuring wants and attitudes not readily discernible through more direct methods. Consists of the presentation of ambiguous materials (e.g., ink blots, untitled pictured, etc.). In interpreting this material, the viewer "projects" tendencies of which he or she may be unaware or may wish to conceal. Diagnostic devices in which interpretation of ambiguous stimuli is taken to reveal something about the observer, based on previous experience and motivations, needs, and interests in play at the time.

proximity The tendency to group stimuli by proximity means that one object will be associated with another based on its closeness to that object.

psychoanalytic theory Theory developed by Sigmund Freud that emphasizes the conflict among id, ego, and superego in childhood and the resolution of these conflicts in adult behavior. The dynamic interaction of these elements results in unconscious motivations that are manifested in observed human behavior.

psychographic characteristics Consumer psychological characteristics that can be quantified. Represented by two classes of variables: lifestyle and personality.

psychological set The consumer's state of mind toward an object; that is, his or her needs, attitudes, and perceptions relative to various brands. The psychological set is represented at a given point in time prior to the decision process. It will change during the decision process when the consumer process new information, resulting in changes in needs, attitudes, and perceptions.

rank order of preference scale A nonmetric scale in which objects are ranked by order of preference. Values have ordinal meaning only.

rate of diffusion A time-oriented measurement that reflects the cumulative level of adoption of a new product over time.

reach The number of people exposed to the message that the marketer sends.

reactance When group pressures to conform become too intense, the consumer may be encouraged to reject group norms and to demonstrate independent behavior.

reference group Any group with which an individual identifies such that he or she tends to use the group as a standard for self-evaluation and as a source of personal values and goals. A group that serves as a reference point for the individual in the formation of beliefs, attitudes, and behavior. Such groups provide consumers with a means to compare and evaluate their own brand attitudes and purchasing behavior.

reference/standard price The price consumers expect to pay for a certain item that serves as a frame of reference by which consumers compare prices of alternative brands.

referent power Power based on the identification of the individual with members of the group. The greater the similarity of the individual's beliefs and attitudes with those of group members, the greater the referent power of the group. A salesperson has referent power if the consumer sees him or her as similar.

reinforcement strategies Used by marketers to reinforce positive attitudes rather than attempting to change them. Can be used to attract new users or appeal to existing users with new or existing products.

reservation price In the context of comparing prices of alternative brands, the higher end of the acceptable price range or the upper limit above which consumers would judge an article too expensive.

response elasticity Measures consumers' sensitivity to a particular marketing stimulus by associating a percentage change in the stimulus with a percentage change in the quantity purchased. Provides a basis for defining consumer segments by degree of sensitivity to marketing stimuli. The most common example is price elasticity.

retain Remember; consumers are most likely to retain messages that are most relevant to their needs.

reward power Power based on the ability of the group to reward the individual.

risk barrier Represents the consumers' physical, economic, performance, or social risk of adopting an innovation.

risky shift phenomenon The hypothesis that joint decision making encourages the group to take riskier decisions because in this way, all members of the group can share the failure of a wrong decision.

ritual A series of symbolic behaviors that occur in sequence and are repeated frequently—for example, those that occur in grooming and gift-giving and during holidays.

ritual artifacts In rituals, these are often in the form of consumer products. For example, colored lights, mistletoe, wreaths, and Santa Claus are artifacts of Christmas rituals.

roles Functions assumed by or assigned to individuals by the group in the attainment of group objectives.

sacred consumption Consumption of goods that promote beauty, the preservation of nature, and cooperation.

scanner data Data collected from scanners that link consumers' exposure to advertising and subsequent behavior.

schema A cluster of concepts or beliefs that represent an individual's perception of an object or situation.

script In rituals, a script prescribes how, when, and by whom products will be used—e.g., the use of the ring, cake, and photographs at weddings.

secondary/extrinsic stimuli A stimulus that is repeatedly linked to a primary stimulus to produce a conditioned response. Communications designed to influence consumer behavior are secondary stimuli that represent the product or stimuli associated with the product (price, store in which purchased, effect of salesperson).

secondary formal group Group with some formal structure with which the consumer meets infrequently (e.g., alumni groups, business clubs, and tenant organizations). These groups are likely to have the least amount of influence on the consumer.

secondary informal group Group with no formal structure with which the consumer meets infrequently (e.g., shopping or sports groups).

secular consumption Consumption of goods that promote technology, the conquest of nature, and competition.

selection The first component of perception. Consumers pick and choose marketing stimuli based on their needs and attitudes (e.g., a car buyer will be more attentive to car ads).

selective perception Consumers perceive marketing stimuli selectively to reinforce their needs, attitudes, past experiences, and personal characteristics. Selective perception means that two consumers can perceive the identical ad, package, or product very differently.

self-concept/self-image theory A person's self-concept causes the individual to see herself or himself through the eyes of other persons. In doing so, an individual takes into account the other person's behavior, feelings, and attitudes. This evaluation is closely related to the perceptions of whether other persons in the reference group will approve or disapprove of the "self" presented to the reference group.

self-designating technique A set of techniques used to measure opinion leadership, innovativeness, perceived risk, or other marketing constructs. The method requires consumers to categorize themselves in a given topic area.

semantic differential A seven-point metric scale anchored by bipolar adjectives and used in marketing to measure beliefs about brands.

semantic memory Words and sentence stored in long-term memory that reflect facts and concepts that we remember.

semiotics A field of study established to study the interrelationship among three components: object (brand), the signs and symbols associated with the object, and the consumer who does the associating. To understand how people derive meaning from symbols, researchers must understand the shared meaning of various signs in a culture.

short-term memory The place where a consumer briefly evaluates perceived information to determine whether it is to be stored in long-term memory.

similarity A principle of grouping that suggests stimuli will be grouped together by similarity in their characteristics.

situational involvement Temporary involvement with a product only in specific situations, such as when a purchase decision is required.

skimming policy A strategic option establishing a high price for a new product entry and "skimming the cream of the market" by aiming at the most price inelastic consumer. Advertising and sales promotion are limited to specific targets, and distribution is selective. The most relevant strategy for discontinuous innovations.

social class A division of society made up of persons possessing certain common social and economic characteristics that are taken to qualify them for equal-status relations with one another and that restricts their interaction with members of other social classes.

socialization The process by which an individual learns the norms and values of the group and of society.

social judgment theory Sherif's theory that describes an individual's position on an issue based on his or her involvement with the issue. Sherif identified a latitude of acceptance, a latitude of rejection, and a latitude of noncommitment to operationalize this concept of involvement. The greater the involvement, the narrower the latitude of acceptance and the wider the latitude of rejection on various positions.

socially dependent consumer A consumer who scores low on opinion leadership but high on information seeking. This consumer represents the traditional view of a follower—an individual who is socially active in soliciting word-of-mouth information but is not an influencer.

socially independent consumer A consumer who scores high on opinion leadership but low on information seeking. This consumer represents the traditional view of opinion leadership—a consumer who transmits information and influence but does not solicit them.

socially integrated consumer One who scores high on opinion leadership and information seeking. This consumer is the most socially active in both transmitting and receiving word-of-mouth communication.

socially isolated consumer One who scores low on opinion leadership and information seeking. This consumer is a passive individual who may receive but does not actively seek information. He or she is not socially active and may avoid personal influence.

social multiplier effect As a result of the demonstration principle, ownership increases in multiples as consumers come into contact with and acquire new products. The social multiplier effect illustrates the volatility of group influence in the American economy. (See also *demonstration principle*.)

social system A set of people with a shared set of norms who tend to interact over time.

socioeconomic factors Consumers' income, education, and employment status. A key set of demographic variables that defines consumers' current and future purchasing power.

sociogram The diagram of a network of communications among individuals. A sociogram is developed by using a sociometric technique (see definition) to identify communications.

sociometric technique A method developed to describe the patterns of communication and influence among members of a group. Members of a group are asked from who they get advice and to whom they go to seek advice or information in making a decision. Specific individuals are identified and can, in turn, be interviewed to trace the network of communication. Individuals with the most frequent communication links are identified as opinion leaders.

source bolstering When viewing ads in low involvement situations, the tendency for consumers to react positively to the source of the message as opposed to the message itself.

source credibility The level of expertise and trustworthiness consumers attribute to the source of the marketing message.

source derogation When viewing ads in low involvement situations, the tendency of consumers to react negatively to the source and, therefore, tend not to believe the message.

source of communication The marketer who develops the marketing message and identifies the objectives and target for its communications.

status The rank of an individual in the prestige hierarchy of a group of community. The position the individual occupies within the group. High status implies greater power and influence within the group.

stimuli Any physical, visual, or verbal communications that can influence an individual's response.

stimulus generalization Consumers' ability to perceive differences in stimuli. Allows consumers to judge brands selectively and to make evaluative judgments about preferences of one brand or another.

subcultural influences Differences in norms and values among subcultures within a society.

subculture The part of the total culture of a society that is distinct from society in certain respects (e.g., an ethnic group, a social class group, a regional group). The ways of behaving that distinguish a particular group from a larger one.

subliminal embeds Tiny figures inserted into magazine ads by high-speed photography or by airbrushing.

subliminal perception Perception of a stimulus below the conscious level. If the stimulus is beneath the threshold of conscious awareness but above the absolute threshold of perception, it is known as subliminal perception. (The conscious level is referred to as the limen; thus, perception below the conscious level is subliminal or below the absolute threshold.)

subtyping Developing a subcategory of a broader category. (E.g., Federal Express established the subcategory, overnight delivery, within the general category of package delivery.)

superego Part of Freud's psychoanalytic theory. The component of personality that is the leash on the id and works against its impulses.

support arguments Thoughts evoked in response to advertising when viewed by consumers who support what is read or said.

symbolic aspiration group A group in which an individual does not expect to receive membership, despite the acceptance of the group's norms and beliefs.

symbolic interactionism The interaction between the individual and the symbols in his or her environment. Consumers purchase products for their symbolic value in enhancing their self-concepts.

teens Consumers who are between the ages of 13 and 17 and who were born in the earlier part of the "echo boom" between 1976 and 1985; together with preteens, this market represents nearly 34 million consumers.

terminal values As defined by Rokeach, terminal values are cultural goals to be attained. Applied to consumers, terminal values are their ultimate purchasing goals.

threshold level Level of sensory discrimination. Ability to discriminate stimuli.

trade-off analysis A technique that provides a basis for determining consumers' optimal combination of product characteristics. A limited number of concepts representing combinations of characteristics are given to consumers for preference ratings. On this basis, an ideal combination of characteristics is determined.

trait theory A quantitative approach to the study of personality postulating that an individual's personality is composed of definite predispositional attributes called traits. The most empirical basis for measuring personality, it states that personality is composed of a set of traits that describe a general response predisposition.

transfer The third of three factors required for retrieval of information from long-term memory. Transfer determines the information consumers will retrieve from long-term to short-term memory. Generally, consumers will transfer information that is most important in making a decision.

transformational effect The effect that occurs when the attitude consumers have toward an ad carries over to the brand. Explains why consumers who cannot tell a difference between soft drinks in blind taste tests have strong brand preferences when they can choose labeled brands.

trickle-across effect The process of diffusion occurring across groups regardless of socioeconomic status. A horizontal pattern of diffusion.

trickle-down effect The process of information and influence traveling from higher to lower socioeconomic groups. A vertical pattern of diffusion.

trickle-up effect The phenomenon that occurs when lower class groups influence the purchases of those farther up the ladder. (E.g., jeans were originally designed for blue-collar workers and made their way up to designer jean status.)

unplanned purchases A buying action undertaken without buying intention prior to entering the store. For types of unplanned purchases are (1) pure impulse, (2) reminder effect, (3) suggestion effect, and (4) planned impulse purchases.

upside price elasticity Sensitivity to increases in price. It is possible that consumers will buy less if prices increase but will not buy substantially more if prices decrease. Consumers are, therefore, elastic on the upside.

usage barrier Occurs when an item is not compatible with the existing practices or habits of consumers.

value barrier A lack of performance relative to price compared with substitute products.

variety seeking The motivation for brand switching is sometimes a desire for change or a search for novelty. It is the result of routinized choice and is a logical expression of consumer boredom.

vocabulary of product attributes and benefits A set of adjectives to describe a product's characteristics and benefits generally obtained from consumer depth interviews. (E.g., a vocabulary for soft drink brands might include terms like mild, sweet, carbonated, thirst-quenching.)

Weber's law A law of psychological relativity: Subjective discriminations are not bound to absolute characteristics of stimuli but to relations between them. The size of the least detectable change or increment in intensity is a function of the initial intensity; the stronger the initial stimulus, the greater the difference needs to be. (E.g., the higher the price of a product, the greater the price difference between two brands of that product must be for consumers to detect it.)

word-of-mouth communication Interpersonal communication between two or more individual such as members of a reference group or a customer and a salesperson. People exert purchase influence through such communication.

N A M E   I N D E X

COMPANY INDEX

SUBJECT INDEX